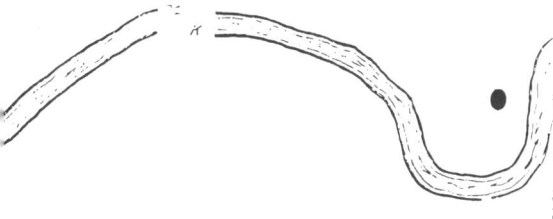

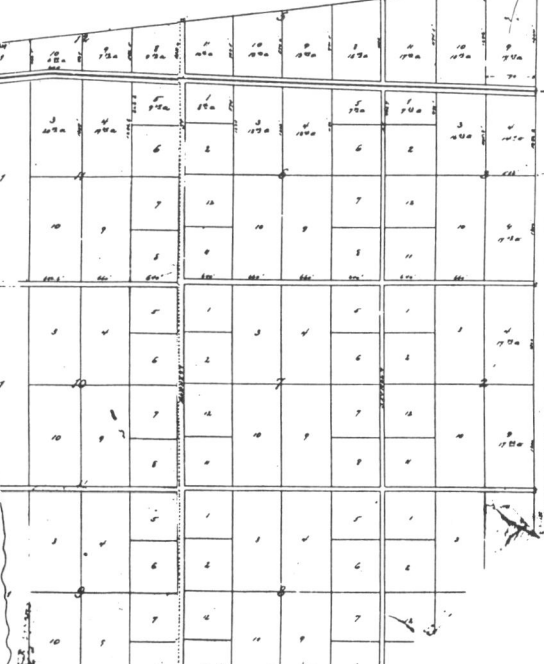

Plat Map

of

PASADENA, TEXAS

filed in Harris County on May 25, 1896.

First land sales executed three years earlier

Pasadena
The Early Years

To W.M. Von-Maszewsky
Enjoy today, for tomorrow
it will be history. Thanks

April 22, 1994

Pasadena
The Early Years

C. David Pomeroy, Jr.

Pomerosa **P**ress
P. O. Box 6266
Pasadena, Texas 77506

*Copyright © 1993
C. David Pomeroy, Jr.
Pasadena, Texas*

*All Rights Reserved
Printed by D. Armstrong Co., Houston*

*Library of Congress Catalog Card No. 93-93686
ISBN No. 0-945010-00-1*

Dedication

Like so many in Pasadena, my perspective of history was of something that simply had occurred before the present and was of little interest. My wife Debbi introduced me to a new awareness of history. From that seed of curiosity and fascination has sprung forth an insatiable desire to know and understand the events and people that have laid the foundations for my Present. It was she that suggested we return home from Ohio and to get to know our grandfathers during their last few remaining years and thus focused me on Local and Family History. As an accomplished writer Debbi has taught me how to put muscle, flesh, feelings, and a soul to the skeleton of facts that make up the story you are about to experience. Her life has so touched mine that I am now able to offer to you what I hope to be, an experience in and an appreciation of our local Heritage.

Table of Contents

Acknowledgements .... *vii*
Introduction .... *ix*

I. Open Ranges (1842-1892) 1
II. Settlement (1893-94) 25
III. Foundations for Survival (1894-99) 45
IV. Renewed Beginnings (1900-1904) 71
V. Community Life (1905-1910) 87
VI. Strawberries (1900-1917) 119
VII. Around Town (1910-1918) 143
VIII. Outside Influences (1900-1920) 187
IX. Roaring Into The Twenties (1919-1924) 205
X. The Struggle to Incorporate (1922-1929) 243
XI. The Eve of the Great Depression (1928-1929) 277
XII. Into The Depression (1929-1932) 303
XIII. Transformation and Recovery (1932-1937) 339

Epilogue *373*
Notes *375*
Bibliography: Public Records *421*
Bibliography: Private Collections *423*
Bibliography: Interviews *427*
Bibliography: Biographies *433*
Bibliography: Books *435*
Bibliography: Publications & Articles *439*
Index *443*

Acknowledgement

This book would not have been possible without the help of so many people. Their names would take a book in and of itself. With the limited space I do have I would like to single out a few to acknowledge.

To my wife Debbi. She lit the fire that all the rest stoked and kindled.

To my scouts who were always looking for information and sources for me: Marilyn Coward, Tommy Hoffman, Anne Nicolardi, and Anne Thomas.

To my invaluable resources: Gordon Black (La Porte's history), Bertha Davis, Mrs. Abbott (who lent me her photo album for many years), Dorothy Weston (lent me Deer Park book), Doris Barnes Howell, Francita Koelsch (Allen Ranch and family), Katherine Russel Daunoy (Munger family and diary), Jim Glass, J. B. Isaac, and, of course, Dick Nichols.

To those that collected and published our histories: Helen Alexander, Jack Lynn, Joe Dollar, Cynthia Saucier (Pasadena Public Library's Pasadena History Collection), the *Pasadena Citizen* newspaper, the Pasadena Early Settlers Association, the Pasadena Historical Society, and Robert and Ann Zimmerer of the Harris County Genealogical Society.

To those who lived the history and shared with me. I will miss those whose final chapter came before I finished that chapter of this book. Some of those who shared with me—Edward Kruse, Catherine Kingsbury, W. S. "Muggins" Parks, John and Gertrude Pomeroy, Loise Pomeroy, Ralph and Winogene Stafford, Lula Pitts, Wesley Pitts, Harry Riley, Sam and Duckie Towles, and Ray C. Williams.

To my parents, Clyde and Marguerite Pomeroy, who shared their memories, encouraged me, and then gave me time off from work to interview, research, and write.

And lastly, to the hundreds of Early Settlers who gave generously of their time, memories, and memorabilia.

Introduction

The first inhabitants of the area that was to become Pasadena were the Amerins (American Indians). For 10,000 years they inhabited the area and except for buried remains and refuse along the waterways, they did not leave a trace. In 1492 Christopher Columbus opened the area to settlement by Europeans. The first recorded Anglo to explore the area was Cabeza de Vaca who had the misfortune of being shipwrecked on Galveston Island in 1528.

No settlement was established in the Pasadena area until Stephen F. Austin received permission from the newly formed Republic of Mexico in the early 1820s to settle 300 families in the area. William Vince of Tennessee laid claim to the land along Buffalo Bayou on both sides of the stream to be named Vince's Bayou. Vince was the first of the cattle ranchers that occupied the land abandoned by the Indians. General Santa Anna of Mexico rode across Vince's land on his way to the plains at San Jacinto. General Sam Houston of the Texian Army followed. The Battle at San Jacinto created the Republic of Texas and the capture of the fleeing Santa Anna in the area to be known as Pasadena completed the victory. For the next 60 years the land would be used for ranching. Sam W. Allen began his legendary ranch that would continue to the 1910s and its remnants to this very date.

The area was opened to farmers in the early 1890s when a railroad was planned to be constructed between Houston and the new community of La Porte. Colonel J. H. Burnett of Galveston bought most of the Vince survey and laid out the townsite of Pasadena. This book chronicles the founding of the community and its growth as a successful farming community in the eastern section of Harris County. The development of the Port of Houston, the petrochemical plants along the Houston Ship Channel, and the demands of World War II moved Pasadena out of the Farming Era and into the Industrial Era. That history will be left for others to write. During its first

50 years Pasadena grew to a population of 3,460 people. She added 120,000 more people over the next 50 years. Upon the firm foundation laid down during the Early Years, Pasadena grew to be the second largest city in Harris County and one of the top 15th in the State.

I

Open Ranges (1842-1892)

The history of Pasadena, Texas, is the summation of the histories of those who settled the area. Pasadena did not have a guiding genius, a determined developer, a financial benefactor, nor even a master plan. Houston's seed was planted firmly by the Allen Brothers. Galveston's destiny was guided by Michel Menard. The Woodlands was the alter ego of George Mitchell. Clear Lake City and Kingwood were the business product of Exxon's Friendswood Corporation. However, Pasadena only began as a grid of lines on the plat of newly purchased property. The concept of a community, and the creation of Pasadena was the work of many individuals. They came to start over, to find an opportunity, or a dozen other reasons. They built their homes, tilled their fields and then began to see what else was appropriate for their wellbeing. They laid the foundation with school and church, then commerce and government. Each evolved as it was needed and only as much as was needed. In the end their labor bore fruit as their community blossomed into the city of "Pasadena."

Before there was a Pasadena the land was unsettled. The Indians had disappeared after roaming the region for ten thousand years. They left behind no visible changes to mark their habitation. For four hundred years the Spaniards had laid claim to the land, but no one had ventured into this area. The French made an ineffective challenge to the Spanish title. The first adventurers who came to try to tame the land arrived in the early 1820s. Stephen F. Austin brought 300 families to colonize the upper coastal region of the new Mexican state of

Coahuila and Texas. The first land grants were issued in 1824. William Vince received title to 4,428 acres along the south side of the Buffalo Bayou. He appropriately named the small creek that drained his property, Vince's Bayou. Seventy years later his land would be the site of the town of Pasadena.[1]

Vince raised cattle and those that followed in title to the land also raised stock. The native prairie grass grew abundantly with the long warm season and ample rainfall. However, between Harrisburg and Lynchburg there were only about six houses and not all of them represented ranching enterprises. Even with the flurry of settlers after the creation of the Republic of Texas in 1836, the future Pasadena area remained basically vacant land. The Ranching Era would continue until the 1890s. During that period of time, one family would rise to dominate the region.

Samuel William Allen came to Texas in 1842 from Tennessee. Although he was only 16 years old, by the standards of the day he was considered a man. Many people were coming to the new Republic of Texas for a fresh start or to seek new opportunities. It was a time of excitement in Texas as dignitaries and reporters toured the republic and sent glowing dispatches home describing the land and the opportunities. The story of the battle at San Jacinto was told and retold. Since the usual route into Texas was through the port of Galveston, up the Buffalo Bayou to Harrisburg and Houston and then on into the interior, Buffalo Bayou and even the Vince tract were mentioned regularly. Immigration from the United States and elsewhere was encouraged and land speculation abounded.[2]

When Sam Allen arrived in Texas there were only a few towns in existence. Galveston was generally the first city a traveller would visit, particularly if he arrived by boat. With a population of over 3,000, it was one of the largest cities in Texas. But the Gulf ports of Galveston, Port Lavaca, Powderhorn (later renamed Indianola), Velasco, and Quintana held little opportunity for anyone other than merchants and stevedores. The opportunities in Texas for a man with little means, other than talent, were inland.[3]

Augustus Chapman (A. C.) Allen and his brother John Kirby Allen (no kin to Sam W. Allen) had come from New York 10 years earlier and had established their town of Houston in 1836. The population of Houston shot upwards after its selection as the capital of the republic on November 30. The following year, on June 5, 1837, Houston was incorporated. At that time it had an estimated population of 1,200 residents. Although Houston lost its designation as the capital of the republic two years later, it was still one of the first places a newcomer visited when travelling to Texas.[4]

Houston was built on the dream of becoming a great port even though it was located inland. Water transportation was the cheapest and fastest way for the cotton plantations of the Brazos River bottomlands to move their product to market in the South and the East. Unfortunately the Brazos River was not always navigable and experienced a recurring sand bar problem at its mouth on the Gulf of Mexico. The Allen brothers pointed out that it was a short overland trip from the Brazos River plantations to Houston and that Buffalo Bayou was an all-season river highway suitable for the transportation of cotton and other commerce. In order to improve the overland route, there was talk of building a wooden road to Houston and of building a railroad line from the Brazos River to Harrisburg. In 1841 the "Port of Houston" was established and funds were raised to remove obstructions from Buffalo Bayou.[5]

Competing with Houston for development was the older village of Harrisburg. Harrisburg was one of the first communities in Stephen Austin's colony and had served as the seat of government for the area before the republic was founded. The Mexican leader, Santa Anna, had burned the village in 1836 and the town was struggling to reestablish itself. Although located more favorably downriver on Buffalo Bayou than Houston, Harrisburg could not compete with the leadership or financial resources of Houston.[6]

All of the settlements in Texas were located on rivers, bays, or the Gulf. Water was critical for general transportation, and survival. In between these cities there was a lot of land and very few people. But many new towns were planned to accommodate the influx of people, or to attract people to Texas, after the creation of the republic. In the area of the future site of Pasadena the promotions were numerous. Germantown, later known as Frostown, bordered Houston. Nearby Hamilton attempted to woo away potential Harrisburg residents. Harrisburg responded with a planned French settlement adjacent to the town with the aim of developing a wine industry. San Jacinto sprang up opposite Lynch's Ferry. Louisville was established down river. Colonel James Morgan tried to reestablish his pre-republic prospective town of New Washington at Morgan's Point.[7]

At the mouth of Vince's Bayou the town of "Buffaloe" was announced on July 8, 1837. Merriweather Woodson Smith had purchased 2,222 acres out of the William Vince survey and laid out his town where Pasadena was to later prosper. His advertisement in the *Telegraph and Texas Register* (published in Houston) read:

> This city, most eligibly situated, and nearly equidistant from the most important towns in Texas, and decidedly the best location in the country, as well as from the quality of its well timbered land and internal productive advantages, with a pure spring of fresh water is now being laid out into lots for public or private sale. The City of Buffaloe is distant from the Brazos about 22 miles, from the mouth of the San Jacinto 10 miles, and from the city of Houston about 8 miles. At the Buffaloe bayou, above its junction with the San Jacinto river, and even up to the levee of the projected city, widens to a considerable extent, vessels that can cross Red Fish bar may sail up, in one day and discharge their caroes[*sic*]. The proprietors of the town have determined as soon as practical to run a rail road to strike the Brazos seven miles above Bolivar and to use every effort, having considerable capital at their control, to rival any city or town in Texas. Applications for lots to be made to Mr. Merriweather W. Smith, on the premises. Houston, July 8, 1837.

Unfortunately, Mr. Smith was more eloquent with his prose than with his sales technique. No lots were recorded as being sold in the town of Buffaloe. Colonel William Fairfax Gray noted in his diary, "Stopt [*sic*] at Wm. Vince's, where I met a man with a harelip, named Merry . . . ." Also travelling the area was Andrew Forest Muir who noted in his magazine article "We found the occupant, who was an old bachelor, with nothing to eat . . . He had plenty of whisky, of which he had drunk so freely that his insolence was insuf- ferable . . . the city of Buffalo, situated upon Vince's farm . . . the sonorous title of Buffalo has been supplanted by the less elegant name of Pokersville, an epithet that originated from the proprietor's superior skill in the game of poker and which has fixed upon him the cognomen of Pokersmith . . . . " Mr. Smith was found dead shortly afterwards, "with his empty bottle by his side."

Whether it was from whiskey, or his poker playing, the cause of death was not revealed. The advertisement for Buffaloe continued to run for several months. Forty-five years would pass before a town would flourish on the William Vince survey.[8]

Sam Allen stopped in the Houston-Harrisburg area where he met Rebecca Jane Thomas, daughter of Ezekiel and Mary Elizabeth Thomas. Rebecca was one of the first children born in Stephen F. Austin's colony in the Harrisburg district. Her father, Ezekiel Thomas and her great-uncle Morris Callahan had been members of Stephen F. Austin's original settlers, commonly referred to as the Old Three Hundred, and each had received land grants along Buffalo Bayou. On August 19, 1824, Ezekiel Thomas received title to a league of land (4,428 acres) situated on the north side of Buffalo Bayou opposite the mouth of Sims Bayou. Two weeks earlier Morris Callahan had partnered with Allen Vince and they received a league of land, on the south side of Buffalo Bayou opposite Thomas's league, and straddling Sims Bayou. The Callahan and Vince league was adjacent to the William Vince league on its western side. According to the Mexican census of 1826 Morris Callahan and Allen Vince were farmers and stock raisers. Within a year Callahan had died. Mary Thomas was his niece and the only relative of Morris Callahan living in the state of Coahuila and Texas at the time of his death. After a lengthy court battle with Callahan's heirs living in the United States, Mrs. Thomas' children received title to the land in the spring of 1843. As her share of the inheritance, Rebecca received 350 acres out of the east half of the Callahan and Vince Survey with frontage on Buffalo Bayou at the mouth of Sims Bayou.[9]

Love blossomed between the Tennessee boy and the Texas belle and they were married May 9, 1844. Five years earlier a yellow fever epidemic struck Houston and killed one-third of the people in town. When "Yellow Jack" returned in 1844 Rebecca and Sam moved out of town to her property. Their house was situated on Sims Bayou at the edge of the tree line that bordered the bayou. Buffalo Bayou was a deep clear river with high banks overgrown with great magnolia trees. The Harrisburg-Lynchburg road ran nearby. Although it was the famous "road to San Jacinto battlefield" it was marked by little more than fading wagon ruts. Public and commercial transportation out of Houston or Harrisburg generally went by boat on Buffalo Bayou. It was rather easy to lose the road and the trail was marked more by landmarks on the horizon that one travelled towards than by a path on the ground. The Harris County commissioners periodically affirmed that the road ran from one point to another, but did not spend any money in marking or improving the road. The largest bayou that one encountered on this road from Harrisburg to Lynchburg was Sims Bayou. Although not as large as the Buffalo Bayou, crossing it could be a problem. Vince's Bayou was to the east and previously had had a bridge, which was destroyed during the battle at San Jacinto. Crossing the bayou was easy during normal weather.[10]

When Sam Allen got into the cattle business he made some valuable friendships with prominent early Texans. Andrew Briscoe had fought at San Jacinto, had served as chief justice of Harrisburg, was married to one of the daughters of the founder of Harrisburg, was promoting the first railroad in Texas, and was already successful in the cattle business. Francis R. Lubbock, ex-comptroller of the republic, and a Houston merchant had gotten in the cattle business on the recommendation of his political friend and fellow merchant-turned-rancher Andrew Briscoe. In 1846 Francis R. Lubbock bought a 400-acre ranch on Sims Bayou, upstream from Sam and Rebecca Allen's place. Sam had already been ranching for a couple of years so he taught the future governor how to rope and round up strays.[11]

The base stock of all Texas cattle was the Longhorn. Its roots went back to Christopher Columbus's return trip to the New World in 1493 when he brought a load of Spanish cattle. The descendants of those cattle finally made their way to Texas in the 1600s as part of the Spanish mission development scheme. Over the years those cattle that escaped from the abandoned missions and from failed ranches roamed and multiplied until millions grazed wild in Texas. The breed had learned to adapt to the climate, the varied vegetation, scarcity of water, the Indians, and freedom. They were free for the taking, if you could catch them.[12]

Allen, Lubbock, and Briscoe often joined the other local ranchers to round up the wild cattle that roamed the area that one day would become Pasadena. A very sizable herd could be assembled for very little cost. Since there were no fences on the range, the only barriers to the migration of the cattle were natural ones such as Galveston Bay, Clear Creek, and Buffalo Bayou. Horse Pen Bayou down near Clear Lake was named for a natural trap where wild horses could be driven and then captured. Many of the cattle were so wild that they would hide from riders in thickets and only venture out at night to graze. Occasionally moonlight roundups were organized and all of the ranchers in the area would participate. If the army needed horses, a special roundup was staged. Most roundups would last for days and would cover large areas of the region. Sam Allen and friends frequently travelled as far west as the Brazos River in search of unbranded cattle and horses.[13]

In those days there was little need for beef in Houston and Galveston since both towns were relatively small and there was plenty of supply in the countryside. There was a slaughter house in Houston that wanted hides and tallow for export shipment. Since it was difficult to preserve the beef in any sizable quantity, the meat was virtually useless. For Allen to survive in the cattle business he had to look for other markets. Galveston offered a slightly better beef market since it was the larger of the two cities, and the cattle could also be shipped by boat to New Orleans and the East Coast. To get to Galveston the cattle had to be driven to Virginia Point and put on sailboats to cross West Bay to Galveston Island. When the winds and tides were favorable only three to seven head could be crossed at a time. Another choice, and a better way to improve profits would be to drive the cattle on a long and tedious overland trip directly to the bigger port market at New Orleans where those that survived would bring a higher price.[14]

Sam was committed to his growing cattle business. He had learned much about commerical dealings from his friends Lubbock and Briscoe and as their interest took them into other ventures, Sam took over their place on the range. Although Briscoe was the first of the three to get into the cattle business, his vision was to introduce railroads into Texas. He turned his attention to the promotion of a railroad from Harrisburg to the Brazos River and ultimately to San Diego, California. Unfortunately Briscoe died in 1849, and never saw his dream come to pass. Allen and Lubbock continued in the cattle business, sometimes partnering and sometimes alone. By 1855 Lubbock claimed to be the largest cattle owner between the Brazos and the Trinity. However, Lubbock's destiny was in government and he reentered the political arena in 1856 when he helped organize the Democratic Party in Texas. The course of his history was reaffirmed with his election to the office of lieutenant governor in 1857 and eventually governor in 1861.

Even though their paths parted for the time being, Lubbock and Allen remained lifelong friends.[15]

Allen prospered and expanded his ranching operations by getting more into the cattle buying and shipping business. He made special arrangements with the Charles Morgan Ship Lines to ship cattle on their steamers out of Galveston. The arrangement with Morgan evolved into an almost exclusive control on the cattle-water shipping business. Many ranchers found it easier to sell direct to Allen instead of trying to drive the cattle overland to New Orleans. Sometimes Allen did not have to go very far to purchase the cattle he needed for shipment. The Dobie brothers, Sterling and Robert, lived on their father's Mexican land grant on Middle Bayou several miles southeast of the Allen Ranch. Sam purchased 2,500 head from them for $8,000 in 1857. Since the Dobies participated in cattle roundups in the area, these cattle were probably some of those that roamed the southern area of what was to be Pasadena a hundred years later. It was Robert's grandson, J. Frank Dobie, that would become the leading Texas author on ranching, cowboys, and the Wild West.[16]

Allen would drive his captured and purchased herds of cattle to Buffalo Bayou where they would be loaded on barges for the trip to Galveston. The loading dock was located just east of his home near the mouth of Sims Bayou. With the proceeds from each sale additional herds were purchased. Those cattle ready for market, called beeves, were shipped and those too young or light were branded and put out to graze until they were marketable. The hides from those cattle that did not survive to be sold were processed at Allen's Tannery, the first on Buffalo Bayou.[17]

Between the roundups and the cattle drives there was something always going on. Colonel James Morgan of nearby Morgan's Point was experimenting with agricultural crops and cattle. He was the first to import a Durham Shorthorn Bull in an effort to upgrade the quality and weight of Texas cattle. Neighbor and then lieutenant-governor, Lubbock was president of the Texas Stock Importing Company during the fifties. He and others were importing various breeds of cattle and occasionally got involved with other animals. For a while Lubbock experimented with Asiatic chickens and although he felt the project was successful, he never sold a chicken. In 1858 he agreed to pasture about 40 camels imported into Galveston. The U. S. Army and others were experimenting with the animal as a beast of burden across the barren southwest. The camels were brought by barge to Allen's place at the mouth of Sims Bayou to be driven to Lubbock's nearby ranch. On a bet from Lubbock's brother-in-law, Allen lassoed one of the camels and brought him down to the ground. The camels were at Lubbock's for about a year and were considered a local attraction. Occasionally their Arab caretakers would ride them six miles to Houston and create quite a sensation in town.[18]

As was the custom in those days, the county commissioners would appoint a committee of local residents, called a jury of view, to designate the location of roads in the area. The Harrisburg-Lynchburg Road was not much more than a set of ruts over the prairie and periodically the county would reaffirm its general location. Sam and others petitioned the county commissioners in 1857 to better mark the Harrisburg-Lynchburg road. As the Olmsted brothers described the road in 1854:

> Leaving Houston, we followed a well-marked road, as far as a bayou, beyond which we entered a settlement of a half-a-dozen houses, that, to our surprise, proved to be the town of Harrisburg. . . . . . . Taking a road here, by direction, which, after two miles, only ran "up a tree," we were obliged to return for more precise information. At noon, we were ferried over a small bayou by a shining black bundle of rags, and instructed by her as follows: "Yer see dem two tall pine in de timber ober dar cross de parara, yander. Yer go right straight da, and da yer'll see de trail somewar. Dat ar go to Lynchburg . . . . " Two miles across the grass we found the pines and a trail, which continually broke into cattle-paths, but by following the general course, we duly reached San Jacinto, a city somewhat smaller than Harrisburg, laid out upon the edge of the old battle-field.

Sam volunteered to build a bridge across Sims Bayou himself since it was the only deep bayou between Harrisburg and San Jacinto. In order to reimburse him for the expenses, the county allowed him to charge a toll. In 1866 he charged 10 cents for a man and horse, 30 cents for a horse and buggy, and 40 cents for a two horse and buggy rig.[19]

The Galveston, Houston & Henderson Railroad (G.H.& H.) was completed in 1860 as the first rail line to connect Houston and Galveston. Since the tracks ran through the middle of his property in the Callahan and Vince Survey, Allen quickly took advantage of this new transporatation alternative. He built cattle loading pens along the track south of its crossing on Sims Bayou. Even though the train only ran between Houston and Galveston, it made shipping cattle to the Morgan shipping docks in Galveston a lot easier than depending on the old Virginia Point ferry, and a lot faster than transshipping them by barge from Allen's dock on Buffalo Bayou. Additionally, by utilizing this convenient and quick transportation system it would be easier for Sam to maintain business offices in Houston and Galveston. Previously he had to travel by horseback or steamboat to get to these cities. Historically, commercial transportation in Texas had centered around access to navigable waters. With the introduction of railroads into Texas, transportation patterns, and later land development patterns, would change. It was the subsequent introduction of another railroad line that lead to the establishment of Pasadena. Sam sensed this important transportation change and moved his ranch headquarters from its Buffalo Bayou location to one nearer to the railroad.

Sam and Rebecca built a large two-story square frame house between Berry Bayou and the new rail line. It was quite a change from their first home. Their children, Flurney, Samuel Ezekiel, Charles Dell, and little Rebecca Jane had filled that little cabin to overflowing. Although the new house was not fancy by Galveston standards, it was a castle to them. They fancied it their plantation home and called it "Dumont." At first the railroad simply referred to the stop at the Allen Ranch as "Allen's Station" but changed it later to "Dumont" to avoid confusion with the Allen Brothers and the depot at Houston. The rail siding continued to be called Dumont even later when the town of South Houston was established at that location. Rebecca Allen also liked the convenience of a train stopping at her front door. She would travel to Galveston to do her shopping there since the Island City was the largest city in the state and the financial and fashion capital of the Southwest. In 1860 its population of 7,307 was almost double that of Houston, which only had 4,845 people.[20]

Sam's business had grown and prospered because of his control of shipping. With Morgan's steamers he had monopolized the water transportation of cattle to New Orleans and other Gulf ports. However, Sam's business slowed appreciably

Open Ranges (1842-1892) 11

when Texas joined the Secessionist movement early in March of 1861. Following the shelling of Fort Sumter, South Carolina, on April 12, the Gulf shipping ports became a target themselves for Union retaliation. Many of the Morgan Ship Line's vessels were impounded in other Southern ports and coastal shipping all but ceased. By July the United States Navy began a series of blockades that hampered all shipments out of Galveston. The city of Galveston came under U. S. naval control in October 1862 but was retaken by Confederate troops three months later on January 1, 1863.[21]

With the war came an increase in the local demand for beef, but a shortage of cowboys to bring the cattle to market. With scarce supplies the price increased to the point that the indigents of Galveston sought civil and military help in obtaining beef. As a major supplier of beef, Allen volunteered to help the indigents by opening a butcher stall in the city on July 1, 1864 and selling beef at 25 cents per pound to certified indigents. Sam had recently formed the enterprise of Allen, Poole & Company with Valentine B. and William D. Poole, both of Galveston. William Poole, 49, was an ex-sailor turned butcher who had moved to Galveston in 1846.[22]

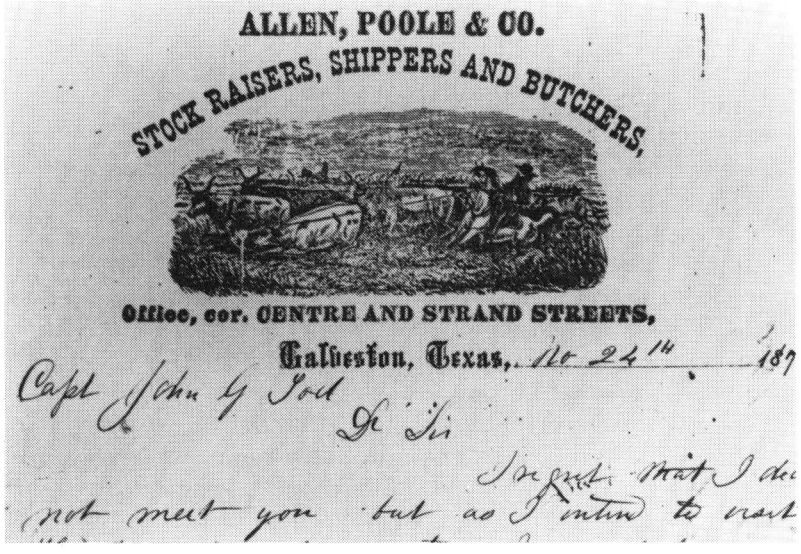

Working through various cattle partnerships, Sam W. Allen greatly expanded his ranching empire.

After the end of the War Between the States in 1865, Allen, Poole & Company began to rapidly expand. The unattended herds in Texas during the war drifted south towards the Gulf and ran wild on the coastal plains. The cattle population in the area increased greatly with this uncontrolled migration and an unchecked birth rate. The old cotton and harvest crop economy of Texas and the South was labor intensive and suffered during the war. With the freeing of the slaves, plantings decreased further and few crops-in-the-field greeted the returning veterans. To raise much-needed cash, many farmers and veterans quickly took to the saddle to round up mavericks and convert them to gold. Many of these new cowboy entreprenuers met Sam Allen.

In the Texas markets the cattle were worth only about $4 a head, but in the beef-hungry booming North they were worth $30 to $40 a head. Allen had the cash and credit necessary to hire the returning veterans as cowboys to round up his cattle, or to purchase cattle from other ranchers. With his knowledge of shipping and the long-estab-lished exclusive arrangement with the Morgan Ship Lines, Sam could ship his cattle directly to the profitable markets at New Orleans and in Cuba. Also, with his extensive grazing pastures, Sam could afford to hold cattle until they were of optimum age and size for market. However, the demand was such that most purchases were loaded directly onto ships that sailed regularly for Allen, Poole & Company.[23]

One of those returning veterans was A. B. "Shanghai" Pierce. Shanghai was a huge man with a booming voice and an ego to match. At six foot five inches and 250 pounds, he was a bigger-than-life individual who worked hard at being a successful cattleman. He began rounding up strays around Matagorda in the Colorado River bottomlands. Although he could sell his cattle to the local rendering plant for their hides and tallow, Shanghai realized that there was more profit in selling the cattle to the meat market at New Orleans. With financial backing from Danny Sullivan of Indianola he would put together a herd and trail it through the Lousiana swamps to New Orleans. He called his cattle "Sea Lions" because they could swim the bays, bayous, and swamps with little trouble. Shanghai soon realized that he was doing all of the work and Sullivan was taking most of the profits. Upon looking around for a better way to get his cattle to market, Shanghai contracted to ship on one of Allen's freighters. The deal worked so well, and the profits, in Cuba, so great, that the shipping firm of Allen & Pierce was formed in 1867. This arrangement greatly increased Sam's area of activity. Pierce would acquire the cattle, by roundup or purchase, and Allen would get them to market. It was not very long before an Allen & Pierce shipment would leave every 10 days from the new docks at Palacios with about every brand registered in South Texas.[24]

Shanghai Pierce estimated that between himself and Allen, Poole & Company, they owned at one time more than 100,000 cattle in southeast Texas. In just a few short years after the end of the war Pierce had struck it rich in cattle. He once claimed to have branded upwards of 20,000 cattle in a year. Naturally he made enemies with other cattlemen chasing the same mavericks. In June 1871 Pierce felt the need to leave the state in order to avoid implication in a Matagorda County hanging. He turned to his friend and partner for a quick buyout and Sam obliged. For $110,000 in gold a quick cattle trade was consummated and Shanghai spent the next 18 months relaxing in Kansas.[25]

Competing with the cattle shipping business were the hide and tallow factories along the Gulf Coast. Since the beginning of the republic the hide and tallow business had been the major export product for the cattle industry. The use of mechanical energy was brought into the South after the war and applied to the cattle rendering business. To these operations beef was a byproduct that was either discarded or some small amount salted down or pickled in barrels for shipment to the West Indies. Seeking to expand the market for the cattle he owned, Sam Allen, with partners Valentine B. Poole and William Poole expanded into the tallow business in 1868. They built a factory in Pooleville, a suburb on the western side of the city of Galveston and used steam to skin and boil the carcasses. Charles Morgan of Morgan Ship Lines provided financing for the construction of the operation. Since this plant only used the tallow and hide of the animal, P. Cone & Company built a plant next door to use the remainder of the meat for packaging.[26]

The Gulf Coast region of Texas was not the only area benefiting from the increased demand for beef. Wranglers and ranchers in central Texas rounded up cattle and trailed them north to Missouri and then Kansas to the railheads there for shipment to the East. It only took about 10 men to drive several thousand head of cattle, so it was cheaper to trail the cattle to these markets and reduce the shipping costs than to load them on the nearest Texas railroad. Since the federal troopers were moving the Indians off the plains and buffalo had become all but extinct, there was plenty of grassland for the cattle to graze on on their way to market. The era of the great trail drives began. This period in cattle history did not diminish the continued growth of the Allen Ranch. In fact, Sam's son would later add another facet to the ranch's operation in order to benefit from the growing cattle ranches of the Great Plains.[27]

Even though Sam's business was growing, he did not forget old friendships. Frank Lubbock had served as governor, gone off to the war, been captured, returned to his burned out home, lost his Negro slaves, had to sell most of his cattle to pay off old debts, and had lost his little remaining money in a beef-packing venture. Allen purchased Lubbock's 1,300-acre ranch in 1871 to provide Lubbock with some working capital, and then hired him to represent Allen, Poole & Company and their New York and Texas Beef Preserving Company. The relationship worked very well and Lubbock secured contracts for the company as the results of a trip to Europe.[28]

Although Allen's dominate business was the buying, shipping, and subsequently selling of cattle his resident herd continued to grow. Pierce and others would provide Allen with branded cattle from yearlings on up. Since the best age to sell cattle was at four years old, Allen's growing herds of necessity contained many too young to go to market. Allen began acquiring more pasture land to graze the cattle on until they were ready for market. He purchased land contiguous to his other holdings or acquired land with water rights. He began a program of fencing some pasture areas so that he could contain and segregate herds for various reasons. Because of the size of his operation, he also obtained grazing pastures in Galveston, Fort Bend, Liberty, Ellis, and Brazoria counties.[29]

By 1872 Sam found it necessary to maintain a residence in Galveston because of his business there. Between Pierce and other Gulf Coast cattlemen providing Allen with an ample supply and Lubbock and other sales representatives arranging contracts, Sam was rapidly expanding his operation. He was even too busy to maintain his toll bridge and sold it to the county in 1871. On September 19, 1873, the stock market crashed and closed for 10 days. By year's end five thousand businesses had failed and soup kitchens sprang up in most of the towns across the nation. To most everyone's surprise, including Sam Allen, Allen, Poole & Company failed in August of 1874. One of the minor interest owners in the company had exercised his check writing authority and had withdrawn $300,000 from the Galveston bank account and left for Honduras. Although Allen had an excellent reputation for honest and fair dealing, the financial drain on the company put it into receivership. The filing for bankruptcy was signed by the copartners at the time, S. W. Allen, Valentine B. Poole, William Poole, James H. Lockhart, and W. O. Tift, and read in part: "whereas said parties of the first part have been engaged in extensive and complicated business and have become embarassed therein and unable to pay promptly all of their creditors . . . ." J. Dyer of Union Marine & Fire Insurance Company of Galveston specifically felt at the time of the bankruptcy that Allen was being duped by his partners.[30]

That same year Colonel Charles Morgan entered into an agreement to take over the dredging of Buffalo Bayou so that his ships could dock in Houston instead of Galveston. Although Morgan had previously enjoyed a preferential relationship with the Galveston Wharf Company, he felt that the company had unreasonably increased their wharfage fees. Several years earlier Indianola had raised its wharfage fees, and Morgan had moved his base for shipping operations to Galveston. He also realized that railroads would eventually offer effective competition to some of his shipping routes and that Houston offered less restrictions to his new plan of developing a transshipping network between rail and ship. Since he had shipped from Allen's docks on Buffalo Bayou near Sims Bayou, Morgan decided to establish his wharf facility opposite the mouth of Sims Bayou so that he could utilize its deep water as a turning basin. He named his docks *Clinton* in honor of the ship that he had most frequently used to pick up Allen's cattle. Morgan's crews finished dredging Buffalo Bayou to 10 feet on April 21, 1876, and by September 11 they had completed the construction of a railroad line from Clinton to connnect with all of the railroads serving Houston. For the first time Houston had direct rail access to coastal shipping without going through Galveston. Slowly the dream of a Port of Houston and a Houston Ship Channel was taking place. The increased railroad activity would result in the founding of the town of Pasadena and the ultimate realization of the Houston Ship Channel's potential would catapult Pasadena into the industrial age.[31]

The failure of Allen, Poole & Company did not put Sam Allen out of business. The processing plant at Poolesville was closed and over the next couple of years cattle and land were sold by the receiver of the bankrupt company. One of the purchasers was Bob Stafford of Columbus. The Stafford brothers were good friends of Sam Allen and ran their cattle operation generally east of Columbus. Bob Stafford purchased some of Allen's land and cattle from the Allen, Poole & Company receiver and then in 1883 sold it back to Sam Allen's son, Sam E. Allen. Within four and a half years the receivership was terminated and a profit returned to the estate. No one had lost money because they dealt with Sam Allen. What was remaining of the assets of the company were conveyed back to Sam W. Allen.[32]

Even during the administration of the bankruptcy estate, Sam Allen continued to operate his ranch. There was constantly a problem with cattle on the tracks of the G. H. & H. railroad that ran through the ranch. Either the train was delayed or cattle were killed. Since the railroad company could not afford to fence its tracks, in 1875 Sam built 19 miles of fence along the east side of the right of way from Harrisburg to League City in order to keep his cattle off of the tracks. Cedar was readily available along Middle Bayou near Clear Creek and it made excellent posts for the type of fence that Sam liked to build; "stud horse high, bull strong and hog proof." It would have four rails built from "Kulkyshoe hert lumber" (heart wood of the Calcasieu pine from Louisiana) and a top rail wide enough that a person could walk the entire distance without stepping on the ground. In fact, Allen had started his fence building program several years earlier when he had his foreman Josh Abbott previously build a wooden fence from Buffalo Bayou to Allen's "Dumont" homestead and over to the Lubbock place. A gate was placed in the fence at the Harrisburg-Lynchburg Road with a large sign above instructing that it should be closed at all times.[33]

The area east of the railroad fence and the fence built in 1869 from Buffalo Bayou to the tracks on Sims Bayou was known as "Allen Pasture" and ran all the way to Galveston Bay. This area contained about 100,000 acres for the cattle to graze on. On the west side of the tracks there was an enclosed pasture called the "Billie McFaddin Pasture." There were loading pens on the railroad at Dumont and at the Old Jackson Place on Buffalo Bayou for shipment on Morgan's ship *Clinton*. There

Open Ranges (1842-1892)

Branding was a spring time chore. Upwards of 1,200 calves were branded at a single roundup.

were also pens at Old Summit (near where Ellington Air Base was later built, south of the future town of Genoa), which were used to brand calves. Ten hands could brand upwards to 1,200 calves at a time there.[34]

Sam was a few years ahead of his time with fencing. Texas was an open range state and a person did not have to own the land in order to take advantage of its grazing capabilities. A landowner was not required to fence his land to keep his cattle contained, so the Allen cattle roamed free over large sections of the upper Gulf Coast. Sam did purchase the land where he maintained watering holes, corrals, and loading pens. Because of his need to separate his herds for branding, shipping, and general pasturing, he began a program of fence building. Barbed wire was introduced into the state around 1876, but was not accepted until after 1880. Some ranchers used the wire to keep other people out, including the rightful owners of the land, and competitors' cattle from water. In about 1883 a Fence Cutting War errupted and it took the state legislature to resolve the issues. Fencing was not required, but the use and abuse of fencing was regulated.[35]

With the move of the Morgan Ship Line to Buffalo Bayou from Galveston, Allen was in a better position to ship cattle. The increased depth of the Bayou could accommodate more ships and more ships could be made available because Morgan now maintained a regular service to his new wharfs. With Morgan's greater reliance on rail and the increasing numbers of railroad lines serving the Houston area, Allen also turned to shipping more of his cattle on the railroads. The G. H. & H. Railroad had been built on a five foot, six inch gauge and northern shipments on this line had to be unloaded and reloaded at Harrisburg into standard gauge cars before they could move to northern and eastern markets. In 1876 the track width was changed to the standard gauge, allowing quick and easy interchange of cars with other railroads. Rail was proving to be the better way to ship cattle since it took less time to get the cattle to market and less damage was done to the stock. For the Allen Ranch, the locomotive would drop off a load of empty cattle cars on its way to Galveston. The cowboys would pull the empties into place by hand and load them out, as many as 25 cars in succession. On its return trip from Galveston, the engine would pick up the loaded cars.[36]

Sam Ezekiel Allen took over the operation of the Allen Ranch in 1881 from his father. Sam W. Allen was 55 years old at the time and Sam E. was 33. Like Shanghai Pierce, Sam E. was a big man, six foot two, and a bit stout. He had been born on the ranch in 1848 and grew up working cattle. In 1876 he married Rosa Chrestie Lum and for a while they lived in the original ranch house near Sims Bayou on the Harrisburg-Lynchburg Road. Later they built a new home nearby. In June Sam E. bought 5,070 acres of the ranch back from the Harris County tax collector for one year's taxes and interest, $58.50. In 1883 he bought back the land and cattle that Bob Stafford had purchased. In 1884 he began purchasing more land because the cattle business was changing.[37]

The Longhorn was the indigenous cattle breed for the Texas ranchers. They were an incredibly durable breed, but they were rather lightweight animals. James Morgan had imported a Durham bull in the early 1840s to try to improve the weight capacity of the local cattle. Unfortunately most non-domestic cattle were suspectible to Texas tick fever and a good crossbreed was hard to establish. With an increasing resident breeding herd, fenced pastures, and easier transportation to market, Sam Allen and others again began considering the upgrading of the breed. With others he looked to the cattle of India that had proven its abilities to survive a broad range of hardships. The "Brimmuhs" sweated all over their body instead of just at the nose and the salt residue discouraged the fever-carrying ticks. In 1878 Shanghai Pierce and Capt. J. N. Keeran purchased the first Indian cattle (Brahmans) to enter the state. The Angus, Hereford, and Shorthorns (with Lavender Viscount breeding) also proved to be good breeds to improve the Longhorn strain.[38]

With good pastures, excellent water sources, mild winters, and a sizable herd, Sam E. expanded his focus to selling younger animals to West Texas ranchers who would themselves graze the cattle out to market weight. In addition to buying and fattening, Sam worked on improving the quality of calves thrown off by his mother herd. This required bringing in blooded stock, cross fencing breeding pens, and pasture rotation. And being on the coast, Allen still could ship beeves direct to Cuba. Annually he would sent 5,000 head south to that market.[39]

Sam E. Allen spent his entire life on the Allen Ranch. Under his control the ranch grew to over 15,000 acres in Harris County. Thousands of additional acres were held in nearby Galveston, Ft. Bend, and Brazoria counties.

Sam W. Allen had capitalized on the opportunities that Texas offered a young Tennessean. He had built an empire and his son was adding to it. By 1888 the Allen Ranch contained 15,000 acres in Harris County, 10,000 acres in Brazoria, and had grazing lands in Galveston and Fort Bend counties. Sam had started the ranch 45 years earlier with 350 acres, a good horse, a rope, and a branding iron. At age 62 he suffered a sunstroke while out campaigning for a political friend. He died in his home on August 8, 1888. He was buried at Harrisburg with many other great and loved Texians. His wife, Rebecca, moved to Harrisburg and then to Washington, D. C., to live with her daughter Rebecca Jane (Mrs. J. A.) Stubbs.[40]

Sam and Rosa Allen's ranch headquarters, named "Oaklawn." It was the center for many social events with its 40-acre front yard.

The Allen ladies stand in front of "Oaklawn." The lady in black is Rebecca Jane (Thomas) Allen, one of the first children born in Austin's colony.

Sam E. and Rosa Lum Allen had built their home near the original Allen homeplace on Buffalo Bayou and Sims Bayou. It was a large 15- room colonial home modeled after the old Lum Plantation house in Natchez, Mississippi. They named their place "Oaklawn" and it became a very popular social center. It was quite a showplace, with its 40- acre "front yard," the extensive landscaping, running tap water in each room (a good 40 years ahead of the times), tennis courts, and a private horse racing facility. Guests would arrive by carriage, or by excursion boat. However it would be awhile before screens for the windows would became available in Houston, so everyone had to sleep under mesquito nets to survive the nights![41]

With an interest in Houston's business community and having a great appreciation for transportation, Sam E. was supportive of the idea for a railroad line along the south side of Buffalo Bayou. Earlier in 1883 the Galveston, Colorado & Santa Fe line had built through Allen's property in the Prentiss and Herrera surveys and had provided an alternate shipper for Allen's cattle. By 1890 there was some speculation concerning a possible Bayline railroad, especially when John H. Burnett, a railroad builder and owner from Galveston, began acquiring land along a probable right of way. L. F. Allien had platted part of the old Colonel James Morgan homesite at Morgan's Point in 1888 and had convinced others to establish a town they called La Porte on adjoining property. Houston and La Porte investors were promoting the La Porte, Houston & Northern Railroad (LP H. & N.) from Harrisburg, through Allen's ranch to the new community on Galveston Bay. At about the same time period a group of Galveston investors were promoting the North Galveston, Houston & Kansas City Railroad (N.G. H. & K.C.) as an alternate route out of Galveston to break Jay Gould's control of the Galveston rail traffic. These two lines were to meet at the mouth of Clear Creek (Clear Lake) on Galveston Bay and provide through service from Galveston to Houston and northward. This new line would even be more convenient for Allen since it would pass near his house at Oaklawn and allow him closer supervision of his shipments. Like his father had done earlier on the G. H. & H. line, Sam insisted that a station be designated at his ranch headquarters so that he could also load his cattle there. Sam would call his station, "El Buey."[42]

The cattle industry had changed in many ways since Sam's father started the ranch 50 years earlier. The changes had been relatively slow and the cowboy in the saddle had hardly noticed the difference. The daily routines were the same, but now there were black cowboys on the ranch. Former Negro slaves and their descendants now worked as cowboys and their numbers were increasing as the Anglo and Hispanic cowboys moved on to ranges in the south and west. Still, Allen's men rode out with their chuck wagon several times a year to work the cattle. If they were rounding up the cattle east of the G. H. & H. tracks in "Allen's Pasture," they would only be out for a few weeks. If they were working the range west of the tracks, they could travel as far as the Colorado River and be out for several months, eating out of the chuck wagon and sleeping on the ground. Allen still regularly purchased herds and his cowboys would round up all of the cattle bearing the purchased brand. Calves and wild cattle collected on the rides would be branded.[43]

No matter where you rode on the Allen Ranch area in the early 1890s, you did not see a lot of people. The area was mostly tall prarie grass surrounded at the water's edge with magnolia, cedar, or oak trees. There were some new faces in the area around the ranch's headquarters, and more fencing. Just to the east of the Allen Ranch house was the old Jackson place were Allen had his ship-loading pen and dock. Next to the Jackson place, the old Evans place had recently changed hands after W. A. "Gus" Evans had ranched there for about 30 years. He had fenced the land north of the Harrisburg-Lynchbrug Road between Vince's Bayou and Cotton Patch Bayou and pastured cattle on it. His daugter, Lizzie Evans Clardy sold the land in 1890 to J. H. Burnett of Galveston. Burnett did not live on the land, but did run some cattle and had the hay cut. There were a few other small ranches along Buffalo Bayou between there and the town of San Jacinto. Dr. N. P. Dolen and his family had been there for 23 years and the Marsh kids had raised themselves on the family homestead after their parents passed away 32 years earlier.[44]

If the cowboys made it to the old battleground at San Jacinto, they could stop at the little town there at the confluence of Buffalo Bayou and the San Jacinto River. Appropriately the town was named San Jacinto. The Allen cowboys had been coming to this area since the days of Frank Lubbock to round up strays. The town of Lynchburg was across the river and could be reached by the ferry that had carried travelers across the San Jacinto River since the early 1830s. With about 178 people and a schoolhouse, Lynchburg was the bigger town. Although San Jacinto had also been in existence since the 1830s, only a few families still lived in the community. Perhaps it did not help that there was another town named San Jacinto located upriver near Huntsville. Living in or near the community were the Wards, Mohrs, Coles, and Habermehls. Stafford Ward was one of the many young men of the area that had worked for Sam W. Allen from time to time.[45]

James Morgan had operated his plantation "Orange Grove" on Morgan's Point, so there was little need to ride up that way. After Morgan's death, Captain L. F. Allien had purchased the property in 1885 and was trying to promote some bayview homesite sales. Captain Nelson, the Edwards, Pizzitolas, Irvins, and Dudleys had places up there. The cowboys now also avoided the area since some investors were laying out a townsite to be called La Porte and erecting a few buildings around Dr. John Beasley's place. Dr. Beasley was a blind doctor who had lived in the area for a long time. Along Galveston Bay, between Dr. Beasley's and the little community of Red Bluff, some cattle might be found. Red Bluff was another town where the cowboys could stop for some supplies. It had a population of about 100, a post office, school, church, and Idlebrook's general store. J. P. Compton, Ed P. Senreau, and Charles Derrick also lived in town. The community just developed several years earlier without any real plan. Downtown was just a couple of buildings and the rest of the town was spread out on nearby farms. The same was true for Morris' Cove a little further down the bay near the mouth of Clear Creek. Ritson Morris settled the area in 1830 and a small community grew up around the homes of his children. Mr. A. Palms had a small store and there was a school for the children. Reverend Peter Nicholson lived nearby along with Alfred Menard, Ed Brantly, Richard Larabee, William Robertson and their families. C. E. Gregory had his old slave plantation nearby, but he lived in Houston.[46]

Morris' Cove was as far southeast as you could go since the area was bounded by Galveston Bay and Clear Creek. Moving westward the cowboys encountered Taylor's Lake and then Mud Lake, both off of Clear Lake. At Mud Lake there was another small community by the name of Killkare. It wasn't much more than a loading point for the farmers in the area. The schoolhouse for the community was located a mile or two north, just off the Harrisburg-Red Bluff wagon trail. It was known as the Middle Bayou school. Thomas Dodson and James Martyn, a couple of Englishmen, and their families were the core of the prairie community. The Ballentines and Gozman brothers lived nearby. Having cleared this community, there was little left to encounter before the wranglers returned home. Jordan and Emily Henry had recently purchased land and lived slightly north of the Middle Bayou community. The Dobie brothers were gone; Robert had drowned in Middle Bayou in 1857 and left a wife with three children and another on the way. Sterling got very despondent over the turn of events about that time and took everyone to Live Oak County where he continued to ranch.[47]

There were several natural traps where cattle could be driven and branded or assembled into a herd. Horse Pen Bayou gots its name for one such trap. It was easy to round up the cattle that had been herded into the U-shaped area formed by Horse Pen and Middle bayous. Further up river on Middle Bayou, just north of Willow Springs Gully and near the Red Bluff road, there was a constructed pen for branding called "Round Point." Allen had purchased the land so that he could build a permanent corral here since the site was about in the middle of the area known as Allen's Pasture. To the southwest there was the larger constructed branding pen at "Old Summit" on the G. H. & H. railroad line. From here the crew could either head north to home if they were through, or cross the tracks and work their way south or west if there were more cattle to collect or to round up. Once a year a large herd was driven to the 10,000-acre pasture in Brazoria to spend the winter. In the spring the herd had to be rounded up, calves branded, and the cattle driven back to Harris County.[48]

To the cowboys, each day was pretty much the same. They lived from sunup to sunset and did not note the subtle changes that were occuring around them. It would be years before ranching would fade from the area, but the events were in motion. It was simply a matter of time before the farmer would claim the land.

II

Settlement (1893–94)

In 1837 Merriweather Woodson Smith tried to start a new town community on the William Vince Survey. He had hoped to capitalize on the flow of immigrants to the new Republic of Texas. He failed, and his town, Buffaloe, never became a reality. Fifty-three years later, Colonel John H. Burnett of Galveston again tried to establish a townsite on the Vince Survey, just east of the Allen Ranch headquarters. It took him three years to get his plan together and with the dedication of Charles R. Munger, Pasadena was founded. The first lot was sold on December 31, 1892.[1]

The opportunity for the creation of Pasadena began when the community of La Porte was conceived in the late 1880s. Captain Leon F. Allien had purchased the old James Morgan plantation at Morgan's Point and adopted Morgan's dream for a new town on Galveston Bay. Morgan's "New Washington" project was effectively destroyed by Santa Anna's forces in 1836. Allien interested the principals of the Interior Land and Immigrant Company of Denver, Colorado, in promoting a new town. Ira R. Holmes (president, and also with the Land and Navigation Department of the Santa Fe Railroad), Col. A. M. York (former state senator from Kansas), J. H. York (brother to A. M. York and a nurseryman from Des Moines, Iowa), Tom Lee (passenger agent for the Oregon Railroad & Navigation Company), and Mr. Thayer (former Governor of Nebraska) were experienced town developers. They were impressed with the beauty and potential of the site. They dubbed their new town, La Porte.

La Porte was to be a commercial town, drawing both upon commercial transportation business and agricultural products. Compared to the Northern states, La Porte was a tropical paradise. The homestead exemption laws of Texas offered financial protection to the Northern farmers who had lost their farms through foreclosure. The availability of cheap land was attractive to immigrants. The climate and soil were ideal for fertile farms. The location of La Porte on Galveston Bay provided better potential port facilities and shipping advantages than either Galveston or Houston. And the developers were experienced with railroads and knew the value of an interconnecting line with Houston, Galveston, and the Northern markets. They proposed the construction of a rail line from Houston, through La Porte, and north across San Jacinto Bay. It was the proposed construction of this rail line that opened the land south of Buffalo Bayou to a new wave of town development in the early 1890s.

John Howell Burnett was born in Tennessee in 1830 and came to Texas in 1846 to fight with General Winfield Scott in the war between the United States and Mexico. He returned to his home in Georgia and was awarded a colo-nelcy in the state troops by the governor for his gallantry in the war. While travelling through Texas he was impressed with the opportunity that he saw there and returned with his family in 1854 after serving two years as sheriff of Chattooga County, Georgia. Two years after his arrival at Crockett, in Houston County, Burnett was elected to the Texas

John H. Burnett knew the value of railroads to land development. He bought 3,328 acres and drew up the plans for Pasadena.

House of Representatives where he served two terms and then was elected to the state senate in 1860. He resigned in 1861 to fight for the Confederacy in the War Between the States with the rank of colonel. He saw action in Arkansas and Louisiana. After the war he returned to Crockett, but moved to Galveston in 1866. He engaged in the commission business with W. B. Wall under the name of Burnett & Wall and then under J. H. Burnett & Co.. By the early 1870s Burnett became involved in the construction business. Beginning in 1875 he built 65 miles of the Gulf, Colorado & Santa Fe Railroad from Galveston to Richmond and then built considerable portions of several other railroad lines. Besides construction, he was active in promoting, financing, operating, and owning railroads. Realizing the economic effect that railroads had on new areas, Burnett acquired extensive land holdings in the Gulf Coast region. In 1877 he completed the construction of the Tremont Hotel and was one of its owners for several years. With the death of his wife in 1886 he began to concentrate more on his real estate business.[2]

When Burnett became aware of the proposed La Porte railroad his interests turned to Harris County real estate. The new rail line would be enough by itself to interest investors in purchasing property along the right of way. However, a group of Galveston and Minneapolis investors were considering a new rail line from Galveston to Kansas City via the city of North Galveston at Edward's Point on Galveston Bay. It would be logical for these two lines to connect at La Porte and thus increase the traffic potential on the Houston to La Porte section of the road.[3]

Beginning in 1889 Burnett began purchasing Harris County real estate. After purchasing several parcels in the city of Houston, he turned his attention to rural land in the vicinity of existing or future railroads. Sam E. Allen owned the largest tracts of land southeast of Harrisburg and Houston and also along the existing railroad tracks. His land was not for sale since he was using it in his Allen Ranch operation and he was living on the piece that Burnett would have wanted. Adjacent to the Allen Ranch and along the probable right of way of the La Porte railroad was the William Vince survey. Lizzie Evans had been raised on the property that her parents farmed and ranched. After her mother died Lizzie inherited most of the property, married, and moved to Kentucky. Burnett paid

$11,000 for the 3,328 acres on March 19, 1890, with $4,000 in cash and $7,000 by notes.⁴

Burnett continued to purchase land in Harris County and over the next three years he had acquired over 16,000 acres. His land holdings that would become the town of Pasadena represented only about a quarter of that total. In fact, the Pasadena project was not of primary concern to him. Colonel Burnett had acquired extensive land holdings along the G. H. & H. Railroad south of the Allen Ranch and was working on plans for another community to be called Genoa. He had purchased about 3,000 acres around the little community of Summit, named such because it was the highest point between Houston and Galveston. In August of 1891 Burnett had pursuaded the G. H. & H. Railroad to relocate its siding from Summit to a nearby location he called Genoa. He also provided an acre for the location of a section house. Beside investment, Burnett had another reason to purchase the land along the G. H. & H. tracks. Burnett's daughter Ellen had been told to move inland for health reasons. Genoa, named for the Italian city of the same name, would be a respectable distance from the coast, yet easily accessible to Galveston and Houston by the railroad. Burnett built a ranch house southeast of the tracks for his daughter, her husband, J. O. Ross, and their two children, Pearl and Burnett.⁵

Meanwhile, Charles Russell Munger was having troubles with his Charles R. Munger Savings Bank in Newton, Kansas. A fi-

Charles R. Munger, who came to Pasadena from Kansas and fell in love with the area. It was his dedication that made the town survive.

nancial panic developed in 1889 with interest rates soaring to 24 percent, some even to 40 percent as a prolonged drought threatened the farming economy. Populist Mary Elizabeth Cylens Lease was urging the Kansas farmers to "raise less corn and more hell" against the Santa Fe Railroad and the loan companies since a third of the farm loans had been foreclosed on in the last 10 years. Munger had survived three runs on his bank by putting all of his personal money into the bank and selling stock to cover cash calls from his depositors. The survival of the bank cost him ownership control and he was forced to "retire" early in 1891. When most men think of retirement, Munger had to think about starting over. He and his wife were approaching 50 years of age, they had two young teenage children and their savings were gone. With a resilient optimism Munger traveled to Texas in the spring of 1891 to see firsthand the opportunity he had heard about.[6]

When Burnett and Munger met, their respective needs merged. Burnett had property that he wanted to sell and Munger needed to make money and believed that the Vince property had a great potential for farming. Munger returned to Newton with a Contract of Agency on Burnett's Vince league property and immediately set about forming a syndicate to purchase the entire property. He felt the land could be packaged and sold for a nice profit to some eastern capitalist. With attorney Spooner they formed a company and then travelled to Texas to look over the project. Since pear orchards were the fad at the time, they investigated the property for the purpose of fruit and truck farming. Munger wrote his wife in July of 1891 that the group was ready to take the land and that he would make $12,000 in commissions on the deal. Unfortunately Burnett was not able to get clear title to the property and did not mention it to his prospective purchasers. Burnett had financed his land purchases by giving notes in part payment and until he paid off the notes he could not sell any of the property. But the notes had been sold to a person who promptly died, and Burnett could not get a release on the land out of the estate. Burnett was forced to procrastinate on signing the contract and thus the project stymied.[7]

Although despondent, Munger stayed and got the rights to harvest hay from the property so that he would have some income. William Johnson had travelled to Texas with Munger and Spooner and also stayed, taking up residency in the only house on the property, possibly Vince's old home. Charles's wife, Avilda, and their children, Russell, age 15, and Edith, age 12, came to visit for a couple of weeks and stayed in the Johnson house, an "old time southern house with a wide hall through the center and a detached kitchen reached by walking a plank." During the hay-cutting operation the baled hay was stored in the house so the Mungers and Mr. Johnson each "shared" their respective rooms with the hay. Avilda and the children returned to Newton in November so that the children could return to school. Charles followed after the hay cutting was finished.[8]

Undaunted, Charles continued to travel between Newton and Texas. He did sell some land in the area and was still trying to make the Burnett deal work. Burnett traveled to New York in July 1892 and stopped in Newton for a couple of days on his trip home. Not missing an opportunity, Charles tried to sell Burnett one of the buildings in town. Like he did on the Vince property deal the year before, Burnett expressed his interest to go ahead but never completed the transaction. Meanwhile Munger continued to push the Kansas syndicate purchase proposal. He put together a marketing program and a brochure. He named his proposed town, Pasadena, for the town of Pasadena, California. Oddly enough, the village of "Indiana Colony" in California had changed its name to Pasadena about 1875 because the Post Office would not accept the former name. The name, PA-SA-DE-NA is a Chippewa (Ojibway) Indian name meaning, "Crown of the Valley." It was stated, that when spoken correctly and as punctuated, the name would "fall pleasantly on the ear." The renamed community promptly experienced a land boom that swelled its population to over 15,000 and began a Tournament of Roses parade in 1890 to emphasize the beauty and productivity of the valley region north of Los Angeles. Although Munger had never been to the town, he had read about its lush vegetation and perfect agricultural climate. This was exactly what he thought about the land in Texas and wanted to convey that same image to others. Even though Burnett stalled, time was on Charles's side. The plans for the railroad and for the competing communities were moving forward quickly and that would force Burnett to do something about his Vince property.[9]

The North Galveston, Houston and Kansas City Railroad (N.G. H. & K. C.) was chartered in June of 1892. The La Porte, Houston and Northern line (L.P. H. & N.) was chartered later that same year in October, with J. H. Tennant of Houston and

A. M. York, J. H. York, T. W. Lee, and A. O. Blackwell of La Porte as the principal backers. Within a month surveying had begun, the necessary right of ways were being secured and grading started for the tracks. Weekly the *Houston Daily Post* was reporting on the progress of both the La Porte and the North Galveston rail lines.[10]

La Porte was already an instant boom town with two hotels, the "Artesian" and the "Ballentine Hotel," under construction. The La Porte promoters had advertised at the Chicago World's Fair and round trip train tickets from the north were available at $15, with full reimbursement if land was purchased. Special excursion trains were organized and a representative of the La Porte Improvement Company would lead the delegation back to La Porte. Since the La Porte railroad was not yet built, getting the prospects to the new townsite took some organization. The excursionists were brought by train to Houston, where they could then be transported down Buffalo Bayou on L. F. Allien's boat, the *Eugene*, to La Porte. If they so decided, the excursionists could change trains in Houston and continue on towards Galveston on the G. H.& H. line. They could leave the train at Summit (now renamed Genoa) where they would be met by horse drawn hacks and travel the final 12-mile trip to La Porte in about two to three hours. Burnett had hoped to syphon off some purchasers at Genoa so he built a hotel for them to spend a night or two as they visited his ventures. Or the excursionists could continue on the train to Galveston were they would be met by Allien and boat up to La Porte, on the *Eugene*. The *Eugene* was regularly travelling between Houston and Galveston, taking a day each way. In addition to delivering mail between the cities, she was offering excursion round trips for one dollar. Naturally she stopped at La Porte on each trip. Although the Galveston side trip provided the travellers with a broader view of the farming potential of the Gulf Coast, it also exposed them to advertisement and promotions from other competing communities such as Websterville (later Webster), League City (also known intermittently as Clear Creek), and Alvin.[11]

City lots in La Porte went on sale January 1, 1892, for $30 each and many sales were recorded. Since the Texas Constitution forbid mortgages on homesteads, all sales were for cash. The developers had built fine homes for themselves in the town and were busy personally promoting the community. A post office had been opened, 22 acres were set aside for a city park, the first church built, a school opened, and the first baby born. The town already boasted a general store, a lumber company, and an attorney. It advertised the principal objectives of the community as: "(1) The building up of a great commercial center and leading harbor on the coast of Texas; (2) The establishing of a natural summer and winter resort; (3) The building of a manufacturing center for the Southwest; and (4) The establishing of an educational center second to none in the Southwest."[12]

Andrew J. Vick of Houston had been blocking up land on the east side of the Vince property by late 1891 for development as a townsite he later called Deepwater. With 5,636 acres to be platted, Vick was planning a community larger than Burnett's. Deepwater was designed around a large round park, which was to be the center of town, some farming plots, and bayou front residential lots. Not only did he pay twice as much per acre as did Burnett, but Vick discovered he had worse title problems. In order to be able to sell his land, Vick had to go to court to clear up the title to the property. Although not public, it was suspected that Burnett had some interest in Vick's project.[13]

News of the proposed railroad reached Simeon Henry West of Illinois early in 1892 and he too was impressed with the investment opportunity in Texas. He began buying land adjacent to Vick's for yet another new town development, his to be called Deer Park. West did not waste time in promoting his new venture. Even before he cleared title to his land he scheduled an excursion train for prospects from Galesburg, Illinois, and personally began selling: three lot minimums, $1,000, cash. On December 14, 1892, he executed over a dozen deeds. He laid out two parks, a depot site, and a reserve for construction of a hotel. In addition to his individual sales efforts, he had committed upwards to one half of his land to A. M. York of the La Porte Improvement Company for him to sell. York travelled to Galesburg early in 1893 and continued to execute deeds for land in Deer Park. Althought West owned much more land, he platted only 1,703 acres for his town. He filed the plats for the outlots of Deer Park on December 31, 1892, and for the town of Deer Park on March 3, 1893. The town of Deer Park was announced and a dozen sales closed before year-end. A hotel was also planned.[14]

Burnett finally paid off the balance of the purchase price on his Vince property on December 22, 1892. Nine days later, on December 31, he signed the first deed. Martin L. Hocker of

Kansas bought 20 acres in Burnett's subdivision of the Vince survey. He purchased Lot 10 in Block 18 per the "plat of the Deep Water Land & Town Company made by J. O. Davis, C. E.." He paid $300 in cash and $300 by note due in one year, with an interest rate of eight percent. As a part of the transaction, Hocker also picked up 42 acres previously belonging to Burnett just south of the Vince Survey for $630. The Pasadena parcel was obviously an investment since it was in the middle of the prairie, in the south central part of the plat, without water frontage and not near any roads or even the proposed railroad right-of-way.[15]

It is not known why Burnett decided to sell his land by the lot rather than in bulk to syndicates. Certainly S. H. West was setting a good example of selling individual parcels, even though afterwards he also sold to several syndicates. Perhaps the Kansas syndicate's offer had expired and Burnett wanted to get the land moving to attract other buyers or syndicates. Instead of requiring spot cash for the sale of lots as was required in La Porte and Deer Park, Burnett agreed to finance the sale of his land by taking a short-term note in part payment. Whatever the reason, Munger's dream of a quick, big commission vanished. If he was to make any money out of Pasadena, it would have to be lot by lot, and spread out over time. Even so, Charles still loved the land and felt that there was a future here for him.

While back in Newton on December 23, 1892, Munger wrote a letter to the editor of the Kansan newspaper describing Texas. That letter was also printed on the front page of the first edition of the *La Porte Chronicle*, on January 26, 1893. It read:

THE COAST COUNTRY

WHAT A PROGRESSIVE KANSAN THINKS ABOUT IT

Newton, Kan., Dec. 23, 1892—
Having just returned from the gulf coast, I thought I might tell your readers something of interest. I am more familiar with that part of the Texas gulf coast lying between Buffalo bayou, which empties into Galveston bay, and the Brazos river, which empties into the gulf about thirty miles west and south from Galveston. The

lands between these two rivers, and as far north as Houston, are known as coast lands. The whole of the land within the limits named is level prairie, sloping to the south; its soil varies from deep black to a whitish gray. The white soil works up nicely, but all such soil needs to be fertilized to produce good crops. The black soil is like the best Kansas soil and the grass appears to be the same. The climate is modified in both winter and summer by the gulf breeze. It is demonstrated that along the coast the climate and soil are right for growth of fruits, flowers, vegetables and grasses. Oats, corn, rice, hemp, flax, cotton and cane, all do exceedingly well, and are paying crops.

Of the fruits the most profitable so far demonstrated are the pear, peach, plum, apricot, nectarine, figs, grapes and strawberries. Blackberries and raspberries grow in profusion. The owners of some fruit farms of 10 acres have been offered as high as $2,000 per acre. Any fruit farm with orchard two years old sells readily at $200 per acres, and very many are changing hands.

Houston is a city of great commercial activity. Almost any business will pay well there.

I left there on the 17th of December. I saw growing in the fields radishes, cabbage, rutabagos, greens, potatoes, okra, peas, beans, onions, lettuce, turnips, and cauliflower. This is truly a land of flowers everwhere. The flower gardens were full of roses, dahlias, chrysanthemums and other varieties. I saw strawberries in blossom on the 11th of this month.

One can not realize all there is to that country without seeing it; seeing is believing. Take advantage of the excursion rates and run down to Houston, Galveston, La Porte or Pasadena or all of them. It will do you good.

I will cheerfully answer any questions so far as I am able.

¶ —Charles R. Munger

Burnett accepted the name Pasadena, and Munger began offering the land for sale and setting up a community. John Richey, Dr. W. W. Murphy, Charles W. Webster, Mr. Hoffman, and John F. Wafer came down from McPherson, Kansas with Munger late in January 1893. William Wiley and May Anderson had moved to the area recently and agreed to board overnight prospects. The Andersons were also from Kansas and had four children: Floyd, Ida M., Pearl, and Lucy. They even stocked a few provisions for a makeshift mercantile store. May was particularly helpful in that she really liked the area and could appreciate its good points. Even so, it would be six months before the Andersons would get around to buying their land. Munger was pleased to have the Andersons there since they were settlers, not investors, and there was now a place to put prospects up on the property since Burnett had not built, or even planned to build, a hotel.

On January 30, 1893, John Richey purchased 20 acres along the west side of Vince's Bayou, just south of the railroad right-of-way. He paid $500, $170 in cash and two notes for $165 each, at eight percent interest, one due in one year and the other due in two years. Officially he bought Blocks 88 and 89, according to the "plat of Deepwater Land & Town Company, being a subdivision of a part of Vince & Seymour Surveys in Harris County, and known as the town of Pasadena." For the first time, "Pasadena" was used legally to describe the area. Even though the deed referred to the plat, Burnett had not yet filed the plat to the town, and it would be several years before he would. Munger was inspired by the sale and knew that he had to at least stake the property so that he would have something better to show his friends and other prospects.[16]

Ira Leander "Lee" Pitts had arrived with his family in covered wagons from the Waxahachie, Texas, area and was looking for farm land. With six children, each barely two years apart, Lee and Lula needed some room to raise their growing family. When the surveyor did not show up on Monday, February 6, Charles headed to town with Lee Pitts to locate some tools to drill an artesian well. The next day the surveyor, Packard, showed up and started his work. Floyd Anderson helped him by carrying the stakes and was paid one dollar per day. Lee Pitts was satisfied with the development and purchased 20 acres for $600, part cash and part with a note. A week later he purchased another 10 acres. This tract was located adjacent on the west side to the first tract, so Lee now owned 30 acres to farm. This second, smaller piece was obviously to be his homestead since he paid $300 cash for the land. He built their house on the northeast corner of Fifth (Shaw) and Vince Streets on the western boundary of Pasadena.[17]

Shortly afterwards, Munger was back in McPherson organizing an excursion trip for area residents to his new project in Texas. He had been in Texas for several months and he was glad to be back home with his family in nearby Newton. Unfortunately, Kansas was in the midst of a blizzard while the temperatures in Texas were ranging from the low forties to the sixties. Thirteen thousand fruit trees were currently being set out in Deer Park. Charles felt that an excursion trip to Texas at this time would surely lead to more sales. But since things were coming together quickly on the Pasadena project, Charles did not stay in Kansas long. Munger felt that if he could get some visible signs of Pasadena on the ground, he might be able to syphon off a few of the buyers out of the excursionists from the north that were frequently touring the area. It had been an uphill struggle to get this far and Munger was determined to make a go of Pasadena.[18]

It was hard for Munger to compete with the other developments in the area since he was working alone and Burnett was not spending any money for community improvements. In Deer Park, Simeon West was preparing to break ground on his hotel and wharf. A 40-foot extension was already being added to the Artesian Hotel in La Porte and there were plans being drawn up for a third hotel, the Crescent. To get to Pasadena you had to be going to Pasadena, or be lost. Although Pasadena was on the Harrisburg-Lynchburg Road, none of the excursion groups used it. To get from Harrisburg to La Porte, you went by water from Houston or Galveston, or by hack from Genoa. It would be awhile before the railroad would be finished through Pasadena so Munger was trying to have something for them to see, a reason for them to stop, look, and buy.[19]

Early in March the Kansas excursion train arrived with A. G. Robb, Mr. and Mrs. Theodore Boggs, John Richey and his daughter, Mr. and Mrs. James Mock and their daughter, Andrew Berggren, Miss Ollie Webster, William Flickinger, Oscar Anderson, W. A. Morris, George McEvain, and Swan Burk, all of McPherson. From the nearby town of Galva, Surd Severtson, A. Knutson, and Claus Larson accompanied the group, as did C. H. Way, M. T. Fletcher and S. C. Lyon of Canton, and Edward Anderson, Elmer Holtgren, J. C. Landers, and F. Linstrom of Marquette. John Lamer of Lindsborg also came with the group. Fletcher, Way, and Severtson each bought 20 acres of land for $500 on March 9, and C. R. Richey bought 30 acres on March 14 for $600. Later that month H. H. Bisbee and J. D. Harrington, both from Michigan, purchased 10 acres each. W. A. Morris was impressed with the area and purchased timberland nearby. While on the trip, F. B. Webster, father of C. W. Webster, took ill and passed away in Houston.[20]

The La Porte Investment Company announced on March 16 that it had acquired the "Vick" tract containing 5,500 acres about five miles below Harrisburg and situated on Buffalo Bayou. Because of the fertility of the Gulf Coast soil, the tract was to be subdivided into farming plots. The "Arcadian Farm" was being laid out on a thousand acres. They reported that "this farm will be given to the cultivation of oranges, figs, olives, almonds, pecan nuts, pears, peaches, plums, strawberries, sweet potatoes, the Cape Jasmine and other flowers, fruits and vegetables, under the supervision of an experienced horticulturist." The season for strawberries had already begun and they were being shipped from southern Texas to Denver and Chicago in refrigerator cars. The early returns indicated that they were being sold for $5 per case and there were 800 cases in each car. The promoter offered that "The farseeing and practical Northern farmer has here ample scope to raise what he will, when he will or how he will; in fact, he has only to work with a will and systematically and success is assured." At the time the scheme sounded impressive, but they had yet to discover that Vick had a problem with the title to his land.[21]

Meanwhile the railroad trestle over Sims Bayou was under construction and the entire line was graded from Harrisburg to La Porte. The L.P. H. & N. Railroad and the N.G. H. & K. C. Railroad entered into a formal agreement to connect their lines at Clear Creek so now there could also be shipments to and from Galveston. Simeon West stepped up his Deer Park promotion by selling a large block of land to the Illinois Deer Park Syndicate of Knox County, Illinois, for resale to northern investors. And families were arriving almost daily at La Porte. Cora Bacon Foster of Houston was advertising in the *Houston Daily Post* that she had 1,107 acres for sale in La Porte. Another investment group had purchased land west of La Porte and started pear orchards in their development called Richland.[22]

After the initial land sales in Pasadena, April and May were quiet. Taking advantage of slightly better land prices, John Richey bought another 20 acres on June 1 and Wiley Anderson also signed on the dotted line for his 10 acres. Munger felt committed to Pasadena and moved his family from Newton, Kansas, to Texas. After 14 years, Munger admitted that he had

Avilda Witter Munger kept a diary of her experiences while the Mungers lived in Pasadena. Witter Street is named for her.

to start over. Unfortunately he had sad news for his wife and children when he meet them at the newly opened Santa Fe train station in Alvin on June 15. Burnett was still having trouble with clearing the title to some of the property, or so it seemed. This would naturally prevent some sales and mean no commissions. Although not evident at the time, Burnett had actually gotten the last of the releases, but the release would not be filed until later that year in November.[23]

The Mungers spent a few nights in Houston and then went to Pasadena to visit the Andersons. It was here that it struck Avilda what a change it would be from Newton and her life as the wife of a banker. It was fortunate for her that May Anderson was as sweet as any sister could be because she was surely helpful those first few days. After a heavy rain Avilda heard sheep baaing outside but could not see them. Upon inquiry she found out that what she was hearing was Texas frogs after a rain. Then she was attacked by mosquitoes, fleas, and red bugs. She was unable to sleep at nights until May dusted everything with flea powder. Shortly afterwards the Mungers went to visit Avilda's brother, Arch Witter who had moved to Dickinson a few years earlier to start a pear orchard for an Easterner named Bartlett.[24]

Charles lasted only a few weeks at Dickinson and he was back at work. La Porte had had a big Fourth of July picnic with fireworks, foot races, basket picnics in Sylvan Grove, and a "first class orchestra" for the dance in the new pavilion. The event attracted people from all around and it was well reported in the *La Porte Chronicle*. Colonel A. M. York had built a four-story Victorian hotel on the bay and it was becoming very popular. York named it the Sylvan Hotel, but it quickly became known as the Sylvan Beach Hotel. Charles visited Houston and a popular new town development called Houston Heights. Actually the Heights had been around for a few years, but it was getting a lot of promotion by the Omaha & South Texas Land Company. It claimed three miles of shelled streets, with artifical stone curbing, 13 miles of graded streets, five miles of an electric street railroad and three miles of steam railway which connected to all of Houston's rail lines. There he met Cora Bacon Foster, a Houston real estate promoter. Since she had represented property in La Porte she was familiar with that area and was likewise impressed with Munger.[25]

Colonel A. M. York built the Sylvan Beach Hotel in 1893. It was the prettiest of the four hotels in La Porte at the time.

On August 15 she purchased 4,142 acres in Pasadena for $62,000 and took over the development of the town. She put down $18,000 in cash and the balance in three notes of $14,666.66 each, payable over the next three years. This represented all but 497 acres that Burnett had purchased in the Vince and Seymour surveys. Burnett had been charging $25 to $30 dollars an acre and Cora had bulk purchased most of the development for $15 per acre. Burnett reserved 30 acres for Charles for his commission but never delivered the deeds, just held them in his safe. The deeds were drawn at a value of $25 per acre, with note payments due roughly at the time that Foster made payments on her notes. Although Foster had paid $18,000 in cash as part of her purchase price, Munger did not receive any land free and clear. Meanwhile Cora sold her first lot 11 days later on August 26, 1893, to Aaron Bakker.[26]

Thus far the only land sold had been in farming lots, that is, in 10-acre tracts or larger. Burnett decided to concentrate his efforts on the downtown section of Pasadena. He needed to get people interested in moving into the center of the townsite, so he sought the support of the Andersons. They lived on the western edge of his property near the Allen Ranch and operated the only retail-type business in the area: a boarding house and grocery store. He offered them a city lot if they could find someone to build in the "downtown" section and serve as the postmaster for the slowly growing community. Jasper F. Hays was the man for the job. He filed an application on September 20 for the establishment of a post office in Pasadena. He stated that there were 25 people in the community and a hundred people in the area. He noted that a railroad line was under construction through the town and that the nearest post offices were those at La Porte, Genoa, and Harrisburg. On September 27 Burnett conveyed city lots to W. W. Anderson, Jasper Hays, and his father, A. Hays. It was Burnett's intention that they would build houses in the city section of the community. The deeds recited that he sold the three lots for a dollar each. Jasper built a small three room "shotgun" style house on the southwest corner of Main and Sixth (Eagle) Street for he and his wife. His parents built a house a block away on the southwest corner of "I" (Munger) and Sixth (Eagle) Street. "Jap" Hays was appointed postmaster on December 6. Officially the "post office" was located 300 feet distant on the south side of the railroad track, which was then under construction. Actually, the fourth class post office was really located in Hays's house; it was a large dry goods box, divided into pigeon hole sections and lettered.[27]

While Hays's appointment was pending, George W. Kuhns arrived on the train from Fort Scott, Kansas, with his wife Elizabeth "Lizzie" and their eight children: May, Charles, Gussie, Nannie, William, Ida, Bertha, and Perry. Their family was the largest single increase in population for the young community. Like so many others, they were fleeing the bitter cold winters of the Midwest. It took George only slightly over a month to find the land he wanted and on December 1 he purchased 16.6 acres on the south side of the railroad right-of-way and on the east side of Little Vince Bayou.[28]

George Kuhns and Jesse Slagle were working for the railroad when they came to Pasadena and decided to purchase land in December 1893. Jesse purchased the lot next to George's. There were no streets yet, only the surveyor's stakes that Munger had arranged for back in February. For roads you simply headed straight across the land for your destination, or followed the appropriate cow path. In wet weather, the cow path was your better choice. Jesse and Charles Kuhns got the job of grading a few streets. They graded Main and "H" (Shaver) Streets and used oxen so that the streets would be straight.[29]

On November 1 John F. Wafer finally bought land from Burnett even though he had been living in the community for a while with his wife Margaret and seventeen year old son Albert. He chose 41 acres fronting on Buffalo Bayou and east of Vince's Bayou. Because he bought so much land it only cost him $25 an acre, and he was able to give Burnett a note for the full amount. John had the prettiest homesite in the community, overlooking Buffalo Bayou on a high ridge, surrounded by beautiful trees.[30]

Cora Bacon Foster was no stranger to real estate developments and knew that land did not sell itself. Buyers were people who had dreams and sought opportunities. To succeed, Pasadena needed to be more than a prairie with a "Lots for Sale" sign on it. She began her program by putting Munger officially in charge. Cora hired Munger as her agent and insisted that he move to Pasadena and live on the property. She built him a house and a stable on the land that Burnett had reserved for him. In order for Charles to properly show prospective purchasers around she also gave him a team and surrey. The horses were named "Queen" and "Riley." Munger arranged to purchase another 10 acres from Burnett and this gave him a total of 40 along the north side of Fifth (Shaw) from "C" (Richey) to "H" (Shaver). Since Harris County was seeking to establish the alignment of its county highway, known locally as the Harrisburg-Lynchburg Road or in the broader sense as the Houston-Cedar Bayou Road, along Fifth (Shaw) Street, Munger would have had a major portion of the highway frontage going through Pasadena.[31]

When Cora got involved with the plat, the streets were unnamed. The east-west streets were numbered and the north-south streets were alphabetized, from A Street on the west to R Street on the east. Only Main and Broad Way (original spelling) Streets were original names. On either side of Main Street she changed the names to Munger and Spooner, the first Kansas people involved in the town's development. Johnson and Wafer Streets were named for the first ex-Kansans to live in the town. Witter Street was named after Alvida Munger's maiden name. Richey Street was named for the first purchaser from the original syndicate group. A street was laid out between Vince's Bayou and Richey Street and called Hoffman for another of the early Kansas investors. Davis was named for the civil engineer that laid out the city, Burnett after the original land owner, and Seymour and Vince Streets for the two surveys on which the town was laid out.[32]

Ever so slowly the town inched forward. Meanwhile La Porte had quickly mushroomed into a booming metropolis. A massive building program had created a downtown section where buildings and shops were separated by feet, not acres. Even a major fire that started out on Main Street in November of 1893 did not dampen the forward rush of the community. Kirkland's two-story building, Seaureau's two-story frame store, Bush & Baker's meat market, and three other buildings were destroyed. Fortunately, the Artesian Hotel was saved by a bucket brigade and lots of wet blankets. The town quickly set about busily rebuilding. With renewed enthusiasm the developers set aside a tract of land for a college campus on First Street, between "M" and "R" Streets. The community ended the year with the first Christmas "get-together," including a hay ride, a songfest, and refreshments.[33]

During 1894 land sales began to pick in Pasadena with Munger in residency and Cora Bacon Foster actively promoting the town. The H. F. Otises, A. G. Redwoods, Albert Hoftsgers, J. W. Lewises, and Parsons arrived in the spring. The Hannas travelled by covered wagon from McPherson. It took them 40 days to make the trip. Sixty-year-old Elias Slagle brought his wife Salomie and son Orlin from Kansas. Leon and Mary Yarnell also came from Kansas with their children: Ethel, Alva, Lennie, and Harly. But increasing land sales was only part

Settlement (1893-94)

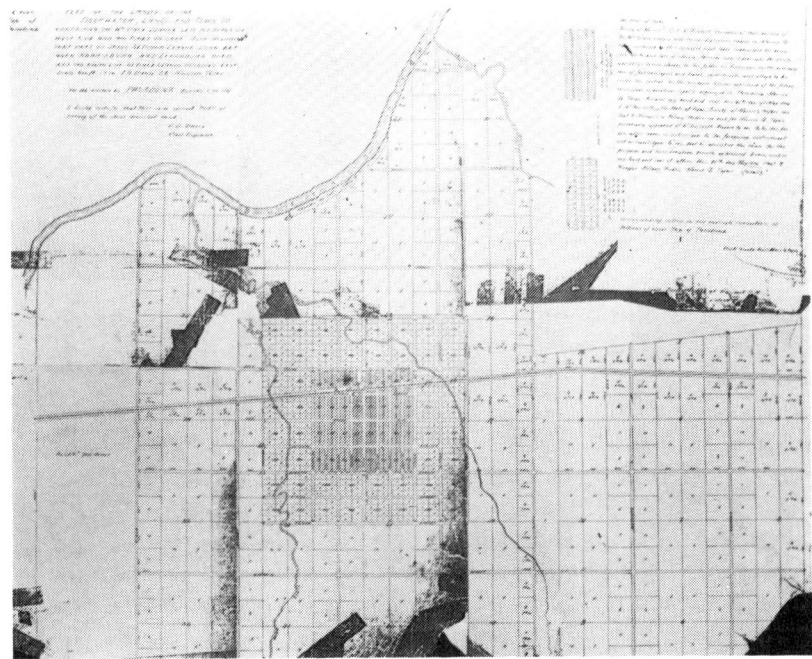

Although the plat to Pasadena was not filed until 1896, the first land sale in the community was made in December, 1892. John Burnett, Charles Munger and Cora Bacon Foster all contributed to the final plat.

of the story for the new community. Spring was the time for plowing, fencing, making gardens, raising chickens, planting flowers, and birthing. Raymond Anderson was the first child born in the community. He arrived on January 19, just four days ahead of the second child, Bernal Howard Pitts. Now the town really had something to brag about. By June there were about 76 people in town with 24 of school age. All of the settlers were from the North except the Pitts. The farmers met at Munger's house and formed the Farmers & Fruit Growers Association and elected J. F. Wafer as the president and Munger as the secretary-treasurer. Enthusiasm was running high and Anderson, Kuhns, and Hays bought additional land so that they could grow more items.[34]

It was also during 1894 that the railroad laid track through Pasadena from Harrisburg on its way to La Porte. Some of the train crew stayed with the Andersons since theirs was the only place in town to rent rooms. Will Palmer was the first engineer and his cousin Bert Palmer was the fireman. Huey A. Neal was the conductor and John McDonald was the brakeman. As mentioned earlier, George Kuhns and Jesse Slagle also worked for the railroad and they bought land in Pasadena and stayed after the railroad job was completed. Elias Slagle and Charles Slagle also purchased land. Because the train engine needed water for steam, Will Kuhns and Jesse Slagle put down the first water well in Pasadena the year before, in 1893. It was an artesian well located on the south side of the railroad tracks on the east side of Main Street. Since the water just flowed when the valve was opened, a pipe was hooked up between the well and the engine tender tank car at nights and the tanks filled. During the day the well served the community. About once a week a family would load their water barrels in their wagon and take them to the well to be filled. Rainwater and bayou water could be used for washing and watering, but well water was used for drinking and cooking. Prior to that they had to travel all the way to Harrisburg or to the artesian well on the Allen Ranch near Sims Bayou for their potable water.[35]

It had taken a lot of work to get a town established on the old Vince Survey. The railroad had not been completed, a hotel or depot had not been built, and the plat had not been filed. Downtown consisted of two single-story shotgun-style houses a block apart. The rest of the community was spread out in small clusters over a couple of miles. But Charles Munger was committed and worked hard with Burnett and Foster to put Pasadena on the map. Small as it was, a town was emerging, and the people were pulling together to make it a community.

Ira and Lula Pitts

III

Foundations for Survival (1894-99)

The economic forces that drove the midwestern farmers into Texas in the early 1890s caught up with them a few years later. The nation's worst economic depression had continued to grow and spread to all parts of the country. The nation struggled with the concept of money supply and the changing roles of business, labor, and government in an increasingly interdependent industrial era. The American farmer was caught in an intensifying squeeze between declining commodity prices and spiraling operating costs. Survival most often meant moving to the cities and working in the new industries. Farming for the individual was quickly becoming obsolete, both as to profitability and opportunity. Since there was little industrialization in the Pasadena area to offer alternative gainful employment, the new settlers either went back to where they came from, or literally, they dug in. Growth in the region stopped, and the survival of the numerous new towns depended upon the commitment and support of those who stayed. Fortunately for Pasadena, Charles Munger and Cora Bacon Foster had understood the importance for creating a feeling of "community" and they were quick to organize the settlement for self-sufficiency. This "coming together to satisfy common needs" created a community spirit that would carry the town through the trying years ahead. Although the young town would be prematurely deprived of the vision and leadership of Munger and Foster, the seeds had been planted. New leaders emerged to carry on with the dream. They took up the responsibility to continue laying a firm foundation upon which the community would ultimately grow and excel.

Every Friday night the Mungers hosted an open house so that the new settlers could meet each other and socialize. Among those regularly attending were the Andersons, Hays, Johnsons, Mungers, Pitts, and Wafers. Included in thoses families were about 25 to 30 young people. The need for an educational program for the children became apparent and a Sunday school was organized late in 1893. Charlie Kuhns served as the first superintendent and "Russie" Munger as the secretary-treasurer. They met originally in Johnson's home and then J. F. Hays and others shared in hosting the group in their homes.[1]

Religious education was just the beginning. A makeshift private school was started in order to instruct the children in the three R's: reading, 'riting, and 'rith-matic. Munger converted part of his new chicken coop into classroom space. The "Chicken Ranch" was located on the west side of Shaver Street near Little Vince's Bayou. Munger's son Russell, then 17 years old, taught the handful of Pasadena children. His students included Pearl Anderson; the Pitts' kids, Lillian, Oliver Claude, and Eula May; and the Kuhns' children, Charles, Ida, Bertha, and Perry. However, it was quickly realized that the children needed formal schooling and that it was too difficult to send them daily to the county schools at La Porte or Harrisburg. Foster contracted with "Professor" L. A. Dowdell in August of 1894 to conduct a proper school. She agreed to give him the use of 20 acres for a school and to loan him $1,500 for 5 years at eight percent interest to build a school house. He agreed to teach school for five years, nine months a year, and to reside on the land and not resell it. As part of the agreement

C. Russel Munger, the first schoolteacher in Pasadena. His first classroom was a converted chicken coop.

he would have an "Academy" to teach in and a cottage in which to live. Between teaching and farming, Dowdell figured that he could make a good living.²

The "Academy" was a fine looking structure. One of the new settlers, Mr. Otis, constructed the large one room school house with a prominent front porch. Inside the front door was an entrance hall flanked by two cloakrooms. There was a bell tower and fancy woodwork trim on the front of the building. It was not anything like the new Opera House just built in Galveston, but it was the fanciest thing in Pasadena. The school house was located at the southeast corner of Wafer and Fifth (Shaw) Streets near Little Vince's Bayou. In October of 1894 Professor Dowdell moved from Houston and started school classes. Pasadena's original teacher, Russell Munger, again became a student and went back to school to finish his education. Young student Charles Kuhns wrote a poem about his life in Pasadena:

> I came from Ft. Kansas in the year of '92,
> And when I came to Texas I was feeling rather blue.
> I went out in the country and went to making hay;
> The wage I got there was only one dollar a day.
> I had to eat a cold supper every night.
> There was no use to fight,
> There was no use to cry,
> The only thing for me to do was root hog or die.³

The Academy quickly became the town's community hall and the first Christmas party was held there in 1894. About 100 people attended the event and a program was presented, which included instrumental and vocal music, along with readings and recitations. There was plenty of candy, nuts, oranges, and naturally, gifts for the children. The holiday celebrations continued when Professor Dowdell hosted a New Year's Eve dance at his home. Wylie and Floyd Anderson provided the music for dancing.⁴

Early the next year Cora Bacon Foster presented the community with an organ. Maybe Wylie and Floyd's New Year's Eve music needed some help. The fine instrument was proudly placed in the school house and Edith Munger was elected to play it. A choir was quickly formed with Mrs. Wafer and Nannie Kuhns singing soprano, Edith Munger alto, Russell Munger tenor, and Charles Kuhns and Albert Wafer as the bass. The new school house got even more use since the Sunday school also began meeting there. At the January 6, 1895, meeting Mr. Noftsyer was elected superintendent and Albert Wafer as secretary-treasurer. Prayer meetings were also started for the adults and they met at the school on Thursday and Sunday nights.[5]

With little to do during the winter, social gatherings became popular in the growing community. Edith Munger and Eva Pollock hosted a party at the Munger house on January 21, 1895. For entertainment they played games, including charades, and held a singing contest. Russell Munger finally won the contest with his rendition of "Seeing Nellie Home." For his vocal victory he received "a large peanut dressed up so grotesquelly as to cause great merriment."[6]

Even though it still was January, plans for the spring planting "began to bloom" when 3,000 fruit trees arrived on the 29th for the (Pasadena) Farmers and Fruit Growers Association. With the amount of commercial planting of fruit trees completed and contemplated in the area, surely this would become one of the prettiest regions in the world. Two years earlier it had been reported that 2,000 acres of pear trees had already been set out in the area and probably 20,000 more acres would be planted before year-end. One subsequent planting included 13,000 fruit trees in Deer Park. The "Richland" project between Deer Park and La Porte included 400 acres in pear trees. Besides the old orange groves originally cultivated by James Morgan for his New Washington project out on Morgan's Point, numerous additional orchards had been recently planted in the La Porte area. Though the 1,000-acre Arcadian Farm project adjacent to Pasadena had been abandoned, the original land owner had platted a new town, Deepwater, and development was beginning to start on this new agricultural community. Naturally, fruit trees were also planned to be a part of this new project. In the spring, the flowering buds from all of the fruit trees in the region were an overwhelming sight, and the fragrance perfumed the air. Promoters of the area had plenty of adjectives to boldface on their sales flyers.[7]

Despite dreams and plans, Mother Nature had a mind of her own. The early spring planting in 1895 had to be postponed when temperatures took a sudden and deep drop. On February 8, 1895, Galveston recorded only 14.8 degrees. A week later, on Valentine's Day, a record snowstorm hit the Gulf region, dumping 24 inches of the rare white powder. Galveston reported an amazing 15 inches on its beaches. Munger knew that the snowfall was a rarity for the area because he had been around since 1891. But the trainload of northern excursionists bound for La Porte that week were shocked. They had travelled to Texas to escape the severe winters in the North. They had come to enjoy the mild winter weather that they had read so much about, and to purchase farm land for a new home. Some never even got off the train.[8]

Just as Pasadena was beginning to take root, La Porte was being pruned. Although the railroad had been completed through Pasadena and the trains were running regularly by February 4, 1895, construction was over two years behind schedule. Back in February 1893 the La Porte promoters proclaimed that the railroad would be completed from Houston to La Porte within the next 60 days! Two years later the railhead was just east of Deer Park, still six miles short of La Porte. At least the hack ride to La Porte was shorter. Both the La Porte, Houston and Northern Railroad and the North Galveston, Houston and Kansas City Railroad were having financial problems and they were consolidated on February 26, 1895, into a newly created company called the Galveston, La Porte and Houston Railroad. The G. L. P. & H. laid the remaining six miles of track into La Porte by the end of the year.[9]

In addition to railroad problems, the original "Nebraska Syndicate" promoters of La Porte had abandoned their development of the city because their financial backers had pulled out. Only Ira Holmes remained and with A. O. Blackwell sought new alliances to keep the development of La Porte alive. Despite Holmes's dedication and effort, many of the original settlers returned to their home states. Even though the growth of the project had slowed, it was still, at least for the time being, the largest town in the area.[10]

With the departure of the York brothers from La Porte, the development of Deer Park also lost its momentum. Simeon West directly oversaw the initial development of the town and then turned over the sales program to several promoters. A. M. York had been involved from almost the beginning. And there was also the Illinois Deer Park Syndicate. Perhaps in connection with the latter, West soon felt that he had been swindled in their promotion of his town. In less than flattering terms he described them as "the most utterly depraved scoundrels I ever came in contact with, their names are not worthy to be mentioned . . . " West had built a beautiful two-story, 24-room hotel in 1893 and had gotten a post office established there on the same day that Pasadena had secured its own post office. Philip P. Hemstreet, formerly of Knox County, Illinois, had purchased land, moved to the community and built a two-story structure. He was appointed the first postmaster and operated the post office in his general merchandise store. He had his residency in the remainder of the building. With the swindlers, the freak snowstorm, and the general economic downturn, the lure of Deer Park waned and its population remained below 100 residents. Although he was approaching 70 years of age, West still periodically visited Deer Park to oversee its development.[11]

Deepwater had gotten a late start in its development as a new town. The La Porte Investment Company had abandoned its Arcadian Farm project on Vick's property adjacent to Pasadena when they discovered a problem with the title. Vick had already begun promotion of his new project, but had to clear up the title to the property before sales could be consummated. Eber R. Bradley had moved to the area and had been appointed postmaster of the community of Deepwater on February 23, 1894. In March Vick filed suit in Harris County district court to clear the title to the property. In anticipation of his successful lawsuit and the filing of the plat, Vick began selling lots in July. Leopold Zlomke purchased the first one on July 27, 1894. Zlomke had moved his family to the South from Grand Isle, Nebraska, because his wife Amelia had developed a respiratory disease. With children Bertha, Will, Lydia, John, and Alvin they moved to Deepwater. Vick subsequently filed a plat for the town of Deepwater on November 24, 1894. By year-end, Vick had executed upwards of a dozen more sales. W. N. "Will" Blakesley, a bachelor who was also from Nebraska and a few weeks shy of his 23rd birthday, arrived at Deepwater on October 30. Calvin E. Parks of New York moved there with his family on November 3. C. B. McNay from Kentucky had also arrived to do some ranching. A hotel was being planned and a lot of excitement was being generated since the railroad had already completed its tracks through Deepwater.[12]

Vick envisioned the community as large farming plots surrounding a picturesque small town with a large, circular central park. All along Buffalo Bayou residential sites were laid out for waterfront estates. Since Buffalo Bayou was still a clear deep canal teaming with fish of all kinds and frequented by river packets, palacial weekend homes for Houston residents would be in demand. Even though Vick listed himself as a capitalist, he was president of the Houston Stockyards and used the land simultaneously to graze approximately a thousand head of cattle. Like the Allen Ranch on the west side of Pasadena, there were no fences and the cattle simply ran free upon the range. No doubt the farmers of Pasadena were glad to see a town being developed on the property instead of them being sandwiched in between two cattle ranches and their free-roaming cattle.[13]

But Vick was not the driving force behind the new boomtown of Deep-water. Martin Tilford Jones had made his fortune in the highly competitive lumber business of East Texas. His competitors called him a "double ender" since he owned both sawmills and lumber yards. He moved to Houston in 1883 and maintained sales offices of his M. T. Jones Lumber Company in Houston, Dallas, Mexia, Laredo, and Monterey, Mexico. In Houston he was also president of South Texas National Bank and vice-president of the Amer- ican Bankers Association. His son, William E. "Willie" Jones, was in charge of the Mexia office. Reluctantly he had hired his nephew Jesse H. Jones to look after his Dallas office. In 1894 Jones became acquainted with Vick's Deepwater community and decided to invest in the project.[14]

Jones was a man who made things happen. First, he needed a man

Robert McPherson Guinn arrived in 1894 to manage the Deepwater town development.

on the site to handle the development. Robert McPherson Guinn had worked with A. J. Vick since 1889, first in charge of Vick's Houston cattle yard, then on a farm owned by Vick in Johnson County. Guinn was appointed overseer of the Deepwater development for Jones and Vick and moved to the community in December 1894. Like the excursionists from the North, Guinn moved his family on the train to Houston, and then on Allien's boat, the *Eugene* down Buffalo Bayou to Deepwater. Then, early in 1895, Jones contracted with E. R. Bradley to publish a weekly newspaper to be called the *Deepwater Enterprise*. Bradley was very familiar with the area since he had been living there for sometime and was serving as the postmaster for the community. Jones began purchasing land from Vick and financed a few of the farming operations by providing seeds, fertilizer, and equipment for a share of the production.[15]

Meanwhile, Colonel Burnett's other community of Genoa was showing little signs of growth. Land sales in Genoa were not going all that well even though Burnett's daughter, Ellen, and her husband, J. O. Ross, were living in Genoa and promoting the townsite. In 1893 Francis and Lilly Gwartney brought their family from Lincoln, Nebraska. They settled in Genoa with their four boys: Harry, Frederick, Clifford, and Frank. The Swedish families of Olsen and Boehm had moved to the area and had just started a church, the First Swedish Baptist Church. The services were conducted in Swedish and the group met in the homes of its nine members. Burnett had built a hotel and a store for the community. The second floor of the store was being used for a school and the county was thinking about taking over its operation. Perhaps the biggest event in the small community was the first marriage in town, that of Burnett's nephew, George P. Burnett, and Minnie Lee Roberts on March 4, 1894. The town had gathered at the hotel for the occasion. Their first child, Bruce, was also the first baby born in Genoa. He arrived on January 8, 1895, a month ahead of the memorial Valentine's Day snowstorm. Roy Thurman was ranching and farming on the western side of Genoa. He had just arrived from Manor, Texas, with his widowed mother and sisters Clara, Josephine, and Lenora. After his father's death several years before Roy had taken over the responsibility for the family. Colonel Burnett was also ranching his extra land and had hired Delbert Ellsworth "Deb" Atkinson to run this operation. Being single, Deb's eyes were turned by the Thurman girls and it would only be a matter of time before a match would be made.[16]

But too much was finally going on in Pasadena for Munger to brood about unseasonably bad weather or get too concerned about other town developments. With the coming of the railroad a regular station had been promised in the near future. A lumberyard was set up and carloads of lumber were being delivered. The Andersons had moved into their new home. The Slagels and Parsons were building. Jap Hays certainly appreciated the train service since he no longer had to spend the better part of a day riding to Harrisburg to pick up the local mail. The train dropped off and picked up mail less than a block from his home.[17]

The previous December Marvin V. Wright, a Houston nurseryman, had purchased 20 acres on the north side of the railroad tracks at Vince's Bayou and was reading plans to plant cape jasmines and other nursery crops. He wanted a local source for the flowers he sold in his shop on Washington Avenue. Albert Noftsyer owned the land on the opposite side of the tracks from Wright's Pasadena property and took advantage of the opportunity to sell his property to Wright at a profit. Sadly, Noftsyer was one of the first of the original settlers to leave.[18]

But adding a commercial nursery to the community was not the only new crops being considered by the farmers. A Mr. Moller held a meeting at the Academy to talk about the benefits of raising tobacco. Philip Hemstreet of Deer Park was having success with this crop and had built drying sheds. The talk must have been convincing, since tobacco was subsequently planted and raised in Pasadena along with an assortment of other crops. Pasadena had already established a reputation back in Kansas City with its "Pasadena Cantaloupe." Sweet potatoes were another promising crop.[19]

The Vanderson's of North Dakota raised wheat for a season and then they were gone. They had arrived the previous November, like a band of gypsies at Munger's gate. They were on their way to La Porte and asked to camp for the night. For unknown reasons, they stayed and built a barracks-type structure for the various families to live in that winter. In the spring they moved into two small cabins nearby and raised some wheat. Only a young girl named Nettie was friendly; the rest kept to themselves. They left after the wheat crop came in, leaving only unmarked graves of those that had unfortunately died during their stay.[20]

Although agriculture was productive, land sales turned out to be fairly slow during 1895. Cora Bacon Foster was having trouble generating enough sales to make her note payment to Burnett. She executed only about six deeds and lost two parcels by foreclosure. In Deepwater the sales were holding their own as M. T. Jones continued to actively promote the project and purchased more land in his name. Jones even tried to purchase the balance of Foster's Pasadena property, but she was not able to deliver the title.[21]

With sales off and commissions down, Munger took a part-time job in Houston with the Valentine & Co. of Chicago, Commission Merchants. When the tobacco crop was harvested that fall Munger also turned the lower floor of his new chicken coop into a cigar factory. Without bragging, Pasadena turned out a fine grade of cigar. Charlie McCullough made the cigars that Munger took to Houston to sell. Since Munger was now making some cash income, one of the best news for the year was that the U. S. Supreme Court declared the federal two percent income tax unconstitutional.[22]

In the spring of 1895 Professor Dowdell taught a high school course with preparation for college. This was particularly useful for Russell Munger who was considering going to college to get his teaching certificate. His try at teaching the year before had whetted his appetite for some formal training. As soon as he could qualify, Russell went to Normal School in Hempstead. He obtained his teaching certificate in the fall and applied to the trustees of the Harrisburg Common School District for a job. In the meantime the Harrisburg District had taken over the responsibility for public schooling at Pasadena and Russell was hired to teach in Pasadena for a four-month term at $30 per month. The term started in October with 27 scholastics (at this period in history it was common to call students "scholastics" and to refer to male teachers as "professor"). Since there was little in the way of school furnishings, Charles Munger, J. T. Wafer, and Willis Hays got together and built what was needed, including a teacher's desk for Russell. The desk survived all of the men.[23]

The slow land sales of 1895 continued on into 1896. With few land sales Cora Bacon Foster was unable to meet her mortgage obligations to Colonel Burnett. Burnett foreclosed on Foster's property and at the sheriff's sale on May 5 bought

Charles Munger, J. T. Wafer, and Willis Hays built furniture for the school in 1895. This teacher's desk was built for Russell Munger and is still owned by the school district.

back the remaining balance of the original 4,142 acres. What he had sold to her two years before at $62,000, he purchased back for $500. The deeds to the land that Burnett had given Munger as the commission on the land sale to Foster were still being held in Burnett's safe. Unless Charles could pay for his land, he would not receive the title to it. Without savings and a regular cash income, Munger faced another hard decision. Reluctantly, he moved to Houston. To meet his basic living expenses, Munger agreed to do some office work for Burnett for a monthly fee. One of the first things Charles did was to help update and complete the plat for Pasadena, which was finally filed on May 25, 1896, three and a half years after the first land sale.[24]

The departure from Pasadena saddened Charles. At least he salvaged something from his real estate adventure, whereas the break in Kansas had left him with nothing. He listed his business in the 1897 Houston City Directory as a Pasadena cigar manufacturer with offices in Houston. He proudly passed around his new product. Lee Pitts was being quite successful growing tobacco and Colonel Jones in Deepwater was growing some of the finest tobacco. A group of Cuban investors set up a cigar factory in Deepwater and hung the tobacco leaves up to dry. Unfortunately a storm blew up and ruined the entire harvest. Thus ended the potential for a tobacco industry in Harris County.[25]

Although Charles had to give up the utopian country life with a community of less than 100 people for the hustle-bustle of a big city whose population numbered about 40,000, he regularly visited Pasadena. Some of his Kansas friends had become good Pasadena neighbors and he wanted to keep tabs on the growth of the community. With a passive promoter and without resident leadership, he knew the future of the community was again in jeopardy. The young community would have to fend for itself. Burnett sold only a couple of parcels in 1896, and only one family came to settle in Pasadena. John L. Perry moved from Kansas with his wife Lucinda and the three youngest of their ten children; Roy H., David, and Ray. Burnett also leased the Academy to Harrisburg School District for its Pasadena school. Since the Mungers had moved to Houston, Professor L. A. Dowdell was hired to teach the 1896-97 session.[26]

While Pasadena was slowing down, La Porte was struggling with new momentum in 1895 and 1896. The American Land Company of Chicago purchased the unsold land out of bankruptcy. Under the Texas corporation name of La Porte Improvement Company, President John Caplan and the only remaining original promoters, ex-railroad man Ira R. Holmes and attorney A. O. Blackwell, promoted their "New Town" on the eastern side of La Porte. The La Porte Wharf and Channel Company also promoted "New Town" as a shipping point and was courting the U. S. Navy for a dry dock project. A second newspaper, the *Herald*, was started. A free pier, swimming, dancing, and picnicking were being promoted at a bay front project called Sylvan Beach at the old Sylvan Grove area. In November M. T. Jones contacted the mayor of La Porte to get the residents of La Porte to petition the Harris County commissioners to have them grade and shell the Harrisburg-La Porte Public Highway. Jones' support of the railroad construction and the public highway was motivated by his ownership of a shell bank at the mouth of Clear Creek. He was selling this shell for ballast for the railroad as well as surfacing for streets. The mayor agreed, but only if the work started in La Porte and progressed west towards Harrisburg.[27]

Deepwater was still booming by comparison in 1896 and boasted of 200 residents, a church, post office, the weekly

Leopold Zlomke moved his family from Nebraska in 1894. This picture was taken about 1915 and includes the entire family.

Deepwater Enterprise newspaper, a physician named Dr. Culpepper, a general store, two groceries, a lumber and hardware store, a sawmill, one barber, two blacksmiths, and three carpenters. The Zlomkes added to the population boom with the birth of their son Ervin in September. Since most of Deer Park's land was bought by investors and not farmers, it was not doing as well. In 1896 there were only 40 people in town, a post office, hotel, general store, and three carpenters. In the *Texas Gazeteer* of 1896 Pasadena was listed, without population, mentioning only Jap Hays (misspelled as "J. F. Ways") as the postmaster. There were about 65 people in Pasadena, all farmers.[28]

The *Deepwater Enterprise* was a weekly newspaper that carried the news of the area to the far corners of the United States for $1.50 per year. It ran a column called "Pasadena Pointers" that reported on the activities of its small neighbor. With the decline in the "Homeseeker's Excursion" railroad trips, Jones began to question the value of the newspaper he was underwriting. Thirty-one residents petitioned Jones not to discontinue the paper late in 1895. They were: J. L. Beadle, W. N. Blakesly, A. L. Bradshaw, Y. H. Bullock, G. W. Cadman, R. D. V. Carr, C. J. Crockett, Mrs. Dr. Culpepper, C. W. DeVoe, Frank Emory, B. F. Extein, L. M. Gililland, George Harris, J. B.

Hill, James C. Hill, R. M. Jan, C. A. Jencks, Ottis Knau, W. A. Mead, N. Moore, Edward H. Norton, C. E. Parks, J. D. Parks, R. E. Parks, J. W. Sallee, J. H. Schmidt, A. B. Snift, J. H. Starkey, S. A. Starkey, W. C.(probably Y.) Starkey, and P. W. Wirt. The editor and publisher, E. R. Bradley, argued that "A town without a local paper does not appeal very strongly to intending settlers and more especially would this be true of a town that once had a paper for a year and allowed it to drop out." The prophetic appeal fell on deaf ears for the paper ceased publication shortly thereafter.[29]

Josiah H. Starkey had fathered twelve children. Four had died early and seven came with him and Mary E. to Deepwater. Spencer A. was the oldest, now 21 years old. Walter and Luther were out of school and working on the family farm with Spencer. Hershal and Wilford were in school and Laura and Bessie O. were too young.[30]

The development momentum in the area had shifted from La Porte to Deepwater. Jones and T. W. House had been appointed receivers of the Galveston, La Porte and Houston Railway Company on January 7, 1896, and were busy trying to build up its traffic. They bought new equipment and completed the line between La Porte and Galveston. They courted C. P. Huntington of the Southern Pacific system to increase traffic over the line. With a rail line and plenty of fertile land, Jones envisioned a cotton industry in Deepwater and considered a cotton gin in the community. W. E. Rodenbough, J. H. Pollard, and E. R. Bradley put in cotton crops. Dr. Culpepper located a ferry that could be used to bring cotton over from growers on the north side of Buffalo Bayou. But cotton was not the only crop Jones was interested in. He contacted the Biering nursery in Hitchcock and the Almeda Town Site and Fruit Farm Company for fruit trees, Bucknout Brothers of Kalamazoo, Michigan, about celery and cabbage, and C. W. Benson of the Texas Fruit Company of Alvin about a 40-acre nursery operation in Deepwater. Benson was impressed with the area and wrote, "There is no better land for berries, pears and nursery stock in the state of Texas than you have at Deepwater . . . ." Besides fertile land, Deepwater had plenty of water for growing, either from shallow artesian wells or by pumpage from Buffalo Bayou. R. M. Guinn was busy "breaking" the prairie and employed Will Blakesley, George Harris, and Burt Harris to help him. But Will was not too busy to notice the Parks girl, Irma, and married her on August 20.[31]

Foundations for Survival (1894-99)

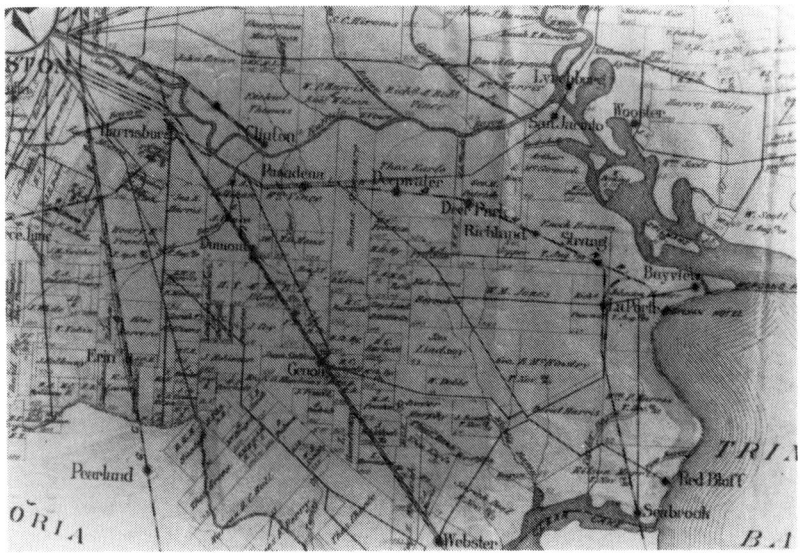

As shown in this 1899 Harris County map, the railroads opened the area to settlement. Many new towns were laid out along the new rail lines in the 1890s.

The void left by Munger and Foster in Pasadena begin to fill late in 1896. Among the new blood that arrived, Oscar and Hanna Kruse came to Texas from Butte, Montana. Oscar was from Sweden and had moved to America in 1888 to take advantage of its promised opportunities. He moved to Montana and married another Swede, Johanna Peterson. Although he prospered as a clothing merchant in the mining district of the state he decided to move his growing family south to a better climate and community. The extravagant advertisements for the Houston district of the sunny South convinced him to sell out, pack up and head to Texas in November 1986. The would-be farmer Oscar, expectant mother Hanna, and three-year-old son Karl, arrived in Houston after four days and nights on the train. It took them a few days to locate the right piece of land for them, 20 acres that would be theirs and their children's for life. Within a year other Swedish descendents purchased in the area and a community was formed less than a few miles from the railroad stop at Pasadena. The Andersons from El Campo, the Larsons from Kansas, the Nelsons from Minnesota, and the Johnsons from Colorado moved to what was now called the Florentine Settlement in honor of the first

The Kruse family moved to the area in 1896 and put down their roots. Oscar and Hannah Kruse stand proudly in front of their house with some of their family.

child born in the community, Florentine Kruse. Unfortunately none of the new residents were accomplished farmers and after a year the Kruses were all alone again, but only temporarily.[32]

The Kruses were located in the country, between communities. At first they had to go to Harrisburg to get their mail. A Swedish-speaking Baptist church was formed in Genoa in 1895 and they found friends there. The Kruse farm was on the trail frequented by Sam Allen and his cowboys and the initial relationship was that of the "American Rancher" and the "Foreigner Farmer," with all of the elements of discord. However it did not take long before mutual distrust developed into mutual respect and then into friendship. Oscar was most interested in education and he turned his attention to Pasadena. The little frame school only had 12 students and not enough tax money to adequately maintain it. As he had proven so many times in just the last 10 years, Oscar only had to apply himself and a solution was possible.[33]

In 1897 several more families drifted into Pasadena. William Benjamin "Will" Bailey was on his way to Deepwater to work as a carpenter. His wife Lydia Catherine "Katie" was a sister to R. M. Guinn's wife Mary Jane, so the Baileys had heard about the opportunities in Deepwater. Unfortunately for Will, but fortunately for Pasadena, he could not find a place to live in

Deepwater. Will, Katie, and nine-year-old son Ben, Jr., found a place for rent in Pasadena and settled in on the corner of Shaver and the La Porte Road.[34]

Woodrow Phillip Coolidge, wife Sadie, and children W. Clyde, Grant Daniel, Irene, and toddler Carrol arrived that same year from Lancaster, Dallas County, Texas. They were looking for some land to ranch and farm on and Pasadena was where they stopped. They rented some ranch land first and then decided to stay and purchased 100 acres out on Eleventh (Harris) Street on both sides of Vince's Bayou.[35]

Will and Katie Bailey were on their way to Deepwater when they decided to settle in Pasadena.

David Daniel McCormick was a section hand foreman for the railroad and in September bought 30 acres on N. Witter street near the Slagles on Cotton Patch Bayou. Land was going for $30 per acre and $12.50 for a city lot. Three months later he purchased 10 more acres. At 54 years of age, Dan was 20 years senior to his wife Belle.[36]

Jap Hays was busy farming and decided to give up the post office since he had moved from his "town" home on Main Street to his farm on Fifth (Shaw) and Richey. He, the Andersons, and Pitts were turning "West" Pasadena green with produce. James W. Lewis agreed to accept the job of postmaster on November 20, 1897, and moved the post office box to his new two-story home on the east side of Munger street, just north of the La Porte Road. Lewis had moved to Pasadena from Kansas in 1894 and had lived around the area. Downtown Pasadena now comprised of the Bailey's residence, the Lewises, a railroad section house at Main Street, and the two old Hays houses south of the tracks. The school house was over towards Deepwater on Fifth (Shaw) and Wafer Street. The Kuhns were a little further east on the south side of the tracks near Little Vince's Bayou.[37]

When Marvin V. Wright's cape jasmine and other plants had grown to sufficient maturity to require full-time care, he sent his assistant, and nephew, Arthur L. Dickerson, to Pasadena. Arthur's mother and 17-year-old brother Wade were working with a florist in Alvin at the time and also moved to Pasadena to help care for the nursery. Wade was happy about the move since he had been riding over regularly to court Lillian Pitts. On one of his horseback trips he met the legendary Sam Allen. Wade had been delayed by a sudden storm on the prairie and stopped to ask for a meal at the Allen's chuck wagon. Allen said no at first, then let the young kid eat his fill.[38]

In January 1898 William Benjamin "Ben" Williams rolled his wagon into Pasadena from Buna, Texas, with his wife Ella and sons Ray, four, and Bryon Fred, three. He counted six families and a section house. There were more families in "greater" Pasadena, but they were so spread out that most people did not realize that the community had as many people as it did. The lack of a downtown area gave the impression of a much smaller community. Ben's younger brother John had considered moving to Pasadena earlier but decided to stay with the family farm in Madison County. He bought out Ben's interest and Ben moved to Pasadena instead. Ben paid $858.90 for 28.6 acres on the La Porte Road at the western boundary of the townsite. He was butt up against the Allen Ranch with the Pitts, Andersons, and Hays as his neighbors on the north side. Ben was on the western side of West Pasadena. Downtown Pasadena was about a mile away to the east, and the Dickerson's nursery was in between. With land to till and crops to put in, it would be a while before Ben would meet everyone in town.[39]

Oscar F. Moore moved his family of 12 to Pasadena by wagon from Harrisburg in 1898. Originally from Georgia, the Moores had drifted into Texas by way of Alabama. They had settled for a while in Webster before moving to Harrisburg and then finally to Pasadena. Oscar rented the old Munger place that was now owned by Mr. Gray of Houston. Wife Emma had her hands full with 10 children, each born about two years apart. Sammie, Zora Lee, Riba, and Floyd were too old for school but Ora Jane, Marion, Dora, Flake, and Verda were of school age. Emma was a year too young.[40]

With more children moving into the area, the issue of adequate schooling was raised. Pasadena was part of the county school system and was under the supervision of the Harrisburg District. Miss Rosa Dellahan was retained for the 1897-98 term and she rode a bicycle each school day, rain or shine, from Harrisburg to Pasadena to teach. The parents in Pasadena felt that not enough county tax money had been allocated to properly run their school and a meeting was called. About a dozen taxpayers showed up and first considered simply supplementing the revenue by private subscription. However, it was decided that the community would be better off to separate itself from the county system and to operate its own public free school. The community would have to incorporate itself for school purposes and to levy its own tax to support the type of school that they wanted. The incorporated city of La Porte had set the precedent in 1893 by taking financial responsibility for its school. The residents of Pasadena did not feel that the community needed to incorporate for town purposes, only for the purpose of financing a free public school. This would also give them more control over who taught their children, what they were taught, and when they were taught.[41]

A school census was taken by the Baileys that spring of 1898 and reported 24 white and three Negro students. Ben and Katie travelled the area by horse and buggy, sometimes going miles out of their way to ford the bayous since there were few roads and no bridges. Katie took along her umbrella to shade her from the sun. Since a Negro family was camping on the prairie and not permanent residents, it was suggested that they send their children to one of the schools for coloreds (a phrase used in those days indicating people of the Negroid race) that was located in the general area. A petition was submitted to the county by J. F. Hays, signed by 26 residents who were qualified to vote, requesting that the area be incorporated for free school purposes. An election was held on March 26, 1898, with Lee Pitts presiding as the election judge, and the issue passed by a vote of 23 to 0. The Pasadena school system became the first independent district in the county. It included approximately 200 inhabitants and was flanked by the county school systems of Harrisburg, Deepwater, and San Jacinto (which included Deer Park).[42]

Although Pasadena had voted to be "independent," County Judge W. N. Shaw did not certify the incorporation that year. During the interim the county superintendent separated Pasadena from the Harrisburg district and designated Pasadena as Common School District Number 42. W. P. Coolidge served as secretary of the first trustee board and Miss Mattie Nichols was hired as the teacher for the 1898-99 school term. The census for the term assigned 23 boys and 25 girls to the district, but the actual enrollment in the school was only 35 students. It fell to Miss Nichols to explain the news of the day: the Spanish-American War, the Alaskan gold rush, and Teddy Roosevelt's Rough Riders. With respect to the latter, Dr. Charles W. Griffith of La Porte had recently left town to serve as the medical examiner for Roosevelt's Rough Riders.[43]

Schoolhouses were obviously important buildings in the community. They served all community functions, from schools to churches, from business meetings to social gatherings. A Sunday school had been in existence for the children since 1893 and with the construction of the Academy late in 1894 prayer meetings were held on Thursday and Sunday evenings. With the growth of Deepwater and the church established in that community, the residents of Pasadena began attending that nondenominational "Union Congregation" church. Neither a Methodist nor Baptist preacher could be persuaded to preach to the group, so a Presbyterian preacher named Ohmstead was persuaded to preach once a month. After about a year Brother McCloud came and took over the preaching for the next couple of years. The Methodists of the community were organized by Pastor Peter E. Nicholson in 1896. The backbone of the group was the R. M. Guinn family. Robert and his second wife Mary Jane had six children. Robert's first wife had died, but most of the eight children from that marriage also were living with him, including son Will and his wife Alice. Mary Jane Guinn's sister, Katie Bailey, and her family undoubtedly rode over from Pasadena to be part of the congregation. Will Blakesley and probably his new bride Irma Parks were among the early Methodists. Reverend Nicholson lived down near Galveston Bay and Clear Lake and had organized the church in Morris' Cove several years earlier. He had also sold 263.3 acres of his land near Morris' Cove to Seabrook W. Syndor for the townsite of Seabrook. Reverend Nicholson continued to live in the new community of Seabrook while he ministered to the Deepwater group for the next two years.[44]

The Deepwater Methodists moved their congregation to Pasadena in 1898 when the schoolhouse was made available for a meeting place. One of the side benefits of Pasadena taking over the responsibility for its school system was the use of the school house for other community functions. No doubt the malaria threat in Deepwater also hastened the decision to move the congregation to Pasadena. Robert Guinn had to move his family from Deepwater to Webster in September in

Organized religion started in Deepwater in 1896 as a "Union Congregation" nondenominational church. Within two years both the Methodists and the Baptists organized their own churches.

an effort to cure them of the fever. To make matters worse, yellow fever had been discovered in Houston and rigid measures were established there to prevent the spread of the disease. Will and Katie Bailey were so glad that they no longer had to make the buggy trip to Deepwater to attend church that they purchased five acres on the La Porte road at Richey that September for their future homestead. Reverend S.W. Warner took over in 1898 as the first pastor assigned by the annual Conference of Methodist Churches. The Pasadena church was called the Methodist Episcopal Church, South and shared its preacher with a circuit composed of Harrisburg, La Porte, Seabrook, and Pasadena. The Methodists of La Porte had organized back in August of 1892 and called themselves the First Methodist Episcopal Church South of La Porte. Although the La Porte congregation immediately began raising money for a sanctuary, it was six years before they got their building. In 1898 the La Porte Methodists purchased the old school house for their sanctuary.[45]

After the formation of the Methodists in Deepwater, the Baptists began to think about organizing. By 1898 they had formed the Deepwater Missionary Baptist church. Pasadena Baptists included W. P. and Sadie Coolidge, Ben and Ella Williams, and Mrs. M. E. Dickerson and son Arthur. All of them had just recently arrived to the area and probably influenced the movement of the church to Pasadena in 1898. Other than their name, there was little else formal about the group. They met at various times and places, no doubt utilizing the school house on non-Methodist preacher Sundays.[46]

County Judge E. H. Vasmer finally certified that the community had "incorporate(d) for free school purposes only, and assume(d) control of the Public Free Schools within it's limits" on June 15, 1899. The newly elected school board members were J. T. Hanna, J. F. Hays, G. W. Kuhns, J. L. Perry, I. L. Pitts, L. J. Yarnell, and J. F. Wafer. Wafer was elected president, Yarnell secretary, and Pitts treasurer. Although they continued to report, for the time being, as District 42 of the county system, they were now recognized by the State Department of Education as an independent district. Under the county system there were three trustees that administered each district, and there were seven board members under the independent system. The board hired L. M. Thompson for $200 to teach the 1899/1900 school term. Although the annual census fell by eight from the year before to 40 students in the Pasadena district, the enrollment was probably the same as the previous year, 35 students.[47]

Teaching in a country school was a challenge because there were so many grades and so few students. The school day started with the school bell. Discipline was important. The children would enter the school, quietly and take their assigned seats, according to the grade they were in. At the front was the recitation bench. Following that was the first grade row, second grade row, and so on. Since there was no real grading system, they were moved from row to row when the teacher felt that they had mastered the material and skills appropriate for each grade level. The first lesson was a chapter from the Bible, which was read by the teacher. Following that the teacher would lead the class in a song and then the prayer. Three recesses were allowed during the day, with the girls playing on one side of the school and the boys on the other. The water bucket had to be filled regularly from a nearby well. Since there was only one dipper, everyone used it to drink water from the bucket. The children brought their lunches in syrup pails and ate biscuits with butter or syrup, or potatoes and bacon out under the trees. Later everyone participated in the cleaning and dusting of the class room.[48]

The creation of the school district gave the residents of Pasadena a common focus. The movement of the Methodist and Baptist congregations to town established more social connections for the people. The momentum that had been temporarily lost when Munger left earlier in 1896 was beginning to reestablish itself. Although still not aggressive in the development of the town, J. H. Burnett had moved from Galveston to Houston in order to be closer to his real estate interests. Over the next year the Clines, William McBurneys, and Will Spacie moved into town. William and Minnie McBurney came from the Rosenberg area and bought a farm in West Pasadena. Children Lucy and Francis "Frank" would be additions to the family shortly. William W. and Emma Spacie arrived with 26-year-old Ellen and 14-year-old William, Jr. Their other three children did not come with them. The Gwartneys (sometimes referred to as Gartney) of Genoa were the first of several families that eventually moved over to Pasadena. But while in Genoa, they had increased their family of six with another son, Stanley, who was born there in 1897. Francis and Lilly Gwartney rented a house and moved their family to Pasadena, along with a niece named Leora. Louis and Clemis Haller brought her children for the new school system, Gerald William Conrad and Warren Conrad. Scipio Shoulders moved his family to Pasadena from Arkansas. His wife Addie V. had her hands full with their five children: Lollie, Mattie, Ruby E., Renie, and Johnie Clara. Dr. Virginius St.Clair MacNider of Houston purchased 10 acres and began his semiretirement to Pasadena. For the first time Pasadena had a doctor living in the area, and ill patients or expectant mothers did not have to travel to Harrisburg, or La Porte for medical attention. Addie Shoulders was probably one of his first Pasadena patients since she named her son born in Pasadena, Robby "McNider." He probably delivered Scipio, Jr., in 1906. The other doctor in the area, Dr. Culpepper, had since departed Deepwater.[49]

Robert Guinn returned to Deepwater in July 1899 to harvest the crop that had been deserted by his renter. Things were changing in Deepwater. Colonel M. T. Jones had died the year before on June 22 after a year or so of ill health. With him the momentum also died. Although the tax rolls for the last several years had listed Vick and Jones as the owners of 5,681.7 acres in Deepwater, Jones's probate records revealed that he personally owned 5,161.98 of those acres. The railroad had finally been sold. The newly chartered company was the Galveston, Houston and Northern Railway Company. J. C. Hutchinson of the Southern Pacific Railroad had been helpful to the infant railroad under Jones and House's control and was the true owner of the new railroad company. The officers of the G. H. & S. A. ran the new railroad for the Southern Pacific.[50]

This change of railroad ownership and control severed the interest for direct development of Deepwater. Jones's son, Willie, inherited a life estate in the Deepwater property and took over management of the project. Unfortunately, he was not the man that his father was and he did not have control of all of the assets that his father had owned. Willie's cousin, Jesse H. Jones, had moved down from Dallas to take over operations of the M. T. Jones Lumber Company. Jesse possessed the talent that Willie was lacking, and, in time, would take over complete control of the M. T. Jones estate.[51]

After finishing his harvest at Deepwater, Guinn moved his family to Pasadena on October 2, 1899. The Pasadena postmaster, Jim Lewis, wanted to move back to Kansas and sold his two lots and his two-story house to Guinn on September 16 for a value of $125. Guinn paid him off with a pair of mules. Lewis hitched them to his wagon and headed home. Guinn, now 54 years old, applied for the postmaster's job and was sworn in on December 4.[52]

Eighteen ninety-nine had proven to be an eventful year in several ways. In February Galveston Bay froze solid as temperatures plummeted to seven degrees and snow drifted to 10 feet in Galveston on Sunday, the twelfth. Deer Park reported eight degrees. In April excitement ran high as a Mexican, claiming to

Foundations for Survival (1894-99)

Robert Guinn moved his family to Pasadena in 1899 from the nearby community of Deepwater.

be an aide to Santa Anna, said that a fortune in gold was hidden somewhere in the banks of Buffalo Bayou near Sam Allen's ranch headquarters. On the Fourth of July Wade Dickerson and Lillian Pitts were the first to get married in Pasadena. Following in the theme of Texas Independence, the state began condemnation action in November to acquire the first lands for the new San Jacinto Battlefield park.[53]

Pasadena was a collection of scattered clusters of farms. Local demand for agricultural products was increasing. Houston was now a major market since it had grown from a population of 2,396 in 1850 to 44,633 in 1900. And Galveston was even larger. Harris and Galveston counties contained slightly over 100,000 people, 80 percent of which lived in the cities of Houston and Galveston. The ever expanding railroad lines were providing access to markets in other parts of the nation. The wagon road to Houston was now paved with shell. Unfortunately for Deer Park and La Porte, the paving ended at Deepwater. From there east it was a dirt rut road. Lee Pitts in West Pasadena had perhaps the oldest pear orchard around in the community. Most of the other fruit orchards had been wiped out by the two uncommonly bitter winters. After the rain storm of a few years back Pitts, and others, had given up raising tobacco. Some wheat, sweet potatoes, cantaloupes, and cucumbers were being grown. Jap Hays was growing the largest cabbage you ever saw. In the entire region there were maybe two strawberry farms. Most every family in the Pasadena area had a couple of horses and a buggy. A few had mules and others had small herds of cattle. "Farmer" Edwin Rice Brown knew nothing of farming and had proven it a few years earlier in Brazoria. He moved to Pasadena with his wife Myra and young daughters Katharine "Kate" and Adele. With memories of earlier successes in ranching, Farmer Brown got back to cattle raising. The Wright/Dickerson nursery was producing a lot of cape jasmine flowers for market. Likewise Mr. Kruse produced a little cotton.[54]

Since most of the farmers were from up north they had to adjust to southern climate crops and so there were a few failures along the way. Once they developed some experience, their crops improved and their success increased. But nothing had prepared them for what was to come next.[55]

George and Elizabeth Kuhns brought their family from Kansas by rail to get away from the cold weather.

IV

Renewed Beginnings (1900–1904)

At the height of the storm the wind roared over Galveston Island at an estimated 120 miles an hour. The official weather gauge had been blown away earlier at a reading of 100 miles an hour. The entire island was under at least eight feet of water. At first most people thought that it was a typical coastal storm, but it became the last thing that over 7,000 people ever experienced. The Galveston Hurricane of 1900 was to become the worst natural disaster this nation has ever experienced. And the futures of several cities were changed by that storm. Just 35 miles away, Pasadena not only survived, it began to grow. The second wave of settlers held firm and the next group built upon their spirit. In this fertile environment the seeds for future successes were planted.

On Friday, September 7, 1900, the day began with a fairly stiff breeze. The Washington weather office had been sending out warning about a hurricane in the Gulf for several days, but few along the Gulf Coast paid much attention. A storm had not hit this area since 1867 and only a few of the current residents could even remember that one. The Port Arthur storm of 1897 was the most recent on the coast and it did very little damage. Besides, many of the new residents were from the North and they did not have any idea what a hurricane could do. Many people were still vacationing on the island, trying to get the last of the summer fling. Others had not yet returned to Houston after summering on the water. The weather deteriorated slowly and was only noted by the sailors and shipping merchants.

Bathers were enjoying the stimulating surf until Friday afternoon.[1]

On Saturday it was just the beginning of another weekend in Pasadena and no one had any idea of the drama that was beginning to unfold. Lee Pitts was in Houston on business. His wife, Lula, had stayed in Pasadena and was visiting with her daughter, Lillian Dickerson, and her infant son, Russell, when the winds began to rise. Before anyone realized that a killer hurricane was in the wind it was almost too late to take precautions. The three of them hid behind a hay stack to avoid the fury of the storm and were forced to stay there until the worst had passed. At home, the Pitts children took shelter in a nearby new barn. They felt that their own house was unsafe. Ella Williams watched as the winds pushed railroad cars along the track back towards Houston. Hanna Kruse made a mad dash to a neighbor's house, only to lose her grip on infant son, Oscar. She retrieved him only when a barbed wire fence stopped his roll. The Kruse house was then blown off of its foundation blocks by the force of the wind. Mr. and Mrs. H. L. Gibbs of Deepwater were returning from a trip to Houston when the storm grew too fierce. They took shelter in the Pasadena schoolhouse on the La Porte Road at Wafer. But fearing that the school would not weather the storm as it worsened, the Gibbs retreated to the railroad section house at Main Street, which was promptly blown from its piers and moved 15 feet. W. C. (probably P.) Coolidge's house and barn were wrecked and he spent harrowing hours in the wind and rain. Jap Hays's house was blown flat to the ground and his barn unroofed.[2]

Residents of Genoa had taken shelter in their depot but fled when the structure began to shake and tremble. They had just cleared the doorway when the building collapsed. The hotel was totally demolished and its occupants took shelter in the railroad section house. The new schoolhouse was also damaged. The roof on the Thurman house collapsed and then the wreck was blown off its piers. Roy Thurman tied his mother and his youngest sister, 13-year-old Clara, to a tree so that they would not blow away. Later the preacher came by and took them to the church for protection. The church building had sustained damage but still provided shelter for the needy. Colonel Burnett's barn was blown down and his house badly damaged.[3]

The story was much much worse in Galveston and along the bay. Caught unawares the residents and vacationers were trapped in their homes, unable to safely retreat to higher ground and safer structures. Nearly 4,000 Galveston homes were destroyed in the night of Saturday, September 8th. The stories were legion with tales of horror and heroism. When 11-year-old John Pomeroy peered out the second-story window of his bedroom on Sunday morning he could see the Gulf. The day before there had been rows of houses blocking his view. The rubble was piled high everywere, most concealing the bodies of the less fortunate. The *Houston Daily Post* headlines on Monday, September 10 blared: **THE FATE OF GALVESTON - ONE THOUSAND PERSONS DROWNED, KILLED OR MISSING, IT IS ESTIMATED.** On Tuesday the headlines continued: **LISTS OF THE DEAD - THE LATEST AND A CONSERVATIVE ESTIMATE OF THE NUMBER OF DEAD PLACES IT AT EIGHTEEN HUNDRED TO TWO THOUSAND, PROBABLY MORE.** By Wednesday the full impact of the devastation was beginning to be realized: **5000 IS NOW ESTIMATED - MANY BODIES ARE STILL IN THE RUINS OF THE BRICK BUILDINGS; OTHERS HAVE BEEN BURNED, AND STILL OTHERS BURIED AT SEA.** For the next several days interior pages were captioned: **A LIST OF THE DEAD** and **SOME PEOPLE WHO SURVIVE**. Robert and Ann James survived. Pearl Robertson rode the storm out with her family and 16 others in the attic of a neighbor's house. Colonel Burnett had moved from Galveston about three years previous, but at least six of his relatives perished. Everyone lost someone they loved, or knew.[4]

On Monday, September 10, 1900, the following article appeared in the *Houston Post*:[5]

> At Pasadena the old story was repeated. The section house of the Galveston, Houston and Northern was torn from its blocks, badly wrenched and forced to a position at least fifteen feet away from that it originally occupied. H. E. Gray's barn was ruined. The buildings belonging to Postmaster R. M. Guinn were not badly damaged, luckily, and Mr. Guinn was enabled to give his assistance to his more unfortunate neighbors, a number of whom accepted his hospitality for the night. The barn and residence of W. C. (P.) Coolidge were both damaged, as was the buildings occupied by F. M. Gartney and owned by a company of which E. L. Dennis of this city is the representative. A house belonging to the J. L.

Watson estate was badly twisted. Only a small amount of damage was done the Pasadena school house.

* * *

Deepwater was one of the worst sufferers along the line. The principal damage was done to the property of Mr. W. E. Jones, who owns a large plantation there . . . . Among the other buildings damaged were two sheds belonging to F. W. Lewis and the house occupied by Mr. Parks, which was blown off its blocks. Mr. Parks' barn was also badly twisted . . . . The barn of J. H. Stark(ey) was damaged considerably, as were the barn and sheds of W. M. Casteel and the barn of Mr. Zlomki. It was reported here that the hay barn of a man named Collins near Genoa had been destroyed and a number of head of stock killed.

Fortunately the damage was slight in the area. A *Post* reporter noted that there was general flooding from Houston to Morgan's Point and that the crops were destroyed or damaged to a great extent. He observed that the hurricane apparently moved in streaks, as damage seemed to follow lines. Had he been a Kansan he would have recognized the tornado pattern. He concludes his article: "after viewing the wreck and ruin between Houston and Deepwater one can scarcely conceive how death or injury was so generally escaped." Sam Allen's house and ranch suffered only about $1,500 damage, while the Kirby Mansion in nearby Harrisburg suffered $11,000.[6]

The worst damage and the greatest deaths occurred adjacent to the water. Thirty houses were down at Morgan's Point with only four buildings left standing. Several died including Louis Braquet who gave his life to save two women. Mr. Black was credited with saving numerous lives. Every bath house and pier between Morgan's Point and La Porte were completely destroyed. There was extensive building damage in La Porte, including the Methodist church that was blown down, McNeil's mercantile store, and Muldoon's saloon. On the Bay, the Sylvan Hotel, the pier, bath house, and dance pavilion were wrecked. The hotel was promptly sold to the Catholic Diocese of Galveston and St. Mary's Seminary was established in the repaired and enlarged structure. Most of the other buildings in town also sustained damage. Many of the people living in

Houston maintained summer homes on the Bay. Even W. E. Jones of Deepwater had a place in La Porte. He had purchased J. H. York's house, the first one built in the new community of La Porte. Like most of the others, it too was damaged and watersoaked. Only the Hamilton cottage survived in Seabrook, all other structures were destroyed. Many lives were lost in the community. The railroad bridge across Clear Creek was washed away. Mrs. Lena Flayer (Phleuger), Mrs. Sam K. McIlhenny and her daughter and two granddaughters, and the Repsdorph family all lost their lives. A steamer from Galveston and three cotton laden schooners were beached and their crews missing.[7]

The bay relief trains travelled through Pasadena and the stories of the disaster were on everyone's lips. One trainload of husbands and fathers from Houston was happily reunited at Deepwater with bayside vacationing family members who had survived the harrowing ordeal. The bodies of those less fortunate rode silently in the baggage cars. The depot at Deepwater was in ruins and the road to La Porte was impassable. Fortunately long distance telephone service between Deepwater and La Porte was in working order and reports from that city could be received.[8]

No one died in Pasadena, but a few were hurt. George Kuhns' oldest daughter fell out a window and permanently injured her hip. Most were just scared. But after the killer freeze of 1899 and the hurricane of 1900 some of the settlers from the North decided to pack it up and head home. The Kuhns decided to move to California but left 16-year-old Bertha, their youngest daughter, behind to marry Arthur Dickerson.[9]

The freeze had taken out many of the fruit trees the year before and now the hurricane had destroyed crops just before harvest time. The plight for the Gulf Coast farmer was a serious matter, but did not go unnoticed by those spearheading the relief program. Clara Barton, then 78 years old, took charge of the American Red Cross relief program for Galveston. It was the last project that she actively participated in, but she gave it her all. She realized that the loss of crops to the Gulf Coast farmer could mean disaster even to those who survived the direct impact of the storm. She quickly arranged to have 1.5 million strawberry plants shipped and distributed. Previously strawberries had been grown successfully in the region. If new plants could be put in immediately, they would yield a cash crop early the next year. The short growing season for strawberries and the mild climate meant that the Gulf Coast berries could be the first crop to the Northern and East Coast market in the spring. Those early berries would demand a premium price. By February the farmers could be receiving much needed income. Prior to the storm only two farms had been growing strawberries in Pasadena. After the hurricane, pears, figs, cantaloupes, and other late blooming or long cultivation crops took a back seat to the quick growing sweet red strawberry.[10]

Farming was a family affair and everyone had a job to do. This was one of the reasons why the community decided to take control of the education of its children. The children were needed to help plant and harvest. School would have to take second place to farming when the children were needed in the fields. The Harris County school system started classes in September and let them out in May. As an independent system, Pasadena could structure the school days around the planting and harvesting days. In the aftermath of the hurricane and the gift of the strawberry plants from Miss Barton and the American Red Cross, school was suspended until the crops were put in.[11]

The hurricane not only blew strawberries to Pasadena, it also spurred a population boom of sorts. Those that left Pasadena and the area in search of a safer environment were replaced by others moving inland from the coast, for the same reason. However, the coastal people felt that Pasadena was far enough inland for them to feel safe. Edward Payson Pomeroy of Galveston had decided to move his family and dairy back to Brenham where they had lived several years before. Payson had had a dairy in Galveston with cows in Galveston and in Hitchcock. Anna's sister and brother-in-law, Rosa and Otto Mangeliers, operated the Hitchcock dairy and Otto would bring milk daily to Galveston to be bottled and sold by Payson. Payson had introduced glass milk bottles into Galveston, and thus Texas, a few years earlier and his Metropolitan Milk Company was quite successful. Otto was lost in the storm and Rosa miscarried unborn twins. The Pomeroys moved to Hitchcock for a brief period to help Anna's sister. Anna then took what was left of the cows by rail to Brenham to relocate the dairy there. Payson and his son John were driving the dairy wagon to Brenham when they came through Pasadena in January 1901. They stopped at Deepwater to dig a water well for one of the farmers, Oscar Starnes. Payson had noted the prairie grass as had Munger almost ten years earlier. After having survived the watery deluge just a few months earlier, the Pomeroys were now faced with a drought in Brenham. Remembering the grasses of Pasadena Payson returned in April to harvest some hay and shipped ten car loads to the U. S. Army in San Antonio for $3.50 per ton. He was impressed with the lush vegetation and decided that his dairy would do better in Pasadena. He immediately purchased the old Jasper Hays house which had served as the first post office in town. The price was cheap since the house had been blown off its piers in the storm and was laying unceremoniously on its side. Located on Main Steet, the site was also across the street, one being generous with the definition of street, from the public water well that the railroad had dug eight years earlier. Payson paid $42.75 for the city lot. Although he only bought one lot, the nearest house was a block away, and all he could see from horizon to horizon was perhaps a half a dozen other houses. Like Sam W. Allen had done when he started his great ranch, one did not need to own the land to use it for grazing his cattle. After righting the little three-room structure, Payson, Anna, and John moved in.[12]

What a change it must have been from Galveston, the social and financial capital of Texas, or even Brenham, with its cultural and historical heritage. Galveston and Houston had electric lights, electric trollies, automobiles, daily newspapers, hospitals, magnificent churches, colleges, opera houses, theatres, and civic organizations. Payson even had to give up his telephone when he moved to Pasadena. Pasadena contained only the Guinn Post Office stocked with a $100 worth of grocery supplies, a section house, and a one-room school. The streets were dirt paths and the only mechanical device in town was the train when it rolled through a couple of times a day. From their porch, the Pomeroys could see only a few neighbors.[13]

James and Sula Conn Williams of Madisonville, Texas moved to Pasadena about the same time. Since all but one of their children had married or passed away, they decided to move south to live near their oldest son Ben and his family. They brought 16-year-old Chester with them. By October Frank and Louise "Lou" Harwell had moved to Pasadena with their six children to add to the school population: Frank, Mary, Betty, Annie Z., Allie, and Odie. Charlie and Lucy Saderwhite also came by then, but without any children in tow.[14]

On June 24, 1901, "Colonel" John Howell Burnett passed away in Houston. He was two weeks short of 71 years of age and had lived a full life. He had fought in two wars, served in the Texas Legislature, been a successful businessman in the mercantile trade, construction, transportation, finance, and land development, and at the time of his death was President of the Planters and Mechanics National Bank of Houston. He had outlived his wife, Catherine, and both of their sons, Oscar and Walter. From a family of ten children, he left only one surviving brother and one sister. After allowances for some land and other items to relatives, the bulk of the estate went to his daughter, Ellen Ross. The task of handling his real estate and promoting his towns of Genoa and Pasadena fell to his only surviving child, Ellen and her husband, James O. Ross. Fortunately James had been working with Burnett for several years, so the transition was smooth.[15]

With a few more people moving into Pasadena, the Baptists got together to restructure the Deepwater Missionary Baptist Church. On October 28, 1901, they reorganized the group with the help of Rev. P. M. Murphy and changed the name of the group to the Pasadena Missionary Baptist Church. The 17 charter members were: W. P. and Sadie Coolidge, Arthur L. Dickerson and his mother, Mrs. M. E. Dickerson, Ben and Ella Williams and Ben's parents, James and Sula Williams, Payson and Anna Pomeroy, Frank M. and Lou Harwell with two of their daughters, Betty and Zeola, Charlie and Lucy Saderwhite, and Mrs. Minnie Starnes of Deepwater. It was agreed with the Methodists that they should share the use of the school house, with each using it on alternating Sundays. However, they continued to cooperate on a Union Sunday School for the children each Sunday. Since the Methodists still used a circuit rider preacher who made Pasadena once every four weeks, the Baptists quickly moved to retain a minister on a half time basis, or once every other week. Reverend W. F. Smith was hired in May, 1902. He was paid $100 for seven months of half time service. The Methodists were now on their third preacher as Reverend L. L. Hursey took over from Reverend S. W. Warner in 1901. Maybe the Baptists thought that they could get a few Methodists to attend some sermons and convert, or at least contribute to the collection plate. The Baptists certainly liked to live up to their "missionary" name. In fact, the Baptist Young People's Union convention that year was held at nearby Sylvan Grove (Sylvan Beach) in La Porte.[16]

Gustov "Gus" Edming decided to move his family south from Wisconsin in 1902. He was 38 years old and a mechanic by trade. Leaving his family in Wisconsin he travelled alone to Galveston in search of a job. In Galveston he learned that a Swede by the name of Oscar Kruse lived near Pasadena. Gus moved to the Florentine Settlement and worked at raising and cutting hay. Finding the area to his liking, he sent for his family.[17]

One by one the Williams family of Madisonville moved to Pasadena. Ben brought his family in 1898 and was followed by his parents and youngest brother Chester in 1901. Brother Walter F. Williams arrived in 1902 with his wife Cynthia and children, Roy and Ardell, in a covered wagon. Ben had been here four years and highly reccommended the country. There were still more Williamses and other relatives back in Madisonville. It would only be a matter of time before they would move to Pasadena.[18]

The Starkey boys had moved over from Deepwater starting in 1901 and farmed on the east side of town. Their father, J. W. (Josiah H.) Starkey was one of the first land purchasers in Deepwater, having bought just two months after the Zlomkes in 1894. Following the Starkeys were the Blakesley and Parks families. Father Calvin Emerson Parks bought ten acres of Harris County land at the Chicago World's Fair in 1893. He tried the farming out first, and after two years, returned to Union County, New York and brought his family back to Texas. Their oldest son did not come, but Calvin and Flora Irene Parks brought the rest of his children, now all adults: Ralph Emerson, William Sullivan, Irma, and James Devere. They settled in Deepwater and it was not long before both Irma and J. D. were married off. In 1902 the Parks started their migration to Pasadena when son-in-law Will N. Blakesley, who bought land in Pasadena in 1900, moved to town in January 1902. Will and Irma moved over with their three children; Ethel, Elson, and Glen. Later that same year, Calvin's son, J. D. Parks, bought in Pasadena and in January 1903 Calvin and his other son, Ralph E., also bought in Pasadena. Calvin moved to Pasadena that same year with his two unwed sons, Ralph and Will. J. D. was the last to move over. With their one-year-old daughter Carrie, J. D. and Nora (Thurman) Parks moved to Pasadena in 1904. Blakesley and the Parks all ran dairy cows and grew strawberries on the side. Blakesley lived north of the railroad track between Witter and Bruner (Tatar) and all of the

Will and Irma Blakesley moved to Pasadena in 1902 from Deepwater and built on the La Porte Road near Witter Street.

The Blakesleys operated one of several dairies in Pasadena in the early 1900s.

Parks were south of the track, in several parcels from Witter west to Richey Street.[19]

By 1904 the Pomeroys, Blakesleys, and Parks had dairies within a mile of each other. With an improved road to Harrisburg and Houston, each had its own milk route and customers. Twice a week Payson Pomeroy would leave before sun rise with his milk wagon and head for the South Main Street section of Houston. In addition to milk he took upwards to 300 pounds of butter in one pound packages. During the summer he would raise 13 hogs on the leftover skim milk and then slaughter one each week during the winter. He made sausage and sold it on his milk route. Kruse came over from time to time and used the milk separator so that he could also make butter. Payson had constructed a large barn which was 40 feet tall. Each cow knew its own stall and would dutifully go to it for the daily milking. Payson fed them cottonseed hulls, cottonseed meal and bran to increase the butter yield in the milk. This feeding program and the use of the glass milk bottles that Payson had introduced into the state several years before had the full support of the Texas Dairyman's Association. Since there were so few houses in town the cows just grazed nearby. The biggest problem was the railroad tracks. The cows would stand on the tracks at night to get away from the mosquitoes and periodically one would get killed by a train. Fortunately, the railroad was quick to pay off. When questioned about the best type of cow to own, Payson would reply, "A brahma crossed with a Santa Fe (railroad), I've made more money on that type."[20]

Even though some of the earliest settlers to Deepwater were moving over to Pasadena, the community of Deepwater was still very much alive. The Joneses were committed to making the venture a successful operation. However, their energies went more into making their land productive than to the development of a balanced and diversified community. The Galveston storm of 1900 demolished the large hay barn and 4,600 bales of hay had been badly damaged. Combined with the equipment and other structures that were damaged, the total loss came to about $7,000 to $10,000. By 1902 W. E. Jones had repaired the damage and had increased his land holdings to 6,220 acres. Experimental farming was a popular pursuit for those who could afford to try new crops or procedures without risking business failure. Colonel Jones tried introducing tobacco into the region, only to have the crop destroyed by a rain storm. Willie followed in his father's footsteps when he retained the services of J. E. Ross to help him engage in the rice business. Jones had undoubtably met Ross when they both lived in Mexia several years previous. The following year, 1903, Mr. Ross was joined in this endeavor by his son, J. H. Ross, and together they put in the first irrigation plant in the area to be used for rice cultivation. Steam engines were used to pump water out of Buffalo Bayou and into two main canals that ran from the bayou almost to the Lynchburg Road. From these canals various rice fields were flooded. Even though there had been some dredging of the bayou and the canal was cut across Morgan's Point, the waters of Buffalo Bayou were still fresh enough for irrigation. The other benefit of rice farming was that excessive rains would not destroy the crop as it had done to the tobacco.[21]

The concept of rice farming sounded easy enough so one of the small farmers in Pasadena planted his ten-acre tract on Wafer Street in rice and flooded it from the waters of Little Vince's Bayou. But by harvest time the farmer had departed Pasadena, returning to his former northern home. The crop went to seed and shortly became the habitat of numerous wolves. One of Sam Allen's cowboys roped a good specimen and put it on display at the general store in Harrisburg.[22]

With the new influx of families to Pasadena after the Galveston Hurricane the schoolhouse got crowded. In four years the school had grown from 13 students to 30 and more were on their way as younger families were beginning to move into town. By 1901 the trustees felt that the school needed to be moved to a more central location and so, in April, Will Bailey, W. P. Coolidge, Robert Guinn, Harrison McLean, and Ben Williams, as trustees, purchased a two-acre tract on Broad Way Street, between Shaver and Main Streets. Two months before he died, Burnett conveyed the property, restricted for school purposes, for $1. A Mr. Dennis represented Burnett, and later the estate, overseeing land sales and development in Pasadena. Although the need was not immediate nor was the move made until the end of 1904, the board had anticipated the growth of the community and had purchased in advance. This thinking established a precedent for future boards.[23]

Robert Guinn was elected treasurer for the schoolboard in 1900 and reported a district property assessed valuation of approximately $150,000. A special tax of 20 cents per hundred valuation was established for the construction of a new schoolhouse. School receipts for the year totalled $288.35. That year

Miss Ruth Rodman was hired for a six-month term at $40 per month, beginning October 24th. She reported 35 students enrolled during the 119 days of instruction during the 1900-1901 school term.[24]

Pink Ellisor was hired the following year to teach the five-month term beginning in November. He was paid only $35 per month with a student enrollment of 38. Miss Rodman returned and taught a five-month school year beginning on October 10, 1902. This was the first year that specific grade levels were established. The school district showed state and local tax receipts of $616.45 for the year ending on August 31, 1903. Pasadena had complained about the inadequate funding under the county school district system and now that it was completely free of that system, the residents were increasing their commitment to local education.[25]

Although Miss Ethel Ross was hired for an eight-month term, beginning October 4, 1903, she taught only 76 days. Probably since there was a post Spanish-American War depres-

Teacher Ethel Ross stands with her class on the front steps of the school in 1903. Some of the students were: Johnny Pomeroy, Lizzie Hays, Pearl Anderson, Lucy Anderson, Ray Anderson, Irene Coolidge, Carrol Coolidge, Benny Bailey, Katie Guinn, Maggie Guinn, Howard Pitts, Rewell Pitts, Clifton McClain, Verda Moore, May Harwell, Allie Harwell, Odie Harwell, Karl Kruse, Milton Jackson, Ray Williams, and Byron Williams.

sion the trustees cut the term down to less than five months and saved $140 in teaching expenses. The following year, school trustees George Berry, W. P. Coolidge, Robert Guinn, Jap Hays, Mr. Kuntz, Harrison McLean, and Ben Williams rehired Miss Ethel Ross for a four-month session to start in October. She was paid $45 a month for her services. On November 1, the school was suspended for two days "for the purposes of holding a truck growers assistance." Simply put, the parents needed their children to work in the fields and get winter crops, probably strawberries, planted before it got too cold or too late in the season. After school term ended on December 30, 1904, the schoolhouse was moved from the La Porte Road and Wafer to the new site on Broad Way and Shaver Streets. It was fronted on Shaver Street, 120 feet south of the corner.[26]

James Andrew and Effie Jackson moved to Pasadena about 1902 and set up residency out in the country near Eighth (Jackson) Street. Their children were J. Milton, Isa, Eula, and Bettie. George Berry, his wife, and little Jesse Lloyd arrived about 1903 and George was drafted for the schoolboard the next year. George L. and Annie Holbrook came by covered wagon from Dayton, in Liberty County, with five young children: Rose Mae, William L. "Willie", Virginia L. "Virgie", Chester, and Sue "Susie." George and Annie built a large house north of the tracks, where Shaver crosses Little Vince's Bayou. They wanted plenty of room since they were anticipating more children. Before that could happen they had a whole house full of guests. The Holbrooks had been foster parents to Donna Murphy and after her marriage in 1902 to Robert Ace Kingsbury, the Kingsburys lived nearby. When the Holbrooks moved to Pasadena, the Kingsburys followed with baby Effie Mae and Blanche Lee on the way. Robert's parents, brothers, and sisters followed. To add confusion to the move, George Holbrook's parents, John L. and Virginia Ann also relocated to Pasadena. And they were followed by George's brother, William Richard. William and his wife Letha Jane already had two children, Milton and Neppie, and were planning more also.[27]

Noah and Emma Crenshaw brought daughters Bessie and Beula from nearby Genoa around that same time but kept a sizeable farming operation in Genoa with son H. L. in charge. George Horace Plum, widowed father of Mrs. Minnie McBurney, arrived and on October 17, 1903, purchased the old A. Hays place on the corner of Sixth (Eagle) and Munger. He had a

John, Virginia Holbrook (1899)
Son: Will, Lee Holbrook (1906).
" : George, Annie Holbrook (190).
and Families.

George and Annie Holbrook built a big house because they expected to have a large family.

small pear orchard and did general labor work for whomever needed it. Horace chipped in with Robert Guinn and his brother-in-law, Will Bailey to purchase lots for the future Methodist church in 1904. J. O. Ross only charged them one half of the $25 purchase price per lot since the lots were going to be used for church purposes. With Horace Plum came his son and daughter-in-law, Tom H. and Ethel Plum. In the next couple of years they would add Alice and George to Pasadena's population. Physician W. B. Ross moved to Deepwater in 1904 with his family. His daughters Ethel and Minnie were teachers, one taught in Pasadena and the other in Deepwater. J. W. Collins had moved to town earlier and was already involved with the community as superintendent of the newly formed Methodist Sunday School. In October of 1904 he was also appointed to the school tax equalization board. The population of the community was really growing.[28]

Since Charles Munger's departure in 1896 the community floundered and then concentrated on surviving. Pasadenans travelled to Deepwater for their religious satisfaction and fussed with their children's education. Slowly a new leadership began to emerge. The growth and success of the community did not rest with just one person. Leadership was being shown by an ever growing group of outspoken and dedicated settlers. Even though he lived the farthest from town, Oscar Kruse took an interest in education. The Hays, Baileys, and Coolidges took responsibility and spearheaded the drive for local control of the school system. The Guinns and Baileys brought the Methodists to town from Deepwater and Robert Guinn operated the post office as the center of town, with a few grocery supplies and in 1902 installed the first telephone in town. Along with Bailey and Guinn, Ben Williams purchased the new school site in 1901. That same year the Coolidges, Harwells, Pomeroys, and Williams reorganized the Baptists in town. The emotional energy of the settlers began to show up in physical structures and social institutions. Success breeds success and Pasadena was writing a book on how to do it.

Payson Pomeroy moved his Metropolitan Milk dairy to Pasadena after surviving the 1900 hurricane in Galveston.

V

Community Life (1905-1910)

You would not call it a stampede, but the growth in the farming community of Pasadena was gaining momentum. Not since Charles Munger organized his fellow Kansans into an excursion trip to Texas and then convinced them that this was the answer to their farming and financial hardships had the pulse of the community beat so strongly. The Cora Bacon Foster foreclosure and the severe weather of 1899 and 1900 almost stunted the vitality of the loose federation of farms graciously called Pasadena. La Porte had rebounded from its early financial woes and the blaze of two devastating fires. Morgan's Point had rushed to a low peak and had held its own, if not as a town, as a resort center. Richland and its fruit orchards faded. Deer Park was still trying to find the 200 people it boasted of in its application for a post office in 1893. Founder Simeon West threw in the towel in 1905 and sold out. Former Pasadenan Edwin R. Brown moved his wife, Myra, and children, Kate, Adele, and E. R., Jr., into the old hotel and ran cattle. Deepwater recovered from a false start in 1893 and was holding its own at about 250 people even though most of the original townsite was now the "Jones Plantation." About as fast as new people were moving to Deepwater, old residents were moving out to Pasadena. Or so it seemed. Genoa was surviving in spirits, recoiling from the Burnett deaths in 1900 and 1901. Ellen and her husband, J. O. Ross were subdividing adjacent lands in an effort to stimulate interest. The First Swedish Baptist Church, founded in 1895, finally adopted English as the language for its services in 1903, changed its name to the First Baptist Church of Genoa, and built its first sanctuary in 1905 for the 31 members.[1]

Since the Galveston hurricane and the end of the Gay Nineties, some interesting events were happening. A fellow by the name of Lucas discovered oil at Spindletop on January 10, 1901, and it made a real mess on the nearby farms. A poll tax was now required to be paid before people could cast their vote in any election. On April 1, 1903, T. Brady got the first traffic ticket issued in Houston for exceeding the six mile per hour speed limit. It cost him $10. Considering that there were only six miles of asphalt paved streets and 20 otherwise paved streets in Houston, it's not hard to figure out where the speed trap was. But since a horse trots at seven miles an hour and runs at 20 miles per hour, Mr. Brady did not necessarily have to be driving recklessly. At the time there were less than 80 cars in Houston. Later that year the first transcontinental automobile trip "under its own power" was staged and in December the Wright brothers took to the air. But Carrie Nation was more interested in reducing the speed of alcohol consumption. Between her brickbats and hatchets she wrecked many a saloon. As for pollution, it was reported that Houston's public water system was so contaminated by the rank fluid from Buffalo Bayou that it contained 320 percent too much bacteria. And the first major oil discovery in Harris County occurred in Humble in 1904. The ice cream cone was introduced at the St. Louis World's Fair and Teddy Roosevelt was re-elected President.[2]

Taking matters into their own hands, the Baptists in Pasadena decided that it was time that they have a church building of their own. With a membership of 20, Pasadena had joined the Union Baptist Association in September 1902 and immediately set out to get their own church building. A site was selected on Main Street at the northwest corner with Broad Way. Main Street was intended to be the "main" street in the community since J. H. Burnett had laid it out 80 feet wide from Third (Belmont) to Eighth (Jackson) and the other streets in town only had a 60-foot right of way. The corner at Broad Way was selected no doubt to be near the new school site which had been bought in 1901. Although the schoolhouse had not yet been moved to this more central location, the idea of a community downtown was beginning to take shape. But for the time being, however, downtown was a state of mind. Ben

The Baptists were the first to build their own sanctuary.

It would be a few years before the Baptists would get a baptismal installed in their church. Until then, they used the historical method of immersion in Buffalo Bayou.

Proud of their new church, some of the congregation gather for this photograph. Included in the picture are W. P. Coolidge, Sadie Coolidge, Carroll Coolidge, Phillip Coolidge, Irene Coolidge, Bertha Kuhns Dickerson, Rev. J. H. H. Ellis, Mary Harwell, Ida Anderson, Pearl Anderson, Mattie Ross, and Sullivan Ross.

Williams was in on both location decisions. To underscore his commitment, he secured the lot and gave it to the church in 1903. A carload of lumber was needed and the Foster Lumber Company of Fostoria, Texas (west of Cleveland) agreed to give half of it if the congregation would pay for the other half plus the freight charges to Pasadena. Under the leadership of Reverend J. F. McLeod $300 was pledged on March 4, 1904. Since they had hoped to raise $400, a "protracted" meeting was held in a tent during the last week of June. Twenty-one people joined the church, four by letters from other churches and 17 by profession of faith. The meeting cost $9.75, of which $5.50 was spent on the tent. Only $8.89 was received in offerings, so the deacons made up the 88 cents difference. Previously the congregation had agreed to build the church that summer or quit talking about it. This show of enthusiasm and determination was enough to convince the Union Baptist Association to lend the group the final $300 needed to build the church. On August 16, the loan was signed and construction began. Progress was slow since the members volunteered their time to erect the building in order to save money. They erected the building high enough off of the ground so that church goers could step straight from their wagons instead of walking through the mud on rainy days. W. P. Coolidge gave the bell for the tower. Since no baptistry was included in the sanctuary, the days of baptisms in Buffalo and Vince's Bayous were not over yet. A small room was built in the back for a class room. On October 29, 1905, Reverend J. H. H. Ellis replaced J. F. McLeod and preached the first sermon in the facility. The Baptists in Genoa completed their new church building the same year. They had more members in their congregation so they spent $1,500 on their new sanctuary.[3]

The Methodists back in Pasadena felt the pressure to likewise build a sanctuary but, like the Baptists, lacked the funds to make a major commitment. Will Bailey and Robert Guinn had participated with Ben Williams earlier in purchasing the new school building site. When Williams had purchased the site for the Baptist church nearby, Bailey and Guinn purchased a site for the Methodists. Now that both churches were to be located near the future school campus, Broad Way, between Shaver and Main Streets would become the social center of

It took the Methodists a little longer to raise their money, but they built a fancier church than the Baptists.

Pasadena about 1907 as viewed from the west side of town looking east.

town. The Baptists built a simple structure, costing around $600 and valued at about a $1,000. The sanctuary planned by the Methodists exceeded in design the basic building erected by the Baptists, and was reflected in its $2,300 cost. Truly, it was to be the most magnificent structure in town. Because of the amount of money involved it took the Methodists two years longer to complete their fundraising and construction. In the meantime, they continued to meet in the schoolhouse, even after it was moved to the new site in 1905. Reverend O. F. Zimmerman was the Methodist minister when the church was completed in 1907. Zimmerman also served the church in Genoa at the same time.[4]

Once the schoolhouse was moved to its new location early in 1905, a 20-foot shed addition was approved by the trustees. In ten years the student population had doubled to 56 pupils. And by placing a blanket or sheet down the middle of the main room, you could have three classrooms and begin to better separate the students by grade level groupings. One teacher might be able to handle the work load if he or she was good at assigning work to one class and moving to the next one for lecture and assignment at an other level of study, and then on to a third group. In 1904, the session had only been four months long, from September through December. Certainly

Community Life (1905-1910)

Panorama of Pasadena in 1907.

the Pasadena trustees exercised the independence status the community had voted for back in 1898 by tailoring the school term to the immediate needs of the season, circumstance or budget. The 1905 session began in June with a teacher hired on a month-to-month basis.[5]

However, the days of a one-room, one-teacher school in Pasadena ended the summer of 1905. John T. Conn was hired for one month at $50 on May 19 and if attendance justified it, he would be hired for a second month. Interest must have been high for the summer session as Will Blakesley was hired in June to build outhouses at the new school site for $16.75. Attendance obviously justified the second month of instruction. In addition, a six-month contract was given to Professor Conn on August 1, with an increase in salary to $75 per month and the requirement that he provide an assistant. New trustees Oscar Kruse, Payson Pomeroy, and Will Bailey joined Hays, Berry, Coolidge, and Guinn in making school history when they required the hiring of an assistant. Additionally, the board shifted from simply hiring a teacher and maintaining a building to "school administration" when it appointed trustees Pomeroy and Hays to work out a course of study with Professor Conn. Continuing their aggressive posture, they suggested that someone talk to the new Tilley family to see if they would

The old schoolhouse was moved from Wafer and Fifth (Shaw) to Shaver Street at Broad Way in 1905 and enlarged.

send their children to school. With pride for their new school campus in mind they had the school painted two coats of "Pearl Grey" with suitable trim, and even hired a boy to stoke the winter fires and carry water to the schoolhouse. The following July they contracted with Tom Plum to enclose the school ground with a three-plank, "one by six" fence for $20.[6]

John Thomas Conn was a relative of the former school board trustee, Ben Williams. John grew up in Madison County and attended Peabody University in Nashville, Tennessee. He married Annie Lydia Hughes in 1902 and they both were teachers. John and Annie arrived in Pasadena with infant Lucille from Madison County. Annie's brother, Leonard Hughes came with them. Obviously Ben convinced John to move to Pasadena so that the school system could have a first-class education "professor." John's father, John Golden Conn was the brother of Ben's mother, Arsula. A year earlier, in January of 1904, J. G. and Nancy Conn purchased seven city blocks from the Burnett estate for $2,100. It included four blocks on the south side of Broad Way from Main Street to Wafer and the three blocks on the north side of Broad Way from Spooner to Wafer. Since the Conns never moved to Pasadena, John at least had a place to live.[7]

There must have been a chamber of commerce at work for the community in 1905 because two mercantile stores were opened that year, each claiming to be the first in Pasadena. Wade Dickerson had been living in Pasadena for eight years. He had married and was now the proud father of two children, Russell and Beatrice. The only grocery store in town was the miniscule collection of goods at Guinn's post office and there was no general merchandise store in town. It was time for Wade to break away from the family florist business and to get into a business for himself. He built a two-story building just south of the railroad tracks, facing Main Street and opposite the community water well. His store was a general merchandise emporium. Charles Henry Tilley moved to Pasadena with his wife Mary and children, Ola O., Arthur Carl, Charles Albert, and Cecil H., in 1905 from Deepwater. He built his two-story home and business establishment directly behind the community water well on Main Street, just south of the railroad tracks. Besides groceries, he supplied leather goods; from shoes to harnesses and offered cobbling services. Tilley's and Dickerson's stores faced each other across Main Street, sandwiched between the railroad tracks and Sixth (Eagle) Street. The real winner in this new commercial competition was the community of Pasadena. No longer did they have to travel to Deepwater or Harrisburg after they depleted the skimpy supply at Guinn's post office. In keeping with the commercial spirit Guinn increased his services to include Western Union. Now you could mail, wire or call at the post office.[8]

All of a sudden the town was beginning to look different. On the south side of the tracks, Dickerson's and Tilley's stores glared at each other. Payson Pomeroy had built a huge barn next to his house on Main Street for his dairy cows. C. E. Parks had done the same on Shaver plus he built a large two-story home for himself. Horace Plum lived in the old A. Hays' house, about the same size as Payson's and located between the two dairies. As a general handyman, he found work easily. One of his frequent employers was the nearby Pomeroy dairy. The school was on its new campus, and with the nearby Baptist Church and the soon-to-be-built Methodist Church, formed the civic center of the community. The Jackson house could be seen in the distance to the south, with the Coolidge's and other buildings dotting the horizon. To the east was J. D. Parks' new two-story home and dairy buildings and the Kuhn's place. Across the tracks on the north side, there was now a series of

The sign out front read, "C. H. Tilley and Co., Grocer." Tilley's store sat next to the community's artesian water well.

John Pomeroy sits on horseback in the middle of the street between Tilley's and Dickerson's new stores. Dickerson's was on the right with the impressive front porch. In the background is Pomeroy's barn and the Baptist Church is barely visible.

Community Life (1905-1910) 97

"Downtown Pasadena" as viewed from on atop the schoolhouse. The cluster of buildings are around Dickerson's and Tilley's stores at Main Street and the railroad tracks.

single-story structures beginning with the Blakesley's in the direction of Deepwater just across Little Vince's Bayou and continuing back to the west through town with the section house, Guinn's, the old Bailey rent house, another sizable residence and ending on the west end with the A. L. Dickerson nursery on Vince's Bayou. Behind those to the north you could see several structures in the tree line along the bayous. To the extreme north you had the Slagles, Perrys, McCormicks, and Davises. Beyond Vince's Bayou on the western edge of town you had the Williams, Pitts, Andersons, Hays, Baileys, McLeans, and McBurneys. Over in the deep southwest of the community was the Florentine Settlement with the Kruses and Edmings. All of those lived in Pasadena and more. It seemed as if someone new moved to Pasadena every month now.[9]

Nineteen-year-old Katie Guinn helped her father in the post office and just about knew everyone that was in town. After all, daily now she was putting mail into their boxes, or mostly in alphabetical order since most people just called for their mail. In 1900, when she was 14 years old, Katie opened the Wells Fargo office and had witnessed the increasing strawberry shipments. Two years later she was made "official assistant" to her father, the postmaster, and custodian of the new telephone.[10]

Almost without hesitation Katie could rattle off the names of those who received mail in Pasadena. The new arrivals by 1905 included the Glasses. Newlyweds Arvie and Grace Thompson would add Edwin and Fern to the population within a few years. William F. and Elnor Agnes Van Dorn arrived with Maybelle, Hazel A., Raymond Oliver, Bessie, Ivy, and Tyra. They would shortly add the twins, Richard and William, and then Lois to bring their total to nine children. Dean K. and Effie Jones came to town with six-year-old Laura. Jake D. Miller brought his family from Hill County. His wife Belle Credella was stepmother to his two oldest, Bob and Bud. Credella was mother to Thomas L., Betty L., Kirby J., and Ira. The Yerkes came to town from Mississippi with their children Mabel and Emile. Dr. Titus Chauncey Loose and family arrived from Ohio, settled on the western side of town and got involved in the Baptist church. T. C. and his wife organized the Baptist Young People's Union (BYPU) and his father, Eli became the first ordained minister of the young church. Mattie McEvers arrived with children Hugh and Rhoda Elizabeth. John Taylor

Dr. T. C. Loose with wife and son. He was the first doctor to live in the community.

Shine, wife Emma and their three children, James Irby, John Oscar, and Cora Bell arrived from Port Lavaca early in 1904. They bought 35 acres in the heart of the little community. It began at the southwest corner of Shaver and Broad Way and went west to Vince's Bayou. Directly across the street from their new house would be the schoolhouse and the Methodists would build almost catty-corner from them. Maybe there were more around who just were not getting any mail. But Katie did not miss much of the comings and goings of the community since she was literally in the middle of everything.[11]

In fact, when the first automobile came through town, she witnessed the event. The advance word spread like wild fire and the bright eyes lined the La Porte Road as the Charles Milby family of Harrisburg rolled through, probably on the way to the bay. Thomas Forbes of Morgan's Point and C. L. Stable, B. T. Houlks, J. K. Kirkland, and G. L. Ashton, all of La Porte had automobiles in 1904 as did Sam Allen and his wife Rosa. H. A. Paine and J. S. Cullinan, both of Houston were also registered owners. Even J. O. Ross, executor of Burnett's estate and thus Pasadena, owned a car, although his was not the first one to visit the community. John Pomeroy stopped his work and marvelled at the motor car that came through town on November 8, 1905. It was the third such machine he had ever seen in his whole life.[12]

Life was still slow, and tied to nature and the seasons. The dairymen rose early to milk the cows and twice a week loaded

The La Porte Road at the turn of the century. The automobile is heading west near Richey Street.

their wagons for deliveries in far off destinations. They were a tie to the news of Houston and Harrisburg and could be counted on to share the news of the day. Payson Pomeroy used his spare time in Houston to work with lawyers on cases and to mix in politics. When he first moved to Pasadena he had learned that title to certain tracts of state public land could be had simply by settling on it for three years, making improvements and paying the state minimal annual installments which were to benefit the county schools. Beginning as far back as 1895 a series of law suits had been filed against J. H. Burnett seeking to cancel his title to four tracts of land for failure to meet the settlement requirements. Hays and Pomeroy were misled by one of the attorneys involved who claimed that he could get the original grants dismissed and new ones issued to Hays and Pomeroy. Hays and Pomeroy began staking their claims by settling on the land. When they refused to pay the attorney what they thought was an exorbinant fee for his services, the attorney had the state's action against Burnett dismissed by misrepresentation of the facts. The whole experience fasci-

Sam and Rosa Allen each had an automobile according to the Automobile Directory of 1904.

nated Payson and even though he was over the age of 70 he considered beginning the apprenticeship program to get an attorney's license.[13]

Like so many people who take to the legal profession, Payson turned to politics. In 1906 he filed for the State House of Representatives, Harris County Position Number Three. He ran his campaign as "The People's Candidate." Since the race was county wide, former Representative John T. Browne won handily with his strength in the Third, Fourth and Fifth Wards of Houston. Naturally Pomeroy won in the Deepwater and La Porte precincts. No one in Genoa voted either way in the Representative race. O. B. Colquitt won the governorship race

Payson Pomeroy ran as "The People's Candidate" for the state legislature.

in Harris County but lost to T. M. Campbell in the final state returns. Colquitt would have to wait four years to get his turn as governor. And Pasadena's first teacher, L. A. Dowdell lost out to incumbent L. L. Pugh in the county school superintendent's race.[14]

The farmers of Pasadena spent much less time in Houston and more time at home. They were into the fields early and the work schedule depended on the weather and the season. No one depended on one job, or crop, to provide for their needs and no one was idle when the main chore was done. During winter there was the butchering of hogs and the curing of meat or stuffing of sausage. Late harvest crops like cucumbers were pickled as were a variety of other products. If the weather was dry and warm there would be outside painting of the buildings with whatever paint was available or using one's own recipe of lime and water to make "white wash." Fences were built to keep cows and other roaming animals out of gardens, and a few yards. Everyone had a cow or more and all of them roamed free on the range. Unless you wanted your greens, strawberries, cucumbers, beans, or other tempting vegetation turned to milk, beef or simply trampled flat, you fenced the offender out. From time to time the fences needed mending. Chicken houses had to be built, repaired, cleaned and the nests robbed daily. Like eggs, honey had to be "robbed." Cows had to be milked daily and butter churned on the back porch. When the churning was done, the separator had to be cleaned. Then there was firewood to cut, ashes to clean out of the stoves and ice to haul. John Pomeroy noted in his diary on Thursday 30, 1905: "This was THANKSGIVING DAY. I worked in the garden a while. Then I shoveled manure from betwine[sic]the barn and the manure pile. After dinner Walter William and I went to Deep Water and got a load of rice strow[sic] from our hogs. I went to bed about 7.30 p.m. and slep[sic] sound." [15]

If a cold snap hit, or a freeze set in, everyone, and that was everyone, in the community turned out to cover the strawberry plants with hay. If it went on into the night, the littlest child carried the lattern to light the way and the others nestled the delicate plants in their blanket of dried grass. Uncovering them after the danger passed was easier since there was no deadline to get that job done. This routine of cover and uncover could be repeated several times a winter. Once you got your berries covered you checked with your neighbors to see if they needed help. Neighbors would do the same for you.

Everyone helped everyone. And even before the threat of frost was over, strawberries started ripening and were picked from January until May. School let out in February or March so that the children would be available to help during the height of the season.[16]

When the weather warmed there were crops to put in. Cantaloupes went in in February; beans, peanuts, cane, and onions in March. Cucumbers, watermelons, and tomatoes were planted in between the strawberry picking. Weeds always grew faster than the plants and had to be hoed out so that your livelihood would survive. And about the time you got your fill of planting and hoeing, the beans started coming off. As the last plant faded, it was pulled and replanting began. Despite the amount and variety of work that had to be done, generally it was not constant. When you had the time, or were needed, you traded your time to another farmer. You might help with someone's harvest and then borrow their team to put your next crop in. Sometimes your neighbor would help with the milking in exchange for milk, or lend a hand with building a fence or an outhouse. Someone was always putting up a barn, or tearing one down. And when it rained, you were digging ditches to get the water to drain off. Strange, it seems that water and gumbo made glue and thus your shovel became a lead club that could not be cleaned or stuck back into the ground. At this point it was only good for making sore muscles.[17]

Summer slowed down with the heat, or rather the work pattern shifted. You rose earlier to get the chores done before it got too hot, or you stayed out later in the evening trying to finish before it got too dark. If you could plan it, during mid day, you were under a tree or snapping beans on a porch, or inside in a cross breeze. Sometime you could just kick back and get caught up on your *Star Monthly* magazine. Washing the buggy was rather pleasant in warm weather. Clothes washing was more of a chore and making the lard/lye soap was a smelly pain. Regularly you had to haul water barrels from the well in front of Tilley's for drinking and cooking purposes. Taking a bath, usually once a week, would be done with cistern water, or a dip in a nearby swimming hole.[18]

Naturally the children all had their favorite swimming holes. Some were in Vince's Bayou, others in Little Vince's, and for the ruffins, Buffalo Bayou was the fun place to take a swim. Each year it was the challenge to see who would "Break the water." Easter Sunday was a good time to issue the challenge and anyone who did not participate was a sissy, regardless of the weather. The honor of being the first to brave the cold water and jump in did not last long and soon the swimming holes were fully occupied. Being raised in Galveston, 16-year-old John Pomeroy took pride in his swimming ability. With witnesses in tow on August 20, 1905, he and Perry Kuhns swam Buffalo Bayou 20 times straight. John figured that was about 2,000 yards.[19]

A Coming Men of America lodge for young men was formed and held monthly meetings on Wednesday evenings. Chester Williams and John Pomeroy got the group together. Perry Kuhns and Hugh McEvers were a part of the original group. Johnie Bryant, Leonard Hughes, Milton Jackson, Warren Rawlins, Ralph Pickett, and William Spacie, Jr. joined up once the group got going. A literary society was also organized and was open to adults and students. The society met on Saturday evenings from September to January. Attending schoolboard meetings was always interesting, if you went for that type of thing.[20]

On Sunday afternoons in warm weather there were a lot of church socials. Sometimes it was a picnic on Buffalo Bayou near the Holbrook place. The Baptists had their favorite spot in Buffalo Bayou for their emersion ceremony and the entire congregation would line the bank in their Sunday best to view the event. At other times church socials would be on the school grounds and contests and games would be held. There was always plenty of food and a wonderful time. The young boys often broke away and went swimming. Eating watermelons was always a fine way to spend some time. There were enough teenagers in town so that walking to and from socials was a good time to court. Some say that Spooner Street earned its name for the "spooning" that went on. Dances were held at some parties and on special occasions. Someone was always hosting a party. Wade Dickerson invited everyone over to show off his new house on August 31, 1906. The Ladies Aid Society hosted chicken dinners for their fund raiser. Sunday supper was usually after the preaching and the congregation took turns inviting the preacher to eat. Pasadena fielded a baseball team by 1906 and if you weren't playing, you went along to watch. It was an exciting game when they beat Harrisburg 16 to 15 on June 30, 1906. And then there always was time to stop and just enjoy nature.[21]

La Porte offered many opportunities for enjoyment. Sylvan Beach or Morgan's Point had good surf to swim in. A rollerskating rink would be set up and you could learn, or show off. Going the other way you could travel to Houston. Not that it really affected anyone from Pasadena, but Houston did pass a no flirting ordinance. And certainly you did not want to be in town when Carrie Nation was around. She did $750 worth of damage on December 30, 1905, to a bar in Houston that had boldly named itself the Carrie Nation Bar. The bar did change its name after that. Getting to Houston was no problem. There was always the daily train to get you there and back, or you could catch a ferry on Buffalo Bayou and steam to Harrisburg or Houston. It had taken them three years but the dredges had finished deepening the bayou to 18 feet so that even larger ships could steam up to Clinton and slightly beyond. For those that did not want to ride their horse or buggy/wagon all the way to Houston, there was a clump of trees at the Pasadena end of the Harrisburg to Houston trolley where you could hitch the animals. Usually you would hitch up next to another animal you recognized, that is, one from Pasadena. After a while it got to be that certain areas became informally known as the Pasadena spot, or the Genoa spot, or whom evers. You could also walk to Houston or La Porte, but that was not very popular. But anyone going in either direction could hitch a ride with anyone heading in that direction. There was a good chance that you would know them or of them, since there were not that many people in the area. Even if you did not know them, there never was anything to fear and everyone helped everyone else.[22]

One thing people do not normally think a lot about is death. Unfortunately it is a fact of life and you must make a place for it. None of the new town developers ever laid out a cemetery. Cemeteries were something that the residents had to come up with. And usually its need would be felt several times before the citizenry accepted the responsibility. Little Ruth Johnson was the first to pass from this life in the struggling community of Pasadena. Malarial fever visited the early settlers and little Ruth was laid to rest under a large oak tree near Buffalo Bayou. The Vanderson clan from North Dakota lived in Pasadena for about a year around 1895. Many of their people died while they were here and they were buried in unmarked graves in the direction of Harrisburg. They left no visible record of their having travelled this way nor the misfortune they suffered.[23]

Edward Payson Pomeroy, 74, passed away at 6:15 A.M., Wednesday, October 24, 1906, at his home on Main Street in Pasadena. Although he had been ill for a couple of weeks and had just returned from a week and a half at St. Joseph's Infirmary in Houston, his death was not expected. Ironically, he had been working with fellow school trustees J. L. Holbrook and J. A. Jackson and several others on establishing a cemetery in the community. They had discussed various sites but had not purchased any land. Upon hearing of Mr. Pomeroy's death, J. L. Holbrook immediately travelled to Houston and purchased a tract of land on the north side of Vince's Bayou, just above its junction with Little Vince's Bayou. R. Guinn, J. A. Jackson, J. T. Shine, C. H. Tilley, and J. L. Holbrook took title to the land that day as trustees for the cemetery association. The six acres cost $200, but J. O. Ross gave them six months to pay for the land due to the immediacy of the need. That afternoon widow Anna Pomeroy and her son John picked the location for Payson's final resting place. Arrangements were made with undertaker Sid Westheimer of the Westheimer Livery and Funeral company of Houston. The traditional pine box with glass viewing panel was brought and a special service performed at the Baptist Church. E. P. Pomeroy was laid to rest in the northeast corner of the new cemetery, in Lot 4, Block 1. Anna paid $10 dollars for the family plot which contained six grave sites. The undertaker got $28.50 for his services. Regardless how dubious the honor, Payson was the first person buried in the new cemetery. Two days later, on Saturday, the 27th, the Pasadena Cemetery Association was organized with J. L. Holbook as president, C. H. Tilley as secretary, R. M. Guinn as treasurer, and J. A. Jackson and J. T. Shine.[24]

Before year's end, Clyde and Emma McMaster of Deepwater purchased the adjoining lot and buried their first born, infant Emma. The following year, trustee J. A. Jackson buried his wife Effie. While in Pasadena Effie had birthed Mollie, Joseph M. and Susie. Susie was the seventh, and shortly after her birth Effie passed away. Horace Edward and Bertha Ford had recently arrived in town when they had to give up their year-old Winnie Lee to the likewise new cemetery. These were sad stories, but paid testimony to the need of the growing community. W. L. Wilson understood how to draw plans so he volunteered to draw up a map of the cemetery. Since the map needed to be large enough to write the names of the owners of the plots on and to locate the grave sites, he used a window shade for his drawing paper. Jim Hughes helped with the project and they marked the shade map, "Pasadena Crownhill Simatry[sic]."[25]

Horace E. Ford had brought his family to Pasadena from Madison County to work with Walter Wilson in 1907. Walter had arrived first, also from Madison County, as a "box car" cowboy. He had been hired to deliver cattle to Pasadena and he rode down with them in a railroad box car. Since the Williams and Conns were also from Madison County, he felt right at home and decided to stay. The Pitts had moved, as it turned out temporarily, to Hondo late in 1905 and sold their place in West Pasadena to the Fords. It worked a real hardship on the budding romance of Jewell Pitts and John Pomeroy. By early 1907 Lee Pitts returned with his family and bought ten acres at the southwest corner of Shaver and Third (now the Southern Pacific railroad bypass tracks). Baby Bert was born while the Pitts were in Hondo.[26]

After the death of Payson Pomeroy in October of 1906, the widow Anna Pomeroy applied for the administration of his estate. The estate consisted of the homestead property on Main Street, valued at $400, the personal property which included the dairy business and its debt of about $400, and about two and three quarters acres of land nearby, valued at $150. The whole estate was valued at approximately $700. Anna was appointed administrator and required to put up a $1,000 bond. J. L. Holbrook and Louis Haller provided the surety for the bond. The court set aside a value of $600 for the widow's "one year's maintenance and support." In addition to the business debt to Mr. J. E. Newton, other debts of the estate totalled $272.40. Anna hired Bama Scroggins in February to help around the house and with the dairy for $10 per month plus room and board. Although most of the debts could be paid off out of the operation of the dairy, the dairy itself had to be sold to pay off all of the debts of the estate. In May of 1908 the dairy was sold for $1,200 to Allen Carpenter and was moved to Crosstimbers.[27]

With more than comfort in mind, Anna had her son John build them a new house in June of 1908. Russell Wallace had been working at the dairy before it was sold and he stayed to help John build the new house. Along with his brother Homer it took them two months to build the six-room house. It had porches front and back, was wallpapered on the inside, guttered all round and had a 224-feet concrete sidewalk. The lumber cost $622.25 and the total job came to $1,081.62. As soon as the job was completed in August, Anna rented out their old house for $5 a month to Mrs. Bryant and took in roomers and boarders at their new house. The new school teachers Gertrude McMasters and Sue Hall boarded for $12 a month. Thus began a long tradition for Anna of boarding teachers and one which would get her a daughter-in-law and a granddaughter-in-law.[28]

Under the tutalege of Anna's attorney, retired County Judge Ernest H. Vasmer, she converted her unspent widow's "maintenance" allowance into land. In addition to her homestead on the west side of Main Street near Sixth (Eagle) Street, she acquired almost three acres on the south side of the railroad tracks between Randall and Wafer. Anna began paying the taxes on the block of land opposite her homestead and acquired title to it by adverse possession. Although the land was held as an investment, it was put to immediate use raising strawberries and other crops.[29]

When John Pomeroy began building their new house he had borrowed some "rollers" in Houston in order to move their old little shotgun-style house across the street to its new location. Moving houses this way was a common occurrence. The rollers

John Pomeroy built his mother a new home for $1,081.62 in 1908.

were a lot easier to use than some of the other methods used earlier. Andrew Jackson acquired a house in Deer Park and moved it on logs from there to his farm on Eighth (Jackson) Street. It was a dog trot style house that had been used as a halfway house for wagon drivers and passengers.[30]

The first doctor to live in Pasadena was Dr. T. C. Loose. He was 30 years old in 1905 when he moved into the southwestern side of town. He had graduated from Starling Medical College in Columbus, Ohio nine years earlier. A year after he arrived in Pasadena he passed the Texas State Board's medical examination and registered to practice in Harris County. Dr. Virginius St. Clair MacNider of Houston had purchased 50 acres of land in Pasadena back in 1898 but had not moved to town. He would visit on occasion but did not maintain a practice in Pasadena. For additional medical attention you had to travel to Deepwater, Harrisburg, Houston, or La Porte. Dr. H. W. Culpepper had lived in Deepwater in 1895 but had moved about a year later when his farming venture did not succeed. Dr. W. B. Ross moved to Deepwater in 1904 with his 11 children and practiced there until 1907.[31]

Doctor Juliett C. Marchant was the first physician to move to La Porte. She was 50 years old when she arrived in 1893 and quickly established a good reputation. Like so many of her patients, she did what she had to, regardless of weather or time of day. She rejected any sympathy that might be offered for the hardships she endured in the course of her treating any emergency, stating "that was part of the bargain when I learned the profession." Dr. H. T. McCoy moved to La Porte in about 1895, and built one of the first brick buildings, the McCoy Building, in that new community. Dr. Charles Wesley Griffiths came to La Porte in 1898, fresh out of the same medical school in Columbus, Ohio that Pasadena's Dr. Loose graduated from the year before. Perhaps it was he who encouraged Dr. Loose to later move to the area. Shortly after arriving in La Porte, Dr. Griffiths left to become the medical examiner for Teddy Roosevelt's Rough Riders. He returned to La Porte in late 1905 to get married and to set up a long delayed medical practice.[32]

Although there were always several doctors in La Porte, there were no clinics or hospitals. If one got so sick that hospitalization was required, they had to travel to Harrisburg or Houston. Dr. Loose lived on the Harrisburg side of Pasadena for that reason. Besides Dr. MacNider, Dr. I. P. Poynor maintained his practice in Harrisburg. He arrived in 1904 from Palestine and was soon also tending to the needs of those in

Pasadena. But because medical care was not convenient, most people simply did without, depending instead on folk medicine traditions passed down from generation to generation. There was always a woman in town with a remedy for persistent ailments, or you could purchase a variety of patent medicines which were touted in most tabloids. Since most babies were born at home and the doctor had to be sent for as the time for birthing grew near, midwifery was a common calling among the women of the community.[33]

After a successful school term in 1905, John T. Conn was again appointed teacher for the 1906-07 school term to start the July 16. He was to receive $100 per month for an eight-month session. The school enrollment had grown from 56 in 1904 to 109 in 1906. Only 56 days of instruction was given in 1904 and that was expanded to 160 in 1906. In addition, Professor Conn was offering some high school level work for the two boys and one girl that were interested in getting more education beyond the 7th grade certificate level. After three years of teaching, John was elected to the school board in 1908 along with J. E. Brooks. They replaced retiring trustees W. P. Coolidge and J. L. Holbrook. At 51 years of age Coolidge had fathered another son. "Woodie" Jr. had surprised them seven years ago and now Byrd gave them another surprise. Other members of the board included J. W. Collins, Robert Guinn, Will Guinn, J. A. Jackson, and Oscar Kruse. It was at about this time that Conn opened a small mercantile store. It was a two-story structure, located on the same intersection with Dickerson's and Tilley's stores. Some thought that Conn and Tilley were in cahoots, sort of ganging up on Dickerson. Since Tilley owned the land, there might have been some truth to that rumor. Zora Lee Moore took care of the Conn's children before her marriage to Robert A. Kingsbury in September 1910.[34]

On May 29, they elected Myrtle McMaster as principal for $100 per month and her younger sister Gertrude as her assistant at $40 per month. Their brother Clyde was postmaster in Deepwater and ran the mercantile store in that town. Shortly after the term started on July 6 Myrtle resigned. J. T. Conn stepped down from the board and was again elected principal. After some squabbling and misunderstanding, Gertrude McMaster was retained as his assistant, and a third teacher, Susan Hall, was hired. W. W. Anderson took Conn's place on the school board, and for a brief period during the squabble, Ben Williams was elected principal. The student

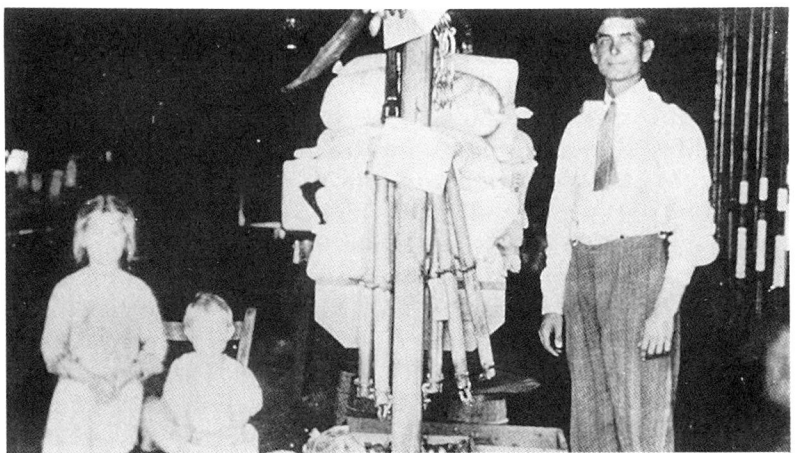

Professor John Conn supplemented his teaching income with his small mercantile store. Lucille and Annie pose with their father.

population of the district had now increased to 104 pupils with enrollment at 92 students. A 60-volume library was started in the school and ten grade levels were being offered. In addition to the three "R's", music was being offered for the first time as part of the curriculum. "Modern Music Series" primers were bought for the classroom. Naturally the increasing demand upon the school structure was taking its toll and by the end of the term the trustees were considering increasing the school tax rate to pay for improvements.[35]

As usual the school term ended in February so that the children would be able to help pick strawberries. Although Gertrude McMaster's brother lived in nearby Deepwater, Gertrude and Susan Hall had boarded at Mrs. Pomeroy's. Young John had been dating Lizzie Hays but soon turned his attention to Miss "G." When the school finished, Gertrude took over for a teacher in Houston Heights. John visited her regularly on Sundays, dropping his buggy off at Harrisburg and riding the street car to the Heights. Between the visits, letters, post cards, and postals, they were not often out of contact.[36]

Miss Ella Wood Hill was elected principal for the 1909-10 term at a salary of $85 per month, assisted by Gertrude McMaster as teacher of primary school at $50 per month and Mrs. Floyd Anderson as assistant teacher at $50 per month.

Ella Hill had previously taught at League City and when she came to Pasadena John Conn went to League City as its superintendent. Ella boarded at Mrs. Pomeroy's for $15 per month and Gertrude stayed with her brother Clyde who had recently moved to Pasadena with his wife Emma and infant Myrtle. Mrs. Floyd Anderson was the former Minnie Ross who had taught in Deepwater and whose sister, Ethel Ross had taught two years in Pasadena. Fifteen-year-old Karl Kruse had started under Ethel Ross when she was the only teacher. The student population had doubled and now there were three teachers. Sisters Florentine and Selma and brother Oscar Kruse were now in school with him. They, and Maurine Collier shared two donkeys to ride to school on. This was a fairly common practice for the children that lived more than a few miles from the schoolhouse. Virgie Holbrook only lived about a half mile from the school so she walked it, carrying her biscuits and jelly for lunch. With more students and thus more teachers, one might not be surprised to learn that the "itch" broke out in school in July and Dr. Byars of Harrisburg was called in to examine the situation. Fortunately only seven cases of the rash were confirmed and the students were excused from classes for about a week.[37]

And there was also a rash of new residents by 1910. Young families were moving into the area with a greater frequency and the school was getting overcrowded. Francis Devier and Martha Jane Newell moved from La Porte to Pasadena early in 1907. They moved from Georgia to Texas for Martha's health. Frances worked as a millwright and they lived in Cleveland for a while. But it was better for Martha

In 1907, Martha Newell informed her husband she had purchased a strawberry farm in Pasadena so he should quit his travelling job and come home for the harvest.

to live near the coast so he moved her and the children to La Porte. Frances travelled a lot because of his job so he would not be at home for periods of time. Early in 1907 Martha informed him that she had bought a ten-acre strawberry farm in Pasadena and he was needed to help harvest. He quit his job and settled down in Pasadena with his family. Despite Martha's ill health they had eight children when they moved to town: Effie Eugene, Buelah Colesta, Bannah Lee, Thomas Vernon, Ila Myrtle, Fontis Eugene, Bertrum F. "Burt", and Earl Lester. They would add Ernest Theodore, Annie Elizabeth, and Wesley Osborne shortly. Shortly afterwards George Pendleton and Minnie Selena Dowell also moved to Pasadena from La Porte with their family. Edgar was eight years of age, followed by Rosa, Mack, and infant Jane. Gus Edming travelled back to Wisconsin and brought his family to Pasadena, including wife Anna and the children: Clarence, Hulda, Selma, and Eva. All except for Eva had been born in Sweden. And Lillie M. would be born in Pasadena. Aldoph F. and Matilda Wallman were also from Sweden. They brought eight of their nine children from Wisconsin. With them came Eva, Ester, Ella, Fred, Freda, Hilda, Henry, and baby Ruth. Eva and Ester were also born in Sweden. Mrs. Lola Emma Long Hargrave was terrified of the cyclones in Oklahoma and persuaded her husband Lester Leroy Hargrave to move to Pasadena because they had relatives there. John Holbrook was Lola's uncle. Besides, Lester's family lived in nearby Dayton. With three-year-old Gladys May and infant Ruby Lee they arrived in December of 1908. Also influenced by the Holbrooks to move to Pasadena, Edward A. and Apha Neppie Olson moved over from Dayton with their young daughters, Rosa and Lottie. From the piney woods of Louisiana, Mrs. Talitha Barnes came to grow strawberries with her son Edgar, an orphaned niece named Lena Barnes, and Talitha's daughter Annie with her husband J. L. Hearn and their three little children, Asa Wilbert, Bobby, and Iza Sue.[38]

In December 1909, Roy M. and Effie Mae Glasgow arrived from Hannibal, Missouri. They were trying to get away from the cold and were heading to Deepwater. Since they could not find a small tract of land for sale, they bought the Ben Williams place in West Pasadena. Ben had given up farming and had gotten into the real estate business that year. He had just purchased land from his uncle, J. G. Conn. Conn had purchased seven city blocks in 1904 but never moved to Pasadena. Ben purchased some of Conn's land in 1909 and built a

Ben Williams built this fancy house about 1910 after selling his West Pasadena farm to Roy Glasgow.

beautiful two-story frame house at the corner of Main and Broad Way. The timing was perfect for Glasgow who needed a little land for his five children. Mary Ellen, Roy, and Cecil were of school age. Kevin and Nora Lee were much too young. No doubt the quality reputation of the school was a factor in their coming to Pasadena, in addition to the reputation of the growing strawberry economy. Thirty-seven-year-old "Professor" Glasgow had been a teacher for 21 years but had decided to try his hand at raising strawberries. It did not take the community very long to realize the potential of this new farmer. Within the year he would be elected to the school board and shortly after that he would return to the classroom.[39]

While new families were moving to Pasadena, marriages were laying the groundwork for future school needs. Cornelius "Neal" Williams, one of the Williams boys that had moved to Pasadena from Madison County, tied the knot with Zeola Annie Harwell in 1904. Hershal Gregg Starkey married Mary Harwell in 1906 and already had Bryan and LaVerne working towards school age. Gregg's brother Spencer was married to Sula A. but she was making her contribution as a teacher. Tom Plum had lived in Pasadena three years before he took Ethel as his bride. Claude Pitts took a liking to Bama Scroggins and they got married in the fall of 1908. The fever must have been going around since Claude's sister, Jewell had just married Gerald Conrad that September. Helge Gigstad was born in Norway but found his way to Dayton, Texas in time to become friends with the Holbrooks before they moved to Pasadena. Based upon their good reports he purchased land in Pasadena, but he rented it out until he decided to move over in January of 1908.

It wasn't big, but it was their home. Gregg and Mary Starkey started their family in 1906.

Perhaps it was the pretty Lydia Zlomke who lived in nearby Deepwater that caught his eye, because they were married in December of that same year. Walter Lee Wilson had been courting Clara Thurman from Genoa. Clara's sister Lenora had married J. D. Parks back in 1901, so Clara attended some of the parties in Pasadena. Lee met her at Wade Dickerson's and took her home after that party. A lot of romances had their roots in the long walk or ride home after the frequent parties in Pasadena. Sure enough, this romance also grew into marriage in 1908. Clara's other sister, Josephine had married neighbor D. E. "Deb" Atkinson in 1902 and they would bring their growing family to Pasadena in 1912. Bessie Crenshaw was another Genoa girl who caught the eye of a Pasadenan. Ray Guinn spotted her and they got married in 1907 and immediately began on their family.[40]

School opened on Monday, July 5, 1909, and Gertrude McMasters had 28 students in her room. She taught the first three grades. On Tuesday she enrolled five more students. On Thursday another student arrived. The student population of Pasadena was growing and setting records each year. The trustees had been wrestling with the crowding problem and the increased operating costs. The Texas State Legislature had just passed a new law allowing rural school districts to issue bonds to raise funds for permanent improvements. This would allow a community to upgrade and expand its school property and equipment without appreciably increasing the tax burden on its residents. Effie Jones, wife of Trustee Dean K. Jones, became very involved in promoting the use of these new bonds to build a large brick school house for the growing community. And when the quality of education was the topic, Pasadena was always quick to act. J. T. Conn, H. E. Ford, W. H. Guinn, J. L. Holbrook, J. A. Jackson, D. K. Jones, W. McBurney, W. C. McMaster, J. D. Miller, F. D. Newell, S. S. Palmer, J. D. Parks, Horace Plum, T. H. Plum, J. I. Shine, J. T. Shine, C. H. Tilley, W. F. Van Dorn, A. F. Wallman, W. B. Williams, and W. F. Williams signed a petition on January 3, 1910, calling for a school bond election. The petition was submitted to the school trustess and the next day, January 4, 1910, J. D. Parks made the motion to build a new brick school. The election, for $10,000 worth of bonds, and a tax increase to support it, passed on February 14 by a vote of 30 for and two against. By comparison, the South Houston and Seabrook Common School Districts of Harris County each authorized $2,000 in bonds. South Houston was the larger school with 89 students and three teachers compared to Seabrook's 58 students and one teacher. Deer Park, as a part of the Lynchburg Common School District, had 25 students with Mrs. S. A. Starkey as the teacher.[41]

Effie Jones pushed for a new brick schoolhouse for Pasadena. It would contain six classrooms and an auditorium.

By April the school bonds were sold and construction began on the new two-story brick schoolhouse. It contained six classrooms and an auditorium. A distinctive architectural feature of the new school was the bell tower or cupola on the top of the roof. Trustees W. N. Blakesley, J. W. Collins, H. E. Ford, R. M. Guinn, J. L. Holbrooks, D. K. Jones, and J. D. Parks accepted the new school on August 23, 1910. With a new building to pay for the trustees turned into businessmen. They first agreed to rent out the auditorium to the "Homesteaders" for 50 cents for each time used. Next they established a $1.50 out-of-district fee for students. The following March they rented the hall for a Valentine's Party, $2.50, and allowed the Mexicans to hold Sunday School in a schoolroom for $1.00 per month. Joe D. Hall was elected principal to start the slightly delayed six-month school term beginning in September 1910. His sister, Susan Hall had taught two years before. Assisting Mr. Hall was Miss Annie Henson and Mrs. Elizabeth Gutherie. Elizabeth Guthrie was well known to the community by her maiden name, Lizzie Hays. She had attended school in Pasadena from its beginning and was now married to John C. Gutherie who had arrived in the community in 1908.[42]

Josiah and Martha H. Rawlins moved to Pasadena in 1909 from Deepwater to be closer to relatives. Robert and Mary Jane Guinn had moved to Deepwater in 1894. In 1897 Mary Jane's

The new school was constructed in five months while the students were on vacation working the strawberry fields.

widowed sister-in-law Sarah V. Hogge and her two sons, Ivan and Erwin, moved to Deepwater and Sarah became the postmistress in June. That same year Mary Jane's other sister, Katie Bailey and husband Will and son Ben Jr. tried to move to Deepwater, but there were no houses to rent so they stopped at Pasadena. Will and Katie decided to stay in Pasadena so they bought 12 acres on the northwest corner of the La Porte Road and Richey. Will sent for his mother who had married Josiah Rawlins after the death of Will's father during the War Between the States. Martha and Josiah arrived with son Warren M. and grandson Eric Strengths by 1900 and settled in Deepwater where Josiah subsequently took over the postmaster's job. Meanwhile Robert and Mary Guinn moved over to Pasadena and Robert took over the postmaster's job in Pasadena. Josiah and Martha finally moved to Pasadena and settled in across Richey Street from Matha's son Will Bailey. The pattern of relatives and friends moving to Pasadena was repeated many times.[43]

Pasadena had indeed come a long way since the turn of the century. Although the Galveston Hurricane of 1900 had run a few families out of town, the population of the community had grown from about 200 to a bustling 500 persons. Guinn's box of groceries was now replaced by three retail establishments. And late in 1910 C. L. and Lizzie Whitten opened the fourth mercantile store in town. They built on the northwest corner of Spooner and the county shell road to La Porte. A new two-story brick schoolhouse had replaced the single-story frame structure and both the Baptists and the Methodists had brand new sanctuaries. Charles Munger would surely have been proud and Colonel Burnett amazed at the town that now straddled the La Porte Road. The delicious pear tree had been the inspiration for the earliest Kansan settlers, and now the sweet strawberry was blossoming from the fertile soil.[44]

VI

Strawberries (1900–1917)

For those that thought the strawberry boom had reached its peak in 1907, they obviously had not travelled to Pasadena.[1]

The land promoters of Gulf Coast Texas in the 1890's focused heavily on the favorable climate and the possibility for agriculture, especially fruit production. The *La Porte Chronicle* repeatedly told the story:

> January 26, 1893–
>
> There seems to be an impression abroad that the climate of Southern Texas is exceedingly hot. Nothing can be more remote from the truth . . . . The climate is the most uniform, equable and mild temperature of a State in the Union.
>
> . . . the temperature on Galveston Bay at La Porte, and for many miles inland, never runs above 90 degrees in the summer, or falls below 25 degrees above zero in winter . . . .
>
> The land surrounding La Porte for 20 miles west and northwest will in five years be the great fruit and garden section of the country and as far famed as the fruit lands of Southern California. It is high and can be most cheaply drained.
>
> . . . home of the strawberry, and immense crops are raised in the vicinity.

In 1898 Oscar Kruse felt that he had struck it rich when he sold his first strawberries for $12 a crate. At the turn of the century strawberries were a minor commodity for the farms in Pasadena. Clara Barton's introduction of strawberries as a major late winter/early spring cash crop after the September 1900 Galveston hurricane, changed the devastated farmers' attitude towards the fast-growing berry. They could begin harvesting this new cash crop within a few months. Being available earlier in the season than even California berries, the shippers bought up the crop and sent them to still-frozen Northern markets. Since success bears repeating, Pasadena farmers stuck with their strawberries. Even though they replanted other crops, the berries were here to stay.[2]

The season began as early as January. In 1906 the Pomeroys sold their first berries for about 40 cents per quart. The peak of the season was in April when they sold 413 quarts for $111.25 (about 27 cents per quart). The last berries were sold in May for about 25 cents per quart. The 1907 season was dropped to a range of 20 cents down to a low of 11 cents per quart. Fortunately the dairy brought in $2,542.20. Prices improved in 1908 slightly with the top price back to 30 cents. In

The Cooks, Davises, and Duffields hitch up their horses to plow Pasadena gumbo soil to produce those famous sweet strawberries.

1909 the Pomeroys set out 6,000 Klondike strawberry plants and 4,000 Excelsior plants.[3]

The favorite strawberry variety was the Klondike. It grew large and consequently fewer were needed for each pint container. The Excelsior variety was smaller and sweeter, so it was normally grown for home use and to share with friends. For those that did not know how to grow berries when they came, there were plenty of teachers around. Ray Williams taught "Foots" Wilson the tricks of the trade and Anna Pomeroy took Edgar Barnes under her wing. Archie G. and Nettie D. Thomasson arrived in 1909 to grow strawberries. Six years later they would be surprised with a little girl, Dagma. Robert Kingsbury returned to Pasadena with his three young children after the death of his wife Donna and rented the MacNider place. The Moores lived nearby and daughter Zora Lee pitched in to help the widower with his kids. They were married in 1910 and began also raising strawberries. Joe and Lillie Cook came from Kansas as did Sam and May Davis and their two small children. Thomas and Nellie Annie Duffield were originally from Kansas but their children's birthplaces indicated the circuitous route they took to get to Pasadena. Clyde M. was born in Nebraska and Elvah M. in Missouri. James and Lillie Cook came to town in 1910 to make their living growing strawberries. Unfortunately, Pasadena early settlers Anderson and Shines decided to move on and they moved to California that same year. Deb and Josephine Atkinson moved their family from Mecca, Texas, in 1912 to farm strawberries. Actually they were early settlers to the Genoa area and had lived there for over 15 years before briefly moving to Mecca.[4]

Even with relatively mild winters in Pasadena, the thermometer usually pushed freezing temperatures a couple of times each winter. In order to protect the early spring, or actually, the late winter crop, it would be necessary to cover the strawberry plants with hay. The weather bureau would mail out post cards with the weather prediciton for the next day or two. However, the more reliable predictor, would be a telephone call from someone in Conroe to Wade Dickerson's store reporting that it was freezing there in Conroe. Unfortunately this did not give a lot of warning, but the word would spread fast and everyone—every man, woman, and child—would be out in the strawberry fields covering the crops with the hay that was purposefully left in the paths between the rows. During the cold weather a grower had to be prepared to respond quickly.

Even non-strawberry growers would turn out to help, usually for a fee for the time spent, or for a return favor. If the call came early in the day, the school children would be excused from classes to go home and help with the covering. As soon as the weather warmed up the hay was removed so that the plants could continue to grow.[5]

Charles Munger and Payson Pomeroy both noted the lush prairies south of Buffalo Bayou. Allen Ranch cattle had grazed these grasses for 70 years unrestricted. With the growth in the strawberry industry, hay from these grasses was also needed to protect the plants from the frost. To insure a continuing supply of good grass the ancient technique of "slash and burn" was used. By controlled burning of the prairies every couple of years the fields would not get matted with dead grasses and thus inhibit the new growth in the following years. Additionally, this would return much needed potash to the soil. Cleared, and thus fertilized, new grasses would grow and replish the prairies. Sometimes nature would provide her own match and set the prairies ablaze. To make sure that any of the fires did not get out of hand, tubs of water with feed sacks soaking in them were a common sight. By dragging or patting the wet sacks over the burning grass, the fire could be confined to the appropriate areas. Sometimes the fires were so prevalent that the nights were lit up with the flames illuminating the horizons on three sides.[6]

Joseph Stephen Cullinan, organizer of the Texas Company and its president from 1903 to 1913, purchased a farm in Pasadena in 1908 and added to it in 1909. The inventory of his property in 1911 listed the following plants and trees: orange, peach, pecan, fig, and persimmon. By 1913 he had hired Joseph Cruse to oversee his farm and had increased his fig tree orchard four and a half times to 770 trees, his persimmons doubled to 220, his peaches and pecans up 50 percent to 79 and 212 respectively, and his oranges, mostly satsuma, constant at about 700 trees. He added 82 lemon trees, 100 plum trees, 10,000 trifoliata plants, and 61,000 strawberry plants. By local standards, Cullinan's 92-acre farm in northern Pasadena and on the banks of the Buffalo Bayou was huge. Most farms in Pasadena were about 10 acres, with a very few exceeding 20 acres. But there was one thing that they all had in common, strawberries.[7]

The public school would end its session in February or March so that the children would be available to help pick strawberries. Early picking began in January and increased in February and reached its peak in March and April. Picking the first few berries required less time and more judgement as to which ones to pick. These initial berries demanded a premium price. The price began to fall in March and April as more strawberries reached the market. Profit margins disappeared sometime in May. In 1913 Cullinan sold his first two crates (24 pints) on January 23 for $9.17 each. A month later, through the Pasadena Exchange, he received $7.57 per crate. By March 25 the rate was down to $3.95 per crate. In May the rate was down to $1.15. The pickers were paid 60 cents per crate and the 24-pint cartons cost 16 cents. The commission house took 15 cents per crate. The cost of the plant was insignificant, one hundred plants for 15 cents. By May the cantaloupes were ready for market so the remaining strawberries were used for canning or making wine.[8]

Unfortunately the price varied from year to year, depending upon the quality of the berry, when it went to market, the demand, and how many crates were for sale. The following year, 1914, Cullinan's January and February pickings were up substantially, and the average sales price dropped to about $2.50 per crate. The March average fell slightly to $2.43 and

George Dowell and his family turn out to pick strawberries.

Helge Gigstad rounds up all hands to help with the strawberry picking. Neighbor helps neighbor until the job gets done.

April to $1.95. May berries were less than a dollar and barely broke even. A grower tried to average $2.00 to $2.50 a crate for the season. Although this was not one of those years, Cullinan ordered 35,000 additional Klondike plants for the 1915 season.[9]

However, there were exceptions. Oscar Kruse's $12 per crate in 1898 sure sounded good. However, being at the right place at the right time can also improve your profits. Edgar Barnes was working for Jesse H. Jones in May of 1913 when Mr. Jones had just completed building the 17-story Rice Hotel. Jones had built on the site of the old Capitol Hotel, which had been used as the capitol of the Republic of Texas from 1837 to 1839. For the grand opening of the hotel on May 17, Mr. Jones wanted fresh, large strawberries with stems left on for holding and dipping in powdered sugar. Edgar, with the help of sister Cumi and her husband Jacob Lanis Hearn, obliged and delivered the berries by flatbed wagon. Mr. Jones gladly paid Edgar a dollar per pint or $24 per each crate![10]

At picking time, everyone got into the program sooner or later. On the family farm, the children were pressed into service. On Cullinan's farm, and other production farms owned by produce companies, migratory workers were employed. The routine was the same. You picked up your berry carrier and headed to the fields. The carriers were homemade wooden trays with handles and would hold pint or quart containers. Pickers at the Walter Williams 20-acre strawberry farm would use eight or ten pint carriers. The smaller carrier would weigh about two and a half pounds and measured 9" by 18". At the Baldwin Farm on Twelfth (Southmore) Street, the carriers were larger and would contain anywhere from eight to 12 quart strawberry containers. The 8-quart size measured 18" by 18" and would weigh about five pounds empty. Because of the shape of the quart containers, they were sometimes referred to as berry coffins.[11]

Will Parks and Leora Gartney (sometimes spelled Gwartney) tied the knot in 1906 and went to work on raising strawberry pickers. They built a two-room house to live in. By 1915 Elmer Calvin, Ima I., and Bessie were old enough to help. Irma Leora and Everett R. were too young, but would take their turn in years to come. W. S. "Muggins," Jr., would be along later. The house grew with each successful strawberry season, and probably because the children were overflowing the rooms. A kitchen was added on the back of the house. Then a second story was added with two bedrooms. Finally a room off of the kitchen. And if there was a shortage of children to help pick, Will's brother J. D. had his batch of kids. Carrie, Flora Irene, and Alice were already picking. Gladys Angeline and James D., Jr., would be out there shortly. When they finished with one patch they could move to the others.[12]

With each successful strawberry crop, Will and Leora Parks added to their house. Figuratively, it was "the house built by strawberries."

The Parks families had a bunch of little pickers in the group.

There were not any special clothes for the job. Normally you had a hat or bonnet for your head to keep the sun off and maybe long-armed gloves with the fingers cut out. It was easiest to sit on the ground and scoot along as you picked the berries. At the family farm on Eleventh (Harris) Street, or as it was known locally, Strawberry Lane, Ima Parks would get on her hands and knees and work her way down the row until her carrier was filled. Usually the younger the picker the more problem you had with more berries going into the mouth instead of the carrier. But you never, never put the pretty strawberries in your mouth, only the ugly ones! When you finished, you would take your carriers to the berry shed and received a token if you were hired help. The tokens were in several sizes or denominations and you would get the appropriate one for the quantity of berries that you turned in. The tokens were redeemable in cash at the end of the day, or the week. Or the tokens could be used like money at the local mercantile store to purchase goods. Emma Moore's parents did not raise strawberries but she picked them for two and a half cents a pint, which would be 60 cents a crate.[13]

At the berry shed the strawberries were put into 24 pint/12 quart shipping crates. The largest, prettiest berries would be separated and put aside. These gems were called the "toppers" or "cappers" and would be placed on the top of each pint to

Strawberries were taken to the railroad loading sheds and prepared for shipment to northern and eastern markets.

finish off the crate. To eat a topper, or rather to get caught eating a topper, would be very bad for the offending child. At the end of the day, or some other appropriate time, the crates were taken down to the railroad berry loading platforms between the railroad tracks and the La Porte Road. There were several covered platforms from Munger to Wafer.[14]

At the loading station buyers and inspectors would review the crates. Once everything was in order the crates would be loaded into the refrigerated cars. Each car held about 700 crates, and 12 tons of ice. Loading the strawberries was everyone's job, but the loading of the ice went to the biggest guys. The ice had to be lifted to the top of the car and placed in an compartment that was loaded through a trap door on the top of the car. In this way, the coolness of the ice would waft down over the berries and keep them cold for the long trip. Wagon loads of ice had to be brought in from Harrisburg from the Texas Ice Company and Butcher Brothers. The railroad locomotive came by late in the afternoon and picked up the loaded cars on the Pasadena siding and sent them on their way to various northern markets. Due to their quality, the Pasadena berries commanded premium prices in those distant destina-

Deepwater had its own loading shed, but all of eastern Harris County was called, "Pasadena Acres" when it came to strawberries.

tions. Those strawberries that were not received in time to be loaded in the railroad cars would be taken to Produce Row in Houston and sold the next day. Since the refrigerated cars were only loaded during the week, the farmer's access to a market dried up for the weekend.[15]

At first the only opportunity to sell produce on the weekend was at Produce Row on Saturday morning. However, a Hous-

Seven hundred crates of strawberries and 12 tons of ice filled each refrigerated railroad car.

ton investment group headed by G. D. Samuells purchased the park at Sylvan Beach in about 1909 and began fixing it up and promoting its use. Each year the season opened on San Jacinto Day and the crowds began to swell at the park. Initially most of the visitors went by daily trains or excursion boats to the park, but a few travelled the La Porte Road through Pasadena. As the traffic on the La Porte Road began to increase—some wagons, some automobiles—Pasadena farmers started setting up roadside stands to sell their excess berries. Since the traffic was heaviest on the weekends, and lasted all spring and summer, the roadside stands continued and expanded the produce that they sold. Picnicking foods were very popular, especially watermelons. Generally, the churches did not take too kindly to "working" on the Sabbath. However, if the Baptists had an emergency, they would refer to the biblical permission granted in the case of an "ox in the ditch."[16]

The routine of planting, protecting, picking, and shipping did not change much over the years, but other aspects of the business were modified in response to changing needs. Most of the berries were sold through or to commission houses. They were the ones that arranged for the refrigerated railroad cars and sent them on their way to remote markets. Desel-Boettcher Company and Baldwin & Cargill were two of the bigger wholesalers purchasing Pasadena strawberries. They were responsible for grading, inspecting, and supervising the loading of the berries. However, the Pasadena farmers did not like leaving their fate and fortune in the hands of outsiders. The Farmers and Fruit Growers Association had been formed by Charles Munger in 1894 and Robert Guinn was involved in the successor organization, the Pasadena Fruit and Truck Growers Association, shortly after the turn of the century. As was the case with the 1898 incorporation of the school system, the residents took more control over the selling of their strawberries by organizing the Pasadena, Texas, Producers Exchange in 1913. The charter members were: W. B. Bailey, Sr., W. B. Bailey, Jr., W. N. Blakesley, G. W. Conrad, H. Gigstad, Guinn Brothers, George Holbrook, Jim Hughes, C. P. Malloy, W. C. McMaster, W. B. Thornton, and W. H. Wagoner. Also active in the group was R. E. Parks, C. L. Garfield, and J. E. Pomeroy. In addition to strawberries listed on their printed form, they also handled dewberries, cabbage, cantaloupes, cucumbers, tomatoes, radishes, and miscellaneous "vegatables [sic]." The Association purchased the old Whitten mercantile store across from the depot and on the corner of the La Porte Road and Spooner. W. C. McMasters was the President of the Association and R. E. Parks was the secretary and treasurer. Actually the Association got more than it needed when it bought the building. George Hunken had purchased the store from C. L. and Lizzie Whitten a couple of years earlier and it was still stocked as a mercantile store. Later on J. M. Cruse would take over the operations of the grocery store for the Association.[17]

Strawberry farming grew beyond the small plots of the Pasadena and area farmers. Several of the produce houses in Houston purchased property and began farms of their own. Scherman Produce acquired a lot of acreage around Genoa and brought in Mexican pickers. In 1913 Baldwin & Cargill purchased 320 acres in the Pasadena area. The property fronted on the south side of Twelfth (Southmore) Street, between Main and Richey Street. Since Twelfth Street was the southern boundary of Burnett's plat of the town, the Baldwin property was outside of the original community and thus represented the first major expansion of its limits. A full-time caretaker's house was built and pickers' cabins erected. Although the main crop was strawberries, other crops were also grown. The company continued to maintain a good relationship with the

Cullinan and Bernart farms ran production operations in Pasadena that required seasonal laborers to help plant and harvest.

community and purchased strawberries to ship along with theirs. Their main source of water was from Vince's Bayou, which bordered the property. By 1919 they turned to McMaster and Pomeroy for water wells to supply their needs. [18]

Probably Baldwin & Cargill's first caretaker was Deb Atkinson. He had moved his family to Pasadena on Columbus Day in 1912 to farm after living eight years in Genoa and then two in Mecca. In Genoa he had married one of the Thurman girls. Since the other two sisters had married men from Pasadena it was natural that he would settle his young family down here. He and Josephine brought their strawberry picking helpers; Delbert LeRoy, Urvine, Nadine, and Melvin. Around 1915 Adolph Herrera arrived with his wife and daughter Julia. They worked on the farm off and on until it was sold in the early 1940s. The farm went by several names over the years, from Baldwin's Farm, to Benart Farms ("Ben" from Benjamin Baldwin and "art" from Arthur Cargill), and then as Bolin Farm (after the caretaker in the 1930's).[19]

Payson Pomeroy first saw the Pasadena area early in 1901 when he travelled to Deepwater to hand dig a water well for one of the farmers. Son John, then 12, accompanied him on the trip. As the Pomeroy farming enterprise expanded and watering of the crops desirable to increase the yields, John Pomeroy drilled a water well for the property he and his mother were farming out east Eleventh (Harris) in an area called Satsuma Gardens, which had recently been platted in 1908. He took the pressing mechanism off of his cane press and used the long turning portion to rotate an auger to drill the hole. Although easier than hand digging a well like his father had done in Brenham in 1896, drilling with mule power was slow and tedious. However, his success was noted among the other farmers. John married one of the school teachers, Gertrude Lucinda McMaster, on June 6, 1911, in the home of her brother, William Clyde McMaster, on North Witter Street. Clyde McMaster had moved to Deepwater in 1906 from High Island to run the steam engines for irrigation at the new rice fields in Deepwater. Clyde had gained his experience with steam engines on oil drilling rigs. He also served as the postmaster of Deepwater from April 1907 to February 1909. Late in 1908 he built a two-story house in Pasadena, on the Deepwater side of town, and began threshing rice. With his knowledge of machinery and drilling, and John's drive and water well experience, the water well drilling firm of McMaster and Pomeroy was formed in 1912.[20]

On July 24, 1912, Clyde McMaster and John Pomeroy, with the help of F. D. Newell, started the first well. Located on John's property, they built the wooden derrick and started drilling July 27 and four days later completed the well at 247 feet. The well came in at about 100 gallons per minute. Mr. E. A. White helped with setting the casing and J. D. Parks helped finishing up the pit around the well. From their first success they drilled the next well for Mr. Moore of Kansas City on his land near Buffalo Bayou and for W. F. Van Dorn the following year. Fortunately Clyde and John were still farmers and continued to rely upon that livelihood since the drilling business only provided supplemental income. Late in 1915 they drilled two wells for J. S. Cullinan. The first well was opposite Vince's Bayou at the Texas Company project on Buffalo Bayou, now renamed or proclaimed by Houston, as the Houston Ship Channel. The second was also on the Channel, across from Pasadena. The Texas Portland Cement Company of Houston contracted for a well in April of 1916 at its clay pit operation in Pasadena.[21]

With the town growing, strawberries blooming, and the waters of Buffalo Bayou, now called the Houston Ship Channel getting more brackish due to the constant dredging and deepening, the demand for McMaster and Pomeroy water increased. W. N. Blakesley ordered up a well in 1916. The Pasadena school district had one put down in 1917 as did S. A. Starkey. This was the same year that the company began drilling outside of the area, travelling to Humble for a couple of wells. The following year they started drilling water wells for the railroads, like Kuhns and Slagle had done in Pasadena 25 years earlier in 1893.[22]

By now strawberries had become the main crop of the community, but not the only one. The surviving fruit trees of Munger and the Kansas settlers' era continued to produce. James Jackson kept an orchard even though he also farmed strawberries. Edward Teas bought 10 acres in 1908 from A. L. Dickerson and 10 acres from Harmah Poyser for a nursery. John Pomeroy and Dean Jones dug a water well for him on the Poyser tract in 1909. Unfortunately a bad winter froze out his citrus trees and Teas moved to a newly developing area called Bellaire. He would be successful there. Ironically, Pasadena's Charles Munger was part of the Bellaire development. Satsuma oranges were popular and their reputation used with the platting of Satsuma Gardens in 1908. The Garfields traveled originally from Ohio and arrived in Pasaden in 1913 "to get rich raising oranges" as promised by the many flyers they read. Although Satsumas were very delicious, they did not make a good commercial fruit since they deteriorated too quickly after picking. Pears never reached the prominence that was forecast before the turn of the century, but orchards dotted the area. Figs did quite well and Pomeroy and Cullinan both maintained orchards. Another orchard was west of Shaver at Eighth (Jackson) Street. However, major cultivation was south of Pasadena in the Friendswood and League City areas. A canning plant was opened in League City.[23]

The commerical success of the "Pasadena Cantaloupes" was established before the turn of the century and cantaloupe production continued, now as the second largest commercial crop. Cantaloupes came into season as the strawberry season ended so the pickers would continue over into the cantaloupe fields. Since there was less picking work with cantaloupes, which was then followed by watermelons, the migratory population decreased. As the amount of farming work exceeded the

Clyde McMaster's silo

family work force, year-round resident workers were brought in. Operations such as Baldwin & Cargill and Cullinan began to maintain year-round work crews, predominately Hispanic-American in origin. Baldwin and Pomeroy provided housing for its caretaker/laborers, whereas Cullinan hired from the nearby community.[24]

Another summer crop, cucumbers, was very prolific in Pasadena. The children played a game where they would see how far across a field they could get, stepping from giant cucumber to the next, never walking on the ground. Potatoes and sweet potatoes were also taken to market in Houston as they came off in the summer and early fall, as were peaches. Pecans then came into season and were harvested. W. H. Dickerson was particularly fond of pecans and promoted their cultivation. At various times during the year peanuts, corn, and even cotton, were hauled into market. Cullinan considered raising loofahs, the vegetable sponge of the gourd family, for the German market in 1915. The proposal that he considered, and subsequently declined, was to start with 15 acres the first year and if successful, plant 200 acres within two years. However, sugar cane was grown in Pasadena. George A. Brown arrived with wife Pearl in 1912 from Cedar Bayou and grew sugar cane in addition to strawberries, dewberries, sweet potatoes, peas, beans, peanuts, and tomatoes. With six children, he had plenty of help. Addie was the oldest at 15. Allie Gertrude

A rice thresher harvests a bountiful crop

George and Pearl Brown grow dewberries on their 20-acre farm on Main and Eighth (Jackson) streets.

"Gertie", Valerie, and La Clere followed. Eugene R. and Ferrell G. were just babies. Daniel Glenn would be along in a few years. George also operated a cane syrup mill on his 20-acre farm east of Main at Eighth (Jackson) Street. John Pomeroy brought his cane there for pressing as did others in the community.

Gertie Brown (in white skirt) and friends sit on the sugar cane press. The Browns pressed cane for many neighbors.

Although Brown had the main sugar mill in town, his was not the only one. Harrison McLean had a good size sugar mill on his place off Tenth (Thomas) Street at Vince's Bayou. Lee Pitts had a mill down stream on his new place between Third (Belmont) and Fifth (Shaw) Streets.[25]

There was a sizable German immigrant farming settlement out Shaver just south of Twelfth (Southmore) Street. Samuel and Mary Garnuch arrived about 1906 with children Hattie, Arthur F., Otto W., and Curtis Samuel. Robert K. was born in Pasadena. William and Frida Laschinsky moved nearby about 1908. They had one daughter, Alma. Frida's parents, Dr. Michael and Eva Wizoreck, were living with them with their son Emil and Emma Louise. Eva had always had a hard time having babies and had lost six out of the nine she carried. It was not surprising that her daughter Emma Louise was sickly. Anna Pomeroy, herself an Austrian, would feed her fried grits to give her strength. Eva passed away in 1917. Harry and Erntine Peltz were born in Illinois, but their parents had come over from Germany. Like the others, Harry farmed whatever was in season. He was glad that he had five sons to help him: Milton, Harry, Jr., Earl, Lawrence, and Lester. Florian and Amalia "Mollie" Beusch moved to Pasadena in 1915 from League City with their 11-year-old son Gilbert Florian "Gib." They also had Elizabeth Pauline Boeske and her brother William with

A. L. Dickerson's nursery was located on the La Porte Road at Vince's Bayou.

them. Elizabeth and William's mother was Mollie's sister and had died in League City five years earlier. The Beuschs were originally from Kansas and the Boeskes from Massachusetts. They bought farm land along Little Vince's Bayou just south of Twelfth (Southmore) Street.[26]

Minnie McKnight was German, but her husband, Robert McKnight was Irish. Their children, Robert A., Elizabeth and Gertrude, were Texans. The widow Martha Morris had her own place with teenage children Reina, Kate, and Joe. Martha was originally from Illinois. Daniel E. and Jeane Nashold were also fresh from Illinois, and they had five children to help with the strawberry picking. Harry, Bessie, Gladys, Marion, and baby Helen were all born in Illinois and probably enjoyed the pleasant Pasadena weather. Myron C. and Myrtle Vaugh moved in from Missouri with their girls Grace and Gertrude. Myron's older widowed brother Marshall came along to help on the rented farm. But Pasadena was not just a retreat for northerners. John W. and Ann Sweeney moved over from Louisiana with Katie, Ernest and Earl. Six other children were older and stayed behind. William H. and Sara Caroline Thornton were also southerners, hailing originally from Alabama. The brought their son Whitt Brownelle and their daughter Alma. The middle child, L. Ward, did not settle in Pasadena. In fact, Alma married Elmer B. Jones and started their family with Walter W. "Bud" and Nina. Shortly afterwards Alma was widowed and returned to Pasadena with her children. Although the Thorntons farmed, they did a lot more land dealing than strawberry picking. Stokey S. and Lucy Palmer settled into their farming operation with Edna, Johnie, and Connie by 1910.[27]

Most of the rice grown in the area was east of Pasadena. As mentioned earlier, W. E. Jones had introduced it into the area in a big way in 1902 and a few smaller operations had been established. At the encouragement of the Houston Chamber of Commerce in 1903, 42-year-old Seito Saibara, a native of Japan, settled a Japanese colony at Webster and introduced the higher producing skinriki strain of rice into the area. John T. Jones, cousin of W. E. Jones, used some of the Jones land in Deepwater and in about 1912 sponsored approximately one hundred Japanese families to experiment with rice cultivation at the Jones farm. Jake Miller's boys raised rice at various locations between Pasadena and La Porte. The Olive families arrived and also grew rice. Even John Pomeroy tried his hand at growing rice. The repeated dredging of Buffalo Bayou allowed the salty water from Galveston Bay to encroach more and more upstream and the pumpage of water from the bayou ceased when the water became too brackish for rice cultivation. In order to raise rice, large deep water wells had to be drilled to provide the necessary fresh water. Due to the costs of drilling and operating the wells, only a few farmers in the area could afford to raise rice.[28]

When A. L. Dickerson took over his uncle's nursery at Pasadena he was growing cape jasmine. David Holloway came to Pasadena in 1912 from the Alvin and League City area. Although he was 63 years old at the time, he also started a nursery in Pasadena. Of the ten acres of land he purchased near the Browns on Main Street at Eighth (Jackson), he planted five acres in strawberries and five acres in cape jasmines. The price of land had certainly increased since 1893 because Holloway paid $130 per acre for his land. Four of his six children came to help him get started. Anna, Raymond, and Vick left after several years. The youngest, Albert G., stayed a bit longer. Before Memorial Day the Dickerson and Holloway would hire helpers to pick and wrap the the flowers, also known as Gardenias. Wade Dickerson and some of the Starkeys also raised cape jasmines. When the bud began to show some color, the fragrant flower would be cut with a 12-inch stem. Some said it was best to pick them before sunrise so the bud could be taken before it burst into a full blossom. A dozen stems would be rolled in newspaper, dipped in water and drained, then boxed for shipment by rail to northern markets. They were paid 25 cents per bloom and were sold on the streets of New York for a dollar. The tropical-looking flower was ready for market from mid-spring to early summer.[29]

As the strawberry industry blossomed, the cattle industry began to decline. Sam Allen had continued to run large herds upon the range. He partnered on herds with his brother C. D. Allen, his son S. M. Allen, his son-in-law E. N. Drouet, and friends Joe Davis and N. T. Masterson. Because of the size of his operation, Sam hired a lot of Negro cowboys. They went by names like Big Six, Coon, Nat, Old Red, and Bones. Steve Ray was perhaps one of the best wranglers to ride the range in later years. The cowboys lived over towards Harrisburg on land provided by Sam. Smaller ranchers such as Coolidge, C. B. McNay of Deepwater, and Edwin Rice Brown of Deer Park,

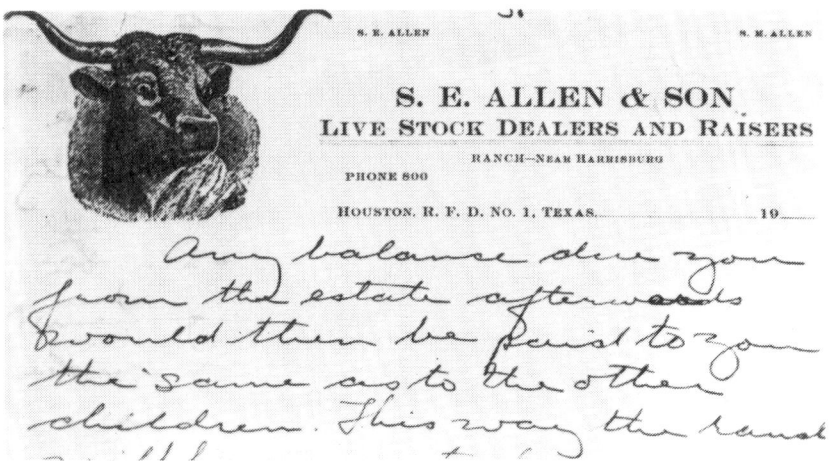

The Allens were always "partnering" with others to expand their cattle business. Like his father before him, Sam E. Allen partnered with his son, Sam M. Allen.

formerly of Pasadena, also ran cattle. In 1911 the open range of Texas ended. It now became the responsibility of the cattlemen to fence their cattle in, rather than for others to fence the cattle out. The last large roundup was staged and ranchers from as far away as Victoria and McFarland rode with the group to end an era in Texas history. Two years later, on June 23, 1913, Sam E. Allen died of complications from a bruise to one of his toes caused by a tight boot. Such a big man, both in stature and in reputation, brought down by such a small and senseless injury. His widow, Rosa Allen, decided to dismantle the huge ranch and in 1917 sold a 712-acre tract that included the Allen Ranch headquarters to the Simms-Sinclair interests.

C. B. McNay of Deepwater was a lawyer, rancher, farmer, and lay preacher.

Louise Davis, daughter of Joe Davis, lunches with the Allen Ranch cowboys at their chuck wagon.

Son Sam M. Allen continued the ranching tradition, but on a much smaller scale gradually shifting the main herd to Brazoria County.[30]

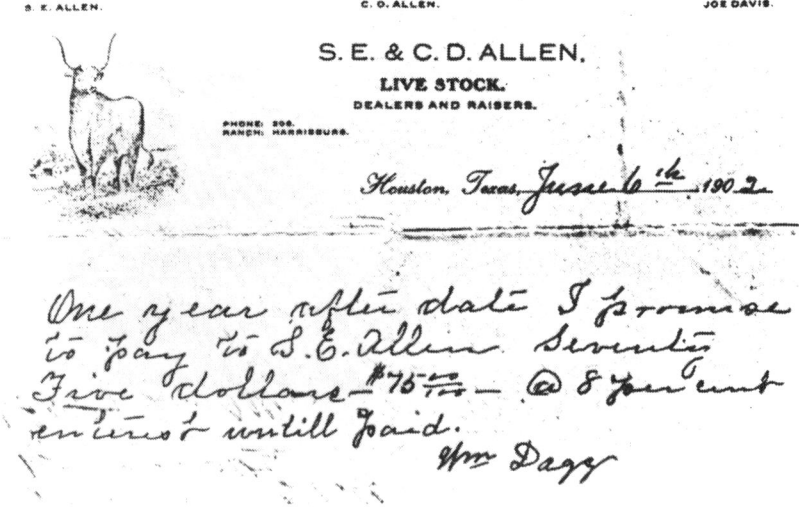

Another Sam E. Allen partnership in cattle raising was with his brother C. D. Allen and a Houston friend, Joe Davis.

The Ranching Era had ended, and the Farming Era was in full bloom. Nature had yielded to the hand of man and the land had become, as described later by Ralph Stafford, "a strawberry farm with the railroad running through it." It was described to J. S. Cullinan in a letter, "you augh[sic] to see the Klon- dike Berries, tha[sic] look like a flower garden." The word about strawberries continued to spread and farmers regularly migrated to Pasadena specifically to grow the sweet little fruit. Charley Cook and Bill Carlisle brought their families to Pasadena about 1917 and almost immediately sent word to their friend Sam Quinn in Beeville, "plenty of work for the boys and everyone was getting rich raising strawberries." The Pasadena National Farm Loan Association was organized in 1917 to help Pasadena residents purchase farm land and finance their operations. The whole of southeast Harris County became known as Pasadena Acres and a thousand acres were dedicated to growing the sweet red fruit. For whatever the word "Pasadena" meant, it was not a surprise that most people began to think of it as "Land of the Flowers."[31]

With the berries came a prosperity that the community well deserved. Success was due to hard work and dedication, not promotion and pipe dreams. Munger's dream had become a reality as the community worked its way slowly to viability. An ongoing economical base had been established. A strong school system had been created. Spiritual education had been addressed. Some semblance of a mercantile base had now been established. However, it was not all work and no play.

Jasper Hays moved to West Pasadena to grow his strawberries. He had one of the first strawberry farms in Pasadena.

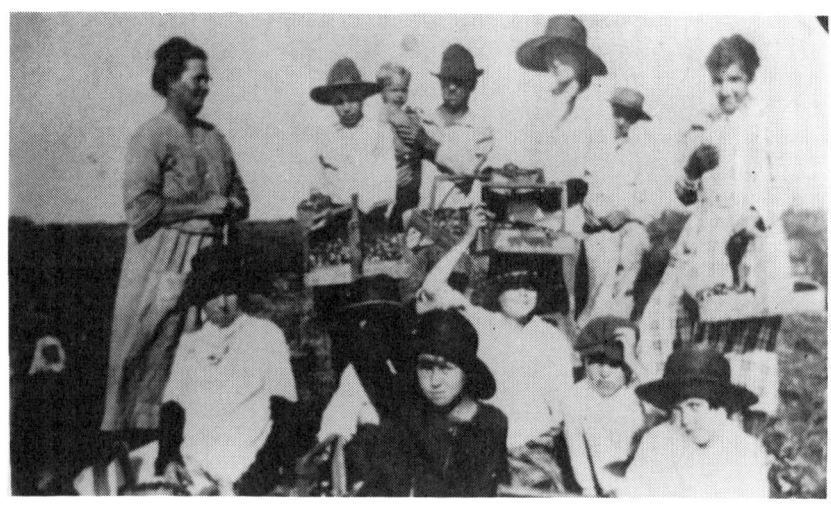

Deb and Josephine Atkinson turned out with their strawberry picking family. Little Delbert would later become mayor of Pasadena.

VII

Around Town (1910-1918)

Leave it to the boys to find things to do. Even with a full schedule of chores, time can be made for more enjoyable pursuits. It's all a part of growing up. Although The Coming Men of America Lodge was an educational organization, it gave the young men an opportunity to socialize without adult supervision. On the weekends when the scholastic and work

Front row (l to r): Howard Pitts, Walter Davis, Sidney Starnes, Rewell Pitts. Jimmy Starnes is in the middle. Top row (l to r): Chester Guinn, Ben Bailey, Mr. Steel, Whitt Thornton and Gary White.

load lightened, the boys occasionally "bumbed[sic] around." After the first of March, this usually meant hitting the swimming hole on Buffalo Bayou. After strawberry season a baseball team was put together and played other area teams on Saturdays. Foots Wilson headed up the first organized team and by 1910 they had acquired uniforms and had a formal playing schedule. In 1911 the team included Howard Pitts, now 17 years old; his brother Rewell, 19; Ben Bailey, Jr., 23; Walter Davis; Chester Guinn;Whitt Thornton; Garrett White; the Starnes brothers from Deepwater (Sidney played, little Jimmy was the bat boy); and Mr. Steel. When he could slip away from the ranch, "Little Sam" Allen would play.[1]

However, the churches provided most of the social contacts in town. Sundays began with the ringing of the church bells, which signalled the call to worship. In the beginning, each congregation could only hire part-time preachers. Visiting was common between the denominations as the worshippers went to the church that had the preacher that Sunday. Edgar Barnes was a Methodist and his new bride, Eula, was a Baptist. The differences in the Sunday schools were not discernable by the children so friendships and programs influenced which class they attended each Sunday. After all, the churches were only two short blocks apart. Besides, the Methodist Church was higher off the ground and the smaller children could play and hide under it better than under the Baptist church. Church socials were a community affair and Sunday afternoon picnics were very popular. Plenty of food, games, and prizes were the only requirements.[2]

By 1910 a small group had organized a Pentecostal church. Mrs. Lillian Dickerson was instrumental in the establishment and growth of the new church. Lillian's husband Wade had purchased the old school house for their home and had it moved to Munger Street near Sixth (Eagle). Before the group could afford a building, they met under an arbor Lillian had erected near her home. Reverend W. A. Mercer was the first minister to the group. The Pentecostals were less formal in their churching and drew members and attendees from both the Baptists and Methodists. Some people called them the "shouting" Baptists and J. L. Hearn thought they were more like the Methodists back home in Louisiana.[3]

Perhaps the Pentecostals located on Munger because it was near the heart of the community. All three churches and the school were located within one block of the intersection of

LOUIS PAULHAN IN A BERIOT BIPLANE.

The Post yesterday completed arrangements for the appearance of Louis Paulhan, the French aviator, in Houston. The flights will take place at South Houston February 18 and 19. The great interest in aerial navigation has made everyone familiar with the accomplishments of Paulhan, who has recently performed some wonderful stunts in biplane and monoplane.

The Frenchman, Louis Paulhan was the first person to fly an airplane in Texas. For $20,000 he braved sleet, wind, and gravity.

Broad Way and Munger Streets. Unless it was raining, it was an easy walk between all of the centers for social contact within the community. However, people turned out for special events regardless of the travel time involved.

Never long on words, John Pomeroy noted in his diary entry of February 18, 1910, "I saw an airship fly at South Houston." What he reported was the very first flight of an airplane in the state of Texas. Just six years before, the Wright brothers had made their historic heavier than air flight at Kitty Hawk, North Carolina. Europe responded more quickly to the achievement than did the United States, and by 1907 the center of interest in aviation shifted to France. The first international air meet held in the United States, was in Los Angeles in January 1910. Louis Paulhan, a 27-year-old French pilot, set the world's altitude record at 4,167 feet. Top speed at the meet was 55 miles an hour. Paulhan crated up his Farman biplane and headed by rail to the east coast. He stopped in Denver for a demonstration flight and another in New Orleans. With an offer of $20,000 from the *Houston Post* and the Western Land Company, Paulhan headed to Houston. Western Land Company was developing a new town called South Houston and provided an "air field" at the G. H. & H. railroad siding adjacent to the South Houston industrial section. Sleet, which covered the ground like snow, on Thursday, February 17, prevented the first scheduled flight. The first aeroplanes exhibited in Texas had occurred in September 1909 at the Dallas Fair Park. An air show was organized for February 1910 but the wind was too gusty for the fragile biplanes and "Wind Checks" were given to the spectators. Meanwhile, the weather cleared in South Houston and Paulhan lifted off before 3,500 witnesses into Texas history on February 18. Spectators paid $1.25 for a round trip train ticket from Houston and admission to the exhibition air field. For one dollar automobiles were "permitted to line the aviation field, giving the occupants an opportunity of not only witnessing the flights from the best possible view point, but utilizing their machines as private boxes." But Frank Meador of South Houston could watch the show free with his brothers and sisters from the steps of the family grocery store on Highway 3.[4]

The following afternoon, with mother Anna and girlfriend Gertrude McMaster, John Pomeroy witnessed the birdman fly again, this time in a 25 mile-an-hour gale. It was reported that over 5,000 people watched "the dapper little man with the curied mustachios, clad in oil skins and puttees, and manipulating the levers of the craft of canvas and silk and wire" brave the elements and take to the air. Only one flight was completed that day due to the weather. Not surprisingly it was reported that he declined to make a flight over Houston or to fly the 50 miles to Galveston. From Texas Paulhan crated up his aeroplanes and travelled to England and in April won the first long distance race in that country. What noisy things those machines were, but what a marvel.[5]

In April the weather was much better when John Pomeroy took his mother and girlfriend to the San Jacinto Battleground for the San Jacinto Day celebration. The Daughters of the Republic of Texas had tried for many years to preserve the battleground as a state park. Over 330 acres had been purchased by the state and a permanent grounds keeper assigned to the park. In 1894 a committee of veterans, including survivors of the battle, located many important sites of the Texan victory. In 1910 the Daughters erected granite boulder markers on these sites. The two remaining survivors of the Texan army were honored guests. Alfonso Steele, 93, was one of the 34 Texans wounded in the battle. William Zuber, 89, was actually stationed with the rear guard opposite Harrisburg when the battle was fought. John Pomeroy shook the hand of both of these men and reflected back upon the significance of the battle fought 74 years earlier. Steele died the following year and Zuber in 1913.[6]

Another change in the area was occurring at Dumont Station. In 1907 The Western Land Corporation had purchased land around Sam W. Allen's Dumont Station on the G. H. & H. railroad between Houston and Galveston. C. S. Woods of La Porte was the president of the company and he envisoned an industrial community south of Houston. During June, July, and August of 1907 N. G. Kolb surveyed the land, setting out sites for public lands, a city square, public parks, a school ground, school play grounds, a college square, a college park, and a railroad oriented industrial district. Allen Street was the northernmost street and Genoa was the southernmost. Most of the streets were named for states of the Union with College, Main, Washington and Dumont as extra wide roadways. The plat for the town of South Houston was filed in April.[7]

By the time of Paulhan's flight South Houston boasted a county school district, college, post office, depot, full line grocery store, 24-room hotel, Baptist church, medical doctor,

The 24-room South Houston Hotel was located between the railroad and the Interurban tracks.

five manufacturing plants, shelled streets, cement sidewalks, and a population of over one thousand people. One of the first thing that the developer did was to construct a beautiful two-story frame school house. Dr. J. L. Dickens had served as the first principal in 1908 and then opened the Asgard College for Girls in town. E. E. Werner took over the county school in 1909, added a second teacher and taught 89 students. R. L. Bunting became principal in 1910, supervised three additional teachers, oversaw a library of 100 volumes, and educated 124 students. Benjamin Franklin and Ann Elizabeth Meador had operated one of two grocery stores in little Milam, Texas. They decided there would be a better opportunity in the booming new town of South Houston so they arrived in 1908. They opened a grocery store and contributed 13 children to the school system. Mr. Aldrich served as the postmaster and used a converted box car for his office. Another box car nearby served as the depot which, to the irritation of the community, continued to carry the name "Dumont." George E. McDaniel was the first preacher of the Baptist Church that claimed 23 members.[8]

Aware of the experiences of Pasadena and other area communities, Woods knew that the community had to have a strong economic base. He chose manufacturing instead of strawberries. Woods attracted industries to South Houston with free land and a cash bonus. The industrial park along the railroad tracks contained the South Houston Iron Works (foundry and manufacturer of stoves), a gasoline engine plant that provided engines for rice field pumps, and a candy factory. They were joined by a brickmaking plant, a toy factory, a bottling works, a cement plant, and a lumber yard.[9]

Working as a machinist at the new foundry was Louis F. Smith. Smith had worked at a saw mill in Groveton before moving his wife Lelisa, their children Loire, Mollie, and Lozene and his mother-in-law Matie Glazener to South Houston. L. F. was very mechanical and would become a prolific inventor with over 40 patents. "Greasy," a nickname he obtained because of his mechanical tinkering, was present at the Paulhan flight and became fascinated with constructing airplanes. Also present at the demonstration was Leslie Lewis "Shorty" Walker who was at the time constructing an aeroplane on the top floor of the Auto and Motorboat Works building in Houston where Walker worked as the foreman. Walker had never seen a plane fly and was constructing his plane from plans he had acquired. The

40-horsepower monoplane was finished by August of 1910 and was taken to the South Houston airfield to be tested. Unfortunately the plane was a single seater and Walker did not know how fly. By trial and error he learned to successfully pilot his plane.[10]

Because of their common interest, Greasy quickly became friends with Walker and worked on airplane designs. He also befriended Guy Hahn, a bookkeeper at the lumber yard and the son of a wealthy South Houston resident. Guy, his wife May and son Douglas also lived in South Houston. Smith and Hahn spent $13,000 constructing their own airplane, a variation of a Curtiss biwing pusher. Since neither Smith nor Hahn had piloted a plane they probably hired Fred DeKor, a professional birdman then operating out of Houston. Early in 1911 the aeroplane triumphantly took to the air. Spurred on by their success Smith and Hahn established a factory in South Houston and quickly began building aeroplanes. At the Cotton Carnival in Harrisburg on November 14, 1911, five Houston-made planes took part in the air show.[11]

Dr. James Edison McWhorter had contracted tuberculosis while treating patients at the Southern Pacific Railroad hospital in Houston. He, his wife and three sons moved to South Houston in 1909 so that he could get the proper treatment for his condition: clean country air and a lighter work load. They settled on the north edge of town, near the old Sam W. Allen homestead on Berry Bayou. The old Allen house was deserted and some thought haunted. It was rumored that someone was killed in the house and that there was blood still on the floor. McWhorter, then 41 years old, opened an office in his home and brought with him one of the few X-ray machines in Houston. Unfortunately there was no electricity in the area and the little generator that he bought put out inadequate electrical power to make the machine work properly. The Western Land Corporation began working on a solution, that is, to bring electrical power to the new community. They also knew about the plans for the new Galveston-Houston Electric Railway which was to be built through the area.[12]

On March 28, 1910, about five weeks after Paulhan's flight, work began on the Galveston-Houston Electric Railway between Houston and Galveston. As early as 1903 the idea of an electric railway connecting Houston and Galveston had been considered. About February 1906 construction was begun at La Porte for a Bayshore line through Seabrook and on to

Galveston. However, with an ownership change in June the shore route construction was abandoned and a direct route was selected instead. The platitudes of the earlier land promoters proclaimed:

> The first and perhaps the most important effect of the interurban will be the settling up of the vast section of country between Galveston and Houston . . . capable of support(ing) several thousand population. The interurban will afford quick and easy transportation to these people; they will dispose of their garden produce and fruit in Galveston and Houston, and in these cities will do their trading, thus bringing added prosperity.[13]

However, the quicker travel time afforded by the direct route meant that it missed the communities between Houston and Galveston by a couple of miles and thus was of questionable short-haul value, at least for the existing communities.[14]

The Galveston-Houston Interurban Land Company was organized to promote the new land opened for development because of the new alignment of the Interurban. The directors and managers of the company read like a Who's Who of Houston and indicated their special interest in the project. W. E.

In 1911 the first intercity commuter train took only 100 minutes to travel between Houston and Galveston.

Richards, president of American National Bank headed up the group that included J. O. Ross and Jesse H. Jones. As heir to the J. H. Burnett estate, Ross owned extensive land holdings in the Genoa area. By May a "revised map" of Genoa was filed showing not only the Genoa town site, but also Orange Grove Addition, Acre Home Addition, Interurban Heights, Eucalyptus Park and Genoa Gardens subdivisions. James H. Bute was the owners of the Bute Fig and Orange Orchards in Genoa, and a large land owner and developer. F. E. Beatty was president of a Michigan strawberry plant growing company. Jesse Jones was only one of a dozen who represented financial and real estate oriented businesses. Eight banks and trust companies were represented. Over 7,000 acres had been assembled for a company directed, cooperative magnolia fig and satsuma orange orchard as well as for strawberry cultivation. While the trees were maturing, peanuts and sweet potatoes were to be planted.[15]

The Stone and Webster Engineering Corporation of Boston was a nationally known owner and operator of electric railway systems from coast to coast. They had previously acquired the Houston Electric Company and then the Galveston Electric Company. The Interurban was to be the link between these two electric street car companies. The last spike for the Interurban railway was driven on October 19, 1911, and the public opening occurred on December 5, 1911. The 50 mile right-of-way was fenced. A steam turbine plant had been built at Webster and a substation constructed at South Houston. Hourly service from both ends were provided from 6:00 A.M. to 11:00 P.M. and the trip took only 100 minutes. Through fares were $1.25 for one way, and $2.00 for round trip. A new, nonlift bridge, The Galveston Causeway, was built, replacing the old wagon and railroad trestle constructed after the 1900 hurricane. Boarding stations convenient to Pasadena were at South Houston and Genoa. Galveston was now less than two hours away from Pasadena. The million-dollar Galvez Hotel had opened earlier that year in June. Naturally, Pasadena would have preferred the original alignment of 1906, which would have put the Interurban through Pasadena and made Houston and Galveston even more convenient.[16]

Other forms of transportation were also improving. The Interurban had greatly reduced the time to travel to Galveston, and greatly increased the number of scheduled runs. The regular train through Pasadena had also improved its service over the years. The La Porte, Houston and Northern Railroad had gone through several receiverships and mergers since it had been established. In 1905 the railroad was acquired by the Southern Pacific, which then leased the operation of the line to the Galveston, Harrisburg and San Antonio Railroad. A spur line had been built to East La Porte, called originally, New Town, and then the line was extended to the bayside resort of Sylvan Beach. Because of the increased popularity of the general bayside area a branch line was built in 1914 from the Strang switch to Seabrook along the edge of Galveston Bay. But railroads ran on schedules and missing the last train back to Pasadena for the day could mean a long walk. The problem was not uncommon, especially for those travelling to Houston. Time just seemed to get away while you were visiting in the big city. More than once John Pomeroy and his friends hiked their way back home. You could walk the railroad tracks or on the shell-paved road. No matter which you took, it would be after midnight before you saw your bed.[17]

The county had gotten good at paving their roads, especially the main ones. Anna Pomeroy's friend, Judge Vasmer, had been a strong advocate of good county roads while he was county judge in the 1890s and the fruits of his labor showed. The paving made rainy weather travelling much easier since there were less ruts and standing water in the road. The county hired local labor to help with its program and John Pomeroy earned $442.50 in six months hauling and spreading shell. The improved roads were more of a benefit to wagons and buggies than to regular horseback traffic. Although Pasadena and its neighboring towns had a few blocks of paved streets, most streets were wagon rut roads that were next to impassable in wet weather. Only a horse could be counted on to get through all of the time. Then again, most everyone walked if the distance was only a mile or two. For school children living further away, donkeys were popular. The Kruse, Edming, and Collier children came in from the Florentine Settlement on donkeys. The Glasgow children were to travel this way to both school and church. The Ostendorf children out on Red Bluff Road travelled to Deer Park that way. A stable was built at the Pasadena School in 1912 to shelter the animals ridden to school by the students.[18]

Besides classes, the school provided more social contacts for the community. The Literary Society was organized before 1905 and met during the school year on Saturday nights. With the construction of the new building in 1910, more students, three teachers, and a more consistent academic regime, it was logical that additional school activities developed. Two literary societies were meeting in 1912 and the Pasadena Public Library Association was given a room in the school and placed its collection of over 500 volumes at the disposal of the school. The library was "open daily and read largely," according to Principal W. C. Williams's report to the Harris County Board of Trustees. A set of encyclopedias had been purchased with money earned by the students and Mrs. W. C. Williams's class won a *Farm And Ranch* library set. The class sent a thank you note to *Holland's Magazine*, thanking it for its "liberality" and noting that there wasn't a single "weak" author in the collection. Thirty "scholars" signed the letter. Miss Stewart taught art during her tenure in 1911 and the well-known La Porte music teacher, Mrs. Marsh, was hired to teach music in 1912. Pasadena even hosted a Teachers' Institute for Harris County rural schools in November. That same year the *Titanic* sank, with 1,513 lives lost, and New Mexico and Arizona were accepted into statehood as the forty-seventh and forty-eighth states. In fact, since Pasadena had been first settled in 1893, Utah and Oklahoma had also become states.[19]

Arbor Day tree plantings and patriotic open air programs were presented and exercise classes were also held in the auditorium. The auditorium was upstairs in the school and occupied one half of the second floor. Mrs. Williams played the piano at assemblies and Mr. Williams lead the singing. Also attending were teachers Miss Fleta Williams and Miss Stewart. In addition, the auditorium was used by the community for box suppers, pie socials, plays, and spelling bees. Besides the Homesteaders group, the Woodmen of the World used the auditorium for their meetings. Four wooden water coolers with nickel faucets were donated by C. A. Elmen & Co. of Houston to replace the old pail and common dipper. Each child now had to have its own cup to drink from. However, water still had to be brought daily from the well in front of Tilley's, usually by a couple of the larger boys. But there were always volunteers since it meant missing some of the classwork. Pearl Ford finally got old enough to take her turn fetching the water.[20]

After seven grades of schooling a student was given a graduation certificate. Additional education was available in the high school program for those students who passed the final seventh grade examination. A high school graduation certificate required four more years of school, for a total of 11 in all. Pasadena offered several high school grade levels, depending on the need and the district's capabilities each year. A consolidation of Pasadena and Deepwater for high school purposes failed when Deepwater declined to go along with the plan. That refusal would ultimately cost Deepwater population. In 1912 nine grades were taught, with 10 students in the ninth grade. W. C. Williams was back with his wife to teach. Irma McMasters, whose sisters Gertrude and Myrtle had taught several years earlier, and whose brother had served as a school trustee, was also hired along with Mrs. Mary Jeter of Houston Heights. In addition to Pasadena, Seabrook and South Houston also offered a two year high school program. Harrisburg was the only school in the area providing a full four year program. The primary grade schools were now called intermediate schools and the county system reported schools at Lomax, Middle Bayou, Morgan's Point, Lynchburg, Deer Park, Deepwater, and Genoa. La Porte had taken Pasadena's lead and had elected to be an independent system by 1912. Houston and Brunner followed. In 1913 Pasadena reported 167 students in school, comprised of 92 males and 75 females. No Negro children were reported in the district. Some considered this as

Shortly after the new school opened, the town turned out for group pictures. Professor Glasgow sat with the parents and younger students.

Around Town (1910-1918)

the year for the first graduation class from the high school at Pasadena. Three boys and four girls were in that class. Trustee Oscar Kruse must have been very proud of himself because his son Karl was in the class. It would be 11 years before the next class would claim that honor. In 1914 Pasadena reported 112 males and 106 females, for a total of 218 students. La Porte reported 222 students, including 33 Negroes.[21]

John Holbrook resigned as a school trustee and Roy Glasgow was appointed in March 1911 to take his place. However, like Conn before him, Glasgow's experience as a teacher compelled him to resign as a trustee in April 1913 to be elected principal of the school. Glasgow quickly came to be considered as one of the greatest educators in the area. Mrs. Justa E. David and her daughter Nannie were elected to assist him. Mrs. David, 55, had served as a Baptist missionary in Africa for 15 years with her husband Reverend W. J. David, and they were now living on a farm near South Houston. Her husband was to serve as the pastor of the South Houston Baptist Church for about a year in 1915.[22]

The widower Frederick G. Deane moved to Pasadena with his children so that his sister-in-law could help with the family.

Teachers Justa and Nannie David stand behind the students in an early group picture at the new schoolhouse.

Belle McCormick and her husband Dan had moved to Pasadena in 1897 and did not have any children. Dan passed away in 1913 and was buried in Crown Hill Cemetery. Although widowed at 50, Belle married Deane shortly afterwards. Minister A. L. Conner of the Methodist church performed the ceremony. Both Dan McCormick and Fred Deane were naturalized Irshmen. Fred was a tinner and shortly afterwards opened a repair shop in Pasadena.[23]

Pasadena in 1915 had an estimated population of 600. Joe Cullinan had a hollow wire gasoline illuminating system installed at his farm house since electricity was not yet available in the Pasadena area. He had also approved the placement of a granite historical marker at his farm to commemerate the capture of General Santa Anna by the soldiers of the Texas army in 1836. Previously a marker had been placed at the site of Vince's Bridge, which had been destroyed to prevent reinforcements to General Santa Anna's army at San Jacinto. Jason Robert and Josephine Moechel moved their family to Pasadena from Missouri by 1910. Renee Marie was 13, Yvonne five, and J. Robert, Jr., only three. Jason bought land at the north end of Main Street, just across Vince's Bayou. The family lived there and rented out several smaller structures located on the property. Although Jason farmed part time, he was in the same

J. M. Cruse managed the Cullinan Farm at the time that the Santa Anna Capture Site historical marker was placed there.

Josephine Moechel with her children Renee Marie, Yvonne, and Robert, Jr.

business as Cullinan, oil. He had a PhD degree in geology and was in the thick of things. George Milton and Serena E. Lakin came to farm with their school-aged children Olive "Ollie" and George, Jr. In addition, George's widowed father Milton H. Lakin came with them.[24]

Alma D. Thornton Jones, the widow of Elmer B. Jones, had taken over the post office from C. H. Tilley the year before and had moved the post office from Tilley's store to a little 12' by 12' building at the corner of Shaver and the La Porte Road. Her father, William H. Thorton had arrived in Pasadena about 1907 and the little post office was located in front of his house. A. L. Dickerson listed his business as a florist and his brother W. H. Dickerson had his general store

The first freestanding post office was operated by Alma Jones as postmistress from 1914 to 1920. It was located on the La Porte Road in front of her parents' (W. H. and Sara Thornton) home.

on Main Street on the south side of the track. Tilley was across the street from Dickerson and sold groceries and leather goods. J. T. Conn had moved to Austin to become the superintendent of the state of Texas rural school system and the widow Zora Lee Kingsbury was buying his old mercantile building to operate a grocery store, and to live upstairs. Ironically Zora Lee used to babysit Conn's children in the same building before her marriage to Robert Ace Kingsbury. Robert had been widowed with three children when they married in 1910. Zora Lee gave him two more, lost one, and a fourth was on the way when Robert died. He had built them a nice home on Spooner at Broad Way a few years earlier, but died early in 1915 while he was working to pave the street with shell. Zora Lee was left with the children and a need to make a living. Effie Mae, Blanche, and Richard were in school, but Catherine and Rayburn were too young. Robert Ackley was about to make his appearance.[25]

Anna Pomeroy should have listed herself as a rooming house since she boarded most of the unmarried teachers. In July she took in three new teachers, Miss Kate Smith, Miss Kilgore, and Miss S. Hager. Her house was now getting crowded since her son John had married the teacher Gertrude McMaster in 1911 and they were living there with their two young children: Marguerite and Edward. Gertrude's father, David Clarkson McMaster, had moved to town in 1911 and enjoyed his new grandchildren. His son Clyde McMaster and wife Emma Alice also presented him with two more grandchildren, Myrtle and Credella, while he was staying in Pasadena. But, when

Miss Kate Smith taught for a year, married, and returned to teach for many more years as Mrs. Kate Smith Bishop.

Baby Edward Pomeroy and sister Marguerite delighted their grandfather, David Clarkson McMaster.

David was accepted into the Confederate Rest Home in 1914, he moved on to Austin. Robert and Ann James had survived the Galveston Hurricane of 1900 as had Anna Pomeroy. They also moved inland, but did not finally arrive in Pasadena until 1911. They bought five acres on Buffalo Bayou near Cotton Patch Bayou and settled in with a few of their children: Mildred Lillian, Annie, Edith, and Robert J.[26]

Back on the north side of the track the Guinns ran the railroad depot. Robert Guinn was the express agent and his daughter Katie was the railroad agent and ran the Western Union office. Twice a day the train travelled to Houston and twice a day it returned, on its way to La Porte, Seabrook, and Galveston. Across the street the Pasadena, Texas Producers' Exchange occupied the corner of the La Porte Road and Spooner.[27]

And of course, the town grew as the families grew. William and Letha Jane Holbrook added Johnie, George Ann, St. Clair, and finally Wesley. That brought their family to six children. George and Annie Holbrook increased their five to eight children with Jewell, Lillian, and Ann. Robert Kingsbury's brother, George Clyde, drifted into town, spotted Rhoda McEvers, married, and they added Ralph C. to the population in 1908. Baby George R. died before his first birthday and was buried at Crown Hill Cemetery. John H. and Allia M. Strope moved to Pasadena early in the century with their daughter

Julia Loomis and her new husband Robert W. King. Robert and Julia began on their family, which grew every other year. Martha Elizabeth was first, followed by Inez M., Esther E., Martin H. and finally Robert. Allia Strope witnessed the birth of all of her grandchildren, then died in 1919 and was laid to rest at Crown Hill. Presley Young Howell moved to Houston with his family and was working at a laundry when he got acquainted with Effie Newell. Effie was working at a millinery in Houston. They courted by rented horse and buggy out South Main and married in 1912. They were living in Victoria when Francie Edwin was born in 1913 and then back to Pasadena for Ila Mae in 1915. W. M. and Lillie Davis bought 20 acres from John Strope and built an impressive two-story house for their daughter Hazel and her impending wedding. The wedding did not happen and the Davises sold the house to Sam Milton and Ann Jane (Glass) Allen in 1911. Little Sam had married in 1907 and was still living at the Allen Ranch with his wife when the property became available. Father Allen bought the house as his wedding present to the couple.[28]

Sam Milton Allen ran the Allen Ranch from his elegant house on Richey Street.

The children of Deepwater now had a schoolhouse of their own and they did not have to travel to Deer Park for their education.

Egbert P. Miller was the postmaster in Deepwater and ran the general store in town. The store was in the old hotel and rooms were rented out upstairs. Myrtle McMaster had been born up there back in 1908 as was Doris Barnes in 1913. The McMaster and Barnes families had since moved to Pasadena. Bessie Starkey was the railroad and express agent for the town. J. H. Starkey, E. H. Bisbay, and C. B. McNay served on the board of trustees of the County Common School District back in 1912. F. J. Martin was now on the board and a new schoolhouse was built in 1915. McNay was interested in the school system since he and Bertha had four children: Lavera E., Laurel Eugene, Lockridge D., and Elizabeth Araverne. Oscar Starnes had three children in the school. His wife, Minnie, had been previously married and Oscar adopted her children, James Q. and Lometta. Roy was theirs and was just starting school. It might have helped that Oscar's brother, Sidney, was living with them, and was a public school teacher.[29]

Deer Park was quickly becoming a ghost town as its population dwindled to about 25. Edwin Brown had moved first from Houston to Pasadena and then on to Deer Park in 1905. The Browns leased the 24-room hotel for their home and ran one of the largest ranches in the area. Their oldest child, Katherine, became postmistress in 1914 and would be followed by the next child, Adelle, in three years. The former postmaster, John Hallburg had passed away in 1914 and his wife and some of the Olson family returned to Illinois. George and Rose Olive lived on the east side towards La Porte with their five-year-old daughter Irma. Charles and Emma Hagberg lived near the Browns with their daughters Hildur "Hilda," Lillie, Amy, and Mildred. Charles carried the mail from Deer Park to Lynchburg.[30]

La Porte was still the largest town in the area with an approximate population of 700 people. William T. Hall, the local Presbyterian minister and staunch Democrat, was serving as the postmaster. G. D. Samuells and Associates of Houston had acquired Sylvan Beach Park in 1909 and had really improved the facility. A large entranceway was built, the dance area improved, and the east depot moved to the front entrance of the park. The Texas State Rotary annual picnic was held at the park in 1914 and the giant picnic table, shaped like a wheel, could seat over 4,000 people. The park was being electrified with lighting from its own generating plant. Cottages had been built and were rented by the weekend or the summer. The summer vacation traffic was a real boom to the economy of the community. Unfortunately, during the summer of 1915 La Porte experienced another of its disastrous downtown fires. Almost three blocks were destroyed, including the post office, the three-story Bisson Building, and the Seureau building.[31]

Genoa was doing quite well in 1915. It boasted of a population of about 200 people. John J. Davidson ran the general store and also served as the postmaster. Davidson had taken over the post office from "Deb" Atkinson several years earlier. Atkinson had subsequently moved to Pasadena. W. L. Moberly was the railroad and express agent, C. E. Vauters was the local water well driller, and H. W. Boehm was the blacksmith. The J. C. Carpenter Fig Company was located in town and there was an assortment of dairymen, fruit growers and nurserymen. School trustees R. S. McGowen, H. L. Crenshaw, and Stanley Anthony were proud of the new red brick schoolhouse with its three classrooms and basement below.[32]

Rivaling La Porte, South Houston also claimed a population of approximately 700 citizens. The town had recently been incorporated as a village and Mr. Throp elected the first mayor. Although the town boasted of 1,200 residents, they had problems in naming 600 people to satisfy the incorporation requirement. It was suspected that the cows that roamed the area were "named" and their pastures given "addresses" for petition purposes. Ironically, the first order of business for the newly incorporated village was to build a fence around the town to keep the cattle out. F. B. Russell published the *South Houston Times* and ran a printing company. J. H. Grannis was the postmaster and J. K. Busby was the railroad agent, express agent, and telegraph operator. No matter how hard the developer or the residents of the town tried, the railroad still called the station "Dumont" and not "South Houston." Even so, South Houston was becoming a town of industries with the Lincoln Machine Company, Texas Fireworks Company, and Twyford Automobile Company. J. L. Dickens was the secretary of the South Houston Commercial Club and also operated a college for ladies. Dr. McWhorter was the town physican and Mrs. Durman ran a sanitarium. B. F. Meader had served on the school board with first M. J. Bass and T. R. Martin and then Bass and L. Peterson before his untimely death. Some of B. F.'s sons continued the grocery business under the name of Meador Brothers Grocery and General Store. B. F. "Frank" II worked as the manager, Joe looked after the vegetables, Rex did the accounting, and Horace did whatever else was necessary. Dumas and Harrala operated a general store.[33]

With a force greater than that of the 1900 storm, another hurricane struck Galveston and the Pasadena area on Monday, August 16, 1915. Fortunately the West Indies disturbance had been monitored for days and people had begun taking precautions. However, the force of the storm was greatly underestimated. The *Galveston Daily News* reported on its front page that Monday morning, "**GULF DISTURBANCE CAUSES UNEASINESS.**" The morning edition of the *Houston Post* reported in a small front page article, "**TROPICAL STORM SWEEPS GULF.**" By Monday afternoon, the *Houston Chronicle* ran its headline: "**STORM HEADS INLAND; TEXAS COAST VISITED BY WINDS AND RAINS.**" During Monday morning the wind began to rise, and by afternoon water was in the streets of Galveston. The barometer reached its lowest point at 2:00 P.M. with a reading of 28.66, but the winds increased until 3:00 P.M. to its highest official reading of 90 mph. Estimates put gusts to 120 mph as the storm inched its way inland. Dr. William Clark of Kemah reported the lowest reading of 28.65 occurred in his town twelve hours later at 3 A.M. Tuesday morning. The might of the storm struck Houston about an hour later, with winds of

80 mph recorded at both 5 A.M. and 6 A.M. Rain began in Houston Monday evening about 6 P.M. and lasted about 14 hours, until 8 A.M. the next morning. The winds gentled to 50 mph and took another eight hours to fall to 26 mph.[34]

Awareness and preparation were credited for the significantly reduced lose of life. The hurricane claimed only a total of 275 lives compared to the 1900 storm's total of nearly 8,000. Only eight people lost their lives in Galveston. The 1900 storm claimed over 6,000. Besides general preparation, the 18-foot-high concave concrete seawall at Galveston diverted the force of the sea that had previously swept the island almost clean. Stories of great courage and sacrifice filled the newspapers for days. Ironically the damage was nearly twice as much as the 1900 storm, with coastal cities suffering the most. The *Houston Chronicle* proclaimed, "Seabrook is gone." Only three buildings were left standing. "La Porte Wiped Out" with all of the bathhouses along Bay Ridge at Morgan's Point destroyed as well as the bathhouse for Sylvan Beach at La Porte. The Seminary suffered. The Second Division, U. S. Army campsite at Texas City was covered by eight feet of water and over a dozen soldiers perished.[35]

Inland, Webster lost its fig factory and South Houston its $7,000 public school and J. C. McDearnor's (or McDurman's) sanitorium. The emerging industrial development in South Houston was terminated that day as the railroad equipment company, masonry manufacturer, candy maker, and walking toy company were all destroyed. Only the Gulf States Asphalt Company and the Texas Fireworks Company survived. Even the hotel was gone. The 1900 storm had done considerable damage to the town of San Jacinto across from Lynchburg and the 1915 storm finished wiping it out. Like the semi-annual visits by the Allen Ranch cowboys, San Jacinto became a permanent part of history. The ferry at Deer Park was destroyed also never to exist again. In Genoa, Pearl Robertson Crenshaw, wife of H. L. Crenshaw lost almost all of the souvenirs that she had saved from her survival of the Galveston Storm 15 years earlier. Like the Pomeroys, the Robertsons had survived the storm in Galveston and moved inland in 1901. About 50 people in Genoa sought refuge in railroad boxcars to escape the fury of the storm as numerous houses were blown down and several people seriously injured. The rest of the season's baseball games for the Houston Buffs had to be transferred when the Houston Ball Club's grandstand roof was demolished and all of its fencing blown away. And also gone with the wind was the roof of Pasadena's new schoolhouse.[36]

The *Houston Chronicle* reported that Pasadena was a heavy sufferer of the storm with practically half of the town in ruins. The roof of the new schoolhouse had been blown off, but only minor damage had been done to both nearby churches. The Pomeroy barn a block away on Main Street was almost demolished as was the Shine two-story house across Shaver from the school. Farther south on Twelfth (Southmore) Street the Atkinson house at the Baldwin and Cargill farm was blown off of its blocks. Members of the family tied themselves to trees to keep from blowing away. Baby Willard was only four months old. Maybe the Atkinsons had learned to depend on trees when they had lived in Genoa where the Thurmans had tied themselves to a tree during the 1900 storm. Adolfo and Santos Herrera lived nearby on the farm and with their four-year-old daughter Julia, they abandoned their home for the shelter of a neighbor's house. J. D. Parks and family abandoned their home on Wafer in favor of his parents home a couple of blocks away on Shaver. More than 30 people crowded into the larger

The school house in Pasadena suffered the most damage in the community during the 1915 Hurricane.

The distinctive cupola on the roof of the school was gone forever after the 1915 Hurricane.

The Pomeroy barn was almost destroyed, but the house was undamaged.

The John Shine house lost its roof but was rebuilt.

Pomeroy home to ride out the storm. A couple of blocks south on Main Street the Browns lost part of their house during the night to the high winds. Mr. Brown tied all of the children together with ropes and led them through waist-deep water to the Holloway house next door. Although the Holloway house eventually lost all of its windows, the people inside were unhurt. Forian and Mollie Beusch were in the middle of moving to Pasadena and were in League City getting their furniture. Their son Gib and Elizabeth and William Boesch were in their Pasadena farm house and fled to the Garnuchs to weather the storm. The McMasters also lost the windows in their home in addition to having ankle-deep water in the house. Mrs. Emma Alice McMaster's parents, Doc and Sarah Webb, were living with them at the time. Up the road the Gigstad children spent the night thinking their house was going to explode with the force of the wind. Lee and Bertha Dickerson had lived through the 1900 storm in Pasadena and took precautions. With the help of a relative, Eddie Artusy, Lee had dug a shelter trench along the high bank of Vince's Bayou near their home and had evacuated the family to the shelter

Monday as the wind rose. They spent the night safely in the shelter. Their barn blew away as well as the front porch of their house. Except for water damage, the house was otherwise okay. Walter and Clara Wilson lived on the other side of Vince's Bayou from Dickerson and had a couple of inches of water in their kitchen. Baby Estelle had arrived just two days before and Mrs. Savage (the former Mattie McEvers) was staying with them to help Clara with the new baby and little Thurman and Sylvia. When the barn was blown down and the pieces settled up against the house, Walter felt that the family should leave. When they woke Mrs. Savage she disagreed, saying that the Lord would protect them. She then went back to sleep. Walter

The Dickerson store on Main Street, on the right, did not replace its front porch after the hurricane destroyed it.

did go outside and helped Mr. Garfield get the cows out of the bayou.[37]

Southwest of Pasadena near the Florentine Settlement, Gus Edming prepared for the storm by bracing the house to fortify it against the anticipated winds. However, he had to spend the entire night holding the door closed. His neighbor Oscar Kruse lost all of the windows on the west side of his house and both of his barns were blown down. Kruse had recently purchased an old house in Houston and used the lumber to build a large barn for his growing dairy business. And to make

The Deepwater berry shed was levelled.

matters worse, Houston now required a license to sell butter and eggs in the city. The inspector came out after the storm and upon seeing the extent of the damage, he told Kruse to do the best that he could since it was obvious that it would take months to rebuild the barn.[38]

Prior to the storm, the Hearn and Barnes families of Pasadena had moved to the Garvin Dairy. The dairy was located between the communities of Lomax and La Porte, at the intersection of Sens Road and the South Houston-La Porte Road (Spencer Highway). Annie Hearn was expecting and her son Asa Hearn went for the doctor as the weather turned ominous. Edith arrived that night, August 16, in the middle of the hurricane. Not surprisingly, the doctor was forced to spend a few extra days at the house because he could not get back to his home.[39]

The road and railroad through Pasadena remained opened and was used to provide evacuation for the refugees and emergency aid for the victims. The railroad engine house at Allen's El Buey rail siding was blown into the nearby field, but did not prohibit the operation of the trains. The recently opened Houston Ship Channel also continued to operate. A monster celebration had been planned for August 19 to honor the arrival of the Southern Steamship Company's vessel, the

The Satilla *was the first ocean going ship to visit the new Port of Houston and had to wait for the hurricane to pass.*

Satilla. Southern had promised to start regular ocean service to the new Port of Houston and the *Satilla* from New York was to be the first arrival. The hurricane delayed the arrival and put a damper on the huge celebration.[40]

With relatively little loss of life, the people turned their energies to rebuilding. In Pasadena, school classes were held in the Baptist and Methodist churches until the damage to the school could be repaired. The school had cost $10,000 to build just five years earlier and it took approximately $5,000 to repair the damages of the storm. The distinctive cupola on the roof was not replaced. Barns were rebuilt and crops planted. For a while the Great War in Europe and the sinking of the *Lusitania* three months earlier were forgotten.[41]

War had been brewing in Europe since 1912 and the assassination of the heir to the Austrian throne on June 28, 1914, was the spark that ignited the world in flames. The Austro-Hungarian government declared war on Serbia on July 28 and a domino effect of declarations triggered by mutual defense pacts embroiled continental Europe, Britain, and Russia in war. Japan joined the war against Germany on August 23 and widened the conflict to a global scale. Europe was quick to grasp the military advantage of aeroplanes (airplanes) and the first German air raid struck Paris August 30, 1914, with two four-pound hand-dropped bombs. The following month a German underwater boat ("U-boat") sank three British cruisers. Germany continued its introduction of new warfare weapons with the use of chlorine gas at the Second Battle of Ypres on April 22, 1915. The Cunard Line passenger ship S. S. *Lusitania* was sunk May 7 off the coast of Ireland by a German U-boat. One thousand, one hundred and ninety-eight people died, including 128 U. S. citizens. U. S. public indignation was ignited even though the unescorted ship carried 173 tons of contraband weapons and food for the war effort, knew that U-boats were operating in the area, and did not change its course. President Woodrow Wilson loudly protested, but stuck to the U. S. policy of neutrality. American volunteers went to Europe to fight and by April 1916 a special French aviation group was formed with American fliers, called the Lafayette Escadrille. They painted an Indian head, complete with war bonnet, on their planes for identification.[42]

Meanwhile at home the U. S. Army vented its frustration on the Mexican revolutionary Pancho Villa. Villa was displeased with the U. S. recognition of the Carranza administration that had ousted him from his dictatorship of Mexico. On March 8, 1916, Villa raided Columbus, New Mexico, and killed 17 U. S. citizens. General John J. "Black Jack" Pershing was sent to deal with the bandito. For the first time, military airpower was utilized. While Germany entered the Great War with approximately 1,200 combat planes and France and Britain could muster 1,000 between them, the U. S. inventory consisted of only 20 flying machines in the newly organized First Aero Squadron. Eight aircraft were assigned to the anti-Villa force and promptly proved inadequate. Only two survived to April and they were scrapped as soon as equally inadequate replacements arrived. Congress responded with a $13 million commitment for the development of an effective and adequate military aviation branch. Unfortunately, neither the technology nor the manufacturing capability existed in the United States. When the U. S. finally entered the Great War in Europe on April 6, 1917, there were less than 250 aircraft and balloons in inventory. The gross inadequacy of the U. S. aircraft inventory and industry was put into perspective when French Premier Ribot asked the United States in May 1917 to provide no less than 4,500 combat aircraft for use on the western front by June 30, 1918, plus another 18,000 training aircraft.[43]

In the rush that followed Texas was selected as a key training area. First, because of its weather and secondly, because its flat lands and relatively few protrusions, either human or geological, were necessary for training, fledgling pilots. The first fields and training school were established near Fort Sam Houston at San Antonio. Camp Kelly was established on June 11, 1917, and officially opened as Kelly Field two months later. Austin, San Antonio, Dallas, Fort Worth, El Paso, Waco, Wichita Falls, Port Arthur, and Houston all contained aviation military facilities. The Houston Chamber of Commerce proposed many sites, but 1,280 acres near Genoa were selected as the site of a flying field early in September. Included in the site was one of the parcels that Payson Pomeroy had tried to homestead in 1901 and had sued J. H. Burnett over. Burnett had prevailed and his heirs would benefit from the new airfield. The land was initially leased to the goverment with a performance bond posted by the Chamber of Commerce. Construction of the base began September 14, 1917.[44]

It had only been seven and a half years earlier that the first airplane flight in Texas occurred just a few miles north of this site. Shorty Walker, Greasy Smith, and Guy Hahn continued to use the airfield constructed at South Houston for that event. Smith and Hahn even started manufacturing airplanes in South Houston and many people thought that this was why the new airbase was located nearby. There was also another reason why the Gulf Coast area was chosen.

Two years after that first flight, or 10 years after the Wright brothers' initial powered flight, the First Provisional Aero Squadron of the U. S. Army arrived at Texas City in March of 1913 to set up a flight training facility. They and their airplanes arrived by train. The Second Army Division had already set up a "training maneuvers" camp at Texas City because of the unrest in Mexico with Pancho Villa. Since the Signal Corps was interested in considering adding seaplanes to its squadron, the nearby beach location was important. The farmers and residents of the area were understandably startled by the flying contraptions, as many as seven at a time, that now roamed and roared in the sky above. By June 14, just three months later, most of the squadron had been moved to San Diego, California, where the weather was more predictable. On November 14, 1913, instructor Lt. Eric Lamar Ellington of North Caro-

Airplanes were manufactured in South Houston.

lina died at San Diego when his Wright biplane took a nose dive from 800 feet. Four years later the new airfield south of Genoa, Texas, was named in his honor.[45]

Ellington Field became operational November 27, 1917, as an advanced pilot training facility with the first aerial bombing school in the army. It took only 73 days from ground breaking to field completion despite numerous change orders and recurrent strikes. Ben Bailey of Pasadena did his share in the

In 73 days the prairie south of Genoa became a military aviation training field.

construction of the new base. Because of his carpentry skills he was drafted into the 461st Aero Construction Squadron and put to work at Ellington. Airplane mechanics were the first to arrive and began assembling the planes that were shipped in by train. The first plane took to the air on Tuesday, November 27. The first formation was flown on Wednesday, December 5. Ten ships flew over Houston, dropping Red Cross literature. Sirens shrieked and bells rang in welcome to the pilots above. A few days later the same Red Cross formation flew over Galveston. If a person had not seen an airplane by 1917, the next few months would remedy that. The first detachment of cadets arrived December 17 and more planes were shipped in and assembled. The sky quickly became filled with the latest training ships and the greenest pilots, attempting to balance the forces of gravity, lift, rudder and propeller.[46]

Cross-country navigation training sent them over the farms of Pasadena. Inexperience or surprise sent some of them to the ground. The first fatality occurred near Genoa in January 1918. In order to retrieve and treat crash victims, the first flying ambulance was created at Ellington. Since runways were little more than smooth fields and occasionally a plane was forced to land in a pasture away from the field, pilots and planes were accustomed to setting down most anywhere. More than one plane used the streets of Pasadena for a landing strip. A group of aviators once parked their planes at Little Sam

The sky filled with airplanes for the opening of the airfield at Ellington.

Around Town (1910-1918) 175

Not all of the airplanes got off of the ground.

Allen's place on Richey Street for a quick party. Sticking to the streets, roads, and wagon trails was easier on the landing and saved on the fuss that a farmer would raise if you landed in his strawberry patch. J. D. Parks was one of those who hosted an airplane in his field. The first time Addie Brown saw an airplane up close was when it was sitting in a strawberry patch. Dive bombing and ground-level surveillance fly-bys were also on the no-no list, especially if there was a farmer's daughter or animal involved. However, after 4:00 P.M. on Fridays, the cadets headed to Houston and other points of female habitation for relaxation. Pasadena was not on the list of hot entertainment spots, but the dust rose

Not all airplanes came down from the sky.

as the dar- ing young men headed through town on their way to Sylvan Beach.[47]

Houstonian G. D. Samuells had taken over Sylvan Beach Park around 1909 and had greatly improved it. Unfortunately the 1915 hurricane laid much of the park to waste. Ed Eisemann, another Houston businessman bought the park and with the help of Cecil Sisson of Houston and Fred Baker of La Porte he rebuilt and improved the pavilion and increased the cottages to a hundred. The grand reopening was on San Jacinto Day, April 21, 1916. A 16-coach holiday excursion train from Houston called the Sylvan Beach Special rolled in with more than 1,000 people. Round trip fare from Houston was 50 cents. More celebrants arrived by automobiles, ready to picnic, dance and/or swim. You did not have to worry about packing your swimsuit to go to Sylvan Beach, you simply rented them. They were wool, and for the ladies they included pleated skirts with bloomers underneath. Coca Cola soda water sold for 5 cents and the dance floor was so large that amorous young people could easily waltz out of view of chaperoning parents. Not afraid of the lime light, Pasadenans Blanche Mitchell and Lewis Garfield won the waltz contest one night. With young men off to military service elsewhere, cadets from Ellington and soldiers from Camp Logan in Houston were willing substitutes. The first permanent rides were installed about 1917, including

During the hot summer months, a cool dip at Sylvan Beach was a relief.

Around Town (1910-1918)

You could get "high" on the Ferris wheel.

a ferris wheel, kiddie rides and the jeweled carrousel. Some adventurous girls were bobbing their hair at the barber shop in the pavilion. Again, taking the fashion lead, Blanche Mitchell, along with Carrie Parks trimmed their locks. Anna Pomeroy so disapproved of the haircuts that she stopped giving Blanche fresh cut roses from her garden.[48]

The merry-go-round was fun for children and those young at heart.

Truly a wonderland with fun things to do.

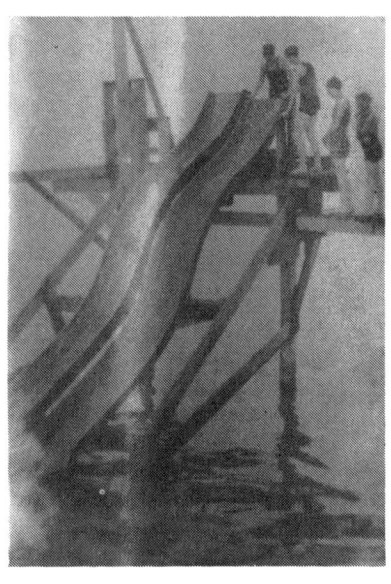

The super-slide was a quick way to get wet

Edna Mae Irwin was fashionable with her bobbed hair and boyish looks.

Bobbed hair became the rage.

Although the army was trying to mechanize, horses and mules were still part of the inventory. Twice a day they came to Lester Leroy Hargrave's flowing well on the west side of Pasadena to be watered. A small army camp was located near the old Allen Ranch headquarters on Sims Bayou and the Ship Channel. Across the Ship Channel, the Universal Shipbuilding Company was constructing 300-foot long wooden ships for the Emergency Fleet Corporation as its part for the war effort. Construction began in August 1917 with a contract for 12 ships, which were to be used to transport provisions to the U. S. soldiers overseas. Up river, Midland Bridge Company was to construct six at its facility at Fidelity, across the channel from Manchester. Pan American Shipbuilding was down river from Universal, located at Penn City and opposite Deepwater and Deer Park. McMaster and Pomeroy drilled the water well for Universal and Pan American. Jess T. Brammer came to work as an electrician at one of the shipyards. He brought his wife Eunice, and children Irma and Paul from Wise County and settled in Pasadena. Pasadenans Edgar Barnes, P. Y. Howell and Ray Williams worked at Universal where the first of the wooden ships launched in the Gulf Coast occurred on April 7, 1918. It was christened the *Nacogdoches* by Houston Chamber President J. S. Cullinan's daughter, Nina. Approximately 1,500

Lester Hargrave provided water for the U. S. Army mules quartered nearby.

people turned out for the event and lined the banks of the channel on both sides. Fifty-four years earlier the channel had witnessed another launching: The *Bagdad* had been christened for Confederate service by Miss Ella Mason, granddaughter of James Morgan. Capitan John Cubb and Thomas Cubb had their shipyard nearer Galveston Bay, at the mouth of Goose Creek.[49]

Also doing her part as a civilian for the war effort, Addie Brown served in the Pasadena Red Cross unit. Among other things the unit raised funds for the Red Cross by putting on entertainment programs at the school house. On September 12, 1918, Pasadena held its selective service registration. Although many had already gone to serve, 83 signed the roll. Six were unnaturalized citizens (two Germans, two Swedes, one Norwegian and one Swiss), nine were Mexican and three were Negro.[50]

Quite a few Pasadenans served in the military. Houston held its first call to arms in May 1917 and by the time of the selective service registration in Pasadena, Robert Guinn, Jr. and Chester Guinn were already in Europe. Karl Kruse was off to Europe. Carl Tilley went to war but brother Charles Albert was left at home. Carrol Coolidge, Grant Coolidge, and Cleveland Pitts served their time. John Ellis went into the Navy. Walter Williams' only son, Roy, was also off to war. Vernon Newell went to the Army and was followed later by his younger brother

Addie Brown served in the Pasadena Red Cross.

Frontis. Fortunately, Frontis went in November 10, 1918, and the Armistice was signed the next day. Vernon returned in 1919 to marry his fiancee Allie Brown, Addie's younger sister. Lester Hargrave's brothers Alfred, Mack, and Wilbur went in the Army. When the trains of troops left Houston for their ships at Galveston they travelled through Pasadena. Mildred Tabor was fascinated at all of those soldiers hanging out the windows and wildly waving as they rolled through town on their way to "The Great War."[51]

Neighbor "Little Sam" Allen also served, stationed out at Ellington. In fact, a lot of the Pasadena boys fulfilled their service requirements at Ellington. George C. Thornton had just moved to Pasadena with his wife Ray and in-laws Sam and Edna Quinn, when he checked into Ellington as a Chauffeur First Class. Jake Miller's boy, Ira was a Private First Class and Robert S. Bayless was a Private. Also serving at Ellington from the area were First Class Private A. Everett Stephens from South Houston. Seabrook residents Louis E. Chapman and Joseph P. Schwandee were chauffeurs and Charles L. Chapline was a cook.[52]

As if it was not enough that the sky should now be constantly full of daring young men in their fragile noisy flying machines, that might swoop down, or crash down at any minute, day or night; the first live bombs were dropped in practice in April

Wilbur Hargrave was stationed in Maryland.

Another of Pasadena's boys gets ready for war.

Men and women served in the armed forces.

Around Town (1910-1918) 183

Returning veteran Vernon Newell marries Allie "Gertie" Brown.

1918. As the program expanded into night bombing, giant calcium spot lights fingered the dark skies for yet another new experience for the Pasadena residents. Fortunately the aerial gunnery school established during May was at distant San

Night flying practice added to the round-the-clock training.

Ream field was a practice field established at Park Place.

Leon. Engines barking, propellors humming and the rat-a-tat-tat of machine gun fire became an ever present background noise. Civilians learned to exercise care while sailing off Red Fish Reef in Galveston Bay in order to avoid becoming mistaken as part of the decoys in the firing range. The more adventuresome aviators would try their hand at close-range duck and geese hunting to sharpen their maneuvering and marksmanship skills. The Second Provisional Wing set up an outpost aviation camp at Park Place and designated the camp Ream Field.[53]

For all the inexperience and risk, there were surprisingly few casualties. The flying machine usually got the worst end of the crash experience. Most pilots walked away, and those that did not, were generally from the earlier training classes. Ironically almost as many men at Ellington died from the "Spanish Influenza" that swept the world that year. In the worst world wide epidemic since the Black Death of the mid-14th century, more than one percent of the world's population, almost 22 million people, died. The Great War only claimed 10 million lives. The flu started in China and reached the United States on August 27, 1918. Over 600 cases were reported at Camp Logan in Houston by September. Half of Houston had the flu by October and 111 were dead by October 14. Twenty-six-year old Emma Moore Cruse described its effect on many people; "You were alive one minute and dead the next." Most of her family caught it, as did many others in Pasadena. Ted Newell, D. E. Atkinson and one of the Holbrook boys almost died from it. Agnes Garfield was less fortunate. Her husband, Charles Lewis and son, Lewis Edgar, got sick but eventually recovered. Her four-year-old Mary stayed with the Thomasons until her father and brother got well. Her eight-year-old sister Cecelia went to the W. S. Parks' family. Newlywed Leona Roberts Burch (Richburg) wanted to adopt the girls. Although they did not suffer a death in their family, Will Parks' brother Ralph had to help out with the dairy and strawberry farming until Will and Leora got back on their feet.[54]

Donald Gregg was the first soldier from Pasadena killed in the war. Jasper Gordon and Effie Averalla Gregg had moved to Pasadena with children Donald and Etta because Jasper's sister Zella was married to Joseph Cruse. Donald died before he could see his sister Etta married to John Franklin Johnson who worked with Joseph Cruse at Cullinan's farm. Ironically Jasper and Effie Gregg had met in Joseph and Zella's home and now their daughter had met her intended in another of the Cruse's homes.[55]

Too old for the draft, John Zlomke volunteered. He was also one of the gallant patriots who gave their lives in the "war to end all wars." His body was put to rest next to his father, Walter in Crown Hill Cemetery. Crown Hill was also the final resting place for Sidney G. Robertson who left his wife, May, and two young children, Blanche and Sidney J. La Porte residents Cecil Bethea and LeRoy Hovey also did not come back from the war.[56]

The armistice was signed November 11, 1918, and the Great War ended. The announcement hit the streets with the 4 A.M. "Extra" edition of the *Houston Post*. Soon the newsboys' shouts were joined by a crescendo of horns, whistles and sirens. Myrtle Blakesley was already in class at Harrisburg High School when the word reached the area and the jubilant students were let out to join the celebration. Ten-year-old Ima Parks was on the way to school when she heard the news. Being too young to understand the meaning she continued to school where she was told that there would be no school that day. That, she understood. At Ellington, 5,000 men and 250 planes assembled on the runway to stand at review in honor of the occasion. John Pomeroy loaded up his car and took everyone to Houston for the big parade.[57]

Although the war had lasted for slightly over four years the United States was not officially involved until the last 19 months. However, the economy and spirit of the American people were involved from the beginning. Even before the men went into military service, the demand for goods opened up jobs for women in the work force. Many new jobs were created in the Houston area as shipments through the port increased. When the United States declared war the influx of military personnel into Houston further heightened the demand for goods, services and finances. But the lasting effect of the war was the accelerated recognition of the usefulness of the internal-combusion engine. To Texas, that meant oil fields. To Houston and its ship channel, it meant refineries. To Pasadena, it would mean a different future.[58]

Doris and Eugene Barnes examine one of the airplanes that made an unscheduled, abrupt stop in a Pasadena strawberry patch.

VIII

Outside Influences (1900–1920)

The development of Buffalo Bayou into a shipping channel was basically ignored by the farmers of Pasadena. The town had been conceived as a farming community and it had evolved exactly that way. Life focused on the soil, the seasons, the weather, planting, harvesting, and selling. Social and commercial institutions developed as an adjunct to that lifestyle. Commission houses, mercantile establishments, manufacturing concerns, and government was the business of Houston. Galveston was the golden lady of business, finance, society, and pleasure. La Porte and the Bayshore was an unclear mixture of fishing, farming, mercantile, and leisure. The commercial battles between Houston and Galveston, and the oil boom, only made occasionally interesting reading.

Since their very beginnings, Houston and Galveston fought over dominance of Texas agricultural shipments. Galveston possessed the best of the Texas coastal ports and quickly took the lead. The Allen brothers, and other Houston promoters pointed to Buffalo Bayou as the best internal waterway system in Texas and that Houston was the closest and most reliable shipping point for the dominate cotton industry. Unfortunately, sections of Buffalo Bayou and Galveston Bay were only deep enough for barging and not adequate for the deepwater vessels necessary for shipments to the eastern textile markets, and especially to Europe. As early as 1851 Galveston was favored by the federal government for the development of a deep- water port. Without conceding the water transportation debate, Houston took the lead in railroad development. The objective was to first get the freight to Houston instead of Galveston. In fact, Merriweather Smith proposed a railroad from the Brazos River to his new town of Buffaloe (later the town site of Pasadena) in 1837. Sam W. Allen's friend Andrew Briscoe of Harrisburg was the first to start construction on a railroad in Texas. He chartered the Harrisburg Railroad and Trading Company in 1841 for a railroad between Harrisburg and some point on the Brazos River. His dream was to extend the line to the Pacific Ocean at San Diego. Construction began, but was not finished.[1]

Sidney Sherman was the first to build a railroad in Texas. The Buffalo Bayou, Brazos, and Colorado Railway was chartered in 1850, nine years after Briscoe's Harrisburg Railroad and Trading Company and a year after Briscoe's death. Twenty miles of track was laid from Harrisburg to Stafford's Point on the Brazos and biweekly service began September 7, 1853. Nearby Houston had been slow in supporting railroads as it focused upon wagon freight and thought that improved roadways, or even turnpikes, would be the quicker and cheaper alternative. Galveston chose to ignore railroads and began building a canal from the Brazos River to Galveston Bay in 1850. In 1855 the Galveston intercoastal canal was finished, as was the extension of the Buffalo Bayou, Brazos, and Colorado Railway from Stafford's Point to Richmond on the Brazos River. Houston woke up, and literally got off of the wagon and onto the railroad. The Houston and Texas Central built northward from Houston and a 25-mile line from Houston to Cypress opened in 1856. That same year the Houston Tap tied Houston into the Buffalo Bayou, Brazos and Colorado line. Seeking to tie into the new rail lines and to bypass the wharf at Houston, Galveston interests chartered the Galveston, Houston and Henderson Railroad Company in 1853. In 1860 that line linked Galveston with the interior of Texas, through Houston.[2]

Being the hub of the Texas railroads still did not mean that Houston would reap the benefits of a shipping port. The contest continued like a ping pong game. In 1873 Galveston sponsored construction of the Gulf, Colorado and Santa Fe Railroad (G. C. & S.F.) through Alvin to Richmond so that Galveston freight did not have to pass through Houston. Beginning in 1875, John H. Burnett (later the founder of Pasadena) built the line to Richmond, finishing it in 1879. Houston attracted shipping magnate Commodore Charles Morgan and his Morgan Ship Lines from Galveston to Houston in 1874. Morgan agreed to dredge a waterway to a depth of nine feet to accommodate steamers of the day. Galveston finally won the federal River and Harbors appropriation in 1890 for the improvement of its port and the Galveston jetties. Houston lobbied hard in Congress but did not receive serious financial attention until the Galveston Storm of 1900. Acting quickly, Houston Representative Thomas Ball pressed for sufficient funds to restore Galveston to its previous condition *and* unconditional recognition of and funding for Houston's channel.[3]

The focus of federal funding was to increase the depth of the channel from Bolivar Roads, opposite Galveston Island, to a designated terminaling point. Although few heard it, La Porte thought the port should be placed there. Morgan had chosen a point opposite Sims Bayou (he named it Clinton). Harrisburg pushed for Brays Bayou. Houston, the prime mover in the program, wanted it at the foot of Main Street. The government engineers selected "Long Reach," the longest and straightest section of the bayou above Lynchburg. Buffalo Bayou was a beautiful canal-like river with steep banks and heavy foliage. Depth in the bayou had not been the initial problem. Red Fish Bar in Galveston Bay was a major depth barrier as was Clopper's Bar at the mouth of the San Jacinto River. Charles Morgan cut a canal across James Morgan's Point (no relation) in 1870 but extracted a toll for its use until it was taken over by the federal government in 1892. With each deepening project, the channel was also widened to allow for better maneuvering of the ever-increasing-in-size ships. Meanders in the bayou were straightened out when cuts were completed at Irish Bend in 1905, Clinton in 1906, and Harrisburg in 1907. The Turning Basin was completed 1908. The upper Clinton, or Fidelity, cut was completed in 1911.[4]

Congress had approved an 18 1/2 foot depth project. However, the magical depth for "deep water" ports by this time was 25 feet. With that goal so close in sight, Houston headed back to Washing- ton. A navigation district had been formed with the authority to initiate improvements and raise money by issuing bonds with voter approval. The Rivers and Harbor Committee approved the project when Houston offered to pay for 1/2 of the cost of the dredging. The Houston Plan, of matching local monies with federal grant monies, was the first of its kind in the nation and set the precendent for future government funding programs. Harris County voters approved the necessary bonds in 1911 and the turnkey contract was let in June, 1912 to the Atlantic, Gulf and Pacific Company. Simultaneously with the Houston Ship Channel project, the Gulf Intracoastal Waterway project was reviving the old Galveston-Brazos canal, tieing Corpus Christi into the Houston Ship Channel in 1913. Further south, the Panama Canal was also being dug at the same time.[5]

To the farmers of Pasadena this history and activity meant very little. Pasadena was neither designed nor settled to take advantage of water transportation. The original plat did provide for a 200-foot-deep "reserve" along the water's edge at the end of Shaver Street, but the abutting land was used for farming, not commerce. There was not even enough interest for a ferry to cross the bayou. Deepwater had a hand-pulled ferry and Deer Park had a wharf of sorts, and a raft for crossing. Waterfront lots in Deepwater were laid out for summer-type estates along the idyllic bayou. Only San Jacinto, Lynchburg, and La Porte were water commerce oriented. Pasadena's markets were reached by wagon to Houston or rail to far off markets. The bayou was for fishing, swimming, and a possible source for irrigation. Jones's rice farming operation in Deepwater initially utilized large pumps to lift the bayou water into a network of irrigation canals. With each dredging the salty bay water encroached further upstream, increasingly making the bayou water unfit for irrigation purposes. Eventually, Jones had to drill water wells to obtain fresh water for his rice crops.[6]

The old riverboat days had passed before Pasadena was settled and the packets and once-proud steamboats were gone. An occasional excursion boat plowed the waters, docking a party at the Allen Ranch, Poole's Rest, San Jacinto battlefield, or Sylvan Beach. Sam Allen was a fancier of horses and held horse races on his ranch. He also hosted some fancy parties at his ranch house. Poole's Rest, sometimes called Moore's Park, was located between Allen's Ranch and Pasadena. It was a place to rest, fish, or party. It contained a 30-foot-square covered building on the edge of the bayou called the Buffalo Bayou Fishing Club. Patrons could sit inside and crab without getting hot or dirty. There was also a restaurant and a dancing pavillion. Some said that there were cock fights and a lot of boozing. Another favorite stopping spot was the San Jacinto State Park. Slowly the state was fixing up the site of the famous battle and it was fashionable to picnic on the grounds and visit the various markers and monuments that were being erected. The historic towns of Lynchburg and San Jacinto were nearby. However, the most popular destination became Sylvan Beach and Park. L. F. Allien's steamer *Eugene* was a familiar sight before the turn of the century. The double decker cruise ship *Nicholas* and the *Ethel B* appeared afterwards. Freighters, tugs, and barges were becoming a more frequent sight. Still this meant nothing economically to Pasadena. However, other outside forces would combine with the channel to make it more than just a canal through Pasadena.[7]

Sam E. Allen was raised with horses and appreciated them for their work and pleasure qualities.

The devastation of the 1900 Galveston Storm brought with it literally the seeds for a new success to Pasadena. While Pasadenans were picking the first fruit of their new strawberry plants, another harvest was beginning at Big Hill near Beaumont. Pattillo "Bud" Higgins had had a vision 10 years before about oil derricks on that hill and had spent those years trying to find oil. He never gave up hope although he had lost most everything else. In 1899, he convinced Captain Anthony F. Lucas of Louisiana to underwrite another try. When Lucas ran short on money he got backing from Guffey and Galey, the

Next to his ranch headquarters, Allen built a horse racetrack.

Pittsburgh oil firm that had invested in the Corsicana (Texas) field. With new money and the Hamil brothers as drillers, another well was started. Higgins was right. The Lucas gusher blew in on January 10, 1901. Seventy-five thousand barrels of oil daily spewed uncontrolled in the air until the well was finally shut in nine days later.[8]

Joe S. Cullinan had visited the site less than a year before when Standard Oil declined to invest. He returned and assisted as the well was capped. The gushing was over, but the boom

One of the popular excursion boats was the Nicholas. *Loading at Harrisburg, the boat would make numerous stops on its way to Sylvan Beach.*

had just begun. The well had broken the world's record and catapulted Texas into the forefront of the petroleum industry. Everyone interested in oil, and in making money, came to Beaumont and bought, sold, or developed leases at Big Hill, now called Spindletop. Oil was produced in unprecedented, undreamed of amounts. The ramifications were limitless. The four railroads in the area immediately converted their coal-fired locomotives to oil burning. Oil drums were too small and cumbersome to handle the flow of oil from Spindletop, so railroad tank cars and pipelines were created. Tank farms and refineries sprung up in the area. Fortunes were made and new companies formed. Prospectors combed the countryside looking for other likely prospects. Before his death in 1901 John H. Burnett leased the oil rights to Pasadena to the Guffey, Galey and Lucas's company. California's gold rush was small potatoes compared to the Texas "black gold" rush.[9]

There were many men who came to prominence and wealth because of the oil boom, but none affected Pasadena like Joseph Stephen Cullinan. Born and raised in Pennsylvania he learned the oil business by working his way up in a Standard Oil affiliate. The first oil boom in Texas came to Corsicana in 1894 when oil was discovered during the drilling of a water well. Respectible production was achieved by 1897 when Mayor James E. Whiteselle invited Cullinan to Texas. Liking the prospects, Joe formed the partnership of J. S. Cullinan and Company and began constructing a gathering pipeline system, storage tanks, and a refinery. Then he set out to create customers for the refined product. He persuaded businesses to covert their furnaces and boilers from coal fuel to oil. Corsicana became the first of many towns to start oiling their streets to cut down on dust. Corsicana was also the first to use natural gas for

J. S. Cullinan was the visionary that made Houston the "Energy Capital of the World," and filled Pasadena's backyard with refineries.

illumination. With Cullinan's leadership, Corsicana soon became the premier city of the fledgling Texas oil industry.[10]

Later, in their book, *Spindletop*, James A. Clark and Michel T. Halbouty described Cullinan as follows:

> "Joe Cullinan, sometimes known to his friends as 'Buckskin Joe,' was a man who believed that doubts and fears are man's worst enemies, and that as long as a man doesn't know he can't do a thing, there is nothing he can't accomplish.
>
> Cullinan was a daring and restless man, a gambler who mixed caution with boldness, and who was probably the nearest to an all-around oil genius ever born. Athletic and agile, with quick, searching eyes and a clear, vigorous voice, his very handclasp inspired confidence. He was tall, handsome and distinguished, with cleancut features, a short-cropped moustache and a head of thick, well-groomed hair. A man of decision, he possessed an active, intelligent mind of the type given only to leaders."[11]

Having developed a proven, profitable program of commercial refining and successful marketing, Cullinan was ready for the opportunity that Spindletop provided. The Lucas gusher was drilled by the Hamill brothers of Corsicana so Cullinan was on top of the well's progress. When the well blew in he was one of the first to arrive. He organized the Texas Fuel Company two months later to purchase and transport Spindletop oil. Realizing the potential of the Gulf Coast, he soon severed his Corsicana connections and moved to Beaumont when the price of oil hit three cents a barrel due to excessive overproduction. Cullinan started purchasing oil contracts for future delivery and arranged financing of his operation by bringing in partners, including ex-Governor Stephen Hogg and John W. "Bet-A-Million" Gates of New York. Shortly the price of oil shot up to 75 cents a barrel. The Texas Company was chartered in April 1902 and took over the assets of the Texas Fuel Company. With Cullinan as president, the company began to rapidly expand beyond Spindletop.[12]

Oil fields located on salt dome structures are limited in geographical area. If you don't get a lease on the "hill," you were out of the production. Since Pattillo Higgins proved that salt domes were good locations for oil fields, prospectors began searching for similar structures. In fact, any spot that had mysterious bubbles coming up in bodies of water, or had a rotten egg odor in the air, became suspect. In quick succession, nearby Sour Lake, Saratoga, and Batson responded to the rotating bit. Cullinan had taken a position at Sour Lake before the boom hit and presold a lot of his oil at 60 cents a barrel. When the field began to flow huge quantities of oil like Spindletop, the market price dropped quickly to 10 cents.[13]

Once the news of a new field was out, the boomers came roaring in. Leases were bought and sold in an ever increasing spiral of ridiculous values. Wells were put down, often a few feet from each other and the oil blew out the crown blocks and ran down the ruts. The price of oil fluctuated wildly, depending directly on how much oil was flowing. Explosions, fires, and even sudden death were everyday occurrences. Everyone thrived on the excitement. Conservation and controlled production were unheard of. You produced as much as you could and as quick as you could, because there was always another lease and another gusher to be drilled. As wells fell off in production and the field output declined, the prospectors went looking elsewhere. Fifty miles to the southwest, the village of Humble was the next on the boom town list. The first wells were drilled on Moonshine Hill in May 1904 and were disappointing. However, there was enough "smell of oil" that the boomers started coming from Batson. By the end of the year people were living in tents and the yet-to-be defined field was alive with activity. On January 7, 1905 the Beatty #2 well blew in at 8,500 barrels a day. Within six months the Humble oil field was producing more oil than any other field in the state. The Texas Company took a position in the field through Walter Sharp and Howard Hughes's Moonshine Oil Company. And the first pipeline to Houston was completed in April.[14]

Seeing the trend of the new fields developing southwest along the Gulf Coast, Cullinan began to move his base of operations to Houston in 1905. By then the Texas Company owned numerous production leases, extensive pipeline operations, a refinery at Port Arthur, and an asphalt plant at Port Neches. Being strong on sales, Cullinan had established marketing facilities throughout the United States and had expanded into Belgium, Luxembourg, and Panama. By 1908 the general offices of the company had been moved to Houston and Cullinan began promoting Houston as the center of the petroleum industry in Texas.[15]

Joe Cullinan was a man of action, who put his plans into motion. He understood the petroleum process from production to consumption. He understood the men that were driving Houston into a major transportation center with its railroads and ever deepening ship channel. Not only was Houston convenient to current abundant crude-oil supplies, but would also be central for additional supplies that would surely come from Mexico and Central and South America. The deep water ship channel had the added advantage of being protected from floods and tropical storms. There was also an abundance of fresh water that was necessary for the refining process. And large acreages were available along the course of the ship channel that would be well suited for construction of refineries. To demonstrate his belief, he began acquiring property on both sides of Buffalo Bayou in the area of Pasadena in 1908. Wafer had purchased the land 15 years earlier for $980 and Cullinan acquired it for $5,500. This was the first financial contact Pasadena had with the new petroleum industry, and locally it only perceived the action as just another farm changing hands. After all, Pasadena was also beginning to boom, or rather bloom, with strawberries.[16]

However, oil production was getting closer to Pasadena and it would only be a short time before the residents would get a first-hand glimpse of the boomers and a wilder land speculation than they could imagine. Some of those strange gas bubbles had been coming up in Tabbs Bay near Goose Creek and the San Jacinto River, opposite Morgan's Point. John Gaillard thought that it had meant that there were feeding fish on the bottom, but he never caught any. An oil scout from La Porte realized that there might be a gas field there when the bubbles flamed when put to the match. The first producing well was drilled on shore in January 1907 but the production was disappointing. In June 1908 a Houston syndicate struck oil at the water's edge, testing out at only 720 barrels per day. Cullinan's Texas Company bought the lease, but abandoned it 18 months later. Oil was there, but it was elusive and would defy the wildcatters for a few more years.[17]

Meanwhile, Cullinan added acreage to the "Pasadena Farm." To the 41-acre Wafer tract acquired in 1908, he added 50 more in 1909. He got a nice residence, a large barn, some outbuildings and two other houses in the deal. Not to mention all the other items that go along with an active farm. Being a practical man, he hired an overseer and kept the farms running. Across the bayou he purchased more land, but this was only for investment and promotion.[18]

The first five years of the twentieth century had been frantic with Texas oil discoveries and production. The wildcatters moved from one discovery to the next without regard for responsibility or conservation. Promotion money quickly flowed to the hot spots and no one thought of long-range planning and production. The price of oil rose and fell with daily discoveries and production rates. Despite Spindletop and the subsequent activity, by 1910 the state of California was the largest producer in the nation. Meanwhile, the Texas wildcat play shifted to North Texas along the Red River. In January 1911 one of Cullinan's crews brought in a well on the Tom Waggoner ranch just west of Wichita Falls. In typical fashion, they tried to keep the discovery a secret until they could gain control of more acreage. The Texas Company did gain control and the Electra field was one of the first orderly developed fields in the state. However, the bigger "play" was in Oklahoma for the next few years.[19]

Meanwhile, in 1911 Ross Shaw Sterling organized the Humble Oil Company at Humble, Texas, after prospering with feed stores and banks in the Gulf Coast boom towns. He felt that the rampant competition was hurting the smaller oil operators and that he could create a profitable company by buying them out and controlling the excessive production. To add to his new production purchases, he also acquired a small refinery at Humble. Following the lead of Cullinan, Sterling moved the headquarters of his new company to Houston in 1912.[20]

Cullinan and others realized that it was cheaper to haul or pipe- line crude oil to a seaport, refine it there, and ship the finished product by water transportation to distant markets. The Texas Company had built a refinery at Port Arthur as had the J. M. Guffey Petroleum Corporation (Guffey had backed Lucas on his Spindletop well, and his company was soon to be reorganized as the Gulf Oil Corporation). The Pierce-Fordyce Oil Association built a refinery at Texas City. The first pipeline to Houston was built in 1905 from the newly discovered Humble oil field. However, the pipeline only carried crude to waiting ships, not to any refineries. Houston and its channel were to wait a few more years before it benefited from the new industry.[21]

John Harris, Nathaniel Lynch, and Lorenzo de Zavala had each built wharfs and sawmills along Buffalo Bayou by the 1830s. The Allen brothers built their wharf at Houston and had the "Port of Houston" declared by city ordinance in 1841. Except for a few small operations around Goose Creek and La Porte, there were only five cotton compresses, a grain elevator, and a few wharfs along the bayou in 1910. The major waterside facilities were located between the foot of Main Street at Houston and the old Morgan docks opposite Sims Bayou. Joe Cullinan began purchasing property along both sides of Buffalo Bayou in the Pasadena area because he could see a far greater potential for the developing ship channel than either the Allen Brothers or the subsequent businessmen of Houston. Houston thought of a channel bringing ships directly to their town and the various loading facilities there. Harrisburg and La Porte each thought only in terms of docks and industries in their cities. Cullinan saw more than a dock at the end of a water course, he saw the entire length of the channel as miles of water frontage on both sides, and thousands of acres available for development. The Texas Company purchased a large block of land on Buffalo Bayou opposite Pasadena in 1912, but it was not the first to build a refinery.[22]

When the Texas Company was formed, the name meant its origin, Texas. The charter members informally agreed that the headquarters of the company was always to remain in Texas. The company had prospered with Cullinan as president, but the Board of Directors voted in 1913 to move the corporate headquarters from Houston to New York. Cullinan resigned in protest. He formed Farmers Oil Company and struck out on his own again. Almost as if by premonition, he had hired Joseph M. Cruse earlier that year at $60 per month to oversee his Pasadena Farm. W. H. Waggoner owned land nearby and had been looking after Cullinan's place. With a new challenge before him, Cullinan quickly found his opportunity. He had "struck it rich" at Spindletop when he contracted for future delivery of cheap crude oil, stored it, and then sold it when the price of crude rose. In mid-1914 a deeper oil zone was discovered in the nearby Humble oil field and a second boom began. Again, Cullinan purchased crude as the price fell with each new well. He quickly built oil storage tanks on the old Norsworthy property on the ship channel. The Gigstads could walk to the channel, and there at the mouth of Cotton Patch Bayou watch the tanks go up across the water. Wade Dickerson even worked for a while at the Norsworthy Terminal.[23]

When the price of crude recovered, Cullinan profited. By 1916 he organized the American Republics Company and reformed Farmers Oil Company into the Republic Oil Company. With an inventory of cheap crude and a ready source of future supply, he organized the Galena-Signal Oil Company and built the first refinery on the newly renamed Houston Ship Channel. Cullinan committed a million dollars to the project. New production was also discovered at deeper zones in the Sour Lake field. On August 23, 1916, the first big strike in the Goose Creek field came in, gushing at 8,000 barrels of oil per day. Others quickly followed as the oil boom returned to the Gulf Coast.[24]

The Goose Creek field was just a few miles down river from Pasadena and gave the farmers of Pasadena their first look at those crazy boomers. After oil was first found at Goose Creek in 1907 the Houston Deepwell Company had been formed and shares sold to Wade Dickerson, John Pomeroy, Clyde McMaster, and others in Pasadena. Since little oil had been found at Goose Creek, the venture was forgotten. This time the farmers of Pasadena just witnessed the activity. A community of sorts had been established along Tabbs Bay as a result of the earlier drilling activity and at the time of the 1915 Hurricane, at least 25 wooden derricks dotted the landscape. When the new boom hit, workers and promoters travelled through Pasadena on the train to La Porte or by jitney to the Lynchburg ferry. From La Porte a water taxi could be arranged to cross the channel to the oil field. The wild excitement of the field was in stark contrast to the tempo of Pasadena's life style. Like going to a circus and its sideshow, weekend sightseeing tours amazed and fascinated the excursionists. But with World War I just around the corner, this was just the beginning of many new experiences for the Pasadena farmer.[25]

Gulf Oil Company also moved its headquarters to Houston in 1916. Humble Oil bought the Southern Pipeline Company to tranport oil from the Goose Creek field to a new ship loading facility built on Hog Island in the Ship Channel. Two years earlier Gulf had built a pipeline loading facility at Lynchburg. With the construction at Harrisburg of the Armour Fertilizing Works in 1913 and the Texas (Portland) Cement plant in 1914, the character of the ship channel was beginning to change. And the impact was slowly beginning to be felt in

Pasadena. Texas Cement purchased land in Pasadena on the west side of Vince's Bayou and south of the railroad tracks. The clay in the soil at that spot was beneficial to the cement manufacturing process. They began a mining operation that would last almost 50 years. With the United States entering the war in April 1917, at least three shipbuilding facilities were constructed along the ship channel. Clyde McMaster and John Pomeroy drilled water wells for two of them. In August the Simms-Sinclair interest brought in the largest oil well in the United States, at Goose Creek. At 35,000 barrels of oil per day, the *Houston Post* calculated it was flowing at $33 a minute. In September the Simms-Sinclair group purchased the 712-acre Allen Ranch headquarters on the ship channel at Sims Bayou for a refinery site.[26]

The first major refinery on the Houston Ship Channel was the Sinclair Refinery next door to Pasadena. The plant was built on the old Allen Ranch land at Sims Bayou.

By year-end, Pasadena had some new neighbors. It had fought off the competition of new towns at the turn of the century and won. There was so much potential farming that any new farms in the area only improved the economy instead of detracted from it. But Pasadena's new neighbors were not in direct competition with the life and livelihood of the community. It was more of a challenge to change. The town of Pasadena was planted in a cow pasture and grew to change the landscape. A new crop was beginning to literally break ground. A "plant" here and a "plant" there did not make much of an impression at first, nor did it impact much upon the community. But like seeds blown on the wind, more industrial "plants" began to sprout.

Some of the new companies were small, like the Magnolia Oil Mixing Plant and the Hoffman Oil & Refining Company facilities. Fidelity Cotton Oil & Fertilizer Co. and the Texas Chemical Company continued the trend away from cotton compresses, grain mills, and general wharfs. However, phase one of the Sinclair Gulf Refinery next door to Pasadena would require $6 million to build and could process 20,000 barrels of oil per day. Although not the first refinery on the ship channel, it was the first for a large oil company, and the biggest refinery by far. Its construction and subsequent operation would provide jobs for any of the Pasadena farmers who wanted a steady income. While Sinclair was under construction in 1918, Humble Oil purchased 1,500 acres near the Goose Creek field for a refinery site. Empire Oil & Gas Company had also purchased 1,000 acres on the ship channel near San Jacinto.[27]

About the time Sinclair came on stream late in 1918, Crown Oil & Refining Company purchased 65 acres in Pasadena from William Blakesley, E. A. Olson, M. Bennett, and Jack West. Crown broke ground in February 1919 for its $750,000 refinery. Jim Hughes had moved to Pasadena in 1908 to farm strawberries. His sister Annie (Mrs. J. T. Conn) was there and his younger brother Leonard had lived there for a while. Jim's sister Mamie subsequently moved to Pasadena in 1915 when she married Howard Pitts. Jim continued to farm his 20 acres across the street from the new refinery site, but hired out with his mules to move dirt and heavy equipment during the refinery construction. With Sinclair, and then Crown under construction, it meant the farmers had to work harder to bring in their normal crops since they also hired out for construction labor. Clyde McMaster and John Pomeroy prospered that year in their new water well drilling business. In March they drilled a temporary well for Crown so that Crown could have water for construction. After the strawberry crop came in Clyde and John came back in May and drilled three production wells for the new refinery. At first they only thought of drilling water wells for farmers. The ship building boom during World War I called upon them for their first industrial water wells. Drilling

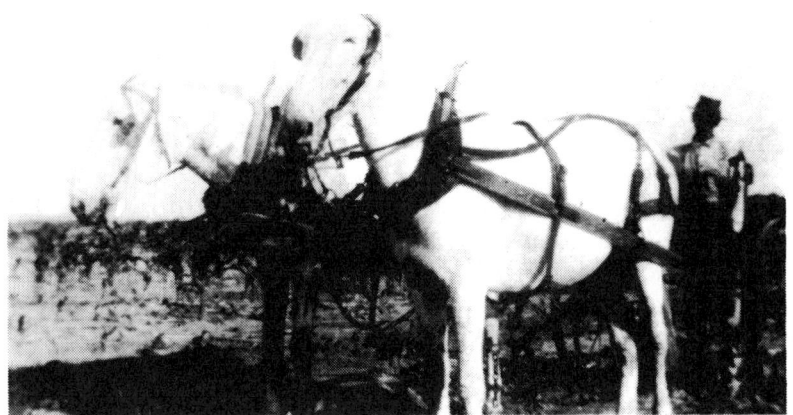

When Crown Refinery was being built in Pasadena, Jim Hughes rented out his mules to help with the construction.

wells for Crown, and then Cullinan, continue their drift in the direction that the community would later take. But they still drilled farm wells. And both Clyde and John drilled a well in their own backyards.[28]

J. S. Cullinan continued to farm his land next door to the Crown Refinery for almost another 20 years.

Crown went on stream in 1919. It was a different kind of plant growing in the fertile strawberry fields of Pasadena.

Under the leadership of its president, Ross Sterling, the recently reorganized Humble Oil was entering an era of rapid growth and expansion. In 1919 Standard Oil Company of New Jersey purchased 50 percent of the company, and with the new capital, Humble began construction in June of its refinery near Goose Creek. At a cost of a million dollars, the new refinery was designed to process 4,000 barrels of oil per day. Sixteen-year-old Earl Newell of Pasadena worked as a riveter on the oil storage tanks. By 1921 the plant's capacity had been expanded so that it could now process 10,000 barrels per day. The rapid oil pumpage from the Goose Creek field created subsidence of the surrounding land and resulted in a lowering of the land elevation by over 16 inches in some areas. The only known earthquake in the Texas Gulf Coast region occurred as a consequence of this activity. The tremors, which rattled dishes, cracked the ground, and disturbed the residents, were only felt locally. It would be almost 30 years before the small communities of Goose Creek, Pelly, and Baytown would combine under the single name of "Baytown."[29]

Also during 1919, E. A. Peden of Houston, and others announced the construction of their Deep Water Refinery in Harrisburg. Their plant would be able of processing 1,000 barrels of oil a day, with the help of McMaster and Pomeroy water. The Keen & Woolf Refinery at Clinton also depended on McMaster and Pomeroy water. The United States Congress approved funds to again deepen the ship channel, this time from 25 feet to 30 feet in order to accommodate the larger oil tankers. And oil production was increasing in Texas with new discoveries, and expansion of older fields. Although Oklahoma had captured the top oil producer title from California, Texas was back in the race.[30]

Joe Cullinan must have been proud of himself as he sat on the second-floor screen porch of his Pasadena farm house, overlooking the ship channel. He chose Houston as the center for the oil industry and moved his Texas Company there. Now all of the big Texas players were represented in Houston. He had also felt that the Houston Ship Channel was the prime location for oil industries and he made the first move. From his rocker he could see three refineries and knew that three more existed beyond his view. Others were planned. Although he was a man of industry, he dabbled in farming at his place in Pasadena. On the other hand, Pasadena was still a community of farmers, but they were beginning to dabble in industrial jobs. Being close to Houston, Galveston, and Galveston Bay, Pasadena had opportunities that more remote farming communities did not have. And taking advantage of opportunities was something Pasadena was good at. So with a postwar boom in place, Pasadena headed into the Roaring Twenties.

IX

Roaring into the Twenties (1919-1924)

"How 'Ya Gonna Keep 'Em Down on the Farm? (After They've Seen Paree)."

The mood in 1919 was reflected in the popular song by Walter Donaldson. Many changes had occurred during the war years and there would be no going back, for the nation, and for Pasadena. The emphasis on production brought more mechanization into the factories as abundant crude oils provided fuel for the internal combustion machine. The benefits of mechanized transportation had been proven by the military and Henry Ford turned this into automobiles for everyone. The practical aspects of now-familiar aviation resulted in airmail and commercial passenger service. Women had been pressed into the work force to help with the increased production, and to replace the men who had gone into military service. They had gained a new sense of freedom along the way that could not be reversed. Texas granted women the right to vote before it was required by U. S. constitutional amendment. Prohibition sentiment during the war resulted in the Eighteenth Amendment in 1919, but the observance would be tenuous and temporary. However, it would take 13 years before the Twenty-first Amendment would officially end Prohibition on December 5, 1933. Having endured the strain of war, the people were ready to relax and be rewarded for their noble, herculean, and successful effort.[1]

But first, the strawberry crop had to be brought in. Mechanization had revolutionized the factories, but it still took hand labor to harvest most agricultural products. And what a bumper crop there was in 1919. Over 110 carloads left the Pasadena siding. One of the shippers complained about the "whiskers" on the strawberries and wanted the berries to be "shaved" so they would look better to the buyers. Translated to the Pasadena farmers, this meant that the shipper was trying to get a special discount on the price of the strawberries. To avoid any "misunderstandings" about price once the berries were shipped, it was decided that a local bank had to be established so that the farmers could immediately convert their bills of lading into cash before the boxcar left the siding.[2]

On Saturday, July 19, 1919, two banks opened for business in Pasadena. Since most people began to loosen up their work load for the weekend, Saturday was a good time to catch them in "downtown" Pasadena. The commissioner of insurance and banking of the state of Texas issued charter number 1191 to Guaranty State Bank with an initial capitalization of $10,000 and authorized stock of 100 shares. The initial directors were: W. H. Dickerson, W. B. Thornton, and G. M. Olive, all of Pasadena; C. E. Truelove, R. L. Young, and A. W. Perryman of Houston; and Dr. I. P. Poynor of Harrisburg. E. F. Defee, W. H. Dickerson, G. C. Olive, G. M. Olive, W. J. Shelton, W. B. Thornton, and W. L. Wilson were the Pasadena-area stockholders. Robert L. Young of Houston was the largest stockholder with 40 percent of the stock. He was president of the People's State Bank in Houston and the manager of Crown Oil & Refining Company, whose refinery was then under construction in Pasadena. Charles E. Truelove, who moved to Pasadena for a short while with wife Minnie Lee to run the bank, had the second largest number of shares. Charles was the assistant cashier of the American State Bank in Harrisburg and continued to show his home address as Houston. Alexander W. Perryman of Houston also owned the same number of shares as did Dickerson and Thornton. Perryman was the vice-president of the American State Bank, president of Houston Oil & Refining Company, general manager of both Humble Cypress Oil Company and Security Oil Association, and president of Perryman Investment Company. Dr. I. Patrick Poynor was president of the American State Bank and was also a medical doctor. Of the non-Pasadena investors, he was the best known since he had lived in Harrisburg for 15 years and had attended to the medical needs of many Pasadena patients.[3]

Guaranty opened for business in Wade Dickerson's two-story frame mercantile store on Main Street, just south of the railroad tracks. Dickerson served as vice-president of the American State Bank of Harrisburg and was familiar with the operation of a bank. It was logical that he was selected as president of the new Pasadena bank. Locally Wade had obtained the moniker "Judge" because he was always dispensing his decisions about various matters from behind the counter at his grocery store. Blanche Roberts was hired as the first female

The first brick building in Pasadena. Built in 1920, Guaranty State Bank occupied one side and Pasadena Drug Store the other.

window teller in Pasadena. Dickerson promptly sold his group the corner lots at the La Porte Road and Munger Street and the first brick commercial building was constructed by W. C. Hedrick, the contractor for Young's new Crown Refinery. Precisely because of the "Houston connection" of Guaranty, another group of Pasadenans simultaneously organized Pasadena State Bank.[4]

Charter number 1192 was issued to Pasadena State Bank on the same day that Guaranty State Bank was chartered and it also opened on the same day as Guaranty. Pasadena State Bank began business in the old Whitten/Hunken mercantile store on the La Porte Road at Spooner, two blocks from Dickerson's store. The building was owned by the Pasadena, Texas Producers' Exchange and many of its members were also stockholders in the new bank. The initial board of directors were: W. N. Blakesley, Charles L. Garfield, W. C. McMasters, C. E. Parks, and R. E. Parks, all of Pasadena, and J. M. Jackson and S. A. Starkey, both of Houston. The list of stockholders included many of the farmers of Pasadena: D. E. Atkinson, W. B. Bailey, Jr., W. N. Blakesley, G. A. Brown, Aubrey R. Cruse, J. M. Cruse, H. E. Ford, Charles L. Garfield, H. Gigstad, Earl Guinn, Oscar Kruse, W. C. McMasters, F. D. Newell, C. E. Parks, J. D. Parks, R. E. Parks, W. S. Parks, Peter J. Peterson, O. C. Pitts, J. E. Pomeroy, James Williams, J. R. Williams, and W. F. Williams. Houston stockholders were the produce firm of Baldwin & Cargill, J. M. Jackson, J. O. Shine, and S. A. Starkey. Jackson, Shine, and Starkey had lived in Pasadena but moved to Houston for jobs. J. Milton Jackson owned 15 percent of the stock and was the only banker in the group. He was the assistant cashier at State Bank & Trust Company of Houston. Ralph Parks also owned 15 percent of the stock. Houston interests, including Shine and Starkey only owned 25 percent of the stock in Pasadena State compared with 67 percent for Guaranty.[5]

Fifteen-year-old Delbert Atkinson plowed early that morning before going to Pasadena State Bank's opening about 10:00 or 11:00 A.M. He was the first customer and deposited $3 by presenting his passbook from another bank. About 30 customers showed up that day and deposited about $9,000 in the new bank. J. M. Cruse sold groceries on one side of the middle aisle, and the bank did business on the other. R. E. Parks was the president and college-educated Aubrey Cruse was the cashier. Aubrey had moved to Pasadena with his parents in 1913 but had returned to Texas A & M for his education. He was around Pasadena long enough to meet and subsequently marry Emma Moore. They moved to Austin where Aubrey worked as an assistant entomologist for the Department of Agriculture. Emma lost her first child at birth but brought infant Aubrey Junior home to Pasadena after a brief stay in Baytown. Emma was again pregnant when they arrived, but had to surrender that child to Pasadena's cemetery after only three months of life. The move back to Pasadena proved fruitful as she was later blessed with four more healthy children.[6]

Since Pasadena only had about a thousand people, it was not a two bank town. Guaranty Bank promoted its financial expertise and the Houston/industry connection. Pasadena Bank emphasized the local farmers' interests and orientation. Guaranty moved into its new brick building, the first in town, to illustrate its progressiveness. Pasadena touted friendliness. After two years of competition, the two banks consolidated on November 2, 1921. Pasadena State Bank absorbed Guaranty and moved into its new bank building. A special certificate of dissolution was issued by the secretary of state for Guaranty on November 15, and Pasadena was united under one bank. Ralph Parks continued to serve as the president, J. Milton Jackson as vice-president and Aubrey Cruse as cashier. Parks was 52 years old and Cruse was about 30. Jackson was also still with State Bank & Trust of Houston, now renamed State National Bank, where he had been promoted to trust officer. Naturally, State National was the bank's Houston correspondent, or contact. In 1922 total deposits of Pasadena State were reported at $28,000.[7]

The successful strawberry crops, World War I, the ever increasing popularity of automobiles, and the new refineries were forcing the village of Pasadena into becoming more of a town. Besides having the only bank on the ship channel between Harrisburg and La Porte, Pasadena started getting gasoline service stations. Since automobiles only had a 10-gallon gas tank, they were required to regularly fill up. In 1917 Lester Hargrave took advantage of the long distance between Harrisburg and La Porte/Sylvan Beach by putting up the first filling station in Pasadena. His station sold Gulf gasoline and

Lester Hargrave opened the first automobile service station in Pasadena in 1917.

Heading east along the La Porte Road into Pasadena in 1917. Hargrave's service station is on the left.

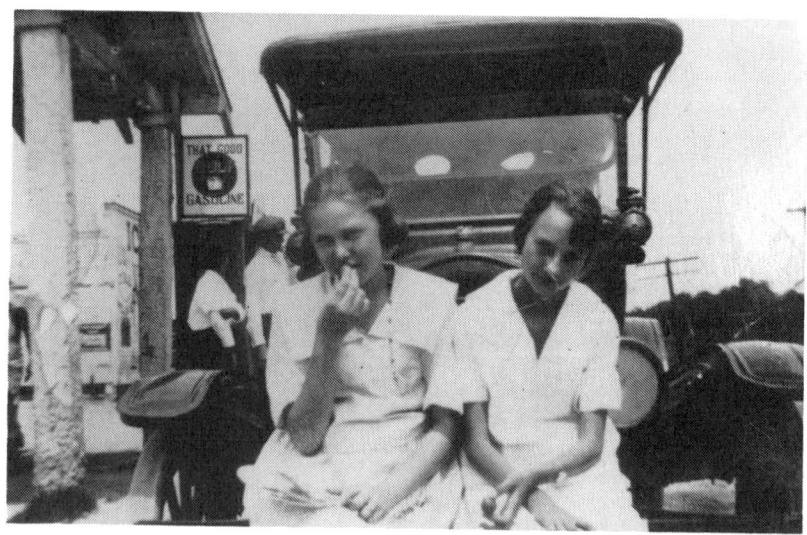

With a fan in one hand, Della Williams munches on candy with Ermine Brammer in front of Hargrave's service station.

was located on the La Porte Road just west of Vince's Bayou. Jess Brammer purchased the station about 1918 and then sold it late in 1921 to Gus Watson. At some point it became a Texaco dealership. Ralph Parks had a keen eye for good real estate investments and with an investment group purchased most of the block fronting on the La Porte Road between Walters and Shaver in 1921 from Whitt Thornton. He apparently acquired a service station, probably a Crown outlet, near the Shaver corner on the La Porte Road. "Foots" Wilson operated the station briefly before he started his Pasadena Ice & Fuel Company, also in 1921. Aubrey Cruse would take over the service station later and would operate it for many years under the Texaco and then Sinclair franchise. Wade Dickerson put in a pump for a couple of years outside of his new business in the next block near the Munger Street intersection.[8]

The shape of downtown Pasadena had changed during the later half of the 1910s. In 1910, Dickerson, Tilley, and Conn's faced off on Main Street just south of the railroad tracks. This was the center of "commercial" Pasadena because the public water well was located there. By 1915 Alma Thornton Jones' post office and Whitten/Hunken/Producers Exchange's mercantile building were north of the track on the La Porte Road. But with the advent of the automobile and the increasing popularity of Sylvan Beach, the La Porte Road became a busy thoroughfare. McMaster and Pomeroy were drilling water wells around town and in 1919 John Pomeroy had drilled a well in his backyard on Main Street that provided water for 30 customers in the immediate area. With the decrease in dependency on the community water well in front of Tilley's, the visibility and convenience of a La Porte street address became important. Dickerson was one of the first to recognize this when he moved his business, and building to the La Porte Road to be next door to his new bank building. A part of his new commerical building had been the old Pasadena schoolhouse that he bought in 1910 and had used as his residence. Ralph Parks and other participants in Pasadena State Bank were acquiring the city block at the northwest corner of the La Porte Road and Shaver. Obviously they envisioned a commercial concentration like Dickerson and Guaranty were putting together. However, the need diminished when Pasadena State Bank took over Guaranty and moved into its building. In the interim, cashier Aubrey Cruse had purchased land adjacent to the Parks piece and fronting on Shaver for a home for his parents and another for his growing family. With Parks's backing he continued working towards commercial development of the La Porte Road frontage.[9]

With only the exception of the railroad depot, all of the businesses along the La Porte Road were on the north side of the street. When Whit Thornton sold the west side of Shaver to Ralph Parks, he moved his house and the little 12' by 12' building his sister Alma Thornton Jones used for the post office across to the east side of Shaver. Alma's children, Walter and Nina, thought the post office was their playhouse as they spent many hours playing around with little Marguerite and Edward Pomeroy.[10]

Carrie Eugenia Roberts became postmistress on April 6, 1920, and continued to use the building for a while. Carrie had moved to Pasadena in 1913 with her husband Joseph Richard Roberts and their children Leona Adell, Constance Zola, and Blanche May. They had come to farm, but Joseph died three years later in 1916. Leona married Robert Andrew Burch in 1918 and was followed five months later by sister Constance who married Loyd Jones Ervin. Two days before Carrie became the postmistress, her last child, Blanche married Lawrence Nelson Sippy. The post office had come a long way since Jasper Hays operated it before the turn of the century. Post office boxes were now available for those that did not want to wait for Carrie to sort through the stack of mail to see if there was a letter for them. John Pomeroy was one of the first to take advantage of the convenience of a post office box. In 1919 the Deer Park postmistress Adele U. Brown closed her post office because there were not enough patrons in the area, and what mail there was transferred to the Deepwater post office. Two years later, in October of 1921, the Deepwater post office was also closed and postmaster Lorenza Keizer transferred his mail responsibilities to Pasadena. Not quite 30 years after the near simultaneous beginnings of the three towns, only Pasadena flourished. Charles Munger's dream was coming true as he quietly passed away in nearby Houston in 1918. It was estimated that there were now about one thousand people in Pasadena. The 1920 census reported 889 people in incorporated La Porte. Deepwater, Deer Park, Genoa, and South Houston were too small to be reported separately.[11]

Continuing east from the post office, Wade Dickerson's collection of stores were a half-block away. He now operated a

Myrtle Blakesley poses in front of Wade Dickerson's stores.

cafe, an auto supply store, and a grocery. He advertised a public telephone and restrooms. Frank and Lillie (Williams) DeFee had moved from Madisonville early in 1919 to both work in Dickerson's grocery. Four-year-old son John A. was cared for by Lillie's mother, Mary Williams. Preston Phillips moved from Arp, Texas, to work in Dickerson's drug store in 1921. It did not take him long to discover Carrie Parks and wed her. Adjacent to Dickerson's and on the corner of Munger was the new brick building with Pasadena Drug, a branch of Harrisburg Drug Company, on one side and Pasadena State Bank on the other. Eighteen-year-old Delbert Atkinson worked in the drugstore as he finished up his high school education at Harrisburg High School. The building had been built for Guaranty State Bank and the word "Pasadena" had been crudely overlaid on "Guaranty" over the doorway.[12]

On the northwest corner of Main and La Porte was the old railroad section house that had been used to house railroad employees. George P. Dowell rented the house about 1918 to accommodate his growing family. They had been living in the Pomeroy's rent house (the old Hay's post office building) for

$5 per month but the family had now grown to nine and the three-room house was just not big enough. L. Stella, Daisy A. "Dixie," and Georgie Pearl had been born since the Dowells had moved to Pasadena 12 years earlier. Two others had died in infancy. The eighth child, Willie Louise, was born in the new home on May 21, 1920. Diagonally across the street on the south side was the railroad depot that was the center of activity during the late winter/early spring strawberry shipping season. The depot and a few berry loading sheds were the structures on the south side of the La Porte Road. On the north side of the La Porte Road, and on the northwest corner at Spooner, J. M. Cruse still ran the grocery store in the Producers'

The depot and berry loading sheds were the only structures on the south side of the La Porte Road.

Exchange building. Howard Pitts was across Spooner with his new garage. However, it would be a couple of years before he would settle down to the business on a full-time basis. It was pretty quiet on that end of town since Pasadena State Bank had moved to the new brick building. And that was the end of downtown Pasadena in 1921.[13]

All that remained of the old "downtown" south of the tracks was Tilley's store and Kingsbury's store. The Tilley store was now little more that a shoe repair/leather store. On the adjacent corner, Zora Lee Kingsbury was operating a grocery store and boarding house in the old Conn's mercantile building. She had John Gutherie build a concrete porch on the front to dress up the place. The grocery store was in the front on the first floor. Her daughter, Blanche, learned to be a meat cutter by the time she was a teenager and became the only regular butcher in town. She would get up a 4:00 A.M., cut up the meat, take her bath, and then was off to school. The rooming and boarding business was also good. Since the Kingsburys lived at

The widow Zora Lee Kingsbury put all six of her children to work in the store they bought from John Conn in 1915.

the store, Zora Lee rented out their house on Spooner at Broad Way. Wade Dickerson's store was gone because he had relocated north of the railroad tracks on the La Porte Road. And that was the new commercial trend. All of the new businesses in Pasadena looked to the La Porte Road and a new linear downtown district that was forming there.[14]

Bertha Kuhns Dickerson's parents had moved to California after the 1900 Galveston storm. Bertha had stayed behind to marry A. L. Dickerson and now had five children. Since Bertha missed her parents and wanted to show off her family, she convinced A. L. to move to California in 1916. With Bertha, Wynona, Carl, Edwin, and Stella in tow they left, but returned in 1918 because A. L. did not like it there and wanted to get back to his nursery business. Not only had the Kuhns previously moved to California from Pasadena, but so had the Wiley Anderson's. Pearl Anderson had married James Irby Shine and apparently convinced him to move to California because they left for Fresno in December 1919. James's parents sold their home place and went with James and Pearl. James's sister Cora Bell and her husband, Rewell Pitts, tagged along with their two-year-old son Victor Grady. Cora Bell would deliver Charles Aubrey the very next month in California. Brother J. O. Shine had previously moved to Houston and stayed.[15]

George Marvin Olive from Deer Park purchased the J. T. Shine place on Shaver across the street from the school. Although they had lived for six years in Deer Park rice farming and raising cattle, Pasadena now offered more of a community life. George and Rose's daughter Irma had been going to the Deer Park school, but it was closed in 1920 and the children sent to Lynchburg. The travel arrangements for the children were less than desirable. In Pasadena they were now located across the street from the school for Irma and less than a block from the Methodist church. And George had gotten involved with the community when he became a shareholder in Guaranty State Bank.[16]

The last of the Williams clan moved from Madison County to Pasadena in 1919. John Williams had first discovered the area in 1897, but convinced his brother Ben to move here instead. Over the intervening years all of the Williams had moved to Pasadena except John. As he approached 51 years of age, John decided to give up farming and move to Pasadena. He purchased his brother Ben's place on Main Street at Broad Way and brought his wife Mary, son Amos, daughter Lillie DeFee, son-in-law Frank DeFee, and grandchild John A. DeFee. They had arrived in time to invest in the new banks in town; John Williams bought stock in Pasadena State and Frank DeFee, because he worked for Wade Dickerson, bought stock in Guaranty State Bank. Although John and son Amos dabbled with farming, John began thinking about opening a mercantile store. Meanwhile his brother Ben had purchased some of David Holloway's land on the La Porte Road at Main Street. Ben built his third house in Pasadena on the east side of Main, between the La Porte Road and Fifth (Shaw) Street. Meanwhile, Holloway continued to operate his nursery and farm at the corner of Eighth (Jackson) and Main. His son Albert G., had married Ila Newell.[17]

Ben's son Ray Williams had been renting and farming in West Pasadena near the new Sinclair Refinery. Ray had married schoolteacher Irma McMaster in 1916 and they had already completed their family with little Everett and "R. C." Probably Ray's neighbors got him a job at Sinclair. Alexander Jacob was born in Russia and had moved to Pasadena with Texan wife Anna and infant Wanda to work as a riveter at the oil refinery. Charlie B. "Chink" would be added to the family shortly. They lived with Snoden Boyd and his wife Rose May and children Sydney, Frederick, Junior, Gladis, and Kevin. Horace Ford had lost his wife Bertha in 1915 and was now married to Tommie, who helped him with his children Marion and Pearl. Snoden and his son Sydney as well as Horace and his son Marion also worked at the refinery. With the prospects of a steady income, Ray and Irma Williams purchased a home on Main Street, just across Fifth (Shaw) Street from his parents. The house was owned by Oscar and Emma Moore and A. R. Cruse had been living in it.[18]

Clyde and Emma McMaster's home, built about 1912, was located on Witter Street between the Blakesleys and the Gigstads.

However, the pleasure of the Williams' new home was short lived. Emma Alice McMaster, the wife of Irma's brother Clyde, died in July of 1920. The Williams moved into the McMaster house and for the next four years took care of Clyde's children, Myrtle and Credella. Emma's parents, "Doc" and Sarah Webb, were still living with the McMasters, but were too old to help with the children. In fact, Sarah passed away the following year in 1921. Ray and Irma left the care of their new home to renters William O. Stafford and his wife May Effie. The Staffords were new in town. About the time they got settled in, William's brother, Leonard J. Stafford, arrived with his family and settled into one of the Moechel's rent houses about a block away, at the end of N. Main Street. Leonard and Belle Adell had three children: Ralph, Eulas, and Marybell.[19]

Emerson Ross Kelley moved to Pasadena in 1918 to work at Sinclair. He and his wife, Olive Maude, rented one of the houses on Richey Street in West Pasadena. They brought six-year-old Olive Mozelle, three-year-old Evelyn Lake and the two-month-old twins, Martha Maxine and Marvin Ross. In 1922 they bought the Rawlins house on the corner of Richey and the La Porte Road. Daughter Anita Maude would be born there a couple of years later. Josiah Rawlins had passed away and his sons Marcus L. and Warren were taking care of their mother, Martha. Marcus had moved to town recently with his wife Alice. Warren had married Nettie Carey and they had daughter Ruth Aline. Their first child, Lonnie Edward, died at birth.[20]

South of town, Emory Congor Goodman purchased acreage below the Baldwin Farm by 1918. He and his wife Jessie M. farmed the land with the help of their four children. Roy H. was born in 1902 and was the oldest. Clyde C. was two years younger and sister Jessie M. was three years behind Clyde. James E. rounded out the crew. Like Emory, Samuel Augustus Quinn came to Pasadena to farm. Good friends Bill Carlisle and Charley Cook had settled here first and sent for their friend. Sam had been a Texas Ranger, photographer, and rancher, but the drought in Beeville pushed him to Pasadena. He arrived in 1917 with his wife Edna Alice and children Rex Clifton, Ray Marian, Samuel Adolphus, Aldy E., Irma Inez, Asa Rogers, and Glen Colquit. They came in two covered wagons, ready to strike it rich in strawberries. First, the oldest child Rex had a sweetheart back home, so he promptly moved back to Beeville and married her. The next oldest, daughter Ray Marian, had just married and brought her husband George

Thornton with them. But George was in the military service. Son Samuel went to work building tanks at Sinclair and Crown and tied the knot with Fern Dow and moved to Houston. And Aldy got a job with Chicago Iron & Bridge Company building refinery tanks and riveted a marriage with local girl Vera Jones in 1923. With only three left to help with the farming, Sam decided to get a job at Sinclair.[21]

When Sam M. Allen, "Little Sam" to most of his friends, moved out of Pasadena after World War I the ties to the great ranching era ended. Sam, like his father before him and his grandfather before that, was a cattleman. Although the cattle range was decreasing, Sam continued the family tradition after his father died. Before the war he ran the ranch from his house on Richey Street. Shortly after the war he and his wife Anna Jane, divorced. Sam moved to Park Place, married Bessie Smith, and continued the ranch. Anna got the house and began taking in boarders. She subsequently married Mr. Waycott of Houston. F. D. Newell sold his small ranch over on Fifth (Shaw) Street and Witter and moved his family into the Allen house until they moved to the valley in 1922. The Newells would eventually move back to Pasadena.[22]

Prior to World War I, most of the people travelling to Houston would take the train or ride their horse or wagon to Harrisburg and then catch the trolley to Houston. The streetcars had been converted from mule drawn to electricity in 1890 and the nickel fare made traveling the fixed routes very popu-

Sam M. Allen was the third generation to operate the Allen Ranch.

Roy Glasgow took high school students into the school at Harrisburg. Picture includes Glasgow, Lewis Garfield, Pearl Ford, Ruth Anderson, Thelma Anderson, Evelyn Lyons, Myrtle Blakesley, Delbert Atkinson, Dutchie Parks, and U. G. Atkinson.

lar. With the coming of the automobile and the expansion of the war, commuters turned to jitneys (passenger automobiles for hire) as a way to get to specific destinations quicker. In Pasadena the idea caught on and a few of the people that had automobiles began hiring them out to take people to Harrisburg or Houston. In 1918 Wade Dickerson added two long benches and a canvas top to his grocery truck to transport students to Harrisburg High School. He would leave the students and benches at school and continue onto Houston for grocery items. In the evening he would return for the students and his benches. Roy Glasgow used his Model T Ford as a jitney from Pasadena to Harrisburg and in 1919 took over the busing of students to Harrisburg High School where he taught. Aubrey Cruse began hiring his car out, using his service station as his dispatching office. As business improved he started the first bus service about 1921 with a Durant touring car, capable of transporting up to eight passengers on his regularly scheduled round trips to Houston. The Durant, "Just a Real Good Car," was named for the flamboyant William Durant, who acquired the financially troubled Buick in 1904 and with it created

General Motors in 1908. The roundtrip fare was 35 cents to Houston or 25 cents to Harrisburg. Lawrence Nelson Sippy moved to Pasadena in 1919 from Wisconsin because of Blanche Roberts. She was visiting in Wisconsin when he met her and he simply followed her back to Pasadena. They were married April 4, 1920, and before he settled down to a job with Crown, he drove one of Pasadena's jitneys.[23]

Will and Elenor Spacie show off their new car.

With the growing numbers of cars in Pasadena, the inevitable happened. Five-year-old David Hughes, son of Jim and Mattie Hughes, was the first person killed by an automobile in Pasadena. On Friday, May 10, 1918, he jumped off of the wagon he was riding in to pick up a sling shot he had dropped, only to be struck by a car driven by Mrs. H. H. Tofte of Houston. Ironically, it was a few years later that David's father began driving a car to make his living. In 1923 Jim Hughes moved his family from their farm to Harrisburg where Jim operated his Oaklawn, Harrisburg and Ship Channel Jitney. Brother-in-law Howard Pitts was married to Jim's sister Mamie Ellen Hughes and for the previous two years they had lived off of Harrisburg Street while Howard operated a jitney business. Jim obviously took over Howard's business and Howard moved back to Pasadena to run his service station.[24]

Everyone was purchasing an automobile. The Ford Motor Car Company opened an assembly plant in Houston in 1919 and employed upwards of 1,300 people to build 350 Model T's per day. Oscar Kruse, Jr., worked at Ford and purchased his car there. His father had the only mechanical tractor in the neighborhood and helped his neighbors fill their silos. The Southern Motors Manufacturing Association Ltd. opened its plant in 1920 to build the "Ranger Four," a five-passenger car that could travel 50 miles an hour, without vibrations. Unfortunately the company went into receivership just two years later in 1922. From 1,031 cars in Harris County in 1911, the number had grown to 34,869 in 1922. Used cars became increasingly available as people replaced their old cars with newer and fancier versions. Particularly important was the move from an open touring car to a closed, or hard body one. In 1921 the following used cars were advertised in the *Houston Post*: 1920 Ford Sedan, $200; Ford Touring, $100; 1919 Ford Touring, $75; Buick Touring, $275; and a 1918 Dodge, $100.[25]

With the freedom of an automobile, people began to travel as they never had before. Unfortunately, the roads had not kept pace with the trend. Houston had struggled with the problem for years, using shell, gravel, wooden planks, wooden blocks, limestone squares, asphalt, and cement. From the very beginning of the city, mud was the biggest problem. Dust was second. By the time the automobile was introduced, progress was being made. In 1912 the citizens of Houston voted to share the cost of street improvement with the city by way of assessment to adjoining property owners. Traffic control also became an issue as jaywalking was banned in 1914, one-way streets appeared in 1920 and the first traffic signal was erected in 1921. However, the county and the state were responsible for the roads outside of the city of Houston, and they were slow in responding to the need for better roadways. For a while, Pasadenans would have to endure on dusty, bumpy, shell-topped roads and rut-riddled wagon trails.[26]

Long before 1920 the La Porte Road was shelled through Pasadena. However, very few of the side streets were covered with shell. Robert Kingsbury had done roadwork for the county and contracted on the side in Pasadena to work on some of its streets. His death in 1915 left a void that had not been fully filled. Main Street and Shaver were sort of paved for the block south of the railroad tracks to Broad Way. Since Kingsbury lived on Spooner, it was also covered with shell for the block south of the tracks. Shaver was paved north to Crown and Cullinan's farm. George Brown lived on Main Street about three blocks south of the railroad tracks. He purchased a second-hand Oldsmobile about 1915 and then upgraded to a Hupmobile about 1917. The car improved, but the roads did not. Brown was constantly pulling his car out of the mud with a team of horses when it rained since Main Street was not shelled that far south. On a rainy Sunday, they quickly opted for the wagon to get them the three blocks to the Methodist Church. Charlie Garfield and son Lewis would push their Model T with little Cecelia panicked at the wheel. Will Blakesley had bought the first car in town, a Hupmobile, but fortunately he lived on the La Porte Road and did not have as many of the mud problems as George. But ruts remained after the mud dried and presented a new set of challenges. Clyde McMaster used to put his car in the hard ruts and take a short nap as his car drove along as if it was on a railroad track.[27]

Gathering on the banks of Buffalo Bayou was a popular Sunday event. The umbrellas were for shade, not rain.

When Galena-Signal Oil Refinery opened across the ship channel from Pasadena in 1916, Harris County had authorized a free ferry at Pasadena. It was little more than a raft, capable of holding about 2 wagons or cars, and was propelled from bank to bank by the physical labor of the parties using the craft. A slack rope was anchored on each side of the channel and rested on the bottom when not in use. In this way it was not an obstruction to the ships using the channel. The rope ran through pulleys on each end of the "ferry" and along a railing on one side. Using a wooden wrench-type device, the passengers would pull the craft across the channel by latching onto the rope at the front of the vessel and walking to the rear, thus propelling the craft forward. The passengers would then release the wrench, walk to the front and repeat the process again until the ferry landed on the other side. After a while the county added a motor to the ferry, which moved the craft by pulling on the cable. Tony Edgar Hodges was hired to operate the ferry. Similar ferries had been installed at Deepwater, San Jacinto, and Seabrook-Kemah. Unless the passenger had a

A ferry became necessary with the automobile revolution since you could not transport a car across the ship channel in a row boat!

wagon, or less likely, a car, it was understandable that they preferred to swim across or get a boat and row. Eight-year-old "Jay" Riggs would carry passengers across in his skiff for five cents. Deb Atkinson, Edgar Barnes, Richmond Brannen, and "Foots" Wilson worked at Galena-Signal and rowed themselves across. Barnes continued to row when he was joined by Ray Williams and P. Y. Howell while they worked at Universal Ship Yards. With the opening of Crown Refinery, the county was persuaded to replace the rope-pull ferry with a nine car motorized one on December 20, 1921. W. H. Dickerson was one of the first to make the trip across that day, but he was not the only one enjoying the change.[28]

For years the natural slip on Buffalo Bayou due north of town was popular with the picnickers. Nearby, the Daughters of the Republic of Texas had erected a granite marker commemorating the capture site of General Santa Anna in April 1836, thus assuring the independence of Texas. Cullinan had agreed to allow the monument to be placed on his property back in 1916. In honor of the historical event, he would thereafter refer to his Pasadena Farm as the Santa Anna Farm. Sundays were particularly popular days for family outings and church socials on the bank of the bayou that had been turned into a ship channel. The parents enjoyed the cool shade and simply relaxing. As if for inspection by the revellers, an occasional ship or excursion boat would plow by. However, the trip to the picnic site was a form of much-needed amusement, recreation, and enlightenment for the children. Ima Parks loved the big trees and the swings hung from their high branches. James Oliver Riggs lived on the other side for a while with his wife Gertrude and children Joseph Allison "Jay" and Isadore, and frequently hosted Sunday school parties with trips over to his side of the channel. Esther Gigstad was not alone in appreciating the simple pleasure of riding the ferry back and forth. The old favorite bayou swimming holes had been destroyed with the continual dredging work on the ship channel, so the boys used the ferry as a means to explore the other side for new dipping spots. Cecilia Garfield also enjoyed swimming, but once had her clothes stolen and she had to go home wrapped in a bath towel. The ferry also allowed groups to go to the Galena side to pick wild grapes, to find new picnic sites, or to challenge the locals to a game of baseball.[29]

Ben Bailey, Jr., and "Foots" Wilson had kept the baseball team going even though they were now in their thirties. Ray

The 1919 team included Archey Worley, Buck Gore, Russell Dickerson, Fred Baker, Ross Worley, Russell Hargrave, Aldy Quinn, and Sam Quinn.

Williams was pushing his late twenties, but like his mid-teens little sister, Ruth, if there was a game to be played, he also wanted to be there. Oscar Kruse, Jr., got in a little ball, playing second base and occasionally, first base. Bailey would cover

Periodically the baseball team would get new uniforms.

first or catch. Russell Hargrave would take third and double as the pitcher. Glenn "Baldy" Quinn could pitch or play in the outfield with his brother Aldy and one of the Gore boys. George Archibald "Watty" Watkins would play any position and could hit the ball a mile. He was an ironworker who took the game seriously and was always getting on everyone to hustle. Bert Pitts wasn't quite as serious a player.[30]

Sundays was a good day for ball since businesses were closed and the farmers took most of the day off. Besides, more people could come and root the team on against other communities, organizations, and companies. Crown Refinery fielded a good team. South Houston and Clinton also had teams. Genoa was one of the biggest rivals. If a team was short on players, the opponents would fill in the slots and a game started. For a while Pasadena had a ball field on the old Munger place, along Fifth (Shaw) Street just east of Vince's Bayou. It sported a covered viewing stand. The new industies in the area were very supportive and encouraged the competition between company teams. Sinclair provided new suits for the team and some of the industries would let the players out of work early so that they could get a little practice in before they went home. Around 1922 the ball field was moved to south of the railroad tracks on Ralph Parks's land just east of Vince's Bayou. Modestly the

Russell Hargrave played third and substitued for the pitcher.

Pasadena boys admitted that they were hard to beat. However, baseball was not the only game in town.[31]

Before the war, there was a lot of "sandlot" sports going on in Pasadena. A few played at tennis, others at football, and the girls focused on basketball. As early as 1911 there was an organized girl's team, complete with uniforms. Somehow it was always easier for the boys to be excused to practice sports. Since organized sports was not a part of the early school curriculum, practice time always competed with chores. Some girls could work it into their routines, but Addie Brown was one of those that could only daydream about playing. In any event, the single hoop at school got a lot of use and a formidable team was fielded. Selma Kruse, Blanche Roberts, Rosa Dowell, Pearl Ford, Myrtle Blakesley, Evelyn Lyons, Valeria Brown, Carrie Parks, Ollie Lakin, Betty Williams, and Susie Holbrooks represented Pasadena in 1917. One of the teachers, Mr. McKay, acted as the coach. The girls wore white middy blouses and black bloomers. Mrs. Lakin required that her daughter Ollie wear a skirt with her uniform. The girls got in a little softball, with Betty Williams regularly hitting the ball over the schoolhouse. At the time Pasadena was offering a limited high school program, with Mr. Hester commuting from the Seabrook area. High school and basketball abruptly ended when the school board dismissed Mr. Hester halfway through the term. The board thought it was too expensive to try to operate its own high school program. The four high school students had to thumb their way to Harrisburg for the rest of the school year.

Roy Glasgow encouraged sports. Around 1913 Oscar Kruse and Russell Dickerson are pictured on the front row with the baseball players. Florentine Kruse and Mary Ellen Glasgow were on the second row with the tennis team.

Fortunately Wade Dickerson and Roy Glasgow provided transportation after that first year. However, the students from Pasadena considered themselves a school within a school and always kept their Pasadena identity.[32]

The war also interrupted the sports program, and then changed it. During the war, many of the men and boys went off

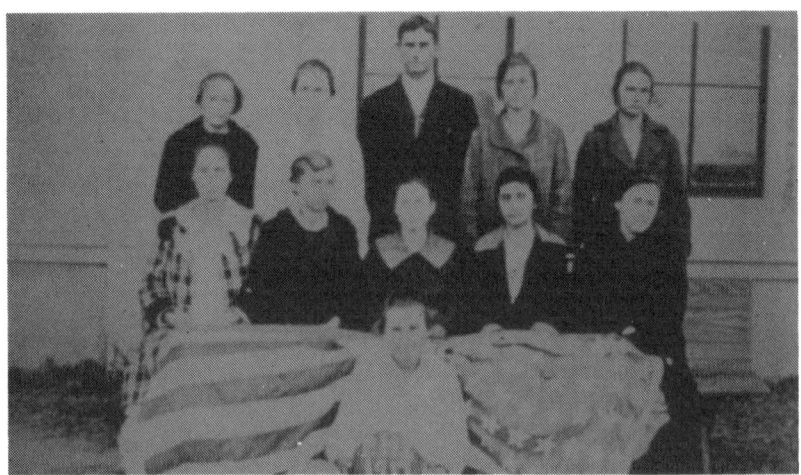

The 1917 Girls Basketball Team, pictured in their overcoats. World War I temporarily suspended Pasadena's sports programs.

to the service or were pressed into new jobs. Women and girls entered the work force, either as volunteers or as employees to fill the vacancies left by the men, or to fill new jobs created by the war effort. After the war many women had to yield jobs back to the menfolk, but they did not forget the new freedom that it had afforded them. Many of the menfolk turned to the new growing industries of the area for employment and did not return to the farms. In Pasadena there was an increase in population, and in children. The school trustees had not been happy with the lack of a high school for the expanding educational needs of its children and recognized the implications of its growing population. With the postwar prosperity, and the addition of Crown Refinery and Texas Cement to the tax base, the board reconsidered its earlier decision. Earlier, education beyond the certified seventh grade was a luxury. Now, a high school diploma was more important if their children were to get ahead. Pearl Ford, Lewis Garfield, Myrtle Blakesley, and Delbert Atkinson had graduated from Harrisburg, as had Mildred James. Board members John Pomeroy, Oscar Kruse, and J. D. Parks had children in the system that would be in high school shortly. After looking at lands along Shaver Street owned by Jackson and Olive, the board purchased the site for a high school building from R. E. Parks for $5,000.[33]

Even before the land was purchased, Pasadena began adding high school course work to its curriculum. Richard T. Gore of Houston was hired as the first high school principal in 1923. Ironically it was the first Pasadena school teacher, Professor L. A. Dowdell, that had recommended that Richard T. Gore of Houston apply for the first principalship of Pasadena High School. Gore was not related to the Gores who already lived in Pasadena. Commencement exercises for the first graduating class of Pasadena High School were held May 16, 1924, in the Methodist church auditorium. Ralph Blakesley, Lillian Brannen, Eva Edming, Anna Kruse, and Ruth Williams received their diplomas. Shortly afterwards ground was broken for the new high school building. A set of plans designed for a northern-climate building had been obtained cheaply so the resulting structure was a bit odd looking with its high window sills. Though the building was not finished, formal dedication of the new Pasadena High School was held December 17, 1924. Superintendent J. O. Davis emceed the evening's program, which included a piano solo by Miss Elizabeth A. McNay and the principal address by Dr. E. E. Oberholtzer. Pasadena had

The Pasadena High School building was formally dedicated in 1924.

not had a school superintendent since 1911, but hired Davis in May of 1923 because of the new high school program. He was also instructed to conduct a summer school session.[34]

Repaired after the 1915 hurricane without its distinctive cupola on top, the Pasadena school became known as the grammar school when the high school building was completed.

With the opening of the high school, the original school building became known as the grammar school. Upon completion of the construction of the new high school, the first of several additions to the grammar school were started. Because

Roaring into the Twenties (1919-1924)

Pictured in front of the grammar school, the high school class of 1924 watched their high school building being built. Members of the first high school class were Ralph Blakesley, Lillian Brannen, Eva Edming, Anna Kruse, and Ruth Williams

The PHS class of 1925 was the first to use the new high school. First to graduate in the new building were Helen Anderson, Otis Boyd, Byrd Coolidge, Iza Sue Hearn, Elise Johnston, and Rex Tabor. The 1926 class did not have a group picture, but included Nadine Atkinson, Lawrence Charlesworth, Janie Dowell, Edward Kruse, John M. Meyer, Alice Parks, Marshall Rhinehart, Ralph Stafford and Mary Witt.

Pictured is the 1927 class, which included Marvin Abbott, Ruby Anderson, Stella Dowell, Richard Elledge, Myrtle McMasters, Irma Olive, Thurman Wilson, and Kitty Witt.

The 1928 PHS graduating class included Mildred Ankele, Ruby and Margy Blakesley, Ferrell Brown, Nauvie Cammack, Ray Coulson, Clarence Coy, Dorothy Darby, Bertha Dickerson, Virgie Freeman, Ferne Freeman, Louis Griffin, J. A. Riggs, Mae Syfan, and Mildred Tabor.

The 1929 PHS graduating class was the first class to go all the way through high school in the new building. It included Ray Abbott, Trannie Bell, Snoden Boyd, Press Brannen, Lillie Edming, Celia Garfield, Glenn Gigstad, Lessie Griffin, J. B. Isaac, Nina Jones, Janette Martin, Credella McMaster, Jack Miller, Addie Nichols, Eletha Pledger, Marguerite Pomeroy, and Jack Rogers.

of his significant contribution to education in Pasadena, the grammar school would later be renamed after school trustee Oscar Kruse. Mae Smythe took over the grammar school program in the fall of 1923 from O. W. Hufstedler who had had the job for two years. Mae had taught 13 years in Fostoria and would put in 36 more in Pasadena. Mae's younger sisters Lillian and Sadye had moved to Pasadena in 1922 to teach. The three sisters would each make a career of educating several generations of Pasadena's youth.[35]

Zora Lee Kingsbury provided room and board in addition to operating her grocery store. She and the children moved into the back of the first floor, rented the upstairs rooms and served meals to the boarders. In addition she divided up her house on Spooner and rented it to several families. When Crown was under construction many of the workers boarded with the Kingsburys. Her apparent success probably encouraged the new banker Aubrey Cruse to build himself an 11-room house on Shaver and rent out rooms under the name of the Old Southern Inn. Jess Brammer purchased the Tilley house about 1921 and his wife Eunice turned it into a rooming house.[36]

Anna Pomeroy liked to board teachers, but her house was getting crowded with her son John's growing family. The third

Baby Clyde completed John and Gertrude Pomeroy's family in 1922. Marguerite was the oldest, followed by Edward, Bessie, and Clyde.

John Pomeroy's family now filled the house John had built for he and his mother 14 years before. So John built a house next door for his mother in 1922. Both houses would be donated to the city of Pasadena in 1986 as historical museums.

child, Bessie Evelyn, arrived in 1920 and the fourth, Clyde David, in 1922. Lillian and Sadye Smythe were boarding in the house when Clyde was born and he was the first newborn they had ever seen. Within minutes Lola Mason gave birth to Ethel

Charles Freeman built Anna Pomeroy's house while she was on vacation visiting her sister.

Marie across the street in the Pomeroy rent house. The proud father was Jess T. Mason. Shortly afterwards, John sent his mother on a trip to Detroit to visit her sister and when she returned he surprised her with a house of her own next door. Now she had more room to rent out and to board other renters in the area.[37]

Charles C. Freeman moved to Pasadena about 1918 from Highlands to work in construction. He brought his wife Bessie and two children: Virgie Mae and Cecil. Francis and Robert joined the family by 1922. Being a fellow Baptist, John Pomeroy hired Charles to build the house for his mother. Like John, Charles regularly hired neighbors as his business grew. Ben Bailey, Mike Coy, Robert Glasgow, and later Bill Pennington worked on and off for Charles. Charles sold Walter Ankele a lot on Pitts Street for $400 and then built him a new home in 1921 for $980. Walter had recently arrived with his wife and daughters Mildred Lou and Moddie Mae. Living nearby was Richmond and Annie Evelyn Brannen. They had arrived in Pasadena in

1914 and were just finishing up their family of six children. Lillian Doris, Grandville La Prell, and Jessie "Woodie" were born before the family arrived. Earlene, Richmond Drulane, and Cecile Maurine "Pokey" were born in Pasadena. All but Earlene were born on Pitts Street.[38]

Living nearby were William J. and Lilly Pearl Shelton. William was a carpenter by trade and probably worked with Charles Freeman. The Sheltons had moved from Madisonville and were renting on the Mochelle Farm. John Payton and William Lloyd were too young to go to school yet. Elvie, Maxine, and Jimmy would be born in Pasadena in the years to come. Mr. Pickett was a furniture repairer with a very good reputation among wealthy Houstonians. He moved his family to Pasadena in 1921 from Houston and lived on Main at Seventh (Park Lane) Street. His wife Ida took care of Henrietta and Luther J.[39]

Masonic Lodge No. 1155 was organized in Pasadena in 1921. The charter members were: W. G. Ankele, D. E. Atkinson, H. C. Barlow, J. M. Boyd, R. Brannen, J. M. Brown, A. R. Cruse, A. B. Freeman, R. Guinn, W. G. Hargrave, J. F. High, D. B. Meyer, R. E. Parks, O. C. Pitts, T. D. Scroggins, L. G. Tabor, G. A. Watson, C. A. Williams, and W. F. Williams. R. Brannen was elected the first Worshipful Master. Originally they met in the homes of the members, and then moved their meetings to the second floor of Kingsbury's store.[40]

Railroad Riley proudly shows off his new son, Harry.

Once he got settled in Pasadena, Archie Columbus "Railroad" Riley would join the Masonic lodge. A. C. and May arrived in 1923 as relative newlyweds from Orange, Texas. A. C. worked for Southern Pacific as a signal maintainer and he would work out of Pasadena until his retirement. His jovial manner would make him and his one-man motorized railroad cart famous from Cleveland to Galveston. At the Baptist church he always had candy for the children. When little Harry E. was born they were living on Main Street, almost across from the church.[41]

Lester and Lola Hargrave's family had increased from two children to seven while in Pasadena. Douglas Lester was child number three, born in 1910. The family moved temporarily to Crosby and Jennie Elizabeth joined the group. Back in Pasadena Carmen Lily, Bennie Abram, and Violet Fern expanded the local population. The Hargraves drifted off to Houston in 1923 and Beatrice Pearl and Wanda Joy would complete the family there. Lester's brother Wilbur had married Ethel Blakesley in 1919 and continued on in Pasadena.[42]

When Houston Lighting & Power announced that they were to build a large electrical generation plant in Pasadena on the Ship Channel, George Thornton saw dollar signs. He contracted to purchase Zora Lee Kingsbury's store and boarding house in 1923. With wife Ray and daughter Glennera along with his in-laws, the Sam Quinn family, Thornton moved into the building. Zora Lee moved her family back into their house on Spooner and took over running Dickerson's Cafe since she had successfully run the first restaurant in town. Daughter Blanche went to work in Dickerson's grocery along with Rosa Dowell. The pretty blond, Iza Sue Hearn also worked there.[43]

Motion pictures were all the rage. Only the Prince and Cozy theatres in Houston still presented live stage productions. The Crown, Iris, Key, Liberty, Queen, Rex, and Zoe theaters offered moving pictures. One dime could get you in. But getting to Houston was still a major task, especially for children. In their usual take-charge manner, a few people in Pasadena began showing movies in town. Aubrey Cruse would occasionally set up a movie in his home for schoolchildren. Whit Thornton rented the grammar school auditorium to display movies. But George Thornton had a movie every weekend. On Saturdays George would clear the downstairs dining room and bring in a two or three "reeler" movie to show. And it was only a "showing" since this was the day of the silent movies. Even so, Mary Garfield hung on the edge of her chair during "The Perils of Pauline." Doris Barnes was a sucker for the Tarzan series, started in 1918 with Elmo Lincoln as "Tarzan of the Apes" and Gene Pollar in the title role in the 1920 version. Tarzan was also popular with Lenora Martinez, who would help her mother clean up the "theater" after the weekend showings. Charlie Chaplin and Harold Lloyd were the popular comics, with Buster Keaton the newcomer. William S. Hart and Tom Mix provided the western excitement, with Will Rodgers commenting on events. Douglas Fairbanks and John Barrymore were top male stars along with Rudolph Valentino who burst all records beginning in 1921. Mary Pickford, Lillian Gish, Gloria Swanson, and Tallulah Bankhead headed the cast of female leads. And introducing the new kid on the block, Chaplin played pan-faced to child star Jackie Coogan in "The Kid." Even though people would travel to Houston to see the current release, it was a lot easier to have the service at home.[44]

When Dr. James Monroe Boyd moved to Pasadena around 1921, the community got its first full-time medical doctor. The first "doctor" to the community was a Dr. Evans. He lived near where Vince's Bayou emptied into Buffalo Bayou around the turn of the century. It was never known whether he was a doctor by education or by practice. And if by education, what area of medicine he was educated in. If a doctor was needed, a doctor was a doctor, regardless of the school of medicine. A veterinarian, dentist, or medical doctor was called upon to help a sick animal or a sick human. Dr. Evans made his rounds on the back of a donkey. When he needed to cross Buffalo Bayou to help those on the far side, he would have Giles Edwards, a huge Negro that lived on the north side, lift his donkey into his boat and row the doctor, and donkey, to the north bank.[45]

Doctor Titus Chauncey Loose was the first recorded medical doctor to live in the community. He arrived in 1905 and stayed only for five years. He was treating Payson Pomeroy when Payson died in 1906. Although Dr. Loose and his wife were active in the Baptist church, there was apparently little medical connection with the community. The Looses left by 1910.[46]

Doctor Virginius St. Clair MacNider of Houston invested in Pasadena real estate in 1898 and 1899 and built a cabin. Although he maintained his practice in Houston for several more years, he frequently tended to the needs of the new community. After a while he moved to Pasadena but kept some of his Houston practice. When they were first married in 1910 Robert and Zora Lee Moore Kingsbury lived on Dr. MacNider's place and took care of his strawberry crop. Robert and Zora had moved to their new house on Spooner where Dr. MacNider delivered Emma Catherine Kingsbury on June 29, 1911. He also delivered Thurman and Sylvia Wilson, Thelma, Stella and Daisy Dowell, and Daniel Glenn Brown. The J. D. Parks and the W. N. Blakesley family were also among the local families that used him. Unfortunately he sold his property to J. S. Cullinan in 1915 and moved out of the area. Years later when little Thurman Wilson was exploring the old MacNider place he found boxes of teeth. None of them belonged to Rosa Dowell because on the long walk over to Dr. MacNider's house to get her tooth fixed, it miraculously got well and she did not finish the trip.[47]

The alternative for medical attention in 1921 was to travel to La Porte or Harrisburg for a doctor. About the only time a person went to the doctor was when they were dying or pregnant. When it came to the delivering part, Anna Pomeroy and Emma Moore often helped as midwives and cared for the newborns. If a person was ill, they often turned to home remedies or patent medicines.[48]

Everyone had hundreds of home remedies for most ailments and only turned to a doctor as the last resort. Turpentine was used for a lot of ailments. Patent medicines were available if homemade were inadequate. "Atlas Compound" was heavily advertised in the Dr. MacDonald's Almanac of 1916, capable of relieving "Constipation, Indigestion, Stomach Trouble, Liver, Kidney, Bladder, Bood and Nervous Disorders." Newspapers were always full of medical tips such as:

> Cough medicines, as a rule contain a large quantity of plain syrup. A pint of granulated sugar with 1/2 pint of warm water, stirred for 2 minutes, gives you as good syrup as money can buy.
> Then get from your druggist 2 1/2 ounces Pinex (50 cents worth), pour into a pint bottle and fill the bottle with sugar syrup. This gives you, at a cost of only 54 cents, a full pint of really better cough syrup than you could buy ready made for $2.50 - a clear savings of nearly $2. Full directions with Pinex. It keeps perfectly and tastes good.
> It takes hold of the usual cough or chest cold at once and conquers it in 24 hours. Splendid for whooping cough, bronchitis and winter coughs.[49]

If formal medical attention was needed, La Porte always had at least a couple of doctors. Dr. Juliett Marchant arrived in 1897 as the first female doctor in the area. Although now in her seventies, she was still popular and practicing. Dr. A. M. Eidson and Dr. C. W. Griffiths had been there for a while. A little closer to Pasadena, Dr. James McWhorter had moved to South Houston from Houston, "a booming community" in 1909 to lighten his patient load and to arrest his tuberculosis by living more outdoors.⁵⁰

However, Harrisburg was the preferred destination for doctoring. Dr. Payton R. Denman came out to Gertrude Pomeroy's home and delivered all of her children from 1912 to 1922. Dr. Moore came out to deliver Leona Burch's son Donald and her sister Blanche Sippy's three girls. From experience he learned to bring his gun so that he could hunt until it was time to deliver the babies. Dr. I. P. Poyner moved to Harrisburg in 1904 and made many trips to Pasadena. He charged one dollar to make the wagon trip to Pasadena. He tended to the Aubrey Cruse family, as well as those of Gerald Conrad, Jim Hughes, F. D. Newell, J. D. Parks, A. L. Dickerson, and Wade Dickerson. He delivered Clara Wilson's third child, Estelle, in 1915. On the side Dr. Poyner was president of American State Bank in Harrisburg and a stockholder in Pasadena's short-lived Guaranty State Bank.⁵¹

Doctor Earl Acker listed his medical address as Pasadena in 1918, but did not stay around long enough to be remembered by the residents. He was probably in town because Sinclair was under construction. He was succeeded by Dr. J. M. Boyd who came to Pasadena by 1921 from Conroe and became the physician for Crown. Dr. Boyd was not related to the Snoden Boyd family that had been living in Pasadena for a couple of years. In addition to his company job, Dr. Boyd also maintained a private practice out of his home on Main Street, just south of Broad Way. Like all doctors at the time, Dr. Boyd made house calls. With him came his wife, Virginia and five of their eight children: J. Otis, Alma, Bueron, John A. and James, Jr. The older three children (Pearl, Bertha, and Una) were out of school and on their own. Dr. Boyd put in one of the few telephones in town and used it almost immediately for an emergency. Eleven-year-old Lillie Edming suffered a ruptured appendix and had to be rushed by ambulance to a hospital in order to save her life. Her older sister Hulda had died at 12 years of age from the same thing. It was not long before he had a regular practice and a good reputation. Since Pasadena was still basically a farming community, he occasionally took strawberries in trade for payment. Dr. Boyd carried his black medical bag with him when he made his calls because he carried all the medicines that he might prescribe. In that way the ill person could immediately get medication and did not have to travel to a drugstore. However, one of his most frequent treatments was for the common cold. He would give the patient a shot of whiskey from the hip flask he carried, have them eat some rock candy, and then go to bed to sweat out the cold. A lot of people swore by that remedy.[52]

The dispensing of alcohol was allowed during Prohibition if it was for medical purposes. Dr. Boyd kept a "Physician's Record" and recorded dutifully his prescriptions of one pint of whiskey in Pasadena. The bedside "shots" were not recorded. While some of the names appearing in the register were Pasadenans, and a few were repeaters, most names were not common in the community. And for a community of approximately 1,100 people, 400 prescriptions (the maximum obviously allowed) per year would indicate that more than the locals were suffering from the flu and were seeking medical attention in Pasadena. The record also identified which pharmacy was to fill the prescription. Although Pasadena had a pharmacy, the prescriptions were directed to about a half dozen different pharmacies, including two in downtown Houston.[53]

In some areas of life there were great changes, frequently called progress. In other areas, improvement moved slower. The family still travelled the 12 miles round trip to Pillot's in Houston for major grocery shopping. You purchased many items in bulk and gave the clerk your list and he went and got the goods. The Pomeroys also picked up their empty milk cans for return. They had reestablished their dairy, and weekly sent full milk cans on the train to Pillot's. Ice was available from Butcher Brothers Ice Company in Harrisburg and there was a bakery across the street. Sunset Coal and Wood Yard off Navigation Street in Houston was where you got coal or cord wood. Usually you had to cut the cord wood in half and then split it for the kitchen stove. If you could afford coal it was better in the parlor pot bellied stove which was used for house heating. When it came to wood, or most anything else not tied down, beware of the "Wood King." Everyone sort of took it in stride, but the white-headed, handlebar-mustached 60-year-old gentleman just roamed around town and picked up anything not tied down. He was called the Wood King because he never bought a stick of firewood, he just stole it. He was considered harmless and certainly did not think of himself as a thief. Mainly he was after food and firewood, just enough for himself and his family.[54]

Most everyone kept chickens so there were plenty of eggs and meat. Besides Blanche Kingsbury at Dickerson's grocery, H. E. Ford would occasionally do some butchering. He would ice down the meat and drive around in his wagon. Peanut butter came in a large paper box with lots of oil on top. Peaberry beans were ground at home for coffee. Most everyone also had some form of vegetable garden and fresh fruits were grown in the area. Children still liked to steal watermelons and chewed tar as gum. As infants, Edward Pomeroy and R. A. "Bob" Kingsbury liked to eat real mud pies. They thought the red clay ones tasted better. Perhaps Edward ate too many pies because he picked up the nickname "Tubby" for obvious reasons.[55]

Homer F. Brammer moved to Pasadena in October 1921 to work at his brother Jess's service station. He earned $18 per week. Homer's wife Ruby D. joined him early in 1922 with three-year-old James Lamoine and three-month, or so, old LaVerne. They lived nearby. Jess sold his service station to Gus Watson about that time and Homer went to work across the railroad track at Lone Star Cement's clay pit operation on Richey. Ruby worked a while for Gus Watson in the little store at the service station. When Houston Lighting & Power began construction of their Deepwater power plant in 1923, Homer hired on. Then Asa Hearn got him a permanent job at Sinclair in 1924. Homer and Ruby bought their first house, on Johnson at Broad Way. They even tied into John Pomeroy's water system so that they could have running water in the kitchen.[56]

Virgil Ernest and Minnie C. Abbott moved their family from Bay City to Pasadena in 1924. Abbott was later quoted as saying that he was "looking for a place that had potentialities and would grow and keep pace with the times. The moment I saw Pasadena, I knew this was 'home'." Sons Marvin and Charles Ray were old enough for school and V. E. went to work at Sinclair. They rented a house at first, and then built a couple of years later.[57]

Thelma Lois Anderson and Delbert Leroy Atkinson had attended the Pentecostal church with their respective families for years and at the ripe age of 21 they fell in love. Thelma's parents, Charles and Maude Anderson had brought the family to Pasadena in 1911 from Oklahoma. Charles farmed for a while and then went to work at Sinclair while his daughters, Floye, Thelma, Ruth, Helen, and Ruby grew up. Thelma Lois married Delbert in 1924 and sister Ruth married another local boy, Lewis Edgar Garfield.[58]

The 1920s proved to be a decade of major growth for the community of Pasadena. Momentum and transition transformed a village into a city.

X

The Struggle to Incorporate (1922-1929)

The 1920s was a period of unusual challenges and changes for the town called Pasadena. Its success as a major farming community continued to grow, and with it, the demands upon its people and structure to produce. The war had exposed its people to new horizons and, coupled with the persistent development of the ship channel, brought new jobs, opportunities, and a new breed of people to the community. Little had changed in the structure of the community since the school and churches settled into place by 1910. Now new growth was requiring attention to the expanding and changing community needs. The school system added more grades to its program, and a new building to handle the increased enrollment. The industries provided cash income jobs and siphoned off the able-bodied men from the fields. Seasonal pickers and resident caretakers became a major component of the farming work force. The increased density of population required more attention to the common needs of water, sewage, and roads. New issues had to be faced and resolved at the same time that the economy was booming.

Day in and day out, it was farming that kept the community alive. Everything else was an add-on to the mandatory daily chores. As the demand for Pasadena berries and other produce grew, so did the population needed to produce the supply. By the 1920s upwards of 1,000 acres were planted in strawberries alone, yielding 25,000 crates of the sweet fruit. One hundred fifty refrigerated railroad cars would roll out in a season with the $200,000 annual crop. Although the whole of southeast Harris County was now known as "Pasadena Acres," the impact was felt strongest at the heart of the area. Before the war most of the farms were simply small family affairs, with all of the work done by the family and on barter with neighbors. As more fields were put into cultivation and the industries began providing year-round jobs and cash, a farm worker shortage developed. However, the greatest demand was seasonal and was specifically critical at picking time. Since the need could not support an increased year-round population, migratory labor was first brought in to alleviate the problem.[1]

Joseph Cullinan did not live in Pasadena nor was his a family farm. By 1911 he was actively cultivating strawberry crops and hired locals and Mexican laborers to work this farm land. Cruse was hired in 1913 as a full-time manager to oversee the operation of the enlarged 90-acre farm. By 1920 the "Santa Anna Farm" included 200 acres of various crops and animals. The need for part-time help had appropriately increased. In Deepwater, Tilford Jones succeeded his father, William E. Jones, in the operation of the Jones Plantation. Like Cullinan, Tilford lived in Houston and visited his country place periodically. Also like Cullinan, the Jones Plantation depended on seasonal help on his large farm and ranch since it was not a family operation.[2]

The Houston wholesale fruit and produce company of Baldwin and Cargill was active in the development of the Pasadena strawberry industry and operated several growing farms in the area. The Baldwin Place was located on the south side of Twelfth (Southmore) Street between the extension of Main Street west to Vince's Bayou. They began developing the property by 1913 and had improved it with two McMaster and Pomeroy water wells by 1920. Delbert E. Atkinson moved his family there about 1912 and farmed strawberries. Adolph Herrera moved there about 1915 and lived there on and off helping supervise the operation. Some of the laborers would be brought in for the picking seasons and others would live year-round on the property, or nearby, and help with the planting and cultivation. In 1914 many of the Montoyas came from Mexico and eventually settled in Pasadena. Juan Montoya brought his eight children, Secundio Montoya brought his family, Francisco Montoya brought his two sisters, and Frajeda Montoya brought his wife Maria and his two sisters. Lorenzo Moruna brought his four children: Felipe, Santiago, Finstia, and Francisco. Mike Reyes and his wife Candilaria had immigrated to the United States in 1901 and their children Roman and Juan had been born in Texas.[3]

Many of the area farms were now taking on Mexicans to help with the farming chores. Jose and Carman Balli Mata started their family in Pasadena with Ignacio and Leonardo. Pedro and Jerza Rosales lived near the Will Parks farm with their children: Agili, Alusa, Dominga, Maria, and Sara. Widow Mary Martinez came to the Pasadena area in 1916 with her two girls, Leonor and Tommie. They worked a while and then moved to Houston. They returned in 1922 and found enough work to stay. They worked for Herrera at the Baldwin Place, and for Walter Williams and the Sam Quinns. Octavino Rocha come from Flatonia in 1917 to pick berries in Deepwater and lived in a bunk house near the McNay's place. He got a job at Sinclair and by 1923 was the proud owner of a new Model T Ford. He paid $100 down, and financed the $400 balance at $25 a month. His reputation with a violin had gotten him several performances with the Houston Symphony and invitations to play at the annual Christmas party at the Burke's place in Pasadena. He courted and then married Lenora Martinez in 1923. Many more Mexicans settled into the community and took over the duties of operating the old Pasadena family farms. With the help of this new labor source, farming continued to prosper.[4]

Some of the old farms and open land were cultivated for a new and more immediately profitable crop, housing. Ralph Parks filed the first subdivision plat on August 25, 1919. Two banks had been opened in town that could finance purchases and Crown was under construction. The R. E. Parks Subdivision was located on Main Street, from Fifth (Shaw) Street northward to Little Vince's Bayou. It extended east to Randall Street and provided for the northern extension of Spooner. The original 150-feet-by-300-feet lots were subdivided into housing lots measuring 50 feet by 135 feet. A home site was now available for someone who worked at Crown and who did not want to farm.[5]

Arthur Dickerson responded nine months later with his A. L. Dickerson Subdivision located on the La Porte Road in 1920. He offered 50-by-100-feet lots, 40-by-150-feet lots, and frontage lots on the La Porte Road. He dedicated two streets with his subdivision filing, Carl and Anderson. Nine months after that, on September 18, 1920, Lester Hargrave subdivided his property into the Hargrave Subdivision and offered even smaller building sites behind his service station on the La Porte Road. Naturally enough, the one road he dedicated through his new development was named Hargrave. With these three subdivision on the north side of the track and convenient to anyone working at Crown, or even Sinclair, refinery, the town was ready for an influx of city folks.[6]

The first residents of Pasadena had been farmers. John Burnett tried to attract "city dwellers" when he gave Wiley Anderson, Jasper Hays, and his father, A. Hays, city lots in 1893. Twenty-seven years later the community was ready to try again to create a city. Surveyor H. L. Patterson drafted his "Map of the City of Pasadena, Harris County, Texas" on June 12, 1920. Basically the "city" section of the community would be located between Vince (Scarbrough) Street on the western edge of the original city plat, to Witter on the east, and from the ship channel south to Ninth (Texas) Street. The Crown refinery site was carved out and thus not within the proposed city limits.[7]

A year earlier in 1919 John Pomeroy had drilled a water well in his backyard on Main Street and was supplying water to 30 families in the immediate area. The new subdivisions would need a source of water for their new homes. Hargrave had a water well but no provision had been made for Dickerson's or Park's. And then there was the problem of sewage and trash. The increase in the number of outhouses, located close together, was raising a literal stink. Although there was little in the way of trash since so much was recycled and reused, the landscape was beginning to get cluttered with various discarded items and the risk of runaway fires from backyard trash burnings was noted. Drainage of rain water was constantly a problem, hampering work, endangering health, and impeding transportation. As the use of automobiles increased, the deplorable condition of what roads there were became more than an inconvenience. Besides, more roads needed to be graded, maintained, or paved with shell and other material. Although dedicated streets existed in the plat of the community, there was no one to take responsibility for them, let alone grant easements to such groups as the telephone company and a proposed interurban to Seabrook.[8]

It took a little over three years for the community to muster enough support to petition the county judge to call for an election. During that period of time Houston Lighting & Power (H.L. & P.), had purchased 92 acres out of the originally platted Pasadena land along the ship channel and broke ground in March of 1923 on a $10 million generating plant. The plant would double the size of the company's generating capacity and would insure continued development along the ship channel. Credit for the site selection had to be given to Joe Cullinan, who worked hard at putting the deal together. His actions were not philanthropic as he owned some of the land that Houston Lighting & Power purchased, and he owned much more, on both sides of the channel, that would increase in value. Over 600 men were working on the project and steady employment would be available for Pasadenans upon its completion. F. M. Blackwell responded to the opportunity by filing his plat on January 22, 1923, for the Blackwell Subdivision on the La Porte Road, adjacent to the H. L. & P. powerline easement. Just west of the Bailey's place, he named his two streets, Blackwell and S. Park. Like Ralph Parks, he laid out the larger 50-by-135-feet lots. Along the north edge of his plat he noted the proposed right-of-way for "The Seabrook Electric Railway" that was under consideration by the Galveston-Houston Electric Railway Company. Although plans were later abandoned, the proposed route was along the ship channel, through Pasadena, San Jacinto battleground, and Morgan's Point, then along Galveston Bay to Seabrook. Charles Meyer and C. Trifon formed the Pasadena Light Company on March 27, 1922, and were negotiating with city fathers for a distribution system to serve the La Porte Road and Shaver, Main, Wafer, Broad Way, and Randall Streets.[9]

On December 6, 1923, a petition signed by 70 residents was filed with County Judge C. H. Bryan and an election called for December 22, 1923. Fifty residents voted unanimously for incorporation. Women had won the right to vote in 1920. Aliens had previously enjoyed the right to vote, but lost that privilege in 1918. Otherwise, a person had to be 21 years old and purchased a poll tax, currently costing $1.50, in order to vote. On January 2, 1924, Judge Bryan authorized the incorporation and after the first city election, held on February 23, Ralph E. Parks was confirmed as the mayor on March 4. E. M. Barnes, Aubrey R. Cruse, Roy Glasgow, and G. M. Olive were certified as aldermen. A. B. Freeman and O. C. Pitts tied for the fifth aldermen's position, so the position was left vacant and neither person certified. When Parks took the oath of office he had to swear that he had "not fought a duel with deadly weapons . . . sent or accepted a challenge . . . nor acted as second in carrying a challenge." J. M. Cruse was appointed secretary-treasurer and city marshall. James G. Donovan was appointed as the first city attorney and was assisted by Homer Stephenson. Although not elected, W. G. Ankele, W. B. Bailey, Jr., Richard Brannen, Max Horsh, J. E. Pomeroy, W. B. Thornton, Ray Williams, and Walter Wilson all offered to serve the infant city.[10]

The incorporation limits of the city had been modified slightly from the original 1920 draft. The formal incorporated limits ran from the western limit of the original city plat east to Witter Street. The northern boundary remained the ship channel and the southern boundary was generally Eighth (Jackson) Street instead of Ninth (Texas) Street. The significant change was that Crown refinery was now included within the city limits and that Houston Lighting & Power was constructing their plant within the city limits. A Board of Equilization was appointed with R. M. Guinn as chairman and W. B. Bailey, Jr., as secretary. Pasadena State Bank served as the temporary city hall. J. S. Cullinan and Crown promptly protested the valuation on their properties and the tax assessed on it. In Cullinan's case an error in mathematics had been made in estimating a tax of approximately $8,000 instead of $800. The rate of 40 cents had been erroneously applied against the valuation of $195,000 instead of 40 cents per $100 of valuation. All land between the channel and Third Street was valued at $1,000 per acre and land between Third and the La Porte Road valued at $750 per acre. Cullinan was only assessed for his land value, with no valuation given to the improvements.[11]

The city of Houston was incensed at the attempt by Pasadena to include the ship channel industries within its corporate limits so that it could tax them. Houston had received state legislative approval in 1913 to include within Houston's city limits, for policing purposes only, a strip of land 2,500 feet wide on either side of the ship channel. The law provided that the strip was not to be taxed. The legislature in 1921 authorized the reorganization of the Navigation District to make it independent of Houston and to give it the responsibility and ability to develop the ship channel. The district could raise funds to develop the channel by the issuance of voter-approved bonds. Even though Houston could not tax Crown and Houston Lighting & Power, it certainly did not want Pasadena to tax them. The Navigation District was silent and Cullinan stood by without public comment.[12]

Houston City Attorney Sewall Myer lead the attack against Pasadena. The *Houston Press* lambasted the "Greedy Village" with hostile editorial reporting. Mayor Parks reported that the total valuation of the newly incorporated town was only 1.5 million dollars and, at the 40 cent rate, would yield the city only $9,000. That was just barely sufficient to operate the new city. The *Press* waved a $26 million valuation, with a $1.50 tax rate, for a greedy take of $390,000. The *Press* speculated that the increased cost to the electric company would cause the light bill of each Houston family to be increased $5 per year. Houston urged State Attorney W. A. Keeling to file suit against the city to force it to unincorporate since it took in too much land, land and businesses that would be taxed and would not receive any benefit for the cost. The *Press* quoted Houston City Attorney Myer in describing Pasadena by saying, "It has a beautiful lighting system and many other municipal improvements that are to be paid for by industries you can't even see with a field glass from the real town."[13]

State Attorney Keeling suggested that Pasadena withdraw their city limits to the 2,500 foot boundary and, after a personal inspection, filed suit when Pasadena refused his suggestion. Not wanting to be involved in a lengthy and expensive lawsuit, the Pasadena Citizens Association was formed and issued a public letter on October 22, 1924, calling for a vote to unincorporate. "Let's get rid of it now and save ourselves any further expense and unfavorable publicity . . . ." G. W. Conrad signed the letter as chairman, with John C. Penn, Jr., as secretary (and spokesman) and W. H. Dickerson, A. L. Dickerson, R. J. James, L. W. Clardy, and E. R. Kelley as committee members. Their plea was acknowledged when a petition was filed on November 1, 1924. Meanwhile Houston Lighting & Power Company had completed construction of its Deepwater Plant and it was put into service on August 24. Myrtle Blakesley was hired in a clerical position as an experiment, the first female employee in the plant. With little subtlety it was made known that the company did not want to be in the corporate limits of Pasadena. Crown had shut down its refining portion in 1923 and was operating with only a few employees as a tank farm and terminal facility. The city of Pasadena filed a contempt and injunction suit against the Association but was unsuccessful in stopping the election.

Dissolution was barely approved on November 29, 1924, with a vote of 36 to 31 as "Pasadena . . . voted itself out of existence . . . ." Of the 200 possible voters in Pasadena, only 75 were qualified since they were resident land owners. All but seven of the qualified voters cast their ballots and the city was abolished by six votes. "Hereafter it will content itself, 'the Pasadenans' said," with raising strawberries instead of taxes." In the midst of the fray a severe winter storm hit on December 19, and was followed by two weeks of record-breaking sleet and freezing weather. After the weather cleared, a motion to set aside the election was denied and after the debts of the town were paid by the property owners, Sixty-First District Court Judge Walter E. Monteith gavelled the city into history on March 11, 1925.[14]

Although the city government had disappeared, the need for regulation remained. The new Deepwater plant of Houston Lighting & Power Company employed 200 and had attracted a few more people to Pasadena. Additionally, the plant would continue to attract more industries, and people to the area. After all, in 1924 the Ford Motor Company had considered adding a ship channel plant even though it already had a Houston assembly facility. Pasadena's new high school had been dedicated December 17, 1924, and would surely attract more residents. Crown refinery reopened after being shut down for two years and would be hiring. And ranching for a livelihood was becoming more difficult with the big freeze and the enforcement of the fencing laws in 1924.[15]

With cars everywhere now, it was too dangerous to continue to allow the cattle to roam the countryside. Although the open

The last big cattle roundup was staged in the early 1920s and fenced pastures became their home. The Ranching Era came to a close.

The Struggle to Incorporate (1922-1929)   251

Not all ranchers were men. Mrs. Bertha McNay knew how to handle a horse and how to trail cattle.

range ended in 1910, enforcement of fencing had been somewhat lax. Now the ranchers were required to fence their pastures and thereby reduce their grazing range. Sam Allen, Tilford Jones, Tom Miller, C. B. McNay, Jim West, and others staged a large roundup and separated and fenced their herds. With fewer acres available for grazing, fewer head were supportable without expensive feed supplements. Unfortunately, some of the herds were quickly reduced in size. Eighty thousand head of cattle froze in the Gulf Coast area when the worst

The winter storm of 1924 claimed 80,000 head of cattle in the Gulf Coast area. The pasture fencing prevented them from drifting with the wind, causing them to freeze.

storm in 30 years hit on December 19, 1924. Thousands were trapped against fence lines and could not drift with the wind. Tilford Jones lost 1,500 cattle, but the McNays saved their 450 head by driving them against the wind back to the barn and packed them in like sardines. Lockridge McNay had his hands and feet frozen and saved them by wrapping them in a paste of lard and buck shot gun powder. Laurel McNay's boots froze solid and Laurel had to soak them in unwarmed water to keep from damaging his feet. Bud Miller told Tilford that he and the 15 other hired hands refused to risk their lives for someone else's cattle. They took shelter in J. A. Meyer's store in Deepwater.[16]

And to rub salt into the wound, hoof-and-mouth disease was brought into the area before 1920 by one steer out of Louisiana, and over the next five years numerous herds in the area were ordered destroyed by the government. For two years there was a quarantine whereby no cattle could be brought in or shipped out of the area. The horses were rounded up and held near the San Jacinto battleground for two years. Sam M. Allen took charge of the destruction of the cattle herds. The government inspector

Irma Williams hated losing her milk cow to the hoof and mouth disease. Although not infected, some cows were slaughtered by the government.

Anna Pomeroy hid her favorite milk cow from the government agents. Several other families did the same.

would specify which herds were infected and then the cattle could be driven to an area near Sam W. Allen's old headquarters. They would be driven into a deep trench and shot. Their bodies were covered with lime by men dressed in decontamination suits and then the carcases covered with dirt. Cars coming in and out of the quarantine area had to drive through a mild acid bath for their tires so that the disease could not be spread by contact with the ground. The government paid top dollar for the cattle selected for destruction, but sometimes that wasn't enough. Edgar Barnes wanted to keep his calf so he hid it in the attic of his house. Foots Wilson lost his good milk cow. She gave five gallons per day and provided about half of the family income. Wilson received $125 in compensation. Oscar Kruse lost 70 head and regardless of the compensation paid, it broke his spirit. Although he continued to serve on the school board, his health deteriorated and he passed away within a few years. Ranchers were being forced out of the area and their land put to more intense use, either farming, housing, or industry.[17]

Within a month of the formal dissolution of the city, John Pomeroy received a franchise from the county commissioners to operate a waterworks for Pasadena. The need for water had expanded since Pomeroy put in his first community well in 1919. Will Bailey had Pomeroy drill him a well on March 10,

John Pomeroy used the rear wheel of his car to help him pump his early water wells.

The sign on the water tower read: For Water, see Pomeroy. It was very visible from the La Porte Road.

1923, and was the first in West Pasadena to provide water to his neighbors. A week later Roy Glasgow had the first of several wells drilled. By the time Pomeroy received his franchise he had two water wells in his backyard and promptly set out running pipe all over town to provide water into the homes of those who wanted it. In order to provide flowing pressure he erected a water tower, using an old 2,000-gallon tin cistern tank. Later he replaced the tank with a wooden one. He used an air compressor to literally blow the water up into the tank. Then the water would flow to the various subscribers by gravity

The Pomeroy children grew up playing with the water well drilling equipment. Sons Edward and Clyde continued the family business.

pressure. Many of the pipelines laid on top of the ground and since there were few valves, some repairs had to be made with the line still under pressure. Water would spray everywhere. At first Pomeroy charged a flat fee but then purchased Buffalo brand water meters and charged by the gallon. Bill Deane was one of the most mechanically minded men in town and he calibrated and repaired the meters. Bill was also the first person in town to have a radio. He found plans for a crystal set in one of the popular-mechanics-type magazines and built it himself. He also helped others build sets, including John Pomeroy.[18]

The first radio transmission was sent in 1900 and the first radio broadcast was made Christmas Eve, 1906. However, it was a dozen years before radios reached Houston. In 1919 the Houston Radio Club was organized and the first commercial broadcast was made in 1922 from a garage, station WEV, to approximately 300 receiving sets. By May the *Houston Post* was sponsoring Sunday radio concerts. Ross Sterling purchased the *Houston Dispatch* newspaper and then the *Houston Post* and merged them into the *Houston Post-Dispatch,* which published its first combined edition on August 1, 1924. Within a year the *Post-Dispatch* purchased a station from theater owner Will Horwitz and reestablished it as KPRC on May 9, 1925. The call letters represented Houston's interest in "Port, Railroad & Cotton." Two months later John Scopes was put on trial in Tennessee over the illegal teaching of evolution in that state's public schools. The "Monkey Trial" was the hot news in July. That fall KPRC broadcast the World Series baseball games where Pittsburgh beat out Washington four to three. John Pomeroy purchased one of the first radios in town, an Atwater Kent, to replace his crystal set. Aubrey Cruse put his new radio outside at his drive-in root beer stand for the Jack Dempsey-Gene Tunney heavyweight boxing championship rematch fight in 1927 so that the patrons could hear the action as Tunney defended his new title with another 10-round decision against Dempsey. At the time there were only a few stations to pick up, and a lot of static in between. But Pasadena was used to static, especially when it came to its desire to incorporate.[19]

A community water system was not enough to satisfy the desire of the people to form a government. They had been scared off the first time for fear of incurring a large legal defense debt and in the end not having a way of paying it off. Houston was getting aggressive with its annexation program and looking in the direction of Pasadena. A cartoon in the March 14, 1925, issue of a Houston newspaper showed "Papa Houston" offering to take over the debts and burdens of Magnolia Park, Harrisburg, and Park Place. A petition was again filed with County Judge Bryan on November 30, 1925, requesting an incorporation election. The petition was signed by 27 voting citizens, although only 20 were required. Attached to it was a map similar to the previous city limits. An election was scheduled for December 19 but was postponed when Houston Lighting & Power Company, Crown Central Petroleum Company, and the port commissioners formally protested. The opponents contended that the city could not provide municipal services to the industries or the channel area, that the boundaries included "industrial sites, farm and pasture land and wooded acres unsuitable for city purposes," and that the 2,500-foot-wide channel strip had already been incorporated by Houston. Speaking on behalf of the citizens committee, James G. Donovan suggested that a mass community meeting be held with the opponents to iron out the differences. A mutually agreeable plan was never worked out and the citizens committee did not push the matter for a while.[20]

Houston annexed Magnolia Park in 1926 and was in the process of annexing Harrisburg and Park Place (all the way to Sims Bayou) when Pasadena again filed for an incorporation

Houston's annexation frenzy was the subject of this cartoon.

election. The proposed Houston annexation plan would have taken land away from the Pasadena Independent School District and put it into the Houston system. The incorporation election was set for December 17, 1927. The petition was signed by 65 qualified voters. A chamber of commerce had been organized during the summer and plans formulated. Augustus Theodore Vick, a well-known and respected owner of a Houston construction electrical engineering firm, contractor on the Crown Refinery job, contractor on Cullinan's new million-dollar Houston residence, and owner of a farm in Pasadena, was elected chairman. A well-thought-out program was developed, addressing the concerns of the community: water service for fire protection, natural gas supply to the community, better streets, a sewer system, and a telephone exchange. In order to get these community needs satisfied, incorporation of the city was necessary. A boundary was worked out that excluded the industries and channel frontage so as to avoid the opposition of the past. Houston Lighting & Power Company had purchased the Pasadena Light Company on February 28, 1927, and was now providing the community with electrical service. Southwestern Bell had promised an exchange office for early 1928 and Houston Gas & Fuel Company was preparing a proposition to furnish gas to the community. A preliminary water and sewer study had been completed by Engineering Service Corporation. This time Crown Oil & Refining Company was very supportive of the program and volunteered to contribute $150 per month towards improvements.[21]

In 1923 and 1925 the opposition to incorporation had been the industries that had been included within the city limits for tax purposes. The 1927 proposition had eliminated that problem and had taken a rather professional approach to the needs of the community and their solutions. The apparent flaw was in the proposed financing of the projects. Vick estimated that the property tax rate would be one dollar per $100 valuation as opposed to the rate of 40 cents used in 1923. The election to incorporate failed on December 17, 1927, by a vote of 63 for and 71 against. It just wasn't time yet.[22]

The city limits of Houston were extended to Sims Bayou by annexation on December 14, 1927. The Allen Ranch subdivisions and Pasadena were now logical targets. Anna Pomeroy, 61 years old and a Pasadena resident since 1901, led the drive to prevent annexation by Houston. Armed with petitions and attorneys representing Sinclair, she boarded the train for Houston. She presented her case to the city council of Houston and persuaded them not to cross Sims Bayou in their annexation race at this time. Perhaps the "Greedy" title affixed to Pasadena by the *Houston Press* during the 1924 city limits battle was salted in Anna's presentation, this time in describing Houston.[23]

Not satisfied that Houston would leave Pasadena alone, and that Pasadena could provide the now necessary community services without incorporating, J. M. Cruse led yet another attempt at incorporation in November of 1928. Joe Cruse, now 63 years old, had supported the move to incorporate from the beginning. Mr. W. W. Moore, general counsel for Fidelity Trust Company, advised Mr. Cullinan in a letter dated December 19, 1928, that "the natives are almost unanimously in favor of incorporation." However he felt that the action could not be defeated on legal grounds, but must be fought by influence of the industrial employers upon their Pasadena resident employees. He estimated that there were 75 votes and that Houston Lighting & Power could control 20, Crown 12, and Sinclair could influence another 12. With these 44 votes the election could be defeated. But Pasadena was growing, not shrinking, and 138 votes had been cast the year before. Crown had supported the 1927 attempt at incorporation and Sinclair was uncommitted. One hundred and ninety-six votes were cast in the election on the day after Christmas. Pasadena was reincorporated by a margin of 8 votes; 102 for and 94 against.[24]

The geographic area of incorporation did not include the industries or the ship channel corridor that had lead to unincorporation in 1925. Less land had been included north of the La Porte Road and more land had been included south of the road. The shape was basically rectangular, centered on the La Porte Road at Shaver intersection, with an arm on the west side that took in the populous "West Pasadena" section that was developing west of Vince's Bayou. Beyond these limits there were only scattered farms and too much distance in between to economically provide "city services" to. Although the city was deprived of the industrial tax base, the school system had been incorporated long before the industries arrived and therefore were blessed with this financial source.

Gerald Conrad had signed the original petition to incorporate in 1923 and had chaired the citizens committee that sought to unincorporate in 1924. Ironically he was selected to serve as the interim mayor. A. L. Dickerson was selected street and bridge commissioner and L. T. Grant as water commissioner. Grant promptly resigned at the first meeting on January 9, 1929, and Clyde McMaster was appointed in his place. Since the mayor was also a commissioner, Conrad assumed the tax and finance responsibility. J. C. Thomas was appointed secretary-treasurer and tax assessor/collector. The first meeting was held in the grammar school and the first citizen's request was for roadwork. Dickerson was instructed to look into it. Previously a landowner would purchase a wagon load of shell and spread it himself on the street in front of his place. Edward Pomeroy and Merle "Mud" Wilson paved Main Street with a wagon by removing a crossways board from the bed and pushing the shell through the slot as the wagon moved forward.[25]

The Houston Natural Gas Company was granted a temporary franchise to provide gas to the residents of Pasadena at that first city council meeting. However, gas had been previously available to some in the community as John Pomeroy was one of the first to have gas installed late in 1927. Several months after he had electricity brought to his home. Reverend Joseph Alfred Chestnut got hot water and gas to his family in the Baptist Parsonage by the middle of 1928. Total cost was $30. Howard Pitts was appointed city marshall on January 26 and was to be paid out of fees collected "as provided for by law." E. A. Gregg and A. A. Ward were appointed depty marshalls. On February 26 a street improvement ordinance was passed and two employees were hired on March 8. Richard J. Griffin was hired as foreman and grader at $5 per day, with assistance from J. R. Huff as tractor driver. The first city council election was held on April 2, 1929, and Conrad was elected mayor over Charles Garfield. Dickerson and McMaster beat out J. M. Larson for the two commissioner positions.[26]

In the course of the struggle for incorporation much had changed in the community. Although strawberries remained the same, the character and texture of the community were different. Had it not been for the popularity of Sylvan Beach, the La Porte Road would probably not have been concrete paved as soon as it was. New dances were the rage, and the sea breeze was cooling to a fast-stepping couple. There were now numerous ways to get to Sylvan. Besides the regularly scheduled train trips, excursion trains were available on many weekends and for special occasions. The Bayshore Suburban diesel motor railroad car made daily trips to and from Seabrook through La Porte. To some it was known simply as the Suburban, but Lillian Smythe called it the "Doodle Bug." The Bayshore bus line was incorporated in 1923. But the Model T provided a more convenient and thus an increasingly popular ride to the bay. The La Porte Road became crowded with the freewheeling weekend frolickers. The first Houston Annual Bathing Girl Revue was held there in 1924 and quickly became a very popular annual event. Many of Houston's influential had built bay homes on Bay Ridge, just north of Sylvan Beach and with the postwar prosperity, more were coming to this coastal "silk stocking row." Just a bit further out on Morgan's Point was the flats, a low-lying area that many used for fishing and swimming.

The village of Seabrook was a popular fishing and summer resort.

The Bayshore Suburban diesel motorcar, "the Doodle Bug" made daily runs from Seabrook, through Pasadena, to Houston and back.

Fashions changed and women could now rent wool bathing suits at Sylvan Beach without pleated skirts with bloomers underneath.

The dredging of the ship channel had earlier ruined the irrigation water for rice farming and the continual dredging was slowing ruining the nice sandy beaches here and at Sylvan.[27]

Houston oilman and Port of Houston Commissioner Ross Sterling built his bay home as a reduced-scale model of the White House in Washington, D. C.. While president of Humble Oil, Sterling and Sylvan Beach park manager Cecil Sisson started the idea of company picnics at the park and now annually it brought thousands for their special day. The county commissioners were finally stimulated into action when in, 1926, the voters mandated a county road improvement program by a four to one majority. The Harrisburg-La Porte Road through Pasadena was paved with shell and asphalt in 1926 and finally concreted in 1928. During paving, 82-year-old Robert Guinn and 38-year-old daughter Margaret "Maggie" Emmeline were hit by an automobile. Robert Guinn, Civil War veteran and past Pasadena postmaster, was killed and Maggie was crippled. Later, the children of Pasadena thought that the finished highway was their private roller-skating rink. By then downtown Pasadena had grown and established itself along the highway.[28]

In 1929 the commerical district of Pasadena began a little further west than it did in 1920. Although the first settlement of the community had begun in "West Pasadena," the commercial development had been concentrated east of there in the center of the plat. The Blackwell and Hargrave subdivisions now provided homesites for those working at Sinclair Refin-

The La Porte Road was paved with concrete at the rate of a mile a day. The two-story Masonic Lodge building is in the background.

ery. By 1929 commerce had jumped Vince's Bayou and a few businesses were located on the La Porte Road near the Richey Street intersection. Will Bailey operated a grocery and service station from his property just west of Richey Street. Living nearby, Ben, Jr., had married Addie Brown in 1920 and now had five-year-old Alden running around the store. Will had

Fred Waring and Ernest Jones in West Pasadena advertised "Our Business is Picking Up."

The Struggle to Incorporate (1922-1929)

W. H. and Lillian Dickerson on the porch of their home between West Pasadena and Pasadena.

some competition from E. D. Boggs, who also operated a grocery in West Pasadena. Gus Watson's service station and garage was run by a succession of operators after Gus bought it in 1921. A race car driver by the name of Willis ran it for a while and burned the garage down. Harry Witt later worked there while his children Mary, Lillian "Kitty," and Harry, Jr., attended Pasadena schools. Ernest Jones and Fred Waring operated it beginning in 1928 as Jones' Garage. The station was destined to change hands several more times in the near future.[29]

Wade Dickerson was still in the middle of things. For years he had been the driving mercantile force. Now he was mostly retired and lived between West Pasadena and downtown Pasadena. In 1927 he moved back to the old homeplace on the east bank of Vince's Bayou

Living nearby, A. L. and Bertha Dickerson pictured with their family. Couples include Bertha and Baldy Quinn, Carl and Loriene Dickerson, and Edwin and Mary Dickerson (with son Royce down front). Wynona Dickerson is in the dark pantsuit.

and enjoyed his pecan trees. As big as his commerical interests had grown, so had his family. When he first got into business in 1905 Wade and Lillian had Russell and Beatrice. Since then they added Leon Eugene, Thelma O., Wade, Jr., Nellie O., Victor, Etta Mildred, Raymond Alvin, and James Alfred. Victor and James died young and were buried nearby in Crown Hill Cemetery.[30]

Downtown Pasadena began on the west at Cruse's Texaco Service Station on the west side of Shaver. Bob Kingsbury got some his first work experience here. Aubrey Cruse had started a jitney service shortly after acquiring the service station and then organized the Houston-Pasadena Bus Company about 1924 when Houston outlawed jitneys. In his new storefront, Cruse also had an insurance agency and a plumbing store. The future *Pasadena Record* newspaper would have an office here and a spare room would function as the first civic meeting room in the community, outside of the school buildings. Perhaps the need for a community civic room was noted while Aubrey served on the school board from 1927 to 1929. It was no surprise that Aubrey had resigned as cashier of the bank back in 1924 to look after his growing business interests. Aubrey's father Joe joined him in running the business by

Bus Service To Houston

In 1927, Houston was a town "a far piece" from Pasadena, but getting there was no particular problem for those who didn't have a car, for they had Aubrey Cruse Sr.'s bus service, which has five modern automobiles for the daily runs to the "big city." Back of the cars are some of Cruse's other enterprises, including an insurance business, a plumbing shop, garage and service station and a weekly newspaper. The Pasadena Record, had an office (under the Texaco sign). The picture was provided by Aubrey Cruse Jr., son of the late Aubrey Cruse Sr., an early-day Pasadena leader and businessman.

Aubrey Cruse was "Mr. Businessman" in Pasadena. Included in his businesses were a bus company, insurance agency, plumbing shop, service station, and garage.

1929. Next door, and on the corner of the La Porte Road and Shaver Street, was the Green Rose Park, a "table service and car service" restaurant operated by W. S. McCrory.[31]

Across Shaver Street Ray L. Coulson brought his wife and children, Ray K. and Carrie, to Pasadena in 1925 and built a drug store on the corner. Coulson's corner was quickly becoming the hangout location for kids, since it was a good spot to hitch a ride into Harrisburg. Next door Whit Thornton had converted the old post office into a storefront and operated his Butterfly Confectionary store there since the early twenties. He added root beer to the menu in the mid-twenties, but then gave the building over to the David-Finger Dry Goods Company. Edward H. David was the son of missionary W. J. David, who had been the preacher at the Baptist church from 1917 to 1920. His mother, Justa, and sister, Nannie, had taught at the Pasadena school from 1913 to 1915. His brother, Reverend V. L. David, was a missionary to Spain and would return to preach at Pasadena. Edward moved to Pasadena early in 1929 with his wife Anna Lou and son Billy. He quickly became involved in the community. Edward helped organize the first American Legion Post and served as its commander. Shortly afterwards he helped organize the Retail Merchants' Association and was elected its president. Aubrey Cruse served as its vice-president and Edgar Henderson as secretary-treasurer. H. A. Carter, O. A. Cook, and T. M. Campbell were the directors.[32]

Just past mid-block the Dickerson buildings contained several stores. Paul Fleming had married "Judge" Dickerson's daughter, Thelma, in 1926 and opened the first barbershop in town. So, naturally, the barbershop was in Dickerson's building. In return, Paul and Thelma gave the Judge a grandchild, Paula. In Paul's shop Mrs. Howard was doing "permanent waving," which had become very fashionable with a new method developed just three years earlier in 1926. Just $5 to get your hair waved. Little Everett Williams picked up spending money by shining shoes. Wade's son Russell operated Pasadena's first radio store. It was probably here that John Pomeroy purchased his Atwater Kent radio. The floor model cost $117, plus the cost of seven tubes to make it work. The table top model cost $84 plus tubes and another $34 for the speakers. Next door, Jess Mason had taken over Wade Dickerson's cafe and called it the Bank Cafe. It became a popular place for the young people to hang out. Wade had opened his grocery store 24 years earlier and had employed many Pasadenans over the years. It was moved from its original site on Main Street to the La Porte Road location in 1920. The store was now associated with the International Grocers' Association (I.G.A) and was being operated by Mr. Hamilton. In front of all of the stores was a wooden sidewalk, just like in front of the Williams buildings in the next block. Next door and on the corner of Munger Street, Pasadena Drug Store was still sharing the only brick building in town with Pasadena State Bank.[33]

Across Munger, beyond the big oak tree and about midblock, E. Frank DeFee operated his general merchandise store. He had moved to Pasadena from Madison County with his wife Lillie and young son John in about 1919 and went to work in Wade Dickerson's store on Main Street. Because Wade was involved in the new Guaranty State Bank, Frank also purchased stock in the bank. About the same time, Lillie's parents, John R. and Mary Williams, joined the rest of the Williams clan in Pasadena. By 1923 John Williams had acquired the old railroad section house at the corner of the La Porte Road and Main Street and opened the J. R. Williams General Merchandise

The Williams General Store, shown here was built by John R. Williams in 1923, and later sold to Walter F. Williams in 1926. KIKK Radio station now occupies the remodeled building.

John Williams opened the first store, then his brother Walter Williams took it over. Walter's daughter Betty (Mrs. Lee Mitchell) continued the business.

Store. Wade Dickerson had farmed out his business interest and the DeFees moved over to the Williams' store. Lillie worked on the general merchandise side of the store and Frank on the grocery side. Three years later, John Williams sold the business to his younger brother, Walter F. Williams. Walter had plenty of children to help run the store, especially daughter Betty, and her husband, W. Lee Mitchell. The store's name was changed to the W. F. Williams Store. Frank and Lillie DeFee opened their own store almost next door. He affiliated with the Red and White grocery association and began plans to constuct a two-story brick building on the old Dickerson store site on Main street, just south of the railroad tracks.[34]

Next door to DeFee, Walter G. Ankele operated an insurance agency. Walter had been active in the incorporation battle and served as an alderman during the first incorporation. Walter also operated the Pasadena Barber Shop with David C. Jackson. D. C. came to Pasadena about 1927 when his father-in-law, Dr. Jim Boyd, sent for him. D. C. was married to Dr. Boyd's oldest daughter Pearl, and they had three children: James A. "Munk", Maxine, and Wanda. Dr. Boyd had bought the Kingsbury store and D. C. operated a barbershop in there for a while. Some say that D. C. was probably the best barber in town. Ankele's building was an add-on to the ever-growing Williams commercial block.[35]

In the middle of the Williams block of buildings, R. J. Good opened his Good's Drug Store. Good had moved to Pasadena about 1921 and probably first worked in the Pasadena Drug Store before striking out on his own. T. M. Campbell was negotiating to purchase the business and was having a six-room house built on Spooner for $2,500. Between Good's and W. F. Williams' Grocery was the post office, with Carroll Coolidge as the new postmaster. Carroll arrived with his parents in Pasadena when he was two years old and he grew up in the

The Lone Star Cement Company dug clay off of Richey Street in Pasadena since the 1910s. It employed just a few men, but it left a big hole.

Channler and Rosa Scannell moved into the Lone Star Cement Company's company house in 1928.

community. At 22 years old he took a job with the post office in Houston. After eight years of experience, he returned to take over the Pasadena post office. He replaced Samuel Hain who had served for less than a year. Hain had taken over from Carrie Roberts who had held the position from 1920 to 1927. Carroll hired Rosa Scannell to help him in the post office. She had arrived in September 1928 with her husband Channler H., who was hired by Lone Star Cement to oversee their clay pit operation in Pasadena. Rosa would work at the post office until she became expectant with her son John Joseph. The east end of the Williams block was W. F. Williams' Grocery store. Walter was very active in all aspects of the community and was taking an interest in the new city government.[36]

Across Main Street and on the corner was the two-story Masonic Lodge building. The building was completed late in 1925. The upstairs was used by the Lodge and the downstairs was rented out. Forrest Fisher was the current Worshipful Master of the group. W. G. Hargrave was the Past Worshipful Master. Forrest and his wife Louise and daughter Dorothy Lee were fairly new in town. Dr. James Boyd had officed for a while downstairs before moving to Mrs. Kingsbury's store on Main Street. He was buying the Kingsbury building when he caught pneumonia while out delivering a baby, and died in 1927. After Dr. Boyd's death there was a rush for doctors to move, or rather offer their services to the little community of Pasadena. Dr. C. V. Beall, Dr. J. M. Beall, and Dr. A. L. W. Tackaberry opened offices and were listed in the first telephone book of

The Struggle to Incorporate (1922-1929)

Dr. Boyd bought the Kingsbury Store for his new offices in 1927.

the community published in August of 1928. If no one answered at the Bealls' office, then you left a message at Coulson's Drug Store. Dr. Oscar F. Portwood came to Pasadena in December 1928 from Texarkana with his wife Cora Iola and son Frank, Jr. The Portwoods bought a home across Main Street from Dr. Boyd's home. Dr. Portwood initially listed his office in the telephone book as at the post office. But within the year Dr. Portwood would move his offices into Dr. Boyd's old office on the first floor of the Masonic Lodge building.[37]

Next door to the Masonic building was a small standup cafe with six or eight stools for those with time to sit. A typical plate lunch meal would set you back about 50 cents. The cafe was run by a steady stream of different operators. A jovial Mr. Scott ran it for a while, but it was called "Jim's Cafe" in 1929.[38]

"Foots" Wilson was a jack-of-all trades and worked at a few over the years. He was a large and likable man with a reddish complexion and a humorous personality. After working for Galena-Signal, Crown Refinery, and operating a service station for a while, Foots started Pasadena Ice & Fuel in 1921. His little building sat parallel to the La Porte Road, about midway between Main and Spooner streets. Since he did not have the ability to make ice, he would drive to Texas Ice & Fuel on Harrisburg and pick up a load. Foots had a little ammonia cooling machine that kept the ice from melting in his Pasadena

Many high school boys earned money delivering Foots Wilson's ice. J. B. Isaac is standing by the truck.

building. The building was rather small and set long wise with the road, with a dock-high covered porch. He would then make deliveries to Pasadena residents, sticking a block of ice in their "ice" boxes to keep its contents cool. Sometimes the icebox would be on the back porch, but most times it was inside. Since no one locked their doors, Foots or one of his boys would take the ice inside and put it in the box. A few electric refrigerators were now beginning to show up in town so the demand for home ice had about peaked. Wilson also put in a supply of cordwood so that people did not have to go into Houston to get stove fuel. He knew everyone in town and was a bit lax in collecting on his accounts.[39]

With his truck, Foots would also move furniture for people. J. Sam and Alice Daily moved their family in from Louisiana with the help of the Wilson truck. J. Marvin, Naomi, Mittie Lee, and Irene now also called Pasadena home. Foots would also haul bricks for the various schoolhouse constructions, haul hay or dirt, and even use it as a hearst to carry a dearly departed friend to their final resting place at Crown Hill Cemetery. Foots dug the graves for free and was always looking for volunteers to help with the work. Teenagers Johnny Meyers and Carey Williams used to run when they saw the old blue truck coming, but Foots would anticipate their escape route and get there first. Clyde Hill and J. D. Parks, Jr., drove the ice truck for a while. Ferrel Brown worked at Wilson's while he was in high school for $1.50 per day. Foots's son Thurman, called by some "Little Foots," would help with the ice delivers as would the lanky J. B. Isaac. Edward Pomeroy was always amazed at how effortlessly Foots and J. B. would handle the 25-pound blocks of ice they loaded into the refrigerated strawberry railroad cars. One or the other would get up on top and the other would pitch the blocks up to him from the bed of the ice truck. They used ice tongs like extensions of their hands and played pitch and catch with poetic rhythm.[40]

Next door to the icehouse was the newly opened Channel Chevrolet Company. Bob Robertson was beginning about 50 years of car dealerships. F. G. Deane's store was on the corner of the La Porte Road and Spooner. The Producer's Exchange had dissolved in 1925 and Deane had bought the building in 1926. Originally Deane had operated his tin smithing business from the building next door, but moved over into the big building and sold some hardware items. Even though the building sat on the corner, it was not all that obvious. Shaver, Munger, and Main streets were fairly well marked. As you progressed in either direction from these streets the side streets were less specific. Most of the side streets were dirt or lightly shelled paths leading off of the La Porte Road. Since there were no street signs to mark the spot, an alleyway or simple path might be misleading as to your location.[41]

Across Spooner, Howard Pitts was back in the service station and garage business. He had started his garage about 1919 and

Pasadena's "first" baby, Howard Pitts, is ready for business at his Pasadena Garage. His sons Glenn and Charles would take over the business location.

Duckie and Thelma Lois play on their father's wrecker while their mother, Mamie Pitts, watches apprehensively.

then went off the Harrisburg to drive a jitney for a while. He came back by 1924 and got serious about the service station business. He got a Gulf dealership and called his place the Pasadena Garage. But never being a person to limit his potential, he sold a little furniture on the side. That furniture business would outlive him. Although Howard was the second person born in Pasadena, he was often considered Pasadena's first baby since Raymond Anderson had moved away to California with his parents about 20 years before. Howard built a nice two-story house next door so that he could work and watch his family grow up.[42]

On the other end of the block, at the corner of the La Porte Road and Randall was the Butcher Brothers Ice House. They had an ice-making plant in Houston and decided to set up one in Pasadena in 1928. McMaster and Pomeroy drilled a water well to provide them with an adequate supply of water for the process. With the exception of the Bank and Pitt's, that ice-making business would outlive all of the other businesses then operating on the La Porte Road.[43]

East of Butcher Brothers there were only two other buisnesses on the La Porte Road. Arthur G. Whitman's Pasadena Lumber Company was located about two blocks away near Wafer. The Whitmans were then members of the Baptist Church, but would later change to the Methodist. Annette, Emmett E., and Ralph Garrison were all in school. Arthur probably had fellow Baptist Mike Coy managing his business. Mike had been around the community for about 10 years with his wife Alma W. and sons Clarence W. and Cullen. The Coys were musically inclined and had a travelling carnival that they took on the road every once in a while. In between trips the carnival equipment was stored behind their home on Broad Way, next to the grammar school. Clarence had graduated in 1928 and was occasionally hauling lumber in from East Texas.[44]

Also working for the lumber company was Robert Andrew Hughes. Robert arrived about 1925 with a family of 10, looking for a job. His wife Fannie had a handfull with Pearl, Marie, Vera, Louella, Jewell, Marvin Edson, Robert Ernest, and Ruby Marcella. They rented all over town and finally built a boardinghouse on the corner of Johnson and Fifth (Shaw) streets. Robert A. only had about a block to walk to work. It did not take son Marvin long to find a cute local girl to court. He convinced Olive Mozelle Kelley to drop out of high school to marry him in 1928.[45]

Across the dirt road from Whitman's was Henry A. Carter's Shell service station. Henry had been in town a few years and his daughter Alice would graduate from high school in 1930. Carl Tilley had operated Tilley's Garage for a couple of years on the La Porte Road and apparently gave the business over to Carter during the summer of 1929. And that was the end of the businesses along the La Porte Road in Pasadena.[46]

There were other businesses around town, but few formal stores. North of downtown Mayor Conrad had a nursery on

Gerald Conrad's nursery was located on North Shaver, just north of Little Vince's Bayou. Crown Refinery is in the background.

McMaster and Pomeroy drill a well for the railroad in 1923 at Devine, Texas. Seated are John Pomeroy, Clyde McMaster, and a pumper for the railroad. Standing are Bob Guinn, Bill Deane, and Pete Glasgow.

Shaver Street just north of Vince's Bayou. The Guinn Brothers operated a pickup laundry on Fifth (Shaw) Street. Earl and Ray were involved and maybe Robert, Jr., and Chester. Ray had married Bessie Maude Crenshaw back in 1907 and had Roy Sidney and Beulah Bernice to show for it. They lived between Pasadena and Genoa. Mr. Shine operated a restaurant across the street from Crown Refinery on land he leased from Jim Hughes. Marion Moore operated a blacksmith shop behind the family home. C. C. Freeman and Will Blakesley were contractors working out of their homes. Ben Williams was the local notary and realtor. He also oper-

McMaster and Pomeroy drilled over 2,000 water wells in the Gulf Coast area. Son Clyde Pomeroy got patents for his numerous water well inventions.

ated out of his home. Although most of his children had homes of their own, Bryon lived there with his wife Nettie Irene and six children: Lula I., Bryon Curtis, Anna Bell, Jimmie L., Alfred G., and Synona Jean. Fortunately son Truett H. lived in his own house on the back side of the property. Clyde McMaster and John Pomeroy drilled water wells all over the Gulf Coast area and ran the business from John's Main Street property. Southwestern Bell Telephone Company bought part of Pomeroy's land facing on Munger Street and opened a switching station in Pasadena on June 30, 1928, with 87 subscribers. In August the new Houston telephone directory had a separate section entitled, "Pasadena Exchange."[47]

John August and Hedwig Paula Meyer moved to Pasadena in the spring of 1926 after their mercantile store in Deepwater burned down. They bought a house from Asa Hearn on the northwest corner of Fifth (Shaw) and Munger. Isabell was their oldest child, but she was away at Sam Houston Normal College in Huntsville getting educated to be a teacher. Their other child, John Maximillian "Johnny" had been traveling to Pasadena for the last two years to attend high school and would graduate that year. John did not go back into the mercantile business, but instead returned to carpentry at 60 years of age. He had built C. B. McNay's 1 1/2-story brick home in 1924. Hedwig took to walking and would be a familiar figure around town, and later at city council meetings.[48]

South down Shaver Street, Samuel Pendegraff Bell sold fruits and vegetables. Sam had brought his wife Emma and children Trannie Estelle, Ollie, Maurice, S. P., Jr., and Norma from Humble, Texas, to work as the caretaker of A. T. Vick's farm. Around them was a small cluster of houses, which included the Will Parks family; L. James and Myrtle Brubaker with their children Helen, Thelma "Mickey," Margarite "Irene," and James "Jimmy;" and the Thorps and their grandchildren Mildred and Jack Casey. A. D. and Minnie Tingle lived nearby with their seven children: A. D., Jr., Juanita, Mary, Billy V. Boyd, Kenneth E., and Jack M. The Sanchez family had eight children. The oldest sons, Tony, Sam, and Phillip worked at the Lone Star Cement clay pits. On the southern edge of town was the Baldwin and Syfan farms. Clarence Edming operated a smelter just west of the Syfan dairy.[49]

Finally, a merchant class had developed in the town and a formal governing body was established to help the town develop. Nothing could go wrong.

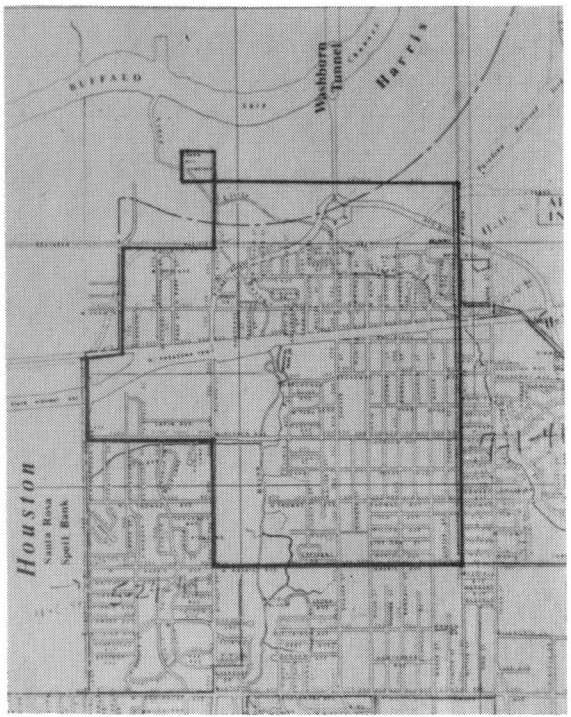

The incorporation limits in 1928 did not include the new industries or the ship channel.

Looking west down the La Porte Road from Main Street, Pasadena's new downtown was taking shape.

XI

The Eve of the Great Depression (1928-1929)

Jesse H. Jones, stepfather to Tilford Jones of Deepwater, convinced the Democratic Party to hold its 1928 national convention in Houston. This was the first time the convention was to be held in the South since the War Between the States. Jones offered the Party $200,000 and a 25,000-seat auditorium and beat out San Francisco for the site of the convention. It took only 64 days to build Sam Houston Hall. Since time was limited and Jones was an old lumberman, it was constructed entirely out of wood. Naturally, no smoking was allowed. Designed for hot-weather gatherings, it opened on all sides to allow for cross-breezes. Air conditioning had been introduced into Houston in 1923 at the Second National Bank, but time and money did not allow for it to be included in the building. The hall cost $200,000 and had a seating capacity for 20,000 people. A section of the gallery was set aside to seat a potential 100 Negro spectators.[1]

The six-story Democratic Building was built as the convention headquarters and two "hospitality" houses were built to accommodate any overflow of spectators. The Rice Hotel became the unofficial headquarters and the Sam Houston, William Penn, the Auditorium, Ben Milam, Milby, Bender, Stratford, Warwick, and Lamar hotels housed the participants. The 37-story Gulf Building was under construction and would be the tallest building west of Chicago. It was expected that

25,000 delegates and visitors would spend $3 million in the city. The anticipated presidential nominee would be Governor Alfred E. Smith of New York and it was suggested that Jesse Jones be nominated for the vice-presidency. Even though Jones owned the *Houston Chronicle*, it was Ross Sterling's *Houston Post-Dispatch* that said," If Smith and Jones isn't a democratic combination of names, then what is?" Jones was nominated for the presidency on the first ballot as a favorite son by the Texas delegation when the convention convened in June. He declined subsequently to be considered as the vice-presidential nominee.[2]

Clyde Pomeroy was five-and-a-half years old when he went to the convention. It was hot and noisy, but he was impressed with all of the state placards. The crowd was more than a bunch of people from Houston, they were thousands of people from every state in the Union! Dressed neatly in knee breeches, he was somewhat afraid of getting a splinter from the wooden benches. The whole family was there, from grandmother Anna, to parents John and Gertrude, and sisters Marguerite and Bessie. Brother Edward was playing in the band. Not yet 14, Edward had been "drafted" by the band director, Vick Kucera, to play in the band for the convention. Kucera taught music and was the director of the 143rd Infantry Military Band of the Texas National Guard. When he was selected for the convention he rounded up as many players as he could find. Edward, Ralph Hodges, and James Goodman were brought in from Pasadena. The group met downtown in one of the warehouses and practiced playing and marching. They were issued World War I uniforms, including leggings, for the occasion. To kick off the convention, the band led a parade from downtown, out Main Street to the Warwick Hotel and back again. Simply blowing their horns was complicated by the uneven streets paved with wooden blocks and crisscrossed with the rails for trolleys. Once inside the convention hall, they played every time someone got up to speak, or sat down. Kucera told them to play loud, even if they lost their place, or their music; it was not necessary that they hit the right notes, just play loud. As Clyde, and many others noted, the crowd was loud, rowdy, and, even though it was during Prohibition, plenty of hip flasks were lifted.[3]

For the first time, radio was a major tool of the election process. With an estimated 10 million receivers in use, the candidates could project their personalities, and argue the issues to a far greater audience. Houston was proud that the national Democratic convention in Houston was the first ever broadcast over the radio. Governor Al Smith was not able to attend the convention, but on June 28 telegraphed his acceptance, which was read before the delegates. Shortly afterwards, station WGY of Schenectady, N. Y., broadcast the first remote pickup of the official ceremony in Albany confirming the Democratic presidential nomination of Al Smith, on television.[4]

Not knowing what television was, nor having the capacity to enjoy it, meant that its significance went unnoticed in Houston. Other media events meant more and were sooner enjoyed. "Wait a minute, wait a minute. You ain't heard nothin' yet, folks; listen to this." Spoken by Al Jolson in *The Jazz Singer*, the age of talking movies was ushered in late in 1927. In 1928 Walter "Walt" Disney's *Steamboat Willie* introduced the cartoon character Mickey Mouse, in the first animated sound track film, and George Eastman exhibited the first colored motion pictures. The first all-electric jukebox was introduced. And on the airways, the radio comedy program, "Amos 'n Andy" began building an audience.[5]

That same year Pasadenans travelled to the newly completed Buffalo Stadium in Houston to watch the Houston Buffaloes beat Wichita Falls for the Texas League championship. Ex-Pasadenan Watty Watkins had moved into professional baseball and was making his mark with the "Buffs." When Watty went to Beaumont to try out for the professional farm club team he tried to get Oscar Kruse to join him. Oscar was too timid and decided to stay at home and get a real job, building oil tanks. Watty was a crowd pleaser and would go on to play with the soon-to-be immortals "Dizzy" Dean and "Pepper" Martin on the St. Louis Cardinals. He would also play against "Babe" Ruth. Ralph Hodges and Edward Pomeroy were among the Pasadena kids who would ride their bicycles to Buffalo Stadium to see the baseball games. They were part of the "Knothole Gang." These were kids who would get free passes to sit in the bleachers instead of watching the game through knotholes in the fences. On some Saturdays Ralph and Edward would bicycle to downtown Houston and sell *Chronicle* newspapers on the corner at the Rice Hotel. With their profits they would spend five cents on a hamburger and 10 cents to get into the Ritz Theater to catch the latest movie.[6]

Meanwhile Hadley and Kizzie White's boy, Tommy, was still knocking them down around the country. Tommy got into boxing when they lived at Texas City and stormed his way through Mexico and South America. By 1926 he held the lightweight, welterweight, and middleweight championship titles in Mexico and the lightweight and welterweight titles in the southwestern United States. Dubbed "Gentleman Tommy" White, the *Baton Rouge State Times* said he was "a polished gentleman out of the ring and a Demon in the Arena." He spoke three languages fluently and served his country in the war. Others called him "Eagle Eye" White for his aggressive and decisive style. He claimed to be half-Cherokee Indian and half-Irish. After only three years in the game he had had 62 professional fights with 23 knockouts and only two losses. In 1925 he had been a contender for the World Lightweight title but was eliminated under a technicality. He was extremely popular on the Latin American circuit and added Venezuelan and Panama Canal Zone titles to his credits. After his folks moved to Pasadena he would roar through town in a style befitting his reputation. Naturally the kids in town, who called him "Bull & Buzz Saw," were awestruck. Not since the Poole boy won the heavyweight Golden Glove championship had there been so much interest in boxing.[7]

Sports had always been popular in the community and the establishment of a high school provided a framework to organize that interest.

Boxer Tommy White was knocking them out all over Mexico and South America.

The Eve of the Great Depression (1928-1929)

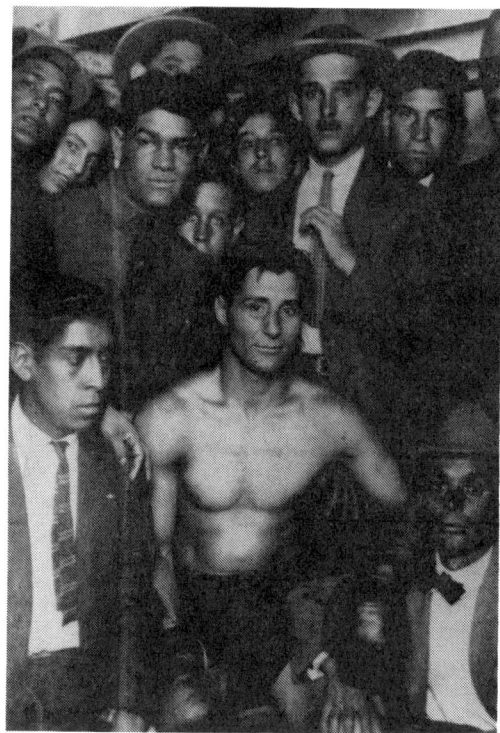

Tommy White was very popular both in the ring and out.

The baskeball hoop at the grammar school was getting a workout when Richard T. Gore hired on to be principal of the new high school in 1923. With the dedication of the new building in December 1924, the school system now had two, two-story brick buildings; one for the grammar school (grades one through seven) and the other for a high school (grades eight through eleven). In the spring of 1925 a track team was organized. The following fall Gore was promoted to superintendent of schools, replacing J. O. Davis. Clara E. Taylor was hired as the principal of the high school. Feeling that Pasadena needed a football team, Gore purchased a football and had the field behind the school levelled for a playing surface. It was rough; a coarse sand paper texture in dry weather, and a mud hole in wet. More than once a game was halted as a player was extracted from the grip of the sticky gumbo. School Trustee Charlie Garfield thought Gore was spending too much money when Gore paid $5 to have the work done. Perhaps as a concession, Gore only bought one complete uniform for each member of the team, no spares. If a uniform got torn, the boy would just have to play with it that way.[8]

Nonetheless, social studies teacher Paul Long was assigned the duty of putting together the first football team. Even though Long was a baseball enthusiast, he had no experience with football. There being less than 20 males in the whole high school, support for the program had to be strong or a team could not be fielded. Twelve came forward and a team was formed. To further complicate the program, only Johnny Meyers had ever seen a game before. Naturally Johnny was appointed captain of the team. Edward Kruse was selected quarterback and almost every boy in school was drafted. Ralph Stafford, Thurman Wilson, Ferrel Brown, Glen Gigstad, Prell Brannen, and Kelvin Glasgow suited up. Marshall Rinehart of South Houston, Jack Gray of Galena Park, and Henry Coffee of Penn City were brought in. Fifteen-year-old Joe "J. B." Isaac had just moved to Pasadena from Galena Park with his parents John Sampson and Mittie Isaac, his younger brother Driscol, and even younger sisters Aleta, Eva Mae, and Doris Jean. Although J. B. had not played before, he knew the signals for the Galena Park team and readily shared them with his new teammates. With barely enough on the team, if two got hurt the game had to be called. Others throwing in with the team from time to time were Marvin Abbott, Ray Coulson, Clarence Coy, Ray Abbott, J. A. Riggs, Snoden L. Boyd, and Ray Kingsbury.[9]

It was dangerous watching the "Green and Purple" play. The playing field took up most of the cleared pasture and the spectators had to crowd along the edges of the field to watch. Occasionally there was more pushing and shoving on the sidelines than on the field. Although the team was spirited, they played terribly. They played six games that first year starting with Harrisburg. They lost three and tied three, a winless season. In fact, they never crossed the goal line that season, only got close a couple of times. Maybe it was the team colors that did not inspire a better performance. Subsequently, when a Houston team rejected a new order of green and white sweaters as not up to specifications, Pasadena quickly changed its school colors from green and purple to green and white and purchased the sweaters at half price.[10]

Marvin and Ray Abbott with their mother Minnie.

After football season other sports were organized. Baseball and basketball teams were fielded and entered the county meet competition. Johnny Meyers and Marvin Abbott represented Pasadena at the county meet in Crosby, each running in the 100 and 220 meter race. The girls were not going to be left out, so the old basketball team was revived for them. Initially long black bloomers and white middy blouses were again chosen as their uniform.[11]

In East Texas, the kids were raised with basketball. Football was an unknown game. When "Stoney" Phillips arrived in 1927 at the ripe age of 12, he had never seen a football game in his life. He was fascinated. J. Barton and Jesse Mae Phillips moved to Pasadena from Arp, Texas, with their children Rodney L., Weldon "Stoney," Herman "Tee Tie," Mary Alice, and Culley "Tut." Barton's younger brother Preston had arrived in 1921 and had given a favorable report on the community. Preston and Carrie were working on their family, which boasted Francis Janette, Lois, and Preston Arland. Caroline would be along shortly. Barton and Preston's youngest brother, Charlie Vernon, also came to town, but it would be a few years before he would settle down in Pasadena. At first, Barton would not let his kids play that rough game of football, only the familiar basketball. But Stoney risked a strapping and joined the team while still in grammar school. You see, there were not enough willing males in high school to fill the roster that year.[12]

By 1927 cheerleaders were chosen to support the school football team. A full-time sports instructor was chosen in 1928.

The Pasadena High School building was enlarged in 1928 and 1929.

Hugo Hartsfield had taken over as superintendent when Richard Gore left in 1927. Gore had married Janie Dowell, a graduate of 1926, and took a job with Houston Lighting & Power Company. Hartsfield was even more dedicated to the development of a sports program and got a gymnasium built in 1928, probably the second one outside of Houston. A girls' gymnasium and auditorium were added the following year. Although A. E. Jackson was the physical eduction instructor for the boys, Jack Horton was assigned the head football coach's job. Jackson assisted. The Phillip boys, Rodney, "Stoney," and "Tee Tie" perked up the football program starting in 1929. Helen Hollinsworth was hired to instruct the girls.[13]

Off campus, Jack Horton organized a Boy Scout troop and was later assisted by fellow teacher Phil Goodrum. W. E. "Pee Wee" Goodwin and Forrest Fisher also worked in the program. Edward Pomeroy joined the Scouts in order to get out of some of his chores. Hugo Hartsfield did not want the girls to be overlooked so he got active in the Masonic-sponsored Rainbow Girls. In fact, Hugo's basic interest was in the overall development of the students. He set up after-hour classes in vocational skills so that the students would have more than book learning. Since he and his wife, Bernice, also a teacher, did not have any children they sort of "adopted" the entire student body. And in addition to the three R's in the classroom, Hartsfield added other programs to the scholastic life of the community.[14]

A community musical program started around 1925 when J. C. Barolet of Houston started Pasadena's French Conservatory of Music. Barolet used a room in Aubrey Cruse's business building on the La Porte Road to teach music lessons and sell musical instruments. He offered singing lessons and some instrument instruction. Marguerite

Helen Hollingsworth re-established the girls' sports program.

Pomeroy was gifted with the piano and soon her brother Edward was given a French horn to join his sister for lessons. Others joined the group and Pasadena's first band was formed. In 1926 Barolet wrote "The Pasadena Band March." It was "dedicated to the Pasadena Band Boys and the General Public of Pasadena, Texas." Cruse was very supportive of the band

J. C. Barolet wrote the "Pasadena Band March" in 1926.

and would provide his Overland jitney on Sundays to take them around to neighboring towns to play concerts. They played Seabrook, Erin, and St. Anne's Catholic Church in Houston. After their performances they would always pass the hat and got enough to purchase a few more instruments, including bass and snare drums. Vick Kucera was more of a band director than a music instructor and took over the group. He would give lessons at Cruse's or the kids would sometimes go to his place in the Heights.[15]

The informal community band was absorbed into the school program in 1928. Kucera was hired to teach music and the "Pasadena Band Boys" donated the instruments acquired by the contributions from their Sunday concerts. Ten strong, the band now had a permanent home. Membership quickly doubled to 20 and black and white uniforms were acquired. Like so many other school activities, they were really community activities. Members for the band were drawn from all of the grades, from the teaching staff, from graduates, and from the community at large. Roy Glasgow played the soprano saxophone, Loise Williams the alto saxophone, and Edward Pomeroy the alto saxophone, baritone saxophone, French horn, snare drum, and bass drum. Billy Shaw played the trombone, Clyde Pomeroy the trumpet, and Ralph Hodges the trumpet, and coronet. Bessie Pomeroy played the trumpet or violin and James Goodman and John DeFee played the clarinet. Johnny Bess Hall played along.[16]

Meanwhile the school library was formalized and a librarian assigned. The first library was a community effort beginning in 1910 and opened in a room of the school by 1912. Over 500 books were available on a daily basis. A central library for the school system was established in 1927 with Mrs. Peggy Cowart in charge. With the growing demand on the school library, a public library system was opened to supplement the inventory of books.[17]

The Harris County library system deposited 100 books at the Pasadena school in 1922 but moved them to the post office the following year. Mrs. S. E. Lakin volunteered to take responsibility for the county books. The books could be checked out on Saturday afternoon, but had to be returned the following Saturday. Up to three books could be checked out at a time on each library card. Regularly the inventory of books was replaced by the county so that new titles would be available for circulation. The books were kept in a metal locker at Carrie Roberts's post office in the Williams Mercantile store on the La Porte Road at Main Street. Since Carrie was always there, she would check the books in and out. Ruth Williams volunteered as the librarian for a while. She lived right around the corner on Main Street and was interested in becoming a teacher. Mrs. Ethel Blakesley Hargrave took over as volunteer custodian of the county library books in 1926. The collection grew to over 200 as demand for the reading material continued to grow. One of her best customers was T. T. "Theo" Shaw. By the time he was a teenager he was collecting library cards from everyone in his family and checking out all of the books that he could for a week's worth of reading. Samuel Hain took over as postmaster in 1927 and then was replaced by Carroll Coolidge in 1928. Carrol had become a family man while working at the post office in Houston. He married Adelia Elizabeth Cammack and together they brought Sadie Dee and Lena Lou back to Pasadena.[18]

The school district also got into food service in the late 1920s. Some of the mothers volunteered to cook a hot meal for the grammar school students. The meal was usually a one-dish meal such as chili or soup prepared in a makeshift kitchen. Finally the trustees had a building erected on Broad Way at Munger and hired Tony Edgar and Constance Hodges to operate the cafeteria. The building had a kitchen, a dining room capable of handling 60 people, and living quarters for the Hodges. For a nickel you could get soup or a piece of pie. Sandwiches and milk were also available. Grammar school students Maurice Bell, Helen and Thelma Brubaker, Mildred and Jack Casey, Regina, Margarite and Opal Follis, Osi Mayo, Juanita and Mary Tingle, and R. C. and Everett Williams all appreciated the fancy dining hall. After a few years, Jessie Dee Thomas took over from the Hodges. Not surprisingly, Superintendent Hartsfield liked the idea of the lunch room and promoted the idea for the high school.[19]

James Cumberland "J. C." and Jessie Dee Thomas moved to Pasadena when J. C. took over as cashier of Pasadena State Bank from Aubrey Cruse in January of 1925. Their boys J. C., Jr. and D. Lamar "Top" were of school age. Daughter Juanita would have to wait a year. The Thomases lived on the northwest corner of Munger and Broad Way and were right across the street from the grammar school. By the time Jesse Dee took over the cafeteria operation all of her kids were in school, and she could make sure they had a proper lunch.[20]

James Cavitt and Gladys Billingsley brought their family to Pasadena in 1925 from Burleson County. James, Jr., and William Harvey were school age and Wanda Ynelle would be shortly. James took a job with Crown and sent word to his brothers about Pasadena. Harvey Cleo arrived the next year and took a job at Houston Lighting & Power. It was there that he met his coworker, Myrtle Blakesley. They were married in March 1927. That was the year that the rest of the Billingsleys moved to town. Mother Claudia had been widowed and remarried to Henry C. Clark. They brought the rest of the Billingsley children: Madge, Tommy Lee "T.L.," Birdie Mae, Oliver M., Irene, and Harry Hudson. Henry Clark was a blacksmith and did handyman worked around town. Oliver got a job at Sinclair and worked until retirement. T. L. worked for Foots Wilson at his icehouse until he graduated from school. He then went to work for Sinclair at 35 cents per hour (no premium for overtime), and it would be several years before he was advanced to 50 cents per hour. From Sinclair, T. L. went to the new Shell Refinery and would put in 41 years there.[21]

Jonah Boyd worked with J. C. Billingsley at Crown. He also arrived in 1925 and helped with the new construction at the refinery. Crown had closed their refining facility in 1923 and had just kept a small crew working at the tank farm and terminal docks. In 1925 they reactivated the refining plant and went back on-stream. Jonah and his wife Frieda Pauline came to Pasadena from Milam with their children Faye, Lawrence, and infant Wilbur. After a couple of years they added Helen Bernice to the family. Helping Jonah at Crown was Jacob Archie Worley. Being a single man when he arrived, it did not take him long to spot a local "pretty." Mildred Gray had moved to Pasadena in 1910 with her parents, Austin S. and Blanche F. Gray. The Grays were from Ohio and had moved south to farm. Arch and Mildred were soon married. Almost in celebration of the reopening, Lawrence and Blanche Sippy added Nathalie to the family. Nathalie was the last of the children, following Jeanette and Dorothy.[22]

What a change of scenery it must have been for the Shaw family! Thomas Thuel Shaw came from the Panhandle region of Texas to Pasadena to get a job at Crown. He moved his family down in 1928 and rented from G. A. Brown. The impact on the school system was immediate. T. T. and Edna Elizabeth had six children and would later add a couple more. With them came Thomas Theodore "Theo," Mary Francis, Buna Constance "Connie," Robert K. "Bobby," Billy Carroll, and Ray.[23]

Crown's reopening also brought Harry Jefferson "Bear" Tacker to Pasadena from Marlin via Freeport. Harry and Ruby Irene rented an upstairs room at the old Sam Allen house on Richey. Dorothy S. was only three and Alvin "Sonny" L. was only one. Edith joined the family a few years later. James B. Larson and his family were living in Galena Park when he quit Galena-Signal and took a job with Crown. His daughter Edyth had just entered the first grade so the family delayed their move to Pasadena. However, in the spring they purchased five acres in the Alta Vista area way out Shaver. James and Victoria Rose moved little Marjorie and James L. into the new house and let Edyth stay in Galena Park with a friend's family to finish the school term. A few years later baby Douglas would join the family. James's brother John Marion Larson was also living in Galena Park with his wife Wilabie when he took a job with Sinclair and also moved over to Pasadena. John might have been influenced to move to Pasadena because his wife was Charles Syfan's daughter. John liked his coffee so much that around Sinclair he became known as "Coffee George." James and John's parents had also been living in Galena Park along with their sister Julia. John Lewis and Lou Larson followed the boys and also moved to Pasadena, but left their daughter and her husband in Galena Park.[24]

Although he had been in town for a few years before he made his choice, Silas W. Brown had picked from the local single female population. He settled down with Lillian Brannen and Doris Evelyn became the apple of their eye. Silas was a superintendent at Sinclair and would put in 38 years there. Adison Basil "A. B." Freeman started with Sinclair in 1923. He and his wife took an interest in their daughter Fern Mae's education. He would put in 25 years with Sinclair and 18 on the school board. Also working at Sinclair was the new hiree Jesse David Downs. Jesse came from Louisiana with this wife Mamie L. and only child, infant Marna Ruth. Jesse would put in 42 years at Sinclair. J. B. Stewart was another employee at Sinclair and would become active in Pasadena's fire department. He and his wife Betty did not have any children.[25]

Nineteen twenty-eight was an exciting year. Roxana Petroleum Corporation purchased 800 acres north of the railroad tracks in the all-but-abandoned community of Deer Park. "Farmer" Edwin Rice Brown was one of the last to leave Simeon West's idyllic town. Like West, Brown had been beaten by the elements and finally moved away in 1927. His large herd of cattle reduced by hurricanes, disease, and ice. Only the once proud Deer Park 24-room hotel, the small depot, and the 1910 schoolhouse remained to mark the location of the former town. Roxana purchased land from several individuals, including Fred Martin. Fred and Floy Mae Martin had been in Deepwater since 1910. Their daughter Janette and son Francis M. had been born in the community and had attended the Deepwater School. Janette was working on her high school degree at Pasadena with good friend Mildred Tabor when Janette's father sold their farm and moved the family to Park Place. Not wanting to give up friends, Janette commuted daily to Pasadena the following year to finish her degree.[26]

Meanwhile Roxana changed its name to Shell Petroleum Corporation and broke ground in November on their $8 1/2 million oil refinery. Within a few months over 2,000 men were busy digging out the winter mud and building the plant. Deer

Park became a tent city overnight and every room in Pasadena was rented out. The traffic on the La Porte Road now daily resembled the summer Sylvan Beach weekend parade. Ford Model T's and Model A's, Chevrolets, Hudson-Essexs, Durants, Plymouths, and Willys-Knight's "Whippets" were bumper to bumper as the workers converged upon and dispersed from the construction site. Wages were 65 cents an hour for a 10 hour, 5 1/2 day work week. A pipeline was built through Pasadena to the new plant and a few farmers made extra money by selling the right-of-way across their property. They also hired out with their mules to help lay the line since the rainy weather had made mechanical equipment useless. McMaster and Pomeroy were hired to drill three wells for the new operation. [27]

Among the first people hired on the construction job at Shell were George Washington Graves and Grover Brown, then of Harrisburg. They were carpenters from Tennessee who had moved to Texas two years earlier in 1926. George had decided to leave Tennessee because jobs were scarce and his friend Grover decided to tag along. It was icy cold when George, his wife Effie, and children James and Rachel loaded into their Model T. Groves went home and got his wife Opha and their two young sons, only telling them that they were leaving and failing to mention where they were going. It was Arkansas before Opha learned of their destination and she broke into tears. She thought Texas was the end of the world and if the Indians and cowboys did not kill them, they would surely starve to death. The two families cooked on the side of the road and camped out the whole way since there were no such things as motels. Opha refused to help and Effie kidded her about her fears. They arrived in Houston on a cold and misty November 11, 1926, about dusk and rented cabins at Camp Dixie on 67th Street near Harrisburg. Homesick and knowing she would starve to death, Opha fell into the bed and cried herself to sleep. She told her husband that he had better take her body back to Tennessee for burial or she would haunt him for the rest of his life. But Opha did not die that night. In fact, with about three weeks of the relatively warm climate, the green trees and blooming flowers, she was convinced of Texas's beauty. She even sent pictures of them in the flowers at the nearby golf course on Wayside Drive back to her old home in Tennessee.[28]

As soon as accommodations could be arranged, the Graveses and Browns moved to Pasadena. They lived on Randall and ate their meals at Mrs. Brod's family diner. There was plenty of work at Shell so George sent for his older brother Ernest back in Tennessee. Ernest built a "room" on the back of his Model T truck and headed south to Pasadena. Besides working at Shell, George, Groves, and Ernest built houses and such. They were regulars at Whitman's Pasadena Lumber Company. Ernest built the first stucco house in Pasadena. It contained five rooms and cost $2,000. And like everyone else in town, when it was strawberry-picking time, all of the adults hired out to help pick berries. On the weekends they would strike out to explore and have fun. Galveston was a popular destination. On Sundays they attended the Pentecostal church. When the construction job ended at Shell, they all decided not to stay on and work in the operation of the plant because they had seen too many accidents and deaths due to gas fires and explosions. Louis Cloutier worked with them on construction and stayed on in plant operation. Five years later he would be killed in a plant fire, leaving his wife Winogene and young daughter Doris Marian. George and Groves were among the very first workers to show up at the start of construction of the plant and they finished the job as two of the last three to leave. They found another construction job at a grain elevator on the ship channel.[29]

James Guy Houston came from Athens, Texas, in 1929 to work on construction at Shell. He rented the shotgun house from Anna Pomeroy on Main Street that had once served as the first post office. Into its three rooms he put his growing family. His wife Alice J. had three girls to tend to: Helen Marie, Bessie Jo, and Clara Belle. Helen and Bessie were in grammar school and Clara was only four. Ashley Earnestine and Jacquelyne "Jackie" would be born in the little house.[30]

Shell Refinery officially "went on stream" on August 13, 1929, with an operating work force of 517 employees. While only about five percent of the work force lived in Deer Park, quite a few lived or would eventually live in Pasadena. Charles Stephen Hodges came from the Indiana/Illionis area to work at Shell in 1929. He and his wife Winona rented one of the Pitts' houses and then Dr. Boyd's place. Son Ralph was entering high school and would eventually be followed by Eloise, Barbara, Juanita, and Philip. Charles would work at Shell until retirement. Harry Jones stayed on after construction and was one of the few who lived in Deer Park. However, he and his wife Johnie Mae would move to Pasadena a few years later. Edward Frank "Hickey" Napp was transferred by Shell from Illinois and took the first cut of oil as the refinery went into production. Hickey and wife Ann lived in Houston at first with infant Donald Edward. It would be five years before they would move to Pasadena and stay.[31]

When Guy W. Butler went to work for Shell he made his home in Pasadena. In fact, he spotted one of Will Blakesley's younger daughters, Ruby, and went to courting. They were married in 1931. William M. Elder moved over from Mississippi to work at Shell and brought his wife Lillie Blum and children: Hazel, Marvin, Ruby and Sadie. Crowded into that pickup trip for the long trip to Pasadena was Lillie's father and mother, William L. and Katie Blum. William also took a job at Shell for a short while. Jimmie and Frances Willard moved in from Longview, Texas, for Jimmie's job with Shell. With them came Frances's mother, Mrs. D. B. Close, and younger sister, Mabel Grace Close. W. T. and Mary E. Hill came to town about that time and W. T. went to work for Shell. Daughter Thelma had just started school and Imagene was a year away. They bought a home on Main Street between Seventh (Park Lane) and Eighth (Jackson) streets. Around the corner on Eighth, Ben and Stella Powell rented a garage apartment from the Gores. Ben got on with Shell and wanted to live nearby. Their son James D. "J. D." was in the sixth grade but it would three years before their daughter Rachel would start her schooling.[32]

George Johan "Tony" Blanyer, Jr., was living in West Texas when Shell began to build a 450-mile pipeline from the McCamey oil field to the refinery. Tony signed on for the Deer Park to Brazos River section. After the pipeline was completed Tony continued to work for Shell. Tony was a photographer and took pictures for Shell and also opened Blanyer's Photographic Studio in Pasadena. While picking up his mail at the post office he met Nauvie Mae Cammack. Nauvie's aunt Adelia, "Aunt Dee," was married to postmaster Carrol Coolidge and Nauvie was living with them and working at the post office. Nauvie was from Madison County and had moved to Pasadena in 1927 to live with the Coolidges and to finish school. But the Coolidges were not the only relatives that Nauvie had in Pasadena. Emma Bell was a first cousin to Nauvie's mother and Emma's daughter Trannie was in school with Nauvie. Nauvie's uncle Houston Thurmand Cammack lived in town for a while and several years earlier another uncle, George W. Thomas, and wife Ella had lived here before moving to Humble. After graduation Nauvie went to Sam Houston State Teachers College in Huntsville. Also from Pasadena in 1929, Ruth Williams was completing her major in history and Virgie Freeman was a classmate. V. W. Miller was an English major from Roscoe, Texas, and would later be superintendent of schools in Pasadena. Helen Hollingsworth was from Leona, Texas, and would be teaching in Pasadena the next year. Phil Goodrum was graduating in vocational Agriculture and would also be teaching in Pasadena the next year. For a brief period Nauvie worked for the post office, met Tony, and the rest became history.[33]

Newton P. Hand moved to Pasadena in 1929 with wife Edith and children Floyd Newton, Wendell Phillip, and Mary Catherine. Newton got on with Shell and the family lived in one of T. A. Scott's cabins near the La Porte Road and Hargrave. Living in another cabin nearby was Robert Edward and Zada Mae Pendleton with their two boys, Robert, Jr., and Bill. Robert came over from Arkansas late in 1928 and got a job with Shell. The rest of the faimly joined him early in 1929. Zada Mae's mother and stepfather lived in nearby La Porte. The Pendletons would rent around town for a few years before building a home. Another Shell family in the neighborhood was the Brittains. George Carroll "Blacky" Brittain started working on the Shell pipeline in East Texas, settled briefly in Pasadena with wife Alice Irene and children Wilma Jean and George, Jr., went off to work on the Brazos line and then returned. By the time they settled permanently in Pasadena, Bryon Glenn had been added to the family. Although he did not work for Shell, Walter Earl "Pee Wee" Goodwin also lived nearby with his eight children: Carter, Truman, Kenneth, Marjorie Nell, Linwood, Walter, Jr., Bennie Allen, and Alfred. Pee Wee worked for Houston Lighting & Power Company.[34]

But not all of the activity in 1929 was associated with the construction of the Shell Refinery. The city government in Pasadena was quickly addressing the long overdue needs of the community whose population was officially estimated at 1,170 people. Besides the immediate need to get streets graded and drainage established, street lights were to be installed, a police force hired, a Board of Tax Equalization established and the city cleaned up. April 13 to April 30, 1929, was declared "Clean Up Days" in Pasadena. The citizens were to rid their property of trash and the city was to provide a truck to pick it up. However, the city did not have any place to dump the trash once they picked it up and it was soon discovered that some people were using Crown Hill Cemetery and vacant lots as a place to dump their garbage.[35]

But garbage was not the only thing in the wrong place in Pasadena. The new city survey showed that all sorts of obstructions were in the street rights-of-way. Houston Lighting & Power and Southwestern Bell were requested to remove their poles from the streets. J. M. Jackson had built his house in the street and he was requested to move it "in order that the City may open said street for traffic." Since Jackson was now living in Houston, his renter, W. O. Youngblood agreed to move the house. The city offered him the help of a tractor and driver for the job. Other residents were requested to remove fences and other obstructions from the streets.[36]

Mayor Gerald Conrad is pictured between Deputy Marshalls Alvin A. Ward and Earl A. Gregg.

However, the city was not the only one complaining about obstructions in the streets. B. B. Thornton, H. A. Carter, A. R. Cruse, D. C. Jackson, B. B. Tilley and others petitioned the city on August 5 to modify traffic enforcement and to remove the speed officers from the streets. The official speed limit in town was 20 miles per hour except on Shaver near the high school and the grammar school, where it was 10 miles per hour. Alvin A. Ward and Earl A. Gregg had been hired as deputy city marshalls. Since a municipal judge had not been hired, Mayor Conrad served in that capacity. As judge of the corporation court, Conrad received $2 for each case he heard. Pasadena quickly developed a reputation as a speed trap since the two motorcycle policeman were vigorous in their enforcement and very creative in hiding out of sight of oncoming motorist. During the first six months of the new city government and its traffic court, over $10,735 had been collected in traffic fines. Local businessmen were up in arms, claiming that the excessive enforcement directed by the mayor was running off potential customers on their way to and from Shell Refinery and Sylvan Beach. In fact, most people felt that the mayor was also using the two motorcycle policeman as personal guards. Claude Beverly, on leave from the Houston Police Department, was appointed to the newly created Office of Special Police on August 26, and O. C. King was appointed deputy city marshall on September 16 and ultimately replaced Ward and Gregg.[37]

Pasadena was still sort of a rough-and-tumble, independent town and the idea of a police force was not well received in some quarters. Mayor Conrad sent his two deputies into the drugstore one day to arrest "Doc" Atkinson and after Doc beat them up he went after Conrad. As Conrad was running down the street with Doc in close pursuit, he was trying to deputize everyone to get someone to stop Doc. No one volunteered for the job. Claude Beverly also had a run in with Doc Atkinson. Claude tried to catch Doc in an illegal poker game and climbed up a ladder to spy in a window. Doc had figured that was what Claude would do, so he sawed the rungs half way through. As planned, the rungs broke as Claude climbed the ladder, and he came tumbling down. Succeeding Claude, O. C. King had bought a big Harley Davis motorcycle and was also the target of some pranksters. They goaded the new motorcycle cop into chasing their car down Shaver Street. The dust from the shell paving was thick and King did not realize that Shaver deadended at Twelfth (Southmore). The motorist turned on Twelfth and King drove through the fence, wrecking his motor. Shortly afterwards he sold his motorcycle so that he would not tempt any more hooligans.[38]

It was about this time that an outhouse appeared on top of Coulson's Drug Store. Some of the young boys in the community decided for Halloween they wanted to do something a little bit different. Arthur Bently and Gertrude Moody moved to Pasadena in 1928 and rented the old Thornton place, located behind Coulson's and facing Shaver Street. A. B. went to work for Crown and Gertrude took care of the three children: Daisy, A. B., Jr., and Margaret. Gertrude was also very involved in the Baptist church and would read the Bible for hours on end while rocking on the large wrap-around porch. They were a distinctive couple; Arthur was little, thin, and quiet whereas Gertrude was very heavy set and outgoing. Despite their "downtown" location, they raised a few goats in the backyard. Since the Moody house, and outhouse, were next door to Coulson's, the mischief makers worked late at night to move the outhouse to its new location on top of the store. In later years, only Edward Pomeroy would admit his membership in the group. For another year, plans were laid to place a Model-T on top of Coulson's. Various pranks would occur over the next 10 years, with a "two-holer" appearing on the corner in front of the store as late as 1936.[39]

In July of 1929 the need for a bond election was acknowledged and 126 voters turned out on August 20 to vote in the first city bond election. Four bonds, totalling $120,000, were approved by over 80 percent of the voters. Twelve thousand dollars were to be used to pay for expenses already incurred by the new city, in particular roadwork. Five thousand dollars were to be used to construct a fire station, city hall, and library building. Fifty-eight thousand dollars were to be used to construct a waterworks and $45,000 to construct a sewer system. Charles Garfield served as the election judge with help from W. B. Williams, Robert Guinn, and Will Bailey. J. D. Parks and Preston Phillips had been appointed to help but did not participate. Like the city council election in April, the bond election was held at the Masonic Lodge building on the corner of the La Porte Road and Main Street. Within a few days land purchases were confirmed: the city hall at the corner of Shaver at Fifth (Shaw), the waterworks adjoining it on the west side, and the sewer disposal plant along the east side of Vince's Bayou on Fifth (Shaw) Street.[40]

A volunteer fire department was contemplated. South Houston had just organized a department with 35 men. R. A. Bell served as the fire chief with William Broussard and Bert Akin as captains. Greasy Smith now was superintendent of the Texas Fireworks Company and had designed a fire truck for the department. His company built and then donated the new vehicle to the community. Unfortunately, it would take another year before a group could be put together in Pasadena.[41]

The city was more successful in passing a fire zone ordinance that focused on the downtown area. The zone included the area bounded by the following streets: beginning on the La

Porte Road at Charles Street, going east to Shaver (misspelled Shaffer), then south across the railroad tracks to Sixth (Eagle) Street, continuing east along Sixth to Randall, then north to Fifth (Shaw) Street, going west on Fifth to Charles, and returning down Charles to the place of beginning. Since the buildings in this area were normally larger and closer together, the chance of fire was greatest. All of the buildings were made of wood except the brick bank building. Even though there had been no disastrous fires in Pasadena as there had been in La Porte, it was decided to require that no new buildings in this zone could be built of wood. The Pentecostals had had a small structure on Munger Street and it was accidentally set on fire when Lillian Dickerson left the heating stove unattended. Anna Pomeroy lived behind the structure, saw the flames, and got the people out before anyone was hurt. The city also adopted the National Electric Code, appointed George Thornton as the electrical inspector, as well as appointing a building inspector and a plumbing inspector. Frank DeFee operated a Red and White grocery store in one of those wooden structures along the La Porte Road. On September 22 he announced the construction of his two-story brick store which was to cost $15,000. The new store was to be built across the tracks on the old Dickerson store site on Main at Sixth (Eagle) Street.[42]

Meanwhile Clifford Bond was interviewing owners along the La Porte Road to see if they would straighten out the storefront building lines and the sidewalks. Pasadena was trying to improve its visual image. On October 2 city council changed the name of the La Porte Road to Sterling Highway. Constance (Mrs. T. E.) Hodges had submitted the name in honor of Ross Sterling. Sterling had been president of Humble Oil Company and one of its founders. He had built a huge home on Galveston Bay at Bayridge, purchased the *Houston Post* and the *Houston Dispatch* and had merged them together, and was chairman of the Port of Houston Commission. Sterling was also chairman of the Texas Highway Commission and probably responsible for getting the La Porte Road paved with concrete through Pasadena.[43]

Thirty-six years after the community was founded, Pasadena finally got a newspaper. Not one, but two. Things just seemed to happen in "twos" in Pasadena. Two townsites were established in the same area; one called Buffaloe and subsequently, Pasadena. Two developers founded the community; John H.

Burnett and Cora Bacon Foster. Two stores opened as the first mercantile store; Dickerson's and Tilley's. Two banks opened on the same day; Guaranty State and Pasadena State. And the city incorporated twice. Although two newspapers started, the competition was brief.

The *Pasadena Sun* and the *Pasadena Record* each sent reporters to the March 4, 1929, city council meeting. The *Pasadena Sun* first published a week earlier on February 28, 1929. It had purchased the subscription list and goodwill of the *Suburban Record* that had been printed in Houston, but claimed Pasadena as its home. The *Suburban Record* was probably an area-wide newspaper that had columnists from each city it served. Mrs. W. G. Anklee and Mrs. R. C. Williams were retained by the *Sun* to continue as local reporters. The masthead proclaimed: "Pasadena-The Coming Industrial City of the Golden Triangle." The *Pasadena Sun* was printed in La Porte, but promised to build with DeFee across the railroad tracks from downtown. The *Pasadena Record* received its second-class mail permit on March 4 and sent a reporter that night to the city council meeting. Both papers were vying to represent the city as the "official publication." On May 13 the *Pasadena Record* was formally selected. Clifford M. Bond was the publisher and he promptly hired Mrs. Ankele to be the society editor of the paper. The masthead proclaimed: (Pasadena) "In the Heart of Houston's Industrial District."[44]

An American Legion Post was formed in Pasadena in the fall of 1929. The application for the appointed submitted the name of the post as "Pasadena," but the approval came with the name changed to the Ben Bailey Post, No. 484. E. H. David was the post commander, L. N. Sippy, the vice-commander and Edgar B. Henderson, the adjutant. Other charter members were: W. B. Bailey, Jr., C. T. Coolidge, G. D. Coolidge, C. M. Davenport, C. C. Guinn, R. M. Guinn, Tom Laymance, Rev. John W. Mills, Jr., T. V. Newell, Preston Phillips, George G. Thornton, and A. C. Tilley. B. B. Brandon of Houston was also a member, and served as the sergeant at arms.[45]

Thomas A. Scott moved to Pasadena about 1924 and started selling real estate for a living. He acquired approximately five acres of the old Wright/Dickerson nursery land from E. M. Barnes in West Pasadena, fronting on the La Porte Road. The land ran north to Fifth (Shaw) Street and was between Lester Hargrave's subdivision on the west and Vince's Bayou on the east. He subdivided the land and filed a plat for Oak Park on

Louise Brown in front of the famous Whoopee.

October 11, 1927. Since Pasadena was unincorporated at the time he had to get the approval of the city council of Houston. He laid out commercial lots along the La Porte Road and residential lots along the newly dedicated street that ran between the La Porte Road and Fifth Street. By simply combining his initials with his last name, he called his street "Tascott." Lots on the east side of Tascott backed up to Vince's Bayou and Scott reserved the bayou frontage for "future wharfs." Nearby, J. S. Cullinan was considering dredging Vince's Bayou near its confluence with the Houston Ship Channel to provide for a wharf facility. Scott obviously envisioned a continuation of that dredging and the creation of the Pasadena Ship Channel with wharf sites from the Houston Ship Channel to the La Porte Road. If this occurred then his residential lots in section B would become commercial lots. However, sales went very slow; in fact, he only sold two lots out of the 29 in the subdivision.[46]

Not daunted, an amusement park was planned. Alton De Young, representing the Armitage Construction Company of Chicago, supervised the construction of a roller coaster type track for people to drive their cars on. The track was a 1,600-foot-long roadway that twisted and turned over 14 wooden hills and dips. One hundred and fifty thousand square feet of lumber was used and the track cost $14,000 to build. Although it was the rage in the North, this was the first one built in Texas. Riders got the sensation of riding waves as they drove their cars over the course. The ride was dubbed "The Whoopee" for the thrill one got as they topped a hill. The Whoopee was to be the first of a number of concessions planned for the amusement

Louise Brown, Selma Tillar, and Mary Brown stand on top of one of the wooden hills on the Whoopee.

park designed to capture some of the weekend and summer trade that travelled to Sylvan Beach through Pasadena. Concurrently, La Porte proudly proclaimed that its population was destined to become at least 100,000 people. To satisfy the food needs of its clientele, a concession stand called the Whoopee Inn was put up at the Whoopee. Edith Hearn worked there with Preston "Bert" Wheeler. In fact, there were specialty restaurants springing up all along the route. Mrs. Scannell in Pasadena was on a telephone party line with the San Jacinto Inn and Ye Olde College Inn in Deer Park. Harvey Fleming had struck it rich in the Alaskan gold rush and settled in Deepwater. He acquired one of the larger houses in town and turned it into a restaurant. Even J. B. Isaac opened a hamburger stand near Pasadena's high school and the La Porte Road. However, he was principally interested in the lunchtime needs of the students. Irma Parks took care of Isaac's place.[47]

But the main attraction at the time was the Whoopee. The Whoopee opened on Saturday afternoon, September 21, 1929, with a formal opening conducted by Mayor Conrad and Commissioners A. L. Dickerson and W. C. McMasters. They also had the honor of driving the first car over the track. Officials of the newly organized American Legion post followed as did a long line of automobiles. What a thrill! Even the most proper of dignitaries grabbed their hats and gasped for air on this stomach-heaving journey that stretched out the length of five football fields in rural Pasadena. Within a week over a thousand motorists had driven the course and could testify to its slogan, "A Thrill on Every Hill."[48]

Naomi Daily screamed every time she travelled over the Whoopee. Screaming did not stop 16-year-old Doris Barnes, who became somewhat of a regular on the loop. Since the trip could be pretty rough on a car, she was always catching rides with other people. Nearby resident Paul Brammer was fearless and regularly loaded up his car with willing thrill seekers. Harry Tacker would take his family and the bravest would ride in the rumble seat. Howard Pitts took his family over the hills and around the bends and permanently imprinted the experience on nine-year-old Julie Estell's mind. Almost everyone else in town had to try it, at least once. Everett Williams, approaching his 12th birthday, loved Saturday mornings when bicycle riders were allowed to run the track free of charge. He could pretend he was on one of the motorcycles that competed in the staged races, only he would not crash and get hurt like one of the policeman did. But speed could present problems. It was very tempting to get up a good head of steam going over the first hills on the straight course, only to lose control at the curve and crash through the fence railing at the far end. Cecelia Garfield, a recent graduate of Pasadena High School, and almost 18 years old, pointed out that a fast trip could mean a short ride.[49]

It was all good news to Gus Watson. He owned the old Hargrave gasoline filling station next to the entrance to the Whoopee on Sterling Highway (formerly the La Porte Road), and he could also make repairs. Estelle Wilson had a front-row seat to all of the excitement with her job at Watson's. Her older sister, Sylvia, thought the whole thing was awful noisy. Sig, Louise, and Collen Montgomery had even a better view of the activity. Their parents, Dewitt Talmage "D. T." and Lois May Montgomery, had purchased two lots in Scott's subdivision and D. T. helped pay for the land and their home by working on the construction of the Whoopee. Going to work was easy since the Whoopee was practically in his front yard. However that convenient location became a problem when the Whoopee opened because of all of the cars and the noise. When the commotion began, newlyweds Raleigh R. and Edna Mae (Irwin) Adams were renting an apartment on Hargrave Street. The Coopers lived on the corner and the Shermans and Brammers also lived nearby. J. M. Sherman had a job with Sinclair and would move over to Main Street shortly. His wife was Mae Hill and they had 12-year-old Wanda. The Pendletons had just moved to Texas from Arkansas to work at Shell and felt lucky to find a duplex on Tascott. George Berry's boy Jesse Lloyd had married another local, Olive Lakin, and they bought a lot on

Hargrave. Sons Jesse, Jr., and Lawrence L. were old enough to watch, and enjoy, all of the excitement at the Whoopee. But before the noise, traffic, and danger of the Whoopee could become a real problem, the world changed overnight.[50]

In his inaugural address on March 4, 1929, President Herbert Hoover echoed the optimism of the country in its continued prosperity. But optimism changed to speculation as millions tried to cash in on the instant riches promised by the stock market. Like the quick thrills of the first few hills on the Whoopee, people got carried away by the excitement of speculation. Racing into the first curve, the economy was travelling too fast to be safe, and, like the indiscrete driver, lost its confidence and crashed. The house of cards built with the glue of speculation came tumbling down on Black Thursday, October 24, 1929, when millions wanted to sell their overvalued stocks, and no one wanted to buy. Like the St. Valentine's Day Massacre six months earlier, they were set up, then mowed down. The panic spread and repeated reasurances by industry and government could not stem the tide. Built on confidence and credit, the economy began to collapse. Even as remote and independent as Texas was from the financial centers, the new trend took hold. The Whoopee was owned by a group from Chicago. It opened in September; the Stock Market crash hit in October. The admission price to the Whoopee fell from one dollar, to 50 cents and the last anyone remembered, maybe a nickel.[51]

Mayor Gerald Conrad would lose his wife Jewel to cancer at the beginning of the Great Depression.

XII

Into The Depression (1929-1932)

First and foremost, Pasadena was still an agricultural community. For 37 years it had made its living from the land, providing itself and others with the bounty of the earth. The Houston Ship Channel had grown in its backyard and crude oil had rooted its way into the neighborhood. Retail trade had flowered, from a single box of groceries at the Anderson boarding house to a respectable commercial district. The community organized itself, first with a school district, then several churches, and finally a city government. With each new enterprise came job opportunities. Families grew and so did the population. In 1930 Pasadena had a population of 1,647 residents. Three generations could now call Pasadena home, with children born here and dearly departed ones laid to eternal rest here. But the primary economic livelihood of the community had not changed. Since people had to eat every day, there was always a demand for Pasadena's produce. Many of those people that worked in the nearby industries also had roots in the farming community, so food and shelter were assured. Few of the industries laid off workers, although wages and hours were occasionally reduced and cash income shrank. Even during the Great Depression, Pasadena's people continued to work and thrive.

The depression did not hit with a bang, but rather as a panic that spread across the land. Life continued as usual in most parts of the country as the economy began to slow down. Banks were among the first to feel the crunch and began pulling back on credit. New house construction and new car purchases began to dry up. New orders and back orders dwindled. With each "contraction" more people lost their jobs. President Hoover was not in favor of government works programs to keep the economy moving, but Congress enacted the Public Buildings Act in March 1930 to provide jobs for the growing unemployed. By the end of the year Hoover finally realized the magnitude of the problem as the whole world began to sink into the depression.[1]

Houston's Mayor Walter Monteith complained that workers wanted more public construction jobs. Taxpayers threatened injunctions if the tax rate was not reduced, and the banks told the mayor to cut the city budget or they would not lend any more money. In Pasadena only a handful of people were on the city payroll and the only public construction was the city hall/fire station building and the sewer system plant. Although the town had committed itself to a bonded indebtedness for basic improvements, there was little other in the way of government expenses. Most taxpayers were landowners who derived their livelihood from the land and as long as people purchased food,

Pasadena's city hall also included the fire station.

there would be a basic flow of income. As long as most of them paid their taxes, the city would survive.[2]

Volunteers, and part-time employees kept the city expenses low. Mayor Conrad and Commissioners A. L. Dickerson and W. C. McMaster served without pay. City Secretary/Tax Assessor and Collector J. C. Thomas, City Attorney Quenton Wright of Houston, Electrial Inspector George Thornton, and Special Deputy Marshall for Animal Impounding J. A. Berry were only part-time employees. Only City Marshall O. C. King and city maintenance employee O. C. Pitts drew full-time salaries. Additional help was hired on a short-term or hourly basis. The major city activities in 1930 were grading and shell paving street, cleaning up the town, passing ordinances, and supervising the expenditure of previously approved bond monies. The first city water well was drilled by McMaster and Pomeroy Water Well Drillers. City hall was completed in June and T. E. Griffin was hired as the city clerk. There was a continual problem with the construction of the sewer plant and sewer lines and the original contractor had to be replaced. The city had grown almost 50 percent during 1929, from 1,170 people to 1,647. Real estate taxable values had grown less than 10 percent during that same period. In order to purchase the Type 99 pump and hose motor car American-La France fire truck (with 80 gallon booster tank) in November, the city issued $5,750 in "time warrants" to the seller. Cash was a scarce commodity for the city as it was for its citizens. By the first of 1931 it became obvious that the city had to watch its expenditures. In a move to reduce expenses, City Marshall O. C. King was laid off and city garbage hauling was discontinued.[3]

Bama Pitts

Mayor Gerald Conrad was personally having even a worse time of it. His wife Jewell was diagnosed with cancer and he lost her just before Christmas in 1930. She left Gerald with their daughters Elva, Hazel, Geraldine, and Doris. Two months later the death angel returned and took six-year-old Doris. To add an even sadder note to the occasion, Claude Pitt's wife Bama had been in treatment with Jewell and she also passed away six months after her.[4]

Commissioner McMaster defeated Mayor Conrad in the city election on April 7, 1931, and Aubrey R. Cruse and W. F. Williams were elected commissioners. Cruse took McMaster's

Mayor Clyde McMaster

place as the water and sewer commissioner and Williams took over Dickerson's job as the street and bridge commissioner. It fell to Clyde McMaster to keep a tight hold on expenses and still provide some form of ongoing city services. He recognized that running the new city government on little or no cash would be difficult, but felt that it was not hopeless. Clyde's jolly, optimistic personality was the type of leadership that the new government needed in order to survive the difficult times ahead. T. E. Griffin was given the city secretary and treasurer's job in addition to his duties as the city clerk, with a salary cut from $150 per month to $125. O. C. Pitts was reappointed, now as the water superintendent and also given the duties of sewer inspector and supervisor of the Street and Bridge Department. His salary was reduced from $175 month to $150. O. C. King was reappointed as the city police officer, but only on a part-time basis. City laborers G. M. Tacker received 40 cents per hour and D. H. McKissick got 50 cents per hour. Dr. O. F. Portwood volunteered to serve as the city health officer, "prompted through a spirit of civic pride for the city, and without pay."[5]

Although the city had a firehouse and a fire truck, it did not have a fire department. Joe Fells was appointed fire marshall in December of 1930 but resigned the following April without a formal firefighting organization. Percy H. Ulmer moved from Savannah, Georgia, in 1929 to take a job with Shell. In May 1931 he and his wife agreed to move into the apartment in the city hall/fire station building, to look after the fire truck and

Into the Deptression (1929-1932)

to set off the fire siren when needed. In order to formalize the group of volunteer firefighters that were trying to organize, the city passed the Pasadena Volunteer Fire Department ordinance on August 24, 1931. Membership had to be approved by city council and the initial members were approved on September 21, 1931. R. E. Dickerson was appointed as fire marshall with Paul Fleming as first assistant chief, Jim Stewart as second assistant chief and T. E. Griffin as secretary. Other members approved were: Ben Bailey, O. M. Billingsley, Horace Bunkley, W. T. Bunkley, Robert A. Burch, Aubrey R. Cruse, L. F. Edwards, Clifford Fain, Charles Griffin, Earl Guinn, Russell Hargrave, W. G. Hargrave, Floyd Hayney, A. W. Hearn, J. L. Hearn, Lance Hill, O. C. King, Lee Mitchell, O. Claude Pitts, Ben Skyes, Fred Spraggins, P. H. Ulmer, and J. A. Worley. Eighteen-year-old Jeff Fleming had to get a waiver of minority signed by his parents before he was allowed to join.[6]

Personal income became an important item during the Great Depression. With the collapse of the stock market, fortunes, both real and on paper, were lost almost overnight. The "spending like there will be no tomorrow" stopped. Unemployment began to rise and credit dried up. Soon savings were called upon to meet financial requirements and banks felt the strain of the drain on their life's blood. Caution became the byword as tomorrow became the unknown. Regionally, Texas was more conservative and not as cosmopolitan as the East Coast and its vulnerability was therefore less. Certainly thousands truly suffered, but most people in this area were able to adjust, improvise, and tighten their belts. Cash came to be in short supply and therefore a more precious commodity. Those that lived on credit, or extended it, hurt. But there was enough cash to keep the machinery of the local economy turning, even though it was in slow motion. And there was always food on the table, with enough to share.

Charles E. Syfan had moved to Pasadena from Galena Park in 1915 and purchased land on Twelfth (Southmore) Street adjacent to Vince's Bayou. His wife, Joessie, was a second cousin to Hugo Hartsfield. Their daughter, Wilabie, and her husband John M. Larson now lived across Vince's Bayou and daughter Mae Evelyn had just married Gentry Alvin Warren in 1930 and they were living at the Syfan home. Gentry's sister Ruby was married to Homer Brammer and probably encouraged her brother to move to Pasadena in 1929. Gentry was able to get a job at Sinclair with the help of Edgar Barnes and Asa

Hearn just before the depression started. And it was probably through fellow Sinclair worker John Larson that Gentry met Mae Syfan. Charles's youngest daughter, Josephine had just entered high school. Charles had served on the school board and was a charter member, and past Worshipful Master of the Masonic Lodge. Although he was manager of Cullinan's American Petroleum Company's plant on the ship channel in 1930 he still operated his Pasadena Pure Milk Dairy. He purchased a new panel body Ford truck in 1931 "to maintain the usual high standard of service that (his) trade (had) been accustomed to getting." Like most people in Pasadena, Syfan would spend money if there was a good reason. Likewise, if someone was in need, he would help out.[7]

Octavino Rocha moved to the Pasadena area in 1917 to pick strawberries. He later got a job at Sinclair, bought a car, and married in 1923. By the time the depression hit, Octovino and Leonor had a family, which included Pedro and Juan. Louis and Anita showed up shortly afterwards. It cost them $35 for each of the baby deliveries. Octovino moved his family to a small farm near the Syfan place and raised a lot of their food. Syfan put Rocha to work at the dairy helping J. W. and Eric Hill so that the family could have some cash income. J. W. and Eric Hill were brothers and nephews of Gentry Warren. R. Q. Mills, Sr., would later work with them and then be joined by his son R. Q., Jr.[8]

The Syfan dairy was not the only one in town during the depression. While living in the Allen/Waycott house on Richey, Harry Tacker operated a dairy in addition to his job at Crown Refinery. When the Tackers moved to Harrisburg for a couple of years, W. S. Dixon moved his family in and took over. His wife Lela M. ran the operation with the help of their eight children. Modine was the oldest girl, followed by Minnie, Hazel, Lela Kay, and Helen. Joe H., C. W., and Harold C. were the boys. The Dixon dairy was more of a family operation than Syfan's. And besides the dairy, Lela also ran a boarding house in the big two-story house.[9]

On his dairy located between Syfan's dairy and Will Parks's farm, Hadley White ran 25 head of cattle. Hadley and Kizzie White had moved to Pasadena in 1927 when Hadley turned in his sheriff's badge in Texas City and began working as the watchman at Crown. Like Syfan, Hadley had the dairy to supplement income and as a place for relatives. All of Hadley and Kizzie's children were married, but most of them would move to Pasadena by the time the depression took hold and help on the dairy. Their oldest son, Thomas C. "Tommy," was the famous boxer and although he frequently toured through town, he did not finally move to Pasadena with his wife Doris and children Josaphine and Tommy, Jr., until 1932. Claud and his wife and William B., his wife, and son Billy were there by 1930. The oldest daughter, Annie Laurie, and her husband William DeWitt Scott and son William Hadley came in 1927 with her parents from Texas City. Hadley and Kizzie's other daughter Thema Myrtle was married to Melvin Ralph Otterside, and they moved over from Harrisburg with son Melvin and daughter Doris. Melvin got a job in Texas City afterwards and moved the family there, only to discover that they liked Pasadena better. The family moved back and Melvin drove to work in Texas City every day.[10]

Gilbert Marvin and Sue Marshall Vick owned the Marvick Dairy Farm just north of Will Parks on Shaver. Marvin's brother A. T. Vick had purchased the farm early in the twenties with his wife, Sue. The Pasadena farm was their "country place" since they lived in Houston. When A. T. died in 1931, his widow married his brother Marvin. Marvin also inherited the electrical contracting business of his brother and continued the family tradition.[11]

John F. Johnson moved over from Cullinan's farm to Sinclair early on. It was a good thing, because he and Etta began working on a family that would total seven children. Mary Evelyn was born in 1919, followed by Leona Winona, Nina Bess, John Lincoln, Anna Mae, and Fred Everett. Sadly they lost Fred at childbirth and Anna in 1930 of appendicitis. It would be a few years before Clyde Franklin would arrive and finish the family. Helge and Lydia Gigstad also had seven children, but Helge just continued to farm instead of seeking a job with one of the industries. Helge arrived in 1908 and farmed, married, and fathered. Their children were all raised to work hard on the farm and taught that chores came before most anything else. Glenn A. was the oldest, followed by Leonard, Esther Amelia, Anna Mae, and Helge. Baby Isabel was stillborn and laid to rest at Crown Hill Cemetery. Ben A. and Iris rounded out the crew. None of the kids were quick to marry or leave home. Seven must have been a magic number for kids. George Edward and Virgie M. Poole moved to Pasadena about 1916 with daughter Virginia and son George. George got a job buildings oil tanks and the family grew with

Aubrey Harold, Irvin, Dan, and finally the twins, Marguerite and Maurine.[12]

Sinclair provided a continuing growth of jobs for the community. Henry Smith arrived in 1925 and weathered the depression here. He bought the McLean house on Tenth (Thomas) Street next to Vince's Bayou. Harrison McLean had built a large two-story house with porches upstairs and down. Harrison and Edith had been in Pasadena since 1900 and raised their seven children in the community. The oldest, Clifton Olive, was 10 when they arrived and he now was a teacher. Mary Lou became a nurse. Junior became an automotive machinist. Ira M. became a machinist for the railroad. William Carrol was the first of the children born in Pasadena on the family 30-acre-farm. Ward L. was traveling the country as a shoe salesman. Edgar L. was the last of the children. When Henry Smith bought the place he kept the 10 acres around the house and sold the 20 acres on the west side of the bayou to the Lone Star Cement Company for their clay pit operation. W. Earl was the oldest child, all of 18. It only took him two years to pick from the local beauties and marry Bertie Florrow in 1927. F. Aaron "Ike" was 10 and promptly went to school. Vera and Sally were younger. Henry's wife, Clara, was a stepmother to the children.[13]

Arriving shortly after Henry Smith and also working at Sinclair was Taylor Florrow. It was his daughter Bertie that married Henry Smith's son, Earl. Taylor and his wife still had 10 more children to deal with: Bertha, Oliver J., Francis, Eva, Vergie, P. A., J. L., Floyd and Lloyd the twins, and Jim Dick. Working with Smith and Florrow at Sinclair was R. E. Yeamans. He and his wife had moved to town and their children Edna and Olin were entering high school.[14]

Sinclair also provided a job for T. E. Griffin who arrived about 1925. His wife's elder parents, Jobe Smith and Sue Francis Thomason, came with them and would remain forever at Crown Hill Cemetery. T. E. and Elma had two sons, Jabe T. and Louis L.. After a while at Sinclair, T. E. tried being a salesman and then settled into working for the city of Pasadena for the next 27 years. Son Louis had not quite reached his 23rd birthday when he married Sena Bell Forrest. Sena Bell's family arrived in 1930 when Phillips Petroleum had transfered her father to the Pasadena plant. James Lee and Sena Larmer Forrest brought four of their six children. The oldest two did not come so Sena Bell had seniority. William P. "Bill," Jim Jr and John Wendell "Chicken" had to listen to their older sister. James Forrest worked with Dowe Wood out at the Phillips facility.[15]

David Winfred "Dave" Shannon arrived in 1918 to help with the construction of Sinclair. He brought his wife, Gertrude Mae, and their young children, Oscar Cleaver, Oley E., Dilla V., and Vina M. from Kentucky. He bought D. K. Jones's place between John Pomeroy and the Baptist church on Main Street in 1921. When Oscar got old enough he also went to work for Sinclair and married Irma Olive. Oscar and Irma made their home out Shaver Street in the new Alta Vista area.[16]

After a while, Gertrude Shannon's mother brought the rest of the Chambers family members to Pasadena. Sister Mollie Green had married Sebe A. Bandy and their family included Elmer J., Arvin E., Otha Dewey, Casper, and Mae. Sister Pearl was married to E. C. Crowe. Bob and Roy were the rest of the Chambers that came down. The Chamberses, Bandys, and Crowes settled down on Spooner Street across from the Shannons. The Shannons, Chamberses, and Bandys were carpenters and Crowe was a plumber.[17]

Elson and Ralph Blakesley had moved to Pasadena with their parents in 1902. Elson married George Brown's daughter, Valeria, in 1920 and got a job with Sinclair. Ralph married Robert James's daughter Mildred in 1925 and also got a job with Sinclair. But Ralph and Mildred took on another job, parenting with Ralph G. and Ann. Al L. and Charlotte Poirrier moved from Harrisburg with their son Louis in 1931. Al had a job with Sinclair and they felt that Pasadena was a better community to live in. They lived across from the high school on Shaver and a block from the grammar school.[18]

Deb Atkinson was glad he took a job with Sinclair in 1927 because his family had grown with the addition of Vernon and Josephine. Son Delbert also worked at Sinclair. Delbert and Thelma Lois's family now included Gerald and newly born Wilma. Interestingly, Deb had served on the school boards of Genoa and then Pasadena. Delbert began his political career by running for the Pasadena school board in 1931. It would take him a few tries before he would be successful. However, the Atkinsons would join the father-son teams of Bailey (Will and Ben), Guinn (R.M. and W.H.), Kruse (Oscar and Karl), and Pomeroy (Payson and John), who both served the school district. Also making it a family affair were a couple Parks (J.D. and W.S.) and Williams (Ben and Walter) brothers.[19]

Delbert Atkinson, right rear, is pictured with his brothers and sisters: Melvin, Nadine, Willard, Urvine, Josephine and Vernon.

John Everett and Nellie Carpenter moved to Pasadena in 1928 and rented in West Pasadena so that John could walk to work at Sinclair. At six years old, Allen was the oldest son, followed by James Ledon "Don" and Everett. John's brother Arlie arrived the next year and also went to work at Sinclair. John's other brother Price arrived shortly after that and stayed in Pasadena during the depression and then moved to Baytown.[20]

John Dearing was in heavy construction and moved to town around 1931. He married Warren Rawlins's daughter, Ruth, in 1931 and moved into the Rawlins' house on N. Shaver Street. John and Ruth started their family with Peggy Louise in 1932. William R. N. Pennington was also in construction, but mainly as a home builder. He had arrived in 1927 so was settled in by the time the depression hit. He and his wife Zelma and daughter Virginia lived on Spooner.[21]

Occasionally John Pomeroy and his brother-in-law Clyde McMaster would find it hard to make cash ends meet in their water well drilling business. John's mother, Anna, would sell a piece of her farming land whenever necessary to help finance the business. Being a good business woman, she would have John and Clyde sign a note for the loan and then make them pay it off, with interest, when they got another drilling job.[22]

Jim Hughes moved his family back to Pasadena in 1932 after living about nine years in Houston. The last six years he worked for the U. S. Department of Engineers on the Houston Ship Channel. Jim returned to take over the cafe Mr. Shine had operated on the Hughes property across from Crown Refinery. Besides providing meals for the refinery workers, Jim and Mattie provided food for the ships docked at Crown. Once they got the hang of the restaurant business Jim took a second job as a school bus driver.[23]

Also moving to Pasadena in 1932 were L. I. (initials only) and Wilma Shore Chapman. Like so many other farmers during the depression, L. I. had lost his farm in Michigan and had moved South to find a job. With little work in Houston, the Chapmans rented the old Whoopee Inn and moved to Pasadena to survive. With four children—Florence Evelyn, Barbara Joy, Lorna June, and George William—the two-room structure was a bit crowded. The family made do while "Dad" contracted to build houses in the area. It was a happy day when "Dad" bought an acre out in the country on Twelfth (Southmore) Street, and a little house to go on it.[24]

Pasadena had made its reputation by the crops that it grew and with an economy still heavily dependent upon agriculture, it entered the depression relatively uneffected by the financial strife growing in the country. Certainly there was a reduction in the demand for strawberries as a delicacy or luxury, but the demand for strawberries and other agricultural products for basic food continued. Friends and relatives who had previously moved to the cities to seek their fortunes began to return to the security of the farms. Some moved in with other families to save on expenses and some bought a small plot of their own. The developments of Golden Acres and Alta Vista began to fill with city folk escaping unemployment, or underemployment. Even those with industrial jobs still moved their families to the country in order to raise some of their food and to reduce their cost of living expenses.

The first section of the community/subdivision of Golden Acres was filed for record on September 28, 1928. Subsequently, two more plats were filed as the community began to fill. The area was generally on both sides of the South Houston-La Porte Road (Spencer) east of Preston Road. Definitely, "out in the country." Compared to Alta Vista, Golden Acres had smaller lots so a family did not have to spend as much money to have a place in the country. Joseph P. and Mary Sue Carlson were one of the first families to move in. They brought their children Margaret, Carolyn, and Ronald. Courtney E. and Blanche Farr followed with their children Byron Enoch, Vera D, Boyd L., Doris Eleanor, and Betty in 1929. James Samuel and Mary Brady Slaton bought one acre on Oak Street because a lot of the railroad employees were buying out in the Pasadena area. Unfortunately, Sam was laid off in 1931, so the family moved to Golden Acres from Houston and grew strawberries. James was the oldest, followed by Charles Elick, and infant M. Eugene. Thomas Ray and, subsequently, Mary Elizabeth were born in Golden Acres. Mr. and Mrs. Frank Hancock moved out and opened the first grocery store in the community. Louis and Winogene Cloutier and daughter Marian lived there while Louis worked at Shell.[25]

Claude P. "Mac" and Wilma McMurry moved from Lake Charles, Louisiana, in about 1929 and settled in South Houston. They brought with them their one-year-old son Robert Charles and Wilma's mother and her family. Avis (pronounced A-vie) Plaisance headed up a family of six children: Wilma (now married to McMurry), Malcolm, Rowena "Ena," Donald, Laura Lee, and Douglas. Mac's brother-in-law, Roy Henderson and his mother lived in South Houston and Roy thought that he and Mac could make a lot of money by opening a garage there. A lot of people were travelling from Houston to Galveston on the highway through town and there were not any garages in the area to service the automobiles. Unfortunately, it was like the Whoopee story; they opened just before the depression hit and their potential business evaporated before their eyes. Mac went to work at Shell Refinery and heard about a service station for sale in Pasadena. A man had taken over H. A. Carter's Shell station, but did not know anything about mechanics and was losing money in the business. Mac went to Pasadena State Bank, borrowed the money, and bought the station. He sold his home in South Houston and moved his family, which now included Wanda Rea, into the apartment at the rear of the station. He also had bought some land in Golden Acres and moved his in-laws there to farm. The Plaisances could raise produce and other food for the table while the boys could help at the service station to get what little cash they needed.[26]

Alta Vista was platted as a subdivision in 1927 and since Pasadena had not yet been incorporated, and the property was literally out in the country, approval was granted by Houston's city council. Pink and Addie Carpenter were the first to move in and bought a company-built house on Fresa at Lafferty. Edith and Mildred were in grammar school in Park Place and transfered at midterm to Pasadena. Milton "Buster" was a couple of years too young for school at the time. Pink worked as a machinist for Southern Pacific Railroad. About six months later Guy H. and Beula Elizabeth Livingston bought four acres on the corner of Shaver and Fresa (the other end of a long, long block from the Carpenters). They moved from Baytown and little George W. started third grade. Guy was a contractor and competed with C. C. Freeman for local jobs. Later on, during the depression, Guy's step-sons Harry and Carl Hillman moved in for a while as did his daughter Edith who had separated from her husband. The third family to arrive was that of Arthur and Carrie Bell Howard in May of 1928. Arthur also worked for Southern Pacific Railroad and thought Pasadena was a better place to raise his children than Houston. Thomas P. and Arthur F. were 11 and nine at the time. The Howards did not realize that the depression was just around the corner. The same was true with James B. and Victoria Larson when they moved over from Galena Park in the spring of 1929. Whitney Patrick was a cotton broker in Houston and he bought near the South Houston-La Porte Road (Spencer).[27]

After the depression hit, Clyde James Strait must have gotten the same message about good country family living, probably from Pink and Arthur, since Clyde worked for the American Railway Express Company in Houston. Clyde and and Mary Strait moved their family to Alta Vista in 1930 and bought the Patrick house. Their kids ranged in age from two to 19. Charles Earl was the oldest, followed by Clearance and Mary Louise. Next came Aruther, Florence, and William Everett "Billy." Christine and Leonard King were too young for school yet. Thomas and Edna Shaw moved out from Pitts Street and located on Westside Drive near the Howards with their six children. The family increased when Albert Howard and Betty Ann were born there. Ed and Mae Williams bought over by the Carpenters on Lafferty and moved there with their daughters Marie and Irene. Andrew Neugebauer and Bessie McCollough tied the knot and moved to the corner of Shaver and Westside. Cleaver and Irma Shannon lived on the other side of Shaver, south of the Neugebauers and near the Larsons. W. D. McDowell was a train dispatcher and moved his family to the country from Houston in 1932. Son Charles "Buddy" transfered from San Jacinto High School and his sister went to the grammar school.[28]

Among those moving, or returning, to Pasadena was Adolph Herrera and his family. Adolph had farmed strawberries in Pasadena from 1915 to the mid 1920s and he returned in 1932 to oversee the field hands that worked at Benart Farms. The 60-acre-farm was located on the south side of Twelfth (Southmore) Street between Vince's Bayou and Main Street and was owned by the Houston wholesale produce company, Baldwin and

Mr. Bolin and family inspect the strawberry fields at the Benart Farm south of town. The Montoyas, Hererra, Adames, Munozes, Sanches, Cardenas, Zepedas and Flores worked the fields.

Temporary help, mostly Mexicans, were brought in to help with the strawberry picking.

Cargill. Adolph had worked there before and several of his children had been born on the place. Tomaso, Conrado, Paul, and Felicia would now divide their time between school and helping to pick the ripe berries. Minnie was too young. The oldest daughter, Julia, would soon start to notice fellow picker Jesse Rivera. Mr. Bolin was the local agent for Baldwin and Cargill, but he also worked at Sinclair so he left the day-to-day operations to Adolph. During this period the place was frequently referred to as the Bolin farm, especially by the pickers. The Herrara family lived in the large two-story house on the

Felicitos Montoya and family were among those that came to pick strawberries in Pasadena and stayed permanently.

property and maintained a large garden nearby. Besides the other families that lived year-round on the property, additional berry pickers were brought in to help from December to April with the harvest.[29]

Because of the depression, everyone in the community turned out during the strawberry picking season to help in order to earn some extra money. Other workers were brought in from Houston and elsewhere to help. Overseeing experienced and inexperienced workers alike kept Adolph very busy during the picking season. Excelsior and Klondike strawberries were still the main varieties raised. They were both round berries with the Klondike the larger and the Excelsior the sweeter. Pickers were given carriers that held either 6-, 12-, or 24-pint containers. Both the carriers and the containers where made on the place. When they filled their carriers, they would turn in the pints and get cardboard tokens, which were exchanged for cash at the end of the week. The tokens could also be used as "currency" at the local stores.

Lawrence Garfield Tabor moved to Pasadena about 1916 with his wife Vina and children Thelma, Rex, Mildred, and Bobbie. L. G. built oil tanks for Petroleum Iron Works in

Tokens were given to the strawberry pickers for the number of pints they picked. At the end of the week the tokens were exchanged for cash.

Oklahoma and was transferred down to the Pasadena area because of the industrial construction along the new ship channel. First they rented from the Moechel's. In 1918 L. G. bought 10 acres from I. L. Pitts at the northwest corner of the future Pitts Street and Shaver. Although L. G. travelled a lot with his tank building job, he operated a strawberry farm. His wife's brother, Calvin I. Barnes worked with L. G. at Petroleum Iron Works and moved to Pasadena with them. While off on a construction job in Arkansas Calvin met his wife to be, Gracie, and brought her back. Together they added Leatrice and Norma Jean to the population of the community. When Calvin was not building tanks, he was helping with the strawberries. Tabor had tokens about the size of silver dollars and in 8-, 12-, and 24-pint denominations. When the strawberries were ready to take to the railroad loading shed, Thelma and Mildred would dress up in their Sunday best and drive them to the shed. It seems that pretty ladies could get a slightly better price for their berries than the boys could.[30]

One of the boys that showed up at the loading shed was Paul Herrera. Ten-year-old Paul helped his father at the Bolin Farm by passing out the tokens and helping to deliver the strawberry crates to the railroad loading sheds on Sterling Avenue (Highway 225) near Main Street (know to the pickers as "Road One"). Although tractors and trucks were now doing a lot of the basic work on many farms, Dolly, a white mule, carried the load around the Bolin farm. Whenever Adolph had to stay at the railroad loading shed, he would put Paul on the driver's seat and instruct him not to touch the reins but to give Dolly her head. With Paul sitting upright and pretending to be driving the wagon, Dolly would return the familiar route home to the farm for another load.[31]

Alfred Marion and Laura Gore moved to Pasadena in 1917 to farm. They had nine children who could help with the work: Wheeler, Boyd Lee, Elwood Buck, Clara, Taylor, Homer, Lester, Mildred, and Velma. The Gores had been struggling to make a living in Milam County. But when their corn grew only waist high, their entire hay crop was only one and a half bales, and their house burned to the ground, they decided to leave. After a short stop in Houston, they arrived in Pasadena and began farming on rented land between Jim Hughes's place and the ship channel. Crown Refinery bought the land they were farming and began construction on its plant. A. M. got enough money hauling gravel for the refinery construction to move his family back to Milam County. After another bad year of picking cotton, they returned to Pasadena. This time they bought 10 acres from Eighth (Jackson) to Ninth (Texas) streets between Randall and Wafer. They had to chop down four pine trees on the ship channel to make utility poles to have electricity run out to their new farm. Six acres went into strawberries. But one by one the children got other jobs as they grew up and moved. Most of the boys worked as boilermakers and tank builders (riveters), but Pasadena was still their home. Lester took a permanent job with Sinclair in 1930 and settled down for the next 12 years.[32]

Samuel D. "Sam" and Louise Boyd moved their family from Houston to the Florentine Settlement in the summer of 1931 to live with relatives. Sam was a dirt contractor and worked all over the county. Since their son George Albert was in the third grade, and daughter Nancy Ann was only four years old, Sam decided to move the family into Pasadena proper to be closer to the school. They bought a house on Eighth (Jackson) and Spooner, with Gores living on both sides of them. Eighth Street was on the southern edge of town with nothing but fields below them.[33]

A couple of blocks away from the "Gore Strawberry Patch" Walter Williams had one of the largest strawberry farms in town with 16 to 20 acres in berries. He also used tokens, but his were metal and sized according to pay, not number of crates picked. Robert Ernest Hughes picked strawberries on the Williams place. But Ernest made off with the sweetest prize, he married the boss's daughter, Jennie Elvira Williams.[34]

The Missionary strawberry was also grown, but it was used for a special purpose. A large, tapered berry, it was picture perfect. The berries were set aside and placed on top of the individual cartons just prior to shipment. They were also picked for special orders where the appearance of the fruit was important, like at restaurants and banquets. Although they were not the sweetest, they were the prettiest. Since the Missionary was a favorite for the children to eat, only special workers were allowed to pick the Missionaries. Many a child got in trouble by eating these "toppers." However, the children were given responsibility on Saturdays to help operate the roadside stands and to sell the berry pints, two for a quarter. With industry workers and weekend travelers on the highway, the roadside stands became a regular sight as they sold whatever was in season. This was certainly easier than getting up at

5:00 A.M. and going to the Farmers' Market in Houston to sell your produce [35]

Unsold strawberries, or unsaleable berries also had a use. Homebrewed wines and beer were not unheard of in Pasadena, even during Prohibition. Wine from strawberries was as popular as that brewed from the wild grapes that grew across the ship channel at the ferry landing. During Prohibition Mrs. Herrera made extra money by selling some of her brew to regular customers from Houston. The men would also use the opportunity to hunt small game while they were out in the country. If they travelled out at night they would get Mrs. Herrera's little son Paul to ride on the fender of their car with a flashlight as they hunted for rabbits. Pasadena was still mostly country, especially south of Twelfth (Southmore) Street and east of Wafer.[36]

Bill Carlisle and Charley Cook had enticed Sam Quinn to Pasadena in 1917 to grow strawberries. After a few years Bill drifted off with his family and Sam took a job with Sinclair. Charley continued to grow strawberries. Charley and Alpha Cook brought plenty of help with them in 1917. Beatrice, Ervin R., and Norman were out of school and could work the farm full time. They also got outside industrial jobs to add cash to the family budget. Virgal J., Thurman B., and Clarence F. were of school age. Curtis N. and Grace R. were too young for school. For a while they moved to Harrisburg, but continued to farm in Pasadena. Charley rented the old MacNider place from J. S. Cullinan and worked it with W. S. Marsh. Mr. and Mrs. J. J. McLaughlin were hired in 1927 to caretake Cullinan's place and were well liked. When the depression hit Charley moved his family to the MacNider house and farmed about 13 acres. But Charley had his own personal depression. His partner, W. S. Marsh, did not work out and had to be let go, the MacNider rent house burned down in the fall of 1931 and they suffered two years of back-to-back crop failures.[37]

Hunting was a popular pasttime and provided ample food for the table for many families during the depression. The marshes along the ship channel were an excellent place to hunt geese and duck. Wild turkey were found across the channel. The prairies were especially good for quail. A person could quickly determine if they had scared up an eating bird by its wing motion. If the bird took off with a steady flap, it was game; if the motion was flap and glide, then the bird was not worth shooting. Rabbit, deer, squirrel, and other small animals were also popular to supplement the dinner meal. Many a Pasadena resident turned to fishing for food and for profit. Earl Newell had a car and he would round up a bunch of single men and they would go fishing. They would rent a cabin down in San Leon for a weekend or longer. Glenn Brown got a commercial fisher-man's license so that they could sell the fish. They would get upwards to a nickel a pound for their efforts. Skinny Dickerson, Rusty Hargrave, Teeler Howell, and T. T. Shaw were a part of the regular gang. The Muecke brothers had been making their living as fishermen in the area since before the twenties so they knew the ropes when the depression hit. Louis John Muecke, Jr., was the oldest and Wesley M. was the younger. Louis and Bertha Mae began their family with Louis A. in 1920 and then added Myrtle Ann, Jewell, and Kenneth. Bertha's younger brother Bert Weinberg was also living in the household. Wesley Muecke lived next door with his wife Amelia and son Wesley, Jr. Their grandfather Fritz Raddue lived with them for a while. Wesley was also a steward in Pasadena's Methodist church.[38]

Another unusual "crop" harvested on the Bolin farm in Pasadena was arrowheads. Adolph had found many arrowheads when he worked on the Baldwin (Bolin) farm earlier, especially near Vince's Bayou. He put his collection in tin cans and would pay the field workers for each one they found. The Brubaker children also found lots of arrowheads along Vince's Bayou when they lived next door to the Will Parkses on Eleventh (Harris) Street. Paul Herrera found a large one, possibly a spear point, near the mouth of Vince's Bayou while his father was cutting the grass at Crown Hill Cemetery with his mule-drawn cutter. It was hard to realize that the only humans in the area 120 years ago were Indians. They had roamed the land for upwards of 10,000 years and all that remained of their occupation were a few arrowheads and some shell mounds that marked the locations of their campsites along the edges of most bayous and lakes. They did not build houses, buildings, roads, or fences. They did not grow crops or domesticate animals. They simply wandered the land, living off its bounty. The French traded with them, the Spanish tried to Christianize them, Stephen F. Austin's settlers fought them, and eventually white man's diseases, such as smallpox, killed them off completely. A large burial mound was discovered in an oyster shell reef near Seabrook in 1896, but the railroad was interested only in the shell for ballast, and the bodies disappeared. It

Into the Deptression (1929-1932)

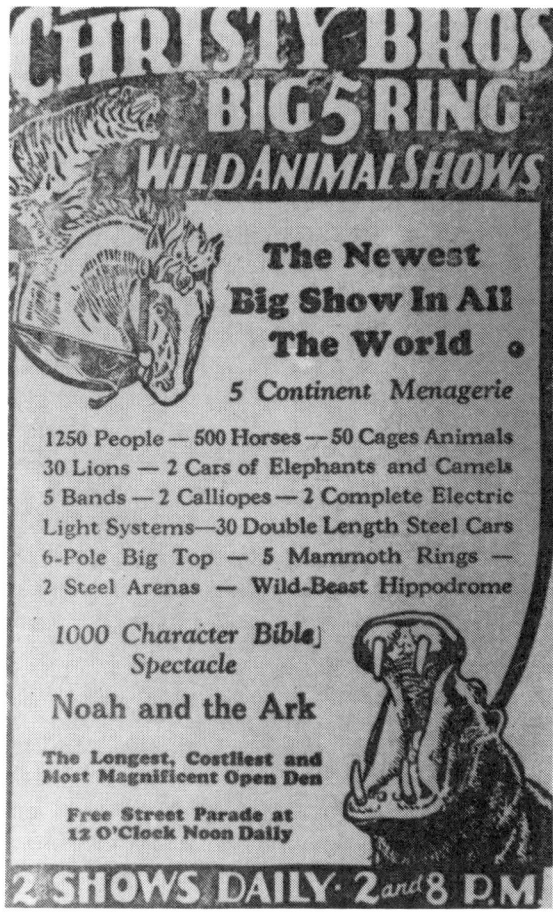

When the circus hit town, flyers were distributed for the Christy Brothers Circus daily performances.

would be several years before any formal archeological investigation of the Indian occupation of the Gulf Coast area would begin. Meanwhile, Paul put the large chipped point in his pocket so that it would never be lost again.[39]

While the souvenir of the Indians in the Pasadena area was saved by Paul, George Christy was distributing artifacts of his colorful past. P. T. Barnum was the inspiration for the circus entrepreneurs of the twentieth century. One such entreprenuer was George Washington Christy, who, at the age of 18 purchased the defunct Son Brothers Circus in 1908 and began his career as a showman. He created the Christy Hippodrome Circus and modernized its image in the 1920s to the Christy Brothers Circus. Even though Christy was the sole owner, it was popular to claim to have "brothers" in the business, like the Ringling Brothers and Cole Brothers. George was quite the showman and was dubbed "The Little Barnum" for his style. At one time he operated the third largest circus in the nation and played to audiences in the states and abroad. After wintering in Beaumont for several years, he moved his headquarters to South Houston in the mid-1920s. He had the largest collection of circus wagons in the world and was the first to introduce the five-ring circus format. It took 20 railroad cars to transport his show from its South Houston home. Even after many other circuses stopped the practice, George persisted in providing a street parade before opening his show in each town.[40]

South Houston was struggling with new-found growth when Christy moved to town. Wallace Warwick Meador was mayor, M. E. Killough and G. P. Black were commissioners and R. C. Adams, and later J. E. Dodd, was the city secretary. Meador was one of the Meador boys that came in 1908. He and others sold Christy several lots in the industrial section along the railroad track beginning late in 1926 and probably discussed some of the changes about to happen in the community. The South Houston Electric Company was given a franchise in January 1927 and then was bought by the Houston Lighting & Power Company in May. A private water franchise had been let in 1925 but failed to materialize. So the community reorganized its city government to give it more municipal authority. Then a bond election was held and $59,500 was approved for a waterworks and $15,500 to pay off prior city indebtedness. Besides attracting Christy to town, the city needed to keep its major industry, the Texas Fire Works Company. The company employed 65 people and because of the potential for explosions and fire, it needed a reliable source of water.[41]

However, Christy's circus made more of a visual impact on the community. At first it was startling to stumble upon Christy's elephants, giraffes, and other exotic animals calmly grazing on the prairies of South Houston and Pasadena. Quickly it became an amusement and a special treat for the children. Most every Sunday there was a crowd making the drive down Spencer Highway to watch the animals in the pasture and then on to the corral west of town to see the zebras and camels. Seventy-five years earlier Frank Lubbock had boarded camels at his ranch on nearby Sims Bayou and they too attracted the curious from Houston and Harrisburg to stare at the strange beasts. As if that was not enough excitement, each Christmas George would give a special free circus performance for the children of the area and gave each of them a gift for attending.[42]

Always the innovator, Christy came to the rescue of the county when it was paving Spencer Highway with shell one wet and muddy winter in 1930-1931. The highway was known as the

South Houston-La Porte Highway at the time and would be renamed in honor of the new county judge, Mr. R. H. Spencer. The carloads of shell were delivered to the rail siding near the circus grounds, but the wagons and trucks could not maneuver in the mud. George rebuilt a few of his circus wagons so that they could be steered from the front, and pushed by his elephants from the rear. With 21 of his pachyderms, they spread the shell along the roadway. Elephants were also used to move the railroad cars into position for unloading. Spencer Highway was probably the only road in Texas paved by elephant power.[43]

Christy could put on a terrific show, but when the depression hit, few could afford the thrill. George tested the waters by sending out a smaller show than usual in the spring of 1930, but it returned home with sad news before the season ended. Although the Christy Brothers Circus never performed again, George did put together a small truck show under the name of Lee Brothers Circus and sent it out for a while. Slowly and reluctantly, he began dismantling his circus. One by one his animals, wagons and equipment found homes elsewhere. He did continue special local performances, in part to keep his spirits up, and also to spread cheer during an unhappy time. And for a long time his elephants continued to graze along Spencer Highway.[44]

George was one of many who helped his neighbors during the depression. South Houston's Texas Fireworks Factory would give free fireworks to the local youngsters for the holiday celebrations. Roy Treadwell put in a large garden and shared all of its bounty with those that were less fortunate. Bill Pendleton was regularly sent to DeFee's grocery to purchase weinies and buns to share with the hobos in town. They would always camp under the Sterling Avenue bridge over Little Vince's Bayou and use the water to brew their coffee and cook their meals. Bill enjoyed eating with them and listening to their stories. Carey Williams would hit the rails regularly with Kelvin Glasgow, and at one time Carey was elected King of the Hobos.[45]

A canning factory was set up in Pasadena at the corner of Johnson and Sterling (La Porte Road) Avenue so that fresh produce could be preserved for eating at other times of the years. Annie Evelyn Brannan worked as one of the supervisors. Bertha Muecke worked there after her husband Louis J. died. In Golden Acres, a Home Demonstration Club was organized to help the city folk adjust to country living. Learning new domestic skills were Mrs. J. P. Carlson, Mrs. Bessie Cuthbert, Mrs. E. G. Dalhaus, Mrs. Mary Everson, Mrs. C. E. Farr, Mrs. S. P. Handy, Mrs. George Jackson, Mrs. Margaret Morris, Mrs. Rosa Morris, Mrs. J. S. Slaten, Mrs. E. A. Stake, Mrs. James Stowers, Mrs. J. I. Stucky, Mrs. John Tognacioli, Mrs. Agnes Williams, and Mrs. Mary Wilson.[46]

Sharing, bartering, and credit were a part of everyday activities. When subscribers on the Pomeroy water system were not able to pay their water bill, they simply bartered a service or product. Paul Fleming gave a lot of "free" haircuts to the Pomeroy children. Little Allen Carpenter delivered the *Houston Press* newspaper around town and also traded Paul for free haircuts. Dr. Portwood had all the food he wanted to eat. Anna Pomeroy always had a basket of freshed baked goods to give to families in need, and it did not make any difference to her if they belonged to her church, or even went to church at all. Many businesses continued to let their customers charge their goods as they had done when farming was the only source of income. Foots Wilson delivered a lot of ice and firewood on credit and Will Bailey sold gasoline and groceries on credit. Most of the customers paid, but Wilson and Bailey would end the depression with a handful of I.O.U.s and almost out of business.[47]

Some sharing was not exactly voluntary. Like their parents in years past, the children still liked to raid watermelon patches and fruit orchards for their sweet treats. Hunger was not the need, just childish thrill. However, they would steal only what they were going to eat. More than that would be sinful according to the Bible. Sometimes the kids would have to prepare their escape in advance if there was a possibility that a caretaker would spot them. John Richey's old pear orchard behind the Lone Star Cement Company's clay pits was a case in point. The caretaker kept his shotgun loaded with bird or rock salt shot and would chase kids out of the orchard. Some of the younger children resorted to raiding the secret storehouse of their older siblings in order to reduce their chances of getting caught by an adult.[48]

Learning to make do, reuse, and to do without was a lot of what it was all about. Experimentation determined how far you could adapt. For gasoline, a person could substitute cheaper kerosene once the engine got hot. On trips you would tank up with gasoline before you went to bed and then crank up the next morning. When you refilled during the day, kerosene worked in the hot motor. In an emergency, kerosene could also be used as antifreeze in the radiator. However, if you left it in too long it would rot the rubber hoses. And if you scratched yourself, or got chigger bites, just rub on a little kerosene for first aid. When travelling and working "on the road" Pomeroy's water well crew would find a service station to fill up at night and then get the operator to let them sleep in the service bay overnight. The men would travel with cots to sleep on. If the night was chilly they would cover up with newspapers and then put a wool blanket on top to keep the body heat in. If their feet got cold, they simply put paper sacks over them and tied them on with a string. They could also use the sacks inside their socks to keep warm during the day.[49]

Luther Pickett would stop at DeFee's and buy yeast cakes on his way to school. The yeast was supposed to supplement the vitamins in his diet. Instead of dissolving the cake in water and drinking it, he would just put it in his mouth and eat. Once in a while he would sort of foam at the mouth. Little Harry Riley would raise a stink around flu time. His mother, May, would make him wear a bag full of a milkweed concoction (*asclepiadaceous*) as a cure for a variety of diseases. Mindful of its smell, Harry would leave the bag hanging on the fence behind Tom Moore's house while he was in school and then put it back on when he returned home. Dorothy Tacker hated to wear shoes to school so she would leave her shoes under the Vince's Bayou railroad tressel while she was at school and then put them on as she returned home.[50]

Children were always being inventive in keeping themselves busy. Bill Pendleton liked to play baseball or hockey (with a can or a rock as the puck) and would steal one of the pickets off of the Pomeroy fence to use as a bat or a hockey stick. They were just the right size. Lawrence Tabor strung a cable between two trees and put a pulley on it so that his children could slide across the yard up in the air. Mildred got her share of thrills and a scar to prove it. Cecille Garfield also took her turn on the tree trolley. Clyde Pomeroy devised a two-chair elevator with a cable and pulley. One child would sit in the chair on the ground and the cable would go up and over the pulley hung from a tree branch. The other child would climb the tree and get in the chair on the other end of the cable up in the tree. The first child would rise and the second child would be lowered to the ground. This worked well until one day "Chicken" Forrest's

Bessie and Clyde Pomeroy borrowed the Glasgow donkey for the two block ride to school.

mother called him home and he bolted out the chair when he was lowered to the ground. Unfortunately Clyde was still in the chair that had been pulled up into the tree and without Chicken's weight to keep him suspended, he came crashing down on top of the surprised Chicken.[51]

Nicknames were quite common and seemed to be particularly popular during the depression. "Foots" Wilson's sons were called "Little Foots" and "Mud." E. R. Kelley worked at Sinclair and was known as "Coke Yard." The Shelton boys were called "Bear Tracks," "Jap," and "Seep." The Phillips boys were "Stoney," "Tee Tie," and "Tut." Stoney and "Nig" Brown both later became Pasadena High School coaches. Nig's sister Maxine was known as "Dinkey." One of Stoney's high school team-mates was Harold "Chew da 'Bacco" Locklin and another was Edward "Tubby" Pomeroy. Running with that crowd was F. E. "Teeler" Howell and Edgar "Bovvie" or "Gensey" Barnes. Bueron Boyd went by "Bruno" and "Booney." Lamar Thomas went by "Top" and his sister Juanita was "Skitter." Brother and sister Wesley and Julie Pitts went by "Sonny" and "Duckie." Edgar Dowell went by "Duke" and his little sister Daisy was known as "Dixie." Sisters Jessie and Maurine Brannen went by "Woodie" and "Pokey" respectively. "Judge" Dickerson's boy, Leon went by "Skinny." Sig "Airplane" Montgomery, Ernest

"Bird Seed" Hughes, Gertrude "Gertie" Brown, and Mrs. "Hat Lady" Larson were also among those with descriptive monikers.

The financial dilemma that tested the stamina of the city was not faced by the school system. Although the city of Pasadena had been unable to include the emerging industry within its city limits for tax revenue purposes, the school system had incorporated those sites long before the industries were built and thus enjoyed the present tax benefits of their improvements. From the very beginning industry had generously supported the school program. During the depression seven industries provided the school system with 90 percent of its income: Houston Lighting & Power Company, Sinclair Oil & Refining, Crown Oil and Refining, Phillips Petroleum, G. H. & S. A. Railroad Company, Lone Star Cement, and Houston Pipe Line Company. Industry paid $59,341.15 of the total $65,528.20 collected in taxes in 1932. By comparison, Deer Park, brought back to life by the construction of the Shell Refinery and Shell's construction of a new eight room brick schoolhouse, collected $17,529.08 in taxes in 1931. Besides the school at Deer Park, the district also operated the school at Deepwater and took in students from the recently burned Lynchburg school. Only six grades were taught at Deer Park, so the high school bound students were bused to Pasadena or La Porte. Seabrook Common District had an income of $6,658, South Houston received $6,631, and Genoa collected $5,951. Some of the best salaries during the depression were paid by the Pasadena school district to its teachers. The district even granted small raises during the period while Houston Lighting & Power cut salaries up to 50 percent and Shell reduced its pay by at least 10 percent. W. J. Cole was one of many teachers that were hired during the depression. Cole came in 1933 with his wife Corinnie and they paid $2,050 for a new house on Wafer Street; $20 per month for the first year and then $25 thereafter. Fleeta Mathews came in from Kirbyville at the request of Hugo Hartsfield to teach in 1931. To keep her in Pasadena the next year Hartsfield gave her a double raise, naturally not to be advertised to the other teachers.[52]

With its finances protected, the Pasadena school system continued to grow. Since schooling was a focal point of the community, social life went on as if nothing much had happened. Most farms now employed Mexican and other migratory workers to tend to the crops and thus the critical need for children to help during the harvest had ceased. Extracurricular activities had grown and replaced Sunday socials as the main community social activity. Although the home might be shared with the family of needy friends, or relatives, it meant another schoolmate and dear friend. Although home cooked meals would include more beans, potatoes, and other backyard garden crops, there was always enough money to scrape together for a new May Day party dress. Madge Billingsley was the May Queen in 1930 with her "lovely white dress, jeweled slippers, and fur trimmed train" and James Darby was the May King in his "white flannel trousers and dark coat." Lavender, green, and pink were worn by members of the Court. And the high school graduating class of 1931 was the first one to wear caps and gowns. Historically the people of Pasadena had provided their own entertainment and the growing school programs simply added more variety to the community life. Since everyone was in the same boat financially, sweet-16 Mary Garfield did not realize how poor they were. They were having too much fun.[53]

As the high school principal Hugo Hartsfield had been very interested in developing a girls' sports program and was instrumental in getting a girls' gymnasium constructed in 1929. The

The May Day festival was the biggest production at the grammar school.

first floor was for an auditorium and the second a gymnasium. Since this was one of the few gymnasiums in the district, many of the county meets were held in Pasadena. The gymnasium was not quite large enough for a regulation basketball court so the half courts were actually "lapped" at the centerline.

Into the Deptression (1929-1932) 331

Everyone had to have a costume for the special event.

Even though it was during the Depression, the Pasadena High School class of 1931 was the first graduating class to rent formal gowns for the occasion.

Helen Hollingsworth coached the 1930 Girls basketball team to a county championship title.

Hartsfield was promoted to the superintendent's position, and his replacement, Jack Horton organized the first boys' and girls' gymnastics teams. However, no one could figure out what to do with the "side horse" apparatus. Jack concentrated on the boys' programs and Hugo promoted the girls' programs.[54]

Helen Hollinsworth was the physical education teacher in 1929 and coached the girls' basketball team. The old long black bloomers and middy blouses were replaced with new gym shorts and tank tops. Although short, junior Doris Barnes was fast and was captain of the team during 1930 when they won the county title. Her teammates included Maxie McNair, Mary Garfield, Sylvia Wilson, Gladys Parks, Para Lee Butler, Dixie Dowell, Oleta King, Sena Bell Forrest, Lorene Follis, and Birdie Mae Billingsley. Alton Ruth Whitaker replaced Hollinsworth as high school coach in 1930. Most of the girls from the championship team returned the following year as seniors and were joined by Edith Hearn, Josie Cockrun, Annie Mae Gigstad, Ila Mae Howell, Velma Gore, and Estelle Wilson. Girls' basketball caught on and industrial teams were fielded much like the earlier boys' semipro baseball teams. Pasadena

State Bank sponsored a team in 1930 with Ruth Williams, Mildred Tabor, Delia Williams, teachers Ruby Reeves and Gladys Jennings, Sena Bell Forrest, and Miss Dewease. Hartsfield was always looking over their shoulders and even organized the Mrs. Young's Bakery (of Houston) team when the bank did not field their team in 1931. Ruth Williams, who worked at the bank, lead the team, which was made up of teachers Marion Mayfield, Catherine Moss, and Loise Williams, and students Gladys Grant, Wilma Grant, and Hazel Sherrill. Dr. Portwood was the team doctor and checked their hearts and blood pressure. This being the depression and cash in short supply, the team was paid with loaves of bread instead of money. Naturally, Hartsfield coached the team.[55]

Young's Bakery (girls basketball) Team was a community team that included any female that could handle a ball.

Whitaker did a good job with the girls' high school team and turned in another championship in the spring of 1933. The team included Eloise Bunkley, Edith Hearn, Gladys Grant, Juanita Tingle, Elizabeth Wright, Edwina Wright, Isabella Rochelle, Marguerite Harris, Earline Brannen, Wanda Sherman, Mildred Sneed, Glenora Thornton, Willie Mae Sherrill, Marie Neal, and Anna Mae Gigstad. For the fun of it, the team played the Young's Bakery team who were the (Houston) City Basketball Champions. The Bakery team was made up mostly of Pasadena women, including Raena Plaisance, Madge Gosch,

Estelle Wilson, Evelyn Kelley, Sena Bell Griffin, Daisy Dowell, Mildred Gore, Wilma Grant, Ada Davis, Gladys Parks, and Emogene Orr. Edith Hearn's brother Dwight coached the team. Both were championship teams; both were from Pasadena. The high schoolers beat the "semipros" 23 to 7.[56]

Not satisfied with double champions, Hartsfield arranged to have Whitaker replaced and hired Doll Harris from Oklahoma in the fall of 1933. He also hired Toka Lee Fields. They were members of the All American Girls Basketball team while at Oklahoma State. The following year he brought in one of their teammates, Coral Worley. Hartsfield gave them jobs at the school and had them also play on the Young's Bakery team. Doll coached the high school girls' team onto an easy county championship in 1934. That team included Edweena Wright, Eloise Bunkley, Mary Tingle, Laura Lee Plaisance, Juanita Tingle, Lillian Roe, Mildred Ely, Mary Alice Phillips, Addie Youngblood, Juanita Thomas, Dorothy Lee Hughes, Wanda Sherman, Babe Wright, and Aleta Isaac. The 1932 Olympic star "Babe" Didrikson of Beaumont dropped by to watch her old teammate Doll Harris coach the Pasadena team. The excitement that night was on the sidelines and not on the court. And for that one game, the whole town turned out.[57]

Although much loved by the students, Hartsfield's parental attitude lead to his termination. The school district had always been mindful of the moral character, and public behavior of its teachers. Off and on it would follow the policy of generally only hiring unmarried females and had special rules for them. They were expected to live in Pasadena, rent rooms in private homes, and be in by a certain hour. They could neither smoke nor drink. They were also expected to go to church and to either teach or attend Sunday school. Shortly after Hartsfield arrived he dismissed three teachers for going out of town and dancing. He went a bit farther with one of his single teachers and suggested that Adella Krenek should stop dating a certain gentleman. The high school home economics teacher took exception to Mr. Hartsfield's position and punctuated her dismay by marrying that young man, Frank Young, in 1931. Policy being what it was, Mrs. Young became unemployed at the end of the school term. She submitted her resignation on May 24, 1932, with no reason given. Fellow teacher Sarah Fowler also submitted her resignation at the same time, stating that she was getting married, "hence the reason for my resignation." Considering, there was a depression and jobs were getting scarce, love extracted a heavy price, $175 a month to be school. At the end of her fourth year she accepted the proposal of her hometown sweetheart, Jimmy Sprott. Ethel Williams and her roommate and fellow teacher, Pearl Durham, both got married on May 31, 1930, in a double wedding ceremony in the home of Mr. and Mrs. Sherman in Pasadena. Ethel married J. B. Sprott and moved to Huntsville, while Pearl married Mr. Townsend of Buchey, Louisiana. The ceremony was not without excitement, as the ring bearer, seven-year-old Clyde Pomeroy, dropped the rings and everyone scrambled on the floor to find them. His sister Bessie performed her duties as flower girl without incident. Ironically Ethel would return with her husband in a few years and teach for another 30 years in the Pasadena school system.[59]

Before Ethel left she got her younger sister, Loise, a job. Naturally, Hartsfield made sure that Loise would play basketball on the semi-professional team. Loise Williams moved to Pasadena in the fall of 1930 to take her sister's place teaching in the grammar school. She shared an apartment with fellow teacher Ruby Fuhlberg, upstairs in the newly opened DeFee's Building. In 1931 Loise took room and board at Mrs. Anna Pomeroy's house and there met Anna's oldest grandson, Edward. Edward had been seriously hurt in an automobile accident in which Mrs. Francis Close Willard had died. Loise agreed to tutor Edward with his school work. Love developed

Edward Pomeroy and Loise Williams began as student and teacher and they ended as husband and wife.

between the high school senior and the grammar school teacher. This was not without precedent in those days. Superintendent Richard Gore had married one of his students, after her graduation, back in 1926. Ferrel Brown secretly dated one of his teachers while a student from 1926 and only upon his graduation in 1928 did they date openly. Matrimony was only a matter of time for them. In 1932 Bill Forrest took a liking to the new girls' coach, Doll Harris, and Payton "Jap" Shelton had eyes for Toka Lee Fields. Both interests led to the altar. Loise and Edward were discrete with their budding romance and married secretly in New Orleans shortly after Edward's graduation in May 1932. In order to keep her job as a teacher they had to pretend to still only be dating. School board trustee Tom Moore discovered the truth while on a trip to New Orleans and afterwards confronted the couple. The situation was even more awkward since Edward's father, John Pomeroy, was on the school board. Not resigning after her marriage was bad enough, but hiding the fact would not reflect kindly on her father-in-law. Loise was allowed to finish out the term and then tendered her resignation in May 1933. Loise and Edward rented a house from his grandmother and opened a kindergarten since Loise had an excellent reputation as a teacher. After 13 years on the board, John Pomeroy did not agressively pursue his reelection the following year so that his daughter-in-law could be rehired as a teacher. Loise was hired as a substitute teacher until a vacancy developed in the teaching staff. She subsequently taught until retirement.[60]

The pace during the depression slowed down from the Roaring Twenties, but "busy" was still a good description. The depression was not even a year old when wildcatter "Dad" Joiner found black gold. After years of searching for a great pool of oil in East Texas, his dream came true. He had trusted a 70-year-old dreamer and a seat-of-the-pants, selftaught geologist named Doc Lloyd. The major oil companies had written the area off as unproductive. But their Daisy Bradford #3 well began the oil boom all over again on September 5, 1930, when it tapped the edge of the world's largest pool of oil. The crude oil flooded an already depressed oil market, but it provided local jobs. School Trustee Thomas Webb "Tom" Moore was glad to hear the news. He was a geologist with Brown & Root. Tom had moved to Pasadena in 1924 with wife Ronnie and sons Carter and Thomas Andrew. With an oil discovery, his job was assured. But like so many entrepreneurial pioneers, Joiner did not get to fully enjoy the financial benefits of his discovery. He had been promoting for too long, and perhaps sold too many shares in his ventures. He was promptly thrown into receivership. Veteran oilman H. L. Hunt purchased Joiner's 4,000 acres of leases for over a million dollars and assumption of all of Joiner's creditors' lawsuits. Joiner went out looking for more discoveries and Hunt made a fortune on his investment. Hunt's new-found crude flowed into Sinclair's refinery and Pasadena employees continued to have jobs during the depression. The following year a pipeline from Kilgore was completed into Shell and East Texas crude began flowing into that plant. Activity in the refineries translated into activity on the ship channel.[61]

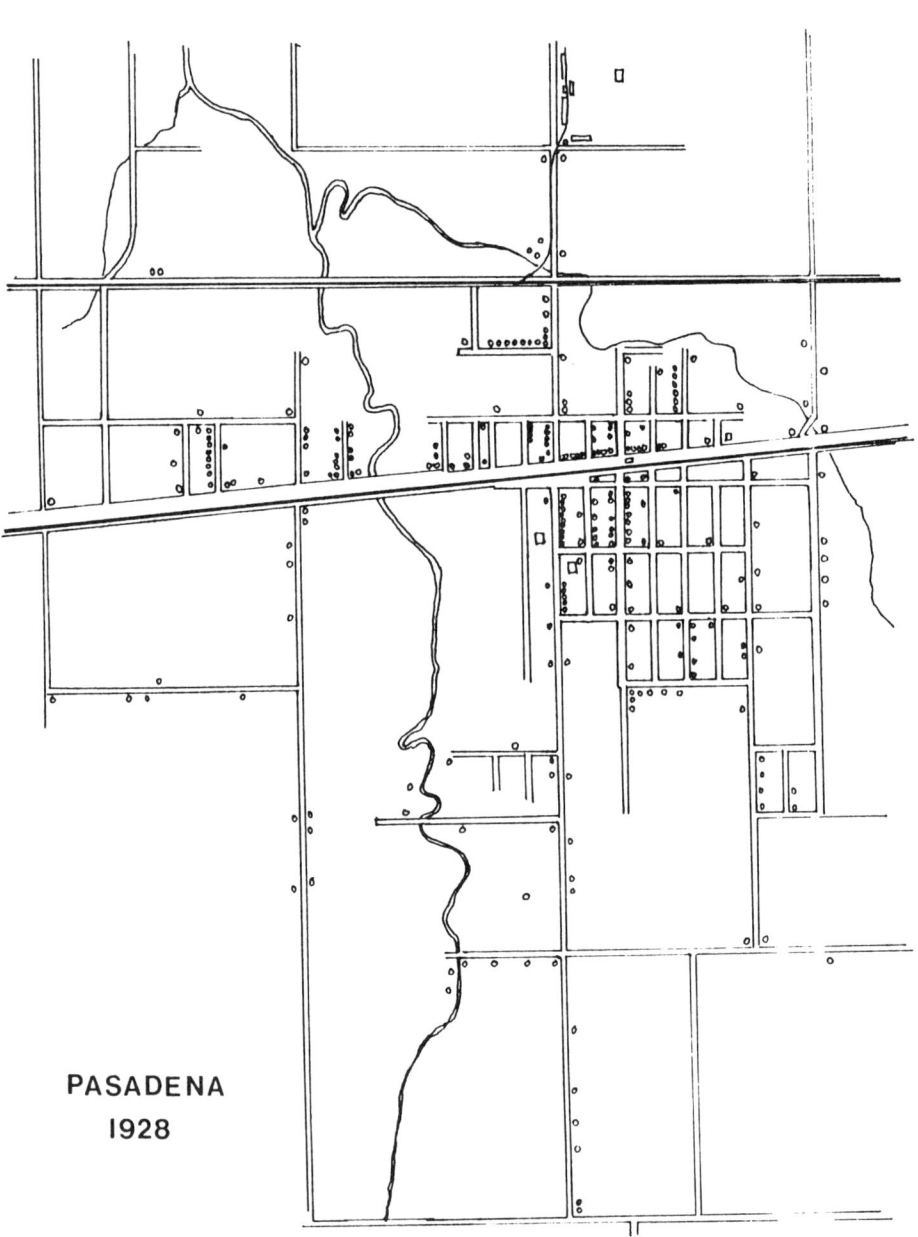

PASADENA
1928

XIII

Transformation and Recovery (1932-1937)

The United States frigate *Constitution*, better known to many as "Old Ironsides," visited the Port of Houston on February 25, 1932. Built in 1797, the three-masted frigate was saved from dismantling in the 1920s by contributions from school children from across the nation. Before the ship was to be permanently berthed in Boston it embarked upon a good-will tour so that as many of the children of the nation as

The U. S. frigate Constitution *is escorted up the Houston Ship Channel*

possible could see the ship their pennies and nickels saved. Although the ship was a day late in travelling up the Houston Ship Channel, over 100,000 people lined the banks of the channel to watch her pass. In honor of the occasion, school let out in Pasadena. Muggins Parks, Clyde Pomeroy, Theo Shaw, and the rest of the children witnessed the passing of the great ship of American naval history. Allie Newell was one of the many adults that came to watch. [1]

Nineteen thirty-two was the crunch year for city government. Fortunately, the credit of the city was still good enough

Almost all of the kids and most of the adults lined the banks of the ship channel to watch the Constitution *go by.*

so that it was able to purchase a Ford dump truck in February from the Jack Roach dealership in exchange for a $500 Pasadena refunding bond. The city purchased the water system owned by John Pomeroy and paid for it with city refunding bonds and water revenue certificates. But cash was in short supply since delinquent real estate taxes were mounting and payments on city water bills were sporadic. The volunteer fire department had to stage benefit programs to raise some of the money they needed to run their operation. J. A. Haacke received permission to erect street marker signs at no cost to the city. The costs were underwritten by the merchants, who hung an advertisement sign under the street name with their business name on it. The city reduced the number of streetlights it could pay to operate to seven: four located on Sterling, one at the school, one at the Baptist church, and one at the Methodist church. Claude Pitt's salary was reduced again, this time to $125 per month, and his assistant, D. H. McKissick's wages were reduced from 50 cents per hour to 40. The services of the city attorney, Judge J. H. Painter were terminated. When O. C. King resigned as police chief, Claude Pitts got that job added to his responsibilities, naturally without increasing his salary. But avoiding costs and cutting expenses was not the full solution. Besides minimal operating expenses, periodic interest payments had to be made on the bonds, warrants, and certificates issued.[2]

In October 1932 Charles Garfield, Ben Bailey, and V. E. Abbott, members of the board of equalization, recommended that there be a blanket reduction of eight percent on the assessed valuations in order to reduce the burden of taxes on the citizens, and to encourage payment of those taxes. Extensions on payment dates were granted so that penalties and interests would not be a burden. With a carrot-and-stick approach, city government went after delinquent taxes. The same applied to delinquent water bills.[3]

Meanwhile, Shell Refinery reduced its salaries 10 percent in June 1932, but then provided free coke as fuel to unemployed families that fall so that they could keep their houses warm in winter. In November J. C. Thomas, president of the newly formed Relief Bureau in Pasadena persuaded the city to help in delivering coke to needy families in the city by supplying labor and the truck for the work. J. L. Hearn helped Thomas in this angel of mercy program.[4]

Mayor McMaster was reelected in April 1933 to serve his second term. Commissioners A. R. Cruse and Earl Guinn were also returned to office. Earl had been appointed in 1932 to serve out the term of W. F. Williams who had died while in office. Judge C. D. Jessup was hired to collect delinquent taxes. Another source of funds was now available from the federal government. Franklin Roosevelt had been elected president of the United States in November of 1932 on the pledge that he would give the American people a "new deal." Roosevelt felt that the federal government should be much more aggressive and involved in helping the country recover from the depression. He took office in March of 1933 and immediately proclaimed a bank "holiday" to prevent the continual drain on their deposits. Pasadena had previously weathered a close call when State Bank Examiner Neal Greer called for a meeting of the directors and they did not show up. Greer got mad and threatened to close the bank if they failed to show a second time. They showed up and the bank remained open.[5]

The Emergency Banking Act, the Federal Emergency Relief Act to create the Civil Works Administration, the Home Owners Loan Corporation, and the National Industrial Recovery Act were all passed within 100 days of Roosevelt taking office. Coupled with the Reconstruction Finance Corporation, the federal government became a source of funds that Pasadena quickly turned to. Grants and financing were available for use on Pasadena's sewer and water extensions and for street maintenance. "Free" labor was available under the Civil Works Administration (CWA). Charles Garfield was hired in July of 1933 at 30 cents per hour to supervise the government free labor, most of whom were Mexicans. For a 40-hour work week Garfield was getting a lot less than the nationally average weekly wage of $17. However, in order to take advantage of the federal programs and funds, Pasadena had to spend money. Understandably, the city only had a limited supply of that commodity. The bottom of the cash reserve was reached on July 29 and the city cancelled the streetlighting program with Houston Lighting & Power in order to save dollars. Some might say that this was the "darkness" before the dawn.[6]

From the bottom of the depression, any movement was progress. Pasadena anticipated the turn and staged a Spring Clean Up campaign in April of 1933 and, as if it swept its troubles out the door, things began to look up. Mayor McMaster quickly took advantage of the new federal assistance programs, and with obvious renewed confidence in the future, almost immediately gave pay raises to McKissick and Garfield. The raise to 45 cents an hour brought their pay within the national average. More importantly, it signalled the end of the pay reductions. Delinquent taxpayers came forward and settlements were reached. Voters approved a $30,500 water and sewer improvement revenue bond issue in July of 1934 by a margin of 84 to 27. The city was taking advantage of Work Projects Administration (W.P.A.) assistance in order to make many improvements. McMaster, Cruse, and Guinn were returned for another term of office in 1935. The local economy was improving so much that Cruse resigned from office in July to attend to his growing business. E. W. Blakesley was appointed to fulfill Cruse's term. Claude Pitts did not get a raise, but his job responsibility was greatly reduced when James D. Wallace was hired as the chief of police in December.[7]

Besides a growing business, Aubrey Cruse had a growing family. Son Aubrey, Jr., had just graduated from high school and was working with his father. Donald, Imogene, and Doris were still in school. Betty Jo had just turned four years old. Aubrey's wife Emma had lost two others. Edgar Barnes, secure with a job at Sinclair, sold five acres of his farm on Bruner (Tatar) Street to get enough money to send Doris and Edgar Eugene off to college. Little Lanis was in grammar school and would still be around to help with the strawberries for a few more years. At the bottom of the Depression, Frieda Boyd passed away, leaving Jonah with four children. As the recovery gained momentum, Jonah married Ruby Odessa Neely and they would add three more to the Boyd family: June Clarice, Jonah, Jr., and David. Harvey Billingsley was secure with his job at H. L. & P. so he and Myrtle continued to work on their family. Erma Claudia came before the depression hit and Norma Ruth came after the recovery begin to show. Margie Marie would be along shortly.[8]

There was something always going on for entertainment. Occasionally a roller rink would come to town and the wooden floor was as smooth as silk compared to the streets and sidewalks normally available to the skaters. A magician brought a tent show to town for a three-day performance. He buried a girl in one of his acts and she almost died before they got her out. That was the talk of the town for a few weeks. The older kids would catch the Galveston train and get off at Sylvan Beach for an evening of fun, music, and dancing. Occasionally they would lose track of time and miss the train back to Pasadena. If they couldn't hitch a ride, they just walked home. Sometimes they would break into the gymnasium and get someone like Marguerite Pomeroy to tickle the ivories on the piano while the others would glide across the floor. And of course there were the "Tin Can" movie matinees.[9]

Will Horowitz was a very successful small movie chain owner in Houston. He owned the Uptown, Texan, Iris, and Ritz

Bessie Pomeroy and friends hang onto Maurine Brannen's "Bored of Education" decorated car.

theaters and always had first-run shows. He was an innovator and connected several of his theaters and a penny arcade together with tunnels and set up radio station WEAY to promote his theaters. By 1925 he had sold the radio station to the *Post-Dispatch* newspaper group owned by Ross Sterling. He demanded cleanliness in the theaters and smiles on the faces of all of his help. When he air conditioned the Texas Theater it was the first one in the state. Beginning in 1926 he gave a Christmas party for children and would give out 5,000 to 10,000 gift baskets each year. He continued that tradition unbroken until his death on Christmas Day in 1941. When the depression hit he refused to go up on the admission price of his movies even though the major studios tried to force him into it. His price remained a nickel. And if the patron brought a can of food to donate to the needy, he would let them in free. John Pomeroy drilled his water wells and son Clyde and his friends took advantage of those "Tin Can" matinees.[10]

Industry tried to help as much as it could. If a plant had to reduce its payroll it would prefer to reduce the numbers of hours worked by each person rather than to lay anyone off. For any new activity, preference was given to hiring more people part time than fewer people full time. The objective was to spread the little money there was around to as many people as possible so that everyone had a little something. Homer Lambert moved to the area in 1920 with his parents because his father and brother got a job building Sinclair. Later Homer also got on there and worked during the depression. When the Ford Motor Company assembly plant closed in Houston in 1931, W. O. Pinkston was out of a job. For a couple of years he did anything and everything, except stealing. In 1933 he got a job with Shell and moved to Pasadena. L. L. "Bill" Hay had moved to Houston from Eddy, Texas, and was living with his brother Albert when he also got a job at Shell. He moved to Pasadena in 1931 and married Mildred Tabor in 1933. Oscar Derrington was transferred in by Shell from Woodriver, Illinois, in 1932. He and his wife Golda bought a house on Randall and Fifth (Shaw) Street for their children, Dorothy Delores and Darrell. Oscar, Jr., was born there a year later. Guy Butler also felt confident enough with his job security at Shell that he and Ruby added Joan to their family in 1933. "Ish" Land worked for Houston Natural Gas when the depression hit and quit in 1930 to return to North Texas. He came back to Pasadena the next year and got a job at Sinclair. He took on odd jobs to supplement his income so that he could get married to Hazel Elder.[11]

Odd jobs and part-time jobs were about all that was available for many. The government Civil Works Administration (CWA), Civilian Conservation Corp (CCC), and then Work Projects Administration (WPA) programs provided a lot of manual labor jobs, most for about 35 cents per hour. The Federal Transient Bureau took over the old Boys Industrial Home in South Houston and housed 520 "transient men and boys" under a federal work program. Joe Cullinan agreed to let the federal government use his 194-acre Santa Anna Farm in Pasadena during 1934 for a token payment of one dollar. The transients were non-residents of Harris County who were given a place to live and who earned their keep and a few coins by performing odd jobs in fixing up the place, raising their own food, and working in nearby communities on federally sponsored projects. Several of the boys attended school in Pasadena while they were at the farm. As Maurine Brannen felt, they were busy, but happy. [12]

The Pasadena city council sent a resolution to the county commissioners in July 1930 requesting a better ferry, asserting that it was necessary in order to "avert a disaster and the probable loss of life in the event the old lop sided delapidated boat now in use should collapse with a load of helpless women and children on it." Nine months later, on March 9, 1931, the 12-car, crude oil burning twin engine *Tex Dreyfuss* ferry was launched by Commissioner Dreyfuss's 3-year-old daughter Rosemary. She used a milk bottle filled with bayou water for the christening. W. H. Cargill got the job operating the new

The old ferry was too small for the increased traffic across the ship channel.

ferry. He and his wife Lelia moved their family to Pasadena about 1927. Son John T. would marry Izadore Riggs and follow in his father's footsteps running the ferry. The girls were Mamie and Norma. The youngest were A. M. and C. Wayne.[13]

The Tex Dreyfuss *ferry could carry 12 cars at a time.*

Likewise, Houston Lighting & Power was confident in the future of the area and continued to upgrade the generation capability of its Deepwater plant in 1931 and in 1932. The plant opened in 1924 with a 40,000 Kilowatt (KW) generating capacity and by 1932 had increased its generating capacity to 151,200 KW, almost a four-fold increase in only eight years. The Deepwater plant next to Pasadena contained over 70 percent of the company's total generating capacity.[14]

While H. L. & P. was powering up, the Port of Houston hit the bottom in 1932. But the growth and potential of the petroleum business convinced the Corps of Engineers that the ship channel had to be deepened to 32 feet in order to accommodate the increasingly larger oil tankers. To provide for night navigation, 32 channel lights were installed in 1933 between Lynchburg and the Sinclair Refinery. This was the same year that the new ferry was established at Morgan's Point. The *Charles D. Massey* carried 24 cars and was the largest one in the county. Merrymakers heading for Sylvan Beach from the north side of the channel saved 20 miles by using the new ferry.

However, they might have to wait in long lines before they could get across. On still afternoons, the mosquitos could be a problem for those who had forgotten to bring their handpump spray guns. It would be a few years before automobile air conditioners, or even radios, would be available. While the national economy was standing still, the foundations for growth were continuing to be laid in Harris County.[15]

On a larger scale, the depression was the era of the gangster and the public enemy. They made great headlines as they roamed the country, robbing banks and shooting it out with lawmen. Will Bailey kept his mouth shut and stuck to business when Clyde Barrow stopped for gasoline at Will's service station in West Pasadena. Barrow roamed Texas, Oklahoma, Kansas, Arkansas, and Louisiana on a two year robbing, kidnapping, and murder spree that ended in a deadly ambush May 23, 1934, in Louisiana. Jessie Plunkett, Ray Kingsbury, and Arthur Hopkins were not as discrete as Bailey.[16]

The three men worked for McMaster and Pomeroy drilling water wells. On one job in East Texas they spent the first couple of days building the derrick for the job and then decided to celebrate before they began drilling for water. Jessie was the small one of the group and had a reputation for starting fights and then letting his bigger buddies finish them. While stirring things up in Cleveland one night they were conned into using the company wench truck to break someone out of the local jail. Destroying the jail and breaking someone out was bad enough, but the criminal was the current Public Enemy Number One. When John Pomeroy arrived the next day to supervise the drilling of the water well he could not find his employees. After a few inquiries, they were discovered in the next town, in its jail. They had been arrested for the jail breaking caper. It took some tall talking to get them out and, of course, their promise to behave in the future. [17]

Horace A. Jackson succeeded Hugo Hartsfield as the superintendent of schools in the fall of 1935. He inherited a much larger school system than Hartsfield had started with only eight years earlier. Although the system had grown despite the depression, the biggest change came during Hartsfield's last year. The depression had placed a financial strain on the Genoa School District and the South Houston School District. In September 1934 trustees of the both districts presented a petition to the Pasadena board asking that they be consolidated into the Pasadena system. Pasadena was considered a rich district since it had several large industries on the property tax rolls and they were good about paying their school taxes. Actually Pasadena had the lowest valuation per student of the three systems, but Pasadena was certainly more solvent. The Harris County school trustees favored the consolidation and on January 1, 1935, Genoa Common School District #43 and South Houston Common School District #44 were merged into the Pasadena Independent School System. The district increased from 27.06 square miles to 56.25 square miles. The student enrollment increased from 940 students to 1,485. The assessed valuations increased from $1,143,507 to $2,094.972. Hartsfield had started eight years earlier with 16 on his payroll and Jackson now inherited about 70 employees. The high school had been expanded twice, the grammar school once, Genoa Elementary acquired, South Houston Elementary acquired, and a junior high building was in the planning stage. And across the board the teachers' salaries were higher. Someone forgot to mention the depression to the school district.[18]

Delbert Atkinson had taken the lead in seeking the merger of the school districts. Delbert was born in Genoa in 1903 and had lived there until the family moved to Pasadena in 1912. He had had to go to Harrisburg to finish his high school education. Upon graduation he was one of the young men that went to work in the nearby industries. He worked at Galena-Signal Refinery for five years until it closed and then moved to Sinclair Refinery after a very brief stay at Crown in 1927. Delbert married his former Pasadena schoolmate, Thelma Lois Anderson, in 1924. He attended night law school and got his degree in 1931. Delbert began his career in politics by promptly running for the school board, but was defeated his first two tries. In 1934 he was elected to John Pomeroy's position on the board. Also serving on the school board at the time of the consolidation was Ben Bailey, Jr., A. B. Freeman, Charles Garfield, T. W. Moore, J. D. Parks, and O. C. Pitts. The Genoa trustees were J. J. Tullis, W. L. Moberly, and O. F. Thompson. The South Houston trustees were Joe B. Massey and B. F. (Frank) Meador. Ironically, Meador's father had previously served on the South Houston board. Now as newlyweds, Frank and his wife Reba wanted to insure the best possible school system for their future children.[19]

Ironically, oil was discovered the following June in South Houston. Despite the pleas of the old South Houston school trustees, Pasadena would not nullify the consolidation to allow the South Houston district its independence. In fact, the Pasadena district had executed an oil and gas lease in May 1935, a month before the South Houston discovery, and had hopes of also reaping royalty income from production on its school lands. [20]

Champion Paper Company of Hamilton, Ohio, was considering Orange, Texas for the site of its new Texas pulpwood mill when J. S. Cullinan intervened. His presentation that the mill

J. S. Cullinan gave up his Pasadena farm so that Champion Paper could build its mill on the ship channel.

should be located on the Houston Ship Channel, sandwiched between refineries and a power generation plant that could provide a variety of low-cost fuel and power, must have been persuasive since Champion redirected its attention to Pasadena. Perhaps it helped that Cullinan owned just the most perfect plant site, and that Champion could acquire it cheaply under a 99-year lease rather than spending a lot of precious cash purchasing the land outright. Whatever the reason, officials from Champion visited with Pasadena's city council on January 25, 1936, and discussed the possibility of constructing a $3.5 million plant that would employ over 1,000 men to build and between 300 to 500 men to operate. Satisfied that Pasadena was the place, Champion entered into the lease with

Cullinan on February 20 and construction began early in March.[21]

Bevis Frazier had moved to Pasadena in 1928 with his parents, Mr. and Mrs. Jesse Frazier, and had graduated from Pasadena High School in 1933. He was working construction at Shell Refinery when he was the first person hired to help build Champion. Bevis married his high school classmate, Earlene Brannen. Ralph A. Davis moved in from Louisiana to work construction and stayed, married Jessie "Woodie" Brannen, and raised a family. Theo Shaw had worked a year with the Civilian Conservation Corps (CCC), then returned to Pasadena to help with the construction of the Pasadena (Movie) Theater and with Champion. Joe McGraw moved to Pasadena in 1936 and lived with his brother Thomas A. McGraw and his wife Nora Lee (Glasgow). They had two children, Tommy Lee and Michael Wayne. Joe got a job with Theo on the construction of the theater and then with Champion. Stoney Phillips had started with the CCC in Arizona, but quit early to go off to college.[22]

With the influx of new people, housing quickly again became a problem. Virginia Lee "Virgie" Holbrook had married Henry Lyles after the death of her first husband, Nolan Harrison.

Bessie Morrison's house is possibly the oldest house in Pasadena.

With the help of Ima Parks, Virgie turned the old J. M. Cruse home on Shaver into a boardinghouse with 21 beds. They did a landslide business with her "35 cents, all you can eat meals." Mollie Beusch purchased Aubrey Cruse's old house next door and with the help of her son Gib ran "Aunt Mollie's" boardinghouse. Around the corner on Fifth (Shaw) Street, Mrs. Pearl Brown built a rooming house for the hoards of construction workers. Mrs. Bessie Morrison converted the old W. W. Anderson house into a rooming house in West Pasadena. In a blink of an eye every vacant house in town was rented and every available bedroom filled with boarders.[23]

Hebert A. Paine had owned land in Pasadena since 1923 and had offered a portion of his 60 acres as the site for a public waterworks during the incorporation struggle in 1927. As a Houston real estate developer and an acquaintance of Cullinan, he quickly capitalized on the housing shortage developing in Pasadena. Paine replatted his Inland Harbor Subdivision a month after Champion broke ground and helped line up federal financing for home ownership in his renewed development. Three hundred homes were to be built at a cost of $300,000. Located between Tenth (Thomas) and Eleventh Street (Harris), from Main to Wafer, Paine's subdivision was out in the country relative to town. Clyde McMaster and business partner John Pomeroy owned a few acres on Sterling and Wafer and filed for their own subdivision that same month. Several farmers began considering the possibility of converting their strawberry fields into subdivisions, if the boom continued.[24]

Nineteen thirty-six was also the centennial year for Texas and the state made big plans to celebrate, and to attract tourist and their pocketbooks. Unfortunately, Houston lost in its bid for the Centennial Fair. Although Dallas won the honors, Fort Worth staged its own competing version with the Frontier Centennial Exposition. Being on the road to the San Jacinto battleground, Pasadena had its own crowd on April 21 as the hordes travelled Sterling Avenue. S. R. "Buddy" Jones, Jr., had just started working at Pasadena State Bank. He had given up a higher paying job as a sacker at Middleton's grocery store in Galena Park. Another ex-Galena Park boy, J. B. Isaac, spent the entire day hauling ice to the drink concession stands so that the liquid refreshment would be refreshing. In June President Franklin Roosevelt travelled to the battlegrounds and announced the construction of a 570-foot monument costing

$1.5 million in state and federal monies. R. E. Parks represented Pasadena on the official reception committee that met the president in Houston. Thirteen-year-old Clyde Pomeroy skipped summer school that day to see Roosevelt up close. *Pathé News* captured his image sitting on the railing behind the president and High School Principal Jack Horton spotted the delinquent student in the newsreel later at the Bluebonnet movie theater in Harrisburg. Horton suggested to the youngster Clyde that the next time he skipped school, he should not get caught by the news camera. Dorothy Tacker also went to see Roosevelt, but she was smart enough to sit behind, not in front of, the news camera.[25]

Construction began on the monument and anyone not already employed, got a job. George Graves first worked on construction at Champion, then hired on as a carpenter on the monument job. Pay was good, 90 cents per hour on both jobs. Adolph Herrera hired on as a laborer and his son Paul also got some part-time work. Since construction of the San Jacinto Monument would take three years, people could again depend upon a steady, regular cash income. Shell expanded its physical plant in 1936 to almost triple the plant's original capabilities, dubbing the project its "New Deal" construction program. The city of Pasadena increased City Secretary Griffin's and Water Superintendent Pitt's salaries in July.[26]

Karl Kruse had weathered the depression with his job at Sinclair and the family farm at the Florentine Settlement. He had married Elizabeth Pauline Boeske in 1924 and entered the depression with little Pauline and H. B. on the way. At the bottom they added Helen and Karl, Jr., was their recovery baby. His brother Oscar married Ruby Lee Waites at the beginning of the depression and they contributed Jean, Shirley, and Judy to the growing population. Sister Florentine had married Axel Emfred "Jimmy" Magnuson. Little brother Edward was in the navy when the depression hit and sent $20 per month home to help his recently widowed mother. When he got out, he came home to help around the place.[27]

John H. and Clara Sabo moved from the coal mines of Ohio in search of a better job. They settled in South Houston with their children Marie, John, and Helen. John sent word home that there were plenty of good jobs to be had. John's brother Michael "Mike" brought his wife Mary and children "Mikey" and Betty Lou and settled in Golden Acres. Sister Mary came with her husband Julius Wesney and their children John "Jack"

George, Mary Marguerite, Delores Jane, and toddler Patricia Gail. They also settled in Golden Acres in 1936. Sister Emma and her busband John Butler and son Robert Lee "Bobby" arrived and likewise settled in Golden Acres. Daughter Judith Dell "Judy" would be along shortly. John's remaining sister Annie and husband Alex Gasper settled on the other side of Houston. John and Clara's fathers, both widowed, were the last of the family to move south.[28]

Luther and Leora Roller came from Kentucky in 1936 because Luther had a job with a contractor at Shell. They rented a house on Spooner, but it would be several years before their young ones, Charles William and Barbara Jean, would be going to school two blocks away. After the construction job, Luther got on permanently with Shell. Already working at Shell was J. E. Tipton. J. E. went to work for Shell in 1935 and was also living in Pasadena. His wife Lenroa Buss had Bill and Charles to raise. Clayton A. Hart brought his family from Illinois to find a job. Wife Faye B. was also working, taking care of the children, O. C., Lucille, Don, and Ralph. While the Harts found a place on Spooner Street, Mr. and Mrs. John Arthur Lohman opted for a place in Golden Acres. John, Jr., and Lenora Louise were in high school and Charles Eugene and Earl were behind them.[29]

Also lucky at finding a permanent job during the depression was Sam A. McCoy. He got on with Sinclair, perhaps because he was boarding at the Hearns and Asa was always getting people jobs at Sinclair. It would take Sam a few years but he would finally spot Naomi Daily and romance her into wedlock. Meanwhile, another of Asa's hirees, Homer Brammer, and his wife Ruby added Larry Arnold to Pasadena's population. Moving over from Houston, George R. "Swaggie" Stroud relocated his family to Pasadena in 1933 while he worked at Sinclair. His wife Aida A. looked after the children G. Russell, Jr., and Mannie May until they reached school age and then she took a job in the cafeteria at the grammar school. Marvin M. Dunaway got on with Crown and his wife Karon got a job teaching. Not that she needed to, but Karon could keep an eye on their son Jack. W. C. Lowe also got on with Crown while his wife Lottie May looked after Charleen. Mr. and Mrs. A. J. Pitre arrived in 1936 with boys A. J., Jr., and Jennings L. "Pete."[30]

The population of Pasadena was growing with the new people moving to town to take jobs with the industries. Employment was shifting from the farms with surprising ease.

Everett Williams had been born in Pasadena. He started life on the family farm, but grew up with his father working at one of the industries. When Everett graduated from Pasadena High School in 1935 he got a job with Shell and married Alma Mason. Since Alma had not graduated from school, they got special permission from Jack Horton for her to finish at Pasadena the following year. Everett and Alma lived upstairs in one of DeFee's apartments while she went to school and he went to Shell.[31]

There was a lot of "New Dealing" going on now. The momentum was returning to the economy, and to the attitude of the people. Apparently having satisfied the need for food, shelter, and clothing, people's interest now turned to more social and civic matters. The Pasadena Early Settlers Club (sometimes called the Pasadena Pioneers Club) grew out of a reception in 1931. A reunion was held at Emma Cruse's for Rewell and Cora Bell Pitts who were visiting from California. Judge Dickerson liked the meeting so much he hosted annual gatherings, which resulted in the organization of the club. The Pasadena Garden Club was organized in January 1936 with the aim of home beautification and civic improvement. In March they appealed to city council to enact a chicken ordinance in order to keep chickens penned up and out of the flower beds. J. L. Hearn lead a group of concerned citizens to city hall to ask that the city require the owner of some "Negro houses" near city hall to place them in a more sanitary condition. Another group of citizens and businessmen raised money to purchase the first traffic signal light for the city so that it could be erected near the school for the protection of the school children. The necessary ordinance and school zone was passed by city council in September 1936. The city had applied for additional WPA funds to develop a city park and to build a community swimming pool. When Gerald Conrad was mayor he identified Pasadena on its official city letterhead as "On the Houston Ship Channel." Clyde McMaster had the entrance signs to the city repainted to read "Welcome to Pasadena" and changed the city letterhead to Pasadena, Texas, "The City of Industries." A real positive mental attitude was taking hold.[32]

Pasadena had a lot to be proud of, chief among which was its school system. Dedicated and capable men, and women, served on the board of trustees. John Pomeroy, Ben Bailey, and Delbert Atkinson were the first of several who would follow in their father's footsteps by serving on the board. These men were also first students of the system before they were elected to lead the district. Many students also returned to become teachers in the system. Doris Barnes, Addie Brown, Elizabeth Hayes, Myrtle McMaster, Renee Moechel, Russel Munger, and Ralph Stafford had been among the first, and more were to follow. Doris and Ralph would stay until retirement. Ralph married fellow teacher Winogene Cloutier and she would also stay until she retired. Others working in the system that would continue on until retirement were Dollie Ruth Buffington, Leta Cornish, the Diven sisters (Greta and Grace), Karon Dunaway, Virgie Freeman, Ruby Fuhlberg, Pearl Hall, Jewell Jennings, Mattie McClung, Loise Pomeroy, Birdie Mae Smith, the Smythe sisters (Sadye, Lillian, and Mae), Lillian Sneed, and Tilman White. Most of these teachers would teach the children and even some grandchildren of their earlier students. And some of those children would also become teachers at Pasadena. Other familiar faces that would continue to put in a life's worth of work in the operations of the schools were Emogene Bunkley, E. A. "Dude" Dowell, T. E. Hodges, and Clara Wilson. Emogene Bunkley was the former Emogene Orr, who married the Shell Refinery worker and Pasadena volunteer fireman, Horace W. Bunkley. With a stable teaching and operations staff, the system just kept on improving.[33]

Hartsfield had retained Vick Kucera in 1928 to direct the new school band. It was a system-wide band since its membership was drawn from almost all of the grade levels. In 1931 the band had grown to 30 members with Edward Pomeroy as its first drum major. His baton was a broom stick covered with green and white paper. The band was complemented with a pep squad of 32 girls headed by yell leaders Eloise Bunkley and Gladys Grant. Andrew A. Davis succeeded Kucera in 1934 for one year and then turned the job over to James Eugene Stuchbery in 1935. The Stuchberys had just moved to Houston because Gene had gotten a job with the Houston Symphony Orchestra when Davis coaxed him to Pasadena. "Gene," or more commonly "Stutts," was a talented, likeable band leader with a colorful background. He played in circuses and for vaudeville, graduated from the U. S. Army Bandmasters' School in Chaumont, France, in 1917 and was playing for a stock theater company in Shreveport, Louisiana, in 1921 when he met, and subsequently married, the leading lady. He was making $35 per week and she was making $150 per week. "Aunt Rill" and "Stutts" settled into Pasadena and, as a team, built

Aunt Rilla and Stutts had a colorful theatrical background before coming to Pasadena and taking over the high school band program.

one of the nation's finest high school band reputations over the next 30 years. Their son Thomas Richard would follow in their footsteps.[34]

Although girls basketball was the most popular school sport in the thirties, football was growing in popularity. Phil Goodrum replaced Jack Horton as the football coach in 1932 and with veteran assistant A. E. Jackson's help, produced an unde-feated season that year. The Pasadena "Eagles" racked up 134 points and allowed only one touchdown to be scored against them. Although no one beat them, they did have two scoreless ties and a third tie with only one TD for each team. Stoney Phillips had played all four years in high school and captained the winning team, which also included Johnny Boyd, Harvey Guedry, and Clarence Whitaker. Stoney played the first year with his brother Rodney, then three years with his other brother, Tee Tie. Nig Brown

The first uniformed band included students from grammar and high schools and wore Kelly green coast trimmed in white and green caps.

would start his four years on the undefeated team. Since there were only 11 grades to schooling at the time, to letter four years meant that you lettered in the eighth grade on the high school team. Stoney would return years later to his alma mater and again lead, as their coach, future teams to victory. Under his leadership as athletic director, Pasadena would become the second best team in the state.[35]

From 1933 to 1936 A. T. "Booty" Johnson coached the team. Stoney's brother, Tee Tie, finished his four years of football in 1933 under Booty. Tee Tie followed Stoney to college and then also into coaching. Nig Brown finished with the 1935 season and after college, returned to be an assistant coach under Stoney. Nig was half-Indian, from his mother's side, and was well liked by everyone. He and his sister Maxine lived with their mother and stepfather J. A. Castleberry. Another Indian on Nig's team was Willis Joe Chapman. Joe was a relative of Russell Dickerson's wife Ruth, so he lived with them on Munger Street. Joe was also a good football player, but did not go on to college. After graduation he married Anna Mae Gigstad and went to work at Crown Refinery.[36]

Besides some great football players, Booty also inherited a newly organized baseball team. Ironically, school baseball never received the popularity that the semipro team had enjoyed earlier. While he was at Pasadena a tennis program was started and tennis courts constructed. Booty would much later receive some notoriety because while he was in college he had roomed with Lyndon Baines Johnson, the future U. S. president. Olin Roberts was coaching at Webster when he got a better job offer from Pasadena about 1934. Instead of sports, he taught math and science. He and his wife Myrtle bought one of A. G. Whitman's new houses on Wafer and settled in with daughter Dorothy. C. P. Wall took over in 1936 and won the Class B's highest honor, the regional championship. C. P.'s wife, "Cy" also taught school. Their daughter was Barbara. Wall, Phillips, and Brown all taught until retirement.[37]

In his eight years Coach Wall turned in several district championship teams. In later years he would pick some of Pasadena's "All Stars" from his early teams, including James Anderson, Harold Dumas, Carl Feazle, Floyd Hand, Francis M. "Harrisburg" Neagle, Clyde Pomeroy, and Boyd Tingle. Sports had quickly become an important part of the school program and good athletes were being recruited to the school. Dumas and Feazle were from Genoa and Neagle was from Harrisburg.

The Chandler brothers, Raymond and Woodrow, were brought in from Highlands and the Hendrick brothers from Lynchburg. Deer Park contributed Jack H. "Mayor" Carswell, Jr., and Harrisburg added Jesse Ray Brobst, Jr. Pasadena was known as a football school. San Jacinto High in Houston was known for its track and field program and Pasadenan Chink Jacobs was recruited for the hurdles.[37]

For 30 years there had been little, if any, change in the religious institutions of Pasadena. A new spirit stirred during the depression. The Mexican Church of Pasadena had been formed in 1933 with Cenobia Ortiz, Abraham Adames, Desideria Mares, and Antonio Rodriguez as trustees. Josephin Cortez and Mr. Carrizal were also involved in creating the mission. Pasadena Baptist church had been working with the Mexican community and in 1932 had allowed them to hold their baptisms at the church. John Pomeroy and Ray Williams were among those who sponsored their mission. The Pentecostal church took a turn to a more formal structure in 1934 when it joined the General Council of the Assemblies of God while under the leadership of Reverend Alton L. Parker. The Golden Acres Baptist Church was organized on May 31, 1936, under the leadership of Reverend D. R. Pevoto. The 17 original members were Rev. D. R. Pevoto, Mrs. Bessie Cuthbert, Mr. and Mrs. W. E. Hurst, Mr. and Mrs. S. P. Mandy, Mrs. J. P. McCauley, Mr. and Mrs. R. B. McCullough, Mr. and Mrs. A. L.

The Pentecostal Church on Main Street was the third church building in the community.

Morries, Mr. and Mrs. J. E. Parks, and J. E. Parks, Jr., Dorothy and Vera Sanders, and Billie Williams. Mrs. G. M. Bailey joined before the charter was issued. In fact, Baptists were coming out of everywhere.[39]

Reverend M. A. Darby arrived at Pasadena Baptist Church in December 1928 and began the longest tenure of any preacher in Pasadena to that date. With him came his wife Alethea and children Dorothy Nell, Jimmy, and Billy. Despite his genetic blindness, Darby oversaw an incredible growth in the church. But rapid growth often brings problems. A sizable membership walked out in 1935 in a dispute over church management. For over a year many of them travelled to Harrisburg for their spiritual satisfaction. In August 1936 a two-week revival was held at the high school. At the end, 120 charter members formed the Pasadena Missionary Baptist Church under the leadership of Reverend L. S. Chambers of Cox's Creek, Kentucky. Most of these members were formerly members of Pasadena Baptist, which was also formerly known as Pasadena Missionary Baptist Church. Since the new church was not a mission of Pasadena Baptist, and in honor of Mrs. T. A. Moore, the name was changed to Memorial Baptist Church. The original Baptist church responded by changing its name to First Baptist Church. Memorial began construction on its new sanctuary, the first brick church building in town. T. E. Hodges, W. Lee Mitchell, and Louy Sims were the first deacons of Memorial Baptist and personally guaranteed the loan for the construction of the new sanctuary. In 1936 the Central Park Presbyterian Church of Houston established a mission in Pasadena.[40]

More businesses moved to Pasadena and specialty stores were beginning to replace the old general merchandise stores. Pasadena's central business district was still located along Sterling Avenue (La Porte Road), stretching from Walter Street to Wafer Street. Shaver Street was becoming the next best business address along with Main Street. Downtown still began with Cruse's businesses. He now operated a garage in addition with his service station. His spare office was still the starting point for many community activities. Cruse now represented Sinclair products. Behind his station and facing on Shaver Street, Jeff Fleming had parted company with his brother and now had his own barber and beauty shop with his new bride Myrtle. He had his eye on a site across Shaver and nearer the new movie house that was under construction. In fact, he was thinking more about real estate as an occupation. His interest in civic affairs was just beginning. Across Shaver and at the corner of Fifth (Shaw) Street, D. P. Rathbone was building Pasadena's first movie theater. It would seat 720 people, or approximately 25 percent of the people in town. The Rita Theatre was bought out before completion of construction by the Long's chain and renamed the Pasadena Theater by the time it opened. Before the Pasadena Theater, the kids would stand on Coulson's corner and hitch a ride to the Bluebonnet in Harrisburg.[41]

Not only was Pasadena finally getting a movie theater, it was going to be air conditioned and could seat 25 percent of Pasadena's population comfortably.

Coulson's Drug Store still occupied the popular corner of Shaver and Sterling. Next door, Leo Karkowski operated a dry goods business and had an insurance agency. He probably took over the David-Finger Dry Goods store when he moved to town in 1933. With Mr. Rubenstein as his partner, they named their business, R & K Dry Goods. The depression just about put them out of business. Rubenstein left and Leo purchased an insurance agency from Meyer Blankfield. Within a couple of years Leo would sell the dry goods side of the business to Sol F. Leff. Meanwhile, Mildred Hay looked after the store. Meyer Blankfield operated his grocery store next to Leo. Across the alley, Paul Fleming still had his barber and beauty shop. He was also trying to operate Crown Cleaners. Mason's Cafe (Bank

Cafe) was shortly destined to change hands and become Crouter's. Walter and Alice Crouter (Crowder?) had moved to town in the mid-thirties with son Billy Bob. Hamilton's I.G.A. grocery was next door. In the bank building, Pasadena Drug was owned by Dr. Boggs of Spring. Although he was not a pharmacist, Dr. Boggs' son Steve ran the store. Within the year Pasadena Drug would move into the Dickerson building with the new ownership of Dr. E. E. Connor, O. E. "Perk" Meyers, and Bill Reno. Johnny Meyer was now married to Sylvia Wilson and would open up a pool hall in the vacated Pasadena Drug side of the bank building. The other half of the bank building was occupied by the Pasadena State Bank. Matt F. Reed had moved to Pasadena with wife Grace and three-year-old Francis Helen in 1932 to take the job of assistant cashier at the bank. He helped guide the bank through the troubles of the depression and now was firmly in charge with the assistance of bookkeeper Ruth Williams and trainee "Buddy" Jones.[42]

Across Munger Street the newly opened Nathan Klien's Ice Cream Store was becoming very popular. Next door was a vacant building where Frank DeFee had started his store. Walter Ankele would be moving his insurance agency within the year into this building from next door. Ankele was no longer in the barbershop business and concentrated all of his energies on his insurance business. Next door to Ankele, Frank Portwood had taken over the Campbell Pharmacy in the old Williams building. Frank was in college when his father, Dr. O. F. Portwood, moved to Pasadena in 1928. Frank was destined to also move to Pasadena when he married Will Blakesley's daughter, Margie, in 1930. Frank's business was doing very well and he was thinking about building his own store on the old Tilley' store site, across Main Street from DeFee's. Cato N. and Nelwyn Nelson had moved over from La Porte with their children Harold, Neal, Donald, Beverly, and stepson Lanny Lamb. Cato was looking for a cafe to operate.[43]

When the post office moved out of the Williams building in 1930 it gave Walter room to expand his business. After his death in 1932 his daughter Betty had inherited the business. Although she ran the general merchandise part of the store as the Pasadena Dry Goods Store, most everyone called it Betty Mitchell's store. Next to Betty's and on the corner her husband, Lee Mitchell, ran Pasadena Grocery and Market. Because of Pasadena's farming roots, grocery purchases could be made on credit. A purchaser would sign the sales slip and then pay their bill at the end of the month, or whenever they got paid. Robert Ernest Hughes worked in Mitchell's store and was married to Betty's sister, Jennie. Ernest had moved to Pasadena as a teenager back in 1925. He grew up working the strawberry fields of Pasadena, especially for Walter Williams. His promotion to the grocery store would ultimately lead him into his own grocery store in the future.[44]

The Masonic Lodge was still located in their two-story structure across Main Street from Mitchell's. A. B. Crumbie was the current Worshipful Master. The small cafe building next door was still in operation, but "Newt" Lucas would turn the building into Pasadena Cleaners shortly and operate his business in Pasadena for the next 40 years. Foots Wilson's Pasadena Ice and Fuel Company was still in operation, but the name on its marquee said it better: Pasadena Ice, Fuel and Transfer Co. The ice and fuel businesses were off after the introduction of electricity and natural gas in the community 10 years earlier. Foots was using his truck more to move people and other items. Besides coffins and shell, Foots hauled manure, bricks, strawberry crates, or whatever needed to be moved from one place to another. His protogee, J. B. Isaac, had learned the business well and was now in competition with his place a couple of blocks east.[45]

Next to Wilson's ice house Jumonville Furniture Store had taken over the old Channel Chevrolet storefront. It shared the space with the Webb Company that sold electrical appliances, including Magic Chef ranges, Philco radios, and Frigidaire refrigerators. Radio reception was real good in Pasadena because KPRC and KTRH radio stations had jointly erected a 375-foot radio transmission tower east of town in the old Deepwater area along the Sterling Highway. The tower was the second of its kind in the world with the ability to transmit both stations simultaneously. Each station now broadcast with 5,000 watts of power. Next door to Webb, and on the corner of Sterling and Spooner, the old Deane store was now occupied by Jo-Mil Stores and H. A. Paine real estate. Jo-Mil had taken over the space from the earlier City Feed & Seed Co. store. Because of the competition from the established Wrights Feed, Jo-Mill would be gone by the end of 1937. The real estate developer Herb Paine would continue on and direct his residential projects in Pasadena from his office.[46]

Howard Pitts's service station sat on the corner across the street at Sterling and Spooner and was taking on more of the look of a furniture and appliance store. The Pitts lived next door and had added Thelma Lois, Glenn, and Charles Alfred to their pack of kids. Charles had just started school. Sonny and Naomi had already graduated and Duckie was in her senior year. Sadly, Baby Vernon never saw his first birthday. Next door, and on the corner of Randall, American Service Company operated an ice making plant. This was originally opened as Butcher Brothers in 1928, changed its name to Home Ice Service in 1931, took over Wilson's ice house phone number, and then in 1934 changed its name to American Service. Whatever the name, the ice plant would operate on that corner for another 56 years.[47]

Across Johnson Street J. B. Isaac operated his ice business out of a small structure with ice brought in from Texas Ice & Fuel in Houston. F. D. Eason and Pasadena Ice & Fuel would join him in friendly competition by operating out of the same office within the year. J. B. had married Lucille "Boots" Skillern in 1934 and little Joe Brian arrived in 1935. J. B. Isaac's ice delivery business eventually would become Pasadena Transfer & Storage and would continue for over 50 years. On the other end of the block and on the corner at Johnson, Wrights' Grain Company had its new building. Morris Jesse Wright

Morris and Jesse Wright found a home in Pasadena and their feed store was very popular.

moved to Pasadena from Livingston, Texas, in 1935 with his wife, Jewell, and 13-year-old son, Morris, Jr., to open City Feed & Seed Company. The business grew quickly and Wright changed its name to Wright Grain Company and relocated it into a new building a couple of blocks east. Although agriculture was on the wane in Pasadena, Wright developed a reputation for taking care of plants and animals and would continue the business for another 30 years. He and his wife often advised the Mexicans of the community on their legal matters.[48]

Arthur G. Whitman's Pasadena Lumber Company was still located in the next block on Sterling near Wafer Street. Whitman was serving on the school board of trustees and had chaired the Methodist board during the construction of its educational building in 1935. Across Wafer Mac McMurry operated his Shell service station. His family still lived in the apartment in the rear of the service station and his in-laws now lived nearby in Blanche Kirk's apartment house. The Kirk's had been in Pasadena since before 1928. Joseph Grant and Rebecca Elizabeth Kirk lived between McMurry's and the Blakesley's. Their son, Birch B., was the first attorney to open an office in Pasadena. He took a room off of the back of Pasadena State Bank in 1931. Their daughters Blanche and Lelah were now school teachers in Houston. Blanche also owned the two-story, four-unit apartment building behind Wright's Grain and next door to Louy Sims on Johnson Street. Louy had moved to Pasadena in 1925 and had gotten a job with Sinclair. Louy and Thelma lived on Johnson with their children Louy Vernon and Jennah.[49]

Other retail businesses in Pasadena early in 1937 included J. C. Thomas's insurance agency. J. C. returned to Pasadena in 1936 after spending five years working for the federal government in its depression relief programs. He helped organize, operate, and then shut down the Regional Agricultural Credit Corporation, which lent money to troubled farmers. He returned to Pasadena to revive the insurance business he had organized back in 1928 while working at Pasadena State Bank. L. S. and Maybelle Locklin brought their family to Pasadena about 1921 when L. S. came to work as a construction supervisor for one of the industries. Gaston, Harold, and Shirley had finished their schooling by 1936 when L. S. opened the Locklin Machine Shop on the corner of Munger and Sixth (Eagle). Charles, Mike, and James were still at home. The business would close within a couple of years and Mr. Locklin would serve as the police chief of Pasadena for many years thereafter. M. F. and Mrs. Norris moved to Pasadena about 1936 and had opened Norris Barber & Beauty Shop.[50]

West Pasadena continued to be almost a separate section of the community with its orientation around the intersection of the Sterling (La Porte Road) Highway and Richey Street. This area would continue to grow rather slowly compared to what was to happen to the south and southeast. Some of the old-timers still lived out there, but most of the residents worked at Sinclair Refinery. Professor Roy Glasgow had retired from teaching at Harrisburg High School, now called Milby High School. His son Roy A. had organized a band, which included Bobby Shaw on the trombone and Clyde Pomeroy on the trumpet. Roy had his eyes on Hollywood. In fact, there was a fair amount of musical talent in Pasadena at the time. Ray Abbott was well known for his guitar playing. Rosa Dowell had married Marion Edwin Ford and their children, Janey Pearl and Marion, Jr., entertained many with their singing. Janey Pearl eventually made it a career in New York City. Although the Abbotts did not live in West Pasadena, the Fords did.

When Ray Abbott was not playing his guitar he was "roughnecking" on one of McMaster and Pomeroy's water wells.

Marion, Sr., worked at Sinclair and his family lived in the old family homeplace since H. E. and Bertha Ford had passed away.[51]

The Kelleys still lived on the northeast corner of Sterling and Richey. Emerson still worked for Sinclair. Anita Maude was the final edition to their family back in 1924. Olive's marriage to Marvin Hughes now added grandchildren to the family, Marvin, Jr., and Marilyn Gay. Evelyn had married Howard William Parker in 1936 and Howard had a good job at Crown. Next to the Kelley's on Sterling was the new Stafford

Lumber Company (not to be confused with Eagle Lumber Company owned by Ralph Stafford several years later). Hill P. White and Herbert "Herb" Tatar purchased land fronting on Sterling and moved their lumber business in 1937 from Stafford, Texas. The lumber company was named for the town, not anyone involved with the business. Like Herb Paine, Tatar was interested in residential development and would leave a lasting legacy in the community. And Calvin E. Powitzky would shortly begin his design and construction business out of Tatar's Stafford Lumber Company's office. Meanwhile, Herb and Eva moved their family to town to keep close tabs on his business. Seymour was a year away from school and Leonard was just one year old.[52]

Gus Watson got his Texaco service station back and was operating it with Gus W. Tips's automobile agency. Watson had leased out the operation for years and now the pumping was back in his hands. A. J. Davis had moved in from Needville, Texas, to operate the station in 1930. Davis's wife Bertha ran the little drive-in sandwich shop that was on the corner at Hargrave. They had lived in one room and the other room was the kitchen. Since there was no other room inside, patrons had to eat outside. The restroom was next door in the service station garage. When Gus wanted to go up on the rent, in the

Hargrave's old service station was now operated by A. J. and Bertha Davis. Besides gasoline, you could get fast food.

middle of the depression, the Davises decided to move in 1933. Coincidentally, the move occurred about the time of the birth of their first child, Shirley. They opened a Crown service station on the east side of West Pasadena, on the northwestern corner of Park Street and Sterling. And with the birth of their second child, A. J., Jr., they moved their service station across Park Street. They rented the structure from teacher Lillian Sneed, and finally had an indoor bathroom. Will Bailey still

The Davises moved west to Park Street and opened a Crown service station.

had his Shell service station and grocery store. He was moving a bit slower these day, being 76 years of age.[53]

Herb Paine, Sr., was a charter member of the Rotary Club of Houston. Since his son, Herb Paine, Jr., was now in business in Pasadena as a residential builder and subdivision developer, Senior suggested that Junior organize a Rotary Club in Pasadena. On October 29, 1936, the Rotary Club of Pasadena was organized with Herb Paine, Jr., as its president. The other charter members were: Walter Ankele (insurance agent), Meyer

The Rotary Club of Pasadena was the first of several businessmen service clubs to organize.

Blankfield (cattle raiser), Aubrey Cruse (gasoline distributor), Euel Graham (railroad station master), Dr. B. C. Hensley (physician), Horace Jackson (superintendent of schools), Dr. O. Harrell Jones (dentist), Leo Karkowski (retail dry goods),

Clyde McMasters (water well driller), C. P. McMurry (service station and garage), Lee Mitchell (grocer), Frank Portwood, Jr. (druggist), Douglas Rathbone (theater manager), Matt Reed (banker), Gilbert Vick (Marvick Dairy Farm), Morris Wright (feed and seed store), and Arthur Whitman (lumber). The membership was a good representation of the businessmen in the community, but certainly not all of them. Douglas Rathbone of Houston was building the first movie theater in the community, located catty-corner to city hall on Shaver at Fifth (Shaw) Street . Doctors Hensley and Jones had maintained part-time offices upstairs in DeFee's building since 1931. By the time that the first group photograph was taken four months later W. R. Crute (Champion Paper mill manager), Reverend Marvin S. Vance (Methodist), J. B. Isaac (ice delivery), Jess Mason (cafe), and Jeff Fleming (barber) had also joined the club.[54]

With the construction of Champion and the resulting excitement in town, Dr. Edwin E. Connor saw an opportunity. Dr. Connor was working in Baytown at the Mutual Benefit Association of Humble Oil when he discovered Pasadena. Pasadena

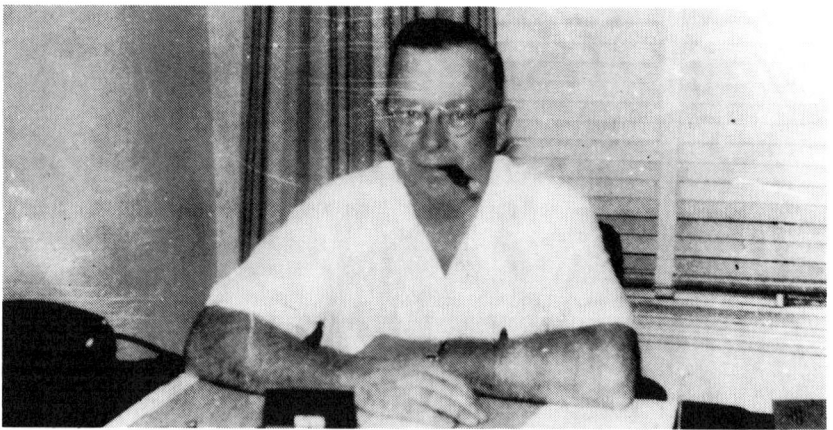

Dr. E. E. Connor built the first hospital in Pasadena and began recruiting many doctors to move to the growing community.

was a community that provided employees to five major industrial plants and a sizable school district. It did not have any medical facilities. There was only an ailing resident physician and a part-time Houston doctor. Harrisburg had the closest hospital for Pasadena, Deer Park, La Porte, South Houston, and Genoa. Dr. Connor was 38 years old, 10 years out of the University of Oklahoma medical school, and two years in

Texas. With a commitment from Champion Paper that he could be their company physician, Dr. Connor decided to move to Pasadena and started construction on the first hospi-

No sooner than Pasadena Hospital and Clinic was completed on Fifth (Shaw) and Spooner streets, it had to be enlarged.

tal in town. He and his wife Inice and young children Jack and Patsy moved into the "last" rent house in town. Connor actively recruited other doctors to come to Pasadena and the flow began within a year with Dr. Clarence F. Osborne, Dr. Catherine Coleman, Dr. James Lawrence DuCroz, and Dr. Everett Parker Veatch. Dr. Coleman was Pasadena's first female doctor. Dr. Connor would become the prime mover in the shape of Pasadena's medical future.[55]

Like Dr. Connor, the opening of the paper mill would bring many people to the community, people who had no ties to agriculture, only industry. Thomas Bryant "T. B." and Hazel Walker would arrive and move into one of Payne's new homes on the southern edge of town. Also moving in from North Carolina would be Samuel Basil Towles. He'd marry one of the Pitt's girls, Julie Estell, and continue the dynasty. Grover Vergil Bradshaw would also come from North Carolina and marry into another early family, Jim Hughes's daughter, Dorothy Lee. In fact, James E. "Red" Porter repeated the same story over with his catch of Mary Agnes Garfield. Sam D. and Edith Ellis would also come in from North Carolina. R. L. Boggs was also transferred in. He brought his wife Catharine and children Elizabeth, Margaret, Wallace, and Kenneth. Jack Beard would come during construction and then send for his wife Estelle when he finally found a place for them to live. John Statts and Ethel Mary Webb would bring little Laura from Louisiana. Edgar Gill and Margaret Bashforth would find their way to town. E. Gilbert Battle would be transferred in from Champion. These new people would make their impression on the community.[56]

Saturdays had traditionally been the busy day in downtown Pasadena as the farmers came to town. During the week they worked their fields and took their harvest to market. On Saturdays they came to town to buy the staples that they needed, to bank, and to visit. On Sundays they went to church and rested. Saturday, February 13 was a special day.

The community pattern had slowly changed over the years as more and more people took jobs off of the farm. At first it was only a single member of the family so the farm life routine was not interrupted. As fathers and sons left, the field work was shifted to hired hands. Life became a hybrid between farm and industry. Saturdays were still the days that the family could "go to town." With the proliferation of the automobile, a quick run

Champion Paper Mill in Pasadena employed 462 full-time employees and signified the end of the Farming Era in Pasadena.

into town was easy and the tradition of the whole family going to town together began to fade. The depression created a mythical step backwards as the farm again became the mainstay. On Saturday, February 13 people were in town to purchase Valentine's cards, and 462 lunch pails. On Sunday, the first sheet of pulp would roll off the new mill machines as Champion and 462 permanent jobs would forever rob the strawberry fields of its workers. It was a clear day, with a low of 46 degrees and a high of 68 degrees. There was no turning back from "progress." The trend had been in motion for a long time and the opening of Champion signalled the end of the depression locally, and the end of farming in Pasadena forever. Henceforth, the work day would start with the sound of the shrill steam whistle instead of the crow of the rooster.[57]

The change had been gradual and few had noticed how great the cumulative difference really was. But early settlers like Anna Pomeroy, now a month over 71 years of age and a resident of Pasadena for the past 36 years, knew that things had changed. No longer could Anna clearly see the billions of stars that speckled the night sky. Her son could no longer hear the corn growing in the fields. The ebb and flow of nature's sounds were muffled by more mechanical noises. She loved her cows, chickens, garden, and chats over the front fence with neighbors. Few people stopped now because so few people walked, but rather sped by in automobiles with the accelerated pace of life. Anna could not say if the change was good or bad, she only noted that people had adjusted. She could sense that an era in the history of Pasadena as she had known it was drawing to a close. Ranching had yielded to agriculture. Now it was agriculture's turn to step aside.

Anna and her kind had not set out to build a town. What they did was to make life easier: schools for their children, churches for their spirit, businesses for their personal needs, and a government for the common good. They did not have a grand design, or pretensions for prosperity. But in their striving, in the satisfaction of their needs, they had built a town, and they knew that it was a town that they were proud of. They knew that things were "better," but Anna and her friends belonged to history and another time. The future was now in the hands of younger folk, to shape and to caretake during their stewardship. Upon the foundations of the past, the future of Pasadena could prosper, and would.

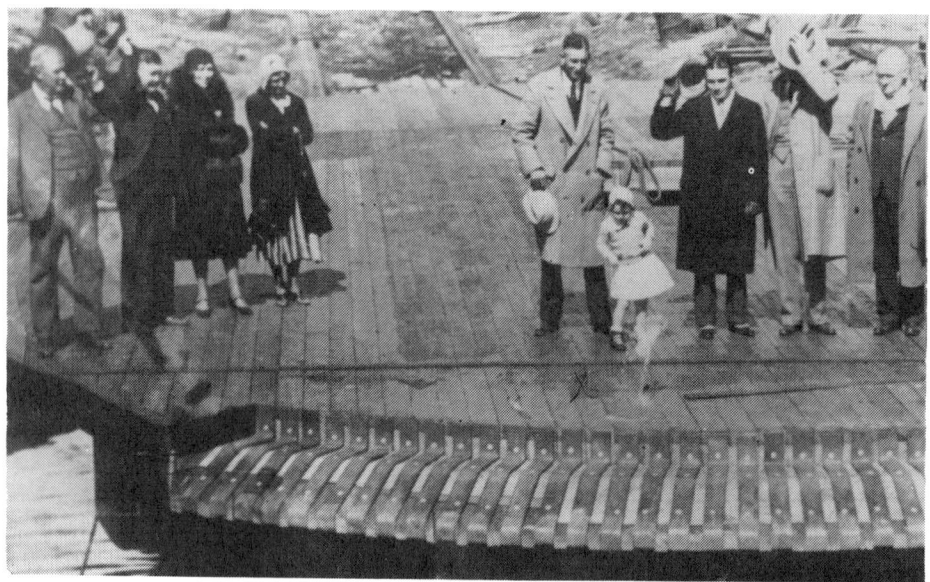

Little Rosemary Dreyfuss christened the new ferry with a bottle of bayou water.

No sooner than the mill was opened expansion plans were started. In fact, all of the industrial "plants" blossomed in the fertile Pasadena soil.

Epilogue

The pace of life in Pasadena got faster as Europe plunged itself into war. Activity on the Houston Ship Channel increased as supplies and materials flowed east, and west. Japan was purchasing every bit of scrap metal if could find. Daily Pasadena witnessed railroad carload after carload go by on its way to the docks, never realizing that it would be turned into instruments of war, and aimed back at us. The United States was drawn quickly into war on two fronts, against the Axis powers in the east and against Japan in the west. The renewed shipbuilding industry employed every able bodied person and tens of thousands quickly moved into the area.

When the shooting stopped and the smoke cleared, pent up consumer demand kept the mills and plants rolling. Those that had moved to Pasadena only for the duration of the war, with every intention of returning "home," stayed. Without realizing it until they had grandchildren of their own, Pasadena was now "home." Pasaden's population leaped from 22,000 to 45,000, then 59,000 and on past 100,000 without breathing. The city began annexing land and Pasadena now touches not only the ship channel, but also Galveston Bay and Clear Lake. The communities of Deepwater, Red Bluff, Middle Bayou, Killkare, Florentine Settlement, Alta Vista and Golden Acres were all absorbed in Pasadena.

In the last fifty years Pasadena has made a success of its industrial economy. Some towns are born and then die. Others flourish, languish and then are revived. Pasadena went straight from a prosperous agricultural period into a prosperous industrial period. That success is due not to the assistance of a benefactor or planning, but to the quality of the people who chose to live and work in Pasadena. They took advantage of the strawberry, and then of a ship channel, and moulded a community upon those products. Some say that Pasadena's future is now in the stars.

Notes

Chapter 1:

[1] Walter Prescott Webb, ed., *The Handbook of Texas*, (2 vols.;Austin: Texas State Historical Association, 1952), 2-844.

[2] Helen Alexander, "A History of Pasadena," *Pasadena News Citizen*, April 16, 1975, Insert p.1.; William Fairfax Gray, *From Virginia to Texas, 1835: Diary of Col. William F. Gray*, (Houston: Fletcher Young Publishing Co, 1965), 148; Edward N. Clopper, *An American Family*, (Cincinnati: Standard Printing and Publishing, 1950); Andrew Forest Muir, ed., *Texas in 1837, An Anonymous, Contemporary Narrative*, (Austin: University of Texas Press, 1958), 23; J. de Cordova, *Texas: Her Resources and Her Public Men*, (1858; reprint, Waco: Texian Press, 1969), 226, 227, 231; Feris A. Bass, Jr., and B. R. Brunson, eds. *Fragile Empires*, (Austin: Shoal Creek Publishers, Inc., 1978), 81.

[3] Webb, *The Handbook of Texas*, 1-662.

[4] David G. McComb, *Houston: A History*, (Austin: University of Texas Press, 1981), 14, 51; Webb, *The Handbook of Texas*, 1-848.

[5] Webb, *The Handbook of Texas*, 1-848.

[6] Webb, *The Handbook of Texas*, 1-778.

[7] Work Projects Administration, *Houston: A History and Guide*, (Houston: The Anson Jones Press, 1942), 37; Looscan, Adele B., "Harris County, 1822-1845," *Southwestern Historical Quarterly*, V.18, (1914-1915), 49, 56.

[8] Houston *Telegraph and Texas Register*, July 8, September 30, 1837; Gray, *From Virginia to Texas*, 148; Muir, *Texas in 1837*, 23; Harris County Probate Records (Family Law Center, Houston), A-103.

[9] Samuel W. Allen biography (unpublished, Pomeroy Collection); Webb, *The Handbook of Texas*, 2-771; Harris County Deed Records (hereinafter cited as HCDR):D-247, 105-152.

[10] M. Russell, ed., *Marriage Records of Harris County*, Vol. 1, 1837-65, #313, Pasadena Public Library, Pasadena, Texas; McComb, *Houston: A History*, 61; Jesse A. Ziegler, *Wave of the Gulf* (San

Antonio: The Naylor Compay, 1938), 88; Frederick L. Olmsted, *A Journey Through Texas* (1857; reprint, Austin: University of Texas Press, 1978), 366.

[11] Webb, *The Handbook of Texas*, 1-217, 2-89; Lubbock, Francis R., *Six Decades in Texas* (Austin: Pemberton Press, 1968), 130, 205.

[12] C. W. Adams, ed., *American Cattle Breeders Hall of Fame* (multiple volumes; San Angelo: Anchor Publishing Co., 1978), 1-266.

[13] Lubbock, *Six Decades in Texas*, 130.

[14] Lubbock, *Six Decades in Texas*, 139.

[15] Webb, *The Handbook of Texas*, 1-217, 2-89; Lubbock, *Six Decades in Texas*, 205.

[16] HCDR, T-125; Richard L. Gregg, "The Wm. Dobie Survey, Harris Cty., Tx.," *Houston Archeological Soc. Newsletter*, Vol. 66 (March 1980):, 22; Vol. 67 (August 1980): 9; Vol. 69 (May 1981): 4, 7; Vol. 70 (August 1981) 14.

[17] Stuart-Allen Collection, Mss 137, Boxes 7, 8, 11, 12, Houston Metropolitan Research Center, Houston Public Libray, Houston.

[18] C. C. Cox, "Reiminscences of C. C. Cox," *Southwestern Historical Quarterly*:6 (Oct. 1902), 129; Lubbock, "Six Decades in Texas," 238.

[19] Olmsted, *A Journey Through Texas*, 366; HCDR: T-49; Harris County Commissioners' Court Records (hereinafter cited as HCCCR), Book C-11.

[20] Ziegler, *Wave of the Gulf*, 29; Stuart-Allen Collection.

[21] Clara M. Love, "History of the Cattle Industry in the Southwest," SWHQ:19 (1915-1916):, 392; Webb, *The Handbook of Texas*, 1-351, 1-662; James Trager, ed., *The People's Chronology* (New York: Holt, Rinehart and Winston, 1979), 502; S. G. Reed, *A History of Texas Railroads* (Houston: St. Clair Publishing, 1941), 242; Earl W. Fornell, *The Galveston Era* (Austin: University of Texas Press, 1961), 10.

[22] Charles W. Hayes, *History of the Island and the City of Galveston* (Austin: Jenkins Garrett Press, 1974), 619; *History of Texas: With Biographical Histories of the Cities of Houston and Galveston* (Chicago: Lewis Publishing Co., 1895); Galveston County Deed Records (hereinafter cited as GCDR):12-784.

[23] Work Projects Administration, *The WPA Guide to Texas*, (Austin: Texas Monthly Press, reprint, 1986), 84; T. R. Fehrenbach, *Lone Star: A History of Texas and the Texans* (New York: American Legacy Press, 1983), 557; James P. Baughman, *Charles Morgan and the Development of Southern Transportation* (Nashville: Vanderbilt University Press, 1968), 128.

²⁴Christopher Emmett, *Shanghai Pierce, a fair likeness* (Norman: University of Oklahoma Press, 1953), 48; Joe Tom Davis, *Legendary Texians* (Austin: Eakin Press, 1982), 154.

²⁵Emmett, *Shanghai Pierce*, 56, 59; Webb, *The Handbook of Texas*, 2-376, GCDR: 8-439; Joe Davis, *Legendary Texians*, 165.

²⁶Rupert Richardson, et al., *Texas, The Lone Star State* (3rd ed., Englewood Cliffs: Prentice-Hall, Inc., 1970), 259; Work Projects Administration, *The WPA Guide to Texas*, 59; Hayes, *Galveston*, 896; GCDR: 1-354, 355; 5-444.

²⁷Richardson, *Texas, The Lone Star State*, 258, 261; D. W. Meinig, *Imperial Texas*, (Austin: University of Texas Press, 1969), 66; Fehrenbach, *Lone Star*, 557; Work Projects Administration, *The WPA Guide to Texas*, 85.

²⁸Richardson, *Texas, The Lone Star State*, 432; Webb, *The Handbook of Texas*, 2-89; Mike Kingston, ed. *The Texas Almanac*, Sesquicentennial Edition, 1986-87 (Dallas: Dallas Morning News, 1986), 206; Francis R. Lubbock, *Six Decades in Texas* (Austin: Pemberton Press, 1968), 595; HCDR:11-48; GCDR:8-440.

²⁹GCDR:14-11.

³⁰*Galveston City Directory*, 1872; HCCCR:C-168; Trager, *The People's Chronology*, 551; McComb, *Houston: A History*, 56; Stuart-Allen Collection; Hayes, *Galveston*, 678, 718; GCDR:12-784; Beers Family Papers, 1777-1925, 36-0670, Box 5, Rosenberg Library, Galveston.

³¹Baughman, *Charles Morgan*, 200; Stuart-Allen Collection, Abbott Deposition; Marilyn M. Sibley, *The Port of Houston: A History* (Austin: University of Texas Press, 1968), 100; George C. Werner, "Magnolia City," *National Railway Bulletin*, Vol. 47, No. 1, 1982, p. 12 (copy at Houston Metropolitan Research Center, Houston Public Library, Houston).

³²HCDR:27-37: Ziegler, IA *Wave of the Gulf*, 30; GCDR:12-784.

³³Stuart-Allen Collection, T. W. Williams deposition, Will Abbott deposition; Robert C. Stuart IV, Oral History by Helen Alexander, 1975, Pasadena Public Library, Pasadena, Texas; HCDR:18-12; HCCCR:C-659.

³⁴Stuart-Allen Collection, Box 7, T. W. Williams deposition, Will Abbott deposition.

³⁵Richardson *Texas, The Lone Star State*, 263; Work Projects Administration, *The WPA Guide to Texas*, 50, 85.

³⁶William F. Rapp, *The Galveston, Houston and Henderson Railroad*, (Crete: J-B Publishing Co., 1987), 2; Robert C. Stuart IV, Oral History.

³⁷HCDR: 22-608: 23-386: 24-311, 314: 27-37, 507.

³⁸Cox, "Reminiscences of C. C. Cox," 129; J. R. Welch, *Riding Fence* (Waco: Texian Press, 1983), 69; J. A. Creighten, *Narra-*

tive *History of Brazoria County* (Waco: Texian Press, 1975), ; Adams, *American Cattle Breeders Hall of Fame*, 100.

³⁹Robert C. Stuart IV, Oral History.

⁴⁰Stuart-Allen Collection, Box 11, Francita Stuart Koelsch, Narrative for Historical Marker, p. 2; BCDR:299-302; Webb, *The Handbook of Texas*, 3-19.

⁴¹Robert C. Stuart IV, Oral History.

⁴²HCDR:42-301; LP-*Bayshore Sun* July 10, 1969.

⁴³Robert C. Stuart IV, Oral History.

⁴⁴Stuart-Allen Collection, T. W. Williams deposition, Will Abbott deposition; Harris County Map Records (HC Map Rec.): 6-9; HCDR:135-366: 303-389, 390, 391; Harris County Probate Records (hereinafter cited as HCPR): J-107; HCDR: 48-457: 303-390, 391: Avilda W. Munger, Diary (subsequently cited as Munger Diary), made available by Mrs. C. Danouy, Houston, 1987; Barbara Y. Weidig, *Deer Park, a History of a Texas Town* (San Antonio: The Naylor Company, 1976), 50.

⁴⁵Lubbock, *Six Decades in Texas*, 131: Webb, *The Handbook of Texas*, 2-97, 554; Jim Glass, "San Jacinto," unpublished abstract of the community, Pomeroy History Collection;*Yesteryears in Pasadena, 1895-1941* (Pasadena: Harris County Genealogical Society, 1987), 224, 228; Weidig, *Deer Park*, 50.

⁴⁶LaPorte community history, Pomeroy History Collection; Red Bluff community history, Pomeroy History file; Margaret S. Henson, *The History of Baytown*, (Baytown: Bay Area Heritage Society, 1986), 58; John C. Eichorn, *God Lives in Our House* (La Porte: La Porte Community Church, 1951), 10; Seabrook community history, Pomeroy History Collection; Ed. Kilman, "Beautiful Shore Estate...," *Houston Post-Dispatch*, May 16, 1926.

⁴⁷Martyn Historic Data File, Armand Bayou Nature Center, Houston: U. S. G. S. Seabrook Quad Map (1932); Seabrook community history; Henry Cemetery report by George E. Wolf, Jr., 1984, Cemeteries file, Pomeroy History Collection; Gregg, "The Wm. Dobie Survey, Harris Cty, Tx," Vol. 70 (August 1981) 14.

⁴⁸Laurel B. McNay, Jr., interview 1988 at notes XV-10; Robert C. Stuart IV, Oral History.

Chapter 2:

¹HCDR:64-528.

²*History of Texas, with Biographical Histories*, 613; John H. Brown, *Indian Wars and Pioneers of Texas* (Easley: Southern Historical Press, 1978), 335; *Galveston City Directory*:1882-3, 1884-5, 1886-7, 1890-1, 1891-2.

Notes

[3] Gordon Black, interviews, various dates, see La Porte file; La Porte community history, Pomeroy Collection; Reed, *A History of Texas Railroads*, 252.

[4] HCPR: S-45, J-107, S-495; Harris County Marriage Records (subsequently HC Marriage), County Clerk's Office, Houston:K-43; HCDR:45-612, 47-164, 48-457.

[5] Harris County Property Tax Rolls, Texas State Library Archives, Austin, 1893; Betty Burnett McGowen, Oral History, Pomeroy Collection, Pasadena; HCDR:56-513; Genoa community history, Pomeroy Collection.

[6] Trager, *The People's Chronology*, 621, 626; Munger Diary.

[7] Munger Diary; HCDR:64-528.

[8] Munger Diary.

[9] Richard T. Colquette, "Early Growth of Pasadena Marks History of Area," *Pasadena Daily Citizen*, September 30, 1962; Trager *The People's Chronology*, 688; *Pasadena Times*, May 13, 1943, Sec.2 p.5; *Houston Post*, May 14, 1943; Munger Diary.

[10] Reed, *A History of Texas Railroads*, 252; *Houston Daily Post*, January 3, 18, February 9, 10, 19, March 9, 14, 30, 1893; HCDR:83-272.

[11] *La Porte Chronicle*, February 16, 1893, p.4 (copies of *La Porte Chronicle* made available by Gordon Black of La Porte); Mary Catherine Lubbock-Evans, "The History of La Porte," *LaPorte-Bayshore Sun* (series ran from July 10 to November 20, 1969), August 7, 1969, p.12, August 14, 1969; Eichorn, *God Lives in Our House*, 14; *Houston Post*, December 16, 1892.

[12] *La Porte Chronicle*, various 1893; Eichorn *God Lives in Our House*, 10; Lubbock-Evans, "The History of La Porte," August 10, 1969.

[13] HCDR:54-355: 55-241,243,244,245; 75-117, 119, 526: 78-290.

[14] HCDR:63-408, 482,494, 521,, 522, 523, 540, 571, 579, 591, 608: 65-177, 284, 290: 66-011, 181, 204; Weidig, *Deer Park*, 57, 62; *La Porte Chronicle*, January 26, 1893.

[15] HCDR: 64-528: 68-43, 42.

[16] Munger Diary, *McPherson Republican Newspaper*, McPherson, Kansas, February 10, 1893; HCDR: 66-106: 68-577.

[17] Munger Diary; Anonymous notes, assumed those of Jack Lynn, Pasadena Public Library, Pasadena; Pearl (Anderson) Shine letter, dated March 1960, copy provided by Marilyn (Towles) Coward, Pomeroy History Collection; Munger Diary; HCDR: 94-289,290.

[18] Lynn Peterson letters, 1988, Pomeroy Collection, Pasadena; *La Porte Chronicle*, February 16, 1893; Munger Diary.

[19] *La Porte Chronicle*, February 2, 1893.

[20]*McPherson Republican Newspaper*, March 10, 1893; HCDR:65-461; 66-419, 420, 576: 68-545, 544; *McPherson Republican Newspaper*, April 7, 1893.

[21]*La Porte Chronicle*, March 16, 23; April 13, 1893.

[22]*Houston Daily Post*, January 3, February 2, 9, 19, 1893; HCDR:66-204; Weidig, *Deer Park*, 66; *La Porte Chronicle* 4, April 27, 1893.

[23]HCDR: 64-528: 68-577: 70-371: 76-492; Mungers Diary.

[24]Munger Diary.

[25]Lubbock-Evans, "The History of La Porte," July 17, 1969; *Houston Daily Post*, January 22, 1893.

[26]HCDR: 71-300: 77-79: 92-550, 551; Mungers Diary.

[27]United State Post Office (subsequently cited as Post Office), P. O. Location Papers, Group 28, Harris County, Texas, National Archives, General Services Administration, Washington, Postmaster Appointments, p. 387; HCDR: 76-141, 217, 218; Irma Williams, "History of Pasadena, Tx" Pasadena Police Officers Association, 1958, reprinted by *Pasadena Citizen*, August 21-28, 1984.

[28]Martin B. Cominsky, ed., *Espiritu*, Pasadena High School Publications Department, Pasadena, 21; United States Census of Harris County, 1900, (subsequently cited as 1900 Census), ED 96, Sheet 19; HCDR: 123-39.

[29]HCDR: 76-614: 123-39; Shine letter.

[30]HCDR:94-275; Munger Diary; 1900 Census; J. S. Cullinan Collection, MSS 69, Houston Metropolitan Research Center, Houston Public Library, Houston, Texas, topographic maps.

[31]Munger Diary; HCDR:92-140, 553.

[32]HCDR:92-140; *Pasadena Times*, May 13, 1943, sec.2 p.5; *Houston Post*, May 14, 1943.

[33]Eichorn *God Lives in Our House*, p. 12; HCDR: 72-4; Lubbock-Evans, "The History of La Porte," August 7, 1969.

[34]HCDR: 76-418: 77-62: 79-428: 80-248: 88-432: 110-276: 114-326: 121-442: 125-451; Munger Diary; Shine letter; 1900 Census.

[35]Shine letter; Anonymous (Lynn) notes; HCDR:77-62; 79-342; John E. Pomeroy personal notes (subsequently cited as Pomeroy notes), Pomeroy Collection, Pasadena; John E. Pomeroy, interview 1979, at notes

Chapter 3

[1]Munger Diary; Irma Williams, "History of Pasadena."

[2]Pomeroy Family Records, personal notes; Shine letter; 1900 Census, ED 98-19-98, 98-19-24; HCDR:75-580, 80-14; Munger Diary.

³Pomeroy Family Records, personal notes.

⁴Munger Diary.

⁵Munger Diary; Irma Williams, "History of Pasadena."

⁶Munger Diary.

⁷Munger Diary; *La Porte Chronicle*, January 26, February 16, p.4, March 9, 16, p.1, April 27, p.4, 1893.

⁸Clarence Ousley, ed., *Galveston in Nineteen Hundred* (Atlanta: William C. Chase, 1900), 77; John Garner, co-ed., *Texas Weather* (Oklahoma City: England and May, 1975), 7; Lubbock-Evans, "The History of La Porte," August 7, 1969, p.12; Erna B. Foxworth, *The Romance of Old Sylvan Beach*, (Austin: Waterway Press, 1986), 17; Eichorn, *God Lives in Our House*, 14; Weidig, *Deer Park*, 83.

⁹Munger Diary; *La Porte Chronicle*, February 2, 1893; C. P. Zlatkovich, *Texas Railroads* (Austin: Bureau of Business Research, University of Texas, 1981), 34, 76, 80; Reed, *A History of Texas Railroads*, 252.

¹⁰Lubbock-Evans, "The History of La Porte," July 24, 1969.

¹¹Weidig, *Deer Park*, 62, 66, 82; Post Office.

¹²Post Office, Postmaster Appointments, p.387 ; HCDR:75-117, 119, 526: 77-397; Leopold Zlomke family biography, Pomeroy Collection, Pasadena; William N. Blakesley family biography; Calvin E. Parks family biography; *Yesteryears in Pasadena*, 151; Charnock B. McNay family biography.

¹³*Houston City Directory*, 1900-01; Harris County Property Tax Roll, 1893.

¹⁴M. T. Jones Lumber Co. Records, 3T566, 4C680, Barker Texas History Center, University of Texas, Austin; Bascom N. Timmons, *Jesse H. Jones* (New York: Henry Holt and Co., 1956), 41 et seq.

¹⁵M. T. Jones Lumber Co. Records, Misc. documents in 3T566 (1888-1898); HCDR: 81-214; Post Office, Postmaster Appointments, p. 387; Howard Stentz, "Katie's Pasadena of 1899" *Houston Chronicle*, March 23, 1969, Sec. 1, p.7.

¹⁶*The Union Baptist Association: Centennial History, 1840-1940* (Brenham: Banner-Press, Inc., undated), 179; Betty (Burnett) McGowen, interview 1987 at notes XI-6A; Rosemary Estes, ed., *Follow the Strawberry Road* (Pasadena: Pasadena Council Parents-Teachers Association, 1976), 50; Carol Williams, "Pasadena Life-Long Resident Recalls Town's Beginnings," *Houston Chronicle*, April 20, 1988; Delbert E. Atkinson family biography.

¹⁷Munger Diary; Irma Williams, "History of Pasadena, Texas."

¹⁸HCDR:110-276, 277; 111-209, 210.

[19] Munger Diary; Weidig, *Deer Park*, 82; Pomeroy Family Records, 1935 newspaper clipping "Townsite First Platted in 1895–Industries Started about 1917"; Irma Williams, "History of Pasadena, Texas."

[20] Munger Diary.

[21] HCDR:80-617: 82-53, 143: 86-407, 489: 87-420: 88-53, 415; M. F. Jones Lumber Co. records, 3T566, March 5 note.

[22] Munger Diary; *Houston City Directory* 1897; Trager, *The People's Chronology*, 647.

[23] Munger Diary; Irma Williams, "History of Pasadena, Texas"; Estes, ed., *Follow the Strawberry Road*, ii.

[24] HCDR:93-21, 635; Munger Diary; *Houston City Directory*, 1897-8.

[25] *Houston City Directory*, 1897-8; Irma Williams, "History of Pasadena, Texas."

[26] Munger Diary; *Pasadena Times*, May 13, 1943; HCDR:91-441: 99-522: 100-632; 1900 Census, ED 96-19; Irma Williams, "History of Pasadena, Texas".

[27] La Porte community history, Pomeroy Collection, Pasadena; Lubbock-Evans, "The History of La Porte," July 24, 1969; M. F. Jones Lumber Co. records, 4C680, letter dated 11-25-95 from Jones to Mayor W. A. Irvin with reply, letter dated 11-26-95 from Jones to J. Waldo re:shell.

[28] 1900 Census, ED 96-18-1; *Texas Gazetteer*: 1896-7.

[29] M. F. Jones Lumber Co. records, 3T566, petition dated 11-30-95, letters dated 12-17-95, 1-9-1896 and 2-20-1896 from Bradley to Jones.

[30] 1900 Census, ED 96-15-67.

[31] M. F. Jones Lumber Co. records, 3T566, numerous letters in file; William N. Blakesley biography.

[32] Kate (Smith) Bishop, "Oscar Kruse as an Educator," Pasadena Reading Club, 1939, p. 3-15; 1900 Census, ED 96-20-47.

[33] *The Union Baptist Association: Centennial History*, 179; Oscar A. Kruse, Jr., interview, 1987; Bishop, "Oscar Kruse as an Educator," 17.

[34] Addie B. Bailey, oral history by Helen Alexander, September 9, 1975: Pasadena Public Library, Pasadena; Alden O. Bailey, interview, September 11, 1989; William B. Bailey family biography.

[35] Woodrow P. Coolidge family biography.

[36] HCDR:101-335, 631: 114-326; 1900 Census, ED 96-19-45; David D. McCormick family biography.

[37] Post Office, Postmaster Appointments, p. 387; HCDR:114-326.

38Thurman L. Wilson, interview, 1988, notes at XIV-4A; Ray C. Williams, interview, 1984, notes at V-5.
39Ray C. Williams, interview, 1984, notes at V-2a, 5; HCDR:104-253.
40Oscar F. Moore family biography; 1900 Census, ED 96-19.
41Irma Williams, "History of Pasadena, Texas"; Bishop, "Oscar Kruse as an Educator," 18; Harris County School Records, Texas State Library Archives, Austin, La Porte, 701-85.
42Irma Williams, "History of Pasadena, Texas"; Pomeroy Family Records, personal notes; HCCCR:H-420, 449.
43HCCCR: H-420; Harris County School Records, Texas State Library Archives, Superintendent Reports, 4-23/273, (1898-1899); Trager, *The People's Chronology* 661, 656; Dr. Charles W. Griffith family biography.
44Munger Diary; Irma Williams, "History of Pasadena, Texas"; First Methodist Church, history provided by Clifton B. Eskridge, material in Pomeroy History Collection; Robert M. Guinn family biography; Jennie Larrabee, "Recollections of the Settling of Morris Cove and the Ritson Morris Family," City Hall Community file, City of Seabrook; City of Seabrook, Comprehensive Plan, p. 20.
45First Methodist Church file, Pomeroy Collection; Robert H. Guinn family biography; Work Projects Administration, *Houston: A History and Guide*, 101; HCDR:106-452; *La Porte Chronicle*, January 26, 1893; Lubbock-Evans, "The History of La Porte," August, 7, 1969.
46*The Union Baptist Association: Centennial History*, 176; "Reflections of Church Growth: 85th Anniv.," and additional material in First Baptist Church file, Pomeroy History Collection.
47HCCCR: H-420, 449; Harris County School Records, Texas State Library Archives, Superintendent Reports, 4-23/273, (1898-1901).
48Pomeroy Family Records, personal notes; Irma Williams, "History of Pasadena, Texas."
49*Houston City Directory*, 1899; Katie (Guinn) Weeks notes, Pomeroy Collection; William McBurney family biography; William W. Spacie family biography; 1900 Census, ED 96-19, 96-19-47; HCDR:106-571: 110-162, 495; Dr. Virginius S. MacNider family biography; Katie (Guinn) Weeks notes.
50Elva Reeves, interview, 1989, notes at XV-54; Robert M. Guinn family biography; HCPR:Film Code 895-64-0030, Vol. 3 p.441, Vol.4 pgs. 201, 215, 399; Reed, *A History of Texas Railroads*, 253.

[51]HCPR:Film Code 895-64-0030, Vol. 3 p.441, Vol. 4 pgs. 201, 215, 399; Ellis A. Davis and E. H. Grobe, ed., *New Encyclopedia of Texas* (Dallas: Texas Development Bureau, 1922).

[52]HCDR:117-159; *Houston Chronicle*, March 23, 1969; Post Office, Postmaster Appointments, p.388.

[53]Ousley, *Galveston in Nineteen Hundred*, 76; Weidig, *Deer Park*, 83; Work Projects Administration, *Houston: A History and Guide*, 101; Marilyn (Pitts) Coward, interview, 1986, notes at IX-16.

[54]United States Bureau of the Census (Washington, D. C.: U. S. Government Printing Office, various dates): Seventh Census, Population, 1850: Twelfth Census, Population, 1900; *Houston Post-Dispatch*,September, 10, 1900; Bishop, "Oscar Kruse as an Educator," 16; Irma Williams, "History of Pasadena, Texas"; Munger Diary; Weidig, *Deer Park*, 106.

[55]Bishop, "Oscar Kruse as an Educator," 16.

Chapter 4

[1]Ousley, *Galveston in Nineteen Hundred*, 28, 29; Garner, *Texas Weather*, 66.

[2]*Houston Post*, September 10, 1900, p.8; *Yesteryears in Pasadena*, 52, 115; Pomeroy Family Records, personal notes; *Galveston Daily News*, September 14, 1900.

[3]Alexander, "A History of Pasadena," p.12; *Houston Daily Post*, September 10, 11, 1900, p.4; *Pasadena Citizen*, February 27, 1966; Clara Wilson, interview, 1983, notes at II-48A; Johnny M.and Sylvia Meyers, interview, 1982, notes at II-27; *Yesteryears in Pasadena*, 235.

[4]*Houston Daily Post*, September 8, 10, 11, 12, 14, 1900; *Yesteryears in Pasadena*, 10; *Houston Post*, September 8, 1957; Betty (Burnett) McGowen, interview, 1987, notes at XI-10A.

[5]*Houston Daily Post*, September 10, 1900, p.8.

[6]*Houston Daily Post*, September 10, 1900, p.8.

[7]*Houston Daily Post*, September 10, 1900, pp.4,8, September 11, 1900, p.4; Foxworth, *The Romance of Old Sylvan Beach*, 21; *Diamond Jubilee (1847-1922) of the Diocese of Galveston and St. Mary's Cathedral in La Porte* (La Porte, Archdiocese, 1922), 114; *La Porte Chronicle*, April 6, 1893; 1900 Census, ED 98-14.

[8]*Houston Daily Post*, September 10, 1900.

[9]Cominsky, *Espiritu*, 21.

[10]Patrick Gilbo, *The American Red Cross, The First Century* (New York: Harper and Row, 1981), 19; Irma Williams,"History of Pasadena, Texas."

[11]Irma Williams,"History of Pasadena, Texas."

[12] *Houston Post*, May 1, 1956; John E. Pomeroy, oral history, 1979, notes at I-5; Irma Williams,"History of Pasadena, Texas"; E. Payson Pomeroy family biography; HCDR:127-471.

[13] *Galveston City Directory*, 1898; *Houston Post*, May 1, 1956; Pomeroy Family Records, personal notes.

[14] James W. Williams family biography; Frank M. Harwell family biography; Charlie Saderwhite family biography.

[15] *History of Texas with Biographical Histories*, 613; Brown, *Indian Wars and Pioneers of Texas*, 335; *Houston City Directory*, 1900-01; HCPR: 10-380; *Galveston Daily News*, June 26, 1901.

[16] *The Union Baptist Association: Centennial History*, 176; "Relections of Church Growth: 85th Anniversary." First Methodist Church file; Lubbock-Evans, "The History of La Porte," July 24, 1969,p.4.

[17] Gustov Edming family biography.

[18] *Yesteryears in Pasadena*, 89.

[19] HCDR: 77-565: 101-161: 123-573: 150-85: 152-44, 45.

[20] John E. Pomeroy, oral history, 1979, notes at I-4; J. Edward Pomeroy, Jr, interview, 1986, notes at X-23; "Proceedings of the Texas Dairyman's Convention, 1908," Barker Texas History Center, Austin, SF232T4T492, pp. 33, 58, 59; Pomeroy Family Records, personal notes; *Yesteryears in Pasadena*, 143; Clyde D. Pomeroy, interview, 1985, notes at VI-25.

[21] *Houston Daily Post*, September 10, 1900, p.8; Harris County Property Tax Rolls, Reel #6 (1897-1900), #7 (1900-1904), Texas State Library Archives, Austin; Davis, *New Encyclopedia of Texas*, 721.

[22] Irma Williams,"History of Pasadena, Texas"; *Pasadena Mirror*, December 3, 1954, p.28.

[23] HCDR:151-485;-*Houston Daily Post*:9-10-00, p.8; Pasadena Independent School District, Minutes of Board Meetings, Superintendent's Office, Pasadena (subsequently cited as School Minutes), July 29, 1904.

[24] Harris County School Records, Pasadena, 701-118, Annual Report, term ending August 31, 1901, Texas State Library Archives, Austin.

[25] Harris County School Records, Pasadena, Annual Report, term ending August 31, 1902, 1903.

[26] Harris County School Records, Pasadena, Annual Report, term ending August 31, 1904; School Minutes, July 19, 1904, October 28, 1904, December 30, 1904.

[27] James A. Jackson family biography; *Yesteryears in Pasadena*, 124, 138; Robert Ace Kingsbury family biography; John L. Holbrook family biography.

[28]HCDR:177-414; First Methodist Church file; *Pasadena News Citizen*, May 26, 1971, Sec. C, p.1; Dr. W. B. Ross family biography; G. Horace Plum family biography; School Minutes, October 28, 1904.

Chapter 5

[1]Weidig, *Deer Park*, 71, 106; *The Union Baptist Association: Centennial History*, 179.

[2]J. A Clark and M. T. Halbouty, *Spindletop* (New York: Random House, 1952), 52; Webb, *The Handbook of Texas*,1-551; James E. Buchanan, ed., *Houston, A Chronological and Documentary History* (Dobbs Ferry: Oceana Publications, 1975), 25; McComb, *Houston: A History*, 71; Trager, *The People's Chronology*, 692, 697, 702; David Wallechinsky and Irving Wallace, *The People's Almanac* (Garden City: Doubleday and Co., 1975, 2 vols.), 1-102; McComb, *Houston: A History*, 79, 91; Walter Rundell, Jr. *Early Texas Oil: A Photographic History, 1866-1936* (College Station: Texas A and M University Press, 1977), 81.

[3]*The Union Baptist Association: Centennial History*, 176, 177, 179; HCDR: 93-21; Pomeroy Family Records, personal notes; "Reflections of Church Growth"; Woodrow P. Coolidge family biography.

[4]Eskridge,"First United Methodist Church..."; *Pasadena News Citizen*, May 26, 1971,C-1; *Pasadena Citizen*, February 27, 1966.

[5]School Minutes, September 1, 1904: February 24, 1905: May 12, 1905; Harris County School Records, 701-118, Pasadena.

[6]School Minutes, May 12, June 5, August 1, September 29, November 10, 29, 1905: July 30, 1906.

[7]Pomeroy Diary, 1905 various entries; HCDR:159-500, 239-516; Maurine (Conn) Vassallo, letter to Marilyn Coward, dated February 12, 1988, copy in Pomeroy History Collection; John T. Conn family biography.

[8]Pomeroy Family Records, personal notes, undated 1932 history; Wade D. Dickerson family biography; School Minutes, September 30, 1905; Charles H. Tilley family biography; HCDR:175-225; *Houston Chronicle*, March 23, 1969.

[9]Pomeroy Diary, various entries.

[10]Howard Stentz, "Katie's Pasadena of 1889," *Houston Chronicle*, March 23, 1969, Sec.1, p.7; Richard (Dick) Nichols, "Grand Lady Reminisces About 82 Years of History," *Pasadena Citizen*, 1969.

[11]*Pasadena Daily Citizen*, May 5, 1961, p.5; Arvie Thompson family biography; William F. Van Dorn family biography; Dean K. Jones family biography; Jake D. Miller family biography; Yerkes family biography; "Reflections of Church Growth"; *The Union*

Baptist Association: Centennial History,177; Dr. Titus C. Loose family biography; Everett and Ray Williams, interview, 1984, notes at V-7; Pomeroy Diary, 1905; Pomeroy Family Records, personal notes, Coming Men of America lodge records; Mattie McEvers family biography; HCDR:167-285; John T. Shine family biography.

[12] Nichols, "Grand Lady Reminisces About 82 Years of History;" Tommy Burns, "Automobile Directory, 1904" *Living Tree Newsletter*, Harris County Genealogical Society, V. 8, Fall 1981, p.127; Pomeroy Diary, November 18, 1905.

[13] *Harris County School Land Frauds* (Smithville: Times Power Print, npd); Texas Land Records, General Land Office, Austin, School Land Files, No. 29439, Abstract 1062, Affidavits in No.27330, Laws of Texas, Vol. 9 (1879-1889), p.881.

[14] *Houston Post*, July 28, 30, 1906.

[15] Clyde D. Pomeroy, interview, various dates; Pomeroy Diary, September 9, 1905.

[16] School Minutes, August 1, 1905, April 13, 1906.

[17] Pomeroy Diary, various dates.

[18] Pomeroy Diary, various dates; Pomeroy Family Records, personal notes.

[19] Pomeroy Diary, August 20, 1905; Pomeroy Family Records, personal notes.

[20] Pomeroy Family Records, Coming Men of America file; Pomeroy Diary, various dates.

[21] Catherine Kingsbury, interview, 1986, notes at VI-47; Pomeroy Diary, September 8, 1905: June 30, August 31, 1906: February 1, June 7, 1907.

[22] Buchanan, *Houston, A Chronological and Documentary History*, 26; George Fuermann, *Peden-1965, 75 Years -and Just a Beginning*, (Houston: Press of Premier, 1965), 36; McComb, *Houston: A History*, 107; Pomeroy Diary: July 15, 1905: February 28, 1909; Robert W. Glasgow, interview, 1987, notes at X-49A.

[23] Irma Williams, "History of Pasadena"; *Pasadena Citizen*, December 11, 1963; Cominsky, *Espiritu*, 10.

[24] Pomeroy Diary: October 24, 25, 1906; Pomeroy Family Records, Abstract C#505602, p.155; HCDR:230-21; Selby Young, interview, 1986, notes at IX-44; Everett and Ray Williams, interview, 1984, notes at V-5A; Johnny and Sylvia Meyers, interview, 1982, notes at II-29; Crown Hill Cemetery, records, Texas State Historical Marker narrative by C. David Pomeroy, Jr., 1989, Pomeroy History Collection.

[25] Johnny and Sylvia Meyers, interview, 1982, 1984; Crown Hill Cemetery, records; James A. Jackson family biography; *Yesteryears in Pasadena*, 85.

[26] Walter L. Wilson family biography; Pomeroy Diary, various dates; HCDR:203-469; Ira L. Pitts family biography.

[27] Pomeroy Family Records, Abstract #502602: p.151, HCPR:31-333: financial records; Pomeroy Diary: February 13, 1907: May 20, 1908.

[28] Pomeroy Diary, June 8, et seq. 1908; Pomeroy Family Records, Account Book.

[29] HCPR:31-333; *Houston Chronicle*, November 8, 1927; Pomeroy Family Records, tax receipts.

[30] Pomeroy Diary, June 6, 1908; Cecila (Garfield) Dickerson, interview, 1984, notes at III-41.

[31] Dr. Titus C. Loose family biography; Dr. Virginius S. MacNider family biography; HCDR:110-162, 533; Joseph S. Cullinan Collection, MSS 69, Houston Metropolitan Research Center, Houston Public Library, Houston, Texas, land ownership file; *Houston City Directory*:1892-3, 1899,1902; *American Medical Association (AMA) Directory*, 1906, 1912, Harris County Medical Society Library and Archives, Houston; Deepwater community history, Pomeroy Collection, Pasadena; Dr. W. B. Ross family biography.

[32] Dr. Juliett C. Marchant family biography; Lubbock-Evans, "The History of La Porte," October 30, 1969; Dr. H. T. McCoy family biography; Harris County Medical Society, records provided by Beth White, 1982, notes at I-69A; Eichorn, *God Lives in Our House*, 15.

[33] Davis and Grobe, *New Encyclopedia of Texas*, 1386.

[34] School Minutes:May 30, 1906: May 7, 1908; Harris County School Records, Superintendent Reports, 4-23/273; Harris County School Department, *Report of Harris County Schools*, located at Houston Metropolitan Research Center, Houston Public Library, Houston, Texas, year ending August 31, 1912; Woodrow P. Coolidge family biography; Catherine Kingsbury, interview, 1988, notes at XII-71, oral history, 1986, notes at VI-56; HCDR:214-200.

[35] School Minutes: May 29, 1908: August 29, 1908: generally July 10, 1908 to February 26, 1909: June 18, 1909;Post Office, Postmaster Appointments, p.365; Harris County School Reports: Pasadena, 701-118, Annual Reports.

[36] Pomeroy Family Records, Gertrude (McMaster) Pomeroy "Street Car" notes, personal correspondence 1909-1910; Gertrude L. (McMaster) Pomeroy Diary, Pomeroy Collection, Pasadena, 1909-1910; Pomeroy Diary, 1909-1910.

[37] School Minutes: April 30, 1909: July, 1909; Marilyn Coward, interview, 1989, notes at XVI-52; Pomeroy Family Records, rent book; Gertrude L. Pomeroy Diary, 1909; E. Payson

Pomeroy family biography; William W. Anderson family biography; Karl Kruse, oral history, by Dick Nichols, 1971, notes at X-19, 22; Irma Williams, "History of Pasadena"; Weidig, *Deer Park*, 100; *Yesteryears in Pasadena*, 124, 125.

[38]Francis D. Newell family biography; *Yesteryears in Pasadena*, 143; Earl L. Newell, interview, 1989, notes at XVI-75; George P. Dowell family biography; Gustov Edming family biography; Ben Hargrave family biography; 1910 Census, ED 110, Family #7, 11, 47, 53, 58, 80; Edward A. Olson family biography; Weidig, *Deer Park*, 146; Jacob L. Hearn family biography; Talitha Barnes family history.

[39]HCDR: 159-500: 239-516; James W. Williams family biography; Thurman Wilson, interview, 1988, notes at XIV-5A; Roy M. Glasgow family biography; 1910 Census, ED 110, Family #42, 67.

[40]1910 Census ED 110, Family #18, 48, 82; Ira L. Pitts family biography; Gerald W. Conrad family biography; Helge Gigstad family biography; Herrington, *Houston Chronicle*, April 20, 1988; Walter L. Wilson family biography; James W. Williams family biography; Delbert E. Atkinson family biography; Robert M. Guinn family biography; George H. Plum family biography.

[41]Gertrude L. Pomeroy Diary, July 1909; *Houston Post*, February 20, 1910, p.14; School Minutes: January 14, February 14, 1910; *Houston Post*, February 20, 1910, p.14; Bishop, "Oscar Kruse as an Educator," 23.

[42]School Minutes: May 23, August 23, September 2, 10, 1910: March 3, 1911; John C. Gutherie family biography.

[43]Josiah Rawlins family biography; William B. Bailey family biography; Robert M. Guinn family biography; Sarah V. Hogge family biography; Post Office, Postmasters, p. 387.

[44]HCDR:264-475.

Chapter 6

[1]*Houston Chronicle*, January 5, 1936.

[2]Bishop, "Oscar Kruse as an Educator," 16.

[3]Pomeroy Family records, Financial Records

[4]Marvin D. Burnett, interview, 1984, notes at III-42, additional notes at IV-39A; Everett Williams, interview, 1982, notes at II-33A; Talitha Barnes family biography; Archie G. Thomasson family biography; 1920 Census ED 107, Family #381; Joe Cook family biography; Sam Davis family biography: Thomas Duffield family biography; Catherine Kingsbury, interview, 1986, notes at VI-48, 53; John T. Shine family biography; William W.

Anderson family biography; Delbert E. Atkinson family biography.

[5] Pomeroy Family Records, postcard; Strawberry file, Pomeroy History Collection; *Yesteryears in Pasadena*, 78; Ralph and Winogene Stafford, interview, 1987, notes at X-38.

[6] *Yesteryears in Pasadena*, 84; Edward Pomeroy, interview, 1988, notes at XV-4A; Thurman Wilson, interview, 1988, notes at XIV-7.

[7] Joseph S. Cullinan Collection, farm records.

[8] Joseph S. Cullinan Collection, farm records.

[9] Joseph S. Cullinan Collection, farm records.

[10] Work Projects Administration, *Houston: A History and Guide*, 250; *Yesteryears in Pasadena*, 78.

[11] *Yesteryears in Pasadena*, 89; Paul Herrara, interview and oral history, 1987, notes at XI-37.

[12] Calvin E. Parks family biography.

[13] *Yesteryears in Pasadena*, 38, 40, 89; Ralph G. Blakesley, interview.

[14] Edward Pomeroy, interview, 1984, notes at IX-7A.

[15] *Yesteryears in Pasadena*, 95, 113, 184; Irma Williams, "History of Pasadena," 6; *Pasadena Times*, May 13, 1943; *Houston Post*, May 14, 1943.

[16] *Yesteryears in Pasadena*, 95, 176; Foxworth, *The Romance of Old Sylvan Beach*, 25; Robert W. Glasgow, interview, notes at X-49; Pomeroy Family records.

[17] Pomeroy Family records, Pasadena, Texas Producers Exchange; HCDR:269-226, 301-141; 1920 Census, ED 107, Sheet 14A, Family 345; *Yesteryears in Pasadena*, 41.

[18] Marvin D. Burnett, interview, 1984, notes at III-42A; HCDR:305-305; Pomeroy Family records, McMaster and Pomeroy Water Well Drilling Co. (subsequent cited as MPWW).

[19] Delbert E. Atkinson family biography; Adolph Herrera family biography; *Yesteryears in Pasadena*, 189.

[20] HCDR:241-585; Clyde D. Pomeroy, interview, 1986, notes at VII-19; Edward and Loise Pomeroy, interview, 1986, notes at IX-2; David C. McMaster family biography; Post Office, Postmaster, p.365; Pomeroy Family records, MPWW.

[21] Pomeroy Family records, MPWW.

[22] Pomeroy Family records, MPWW.

[23] Addie B. Bailey, oral history, 1975, notes at IV-8; HCDR:223-172, 225-290; Pomeroy Family records, financial records; Janis Teas, interview, 1993, notes at XVIII-30B; Charles L. Garfield family biography; *Yesteryears in Pasadena*, 175; Kenyon, *From Arrows to Astronauts*, 41.

Notes 391

[24] Irma Williams, "History of Pasadena," 5; *Pasadena Times*, May 14, 1943; *Houston Post*, May 14, 1943.

[25] Irma Williams, "History of Pasadena," 5; Helen Brubaker, interview, 1979, notes at I-11; Raymond A. Dickerson, interview, 1986, notes at IX-28; Robert W. Glasgow, interview, 1987, notes at X-42A, 49A; Joseph S. Cullinan Collection, farm records; George A. Brown family biography; *Yesteryears in Pasadena* 142; Addie B Bailey, oral history, 1975, notes at IV-3; ; Edward and Loise Pomeroy, interview, 1986, notes at IX-6; Ira L. Pitts family biography.

[26] 1910 Census, ED 110, Family # 88, 89, 90; Samuel Garnuch family biography; William Laschinsky family biography; Helen (Kruse) Shinpaugh, interview, 1993, notes at XIX-41; Crown Hill Cemetery records.

[27] 1920 Cen ED 107, sheet 14A, family 337, sheet 14B, family 353; 1910 Cen ED 110, Family #4, 29, 30, 46, 66; William H. Thornton family biography.

[28] Mary Kegg, "Japanese Heritage in Bay Area Dates to 1903," *The Clear Lake Citizen*, April 7, 1988, p. 10; Kenyon, *From Arrows to Astronauts*, 40; Johnny and Sylvia Meryer, interview, 1982, notes at II-29A; Karl Kruse, oral history, notes at X-14; *Yesteryears in Pasadena*, 100.

[29] David Z. Holloway family biography; Raymond Dickerson, interview, 1984, notes at VI-20A; *Yesteryears in Pasadena*, 53; Raymond Dickerson, interview, 1986, notes at IX-28; John Kriegel, *Houston Garden Book*, (Houston: Shearer Publishing, 1983), 91.

[30] Stuart-Allen Collection; Allen Ranch history file, Pomeroy Collection, Pasadena; Laurel B. McNay, Jr., oral history, 1988, notes at XV-17; Weidig, *Deer Park*, 94; Eldon Branda, ed., *The Handbook of Texas, A Supplement*, Vol. 3 of 3 volume set, (Austin: Texas State Historical Association, 1976), 3-19.

[31] *Yesteryears in Pasadena*, 204; Joseph S. Cullinan Collection, farm records; Samuel A. Quinn family biography; Edward Kruse, oral history and interview, 1985, notes at VI-31.

Chapter 7

[1] Pomeroy Diary, various dates; Carol Williams, "Pasadena Life-Long Resident Recalls Town's Beginnings."

[2] Talitha Barnes family biography; *Yesteryears in Pasadena*, 80.

[3] Doris (Barnes) Howell, interview: 1989, notes at XVII-4: 1983, notes at III-35; *Yesteryears in Pasadena*, 80; Pentecostal Church history, Pomeroy Collection, Pasadena.

[4] Pomeroy Diary, February 17, 18, 1910; Roger Bilstein and Jay Miller, *Aviation in Texas*, (Austin: Texas Monthly Press, Inc.

1985), 11; Alvin Josephy, *The American Heritage of Flight* (American Heritage Publishing, 1962), 123; Walker, "1910: The Year the Air Age Came to Houston," 41, 42; *Houston Post*: February 13, 1910, p.13: February 16, 1910: February 19, 1910, p.1; Ben F. Meador, Jr., interview, 1993, notes at XIX-34.

[5]Pomeroy Diary, February 19, 1910; *Houston Post*, February 20, 1910, p.1; *Houston Chronicle*, February 19, 1910, p.5; Fuermann, *Peden-1965*, 35; Josephy, *The American Heritage of Flight*, 123.

[6]Webb, *The Handbook of Texas*, 2-556, 665, 953; *The Groesbeck Journal*, April 24, 1986; Pomeroy Diary, April 21, 1910.

[7]City Council Minutes, City of South Houston, City Hall, South Houston, May 4, 1922, Vol. 2, p.91; Arland Weise, "A Short History of South Houston." circa 1975, provided by Pat Lapold, South Houston History Collection, Harris County Public Library, South Houston, Texas; Map of South Houston, Houston Metropolitan Research Center, Houston Public Library, Houston, Texas, H-1911. HCDR Plat Bk:2-42.

[8]*Houston Post*: February 13, 1910, p.16, February 20, 1910, p. 14; Weise, "A Short History of South Houston," South Houston History Collection; South Houston community history file, Pomeroy Collection, Pasadena; *Report of Harris County Schools*, year ending August, 1910; *South Houston Press*, January 8, 1976; Estes, *Follow the Strawberry Road*, 56; Ben F. Meador, Jr., interview, 1993, notes at XIX-34; *The Union Baptist Association: Centennial History*, 245.

[9]Weise, "A Short History of South Houston," and South Houston History Exhibit, and Marjorie S. Ward, ed., "The South Houston Metamorphosis," South Houston High School English Department project, circa 1986, South Houston History Collection.

[10]James O. Holly, "Pasadena Board Running Short of School Names" undated newspaper clipping in South Houston community history file, Pomeroy Collection, Pasadena; 1910 Census ED 110, Sheet 18A; Walker, "1910: The Year the Air Age Came to Houston," 45, 47; Work Projects Administration, *Houston*, 147.

[11]Walker, "1910: The Year the Air Age Came to Houston," 50; Work Projects Administration, *Houston*, 147; 1910 Census ED 110, Sheet 18A.

[12]Harris County Medical Society, Archive files; Clara Wilson, oral history, notes at III-77.

[13]Herb Woods, *Galveston-Houston Electric Railway* (Glendale: Interurban Publications, 1976), 21.

[14]Woods, *Galveston-Houston Electric Railway*, 21.

[15] Harris County Map Records:3-32;. Galveston-Houston Interurban Land Co., Barker Texas History Center, University of Texas, Austin, Texas, T6934/G139f, brochure; *Houston Post*: February 17, 1910, p.4: February 20, 1910, p.13.

[16] Woods, *Galveston-Houston Electric Railway*, 21.

[17] Reed, *A History of Texas Railroads*, 253; Zlatkovich, *Texas Railroads*, 44.

[18] Pomeroy Family Records, Account Book; Pearl (Ford) Hickman Schloeman, "School Days in Pasadena, 1910-1921," *The Living Tree*, Harris County Genealogical Society, 1985, Vol. 11, p.1; X-19; *Star News Citizen*, May 6, 1963; Robert W. Glasgow, interview, 1987, notes at X-45A; Weidig, *Deer Park*, 100; School Minutes: January 26, 1912: October 25, 1912.

[19] Pomeroy Diary, October, November, December 1905; *Report of Harris County Schools*, year ending August 1912, p. 79; Mrs. W. C. Williams, letter dated January 24, 1912, to *Holland's Magazine*, copy provided by Anne Nicholardi, Pasadena School history, Pomeroy History Collection; Schloeman, "School Days in Pasadena, 1910-1921"; School Minutes: October 25, 1912: November 2, 1912; Traeger, *The People's Chronology*, 744; Otto Johnson, ed., *Information Please Almanac, 1990* (Boston: Houghton Mifflin Co., 1989), 748, 762, 765, 770.

[20] *Report of Harris County Schools*, year ending August 1912, p. 79; Pasadena School history file, Pomeroy Collection, Pasadena, article provided by Anne Nicholardi, 1988; Schloeman, "School Days in Pasadena, Texas, 1910-1921"; School Minutes, August 17, 1912; Bishop, "Oscar Kruse as an Educator," 26.

[21] School Minutes: October 27, 1911: August 2, 1912: March 8, 28, 1913; Bevis Frazier, oral history by Helen Alexander, 1978, Pasadena History Collection, Pasadena Public Library, Pasadena, Texas, notes in Pomeroy Collection at IV-22; *Report of Harris County Schools*, year ending August 1913, 1914.

[22] Karl Kruse, interview, notes at X-21; School Minutes, April 25, 1913; W. J. David family history, obituary.

[23] David D. McCormick family biography, cemetery record; Frederick G. Deane family biography ; HC Marriage:7-362, Cert.# 260561; 1910 Census, EN 110, Family #49; 1920 Census, EN 107, Sheet 17A, Family #408.

[24] *Texas Gazetteer*, 1914-1915.; Joseph S. Cullinan Collection, Purchase contract with Sterling Anderson, May 24, 1915, farm records file; Jason R. Moechel family biography; George J. Lakin family biography.

[25] Post Office, Postmaster Appointments, p. 367; William H. Thornton family biography; John T. Conn family biography; Robert A. Kingsbury family biography.

[26] Pomeroy Diary, July 12, 1915; E. Payson Pomeroy family biography; David C. McMaster family biography; Robert G. James family biography.

[27] Howard Stentz, "Katie's Pasadena of 1899," *Houston Chronicle*, March 23, 1969, sec. 1, p.7; Robert M. Guinn family biography; *Houston Chronicle*, August 19, 1915, p. 10; Joseph S. Cullinan Collection, miscellaneous notes, farm records .

[28] John L. Holbrook family biography; John H. Strope family biography; Robert W. King family biography; Samuel W. Allen family biography.

[29] *Texas Gazetteer*, 1914-1915; Doris Howell, interview, 1989, notes at XVI-50; *Report of Harris County Schools*, year ending August 1912; Charnock B. McNay, family biography; Oscar Starnes family biography; 1910 Census, EN 110, Family #97.

[30] *Texas Gazetteer*, 1914-1915; Weidig, *Deer Park*, 106, 133, 152; Post Office, Postmaster appointments, p.365.

[31] *Texas Gazetteer*, 1914-1915; Post Office, Postmaster appointments, p. 368; Lubbock-Evans, "The History of La Porte," *La Porte-Bayshore Sun*, October 2, 1969; Foxworth, *The Romance of Old Sylvan Beach*, 25.

[32] Post Office, Postmaster appointments, p. 366; *Texas Gazetteer*, 1914-1915; *Report of Harris County Schools*, year ending August, 1910, 1912; Estes, *Follow the Strawberry Road*, 50.

[33] *Texas Gazetteer*, 1914-1915; Branda, *The Handbook of Texas, A Supplement*, 3-903; City Council Minutes of South Houston, v.2, p.91; South Houston community history; *Houston Press*, January 8, 1976; *Pasadena Citizen*, January 27, 1980; South Houston Exhibit; Pat Lippold, interview, 1988, notes at XIII-28; *Report of Harris County Schools*, year ending August, 1910, 1912; Ben F. Meador, Jr., interview, 1993, notes at XIX-34.

[34] *Galveston Daily News*, August 16, 1915, p.1; Garner, *Texas Weather*, 66; *Houston Chronicle*, August, 18, 20, 1915.

[35] Garner, *Texas Weather*, 66; Woods, *Galveston-Houston Electric Railway*, 59.

[36] *Houston Chronicle*, August 17, 18, 1915; *Houston Post*, August 18, 19, 1915, September 8, 1957; Branda, *The Handbook of Texas, A Supplement*, 3-903; South Houston Exhibit; *Yesteryears in Pasadena*, 225; Weidig, *Deer Park*, 114.

[37] *Houston Chronicle*, August 18, 1919, p.8; Delbert E. Atkinson family biography; Helen (Kruse) Shimpaugh, interview, 1993, notes at XIX-41; *Yesteryears in Pasadena*, 4, 27, 153, 166, 178, 180, 189, 229, 232; Thurman Wilson, interview, 1988, notes at XIV-5.

[38] *Yesteryears in Pasadena*, 113, 137; Karl Kruse, oral history, 1971, notes at X-15.

[39] Doris Howell, interview, 1993, notes at XVIII-43.
[40] Sibley, *Deer Park*, 149; *Houston Chronicle*, August 21, 1915.
[41] *Yesteryears in Pasadena*, 144; Myrtle (Blakesley) Billingsley, interview, 1983, notes at III-23.
[42] Trager, *The People's Chronology*, 758, 765; Josephy, *The American Heritage of Flight*, 161, 178; Bernard Grun, *The Timetables of History* (New York: Simon and Schuster, 1979), 467.
[43] Bilstein and Miller, *Aviation in Texas*, 18, 19, 51; Josephy, *The American Heritage of Flight*, 164.
[44] Bilstein and Miller, *Aviation in Texas*, 51; *Ellington:1918, Yearbook of Ellington Air Base*, 3, 65.
[45] Bilstein and Miller, *Aviation in Texas*, 19, 269; Bob Grafton, "The Texas City Aviators," *Focus*, College of the Mainland, Texas City, Texas, March 1986; Jim Higgins, Ellington," *Houston Chronicle, Texas Magazine*, p.4.
[46] Higgins, "Ellington," 4; Historical Background-Ellington Air Force Base, letter from Department of the Air Force, 147th Fighter Interceptor Group, 1987, Pomeroy Collection, Pasadena; William B. Bailey family biography; *Ellington:1918, Yearbook of Ellington Air Base*, 5.
[47] *Ellington:1918, Yearbook of Ellington Air Base*, 33, 97; Thurman Wilson, interview, 1988, notes at XIV-5; Addie (Brown) Bailey, oral history, 1975, notes at IV-6; Higgins, "Ellington," 4.
[48] Foxworth, *The Romance of Old Sylvan Beach*, 25; Clara Wilson, oral history, by Helen Alexander, 1975, notes at IV-1A; *Yesteryears in Pasadena*, 139; Ruth (Rawlins) Dearing, interview, 1989, notes at XVI-55; Barbara Neal, "Blanche Remembers" *Bayshore Sun*, April 12, 1987.
[49] Marvin D. Burnett, interview, 1984, notes at IV-39A; *Houston Post*, August 5, 1917: April 7, 1918; McComb, *Houston: A History*, 76; Pomeroy Family records, MPWW; Jess T. Brammer family biography; Ray C. Williams, interview, 1988, notes at XII-71A; *Yesteryears in Pasadena*, 78; J. Edward Pomeroy, Jr., interview, 1985, notes at VII-76A; O. F. Allen, *The City of Houston, From Wilderness to Wonder*, (Temple, Texas: n.p., 1936) p.43; Webb, *The Handbook of Texas*, 2-235.
[50] *Houston Post*, April 28, 1918; *News Citizen*, February 27, 1966.
[51] Work Projects Administration, *Houston*, 109; Robert M. Guinn family biography; Thurman Wilson, interview, 1988, notes at XIV-4; Oscar Kruse family biography; Woodrow P. Coolidge family biography; Everett and Ray Williams, interview, 1984, notes at V-2; *Yesteryears in Pasadena*, 38, 90, 142, 145, 233; Ben Hargrave family biography; Mildred (Tabor) Hay, interview, 1993, notes at XVIII-51.

⁵²*Yesteryears in Pasadena*, 84; Thurman Wilson, interview, 1988, notes at XIV-5; *Ellington:1918, Yearbook of Ellington Air Base*.

⁵³*Ellington:1918, Yearbook of Ellington Air Base*, 71, 81, 131; Work Projects Administration, *Houston*, 111.

⁵⁴*Ellington:1918, Yearbook of Ellington Air Base*, 97; Trager, *The People's Chronology*, 784; Work Projects Administration, *Houston*, 109; *Yesteryears in Pasadena*, 38, 41, 48, 125, 145, 178; Cecelia (Garfield) Dickerson, interview, 1984, notes at III-41.

⁵⁵*Yesteryears in Pasadena*, 41; John F. Johnson family biography.

⁵⁶*Yesteryears in Pasadena*, 230; Crown Hill Cemetery Records; Sidney G. Robertson family biography; Eichorn, *God Lives in Our House*, 17.

⁵⁷Work Projects Administration, *Houston*, 111; *Yesteryears in Pasadena*, 8, 37, 233; *Ellington:1918, Yearbook of Ellington Air Base*, 10.

⁵⁸Sibley, *The Port of Houston*, 150.

Chapter 8

¹Webb, *The Handbook of Texas*, 1-779; HCDR:A-418; HCPR:D-536; *Pasadena Citizen*, April 22, 1973; *Telegraph and Texas Register*, July 8, 1837; Reed, *A History of Texas Railroads*, 36.

²Webb, *The Handbook of Texas*, 1-217, 240; Sibley, *The Port of Houston: A History*, 63, 65, 73, 74; Reed, *A History of Texas Railroads*, 77.

³Webb, *The Handbook of Texas*, 1-746; John H. Burnett family biography; Brown, *Indian Wars and Pioneers of Texas*, Burnett; Sibley, *The Port of Houston: A History*, 99, 125; Thomas H. Ball, *The Port of Houston, How it Came to Pass*, (Houston: *Houston Chronicle*, npd), also as a collection of articles in the *Houston Chronicle* so cited both ways, August 16, 1936.

⁴Sibley, *The Port of Houston: A History*, 95, 129; Ball, *Houston Chronicle*, August 16, 1936.

⁵Sibley, *The Port of Houston: A History*, 136, 141.

⁶HCDR:93-21, 75-526; Johnny and Sylvia (Wilson) Meyers, interview, 1982, notes at II-29A.

⁷HC Map Records, OM: 6-9, 10; Robert W. Glasgow, interview, 1987, notes at X-44A, 56A; Doris (Barnes) Howell, interview, 1987, notes at XI-50; Webb, *The Handbook of Texas*, 2-556; Foxworth, *The Romance of Old Sylvan Beach*, 56.

⁸Clark and Halbouty, *Spindletop*, 4-58; James Presley, *A Saga of Wealth* (New York: G. P. Putnam's Sons, 1978), 37.

⁹Presley, *A Saga of Wealth*, 37; Rundell, *Early Texas Oil: A Photographic History*, 37; John S. Spratt, *The Road to Spindletop*:

Economic Change in Texas, 1875-1901 (Austin: University of Texas Press, 1970), 274; HCCCR:10-282.

[10] Rundell, *Early Texas Oil: A Photographic History*, 25.

[11] Clark and Halbouty, *Spindletop*, 144.

[12] Clark and Halbouty, *Spindletop*, 144, 149; Rundell, *Early Texas Oil: A Photographic History*, 37; Presley, *A Saga of Wealth*, 60; Webb, *The Handbook of Texas*, 2-736.

[13] Clark and Halbouty, *Spindletop*, 155.

[14] Nina Smith, ed., *A History of the Humble, Texas, Area*, (Humble: Bicentennial Heritage Committee, 1976), 29, 31, 32; Rundell, *Early Texas Oil: A Photographic History*, 81; Webb, *The Handbook of Texas*, 1-863; Clark and Halbouty, *Spindletop*, 154; Buchanan, *Houston, A Chronological and Documentary History*, 26.

[15] Webb, *The Handbook of Texas*, 1-444, 2-736; Sibley, *The Port of Houston: A History*, 152; Davis and Grobe, *New Encyclopedia of Texas*, 226; John O. King, *Joseph Stephen Cullinan* (Nashville: Vanderbilt University Press, 1970), 182.

[16] Sibley, *The Port of Houston: A History*, 152; HCDR:228-335.

[17] Henson, *The History of Baytown*, 77.

[18] HCDR:229-102; Joseph S. Cullinan Collection, land schedules and farm records.

[19] Presley, *A Saga of Wealth*, 90, 98; Rundell, *Early Texas Oil: A Photographic History*, 94.

[20] Rundell, *Early Texas Oil: A Photographic History*, 120; Smith, *A History of the Humble, Texas, Area*, 23; Work Projects Administration, *Houston*, 63; Webb, *The Handbook of Texas*, 1-863.

[21] Webb, *The Handbook of Texas*, 1-747, 2-736; Rundell, *Early Texas Oil: A Photographic History*, 82, 91; Buchanan, *Houston, A Chronological and Documentary History*, 26.

[22] Webb, *The Handbook of Texas*, 1-848; Joseph S. Cullinan Collection, land records; Ball, *Houston Chronicle*, 8-23-1936.

[23] Clark and Halbouty, *Spindletop*, 221; Webb, *The Handbook of Texas*, 1-444, 2-737; King, *Joseph Stephen Cullinan*, 182; Joseph S. Cullinan Collection, farm operations records ; Joseph M. Cruse family biography; Smith, *A History of the Humble, Texas, Area*, 36; Ball, *Houston Chronicle*, August 23, 1936; *Yesteryears in Pasadena*, 51.

[24] Clark and Halbouty, *Spindletop*, 221; Sibley, *The Port of Houston: A History*, 152; Pomeroy Family Reocrds, MPWW; Virginia Hahn, "This Oil Man Looked East," *Pasadena Citizen*, October 1, 1992, p. 7; *Houston Post*, August 5, 1917; McComb, *Houston: A History*, 80; Webb, *The Handbook of Texas*, 2-639; Rundell, *Early Texas Oil: A Photographic History*, 66, 119.

[25]Raymond Dickerson, interview, 1986, notes at IX-26; Henson, *The History of Baytown*, 78.
[26]Rosa Scannell and Bertha Davis, interview, 1983, notes at II-38A; McComb, *Houston: A History*, 81; Pomeroy Family Records, MPWW; *Houston Post*, August 5, 1917, p.1: September 18, 1917.
[27]Sibley, *The Port of Houston: A History*, 152; McComb, *Houston: A History*, 80; Raymond Klempin, "The Houston Ship Channel: Waterway to Energy World," *Houston Business Journal*, June 15, 1981, p. 1; Ball, *Houston Chronicle*, August 23, 1936; Rundell, *Early Texas Oil: A Photographic History*, 123; Henson, *The History of Baytown*, 95.
[28]Work Projects Administration, *Houston*, 111; Pomeroy Family collection, maps; McComb, , *Houston: A History*, 80; *Houston Post*, February 2, 1919, p.1; Crown Refinery history file, Pomeroy History Collection, Pasadena; David H. Hughes family biography; *Yesteryears in Pasadena*, 86; Dorothy (Hughes) Parker, interview, 1986, notes at IX-41; Pomeroy Family Records, MPWW.
[29]Henson, *The History of Baytown*, 95, 96; Webb, *The Handbook of Texas*, 1-127, 863; Rundell, *Early Texas Oil: A Photographic History*, 122, 123; *Yesteryears in Pasadena*, 145; *Houston Chronicle*, December 26, 1988; W. E. Pratt and D. W. Johnson, "Local Subsidence of the Goose Creek Oil Field," *The Journal of Geology*, Vol.34, Oct-Nov 1926, 577.
[30]McComb, *Houston: A History*, 80; Ball, *The Port of Houston, How it Came to Pass*, 80; Davis and Grobe, *New Encyclopedia of Texas*, 281; Pomeroy Family records, MPWW; Sibley, *The Port of Houston: A History*, 152; Buchanan, *Houston, A Chronological and Documentary History*, .

Chapter 9
[1]Trager, *The People's Chronology*, 791,795, 797, 799, 803, 861, 903; Webb, *The Handbook of Texas*, 1-551;
[2]John E. Pomeroy, interview, 1979, notes at I-4.
[3]Bill Aldridge, Texas Banking Commission, interview, 1985, notes in banking file; Davis and Grobe, *New Encyclopedia of Texas*, 1386; *Houston City Directory*, 1919, 1920; HCDR: 463-126, 491-188.
[4]*Houston Post*, February 2, July 8, 1919; Dorothey (Sippy) Roye, interview, 1988, notes at XIV-8; 1920 Census, ED 107, Family #427; *Pasadena Citizen*, February 27, 1964; HCDR:427-589, 513-274; "Crown Central, the Original 'Made in Pasadena'" history provided by Lori Trina of Crown Central, 1986, copy in Pomeroy Collection, Crown Refinery file.

⁵Aldridge, Texas Banking Commission, interview, 1985; Photograph in *Pasadena Citizen* 1963 Anniversary Section provided by Matt F. Reed, president of First Pasadena State Bank, copy on file; HCDR:301-141; Charter for Pasadena State Bank, dated July 8, 1919, Pomeroy Collection (also filed HCDR, 423-614), Pasadena State Bank file, Pasadena; *Houston City Directory*, 1919, 1920; James A. Jackson family biography.

⁶*Pasadena Citizen*, February 27, 1964; *Yesteryears in Pasadena*, 41, 151; S. R. "Buddy" Jones, Jr., interview, 1982, notes at I-72; Joseph M. Cruse family biography; Doris (Cruse) Hale, interview, 1988, notes at XIV-14A; Judy Cruse, interview, 1989, notes at XVI-62

⁷Aldridge, Texas Banking Commission, interview, 1985; HCDR:522-275; *Yesteryears in Pasadena*, 41; *Texas Banking Directory*, 1920-1921, 1922.

⁸Ben Hargrave family biography; Ruby (Warren) Brammer, interview, 1986, notes at Telcon 20:8-1-86; Larry A. Brammer, interview, 1993, notes at XIX-10; HCDR:489-29, 434-563; Thurman Wilson, interview, 1988, notes at XIV-6; Sylvia (Wilson) Meyer, interview, 1988, notes at XIV-11A; Catherine Kingsbury, interview, 1988, notes at XIV-9A.

⁹Pomeroy Family, records, MPWW; Bishop, "Oscar Kruse as an Educator," 22; HCDR:440-572, 489-29, 490-193, 498-416.

¹⁰Edward and Loise Pomeroy, interview, various dates.

¹¹Joseph R. Roberts family biography; Pomeroy Family records, personal notes; Post Office, Postmaster appointments, 366; Charles R. Munger family biography; 1940 Census, Population, Vol. 1, p.1050.

¹²Bertha (Dickerson) Quinn, interview, 1983, notes at III-24, 24A; Addie (Brown) Bailey, oral history, 1975, notes at IV-8; *Yesteryears in Pasadena*, 46; Weldon "Stoney" Phillips, interview, 1993, notes at XIX-44; *The (Pasadena) Mirror*, September 30, 1953, p.15; S. R. "Buddy" Jones, interview, various dates.

¹³George P. Dowell family biography; Ira L. Pitts family biography.

¹⁴Everett and Ray Williams, interview, 1984, notes at V-6.

¹⁵Cominsky, *Espiritu*, 22; John T. Shine family biography; Ira L. Pitts family biography; Marilyn (Pitts) Coward, interview, 1986, notes at IX-20; HCDR:440-8.

¹⁶George M. Olive family biography; Weidig, *Deer Park*, 135; HCDR:440-8; Clara (Thurman) Wilson, oral history, 1975, notes at IV-2.

¹⁷E. Frank DeFee family biography; HCDR:412-490; Everett and Ray Williams, interview, 1984, notes at V-4A; Catherine

Kingsbury, interview, 1986, notes at VI-54; David Z. Holloway family biography.

[18]1920 Census EN 107, Family #368, #367, #366, #369; Alexander Jacob family biography; Doris (Cruse) Hale, interview, 1988, notes at XIV-15A; Everett and Ray Williams, interview, 1984, notes at V-5; James Williams family biography.

[19]James Williams family biography; David C. McMaster family biography; D. L. Webb family biography; Leonard J. Stafford family biography.

[20]Emerson R. Kelley family biography; Josiah Rawlins family biography.

[21]Emory C. Goodman family biography; Samuel A. Quinn family biography.

[22]Samuel W. Allen family biography; Francis D. Newell family biography; Doris (Barnes) and F. E. "Teeler" Howell, interview, 1984, notes at III-64A.

[23]Robert W. Glasgow, interview, 1987, notes at X-49A and X-57; McComb, *Houston: A History*, 73; *Houston Post*, November 6, 1921; Schloeman, "School Days in Pasadena"; Pomeroy History Records, personal notes; Karl Ludvigsen et al., *The Encyclopedia of the American Automobile* (Secaucus: Chartwell Books, Inc., 1977), 18; Floyd Clymer, *Treasury of Early American Automobiles, 1877-1925* (New York: McGraw-Hill Book Co., 1950), 136; Judy Cruse, interview, 1988, notes at XIV-2; *Yesteryears in Pasadena*, 99, 184; Lawrence N. Sippy family biography; Dorothy (Sippy) Roye, interview, 1988, notes at XIV-8.

[24]*Yesteryears in Pasadena*, 85; *Houston Post*, May 11, 1968; Dorothy (Hughes) Parker, interview, 1987, notes at X-40; Ira L. Pitts family biography.

[25]Oscar Kruse family biography; Karl Kruse, oral history, 1971, additional notes at X-17A; McComb, *Houston: A History*, 71, 75; *Houston Post*, November 6, 1921.

[26]McComb, *Houston: A History*, 70, 73.

[27]Catherine Kingsbury, oral history, 1986, notes at VI-41; Addie (Brown) Bailey, oral history, notes at IV-4; *Yesteryears in Pasadena*, 28, 48; Johnny and Sylvia (Wilson) Meyer, interview, 1984, notes at III-69A; Clyde D. Pomeroy, interview, 1985, notes at IV-10A.

[28]*Yesteryears in Pasadena*, 23, 78; 80, 99, 115, 151, 172; Thurman Wilson, interview, 1988, notes at XIV-2A, 3A; J. Edward Pomeroy, Jr., interview, 1985, notes at VII-79; Clara (Thurman) Wilson, interview, 1975, additional notes at III-78A; J. A. "Jay" Riggs, interview, 1993, notes at XIX-13; Dolores Kenyon, *From Arrows to Astronauts*, (League City: National Association

of Conservation Districts, 1976), 28; J. B. and Boots Isaac, interview, 1986, notes at VII-68A; Vernon Atkinson, interview, 1983, notes at III-12B; Clara Wilson, oral history, 1975, additional notes at III-78A; Ray C. Williams, interview, 1988, notes at XII-71A; S. R. "Buddy" Jones, Jr., oral history, 1988, notes at XIII-5A; *Houston Post*, May 28, 1950, sec.1, p.24.

[29] Joseph S. Cullinan Collection, correspondence; Historical Marker inscription as to placement date; *Yesteryears in Pasadena*, 37, 48, 139, 229; 1920 Census ED 107, Family #386

[30] Oscar Kruse, interview, 1987, notes at XI-41A, 44A; Thurman Wilson, interview, 1988, notes at XIV-2A; Addie (Brown) Bailey, oral history, 1975, additional notes at IV-6A.

[31] Oscar Kruse, interview, 1987, notes at XI-44, 44A; Thurman Wilson, interview, 1988, notes at XIV-7; Addie (Brown) Bailey, oral history, additional notes at IV-6A; Clyde D. Pomeroy, interview, 1979, notes at I-16; Johnny and Sylvia (Wilson) Meyer, interview, 1982, notes at II-28A.

[32] Addie (Brown) Bailey, oral history, additional notes at IV-3; *Pasadena Citizen*, May 26, 1971, p. B-2; Carrie (Parks) Phillips, interview, 1988, notes at XIII-15; Schloeman, "School Days in Pasadena"; Myrtle (Blakesley) Billingsley, interview, 1982, notes at II-26.

[33] Schloeman, "School Days in Pasadena"; Delbert E. Atkinson family biography; School Minutes, 1922; Pomeroy Family records, personal notes.

[34] *Pasadena Citizen*, August 11, 1987, p.1; 50th Anniversary program, April 19, 1974, in Pasadena School history file, Pomeroy collection, Pasadena; Graduation Announcement, in Pasadena School history file; Dedication program, in Pasadena School history file.

[35] Pasadena School history file: teachers, school buildings; Smythe sisters family biography; Estes, *Follow the Strawberry Road*, 47.

[36] Catherine Kingsbury, oral history, 1986, additional notes at VI-53: interview, 1988, notes at XIV-8A; *Bayshore Sun*, April 12, 1987; Doris (Cruse) Hale, interview, 1988, notes at XIV-15; Everett and Ray Williams, interview, 1984, notes at V-6.

[37] E. Payson Pomeroy family biography; Jess T. Mason family biography; Clyde and Marguerite Pomeroy, interview, 1983, notes at III-28A; J. Edward Pomeroy, Jr., interview, 1986, notes at X-25; Catherine Kingsbury, Oral history, 1986, additional notes at VI-49.

[38] Charles C. Freeman family biography; Clyde D. Pomeroy, interview, 1986, notes at VI-38A; Robert W. Glasgow, interview, 1987, notes at X-48; Francis (Freeman) Wales, interview, 1993, notes at XVIII-55; Richard Brannen family biography.

[39] Pickett family biography; William J. Shelton family biography.

[40] Masonic Lodge records, Pomeroy History Collection, notes at XIII-23.

[41] Archie C. Riley family biography.

[42] Ben Hargrave family biography.

[43] Catherine Kingsbury, interview, 1988, notes at XIV-8A; *Yesteryears in Pasadena*, 110, 139; Blanche (Kingsbury) Mitchell, interview, 1979, notes at Telcon 2:December 7, 1979; Doris (Barnes) Howell, interview, 1989, notes at XVI-49; Everett Williams, interview, 1988, notes at XIV-12A.

[44] *Houston Post*, July 19, 1919; J. B. and Boots Isaac, interview, 1986, notes at VII-67; Dorothy (Hughes) Parker, interview, 1986, notes at IX-42; *Yesteryears in Pasadena*, 80, 176; Daniel Blum, *A Pictorial History of the Silent Screen*, (New York: Perigee Books, 1982), 157, 159, 185, 189; Octoavino and Leonor (Martinez) Rocha, oral history, 1986, notes at VII-49.

[45] Alexander, "A History of Pasadena"; Catherine Kingsbury, oral history, 1986, notes at VI-49; *Yesteryears in Pasadena*, 111; Clara Wilson, oral history, 1975, additional notes at III-78A; Addie (Brown) Bailey, oral history, 1975, additional notes at IV-5A; Rosa (Dowell) Ford, interview, 1985, notes at V-26; Joseph S. Cullinan Collection: real estate and MacNider files; Thurman Wilson, interview, 1989, notes at Telcon:7-30-89.

[46] Dr. Titus C. Loose family biography; Pomeroy History Collection, Abstract #502602, p. 155 (HCPR: 31-333).

[47] Catherine Kingsbury, oral history, 1986, notes at VI-49.

[48] *Dr. Mac Donald's Household Almanac, 1916*, (Binghamton, N. Y: J. Mac Donald, M. D. publisher, 1916) 11th edition, copy in Pomeroy History Collection.

[49] Harris County Medical Society, Directory and archive files.

[50] E. Payson Pomeroy family biography; Octoavino and Leonor (Martinez) Rocha, oral history, 1986, notes at VII-50A; *Yesteryears in Pasadena*, 41, 52, 68, 88, 144, 152, 180, 184; Clara (Thurman) Wilson, oral history, 1975, additional notes at III-78A; Davis and Grobe, *New Encyclopedia of Texas*, 1386; Bill Aldridge, interview, 1985.

[51] Harris County Medical Society, archive files; 1920 Census ED 107, Family #366; Dr. James M. Boyd family biography; Bueron Boyd, interview, 1990, notes at XVII-16; *Yesteryears in Pasadena*, 21, 137; Addie (Brown) Bailey, oral history, 1975, additional notes at IV-6; J. Edward Pomeroy, Jr., interview, 1988, notes at XV-1.

[52] Dr. J. M. Boyd material, Pasadena Historical Museum, Pasadena.

[53]VII-77; Robert W. Glasgow, interview, 1987, notes at X-49, 57A; VII-79A; J. Edward Pomeroy, Jr., interview, 1986, notes at X-24, 25 and (1989) XVI-54.

[54]Robert W. Glasgow, interview, 1987, notes at X-49A; Ruby L. (Hargrave) Hartrick, Carman L. (Hargrave) Holderby and V. Fern (Hargrave) Willis, interview, 1986, notes at IX-15; J. Edward Pomeroy, Jr., interview, 1989, notes at XVI-3.

[55]Homer F. Brammer family biography; Larry A. Brammer, interview, 1993, notes at XIX-10.

[56]Virgil E. Abbott family biography.

[57]Delbert E. Anderson family biography.

Chapter 10

[1]*Pasadena Times*, May 13, 1943; *Houston Post*, May 14, 1943; Irma Williams, "History of Pasadena, Texas" (6).

[2]Joseph S. Cullinan Collection, farm records; Jones Ranch file, Pomeroy History Collection, Pasadena.

[3]Baldwin and Cargill farm file, Pomeroy History Collection, Pasadena; HCDR:305-305; Pomeroy Family Records, MPWW; *Yesteryears in Pasadena*, 3; 1920 Census ED 107, Family #435, 436, 437, 438, 439, 447.

[4]Pearson and Macias, eds., *Harris County Birth Records and Delay Birth Records* (Pasadena: Harris County Genealogical Society, 1990), #539, 541; 1920 Census ED 107, Family #352; Octavino and Leonor (Martinez) Rocha, oral history, 1986, notes at VII-48; *Houston Chronicle*, May 13, 1988.

[5]HCDR: 431-58.

[6]HCDR: 451-394, 459-463.

[7]H. L. Patterson, Proposed Pasadena City Limits map, June 12, 1920, Pomeroy History Collection, Pasadena.

[8]Pomeroy Family Records, MPWW; Clyde D. and Marguerite (Wesney) Pomeroy, interview, 1986, notes at IX-4; Pomeroy Diary: May 15, 1907; Woods, *Galveston-Houston Electric Railway*, 24; HCDR: 526-199.

[9]Houston Lighting & Power file, Pomeroy History Collection, Pasadena; Joseph S. Cullinan Collection; HCDR: 526-199; Woods, *Galveston-Houston Electric Railway*, 24; Patterson, Proposed Pasadena City Limits map.

[10]Webb, *The Handbook of Texas*, 1-551; HCCCR: V-281, 303, 365, 366.

[11]HCCCR: V-303; Joseph S. Cullinan Collection, correspondence, letter to Judge W. W. Moore, dated August 15, 1924.

[12]*Houston Press*, October 16, 1924; Sibley, *The Port of Houston*, 156, 157.

[13]*Houston Press*, October 16, 17, 1924.

[14]Pomeroy Family Records letter from Pasadena Citizens Association dated October 22, 1924; *Houston Chronicle*, October 23, November 2, 30, 1924: March 12, 1925; William N. Billingsley family biography.

[15]*Houston Press*, October 17, 1924; Stuart-Allen Collection, correspondence.

[16]Laurel B. McNay, Jr., oral history, 1988, notes at XV-11, 12; Weidig, *Deer Park*, 129..

[17]*Yesteryears in Pasadena*, 182; Joseph S. Cullinan Collection; Laurel B. McNay, Jr., oral history, 1988, notes at XV-15; Karl Kruse, oral history, 1971, additional notes at X-16; Thurman Wilson, interview, 1988, notes at XIV-6; Oscar Kruse family biography.

[18]Pomeroy Family Records, MPWW; W. B. Bailey family information, Pasadena Public Library, notes at III-56; Robert W. Glasgow, interview, 1987, notes at X-57B; J. Edward Pomeroy, Jr., interview, 1985, notes at VII-76; Lee Phillips, interview, 1979, notes at I-25; Edward and Loise (Williams) Pomeroy, interview, 1988, notes at XIII-12A.

[19]Grun, *The Timetables of History*, 461; Trager, *The People's Chronology*, 771, 834; Wallechinsky and Wallace, *The People's Almanac*, 442; McComb, *Houston: A History*, 103; Webb, *The Handbook of Texas*, 2-668; Marguerite Johnston,*Houston, The Unknown City, (1836-1946)* (College Station: Texas A and M University Press, 1991), 244; Work Projects Administration, *Houston: A History and Guide*, 208, 209, 210; *The 1929 World Almanac and Book of Facts* (facsimile edition: Workman Publishing and American Heritage Press, 1971), 776, 821; Edward and Loise (Williams) Pomeroy, interview, 1988, notes at XIII-12A; Clyde D. Pomeroy, interview, 1979, notes at I-14A.

[20]*Houston Chronicle*, December 1, 3, 1925; Joseph S. Cullinan Collection, correspondence from J. Y. Powell to Judge W. W. Moore, dated December 3, 1925; *Houston Post-Dispatch*, December 3, 1925.

[21]Pasadena school history, undated newspaper clipping, circa 1927; Joseph S. Cullinan Collection, correspondence, A. T. Vick to J. S. Cullinan, dated November 28, 1927 and M. C. Ehlen of Crown Oil to Pasadena Chamber of Commerce, dated November 17, 1927; D. L. Smith, *The History of Harrisburg, Texas* (no publishing information, located at Houston Metropolitan Research Center), 61.

[22]Joseph S. Cullinan Collection, correspondence, A. T. Vick to J. S. Cullinan, dated November 28, 1927; Election returns, 1929,

City of Pasadena, provided by Pam Ramey, City Secretary, Pasadena City Hall, Pasadena.

[23] Growth of Houston, Incorporation Area, 1978, publication of the Houston City Planning Department, City of Houston; Annexation Maps, City of Houston, including Fantham and Fanthan map, H-1928, Houston Metropolitan Research Center; Clyde and Marguerite (Wesney) Pomeroy, interview, 1983, notes at III-27A; E. Payson Pomeroy family biography.

[24] Joseph S. Cullinan Collection, correspondence, W. W. Moore to J. S. Cullinan, dated December 19, 1928; Election returns, 1929, City of Pasadena .

[25] City Council Minutes, City of Pasadena, City Secretary's Office, Pasadena, Vol.A, January 9, 1929; J. Edward Pomeroy, Jr., interview, 1986, notes at X-28.

[26] City Council Minutes, Pasadena, January 9, April 2, 1929; JEP; "Reflections of Church Growth: 85th Anniversary."

[27] Johnny and Sylvia (Wilson) Meyers, interview, 1982, notes at II-27A; J. Edward Pomeroy, Jr., interview, 1986, notes at X-27: 1989, notes at XV-64; *Yesteryears in Pasadena*, 199; McComb, *Houston: A History*, 122; Foxworth, *The Romance of Old Sylvan Beach*, 43.

[28] Foxworth, *The Romance of Old Sylvan Beach*, 36; McComb, *Houston: A History*, 70; City Council Minutes, Pasadena, July 22, 1929; Elva (Guinn) Reeves, interview, 1989, notes at XV-56: Robert M. Guinn family biography; Raymond Dickerson, interview, 1984, notes at VI-20A.

[29] HCDR: 459-463: 526-199; William B. Bailey family biography; E. D. Boggs family biography ; Pasadena school history, 1929 graduation program; J. A. Riggs, interview, 1993, notes at XIX-13; Harry Witt family biography; Robert W. Glasgow, interview, 1987, notes at X-55A; *(Pasadena) News Citizen*, February 27, 1966.

[30] Robert Dickerson family biography.

[31] Everett Williams, interview, 1988, notes at XIV-13; McComb, *Houston: A History*, 74; Buchanan, *Houston, A Chronological and Documentary History*, 34; Joseph M. Cruse family biography; Judy Cruse, interview, 1988, notes at XIV-2; *Houston Telephone Book*, Pasadena Exchange, August 1928; Pasadena school history, school board file, 1929 graduation program.

[32] *Pasadena Times, May 13, 1943; Houston Telephone Book*, Pasadena Exchange, April 1929; Pasadena school history, 1929 graduation program advertisements; Clyde D. Pomeroy, interview, 1993, notes at XVIII-33; W. J. David family biography; *Pasadena Mirror*, December 3, 1954, p.1 .

33 Paul O. Fleming family biography; Trager, *The People's Chronology*, 846; Arthur F. Howard, interview, 1981, notes at I-49A; *Pasadena Mirror*, December 3, 1954, p.1; Everett Williams, interview, 1988, notes at XIV-12, 12A; *Houston Telephone Book*, Pasadena Exchange, August 1928, April 1929; Pasadena school history, 1929 graduation program advertisements; *Pasadena Sun*, February 28, 1929; Naomi (Daily) McCoy, interview, 1981, notes at I-55A; J. B. and Boots Isaac, interview, 1986, notes at VII-65 and IX-9A; Johnny Meters, interview, 1988, notes at XIV-11.

34 E. Frank DeFee family biography; Catherine Kingsbury, interview, 1988, notes at XIV-10; *Houston Telephone Book*, Pasadena Exchange, August 1928; Pasadena school history, 1929 graduation program advertisements; Rosa Scannell and Bertha Davis, interview, 1983, notes at II-38A; W. Lee Mitchell family information, Pasadena History Collection, Pasadena Public Library, Pomeroy notes at III-52; Addie (Brown) Bailey, oral history, additional notes at IV-8A; *Yesteryears in Pasadena*, 46.

35 Pasadena school history, 1929 graduation program advertisements; Johnny Meyers, interview, 1988, notes at XIV-11, 12; J. B. and Boots Isaac, interview, 1986, notes at VII-65 and IX-9A; Walter G. Ankele family biography; Robert W. Glasgow, interview, 1987, notes at X-44.

36 J. B. and Boots Isaac, interview, 1986, notes at VI-65 and IX-9A; *Houston Telephone Book*, Pasadena Exchange, April 1929; Catherine Kingsbury, interview, 1988, notes at XIV-10; Johnny Meyers, interview, 1988, notes at XIV-11; Everett Williams, interview, 1988, notes at XIV-12; Naomi (Dailey) McCoy, interview, 1981, notes at I-55A; *Houston Post*, September 22, 1929; *Houston Telephone Book*, Pasadena Exchange, April 1930; Post Office, Postmaster Appointments, p. 368; Woodrow P. Coolidge family biography; Rosa Scannell and Bertha Davis, interview, 1983, notes at II-38A; *Houston Telephone Book*, Pasadena Exchange, :1928; Pasadena school history, 1929 graduation program advertisements.

37 Masonic Lodge records, Pomeroy notes at XIII-23; Dr. James M. Boyd family biography; Forrest Fisher family biography; Dr. Oscar F. Portwood family biography; Catherine Kingsbury, interview, 1988, notes at XIV-9; *Houston Telephone Book*, Pasadena Exchange, August 1928, April and October 1929, April and September 1930; J. B. Isaac, interview, 1988, notes at XIV-14.

38 J. B. Isaac, interview, 1988, notes at XIV-13A; Pasadena school history, 1929 graduation program advertisements.

39 Clyde D Pomeroy, interview, 1982, notes at II-31A; J. Sam Dailey family biography; Walter L. Wilson family biography; J. B.

Isaac, interview, 1988, notes at XIV-14; Clara (Thurman) Wilson, interview, 1983, notes at II-49A: 1975, oral history, additional notes at III-79; Naomi (Daily) McCoy, interview, 1981, notes at I-53A; Johnny and Sylvia (Wilson) Meyers, interview, 1982, notes at II-27A, 28: interview, 1985, notes at V-30A; Edward and Loise (Williams) Pomeroy, interview, 1988, notes at XIII-13A; *Yesteryears in Pasadena*, 29; Thurman Wilson, interview, 1988, notes at XIV-6.

[40]*Houston Telephone Book*, Pasadena Exchange, October 1929; Everett Williams, interview, 1988, notes at XIV-11A; J. B. and Boots Isaac, interview, 1986, notes at IX-9A; Pasadena, Texas, Producers Exchange file, Pomeroy History Collection, Pasadena.

[41]*Houston Telephone Book*, Pasadena Exchange, August 1928; Ira L. Pitts family biography.

[42]*Houston Telephone Book*, Pasadena Exchange, August 1928; Pomeroy Family Records, MPWW.

[43]*Houston Telephone Book*, Pasadena Exchange, August 1928; Pasadena school history, 1929 graduation program advertisements; Catherine Kingsbury, interview, 1988, notes at XIV-9; Mike L. Coy family biography; Arthur G. Whitman family biography.

[44]Robert A. Hughes family biography.

[45]Henry A. Carter family biography; Charles H. Tilley family biography; *Houston Telephone Book*, Pasadena Exchange, April and October 1929.

[46]*Yesteryears in Pasadena*, 86; Pasadena school history, 1929 graduation program advertisements; John T. Shine family biography; James W. Williams family biography; Everett Williams, interview, 1983, notes at III-9; Pomeroy Family Records, MPWW; *Pasadena Citizen*, March 22, 1962, p.2; Mrs. Maribell, Southwestern Bell Telephone Company, interview, 1980, notes at Telcon 3:3-7-80; *Houston Telephone Book*, Pasadena Exchange, August 1928.

[47]John A. Meyer family biography.

[48]Pasadena school history, 1929 graduation program advertisements; Samuel P. Bell family biography; L. James Brubaker family biography; Thorpes family biography; A. D. Tingle family biography; Robert W. Glasgow, interview, 1987, notes at X-47A.

Chapter 11

[1]McComb, *Houston: A History*, 5, 84, 109; Webb, *The Handbook of Texas*, 1-487; Work Projects Administration, *Houston*, 226, 284; *The 1929 Almanac and Book of Facts*, 92, 851.

[2]Webb, *The Handbook of Texas*, 1-487; Work Projects Administration, *Houston*, 117, 226; McComb, *Houston: A History*, 84; *Houston Post-Dispatch*, January 29, 1928.

[3]J. Edward Pomeroy, Jr., interview, 1988, notes at XIII-1, 16A, 17; 1987, notes at XII-12A: 1989, notes at XV-8; Clyde Pomeroy, interview, 1988, notes at XIII-16.

[4]Vince Ryan, speech, Dedication of Texas Historical Marker, June 27, 1988, notes in Pomeroy History Collection, Historical marker file; *The 1929 Almanac and Book of Facts*, 92, 127; Webb, *The Handbook of Texas*, 1-487; Wallechinsky and Wallace, *The People's Almanac #2*, 455.

[5]Paul Michael, ed., *The Great American Movie Book*, (Englewood Cliffs: Prentice-Hall, Inc. 1980), iii; Trager, *The People's Chronology*, 851, 852, 859; Grun, *The Timetables of History*, 497.

[6]Buchanan, *Houston, A Chronological and Documentary History*, 36; *The 1929 Almanac and Book of Facts*, 772; Thurman Wilson, interview, 1988, notes at XIV-3; Oscar Kruse, Jr., interview 1987, notes at XI-41A; J. Edward Pomeroy, Jr., interview, 1988, notes at XIII-16A: 1989, notes at XVI-2 and XVI-53.

[7]*Houston Chronicle*, 3-14-26, p.72; Thomas C. White family scrapbook, in possession of Mrs. T. C. White, provided by T. C. White, Jr., 1988, Pomeroy notes at XIII-7; B. R. Sugar, ed., *The Ring*, (New York: Ring Publishing Co., 1981), 632 et seq.; Clyde Pomeroy, interview, 1979, notes at I-16A; Hadley White family biography; Everett Williams, interview, 1983, notes at III-8A.

[8]Estes, *Follow the Strawberry Road*, 26; *Yesteryears in Pasadena*, 94, 154; Pasadena School records, staff file; Oscar Kruse, Jr., oral history, 1987, notes at XI-44; Ralph Stafford, interview, 1988, notes at XIII-20.

[9]Estes, *Follow the Strawberry Road*, 26; John S. Isaac family biography; Johnny Meyers, interview, 1988, notes at XIII-19; Ralph Stafford, interview, 1988, notes at XIII-19A; J. B. Isaac, interview, 1988, notes at XIII-20A; *Yesteryears in Pasadena*, 23, 94, 236.

[10]Ralph Stafford, interview, 1988, notes at XIII-20; Estes, *Follow the Strawberry Road*, 26, 54.

[11]Johnny Meyers, interview, 1988, notes at XIII-19A; Estes, *Follow the Strawberry Road*, 26, 48.

[12]Weldon "Stoney" Phillips, interview, 1993, notes at XIX-44; *Yesteryears in Pasadena*, 154.

[13]Richard T. Gore family biography; Estes, *Follow the Strawberry Road*, 26, 54; *Yesteryears in Pasadena*, 154, 156; Pasadena School history, staff file.

[14] J. Edward Pomeroy, Jr. interview, 1985, notes at VII-76A: 1988, notes at XV-1A; Doris (Barnes) Howell, interview, 1983, notes at III-36.

[15] J. Edward Pomeroy, Jr., interview, 1988, notes at XIII-1, 16A, 17: 1989, notes at XV-8; with Loise (Williams) Pomeroy, 1986, notes at IX-3; Band history file, Pomeroy History Collection, Pasadena.

[16] Band history file; *Houston Post*, October 30, 1931; J. Edward Pomeroy, Jr., interview, 1988, notes at XIII-16A: 1986 with Loise (Williams) Pomeroy, notes at IX-3.

[17] *Report of Harris County Schools*, year ending August 31, 1910, August 31, 1912; Library history file, Pomeroy History Collection, Pasadena.

[18] *Yesteryears in Pasadena*, 9, 21, 195; "Townsite First Plated in 1895-Industries Started About 1917," unnoted newspaper article, circa 1935, found among Pomeroy Family Records; Ben Hargrave family biography; Post Office, Postmaster Appointments, 367; Woodrow P. Coolidge family biography.

[19] L. James Brubaker family biography; Estes, *Follow the Strawberry Road*, 34.

[20] James C. Thomas family biography.

[21] James C. Billingsley family biography; Claudia (Draper) Tabor, interview, 1993, notes at XVIII-37A; T. L. Billingsley, interview, 1993, note at XVIII-39A.

[22] Crown Refinery file, Pomeroy History Collection, Pasadena; Jonah Boyd family biography; Jacob A. Worley family biography; Austin S. Gray family biography; Lawrence N. Sippy family biography.

[23] Thomas T. Shaw family biography; *Yesteryears in Pasadena*, 194.

[24] Harry J. Tacker family biography; *Yesteryears in Pasadena*, 16; Edyth (Larson) Cope, interview, 1993, notes at XIX-8, 8A.

[25] Silas W. Brown family biography; Jesse D. Downs family biography; J. B. Stewart family biography; Adison B. Freeman family biography.

[26] Barbara Wells, *Shell at Deer Park*, (Deer Park: Shell Oil Company, 1979), 19, 33; Janett (Martin) Schultz, interview, 1993, notes at XIX-58.

[27] Wells, *Shell at Deer Park*, 29, 31, 45; Ludvigsen et al., *The Encyclopedia of the American Automobile*, 103; *Pasadena Sun*, February 28, 1929.

[28] George Graves, interview, 1988, notes at XIII-33; Mrs. George Brown, interview, 1988, notes at XIII-39A.

[29] George Graves, interview, 1988, notes at XIII-33; Mrs. George Brown, interview, 1988, notes at XIII-39A; Catherine

Kingsbury, interview, 1988, notes at XIII-41A; *Houston Post*, September 22, 1929; George Graves family biography; Ralph and Winogene Stafford, interview, 1987, notes at X-38A; *Yesteryears in Pasadena*, 202.

[30]James G. Houston family biography.

[31]Wells, *Shell at Deer Park*, 57; Deer Park community vertical file, Deer Park Public Library, Deer Park, Texas; Eloise (Hodges) Lockey, interview, 1993, notes at XVIII-55; Harry Jones family biography; Edward F. Napp family biography.

[32]Hazel (Elder) Land, interview, 1993, notes at XIX-6; *Yesteryears in Pasadena*, 119; William M. Elder family biography; Guy W. Butler family biography ; W. T. Hill family biography; Ben Powell family biography; *Pasadena Record*, September 4, 1931.

[33]Wells, *Shell at Deer Park*, 45; George J. Blanyer, Jr., family biography; Pasadena school history, staff; DeWitt Chaddick,ed., *The Alcalde 1929*, (Huntsville, Sam Houston State Teachers College, 1929), Vol. 20.

[34]Bill Pendleton, interview, 1987, notes at XI-15A: 1993, notes at XIX-3A, 5; Mary (Hand) McCain, interview, 1993, notes at XIX-2; Walter E. Goodwin family biography.

[35]*Houston Chronicle*, September 22, 1929; Pasadena City Council Minutes: April 9, December 9, 1929.

[36]Pasadena City Council Minutes: June 10, July 1, August 13, 1929.

[37]Percy Ulmer, Pasadena City and fire department records, in possession of Jimmy Barnes, made available in 1993, copies in Pomeroy History Collection, Pasadena Volunteer Fire Department file, see information in ledger, p.16; Everett and Ray Williams, interview, 1984, notes at V-2; *Pasadena Sun*, May 26, 1929; Pasadena City Council Minutes: March 11, August 5, 26, September 16, 1929; *Houston Post Dispatch*, August 27, 1929.

[38]Clyde Pomeroy, interview, 1979, notes at I-14A; Clyde Pomeroy and Rosa Ford, interview, 1979, notes at I-23; Lee Phillips, interview, 1979, notes at I-25A, 26; Johnny and Sylvia (Wilson) Meyers, interview, 1982, notes at II-27.

[39]*Yesteryears in Pasadena*, 19; Arthur B. Moody family biography; Clyde Pomeroy, interview, 1993, notes at XVIII-40A; J. Edward Pomeroy, Jr., interview, 1993, notes at XVIII-40A; S. R. Buddy Jones, Jr., interview, 1993, notes at XVIII-41.

[40]Pasadena City Council Minutes: July 9, August 20, September 4, 1929; *Houston Press*, August 20, 1929; *Houston Post-Dispatch*, August 27, 1929.

[41]South Houston community history.

[42]*Yesteryears in Pasadena*, 51; E. Payson Pomeroy family biography; *Houston Post*, September 22, 1929; *Houston Post-Dispatch*, August 27, 1929.

Notes 411

[43]Pasadena City Council Minutes: October 2, 1929; Webb, *The Handbook of Texas*, 2-668; Sibley, *The Port of Houston*, 171; Richardson, *Texas, The Lone Star State*, 330.

[44]*Pasadena Sun*, February 28, 1929; Pasadena City Council Minutes: May 13, 1929; Newspaper file, Pomeroy History Collection, Pasadena.

[45]Approved Application for Post of The American Legion, dated October 8, 1929, Organizations file, Pomeroy History Collection, Pasadena.

[46]HCDR: 633-130, 725-47, 782-404, 852-385, 926-553; F. E. and Doris (Barnes) Howell, interview, 1984, notes at III-63A; Joseph S. Cullinan Collection, map records, Santa Anna Farm, December 1922.

[47]*Houston Chronicle*, September 22, 1929, RESec.p.2; *Yesteryears in Pasadena*, 190; Bertha Davis and Rosa Scannell, interview, 1983, notes at II-38A; Robert W. Glasgow, interview, 1987, notes at X-51; J. B. and Boots Isaac, interview, 1986, notes at VII-68A; *Houston Post*, September 22, 1929; *Houston Chronicle*, September 22, 1929; *Pasadena Sun*, September 5, 1929; Edith (Hearn) Curry, interview, 1993, notes in Early Settlers file, Pomeroy History Collection, Pasadena; J. B. Isaac, interview, 1985, notes at VI-30.

[48]*Houston Post*, September 22, 1929; *Houston Chronicle*, September 22, 1929; Whoopee file, Pomeroy History Collection, Pasadena; *Star News Citizen*, May 9, 1963.

[49]Naomi (Daily) McCoy, interview, 1981, notes at I-53; Leona (Roberts) Richburg and J. E. "Duckie" (Pitts) Towles, interview, 1982, notes at II-33A; Everett Williams, interview, 1982, notes at II-34: 1988, notes at XIV-13; Johnny and Sylvia (Wilson) Meyers, interview, 1984, notes at III-70; Doris (Barnes) Howell, interview, 1987, notes at XI-50; Robert W. Glasgow, interview, 1987, notes at X-55A; *Yesteryears in Pasadena*, 17, 48.

[50]Johnny and Sylvia (Wilson) Meyers, interview, 1985, notes at V-29A: 1984, notes at III-70: 1982, notes at II-28A; Bertha Davis and Rosa Scannell, interview, 1983, notes at II-38A; Robert W. Glasgow, interview, 1987, notes at X-55A; J. M. Sherman family biography; Edna Mae (Irwin) Adams, interview, 1984, notes at V-10A; Bill Pendleton, interview, 1987, notes at XI-15A; George Berry family biography.

[51]Wallechinsky and Wallace, *The Peoples Almanac #2*, 455; Robert W. Glasgow, interview, 1987, notes at X-55A; Johnny and Sylvia (Wilson) Meyers, interview, 1984, notes at III-70: *Yesteryears in Pasadena*, 48.

Chapter 12

[1] Trager, *The People's Chronology*, 871.

[2] McComb, *Houston: A History*, 115.

[3] Pasadena City Council Minutes: October 28, 1929: June 21, 30, November 17, 21, 1930: January 12, March 11, 1931.

[4] Geraldine (Conrad) Ferguson, interview, 1993, notes at XVIII-36A.

[5] Pasadena City Council Minutes: April 9, May 4, 6, June 1, 13, 1931; *Yesteryears in Pasadena*, 70; Edward and Loise (Williams) Pomeroy, interview, 1986, notes at IX-1A.

[6] Pasadena City Council Minutes: May 6, September 21, 193; Percy H. Ulmer family biography.

[7] Charles E. Syfan family biography; John L. Larson family biography; Gentry A. Warren family biography; Homer F. Brammer family biography; *Pasadena Record*, September 4, 1931, p.7.

[8] Octavino and Leonor (Martinez) Rocha, oral history, 1986, notes at VII-50A; J. W. Hill family biography; R. Q. Mills, Jr., interview, 1993, notes at XIX-32.

[9] W. S. Dixon family biography.

[10] Hadley White family biography; William D. Scott family biography; Melvin R. Otterside family biography.

[11] Augustus T. Vick family biography; , Gilbert M. Vick family biography.

[12] John F. Johnson family biography; Helge Gigstad family biography; George E. Poole family biography.

[13] Henry Smith family biography; Harrison McLean family biography.

[14] Taylor Florrow family biography; R. E. Yeamans family biography.

[15] T. E. Griffin family biography; James L. Forrest family biography; Dowe Wood family biography.

[16] HCDR:491-58; David W. Shannon family biography.

[17] David W. Shannon family biography; Chambers family biography; Sebe A. Bandy family biography; E. C. Crowe family biography.

[18] William N. Blakesley family biography; Al L. Poirrier family biography.

[19] Delbert E. Atkinson family biography; School Minutes: April 7, 1934; Pasadena school history, School Board file .

[20] John E. Carpenter family biography .

[21] John Dearing family biography; William R. N. Pennington family biography.

[22]J. Edward Pomeroy, Jr., interview, 1985, notes at VII-77A; Pomeroy Family Records, personal notes.

[23]*Yesteryears in Pasadena*, 85 .

[24]L. I. Chapman family biography; *Yesteryears in Pasadena*, 35.

[25]HCDR:725-300; HC Map Rec:10-35: 11-60; Golden Acres community history, Pomeroy History Collection, Pasadena; Joseph P. Carlson family biography; Courtney E. Farr family biography; James S. Slaton family biography; Louis Cloutier family biography.

[26]Wilma (Plaisance) McMurry, interview, 1993, notes at XVIII-45A.

[27]HC Map Rec: 8-68, 9-41, 11-53: Alta Vista community history, Pomeroy History Collection, Pasadena; George W. Livingston, interview, 1993, notes at XIX-48; Arthur Howard family biography; Whitney Patrick family biography.

[28]Clyde J. Strait family biography; George W. Livingston, interview, 1993, notes at XIX-48; Arthur F. Howard, interview, 1981, notes at I-48A.

[29]Adolph Herrera family biography; Paul Herrera, interview, 1987, notes at XI-37; Octavino and Leonor (Martinez) Rocha, interview, 1986, notes at VII-48.

[30]Mildred (Tabor) Hay, interview, 1993, notes at XVIII-50A: Lawrence G. Tabor family biography; Calvin I. Barnes family biography.

[31]Paul Herrera, interview, 1987, notes at XI-37; Carol Williams, "Herrara's roots go deep," and "Berry pickings: a way of life," *Houston Chronicle*, April 13, 1988, This Week, SE Sec.; *Yesteryears in Pasadena*, 189.

[32]A. M. Gore, Jr., interview, 1993, notes at XVIII-51A; Alfred M. Gore family biography.

[33]Samuel D. Boyd family biography; George A. Boyd, interview, 1993, notes at XIX-22.

[34]A. M. Gore, Jr., interview, 1993, notes at XVIII-51A; *Yesteryears in Pasadena*, 89; Robert A. Hughes family biography.

[35]*Houston Chronicle*, April 13, 1988; Paul Herrera, interview, 1987, notes at XI-37.

[36]*Houston Chronicle*, April 13, 1988; Paul Herrera, interview, 1987, notes at XI-37.

[37]Charles E. Cook family biography.

[38]Clyde Pomeroy and Bessie (Pomeroy) Stack, interview, 1987, notes at XI-1A; Luther Pickett, interview, 1987, notes at XI-60A; Earl Newell, interview, 1989, notes at XVI-76; *Yesteryears in Pasadena*, 140, 145; Louis J. Muecke family biography; 1920 Census ED 107, Family #465, 467; First Methodist Church

history, information provided by Clifton B. Eskridge, Pomeroy History Collection, Pasadena.

[39] Octavino and Leonor (Martinez) Rocha, interview, 1986, notes at VII-48; L. James Brubaker family biography; *Pasadena Citizen*, September 10, 1987; Adolph Herrera family biography; Kenyon, *From Arrows to Astronauts*, 28; Frank Hole, ed., *Archeological Investigations Along Armand Bayou, Harris County, Texas*, (Houston: Rice University, 1974), 73; H. J. Simmons, letter to James Douglas, dated October 12, 1903, published as "Human Bones Found Near Galveston," *Bulletin of the American Geographical Society of New York*, Vol. 35, 1903; Murat Halstead, *Galveston: The Horrors of a Stricken City*, (n.c.: American Publishers' Association, n.d.), 276.

[40] Debbi Pomeroy, "Remember the 'Big Top'?," *Pasadena Citizen*, Texas Weekly Magazine, October 18, 1981; C. P. Fox and T. Parkinson, *The Circus in America*, (Waukesha: Country Beautiful, 1969), 58, 98, 162; *Pasadena Citizen*:V.38,No.296, 1984.

[41] City Council Minutes, City of South Houston: February 8, 1927 et seq.; *Houston Chronicle*, September 22, 1929, p.4.

[42] Lubbock, *Six Decades in Texas*, 238; Pomeroy, "Remember the 'Big Top'?"; Marvin D. Burnett, interview, 1984, notes at III-43A.

[43] *Harris County School Life*, January 16, 1931, p.6; Foxworth, *The Romance of Old Sylvan Beach*, 68; Pomeroy, "Remember the 'Big Top'?."

[44] Pomeroy, "Remember the 'Big Top'?"; Virginia Hahn, "Elephants, convicts help on highway," *Pasadena Citizen*, June 17, 1993, p.8.

[45] Marvin D. Burnett, interview, 1984, notes at III-43A; *Yesteryears in Pasadena*, 199; Bill Pendleton, interview, 1987, notes at XI-16; J. Edward Pomeroy, Jr., interview, 1984, notes at IX-7A: 1993, notes at XVIII-34.

[46] *Yesteryears in Pasadena*, 24, 140; Bradie Slaten, interview, 1984, notes at V-8A.

[47] *Yesteryears in Pasadena*, 166; Clyde D. Pomeroy, Oral History, 1986, by Ann Zimmerer, published in part in *Yesteryears in Pasadena*, Pasadena Public Library, Pasadena, Texas, with additional notes at VII-24A; E. Payson Pomeroy family biography; Allen Carpenter, interview, 1993, notes at XVIII-39; William B. Bailey family biography; Walter L. Wilson family biography.

[48] Clyde D. Pomeroy, interview, 1986, notes at IV-36: 1987, notes at X-59.

[49] J. Edward Pomeroy, Jr., interview, 1988, notes at XII-66: 1988, notes at XV-7: 1993, notes at XIX-8A; Clyde D. Pomeroy, interview, 1985, notes at IV-10.

[50] Luther Pickett, interview, 1987, notes at XI-61; Clyde D. Pomeroy, interview, 1986, notes at IV-36; Dorothy (Tacker) Bradley, interview, 1986, notes at VI-39A.

[51] Bill Pendleton, interview, 1987, notes at XI-16; J. B. and Boots Isaac, interview, 1986, notes at VII-69; Clyde D. Pomeroy, interview, 1986, notes at VII-71; Mildred (Tabor) Hay, interview, 1993, notes at XVIII-44.

[52] Bevis Frazier, oral history transcript, 1978, made available by Betty Anderson at Champion Paper Mill plant in Pasadena, notes at V-41; *Harris County School Life*, January 16, 1931, p. 5; Deer Park Independent School District, "The Story of Our Community," 1966, publication in vertical file, Deer Park Public Library, Deer Park, Texas; Pasadena school history, School Board file; *Yesteryears in Pasadena*, 180; Wells, *Shell at Deer Park*, 70; Samuel M. Mathews family biography.

[53] *Yesteryears in Pasadena*, 38, 80, 117, 150, 173, 177; *Pasadena Record*, May 1930 (reprinted in Pasadena Historical Society's newsletter, Jan 1980, copy in Pomeroy History Collection, Pasadena).

[54] Doris (Barnes) Howell, interview, 1983, notes at III-34A, 35, 35A; Clyde D. and Marguerite (Wesney) Pomeroy, interview, 1983, notes at III-28.

[55] Doris (Barnes) Howell, donated picture with names and other material, in Girls Basketball file, Pomeroy History Collection,; *Harris County School Life*, January 16, 1931, p.3; Loise (Williams) Pomeroy, interview, notes in Girls Basketball file.

[56] *Houston Post*, March 5, 1933; *Houston Chronicle*, 1933.

[57] School Minutes: April 7, 1933; Girls Basketball file; Clyde D. and Marguerite (Wesney) Pomeroy, interview, 1983, notes at III-28.

[58] Loise (Williams) Pomeroy, interview, 1985, notes at VII-75A; School Minutes: May 24, 1932: April 6, May 17, 1935; Mildred (Tabor) Hay, interview, 1993, notes at XVIII-50A; Frank M. Young family biography.

[59] James B. Sprott family biography; Clyde D. Pomeroy and Bessie (Pomeroy) Stack, interview, 1987, notes at XI-1; *News Citizen*, June 2, 1966, p.7.

[60] J. Edward and Loise (Williams) Pomeroy, interview, 1985, notes at VI-29, 29A: 1988, notes at XIII-44 ; *Pasadena Record*, September 4, 1931; *Pasadena Citizen*, August 11, 1987; *Yesteryears in Pasadena*, 29; James L. Forrest family biography;

William J. Shelton family biography; E. Payson Pomeroy family biography; Loise (Williams) Pomeroy, interview, 1982, notes at II–21A; School Minutes: May 15, 1933: May 24, 1935.

[61]Rundell, *Early Texas Oil: A Photographic History*, 224; Thomas W. Moore family biography; Presley, *A Saga of Wealth*, 117, 122; James A. Clark and Michel T. Halbouty, *The Last Boom*, (Texas: Shearer Publishing, 1984) 69, 96; Shell Refinery file, Pomeroy History Collection, Pasadena.

Chapter 13

[1]Sibley, *The Port of Houston*, 182; *Yesteryears in Pasadena*, 143, 168, 195; Clyde D. Pomeroy, oral history, 1986, additional notes at VII–24A; W. S. "Muggins" Parks, Jr., interview, 1989, notes at XVI–72.

[2]City Council Minutes, Pasadena: February 2, April 19, May 17, June 2, July 5, September 20, 1932.

[3]City Council Minutes, Pasadena: October 18, December 30, 1932.

[4]Wells, *Shell at Deer Park*, 71; City Council Minutes, Pasadena: November 22, 1932.

[5]City Council Minutes, Pasadena: September 29, 1932: April 15, June 13, 1933; S. R. "Buddy" Jones, Jr., interview, 1983, notes at II–62: 1988, notes at XIII–6A.

[6]Trager, *The People's Chronology*, 888, 895; City Council Minutes, Pasadena: July 15, 29, 1933.

[7]City Council Minutes, Pasadena: May 30, 1934: July 6, December 19, 1935.

[8]Talitha Barnes family biography; Jonah Boyd family biography; Harvey C. Billingsley family biography; Doris (Barnes) Howell, interview, 1987, notes at XI–50.

[9]J. Edward Pomeroy, Jr., interview, 1985, notes at VII–78; Clyde D. Pomeroy, interview, 1982, notes at IX–8; J. B. Isaac, interview, 1987, notes at XI–60A.

[10]Work Projects Administration, *Houston*, 210; Johnston, *Houston, the Unknown City*, 244; Clyde D. Pomeroy, interview, 1980, notes at I–29: 1993, notes at XVIII–35; *Houston Chronicle*, December 25, 1989, p.E–1; Work Projects Administration, *Houston*, 210; Webb, *The Handbook of Texas*, 2–668.

[11]*Yesteryears in Pasadena*, 81, 119, 122, 160; Mildred (Tabor) Hay, interview, 1993, notes at XVIII–44: Oscar Derrington family biography; Guy W. Butler family biography.

[12]Joseph S. Cullinan Collection, Santa Anna Farm correspondence; *Yesteryears in Pasadena*, 24.

[13]City Council Minutes, Pasadena: July 7, 1930; Rosemary (Dreyfuss) Parks, interview, 1989, notes at XIII-79; Doris (Cruse) Hale, interview, 1988, notes at XIII-18; W. H. Cargill family biography.

[14]Houston Lighting & Power Company history, provided by Jim Parsons, 1986, copy in Pomeroy History Collection.

[15]Sibley, *The Port of Houston*, 175, 184; George P. Moore, "Ferries of Harris County," 1942 report to Harris County Commissioner Court, Houston Metropolitan Research Center; Foxworth, *The Romance of Old Sylvan Beach*, 82.

[16]Alden Bailey, interview, 1986, notes at VII-35; Trager, *The People's Chronology*, 911.

[17]Clyde D. Pomeroy, interview, 1987, notes at XI-41.

[18]City Council Minutes, Pasadena: Vol. 5, 1934, copy of Minutes of County School Trustees meeting of September 21, 1934, approving consolidation; Pasadena school history.

[19]Delbert E. Atkinson family biography; Benjamin F. Meador family biography; City Council Minutes, Pasadena: April 4, 1931: April 2, 1932: April 7, 1934.

[20]Work Projects Administration, *Houston*, 164; City Council Minutes, Pasadena: May 10, 1935.

[21]Joseph S. Cullinan Collection, correspondence and papers; Champion Paper Company file, Pomeroy History Collection; City Council Minutes, Pasadena: January 25, 1936.

[22]Bevis Frazier, oral history transcript, 1978, made available by Betty Anderson of Champion Paper, notes at V-39A; *Pasadena Mirror*, May 3, 1954, p.28; Jesse Frazier family biography; Ralph A. Davis family biography; *Yesteryears in Pasadena*, 133, 196; Thomas A. McGraw family biography; Weldon "Stoney" Phillips, interview, 1993, notes at XIX-46.

[23]*Pasadena Citizen*, September 21, 1980; Florian Beusch family biography; Bessie Morrison family biography; Addie (Brown) Bailey, oral history, 1975, additional notes at IV-7.

[24]Joseph S. Cullinan Collection, correspondence from A. T. Vick; HCDR:1013-303; Pomeroy Family Records; HCMR:13-3; HC Map Rec:65-87.

[25]S. R. "Buddy" Jones, Jr., interview, 1988, notes at XIII-5A; Calvin E. Parks family biography; Clyde D. Pomeroy, interview; *Yesteryears in Pasadena*, 19.

[26]George W. Graves, interview, 1988, notes at XIII-38; Wells, *Shell at Deer Park*, 77; City Council Minutes, Pasadena: July 15, 1933.

[27]Oscar Kruse family biography; *Yesteryears in Pasadena*, 114.

[28] Julius Wesney family biography; Marguerite (Wesney) Pomeroy, interview, 1993, notes at XIX-37.

[29] M. Luther Roller family biography; J. E. Tipton family biography; Clayton A. Hart family biography; John A. Lohman family biography.

[30] Sam A. McCoy family biography; Homer F. Brammer family biography; George R. Stroud family biography; Marvin M. Dunaway family biography; W. C. Lowe family biography; A. J. Pitre family biography.

[31] Everett and Ray Williams, interview, 1984, notes at V-5A.

[32] Organizations file, Pomeroy History Collection; City Council Minutes, Pasadena: May 26, 1930 (insert stationary): March 19, 1932, August 31, 1935, March 7, September 5, 1936, January 25, 1936 (insert stationary).

[33] Pasadena school history, School Board file, Staff file; Horace W. Bunkley family biography.

[34] J. Edward Pomeroy, Jr., interview, 1990, notes at XVII-58; *Houston Post*, October 30, 1932; *(Pasadena) (Star) News Citizen*, April 17, July 11, 1965; Estes, *Follow the Strawberry Road*, 54; James E. Stuchbery family biography.

[35] Pasadena school history, staff; Estes, *Follow the Strawberry Road*, 26; Sports file, Pomeroy History Collection; *Yesteryears in Pasadena*, 154; Weldon "Stoney" Phillips, interview, 1993, notes at XIX-44.

[36] *Yesteryears in Pasadena*, 156, 212; Allen "Nig" Brown family biography; J. A. Castleberry family biography; Willis J. Chapman family biography.

[37] Estes, *Follow the Strawberry Road*, 26; A. T. Johnson family biography; Olin Roberts family biography; C. P. Wall family biography; *Yesteryears in Pasadena*, 211.

[38] *(Pasadena) Daily Citizen*, October 30, 1959; *Yesteryears in Pasadena*, 155; Clyde D. and Marguerite (Wesney) Pomeroy, interview, 1993, notes at XIX-43.

[39] Mexican Church file, Pomeroy History Collection; "Reflections of Church Growth: 85th Anniversary," see 1932; First Baptist Chruch file, Pomeroy History Collection; E. Payson Pomeroy family biography; Williams family biography; Pentecostal/Assembly of God Church file, Pomeroy History Collection; *The Union Baptist Association: Centennial History*, 181.

[40] "Reflections of Church Growth: 85th Anniversary"; First Baptist Chruch file; M. A. Darby family biography; Louy Sims family biography; *The Union Baptist Association: Centennial History*, 202; Memorial Baptist Church file, Pomeroy History Collection; *The (Pasadena) Mirror*, December 3, 1954.

[41] Jeff E. Fleming family biography; Rotary Club file, with material provied by Murf McCullen, Pomeroy History Collection; *Pasadena Mirror*, December 3, 1954, p.30; Clyde D. and Marguerite (Wesney) Pomeroy, interview, 1979, notes at I-24; J. Edward Pomeroy, Jr., interview, 1985, notes at VII-77A.

[42] Leo Karkowski family biography; John A. Meyer family biography; Matt F. Reed family biography; Jay Karkowsky, interview, 1990, notes at XVII-66; Mildred (Tabor) Hay, interview, 1993, notes at XVIII-44; *Houston Telephone Directory*, Pasadena Exchange, November 1933, December 1937, 1936, 1937, 1938; *Pasadena Beacon*, February 1937, January 1938, October 1939; Newton Lucas, interview, 1990, notes at XVII-66A; Johnny and Sylvia (Wilson) Meyers, interview, 1984, notes at III-68A; Bill Reno, interview, 1982, notes at I-64.

[43] Walter G. Ankele family biography; Dr. Oscar F. Portwood family biography; Cato N. Nelson family biography; *Houston Telephone Directory*, Pasadena Exchange, June 1936, June 1937; *Pasadena Mirror*, December 3, 1954, p.1.

[44] W. Lee Mitchell family biography; Robert A. Hughes family biography; *Houston Telephone Directory*, Pasadena Exchange, June 1936, June 1937.

[45] Masonic Lodge records; Newton Lucas, interview, 1990, notes at XVII-66A.

[46] *Houston Telephone Directory*, Pasadena Exchange, June 1936, December 1936, June 1937, December 1937; *Pasadena Beacon*, January 24, 1938; Work Projects Administration, *Houston*, 210, 231; Morris J. Wright family biography.

[47] *Houston Telephone Directory*, Pasadena Exchange, 1928-38; Ira L. Pitts family biography.

[48] *Houston Telephone Directory*, Pasadena Exchange, December 1937, June 1938; J. B. and Boots Isaac, 1986, notes at IX-9A; John S. Isaac family biography; Morris J. Wright family biography.

[49] *Pasadena Beacon*, February 10, 1937; First Methodist Church file; Joseph G. Kirk family biography; Louy Sims family biography; Arthur G. Whitman family biography; *Houston Post*, May 14, 1943, p.3; *Pasadena Record*, September 4, 1931, p.2.

[50] *Pasadena Mirror*, December 3, 1954; L. S. Locklin family biography; *Houston Telephone Directory*, Pasadena Exchange, December 1936, June and December 1937; *Pasadena Beacon*, February 10, 1937.

[51] Horace E. Ford family biography; Roy M. Glasgow family biography; Clyde D. Pomeroy, interview, 1993, notes at XVIII-33.

[52] Emerson R. Kelley family biography; Robert A. Hughes family biography; Howard W. Parker family biography; Calvin E.

Powitzky family biography; Herbert Tatar family biography; Ralph Stafford, interview, 1990, notes at XVII-41A; *Houston Telephone Directory*, Pasadena Exchange, June 1937.

[53]*Houston Telephone Directory*, Pasadena Exchange, June 1937, December 1937; William B. Bailey family biography; A. J. Davis family biography.

[54]*Houston Telephone Directory*, Pasadena Exchange, March 1932, December 1936, June 1937; Rotary Club of Pasadena, material provided by Murf McCullen, in Pomeroy Histroy Collection.

[55]Medical history, Pomeroy History Collection; C. David Pomeroy, Jr., "Medical History of the Pasadena Area'" Part III, *The (Pasadena Historical Society's newsletter) Pasadena Record*, December 1984; Dr. Edwin E. Connor family biography; *Houston Telephone Directory*, Pasadena Exchange, June 1937.

[56]Grover V. Bradshaw family biography; Thomas B. Walker family biography; Samuel B. Towels family biography; James E. Porter family biography; Sam D. Ellis family biography; R. L. Boggs family biography; Jack Beard family biography; John S. Webb family biography; Edgar G. Bashforth family biography; E. Gilbert Battle family biography.

[57]Champion Paper Company, Pasadena Mill material, provided by Betty Anderson, 1985, notes at V-38A, Pomeroy History Collection; *Pasadena Mirror*, December 3, 1954, p.6.

Bibliography: Public Records

Brazoria County, Deed Records (BCDR) County Clerk's Office, Angleton, Texas.
City Council Minutes, City of Pasadena (Tx) Vol. A & B, Pasadena, Texas.
City Council Minutes, City of South Houston, Vol. 2, South Houston City Hall, South Houston, Texas.
City of Seabrook, Municipal History Collection, City Hall Seabrook, Texas.
Galveston County, Deed Records (GCDR) County Clerk's Office, Galveston, Texas.
Harris County, Commissioners Court Records (HCCCR) Commissioners Court Office, Houston, Texas.
Harris County, Deed Records (HCDR) County Clerk's Office, Houston, Texas.
Harris County, Harris County School Department "Report of Harris County Schools," 1910-14 Houston Metropolitan Research Center, Houston, Texas.
Harris County, Map Records (HC Map Rec.) County Clerk's Office, Houston, Texas.
Harris County, Marriage Records (HC Marriage), County Clerk's Office, Houston, Texas.
Harris County, Mortgage Records (HCMR), County Clerk's Office, Houston, Texas.
Harris County, Probate Records (HCPR), Family Law Center, Houston, Texas.
Harris County, Property Tax Rolls; Reels #4, 5, 6, 7, Texas State Library Archives, Austin, Texas.
Harris County School Records. Texas State Library Archives, Austin, Texas.
Pasadena Independent School District Minutes of Board Meetings (School Minutes), Superintendent's Office, P.I.S.D. Pasadena, Texas.
Texas, Land Records, General Land Office, Austin, Texas.
United States Census, Harris County, Texas, 1900, 1910, 1920.
United States Post Office, P. O. Location Papers, Group 28, Harris County, Texas, National Archives, General Services Administration, Washington, D. C.

Bibliography: Private Collections

Allen Ranch file. Pomeroy History Collection, Pasadena.
Alta Vista community history. Pomeroy History Collection, Pasadena.
Baldwin and Cargill farm file. Pomeroy History Collection, Pasadena.
Band history file. Pomeroy History Collection, Pasadena.
Beers Family Papers, 1777–1925. Location 36-0670, Box 5, Rosenberg Library, Galveston.
Bishop, Kate Smith. "Oscar Kruse as an Educator," Pasadena Reading Club, 1939, Pomeroy History Collection, Pasadena.
Boyd, Dr. James M., material. Pasadena Historical Museum, Pasadena.
Champion Paper Company. Pasadena Mill material, provided by Betty Anderson, Pomeroy History Collection, Pasadena.
Crown Hill Cemetery. Records, Pomeroy History Collection, Pasadena.
Crown Refinery history file. Pomeroy History Collection, Pasadena.
Cullinan, J. S., Collection, MSS 69. Boxes 37, 46, 57, 61, 74 Houston Metropolitan Research Center, Houston Public Library, Houston.
Deepwater community history. Pomeroy History Collection, Pasadena.
Deer Park community vertical file. Deer Park Public Library, Deer Park.
Department of the Air Force. 147th Fighter Interceptor Group, 1987, correspondence, Pomeroy History Collection, Pasadena.
Early Settlers file. Pomeroy History Collection, Pasadena.
First Baptist Church file. Pomeroy History Collection, Pasadena.
First Methodist Church file. Pomeroy Collection, Pasadena.
First Methodist Church, history. Provided by Clifton B. Eskridge, Pomeroy History Collection, Pasadena.
Galveston-Houston Interurban Land Company. Barker Texas History Center, University of Texas, Austin.
Genoa community history. Pomeroy History Collection, Pasadena.
Girls Basketball file. Pomeroy History Collection, Pasadena.
Glass, Jim. "San Jacinto," unpublished abstract, Pomeroy History Collection, Pasadena.
Golden Acres community history. Pomeroy History Collection, Pasadena.

Harris County Medical Society. Library references, Directories and Archives, provided by Beth White, Houston Medical Center, Houston.

Historical Marker file. Pomeroy History Collecton, Pasadena.

Houston Lighting & Power Company. History of the Deepwater Plant, provided by Jim Parsons, November 6, 1986, Pomeroy History Collection, Pasadena.

Jones Ranch file. Pomeroy History Collection, Pasadena.

Jones (M. T.) Lumber Co. Records,. 3T566, 4C680, Barker Texas History Center, University of Texas, Austin.

La Porte community history. Pomeroy History Collection, Pasadena.

Library history file. Pomeroy History Collection, Pasadena.

Lynn, Jack. anonymous notes, Pasadena Public Library, Pasadena.

Map Collection. Houston Metropolitan Research Center, Houston Public Library, Houston, Texas.

Martyn, Jimmy farm data. Armand Bayou Nature Center, Houston.

Masonic Lodge records. Pomeroy History Collection, Pasadena.

McWhorter, Dr. James E, biography. Made available by Beth White, Harris County Medical Society, Archives' Library, Houston, Tx 1981.

Medical history. Pomeroy History Collection, Pasadena.

Memorial Baptist Church file. Pomeroy History Collection, Pasadena.

Mexican Church file. Pomeroy History Collection, Pasadena.

Moore, George P.. "Ferries of Harris County," 1942, Report to Harris County Commissioners' Court, Houston Metropolitan Research Center, Houston.

Munger, Avilda Witter, Diary of. Made available by Mrs. C. Danouy, 1987, Houston, Tx, Pomeroy History Collection, Pasadena.

Newspaper history file. Pomeroy History Collection, Pasadena.

Organizations file. Pomeroy History Collection, Pasadena.

Pasadena school history. Pomeroy History Collection, Pasadena.

Pasadena, Texas Producers Exchange file. Pomeroy History Collection, Pasadena.

Patterson, H. L., June 12, 1920. Proposed Pasadena City Limits, Map Collection, Pomeroy History Collection, Pasadena.

Pentecostal Church history. Pomeroy History Collection, Pasadena.

Peterson, Mr. Linn. Kansas historical background material, 1988, Pomeroy History Collection, Pasadena.

Plat, City of Pasadena, 1923. Courtesy A. J. Pitre, Map Collection, Pomeroy History Collection, Pasadena.

Pomeroy Family Records. including McMaster & Pomeroy Water Well Co., Financial Reports, Water franchise records, Pomeroy History Collection, Pasadena.

Bibliography: Private Collections

Ramey, Pam, City Secretary. election returns, City of Pasadena, City Hall, Pasadena.

Red Bluff community history. Pomeroy History Collection, Pasadena.

Rotary Club of Pasadena. material provided by Murff McCullen, Pomeroy History Collection, Pasadena.

Seabrook community history. Pomeroy History Collection, Pasadena.

Shine, Mrs. J. I.(Pearl Anderson), letter. March 1960, made available by Marilyn (Towles) Coward, Pomeroy History Collection, Pasadena.

South Houston community history. Pomeroy History Collection, Pasadena.

South Houston History Collection. Pat Lapold, Librarian, Harris County Public Library, South Houston.

Sports history file. Pomeroy History Collection, Pasadena.

Strawberry file. Pomeroy History Collection, Pasadena.

Stuart-Allen Collection, MSS 137. Boxes 7, 8, 11, 12 Houston Metropolitan Research Center, Houston Public Library, Houston.

Ulmer, Percy. Pasadena City and Fire Department Records, provided by Jimmy Barnes, 1993, Pomeroy History Collection, Pasadena.

Vassaloo, Maurine (Conn). letter dated February 12, 1988, donated by Marilyn (Towles) Coward, Pomeroy History Collection, Pasadena.

Weeks, Katie (Guinn). notes, Pomeroy History Collection, Pasadena.

White Family Scrapbook. Material made available by Thomas C. White, Jr., 1988, Pomeroy History Collection, Pasadena.

Whoopee file. Pomeroy History Collection, Pasadena.

Wolf, George E., Jr.. Henry Cemetery report, 1987, Cemeteries file, Pomeroy History Collection, Pasadena.

"Proceedings of the Texas Dairyman's Convention, 1908." SF232T4T492, Barker Texas History Center, University of Texas, Austin.

Bibliography: Interviews

Location of notes from interviews are specified in the parenthesis and refers to the collection of bound note volumes in Pomeroy History Collection, Pasadena

Adams, Edna Mae (Irwin). Interview, 1984 (V-10A), Pomeroy History Collection, Pasadena.
Aldridge, Bill, Texas Banking Commission, Interview, 1985 (Banking file), Pomeroy History Collection, Pasadena.
Atkinson, Vernon. Interviews, Pomeroy History Collection, Pasadena.
Bailey, Addie (Brown). Interview and oral history, 1975, taped with Helen Alexander (IV-2, 7), Pasadena Public Library, Pasadena.
Bailey, Alden O. Interviews, various dates 1986 (VII-35), 1989, Pomeroy History Collection, Pasadena.
Billingsley, Mrytle (Blakesley). Interview, Pomeroy History Collection, Pasadena.
Black, Gordon. Interviews, various dates, Pomeroy History Collection, Pasadena.
Blakesley, Ralph G. Interview, Pomeroy History Collection, Pasadena.
Boyd, Bueron. Interview, 1990 (XVII-16), Pomeroy History Collection, Pasadena.
Boyd, George A. Interview, 1993 (XIX-22), Pomeroy History Collection, Pasadena.
Brady, Dorothy (Tacker). Interview, 1986 (VI-39A), Pomeroy History Collection, Pasadena.
Brammer, Larry A. Interview, 1993 (XIX-10), Pomeroy History Collection, Pasadena.
Brammer, Ruby (Warren). Interview, 1986 (Telcon 20:8-1-86), Pomeroy History Collection, Pasadena.
Brown, Mrs. George. Interview, 1988 (XIII-39A), Pomeroy History Collection, Pasadena.
Brubaker, Helen. Interview, 1979 (I-11), Pomeroy History Collectio, Pasadena.
Burnett, Marvin D. Interviews, 1984 (III-43A): 1988 (III-42, IV-39A), Pomeroy History Collection, Pasadena.
Carpenter, Allen. Interview, 1993 (XVIII-39), Pomeroy History Collection, Pasadena.

Cope, Edyth (Larson). Interview, 1993 (XIX-8, 8A), Pomeroy History Collection, Pasadena.
Coward, Marilyn (Towles). Interviews, 1989 (XVI-52), 1986 (IX-16, 20), Pomeroy History Collection, Pasadena.
Cruse, Judy. Interview, 1988 (XIV-2), 1989 (XVI-62), Pomeroy History Collection, Pasadena.
Davis, Bertha. Interview, 1983 (II-38A), Pomeroy History Collection, Pasadena.
Dearing, Ruth (Rawlins). Interview, 1989 (XVI-55), Pomeroy History Collection, Pasadena.
Dickerson, Ceclia (Garfield). Interview, 1984 (III-41), Pomeroy History Collection, Pasadena.
Dickerson, Raymond. Interview, 1986 (IX-28), 1984 (VI-20A), Pomeroy History Collection, Pasadena.
Ferguson, Geraldine (Conrad). Interview, 1993 (XVIII-36A), Pomeroy History Collection, Pasadena.
Ford, Rosa (Dowell). Interviews and oral history, 1979 (I-23), Pomeroy History Collection, Pasadena.
Frazier, Bevis. oral history by Helen Alexander, 1975 (Pomeroy notes IV-21A), Pasadena Public Library, Pasadena.
Frazier, Bevis. Oral history transcript made available by Betty Anderson, Champion Paper Co. 1978.
Glasgow, Robert W. Interviews and oral history, 1987 (X-42A, 48), Pomeroy History Collection, Pasadena.
Gore, A. M., Jr. Interview, 1993 (XVIII-51A), Pomeroy History Collection, Pasadena.
Graves, George Washington. Interviews, 1988 (XIII-33, 38), Pomeroy History Collection, Pasadena.
Hale, Doris (Cruse). Interview, 1988 (XIV-14A), Pomeroy History Collection, Pasadena.
Hartrick, Ruby L. (Hargrave), Interview and oral history, 1983, 1986 (IX-15), Pomeroy History Collection, Pasadena.
Hay, Mildred (Tabor). Interview, 1993 (XVIII-44, 50A), Pomeroy History Collection, Pasadena.
Herrera, Paul. Interviews and oral history, 1987 (XI-37), Pomeroy History Collection, Pasadena.
Holderby, Carmen L. (Hargrave). Interview and oral history, 1986 (IX-15), Pomeroy History Collection, Pasadena.
Howard, Arthur F. Interview, 1981 (I-48A), Pomeroy History Collection, Pasadena.
Howell, Doris (Barnes), Interviews, 1983 (III-34A, 36), 1987 (XI-50) 1989 (XVI-49, 50:XVII-4), 1993 (XVIII-43), Pomeroy History Collection, Pasadena.
Howell, F. E. "Teeler" and Doris (Barnes). Interview, 1984 (III-64A), Pomeroy History Collection, Pasadena.

Isaac, J. B. Interviews, 1985 (VI-30) 1987 (XI-60A), 1988 (XIII-20A, XIV-14), Pomeroy History Collection, Pasadena.
Isaac, J. B. and Boots. Interview, 1986 (VII-65, 67, 68A, 69A: IX-9A), Pomeroy History Collection, Pasadena.
Jones, S. R. "Buddy", Jr., Interviews and oral history, 1983 (II-12) 1982 (I-72), 1988 (XIII-5A), 1993 (XVIII-41), Pomeroy History Collection, Pasadena.
Karkowsy, Jay. Interview, 1990 Pomeroy History Collection, Pasadena.
Kingsbury, Catherine. Interviews and oral history, 1986 (VI-41, 48, 53), 1988 (XIV-8A, 9, 9A, 10), Pomeroy History Collection, Pasadena.
Kruse, Edward. Oral history, 1985 (VI-31), Pomeroy History Collection, Pasadena.
Kruse, Karl. Oral history by Dick Nichols, 1971 (Pomeroy notes at X-14), Pasadena Public Library, Pasadena.
Kruse, Oscar Jr. Interview, 1987 (XI-41A) oral history, 1987 (XI-44), Pomeroy History Collection, Pasadena.
Livingston, George W. Interview, 1993 (XIX-48), Pomeroy History Collection, Pasadena.
Lockey, Eloise (Hodges). Interview, 1993 (XVIII-55), Pomeroy History Collection, Pasadena.
Lucas, Newton. Interview, 1990 (XVII-66A), Pomeroy History Collection, Pasadena.
Maribell, Mrs. of Southwestern Bell Telephone Co., Interview, 1980 (Telcon#3:3-7-80), Pomeroy History Collection, Pasadena.
McCain, Mary (Hand). Interview, 1993 (XIX-2) Pomeroy History Collection, Pasadena.
McCoy, Naomi (Daily). Interview, 1981 (I-53, 53A, 55A), Pomeroy History Collection, Pasadena.
McGowen, Betty (Burnett). Interviews, 1987 (XI-6A, 10A), Pomeroy History Collection, Pasadena.
McMurry, Wilma (Plaisance). Interview, 1993 (XVIII-45A), Pomeroy History Collection, Pasadena.
McNay, Laurel B. Jr. Interviews and oral history, 1988 (XV-9, 17) Pomeroy History Collection, Pasadena.
McWhorter, Cullen, Interview, Pomeroy History Collection, Pasadena.
Meador, Ben F. Jr. Interview, 1993 (XIX-34) Pomeroy History Collection, Pasadena.
Meyers, Johnny M. Interviews, 1988 (XIII-19: XIV-11), Pomeroy History Collection, Pasadena.
Meyers, Johnny M. and Sylvia (Wilson). Interview, 1982 (II-27, 27A, 28, 28A, 29A) 1984 (III-68A, 69A, 70), 1985 (V-29A, 30A), Pomeroy History Collection, Pasadena.
Meyers, Sylvia (Wilson). Interviews, 1988 (XIV-11A), Pomeroy History Collection, Pasadena.
Mills, R. Q. Jr. Interview, 1993 (XIX-32), Pomeroy History Collection, Pasadena.

Mitchell, Blanche (Kingsbury). Interview, 1979 (Telcon @:12-7-79), Pomeroy History Collection, Pasadena.
Newell, Earl. Interview, 1989 (XVI-76), Pomeroy History Collection, Pasadena.
Parker, Dorothy (Hughes). Interview, 1986 (IX-41, 42), Pomeroy History Collection, Pasadena.
Parks, Rosemary (Dreyfuss). Interview, 1989 (XIII-79), Pomeroy History Collection, Pasadena.
Parks, W. S. "Muggins" Jr. Interview, 1989 (XVI-72), Pomeroy History Collection, Pasadena.
Pendleton, Bill. Interview, 1987 (XI-15A, 16), 1993 (XIX-3A, 5) Pomeroy History Collection, Pasadena.
Phillips, Lee. Interview, 1979 (I-25A, 26), Pomeroy History Collection, Pasadena.
Phillips, Weldon "Stoney." Interview, 1993 (XIX-44, 46), Pomeroy History Collection, Pasadena.
Pickett, Luther. Interview, 1987 (XI-60A, 61), Pomeroy History Collection, Pasadena.
Pomeroy, Clyde D. Interviews and oral history, various dates 1985 (IV-10A), 1986 (IV-36: VI-38A: VII-19, 71); 1979 (I-16A, 23) 1980 (I-29), 1985 (VI-25: IX-8); 1982 (II-31A) 1987 (X-59:XI-1, 1A, 41), 1988 (XIII-16) 1993 (XVIII-33, 35, 40A), Pomeroy History Collection, Pasadena.
Pomeroy, Clyde D. Oral history, by Ann Zimmerer 1986 (additonal notes @ VII-24A), Pasadena Public Library, Pasadena.
Pomeroy, Clyde D. and Marguerite (Wesney). Interviews, 1979 (I-24) 1983 (III-28, 28A), 1993 (XIX-43), Pomeroy History Collection, Pasadena.
Pomeroy, John Edward Sr. Interviews and oral history, 1979, tape notes at I-5, Pomeroy History Collection, Pasadena.
Pomeroy, J. Edward Jr. Interviews, 1985 (VII-76A) 1986 (X-24, 25), 1987 (XII-12A), 1988 (XV-1, 1A, 4A: XIII-1, 16A, 17); 1988 (XII-66), 1990 (XVII-58), 1993 (XIX-8A); 1984 (IX-7A) 1989(XV-8:XVI-2, 3, 53, 54), 1993 (XVIII-39, 40A), Pomeroy History Collection, Pasadena.
Pomeroy, J. Edward Jr.and Loise (Williams). Interviews, 1985 (VI-29, 29A) 1986 (IX-2, 3, 6), 1988 (XIII-13A, 44), Pomeroy History Collection, Pasadena.
Pomeroy, Loise (Williams). Interviews, 1982 (II-21A), Pomeroy History Collection, Pasadena.
Pomeroy, Marguerite (Wesney). Interview, 1992 (XIX-37), Pomeroy History Collection, Pasadena.
Reeves, Elva (Guinn). Interview, 1989 (XV-54), Pomeroy History Collection, Pasadena.
Reno, Bill. Interview, 1982 (I-64), Pomeroy History Collection, Pasadena.
Richburg, Leona (Roberts), Interview, 1982 (II-33A), Pomeroy History Collection, Pasadena.

Rocha, Octavino and Leonor (Martinez), Interview and oral history, 1986 (VII-49), Pomeroy History Collection, Pasadena.
Roy, Dorothy (Sippy). Interview, 1988 (XIV-8), Pomeroy History Collection, Pasadena.
Scannell, Rosa. Interview, 1983 (II-38A), Pomeroy History Collection, Pasadena.
Schultz, Janette (Martin). Interview, Pomeroy History Collection, Pasadena.
Shinpaugh, Helen (Kruse). Interview, 1993 (XIX-41), Pomeroy History Collection, Pasadena.
Stack, Bessie (Pomeroy). Interview, 1987 (XI-1, 1A), Pomeroy History Collection, Pasadena.
Stafford, Ralph. Interview, 1988 (XIII-20), 1990 (XVII-41A). Pomeroy History Collection, Pasadena.
Stafford, Ralph and Winogene (Cloutier). Interviews and oral history, 1987 (X-38, 38A), Pomeroy History Collection, Pasadena.
Stuart, Robert Cummins, IV, Oral history by Helen Alexander, 1975 Pasadena Public Library, Pasadena.
Teas, Janis. Interview, 1993 (XVIII-30B), Pomeroy History Collection, Pasadena.
Towles, Julia "Duckie" (Pitts). Interviews, 1982 (II-33A), Pomeroy History Collection, Pasadena.
Wales, Francis (Freeman). Interview, 1993 (XVIII-55), Pomeroy History Collection, Pasadena.
Williams, Everett M. Interviews, 1982 (II-34), 1983 (III-9) 1988 (XIV-11A, 12, 12A, 13), Pomeroy History Collection, Pasadena.
Williams, Ray C. Interview, 1984 (V-5), Pomeroy History Collection, Pasadena.
Williams, Ray C. and Everett M. Interviews, 1884 (V-2A), Pomeroy History Collection, Pasadena.
Willis, V. Fern (Hargrave). Interview and oral history, 1986 (IX-15) Pomeroy History Collection, Pasadena.
Wilson, Clara (Thurman). Interview, 1983 (II-49A), Pomeroy History Collection, Pasadena.
Wilson, Clara (Thurman). Oral History by Helen Alexander, 1975 (additional notes at III-79, IV-1A), Pasadena Public Library, Pasadena.
Wilson, Thurman L. Interviews, 1988 (XIV-3, 4A, 6), Pomeroy History Collection, Pasadena.
Young, Selby. Interview, 1986 (IX-44), Pomeroy History Collection, Pasadena.

Bibliography: Biographies

Biographical Histories in the Pomeroy Collection, by original head of household (children and their families listed under same heading). All citations to "family biography" refer to unpublished biographies created for this project and held in the Pomeroy Collection, Pasadena. Listed below are those cited in the text.

Allen, Samuel W.; Anderson, William W.; Ankele, Walter G.; Atkinson, Delbert E.; Bailey, William B.; Bandy, Sebe A.; Barnes, Calvin I.; Barnes, Talitha; Bashforth, Edgar G.; Battle, E. Gilbert; Beard, Jack; Bell, Samuel P.; Berry, George; Beusch, Florian; Billingsley, Henry C.; Billingsley, James C.; Blakesley, William N.; Blanyer, George J. Jr.; Boggs, E. D.; Boggs, R. L.; Boyd, Dr. James M.; Boyd, Jonah; Boyd, Samuel D.; Bradshaw, Grover V.; Brammer, Homer F.; Brannen, Richard; Brown, George A.; Brown, Allen "Nig"; Brown, Silas W.; Brubaker, L. James; Bunkley, Horace W.; Butler, Guy W.; Cargill, W. H.; Carlson, Joseph P.; Carpenter, John E.; Carter, Henry A.; Castleberry, J. A.; Chambers,; Chapman, L. I.; Chapman, Willis J.; Cloutier, Louis; Connor, Dr. Edwin E.; Conrad, Gerald. W.; Cook, Charles E.; Cook, Joe; Coolidge, Woodrow P.; Coy, Mike; Crowe, E. C.; Cruse, Joseph M.; Dailey, J. Sam; Darby, M. A.; David, W. J.; Davis, A. J.; Davis, Ralph A.; Davis, Sam; Deane, Frederick G.; Dearing, John; DeFee, E. Frank; Derrington, Oscar; Dickerson, Robert; Dixon, W. S.; Dowell, George P.; Duffield, Thomas; Dunaway, Marvin M.; Edming, Gustov; Elder, William M.; Ellis, Sam D.; Farr, Courtney E.; Fisher, Forrest; Fleming, Paul O.; Florrow, Taylor; Ford, Horace E.; Forrest, James L.; Frazier, Jesse; Freeman, Adison B.; Freeman, Charles C.; Garfield, Charles L.; Garnuch, Samuel; Gigstad, Helge; Glasgow, Roy M.; Goodman, Emory C.; Gore, Alfred M.; Gray, Austin S.; Griffin, T. E.; Griffith, Dr. Charles W.; Guinn, Robert M.; Gutherie, John C.; Hargrave, Ben; Hart, Clayton A.; Harwell, Frank H.; Hearn, Jacob L.; Herrera, Adolph; Hill, J. W.; Hill, W. T.; Hogge, Sarah V.; Holbrook, John L.; Holloway, David Z.; Houston, James G.; Howard, Arthur; Hughes, David H.; Hughes, Robert A.; Isaac, John S.; Jackson, James A.; Jacob, Alexander; James, Robert G.; Johnson, A. T.; Johnson, John F.; Jones, Dean K.; Jones, Harry; Karkowski, Leo; Kelley, Emerson R.; Kingsbury, Robert A.; King, Robert W.; Kirk, Joseph G.; Kruse, Oscar; Lakin, George M.; Larson, John L.; Laschinsky, William; Locklin, L. S.; Lohman, John A.;

Loose, Dr. Titus C.; Lowe, W. C.; MacNider, Dr. Virginius S.; Marchant, Dr. Juliett C.; Mason, Jess T.; Mathews, Samuel M.; McBurney, William; McCormick, David D.; McCoy, Sam A.; McEvers, Mattie; McGraw, Thomas A.; McLean, Harrison; McMaster, David C.; McNay, Charnock B.; Meador, Benjamin F.; Meyer, John A..; Miller, Jake D.; Mitchell, W. Lee; Moechel, Jason R.; Moore, Oscar F.; Moore, Thomas W.; Morrison, Bessie; Muecke, Louis J.; Munger, Charles R.; Napp, Edward F.; Nelson, Cato N.; Newell, Francis D.; Olson, Edward A.; Otterside, Melvin R.; Parker, Howard W.; Parks, Calvin E.; Patrick, Whitney; Pennington, William R. N.; Pickett; Pitre, A. J.; Pitts, Ira L.; Plum, George H.; Poirrier, Al L.; Pomeroy, E. Payson; Poole, George E.; Porter, James E.; Portwood, Dr. Oscar F.; Powell, Ben; Powitzky, Calvin E.; Quinn, Samuel A.; Rawlins, Josiah; Reed, Matt F.; Riley, Archie C.; Robertson, Sidney G.; Roberts, Joseph R.; Roberts, Orlin; Roller, M. Luther; Ross, Dr. W. B.; Saderwhite, Charlie; Scott, William D.; Shannon, David W.; Shaw, Thomas T.; Shelton, William J.; Sherman, J. M.; Shine, John T.; Sims, Louy; Sippy, Lawrence N.; Slaton, James S.; Smith, Henry; Spacie, William W.; Sprott, James B.; Stafford, Leonard J.; Starkey, Josiah H.; Starnes, Oscar; Stewart, J. B.; Strait, Clyde J.; Strope, John H.; Stroud, George R.; Stuchbery, James E.; Syfan, Charles E.; Tabor, Lawrence G.; Tacker, Harry J.; Tatar, Herb; Thomasson, Archie G.; Thompson, Arvie; Thornton, William H.; Thorps; Tilley, Charles H.; Tingle, A. D. Tipton, J. E.; Towles, Samuel B.; Ulmer, Percy H.; Van Dorn, William F.; Vick, Augustus T.; Vick, Gilbert M.; Walker, Thomas B.; Wall, C. P.; Warren, Gentry A.; Webb, D. L. "Doc"; Webb, John S.; Wesney, Julius; White, Hadley; Whitman, Arthur G.; Williams, James W.; Wilson, Walter L.; Witt, Harry; Wood, Dowe; Worley, Jacob A.; Wright, Morris J.; Yeamans, R. E.; Yerkes; Young, Frank M.; Zlomke, Leopold.

Bibliography: Books

Adams, C. W., ed. *American Cattle Breeders Hall of Fame Vol. 1*. San Angelo: Anchor Publishing Co. 1978
Allen, O. F. *The City of Houston, From Wilderness to Wonder*. Temple, Tx: n.p. 1936
Ball, Thomas H. *The Port of Houston, How it Came to Pass*. Houston: Houston Chronicle, npd
Bass, Feris A. ed. and Brunson, B. R., *Fragile Empires*. Austin: Shoal Creek Publishers, Inc. 1978
Baughman, James P. *Charles Morgan and the Dev. of Southern Transportation*. Nashville: Vanderbilt University Press, 1968
Bilstein, Roger and Miller, Jay *Aviation in Texas*. Austin: Monthly Press, Inc., 1985
Blum, Daniel *A Pictorial History of the Silent Screen*. New York: Perigee Books, 1982
Branda, Eldon Stephen, ed. *The Handbook of Texas, A Supplement, Vol. 3*. Austin: Texas State Historical Association, 1976
Brown, John Henry *Indian Wars and Pioneers of Texas*. Easley: Southern Historical Press (reprint), 1978
Buchanan, James E., ed. *Houston, A Chronological and Documentary History*. Dobbs Ferry: Oceana Publications, Inc., 1975
Chaddick, DeWitt, ed. *The Alcalde, 1929*. Huntsville: Sam Houston State Teachers College, 1929
Clark, J. A. and Halbouty, M. T. *The Last Boom*. Texas: Shearer Publishing, 1984
Clark, J. A. and Halbouty, M.T. *Spindletop*. New York: Random House, 1952
Clopper, Edward N. *An American Family*. Cincinnati: Standard Printing and Publishing, 1950
Clymer, Floyd *Treasury of Early American Automobiles, 1877-1925*. New York: McGraw-Hill Book Co., 1950
Creighten, J. A. *Narrative History of Brazoria County*. Waco: Texian Press, 1975
Davis, Ellis A. and Grobe, E. H.*New Encyclopedia of Texas*. Dallas: Texas Development Bureau, 1922
Davis, Joe Tom *Legendary Texians*. Burnett: Eakin Press, 1982
de Cordova, J. *Texas: Her Resources and Her Public Men*. Waco: Texian Press (reprint), 1969

Eichorn, John Clifford *God Lives in Our House*. La Porte: La Porte Community Church, 1951

Emmett, Chris *Shanghai Pierce, a fair likeness*. Norman: University of Oklahoma Press, 1953

Estes, Rosemary, ed. *Follow the Strawberry Road*. Pasadena: Pasadena Council PTA, 1976

Fehrenbach, T. R. *Lone Star: a History of Texas and the Texans*. New York: American Legecy Press, 1983

Fornell, Earl W. *The Galveston Era: The Texas Crescent on the Eve of Secession*. Austin: University of Texas Press, 1961

Foxworth, Erna B. *The Romance of Old Sylvan Beach*. Austin: Waterway Press, 1986

Fox, C. P. and Parkinson, T. *The Circus in America*. Waukesha: Country Beautiful, 1969

Fuermann, George *Peden-1965, 75 years--and Just a Beginning*. Houston: Press of Premier, 1965

Garner, John, co-ed. *Texas Weather*. Oklahoma City: England and May, 1975

Gilbo, Patrick *The American Red Cross, The First Century*. New York: Harper and Row, 1981

Gray, William Fairfax *From Virginia to Texas, 1835: Diary of Col. Wm. F. Gray*. Houston: Fletcher Young Publishing Co., 1965

Grun, Bernard *The Timetables of History*. New York: Simon and Schuster, Inc., 1979

Halstead, Murat *Galveston: The Horrors of a Stricken City*. n.c. American Publishers' Association. n.d.

Hayes, Charles W. *History of the Island and the City of Galveston*. Austin: Jenkins Garrett Press, 1974

Henson, Margaret Swett *The History of Baytown*. Baytown: Bay Area Heritage Society, 1986

Hole, Frank, ed. *Archeological Investigations Along Armand Bayou, Harris County, Tx*. Houston: Rice University, 1974

Johnson, Otto, ed. *Information Please, Almanac 1990*. Boston: Houghton Mifflin Co., 1989

Johnston, Marguerite *Houston, The Unknown City, (1836-1946)*. College Station: Texas A and M University Press, 1991

Josephy, Alvin M., Jr. ed. *The American Heritage of Flight*. n.c. American Heritage Publishing, 1962

Kenyon, Dolores *From Arrows to Astronauts*. League City: National Association of Conservation Districts, 1976

Kingston, Mike, ed. *The Texas Almanac*. Sesquicentennial Edition 1986-87 Dallas: Dallas Morning News, 1986

King, John O. *Joseph Stephen Cullinan*. Nashville: Vanderbilt University Press, 1970

Kriegel, John *Houston Garden Book*. Houston: Shearer Publishing, 1983

Lubbock, Francis R. *Six Decades in Texas*. Austin: Pemberton Press, 1968

Ludvigsen, Karl and others *The Encyclopedia of the American Automobile*. Secaucus: Chartwell Books, Inc., 1977
McComb, David G. *Houston: A History*. Austin: University of Texas Press, 1981
Meinig, D. W. *Imperial Texas*. Austin: University of Texas Press, 1969
Michael, Paul, ed. *The Great American Movie Book*. Englewood Cliffs: Prentice-Hall, Inc., 1980
Muir, Andrew Forest, ed. *Texas in 1837, An Anonymous, Contemporary Narrative*. Austin: University of Texas Press, 1958
Olmsted, Frederick Law *A Journey Through Texas*. Austin: University of Texas Press, 1978
Ousley, Clarence, ed. *Galveston in Nineteen Hundred*. Atlanta: William C. Chase, 1900
Presley, James *A Saga of Wealth*. New York: G. P. Putnam's Sons, 1978
Rapp, William F. *The Galveston, Houston and Henderson Railroad*. Crete: J-B Publishing Co., 1987
Reed, S. G. *A History of Texas Railroads*. Houston: St. Clair Publishing, 1941
Richardson, Rupert, et al. *Texas, The Lone Star State, 3rd ed.*. Englewood Cliffs: Prentice-Hall, Inc., 1970
Rundell, Walter Jr. *Early Texas Oil:A Photographic History, 1866-1936*. College Station: Texas A and M University Press, 1977
Sibley, Marilyn McAdams, *The Port of Houston: A History*. Austin: University of Texas Press, 1968
Smith, D. *The History of Harrisburg, Texas*. n.c. n.p. n.d.
Smith, Nina, ed. *A History of the Humble, Texas, Area*. Humble: Bicentennial Heritage Committee, 1976
Spratt, John Stricklin *The Road to Spindletop:Economic Change in Texas, 1875-1901*. Austin: University of Texas, 1970
Sugar, B. R. ed. *The Ring*. New York: Ring Publishing Co., 1981
Timmons, Bascom N. *Jesse H. Jones*. New York: Henry Holt and Co., 1956
Trager, James, ed. *The People's Chronology*. New York: Holt, Rinehart and Winston, 1979
Wallechinsky, D. and Wallace, I.*The People's Almanac #2*. New York: Bantam Books, 1978
Wallechinsky, D. and Wallace, I.*The People's Almanac*. Garden City, NY: Doubleday and Company, Inc., 1975
Webb, Walter Prescott, ed. *The Handbook of Texas (2 vol.)*. Austin: Texas State Historical Ass'n, 1952
Weidig, Barbara Yeary *Deer Park, a History of a Texas Town*. San Antonio: The Naylor Company, 1976
Welch, J. R. *Riding Fence* Waco: Texian Press, 1983
Wells, Barbara *Shell at Deer Park*. Deer Park: Shell Oil Company, 1979
Woods, Herb *Galveston-Houston Electric Railway*. Glendale: Interurbans Publications, 1976
Work Projects Administration *Houston: A History and Guide*. Houston: The Anson Jones Press, 1942

Work Projects Administration *The WPA Guide to Texas.* Austin: Texas Monthly Press, reprint 1986

Ziegler, Jesse A. *Wave of the Gulf.* San Antonio: The Naylor Company, 1938

Zlatkovich, C. P. *Texas Railroads.* Austin: Bureau of Business Research, UT, 1981.

Ellington: 1918, Yearbook of Ellington Air Base. npd.

Harris County School Land Frauds. Smithville: Times Power Print npd.

The 1929 World Almanac and Book of Facts. facsimile edition: Workman Publishing and American Heritage Press, 1971.

The Union Baptist Association: Centennial History, 1840-1940. Brenham: Banner-Press, Inc. npd.

Yesteryears in Pasadena, 1895-1941. Pasadena: Harris County Genealogical Society, 1987

Diamond Jubilee (1847-1922) of the Diocese of Galveston and St. Mary's Cathedral in La Porte. La Porte: Archdiocese of Galveston, 1922

History of Texas, with Biographical Histories of the Cities of Houston and Galveston. Chicago: Lewis Publishing Co., 1895

Bibliography: Publications & Articles

Alexander, Helen. "A History of Pasadena," *Pasadena News Citizen* April 16, 1975 Insert p.1.
Burns, Tommy. "Automobile Directory, 1904," *Living Tree Newsletter*, Harris County Genealogical Society, Vol.19, 127.
Colquette, Richard T. "Early Growth of Pasadena Marks History of Area," *Pasadena Citizen*, Sept. 30, 1962.
Cominsky, Martin B., ed. *Espiritu*, Pasadena High School Publications Dept., Vol. 1, No. 1, Winter 1976.
Cox, C. C. "Reminiscences of C. C. Cox," *Southwestern Historical Quarterly* Vol. 6 (Oct. 1902) 127-129.
Donald, J. Mac, M. D. *Dr. MacDonald's Household Almanac*, Binghamton, N.Y., 11th edition, 1916.
Eskridge, Clifton. *First United Methodist Church, 90th Anniversary*, First United Methodist Church, Pasadena, 1986.
Galveston City Directory. 1872, 1882-83, 1884-85, 1886-87, 1898, 1890-91, 1891-92.
Grafton, Bob. "The Texas City Aviators," *Focus*, College of the Mainland Texas City, Texas, March, 1986, p. 1.
Gregg, Richard L. "The Wm. Dobie Survey, Harris Cty, Tx," *Houston Archeological Soc. Newsletter*, No. 66: March 1980, 22.
Gregg, Richard L. "The Wm. Dobie Survey, Harris Cty, Tx" *Houston Archeological Soc. Newsletter*, No.67: August 1980, 9.
Gregg, Richard L. "The Wm. Dobie Survey, Harris Cty, Tx" *Houston Archeological Soc. Newsletter*, No. 69: May 1981, 4.
Gregg, Richard L. "The Wm. Dobie Survey, Harris Cty, Tx" *Houston Archeological Soc. Newsletter*, No. 70: August 1981, 14.
Hahn, Virginia. "Elephants, convicts help on highway," *Pasadena Citizen*, June 17, 1993, 8.
Hahn, Virginia "This Oil Man Looked East," *Pasadena Citizen*, October 1, 1992, 7.
Harris County Medical. Directory, 1912.
Higgins, Jim. "Ellington," *Texas, Houston Chronicle Magazine*, Nov. 1, 1987, p.4.
Houston City Directory. 1892-93, 1897-8, 1899, 1900-01, 1902, 1919, 1920.

Kegg, Mary. "Japanese Heritage in Bay Area dates to 1903," *The (Clear Lake) Citizen*, Apr. 7, 1988, p.10.

Kilman, Ed. "Beautiful Shore Estate of E. A. Peden...," *Houston Post-Dispatch*, May 16, 1926.

Klempin, Raymond. "The Houston Ship Channel: Waterway to energy world," *Houston Busines Journal*, June 15, 1981, p. 1.

Looscan, Adele B. "Harris County, 1822-1845," *Southwestern Historical Quartley*, Vol. 18, (1914-1915); 195-207, 261-286, 399-409, 37-64.

Love, Clara M. "History of the Catttle Industry in the Southwest," *Southwestern Historical Quarterly*, XIX: (1915-1916), 390.

Lubbock-Evans, Mary Catherine. "The History of La Porte," *La Porte-Bayshore Sun*, series published July 10, 1969 - November 20, 1969.

Neal, Barbara. "Blanche Remembers," *Bayshore Sun*, April 12, 1987.

Nichols, Richard (Dick). "Grand Lady Reminiscences About 82 Years of History," *Pasadena Citizen*, newspaper 1969.

Pearson, M. S. and Macias, I. V. *Harris County Birth Records and Delay Birth Records:1896-1940*, Harris Cty Genealogical Society, 1990.

Pomeroy, C. David, Jr. "Medical History of Pasadena," Part III *The (Pasadena Historical Society's newsletter) Pasadena Record*, December 1984

Pomeroy, Debbi. "Remember the `Big Top'?" *Texas Weekly Magazine, The Pasadena Citizen*, October 18, 1981.

Pratt, W. E. and Johnson, D. W. "Local Subsidence of the Goose Creek Oil Field," *The Journal of Geology*, Vol. XXXIV: Oct.-Nov. 1926, 577.

Russell, M. *Marriage Records of Harris County*, Vol. I, 1837-65 Pasadena Public Library, Pasadena.

Schloeman, Pearl (Ford) Hickman. "School Days in Pasadena, 1910-21," *The Living Tree*, Harris County Genealogical Society, Vol 11, No. 1, 1985.

Simmons, H. J. "Human Bones Found Near Galveston," *Bulletin of the American Geographical Society of New York*, Vol. 35, 1903.

Stentz, Howard. "Katie's Pasadena of 1899," *Houston Chronicle*, Mar. 23, 1969, Sec.1 p.7.

Walker, L. L. Jr. "1910:The Year the Air Age Came to Houston," *The Houston Review*, Houston Library Board, Houston, Tx, Vol. VI:1, 1984, p.41.

Werner, George C. "Magnolia City," *National Railway Bulletin*, Vol. 47, No. 1, 1982.

Williams, Carol. "Berry picking; a way of life," *Houston Chronicle* This Week, Southeast section, April 13, 1988, p.1.

Williams, Carol. "Herrera's roots go deep," *Houston Chronicle*, This Week, Southeast section, Apr. 13, 1988, p. 1.

Williams, Carol. "Pasadena Life-Long Resident Recalls Town's Beginnings," *Houston Chronicle*, April 20, 1988.

Williams, Irma M. "History of Pasadena, Texas," Pasadena Police Officers' Ass'n 1958, reprinted *Pasadena Citizen Newspaper*, Aug. 21-28, 1984.

.. "A Short History of South Houston," South Houston Chamber of Commerce, circa 1982.

Bibliography: Publications & Articles 441

.. "Reflections of Church Growth: 85th Anniversary," First Baptist Church of Pasadena, Tx, 1986.
Bayshore Sun Newspaper. La Porte, Tx 1987.
Galveston Daily News. Newspaper, Galveston, Tx 1900, 1901, 1915.
Harris County School Life. Official County School Newspaper, Houston, Tx, 1931.
Houston Chronicle. Newspaper, Houston, Tx 1910, 1915, 1919, 1924-27, 1929, 1933, 1936, 1969, 1988, 1989.
Houston Daily Post. Newspaper, Houston, Tx 1893, 1900.
Houston Post-Dispatch. Newspaper, Houston, Tx, 1925, 1928, 1929.
Houston Post. Newspaper, Houston, Tx, 1892, 1900, 1906, 1910, 1915, 1917-19 1921, 1929, 1931-33, 1943, 1956, 1957, 1968.
Houston Press. Newspaper, Houston, Tx, 1924, 1929.
Houston Telephone Directory. Pasadena Exchange, 1928-1938.
La Porte Chronicle. Newspaper, La Porte, Tx, 1893-1895.
La Porte-Bay Shore Sun. Newspaper, La Porte, 1969.
McPherson Republican. Newspaper, McPherson County, Kansas, 1893.
News Citizen. Diamond Jubilee Edition, Pasadena, Tx, May 26, 1971.
Pasadena Beacon. Pasadena High School Newspaper, Pasadena, Tx, 1937, 1938, 1939.
Pasadena Citizen. Newspaper, Pasadena, Tx. (intermittently *News Citizen, Daily Citizen, Pas. Daily Citizen, Star News Citizen*), 1961, 1963-66, 1969, 1971, 1978, 1980, 1981, 1984 1987, 1993.
Pasadena Record. Newspaper, Pasadena, Tx, 1930, 1931.
Pasadena Sun. Newspaper, Pasadena, Tx, 1929.
Pasadena Times. Newspaper, Pasadena, Tx, 1943.
South Houston Press. Newspaper, South Houston, Jan. 8, 1976.
Star News Citizen. Sixty-Eighth Anniversary Section, Pasadena, Tx, 1963.
Telegraph And Texas Register Newspaper, Houston, 1837.
Texas Bank Directory. 1920-21, 1922.
Texas Gazetteer. 1896-7.
The Groesbeck Journal . Newspaper, Groesbeck, Tx, April 24, 1986.
The Pasadena Mirror. Newspaper, Pasadena, Tx, 1953, 1954.

Index

A

Abbott, Josh 16
Abbott, Charles Ray 233, 242, 282, 365
Abbott, Marvin B. 233, 242, 282-83
Abbott, Minnie C. 242
Abbott, Virgil Ernest 242, 341
"Academy", The 47, 53, 56, 64
Acker, Dr. Earl 240
Adames, Abraham 358
Adames family 316
Adams, Edna Mae (Irwin) 301
Adams, Raleigh R. 301
Adams, R. C. 324
Air Conditioning 277, 344, 347, 360
Airplane 145-149, 171-175, 181-183
Akin, Bert 296
Aldrich, Mr. 148
Allen & Pierce 13
Allen, Anna Jane (Glass, see Waycott) 160, 219
Allen, Augustus Chapman (A.C.) 2
Allen Brothers (A. C. & J. K.) 1, 3, 10, 187, 198
Allen, Charles Dell 10, 138, 140
Allen, John Kirby (J. K.) 2
Allen, O. Flurney 10
Allen, Poole & Co. 11-16
Allen Ranch 8, 10, 14, 18, 19, 22, 25, 27, 40, 44, 51, 62, 69, 122, 139, 140, 157, 164, 179, 190, 200, 257
Allen, Rebecca Jane (Mrs. J. A. Stubbs) 6, 10, 19
Allen, Rebecca Jane (Thomas) 5, 10, 20.
Allen, Rosa Chrestie (Lum) 18, 20, 21, 99, 100, 139
Allen, Samuel Ezekiel 10, 16, 18-21, 27, 60, 62, 69, 99, 100, 138, 139, 190
Allen, Samuel Milton "Little Sam" 138-40, 144, 160, 175, 181, 219, 250, 252, 308
Allen, Samuel William 2, 11, 16, 18, 19, 23, 77, 83, 147, 149, 188, 253
Allen's Pasture 16, 22, 24
Allen's Station (also see Dumont) 10
Allen's Tannery 8
Allien, Leon F. 21, 23, 25, 31, 52, 191
Almeda Town Site & Fruit Farm Co. 58
Alta Vista 288, 311, 314, 315
Alvin, Community of 31, 38, 50, 58, 138, 188
American Land Co. 56
American Legion 265, 298, 300
American National Bank 151
American Petroleum Corp. 308
American Red Cross 75
American Republics Corp. 199
American Service Ice Co. 363
American State Bank 206, 240
Amusement Park (Oak Park) 299
Anderson, Charles 242
Anderson, Edward 34, 36
Anderson family (from El Campo) 59
Anderson, Floyd 34, 35, 47
Anderson, Floye 242
Anderson, Helen 231, 242
Anderson, Ida M. 34, 90
Anderson, James 357
Anderson, Lucy 34, 83
Anderson, Maude (Shutts) 242
Anderson, May 34, 38
Anderson, Minnie (Ross) 111-12
Anderson, Oscar 36
Anderson, Pearl (See Shine) 34, 46, 83, 90, 216
Anderson, Raymond 43, 83, 272
Anderson, Ruby A. 242
Anderson, Ruth H. (See Garfield) 220, 232, 242

Anderson, Thelma Lois (See Atkinson) 220, 242, 348
Anderson, William Wiley 37, 40, 47, 110, 216, 246, 303, 351
Ankele, Mildred Lou 232, 235
Ankele, Moddie Mae 235
Ankele, Walter G. 235, 236, 248, 267, 361, 367
Ankele, Mrs. W. G. 235, 298
Annexation 256-258
Anthony, Stanley 162
Arcadian Farms 37, 48, 50
Armestice 181, 185
Armitage Construction Co. 299
Arrowheads 322
Artesian Hotel 31, 36, 42
Artusy, Eddie 167
Asgard College 148
Ashton, G. L. 99
Assembly of God (See Pentecostal) 358
Atkinson, Alice Josephine 311
Atkinson, Delbert Ellsworth "Deb" 52, 115, 121, 131, 142, 162, 185, 224, 236, 244, 311
Atkinson, Delbert LeRoy 131, 142, 208, 213, 220, 229, 242, 311, 312, 348, 354
Atkinson, Gerald O. 311
Atkinson, Josephine (Thurman) 121, 131, 142, 311, 312
Atkinson, Melvin Hewitt 131, 312
Atkinson, Thelma Lois (Anderson) 311, 348
Atkinson, Urvine Goddard "Doc" 131, 220, 295, 312
Atkinson, Vernon Thurman 311-312
Atkinson, Vida Nadine 131, 231, 312
Atkinson, Willard Ellsworth 165, 312
Atkinson, Wilma L. 311
Atwater Kent radio 255, 265
Austin, Stephen F. 1, 3, 5, 322
Automobile 209, 290, 314, 322, 343, 345-347

B

B. B., B. & C. RR 188
Bagdad Confederate ship 180
Bailey, Addie (Brown) 262
Bailey, Alden 262
Bailey, Mrs. G. M. 359
Bailey, Lydia Catherine "Katie" 60, 61, 63, 64, 65, 118
Bailey, William Benjamin "Ben" Jr. 60, 61, 83, 93, 118, 129, 143-144, 173, 208, 225, 235, 248, 262, 298, 311, 326, 347, 367
Bailey, William Benjamin "Will" Sr. 60, 61, 82, 85, 91, 118, 129, 253, 262, 298, 307, 311, 341, 348, 354
Baker, Fred 176
Bakker, Aaron 40
Baldwin & Cargill 127, 130-31, 134, 165, 208, 244, 316
Baldwin Place/Farm (See Benart Farm) 125, 131, 218, 244, 245, 275, 316-317, 322
Ballentine family 24
Ballentine Hotel (La Porte) 31
Band, Community 278, 365
Band, School 355, 356
Bandy, Arvin E. 311
Bandy, Casper 311
Bandy, Elmer Jackson 311
Bandy, Mae 311
Bandy, Mollie Green (Chambers) 311
Bandy, Otha Dewey 311
Bandy, Sebe A. 311
Bank Cafe 265, 360
Bank Holiday 341
Baptist, Deepwater 66
Baptist, Genoa 52, 60, 91
Baptist, Pasadena 64, 67, 88-92, 95-96, 98, 104, 106, 118, 129, 144, 170, 292, 311, 339, 359
Baptist, South Houston 148
Barlow, H. C. 236
Barnes, Annie (See Hearn) 113
Barnes, Calvin I. 319
Barnes, Doris Ann 161, 186, 237, 300, 332, 342, 355

Index

Barnes, Edgar Eugene "Bovvie" 186, 328, 342
Barnes, Edgar Monroe 113, 121, 124, 144, 179, 224, 247, 253, 298, 307, 342
Barnes, Eula Lenora (Garner) 144
Barnes, Garcie 319
Barnes, Lanis G. 342
Barnes, Leatrice 319
Barnes, Lena 113
Barnes, Norma Jean 319
Barnes, Talitha 113
Barnum, P. T. 323
Barolet, J. C. 284-285
Barrow, Clyde 347
Barter 326
Barton, Clara 75-76, 120
Baseball (also see Hou. Buffs) 143, 281, 283, 327, 332, 357
Bashforth, Edgar Gill 370
Bashforth, Margaret (Giddins) 370
Basketball 227, 281, 283, 332, 336, 356
Battle, E. Gilbert 370
Bay Ridge 164, 260
Bayless, Robert S. 181
Bayshore Bus Line 260
Bayshore Suburban Motor Car 259-260
Baytown, community of 187, 203, 312, 315, 368
Beadle, J. L. 57
Beall, Dr. C. V. 268
Beall, Dr. J. M. 268
Beard, Jack 370
Beard, Estelle (Aman) 370
Beasley, Dr. John 23
Beatty, F. E. 151
Beaumont, community of 191, 193, 279, 323, 334
Beeville, Texas 218
Bell, Emma (Thomas) 275, 292
Bell, Maurice 275, 287
Bell, Norma 275
Bell, Ollie 275
Bell, R. A. 296
Bell, Samuel Pendegraff 275

Bell, Samuel P. Jr. 275
Bell, Trannie Estelle 233, 275, 292
Benart Farm (See Baldwin Place) 130-131, 316
Bennett, M. 201
Benson, C. W. 58
Berggren, Andrew 36
Berry, George 84, 93, 301
Berry, J. A. 305
Berry, Jesse Lloyd 84, 301
Berry, Jesse L. Jr. 301
Berry, Lawrence L. 301
Berry, Olive (Lakin) 301
Berry Bayou 149
Bethea, Cecil 185
Beusch, Amalia "Mollie" 136, 167, 351
Beusch, Gilbert Florian "Gib" 136, 167, 351
Beusch, Florian 136, 167
Beverly, Claude 295
Biering Nursery 58
Billingsley, Birdie Mae 287, 332
Billingsley, Claudia (See Clark) 287
Billingsley, Erma Claudia 343
Billingsley, Gladys (Pearson) 287
Billingsley, Harry Hudson 287
Billingsley, Harvey Cleo 287, 343
Billingsley, Irene 287
Billingsley, James Cavitt 287-88
Billingsley, James C. Jr. 287
Billingsley, Madge 287, 330
Billingsley, Margie Marie 343
Billingsley, Myrtle (Blakesley) 287, 343
Billingsley, Norma Ruth 343
Billingsley, Oliver M. 287, 307
Billingsley, Tommy Lee "T.L." 287
Billingsley, Wanda Ynelle 287
Billingsley, William Harvey 287
Bisbay, E. H. 161
Bisbee, H. H. 36
Bisson Building 162
Black, Mr. 74
Black, G. P. 324
Blackwell, A. O. 31, 49, 56
Blackwell, F. M. 247

Blakesley, Ann 311
Blakesley, Elson William 79, 311, 342
Blakesley, Ethel (See Hargrave) 79, 237
Blakesley, Glen H. 79
Blakesley, Irma (Parks) 58, 79, 80
Blakesley, Irma Marguerite "Margie" (see Portwood) 232, 361
Blakesley, Mildred (James) 331
Blakesley, Myrtle (See Billingsley) 185, 213, 220, 224, 229
Blakesley, Ralph C. 229, 231, 311
Blakesley, Ralph G. 311
Blakesley, Ruby (See Butler) 232, 292
Blakesley, Valerie (Brown) 311
Blakesley, William N. "Will" 50, 58, 64, 79-80, 93, 117, 129, 132, 201, 208, 223, 238, 274, 292, 361, 364
Blakesley dairy 81
Blankfield, Meyer 360, 367
Blanyer, George Johan "Tony" Jr. 292-293
Blanyer, Nauvie (Cammack) 292-293
Blanyer Photographic Studio 292
Bluebonnet Theater 352, 360
Blum, William L. 292
Blum, Katie 292
Boarding/Rooming Houses 108, 158, 214, 215, 233, 234, 237, 273, 308, 351
Bobbed hair 178, 179
Boehm family 52
Boehm, H. W. 162
Boeske, Elizabeth Pauline (See Kruse) 136, 352
Boeske, William 136
Boggs, Catharine (Saunders) 369
Boggs, Dr. 361
Boggs, E. D. 263
Boggs, Elizabeth 370
Boggs, Kenneth 370
Boggs, Margaret 370
Boggs, R. L. 369
Boggs, Steve 361

Boggs, Mrs. Theodore 36
Boggs, Theodore 36
Boggs, Wallace 370
Bolin Farm (Benart, Baldwin) 131, 317, 319, 322
Bolin, Mr. 316-317
Bond issues, city 296
Bond issues, school 115, 116
Bond issues, South Houston 324
Bond, Clifford M. 297-298
Boy Scouts 284
Boyd, Alma 240
Boyd, Bertha "Bee" 240
Boyd, Bueron "Booney", "Bruno" 240, 328
Boyd, David 343
Boyd, Faye 288
Boyd, Fredrick 217
Boyd, Frieda Pauline 288, 343
Boyd, George Albert 320
Boyd, Gladis 217
Boyd, Helen Bernice 288
Boyd, J. Otis 240
Boyd, Dr. James Monroe "Jim" 238, 240, 267-269
Boyd, James M. Jr. "Jim" 236, 240
Boyd, John A. "Johnny" 240, 356
Boyd, Jonah 288, 343
Boyd, Jonah Jr. 343
Boyd, June Clarice 343
Boyd, Kevin 217
Boyd, Lawrence 288
Boyd, Louise A. 320
Boyd, Nancy Ann 320
Boyd, Otis 231
Boyd, Pearl (See Jackson) 240, 267
Boyd, Rose May 217
Body, Ruby Odessa (Neely) 343
Boyd, Samuel D. "Sam" 320
Boyd, Snoden L. 217, 240, 282
Boyd, Snoden L. Jr. 217, 233
Boyd, Sydney 217
Boyd, Una 240
Boyd, Virginia 240
Boyd, Wilbur D. 288
Bradley, Eber R. 50, 52, 58
Bradshaw, A. L. 57

Bradshaw, Dorothy Lee (Hughes) 369
Bradshaw, Grover Vergil 369
Brady, Mr. T. 88
Brammer, Eunice 179, 233
Brammer, Homer Franklin 242, 307, 353
Brammer, Irma (Ermine?) 179, 210
Brammer, James Lamoine "Jim" 242
Brammer, Jess Tuggle 179, 211, 233, 242
Brammer, Larry Arnold 353
Brammer, LeVerne 241
Brammer, Paul 179, 301
Brammer, Ruby Davis (Warren) 242, 307, 353
Brandon, B. B. 298
Brannen, Annie Evelyn 235, 325
Brannen, C. Maurine "Pokey" 236, 328, 343, 345
Brannen, Earlene (See Frazier) 236, 333, 350
Brannen, Grandville LaPrell "Press" 233, 236, 282
Brannen, Jessie "Woodie" (See Davis) 236, 328, 350
Brannen, Lillian Doris (See Brown) 229, 231, 236, 289
Brannen, Richmond 224, 235, 236, 248
Brannen, Richmond Drulane 236
Brantley, Ed 23
Braquet, Louis 74
Brazos River 3, 4, 7, 33, 188, 292
Brazoria County 14, 19, 24, 140
Brenham, Texas 76-77, 130
Briscoe, Andrew 6, 7, 188
Brittain, Alice Irene 293
Brittain, Bryon Glenn 293
Brittain, George Carroll "Blacky" 293
Brittain, William Jean 293
Brobst, Jesse Ray, Jr. 358
Brod's (Mrs.) Diner 291
Brooks, J. E. 110
Broussard, William 296
Brown, Addie E. (see Bailey) 134, 175, 180-181, 227, 262, 355

Brown, Adele U. 70, 87, 161, 212
Brown, Allen "Nig" 328, 356, 357
Brown, Allie "Gertie" (See Newell) 134, 181, 183, 328
Brown, Daniel Glenn 135, 238, 322
Brown, Doris Evelyn 289
Brown, Edwin Rice "Farmer" 70, 87, 161, 289
Brown, Edwin R. Jr. 87
Brown, Eugene R. 135
Brown, Ferrel G. 135, 232, 270, 282, 336
Brown, George A'delbert 134-135, 208, 222, 288, 311
Brown, Groves 290
Brown, Katherine "Kate" 70, 87, 161
Brown, J. M. 236
Brown, La Clere 135
Brown, Lillian (Brannen) 289
Brown, Louise 298, 300
Brown, Mary 298
Brown, Maxine "Dinkey" 328, 357
Brown, Myra 70, 87
Brown, Opha 290
Brown, Pearl (See Vickers) 134, 351
Brown, Silas W. 289
Brown, Valeria (see Blakesley) 135, 227, 311
Browne, John T. 101
Brubaker, Helen 275, 287
Brubaker, James "Jimmy" 275
Brubaker, Louise James 275
Brubaker, Margarite "Irene" 275
Brubaker, Myrtle 275
Brubaker, Thelma "Mickey" 275, 287
Brubaker Children 322
Brucknout Brothers 58
Brunner, Texas 154
Bryan, Judge C. H. 247, 256
Bryant, Mrs. 108
Bryant, Johnie 104
Buffalo Bayou (also see HSC) 2-6, 8, 10, 15-17, 21-22, 26, 31, 33, 37, 41, 50, 52, 58, 69, 82, 88-89, 91, 103-105, 122, 132, 138, 144, 159, 187, 189, 196, 198, 224, 238

Buffalo Bayou Fishing Club 190
Buffalo Stadium 279
Buffaloe, Texas 4, 5, 25, 188, 297
Buffington, Dollie Ruth 355
Buffs (See Hou. Buffaloes)
Bullock, Y. H. 57
Bunkley, Heloise "Eloise" 333, 334, 355
Bunkley, Emogene (Orr) 355
Bunkley, Horace W. 307, 355
Bunkley, Wade T. 307
Bunting, R. L. 148
Burch, Donald 240
Burch, Leona (Roberts) 185, 212, 240
Burch, Robert Andrews 212, 240, 307
Burk, Swan 36
Burke Place 245
Burleson County, Texas 287
Burnett, Bruce 52
Burnett, Catherine 78
Burnett, "Colonel" John H. 21, 22, 25, 26, 27, 52, 54, 67, 72, 78, 87, 88, 99, 100, 118, 151, 172, 188, 193, 246, 298
Burnett, Ellen (See also Ross) 52, 78
 See also Ross, Ellen (Burnett)
Burnett, George P. 52
Burnett, Minnie Lee (Roberts) 52
Burnett, Oscar 78
Burnett, Walter 78
Bus 220, 260, 264
Busby, J. K. 163
Butcher Brothers Ice Co. 127, 272, 363
Bute, James H. 151
Bute Fig & Orange Orchards 151
Butler, Emma (Sabo) 353
Butler, Guy W. 292, 344
Butler, John 353
Butler, Joan 344
Butler, Judith Dell "Judy" 353
Butler, Para Lee 332
Butler, Robert Lee "Bobby" 353
Butler, Ruby (Blakesley) 344
Butterfly Confectionary 265

Byars, Dr. 112

C

Cadman, G. W. 57
Callahan & Vince Survey 5, 10
Callahan, Morris 5
Camels 8, 324
Cammack, Adelia Elizabeth (See Coolidge) 286
Cammack, Nauvie Mae (See Blanyer) 232, 292-293
Cammack, Houston Thurmand 292
Campbell's Pharmacy 361
Campbell, T. M. 102, 265, 267
Cantaloupes 53, 70, 103, 129, 133
Cape Jasmine flowers 37, 53, 62, 70, 138
Caplan, John 56
Cardenas family 316
Cargill, A. Martell "Red" 346
Cargill, C. Wayne 346
Cargill, Izadore (Riggs) 346
Cargill, John T. 346
Cargill, Lelia (Bullock) 346
Cargill, Mamie 346
Cargill, Norma 346
Cargill, W. H. 345
Carlisle, Bill 141, 218, 321
Carlso, Mrs. J. P. 326
Carlson, Carolyn 314
Carlson, Joseph P. 314
Carlson, Margaret 314
Carlson, Mary Sue (Vance) 314
Carlson, Rondald W. 314
Carpenter, Addie 315
Carpenter, Allen (#1) 107
Carpenter, Allen (#2) 312, 326
Carpenter, Arlie R. 312
Carpenter, Edith 315
Carpenter, Everett 312
Carpenter, J. C. Fig Co. 162
Carpenter, James Ladon "Don" 312
Carpenter, John Everett 312
Carpenter, L. Price 312
Carpenter, Mildred 312
Carpenter, Milton "Buster" 315
Carpenter, Nellie Lucile (Maud) 312

Index 449

Carpenter, Pink 315, 316
Carr, R. D. V. 57
Carrizal, Mr. 358
Carswell, Jack H. Jr. "Mayor" 358
Carter, Alice 273
Carter, Henry A. 265, 273, 294, 315
Casey, Jack 275, 287
Casey, Mildred 275, 287
Casteel, W. M. 74
Castleberry, J. A. 357
Catholic Seminary (St. Mary's) 74
Catholics 74
Cattle roundups 7, 8, 13, 139, 251
Cattle trail drives 8, 14
Cedar Bayou, Community of 134
Cemeteries (also see Crown Hill Cemetery) 105-106
Centennial Celebration (Texas) 351
Central Park Presbyterian Church 359
Chamber of Commerce (Pasadena) 257
Chambers, Bob 311
Chambers, Gertrude Mae (See Shannon) 311
Chambers, Rev. L. S. 359
Chambers, Mollie Green (See Bandy) 311
Chambers, Mrs. 311
Chambers, Pearl (See Crowe) 311
Chambers, Roy 311
Champion Paper Co. 349-352, 368-372
Chandler, Raymond 358
Chandler, Woodrow 358
Channel Chevrolet Co. 271, 362
Chapline, Charles L. 181
Chapman, Anna Mae (Gigstad) 357
Chapman, Barbara Joy 313
Chapman, Florence Evelyn 313
Chapman, George William 313
Chapman, L. I. 313
Chapman, Lorna June 313
Chapman, Louis E. 181
Chapman, Willis Joe 357
Chapman, Wilma Shore 313
Charlesworth, Lawrence "Chick" 231
Cheerleaders 282
Chestnut, Rev. Joseph Alfred 259
Chicago Iron & Bridge Co. 219
Chicken Ordinance 354
Christy Brothers Circus 323-325
Christy Hippodrome Circus 323
Christy, George W. 323-325
Churches (Also see individual) 1, 23, 32, 52, 56, 60, 64-66, 72, 74, 77, 78, 85, 87, 144, 155, 162, 243, 265, 272, 285, 358, 359
Cigars 54
City Feed & Seed Store 362-363
City Hall 304-306, 354, 368
Civil War (See War Between the States)
Civil Works Administration (CWA) 342, 345
Civilian Conservation Corp. (CCC) 345, 350
Clardy, L. W. 249
Clark, Claudia (Billingsley) 287
Clark, Henry C. 287
Clark, Dr. William 163
Clay pit, see Lone Star Cement
Clean up days 293, 342
Clear Creek 6, 16, 21, 23, 31, 37, 56, 75
Clear Creek, Community of 31
Clear Lake 1, 64
Clines family 67
Clinton, community of 15, 105, 226
Clinton steamship 15, 16
Close, Mrs. D. B. 292
Close, Mabel Grace 292
Cloutier, Doris Marian 291, 314
Cloutier, Louis 291, 314
Cloutier, Winogene (Hewlett, See Stafford) 291, 314, 355
Cockrun, Josie 332
Coffee, Henry 282
Cole family 23
Cole Brothers Circus 323
Cole Corinnie 329
Cole, W. J. 329
Coleman, Dr. Catherine 369

Collier, Maurine 112
Collier children 152
Collins, J. W. 74, 85, 110, 117
Colquitt, O. B. 101, 102
Coming Men of America 104, 143
Compton, J. P. 23
Conn, Annie (Hughes) 94, 201
Conn, John Golden 94, 113
Conn, John T. 93-94, 110-112, 116, 157, 201
Conn, Lucille 94, 111
Conn, Nancy 94, 111
Conn's Mercantile 110, 211, 214
Connor, Dr. Edwin Earl 361, 368, 369
Connor, Inice 369
Connor, Jack 369
Connor, Patsy 369
Conrad, Doris 305
Conrad, Elva 305
Conrad, Gerald William 67, 114, 129, 240, 249, 258, 273, 294, 295, 301, 304, 305, 354
Conrad, Geraldine 305
Conrad, Hazel 305
Conrad, Jewell (Pitts) 114, 305
Conrad, Warren 67
Constitution, U. S. Frigate 339, 340
Convention (See National Democratic)
Cook, Alpha A. 321
Cook, Beatrice R. 321
Cook, Charles Ervin 141, 321
Cook, Clarence F. 321
Cook, Curtis N. 321
Cook, Ervin R. 321
Cook, Grace R. 321
Cook, Joe 121
Cook, Lillie 121
Cook, Norman 321
Cook, O. A. 265
Cook, Thurman B. 321
Cook, Virgal J. 321
Coolidge, Adella Elizabeth (Cammack) 286, 292
Coolidge, Byrd W. 110, 231
Coolidge, Carrol Truett 61, 83, 88, 90, 180, 267, 286, 292, 298
Coolidge, Grant Daniel 61, 180, 298
Coolidge, Irene 61, 83, 90
Coolidge, Lena Lou 286
Coolidge, Sadie (Daniel) 61, 66, 78, 90
Coolidge, Sadie Dee 286
Coolidge, W. Clyde 61
Coolidge, Woodrow Phillip 61, 64, 66, 72-73, 78, 82, 84, 90, 91, 93, 110
Coolidge, W. P. Jr. "Woodie" 90, 110
Cooper family 301
Cornish, Leta 355
Cortez, Josephin 358
Cotton crop 34, 58, 70, 134, 314, 320
Cotton Patch Bayou 61, 159, 198
Coulson, Carrie 265
Coulson, Mrs. 265
Coulson, Ray L. 232, 265
Coulson, Ray K. 265, 282
Coulson's Corner 265, 360
Coulson Drug 265, 269, 295, 360
Cowert, Peggy 286
Coy, Alma W. 273
Coy, Clarence W. 232, 273, 282
Coy, Cullen 273
Coy, Mike L. 235, 272
Crenshaw, Bessie Maud (See Guinn) 84, 115
Crenshaw, Beula 84
Crenshaw, H. L. 84, 162, 164
Crenshaw, Noah S. 84
Crenshaw, Pearl (Robertson) 164
Crenshaw, Sarah Emma 84
Crescent Hotel 36
Crockett, C. J. 57
Crosby, Community of 283
Crouter, Alice 361
Crouter, Billy Bob 361
Crouter, Walter 361
Crouter's Cafe 361
Crowder (see Crouter)
Crowe, E. C. 311
Crowe, Pearl (Chambers) 311

Index 451

Crown Cleaners 360
Crown Hill Cemetery, (See Pas. Cem) 156, 160, 185, 264, 270, 309, 310, 322
Crown Refinery 201-203, 206-207, 219, 221, 224, 226, 229, 233, 240, 245-250, 256-258, 269, 273-274, 308, 313, 319, 329, 348, 353, 357, 365
Crumbie, A. B. 362
Cruse, Aubrey Randloph 208-211, 220, 233, 236-237, 240, 255, 264-265, 284, 287, 294, 305, 307, 341, 342, 351, 359, 367
Cruse, Aubrey R., Jr. 208, 342
Cruse, Betty Jo 342
Cruse, Donald Morgan 342
Cruse, Doris Mae 342
Cruse, Emma (Moore) 185, 208, 342, 354
Cruse, Imogene 342
Cruse, Joseph Morgan 122, 130, 185, 198, 208, 214, 247, 258, 264, 351
Cruse, Zella (Gregg) 185
Crute, W. R. 368
Cubb, Capt. John 180
Cubb, Thomas 180
Cucumbers 70, 99, 102-103, 122, 129, 132, 134,
Cullinan, J. S. 141, 156-57, 179, 185, 192-196, 198-199, 202, 225, 238, 244, 247-249, 257-258, 299, 308, 309, 321, 345, 349, 350, 351
Cullinan, Nina 179
Culpepper, Dr. Henry W. 57, 58, 68, 109
Culpepper, Mrs. Dr. 57
Curtis, Mr. 353
Cuthbert, Mrs. Bessie 326, 358
Cypress, Texas 188

D

Daily, Alice 270
Daily, Irene 270
Daily, J. Marvin 270
Daily, J. Sam 270
Daily, Mittle Lee 270
Daily, Naomi 270, 300, 353
Dairies (see individuals) 81, 168, 169, 185, 308
Dalhaus, Mrs. E. G. 326
Darby, Alethea 359
Darby, Billy 359
Darby, Dorothy Nell 232, 359
Darby, Jimmy 330, 359
Darby, Rev. M. A. 359
Davenport, C. M. 298
David, Anna Lou 265
David, Billy 265
David, Edward H. 265, 298
David, Justa E. 155, 265
David, Nannie 155, 265
David, Rev. V. L. 265
David, Rev. W. J. 155, 265
David-Finger Dry Goods 265, 360
Davidson, John J. 162
Davis, Ada 334
Davis, A. J. 366, 367
Davis, A. J. Jr. 367
Davis, Andrew A. 355
Davis, Bertha M. (Perkins) 366
Davis, Hazel 160
Davis, Jesse (Brannen) 350
Davis, J. O. (surveyor) 33, 42
Davis, J. O. (teacher) 229, 281
Davis, Joe 138, 140
Davis, Lillie 160
Davis, Louise 140
Davis, May 121
Davis, Ralph A. 350
Davis, Sam 121
Davis, Shirley M. 366
Davis, Walter M. 143-144, 160
Dayton, Texas 84, 113, 114
Dean, J. H. "Dizzy" 279
Deane, Belle (McCormick) 156
Deane, Bill 255, 274
Deane, Fredrick George 155-156, 271
Deane's Store 362
Dearing, John 313
Dearing, Peggy Louise 313
Dearing, Ruth A. (Rawlins) 313

Deep Water Land & Town Company 35
Deep Water Refinery 203
Deepwater, Community of 32, 48, 50-52, 54-58, 60, 62, 64, 65, 68, 69, 72-75, 78, 79, 81, 85-87, 95, 97, 101, 102, 106, 109, 110, 112, 113, 115, 117, 118, 127, 131, 138, 139, 144, 154, 161, 169, 179, 190, 211, 212, 241, 244, 245, 252, 277, 329, 362
Deepwater Enterprise newspaper 52, 57
Deepwater Missionary Baptist Church 66, 78
Deer Park 32, 33, 36, 37, 48-50, 53, 57, 64, 68, 69, 87, 116, 138, 152, 154, 161, 162, 164, 179, 190, 211, 212, 216, 289, 291, 292, 300, 329, 358, 368
Deer Park Hotel 32, 289
DeFee's Grocery/Building 297, 325, 327, 336, 354, 361, 368
DeFee, E. Frank 206, 213, 216, 266, 267, 297, 361
DeFee, John A. 213, 216, 266, 267, 286
DeFee, Lillie (Williams) 213, 216, 266
DeKor, Fred 149
Dellahan, Rosa 63
Democratic National Convention 277-279
Denman, Dr. Payton R. 240
Dennis, E. L. 73, 82
Depot, Pasadena 130, 212, 214
Depression, 1873 14
Depression, 1894 45
Depression, 1903 (Post Spn-Am War) 83
Depression, 1929 (The Great) 303, 307-310, 312-315, 318, 321, 322, 325, 326, 329, 330, 333, 334, 337, 341-342, 344, 347, 348, 352, 353, 360, 361, 364, 366, 371
Deputy Marshalls 294, 295
Derrick, Charles 23

Derrington, Darrell 344
Derrington, Dorothy Delores 344
Derrington, Golda 344
Derrington, Oscar 344
Derrington, Oscar Jr. "Buddy" 344
Desel-Boettcher Co. 129
DeVoe, G. W. 57
DeWease, Miss 333
DeYoung, Alton 299
De Zavala, Lorenzo 198
Dickens, Dr. J. L. 148, 163
Dickerson, Arthur Lee 62, 75. 78, 132, 136, 138, 157, 167, 215-216, 240, 245, 249, 259, 263, 300, 304, 306
Dickerson, Beatrice E. 95, 264
Dickerson, Bertha Elma (Kuhns) 75, 90, 167, 215-16, 263
Dickerson, Berta Elizabeth (see Quinn) 232
Dickerson, Carl L. 216, 263
Dickerson, Etta Mildred 264
Dickerson, George Edwin 216, 263
Dickerson, James Alfred 264
Dickerson, Leon Eugene "Skinny" 264, 322, 328
Dickerson, Lillian Rhoretta (Pitts) 46, 62, 69, 72, 144, 263, 264, 297
Dickerson, Loriene 263
Dickerson, Marguerite Elizabeth 62, 66, 78
Dickerson, Mary 263
Dickerson, Nellie O. 264
Dickerson, Raymond Alvin "Ray" 264
Dickerson, Royce 263
Dickerson, Russell E. 72, 95, 228, 264, 265, 307, 357
Dickerson, Ruth (Williams) 357
Dickerson, Stella 216
Dickerson, Thelma O. (See Fleming) 264, 265
Dickerson, Victor 264
Dickerson, Wade Hampton "Judge" 62, 69, 95, 104, 138, 144, 157, 199, 206-207, 211-212, 215, 216, 220, 224, 240, 249, 263-266, 328, 354

Index 453

Dickerson, Wade H. Jr. 264
Dickerson, Wynona 216, 263
Dickerson's Building 206, 211, 212, 265, 361
Dickerson's Cafe 212, 237, 265
Dickerson's Grocery/Store 97, 110, 121, 168, 206, 207, 211-213, 215, 237, 241, 266-267, 298, 335
Dickerson's Nursery (also see Wright's Nursery) 53, 62, 91, 298
Dickinson, Community of 38, 168
Didriksen, Mildred Ella "Babe" 334
Diven, Grace Delores 355
Diven, Greta E. 355
Dixon, C. W. 308
Dixon, Harold C. 308
Dixon, Hazel 308
Dixon, Helen 308
Dixon, Joe H. 308
Dixon, Lela Kay 308
Dixon, Lela M. 308
Dixon, Minnie 308
Dixon, Modine 308
Dixon, W. S. 308
Dixon's Dairy 308
Dobie, J. Frank 8
Dobie, Robert 8, 24
Dobie, Sterling 8, 24
Dodd, J. E. 324
Dodson, Thomas 24
Dolen, Dr. N. P. 22
Dolly (the mule) 319
Donkeys 112, 152, 328
Donovan, James G. 248, 256
Doodle Bug (Suburban trolley) 260
Dow, Fern (See Quinn) 219
Dowdell, Professor L. A. 46, 47, 54, 56, 102, 229
Dowell, Daisy "Dixie" 214, 238, 328, 332, 334
Dowell, Edgar A. "Duke" 113, 328, 335
Dowell, George Pendleton 113, 123, 213
Dowell, Georgia Pearl 214
Dowell, Jane "Janie" (See Gore) 113, 284, 231

Dowell, Mack 113
Dowell, Minnie Selena 113
Dowell, Rosa (See Ford) 113, 227, 237, 239, 365
Dowell, Stella 214, 232, 238
Dowell, Thelma 238
Dowell, Willie Louise 214
Downs, Jesse David 289
Downs, Mamie L. 289
Downs, Marna Ruth 289
Dreyfuss, Tex (ferry) 345, 347
Dreyfuss, Commissioner T. H. "Tex" 346
Dreyfuss, Rosemary 346, 372
Drouet, E. N. 138
DuCroz, Dr. James Lawrence 369
Dudley family 23
Duffield, Clyde M. 121
Duffield, Elvah M. 121
Duffield, Nellie Annie 121
Duffield, Thomas 121
Dumas, Harold 357
Dumas & Harrala General Store 163
Dumont (Plantation & Station) 10, 16, 147, 163, 178
Dumont Station (also see Allen's Station) 10, 16
Dunaway, Jack 353
Dunaway, Karon 353, 355
Dunaway, Marvin M. 353
Durham, Pearl 335

E

Eagle Lumber Co. 366
Earthquakes 203
Eason, F. D. 363
Edming, Anna Marie (Anderson) 113
Edming, Clarence 113, 275
Edming, Eva 113, 229, 231
Edming, Gustov "Gus" 79, 113, 168
Edming, Hulda 113, 240
Edming, Lillie M. (See Malmberg) 113, 233, 240
Edming, Selma (See Bogevold) 113
Edward family 23
Edward's Point 27

Edwards, Giles 238
Edwards, L. F. 307
Eidson, Dr. A. M. 239
Eisemann, Ed 176
El Buey (train station) 21, 169
Elder, Hazel (See Land) 292, 344
Elder, Lillie (Blum) 292
Elder, Marvin 292
Elder, Ruby 292
Elder, Sadie 292
Elder, William M. 292
Election, bond City 296
Election, incorporation 1923 247-248
Election, incorporation 1925 256
Election, incorporation 1927 257-258
Election, incorporation 1928 258-259
Election, school district 63
Electric lights/electricity 56, 77, 149
Elephants 324, 325
Elledge, Richard 232
Ellington (also see airplanes) 17, 172-176, 181, 184-185
Ellis, Edith (Davis) 369
Ellis, Rev. J. H. H. 90, 91
Ellis, John J. 180
Ellis, Sam 369
Ellisor, Pink 83
Elmen, C. A. & Co. 153
Ely, Mildred 334
Emory, Frank 57
Empire Oil & Gas Co. 201
Engineering Service Corp. 257
Erin, Community of 285
Ethel B., The (excursion boat) 101
Eugene, The (excursion boat) 31, 52, 191
Ervin, Constance Zola (Roberts) 212
Ervin, Loyd Jones 212
Evans, Dr. 238
Evans, Lizzie 27
Evans, W. A. "Gus" 22
Everson, Mrs. Mary 326
Excelsior strawberry 121, 318
Excursion boats (also see individual)
31, 52, 101, 129, 190, 191, 192, 199
Excursion trains (See Trains, Excur.) 129
Excursionist 49, 52
Extein, B. F. 57

F

Fain, Clifford 307
Farm & Ranch magazine 153
Farmers Oil Co. 198, 199
Farmers & Fruit Growers Ass'n of Pasadena 43, 48, 129
Farr, Betty 314
Farr, Blanche 314, 326
Farr, Bloyd L. 314
Farr, Byron Enoch 314
Farr, Courtney E. 314
Farr, Doris Eleanor 314
Farr, Vera D. 314
Feazle, Carl 357
Federal Transient Bureau 345
Fells, Joe 306
Fences & Fencing 16, 17, 251, 252
Ferry 58, 190, 199, 223-224, 250-251, 321, 345, 346, 372
Fields, Toka Lee (See Shelton) 334, 336
Fidelity Cotton Oil & Fertilizer Co. 200, 334
Fideltiy Trust Co. 258
Figs 122, 133, 151, 162, 164
Fire, (destruction) 162, 246, 291, 297
Fire Department Pasadena (PVFD) 289, 296, 306-307, 340, 355
Fire Department, South Houston 296
Fire Truck 305, 306
Fire Station 296, 304, 306
First Aero Squadron 171
First Baptist Church 359
First Methodist Episcopal Church, South 66
First Provisional Aero Squadron 172
First Swedish Baptist Church 52, 87
Fisher, Dorothy Lee 268

Index 455

Fisher, Forrest 268, 284
Fisher, Louise 268
Fleming, Harvey 300
Fleming, Jeff E., 307, 359, 368
Fleming, Myrtle Virginia (Curtis) 359
Fleming, Paul O. 265 307, 326, 359, 360
Fleming, Paula 265
Fleming, Thelma (Dickerson) 265
Fletcher, M. T. 36
Flickinger, William 36
Florentine Settlement 59, 79, 97, 152, 168, 320, 352
Flores family 316
Florrow, Berdie (See Smith) 310
Florrow, Bertha 310
Florrow, Eva 310
Florrow, Floyd 310
Florrow, Francis 310
Florrow, J. L. 310
Florrow, Jim Dick 310
Florrow, Lloyd 310
Florrow, Oliver J. 310
Florrow, P. A. 310
Florrow, Taylor 310
Florrow, Mrs. Taylor 310
Florrow, Vergie 310
Follis, Lorene 332
Follis, Margarite 287
Follis, Opal 287
Follis, Regina 287
Football 227, 281-283, 356
Forbes, Thomas 99
Ford, Bertha E. (Madale) 106, 217, 365
Ford, Horace Edward 106-107, 116-117, 208, 217, 241, 365
Ford, Janey Pearl 365
Ford, Marion Edwin 217, 365
Ford, Marion E. Jr. 365
Ford, Pearl Flavelin 153, 217, 220, 227, 229
Ford, Rosa Maye (Dowell) 365
Ford, Tommie 217
Ford, Winnie Lee 106
Ford Motor Car Company 221, 250, 344

Forrest, Doll (Harris) 336
Forrest, James Lee 310-311
Forrest, James L. Jr. "Jim" 310
Forrest, John Wendell "Chicken" 311, 327, 328
Forrest, Sena Bell (See Griffin) 310, 332, 333
Forrest, Sena Larmer (Henry) 310
Forrest, William P. "Bill" 310, 336
Foster, Cora Bacon 37, 39, 41, 42, 43, 45, 47, 54, 87, 298
Fowler, Sarah 334
Frazier, Bevis 350
Frazier, Earlene (Brannen) 350
Frazier, Jesse 350
Frazier, Mrs. Jesse 350
Freeman, Adison Basil "A. B." 236, 247, 289, 348
Freeman, Mrs. A. B. 289
Freeman, Bessie E. 235
Freeman, Cecil E. 235
Freeman, Charles C. 235, 236, 274, 315
Freeman, Fern Mae 232, 289
Freeman, Francis 235
Freeman, Robert Edward 235
Freeman, Virgie Mae (See Burns) 232, 235, 293, 355
Freeze, 1895 48
Freeze. 1899 75
Freeze. 1924 250
French Conservatory of Music 284
Friendswood, Community of 133
Frostown, community of 3
Fuhlberg, Ruby 336, 355

G

G. C. & S. F. RR 27, 188
G. H. & H. RR 16, 18, 21, 22, 24, 145, 147, 188. *See also* Railroads
G. H. & S. A. RR 68, 152, 329
G. L. P. & H. RR 49, 58
Gaillard, John 196
Galena (Park), Community of 282, 288, 307, 315, 351
Galena-Signal Oil Co. 199, 223, 224, 269, 288, 348

Galva, Kansas 36
Galveston, City of 2, 7, 10, 11, 14, 15, 21, 26-28, 47, 48, 58, 67, 69, 72, 75-77, 79, 146-147, 149, 151, 153, 159, 163-164, 174, 181, 187-190, 204, 291, 314
Galveston Bay 6, 10, 16, 21, 23, 25-27, 33, 64, 68, 119, 138, 152, 180, 184, 187, 188, 204, 247, 297
Galveston, Houston, & Henderson Railroad (See G. H. &. H. RR)
Galveston, Houston & Northern Railroad (G. H. & N. RR) 73
Galveston Causeway 151
Galveston Daily News 163
Galveston Electric Company 149, 151
Galveston Storm of 1900 (See Hurrican, 1900 Galv.)
Galv.-Hou. Electric Ry "Interurban" 149-151, 247
Galv.-Hou. Interurban Land Co. 150
Galvez Hotel 151
Gardenias (See Cape Jasemines) 138
Garfield, Agnes Cecellia (Thompson) 185
Garfield, Cecelia Newman "Celia" 185, 223, 225, 233, 301, 326
Garfield, Charles Lewis 168, 185, 208, 223, 259, 281, 296, 341, 342, 348
Garfield, Lewis Edgar 176, 185, 220, 223, 229, 241
Garfield, Mary Agnes (See Porter) 185, 237, 330, 332, 369
Garfield, Ruth (Anderson) 242
Garnuch, Arthur F. 136
Garnuch, Curtis Samuel 136
Garnuch, Hattie 136
Garnuch, Mary 136
Garnuch, Otto W. 136
Garnuch, Robert K. 136
Garnuch, Samuel 136
Gartney, also see Gwartney
Gartney, F. M. 73
Gartney, Leora (See Parks) 125
Garvin Dairy 169

Gasper, Alex 353
Gasper, Annie (Sabo) 353
Gates, John "Bet-a-million" 194
Genoa, City of 17, 28, 31, 36, 40, 52, 60, 67, 72, 74, 78, 84, 87, 101, 105, 115, 121, 130, 131, 151, 154, 162, 164, 165, 172-174, 212, 226, 328, 348, 357, 368
Genoa Hotel 52, 72
Georgia, state of 112
Germantown, community of 3
Gibbs, H. L. 72
Gibbs, Mrs. H. L. 72
Gigstad family 167, 198
Gigstad, Anna Mae "Annie" (see Chapman) 309, 332, 333, 357
Gigstad, Ben A. 309
Gigstad, Esther Amelia 225, 309
Gigstad, Glen A. 233, 282, 309
Gigstad, Helge "the father" 114, 122, 129, 309
Gigstad, Helge A. "the son" 309
Gigstad, Iris L. 309
Gigstad, Isabel 309
Gigstad, Leonard 309
Gigstad, Lydia A. (Zlomkie) 309
Gililland, L. M. 57
Glasgow, Cecil W. 114
Glasgow, Effie Mae 113
Glasgow, Kelvin E. 114, 282, 325
Glasgow, Mary Ellen 114, 228
Glasgow, Nora Lee (See McGraw) 114, 350
Glasgow, Robert W. 235
Glasgow, Roy A. 247, 365
Glasgow, Roy Foster 114
Glasgow, Roy M. 113-114, 155, 220, 227, 254, 286, 328, 365
Glasses family 98
Glazener, Matie 148
Golden Acres, Community of 313, 315, 325, 352, 353
Golden Acres Baptist Church 358
Good's Drug Store 267
Good, R. J. 267
Goodman, Clyde C. 218
Goodman, Emory Congor 218

Goodman, James E. 218, 278, 286
Goodman, Jessie M. 218
Goodman, Jessie M. "the daughter" 218
Goodman, Roy H. 218
Goodrum, Phil 284, 293, 356
Goodwin, Alfred 293
Goodwin, Allen 293
Goodwin, Bennie 293
Goodwin, Carter 293
Goodwin, Kenneth 293
Goodwin, Linwood 293
Goodwin, Marjorie Nell 293
Goodwin, Walter Earl "Pee Wee" 284, 293
Goodwin, Walter E. Jr. 293
Goose Creek 180, 196, 198-201, 203
Gore, Alfred Marion 319, 320
Gore, Boyd Lee 319
Gore, Clara 319
Gore, Elwood Buck "Smiley" 319
Gore, Homer, B. 319
Gore, Janie (Dowell) 284
Gore, Laura 319
Gore, Lester C. 319-320
Gore, Mildred 319, 334
Gore, Richard T. 229, 281, 284, 336
Gore, Taylor L. 319
Gore, Velma 319, 332
Gore, Wheeler W. 319
Gosch, Madge 333
Gozman family 24
Graham, Euel 367
Grammar School (Kruse Elem.) 259, 273, 311, 316, 332, 335, 336, 342, 348, 353, 356
Grannis, J. H. 163
Grant, Gladys 353, 355
Grant, L. T. 259
Grant, Wilma 333, 334
Graves, Effie 290
Graves, Ernest 290-291
Graves, George Washington 290-291, 352
Graves, James 290
Graves, Rachel 290
Gray, Mrs. 63

Gray, Austin S. 288
Gray, Blanche F. 288
Gray, H. E. 73
Gray, Jack 282
Gray, Mildred B. (See Worley) 288
Great War, See WWI 170, 171, 181, 184, 185
Green, Rose Park 265
Greer, Neal 341
Gregg, Donald 185
Gregg, Effie Averalla (Moody) 185
Gregg, Etta (see Johnson) 185
Gregg, Jasper Gordon 185
Gregg, Earl A. 259, 294
Gregory, C. E. 23
Griffin, Charles 307
Griffin, Elma (Thomason) 310
Griffin, Jabe T. 310
Griffin, Lessie 233
Griffin, Louis L. 232, 310
Griffin, Richard J. 259
Griffin, Sena Bell (Forrest) 310, 334
Griffin, T. E. 305-307, 310, 352
Griffith, Dr. Charles Wesley 64, 109, 239
Groveton, Texas 148
Guaranty State Bank 206, 211, 213, 216, 240, 266, 298
Guedry, Harvey 356
Guinn, Alice 64
Guinn, Bessie Maud (Crenshaw) 274
Guinn, Beulah Bernice 274
Guinn, Catherine "Katie" 83, 97, 98, 159
Guinn, Chester Carlisle 143, 144, 180, 274, 298
Guinn, Earl Hogge 208, 274, 307, 341, 342
Guinn, Margaret E. "Maggie" 83, 261
Guinn, Mary Jane (Hogge) 60, 64, 117, 118
Guinn, Ray M. 115, 274
Guinn, Robert McPherson 51, 52, 58, 60, 64, 73, 82, 84-86, 91, 93, 95, 106, 129, 159, 248, 261, 274, 298, 311

Guinn, Robert M., Jr. 110, 117, 118, 129, 180, 236, 274
Guinn, Roy Sidney 274
Guinn, William Henry "Will" 64, 110, 116, 311
Guinn Brothers Laundry 274
Gulf, Colorado & Santa Fe RR (See G. C. & S. R. RR)
Gulf Intracoastal Waterway 190
Gulf Oil Corp. 197, 199
Gulf States Asphalt Co. 164
Gutherie, Elizabeth (Hays) 117
Gutherie, John C. 117, 215
Gwartney, also see Gartney
Gwartney, Clifford 52
Gwartney, Francis 52, 67
Gwartney, Frank 52
Gwartney, Frederick 52
Gwartney, Harry 52
Gwartney, Leora (See Parks) 67, 125
Gwartney, Lilly W. 52, 67
Gwartney, Stanley 67
Gymnastics 332

H

H. L. & P. 237, 241, 246-250, 256-258, 283, 293, 294, 324, 329, 342, 343, 346
H. & T. C. RR 188
Haacke, J. A. 340
Habermehl family 23
Haberg, Amy 162
Haberg, Charles A. 162
Haberg, Emma 162
Haberg, Hildur "Hilda" 162
Haberg, Lillie "Lilly" 162
Haberg, Mildred 162
Hager, Miss S. 158
Hager, Susan B. 157
Hahn, Douglas 149
Hahn, Guy 149, 172
Hahn, May 149
Hain, Samuel 268, 286
Hall, Joe D. 117
Hall, Johnny Bess 286
Hall, Pearl 355
Hall, Susan 108, 110, 111, 117

Hall, William T. 162
Hallburg, John 162
Hallburg, Mrs. John 162
Haller, Clemis (Conrad) 67
Haller, Louis 67, 107
Hamilton, community of 3
Hamilton's IGA grocery 266, 361
Hamilton, Mr. 266
Hamilton Cottage 75
Hancock, Mr. & Mrs. 314
Hand, Edith 293
Hand, Floyd Newton 293, 357
Hand, Mary Catherine 293
Hand, Newton P. 293
Hand, Wendell Phillip 293
Handy, Mrs. S. P. 326
Hanna, J. T. and family 42, 66
Hargrave filling station and store 209, 301, 366
Hargrave, Alfred 181
Hargrave, Beatrice Pearl 237
Hargrave, Bennie Abram 237
Hargrave, Carmen Lily 237
Hargrave, Douglas Lester 237
Hargrave Ethel (Blakesley) 237, 286
Hargrave, Gladys May 113
Hargrave, Jennie Elizabeth 237
Hargrave, Lester Leroy 113, 179-181, 209-210, 237, 245
Hargrave, Lola Emma (Long) 113, 237
Hargrave, Mack 181
Hargrave, Ruby Lee 113
Hargrave, Russel "Rusty" 226, 307, 322
Hargrave, Violet Fern 237
Hargrave, Wanda Joy 237
Hargrave, Wilbur G. 181, 182, 237, 268, 307
Harrala (see Dumas & Harrala)
Harrington, J. D. 36
Harris, Burt 58
Harris, Doll (see Forrest) 334, 336
Harris, George 58
Harris, John 198
Harris, Marguerite 333
Harrisburg, City of 2, 3, 5, 6, 7, 9, 16,

Index 459

18, 19, 21, 36, 37, 40, 43, 44, 46, 53, 56, 60, 62, 63, 64, 66, 68, 74, 82, 95, 99, 100, 104, 105, 109, 111, 127, 138, 146, 149, 154, 188-189, 192, 199, 203, 206-207, 209, 219-222, 227, 229, 238, 240, 241, 255, 265, 269, 272, 282, 290, 308, 309, 311, 321, 324, 354, 357-360, 368
Harrisburg-La Porte Road 56, 261
Harrisburg Common School District 46, 54, 56
Harrisburg-Lynchburg Road 5, 9, 16, 18, 22, 36, 41
Harrisburg-Red Bluff Road 23
Harrisburg Drug Co. 213
Harrisburg High School 185, 213, 220, 348, 365
Harrisburg Railroad & Trading Co. 188
Harrison, Nolan 350
Hart, Clayton A. 353
Hart, Don G. 353
Hart, Faye B. 353
Hart, Lucille 353
Hart, O.C. 353
Hart, Ralph 353
Hartsfield, Bernice 284
Hartsfield, Hugo 284, 287, 307, 329-330, 332-336, 347, 348, 355
Harwell, Allie 77, 83
Harwell, Annie Zeola (see Williams) 77, 78, 114
Harwell, Betty 77, 78
Harwell, Frank 77
Harwell, Frank M. 77, 78
Harwell, Louise "Lou" 77, 78
Harwell, Mary (see Starkey) 77, 90, 114
Harwell, Odie 77, 83
Hay cutting 29, 30, 47
Hayney, Floyd 307
Hay, Albert 344
Hay, L. L. "Bill" 344
Hay, Mildred (Tabor) 344, 360
Hays, A. 40, 84, 93, 95, 246
Hays, Elizabeth "Lizzie" (see Guthrie) 83, 111, 117, 355

Hays, Jasper F. "Jap" 40, 46, 53, 57, 61, 63, 66, 70, 72, 77, 84, 100, 142, 212, 246
Hays, Willis 54
Hearn, Asa Wilbert 113, 169, 242, 275, 307-308, 353
Hearn, Annie Cumi (Barnes) 113, 124, 169
Hearn, Bobby 113
Hearn, Dwight 334
Hearn, Edith 169, 300, 332, 334
Hearn, Iza Sue 113, 231, 237
Hearn, Jacob Lanis 113, 124, 144, 169, 307, 341, 353, 354
Hedrick, W. C. 207
Hemstreet, Philip R. 50, 53
Henderson, Edgar B. 265, 298
Henderson, Roy 314
Hendricks brothers 358
Henry, Emily 24
Henry, Jordan 24
Hensley, Dr. B. C. 367, 368
Henson, Annie 117
Herrera, Adolph 131, 165, 244, 245, 316-319, 322, 352
Herrera, Mrs. Adolph 131, 165, 321
Herrera, Conrado 317
Herrera, Felicia 317
Herrera, Julia (see Rivera) 131, 165, 317
Herrera, Minnie 317
Herrera, Paul 317, 319, 321-323, 352
Herrera, Tomaso 317
Hester, Mr. 227
Higgins, Patillo "Bud" 191, 194
High, J. F. 236
High School (see Pasadena & Harrisburg) 54, 110, 153-155, 185, 213, 220, 227-231, 250, 271, 273, 275, 280-282, 287, 291, 300, 301, 308, 310-311, 348, 353, 356, 357, 359
Hill, Clyde 270
Hill, Ella Wood 111, 112
Hill, Eric 308
Hill, Imagene 292
Hill, J. B. 58

Hill, J. W. 308
Hill, James C. 58
Hill, Lance 307
Hill, Mary E. (Slone) 292
Hill, Thelma 292
Hill, W. T. 292
Hill County/Hillsboro 98
Hillman, Carl 315
Hillman, Harry 315
Hitchcock, community of 58, 76
Hobos 325
Hocker, Martin L. 32, 33
Hodges, Barbara 291
Hodges, Charles Stephen 291
Hodges, Constance O. (Magee) 287, 297
Hodges, Eloise 291
Hodges, Juanita 291
Hodges, Ralph 278, 279, 286, 291
Hodges, Philip 291
Hodges, Tony Edgar 224, 287, 355, 359
Hodges, Winona L. (Hendricks) 291
Hoffman, Mr. 34, 42
Hoffman Oil & Refining Co. 200
Hoftsger, Albert 42
Hogge, Erwin 118
Hogge, Iva 118
Hogge, Sarah V. 118
Holbrook, Ann 159
Holbrook, Annie (Williams) 84, 85, 159
Holbrook, Chester 84
Holbrook, George Ann, 159
Holbrook, George L. 84, 85, 129, 159
Holbrook, Jewell 159
Holbrook, John L. 84, 106-107, 110, 113, 116-117, 155
Holbrook, Johnie 157
Holbrook, Letha Jane (Penn) 84, 157
Holbrook, Lillian 159
Holbrook, Milton 84
Holbrook, Neppie 84
Holbrook, Rose Mae 84
Holbrook, St. Clair 159

Holbrook, Sue "Susie" 84, 227
Holbrook, Virginia A. (Cummings) 84, 350
Holbrook, Virginia Lee "Virgie" 84, 112
Holbrook, Wesley R. 159
Holbrook, William Lafayette "Willie" 84
Holbrook, William Richard 84, 159
Holland's Magazine 153
Hollinsworth, Helen 284, 293, 332
Holloway, Albert G. 138, 217
Holloway, Anna 138
Holloway, David Z. 138, 167, 216-217
Holloway, Ila Myrtle (Newell) 217
Holloway, Raymond 138
Holloway, Vick 138
Holmes, Ira R. 25, 49, 56
Holtgren, Elmer 36
Home Demonstration Club 325
Home Ice Service 363
Homesteaders Club 117, 153
Hoof & Mouth Disease 252-253
Hoover, Pres. Herbert 301, 304
Hopkins, Arthur 347
Horse Pen Bayou 6, 24
Horsh, Max 248
Horton, Jack 283, 284, 332, 352, 354, 356
Horwitz, Will 255, 343
Hospitals 77, 109, 368, 369
Hotels (see also individual) 31, 32, 36, 42, 49, 50, 52, 57, 72, 74, 124, 147, 151, 191-192, 277, 279, 289
Houlks, B. T. 99
House, T. W. 58
Houston, Alice J. (Highsaw) 291
Houston, Ashley Earnestine 291
Houston, Bessie Jo 291
Houston, City of 2, 3, 4, 5, 6, 7, 9, 10, 15, 21, 23, 26, 27, 28, 31, 34, 47, 49-56, 58-59, 63, 65, 67, 69, 71-72, 74-75, 78, 88, 100-102, 105-106, 109, 130, 132, 137, 146-153, 161, 163-164, 168, 172, 174-176, 180, 181, 185-187, 189, 190, 195, 196,

Index 461

198, 203, 204, 206, 208, 211, 219, 220-221. 238-39, 244, 248-250, 255-258, 264, 270, 272, 275, 277-279, 299, 304, 305, 309, 313-316, 318-321, 324, 333, 343-344, 351-353, 355, 358, 359, 363, 364, 368
Houston, Helen Marie 291
Houston, Jacquelyne 291
Houston, James Guy 291
Houston Buffaloes "Buffs" baseball 164, 279
Houston Chronicle newspaper 163-165, 278, 279
Houston Deepwell Co. 199
Houston Dispatch newspaper 255, 297
Houston Electric Co. 151
Houston Gas & Fuel Co. 257
Houston Heights community 39, 111, 154, 285
Houston Lighting & Power Co. (see H. L. & P.)
Houston Natural Gas Co. 259, 344
Houston Oil & Refining Co. 206
Houston Pipeline Co. 329
Houston Post newspaper 73-74, 145, 163, 185, 200, 222, 255, 297
Houston Post-Dispatch newspaper 255, 278, 297, 344
Houston Press newspaper 249, 258, 326
Houston Radio Club 255
Houston Ship Channel 132, 169, 179, 189, 190, 199, 200, 204, 250, 261, 299, 303, 308, 313, 319-321, 337, 339, 340, 345, 346, 349, 354.
Houston Stockyards 50
Houston Tap RR 188
Houston-Cedar Bayou Road 42
Houston-Pasadena Bus Co. 264
Hovey, LeRoy 185
Howard, Arthur 315-316
Howard, Arthur F. 315
Howard, Carrie Bell (Pitts) 315
Howard, Thomas P. 315
Howell, Effie (Newell) 160
Howell, Francis Edwin "Teeler" 160,
322, 328
Howell, Ila Mae 160, 332
Howell, Presley Young "P. Y." 160, 179, 224
Huff, J. R. 259
Hufstedler, O. W. 233
Hughes, Annie Lydia (see Conn) 94
Hughes, David 221
Hughes, Dorothy Lee (see Bradshaw) 334, 369
Hughes, Fannie (Ramsey) 273
Hughes, Jennie (Williams) 320, 362
Hughes, Jewell 273
Hughes, James Emore "Jim" 107, 129, 201, 221, 240, 274, 313, 319, 335, 369
Hughes, Leonard 94, 104, 201
Hughes, Louella 273
Hughes, Mamie Ellen (see Pitts) 201, 221
Hughes, Marie 273
Hughes, Marilyn Gay 365
Hughes, Marvin Edson 273, 365
Hughes, Marvin E. Jr. 365
Hughes, Mattie (Lewis) 221, 313
Hughes, Olive Mozelle (Kelley) 273, 365
Hughes, Pearl 273
Hughes, Robert Andrew 273
Hughes, Robert Ernest "Bird Seed" 273, 320, 328, 362
Hughes, Ruby Marcella 273
Hughes, Vera 273
Humble, Texas 88, 132, 195, 197, 198, 293
Humble Cypress Oil Co. 206
Humble Oil Co. 197, 199, 201, 203, 261, 297
Humble Oil Refinery 201, 368
Humble, city & oil field 195, 197
Hunken, George 130
Hunt, H. L. 337
Huntington, C. P. 58
Huntsville, community of 275, 293, 335
Hupmobile automobile 223
Hurricane, 1900 Galveston 71-76,

81-82, 87, 88, 120, 151, 159, 189, 191
Hurricane, 1915 163-164, 199
Hursey, Rev. L. L. 78
Hurst, W. E. 358
Hurst, Mrs. W. E. 358
Hutchinson, J. C. 68

I

Idlebrook family 23
Illinois Deer Park Syndicate 37, 49
Income tax 54
Incorporation, city 250, 256-258
Incorporation, school district 63, 66
Indians 1, 322, 323, 357
Influenza, Spanish 184
Interior Land & Immigrant Co. 25
Interurban (see Gal-Hou. Elec. Ry)
Irish Bend 189
Irvin family 23
Irwin, Edna Mae (see Adams) 178
Isaac, Aleta 282, 334
Isaac, Driscol 282
Isaac, Doris Jean 282
Isaac, Eva Mae 282
Isaac, J. B. 233, 270, 271, 282, 300, 351, 362, 363, 368
Isaac, Joe Brian, 363
Isaac, John Sampson 282
Isaac, Lucille "Boots" (Skillern) 363
Isaac, Mittie (Cox) 282
Itch disease 112

J

Jackson, A. E. 284, 356
Jackson, Bettie 84
Jackson, David C. 267, 294
Jackson, Effie 84, 106
Jackson, Eula 84
Jackson, Mrs. George 326
Jackson, Horace A. 347, 348, 367
Jackson, Isa 84
Jackson, James A. "Munk" 267
Jackson, James Andrew 84, 106, 109, 110, 116, 132
Jackson, J. Milton 83, 84, 104, 208, 294
Jackson, Joseph M. 106
Jackson, Maxine 267
Jackson, Mollie 106
Jackson, Pearl (Boyd) 267
Jackson, Susie 106
Jackson, Wanda 267
Jacob, Alexander 217
Jacob, Anna 217
Jacob, Charlie B. "Chink" 217, 358
Jacob, Wanda 217
James, Ann (Knight) 158
James, Annie 159
James, Mildred Lillian (see Blakesley) 159, 229, 311
James, Robert J. 158, 159, 249, 311
Jan, R. M. 58
Japanese 137
Jencks, C. A. 58
Jennings, Gladys 333
Jennings, Jewel 355
Jessup, C. D. 341
Jeter, Mrs. Mary 154
Jim's Cafe 269
Jitneys 199, 220-21, 264, 285
Jo-Mill Stores 362
Johnson, A. T. "Booty" 357
Johnson, Anna Mae 309
Johnson, Clyde Franklin 309
Johnson, Etta (Gregg) 185, 309
Johnson, Fred Everett 309
Johnson, John Franklin 185, 309
Johnson, John Lincoln 309
Johnson, Leona Winona 309
Johnson, Lyndon Baines 357
Johnson, Mary Evelyn 309
Johnson, Mrs. James F. 309
Johnson, Nina Bess 309
Johnson, Ruth 105
Johnson, William 29, 30, 46
Johnson family (#2) 57
Johnston, Elise 231
Joiner, "Dad" 337
Jolson, Al 279
Jones, Alma (Thornton) 137, 157, 211-212
Jones, Dean K. 98, 116, 117, 132, 311

Jones, Effie 98, 116
Jones, Elmer B. 137, 157
Jones, Ernest 262, 263
Jones, Harry 291
Jones, Jesse H. 51, 124, 151, 277, 278
Jones, John T. 137
Jones, Johnie Mae 292
Jones, Laura 98
Jones, Col. Martin Tilford 51, 81
Jones, M. Tilford 244, 251, 252, 277
Jones, Nina 137, 212, 233
Jones, Dr. O. Harrell 367-368
Jones, S. R. Jr. "Buddy" 351, 361
Jones, Vera (see Quinn) 219
Jones, Walter W. "Bud" 74, 137, 212
Jones, William E. "Willie" 51, 68, 75, 81, 137, 244
Jones' Garage 263
Jones (M.T.) Lumber Company 51, 68
Jones Rice Farm 191
Jones Plantation 87, 244
Jumonville Furniture Co. 362

K

Kansas, State of 13, 25, 28, 29, 30, 33-37, 42, 55, 56, 59, 62, 68, 121, 132, 137, 347. *See also* Fort Scott, Kansas; McPherson, Kansas; Newton, Kansas
Karkowski, Leo 360, 367
Keeling, W. A. 249
Keen & Woolf Refinery 204
Keizer, Lorenza 212
Kelley, Anita Maude 218, 365
Kelley, Emerson Ross "Coke Yard" 218, 249, 328, 365
Kelley, Evelyn Lake (see Parker) 218, 334, 365
Kelley, Martha Maxine 218
Kelley, Marvin Ross 218
Kelley, Olive Maude (Brown) 218
Kelley, Olive Mozelle (see Hughes) 218, 273, 365
Kemah, community of 163, 224
Kilgore, Miss 157
Killkare, community of 23

Killough, M. E. 324
Kindergarten 336
King, Esther E. 160
King, Inez M. 160
King, Julia (Strope) 160
King, Martha Elizabeth 160
King, Martin H. 160
King, O. C. 295, 305-307, 340
King, Oleta 332
King, Robert H. 160
King, Robert W. 160
Kingsbury, Blanche Lee 84, 157, 215, 237, 241
Kingsbury, Emma Catherine 157, 238
Kingsbury, Donna (Murphy) 84, 121
Kingsbury, Effie Mae 84, 157
Kingsbury, George Clyde 159
Kingsbury, George R. 159
Kingsbury, Ralph C. 159
Kingsbury, Rayburn Sinclair "Ray" 157, 282, 347
Kingsbury, Rhoda E. (McEvers) 159
Kingsbury, Robert Richard "Dick" 157
Kingsbury, Robert Ace 84, 110, 121, 157, 222, 238
Kingsbury, Robert Ackley "Bob" 157, 241, 264
Kingsbury, Zora Lee (Moore) 110, 121, 157, 214-215, 233, 237, 238, 268
Kingsbury's Store 214, 236, 237, 268, 269, 287
Kirk, Birch B. 364
Kirk, Blanche 364
Kirk, Joseph Grant 364
Kirk, Lelah 364
Kirk, Rebecca Elizabeth 364
Kirkland, J. K. 99
Klein's Ice Cream Store 361
Klondike strawberries 121, 124, 318
Knau, Ottis 58
Knothole Gang 279
Knutson, A. 36
Kolb, N. B. 147

KPRC radio station 255, 362
Krenek, Adella (see Young) 334
Kruse, Anna 229, 231
Kruse, Edward Eugene 231, 282, 352
Kruse, Elizabeth Pauline (Boeske) 352
Kruse, Florentine 60, 112, 227, 352
Kruse, H. B. 352
Kruse, Helen 352
Kruse, Jean 352
Kruse, Johanna W. "Hanna" 59, 72, 352
Kruse, Judy 352
Kruse, Karl Edgar 59, 61, 83, 112, 155, 180, 311, 352
Kruse, Karl E. Jr. 352
Kruse, Oscar Arthur 61, 79, 85, 93, 110, 120, 155, 159, 168, 208, 221, 225, 227, 229, 233, 253, 311
Kruse, Oscar A. Jr. 72, 112, 124, 221, 225, 227, 279, 352
Kruse, Pauline 352
Kruse, Ruby Lee (Waites) 352
Kruse, Selma 112, 227
Kruse, Shirley 352
KTRH radio station 362
Kucera, Vick 278, 285, 355
Kuhns, Bertha 40, 46, 75
Kuhns, Charles 40, 41, 46, 47
Kuhns, Elizabeth "Lizzie" 40
Kuhns family 43, 62. *See also* Kuhns, George W.
Kuhns, George W. 40, 41, 44, 66, 75
Kuhns, Gussie 40
Kuhns, Ida 40, 46
Kuhns, May 40
Kuhns, Nannie 40, 47
Kuhns, Perry 40, 46, 104
Kuhns, William "Will" 40, 44,
Kuntz, Mr. 84

L

L. P., H. & N. R. R.. *See* Railroads 21, 30, 37, 49, 151
La Porte Chronicle newspaper 33, 39, 119

La Porte, City of 21, 23, 25, 26, 27, 31, 33, 34, 36, 38, 39, 42, 48, 49, 53, 74, 75, 78, 87, 105, 109, 112, 113, 119, 147, 149, 151, 153-155, 159, 162, 164, 169, 176, 185, 187, 189, 190, 196, 198, 199, 209, 239, 260, 293, 297, 298, 300, 329, 361, 368
La Porte Herald newpaper 56
La Porte, Houston & Northern Railroad (see L. P., H. & N. RR.)
La Porte Improvement Company 31, 32, 37
La Porte Investment Company 37, 50
La Port, New Town 56, 152
La Porte Wharf and Channel Co. 56
La Porte/Highway Road (also see Harrisburg-La Porte Road and Sterling Highway) 61, 62, 65, 72, 80, 84, 99, 118, 126-127, 130, 136, 284, 286, 290, 293, 296-298, 300, 325, 359, 365
Ladies Aid Society 104
Lafayette Escadrille 171
Lakin, George Milton 157
Lakin, George M. Jr. 157
Lakin, Milton H. 157
Lakin, Olive "Ollie" (see Berry) 157, 227, 301
Lakin, Serena C. "or E." 157, 286
Lamb, Lanny 361
Lambert, Homer 344
Lamer, John 36
Land, Hazel (Elder) 344
Land, Ishmael Laverne "Ish" 344
Landers, J. C. 36
Larabee, Richard 23
Larson family 59
Larson, Claus 36
Larson, Edyth 288
Larson, James B. 288, 315, 316
Larson, James L. 288
Larson, John Lewis 288
Larson, John Marion "Coffee George" 259, 288, 307, 308
Larson, Julia 288

Index

Larson, Lou (Garrett) 288
Larson, Marjorie 288
Larson, N. Douglas 288
Larson, Victoria Rose (Tipton) 288, 315
Larson, Wilabie (Syfan) 288, 307
Larson, Mrs. "Hat Lady" 329
Laschinsky, Alma 136
Laschinsky, Frida (Wozoreck) 136
Laschinsky, William 136
Laymance, Tom 298
League City, community of 31, 112, 133, 138, 167
Lee Brothers Circus 325
Lee, T. W. "Tom" 25, 31
Leff, Sol F. 360
Lewis, F. W. 74
Lewis, James W. 42, 62, 68
Library, City 286, 296
Library, School 286
Lincoln Machine Co. 163
Linstrom, F. 36
Literary Society, 104, 152
Little Vince's Bayou 46, 47, 82, 84, 97, 103, 106, 137, 245, 273, 325
Livingston, Beula Elizabeth 315
Livingston, Edith 315
Livingston, George W. 315
Livingston, Guy H. 315
Livingston, Texas 363
Lloyd, "Doc" 337
Loading sheds/platform 127, 319
Locklin, Charles 364
Locklin, Gaston 364
Locklin, Harold 328, 364
Locklin, James B. "Jim" 364
Locklin, L. S. 364
Locklin, Maybelle 364
Locklin, Mike 364
Locklin, Shirley 364
Locklin Machine Shop 364
Lohman, Charles Eugene 353
Lohman, Earl 353
Lohman, John Arthur 353
Lohman, John A. Jr. 353
Lohman, Mrs. J. A. 353
Lohman, Lenora Louise 353

Lomax, community of 154, 169
Lone Star Cement (also see Texas Portland Cement Co) 241, 267, 268, 275, 310, 326, 329
Longhorn cattle 18, 19
Long, Paul 281
Long's Theater 360
Loose, Eli 98
Loose, Dr. Titus Chauncey 98, 238
Loose, Mrs. T. C. 98, 109
Louisiana State of 16, 27, 113, 144, 314, 335, 347, 350, 355, 370
Louisville, Kentucky 3
Lowe, Charleen 353
Lowe, Lottie May (Sealy) 353
Lowe, W. C. 353
Lubbock, Frank R. 6, 7, 8, 9, 14, 16, 21, 22, 324
Lucas, A. F. 88, 191, 193, 197
Lucas, Newton A. "Newt" 362
Lusitania, steamship 170, 171
Lyles, Henry 350
Lyles, Virgie (Holbrook) 350, 351
Lynch, Nathaniel 198
Lynch's Ferry (see also ferries) 3
Lynchburg, community of 2, 6, 9, 22, 116, 154, 162, 164, 189, 190, 191, 199, 216, 329, 346, 358
Lyon, S. C. 36
Lyons, Evelyn 220, 227

M

MacNider, Dr. Virginius St. Clair 66, 109, 121, 238, 239, 321
Madison County/Madisonville 62, 77, 79, 94, 107, 114, 213, 236, 266, 335
Magnolia Oil Mixing Plant 201
Magnolia Park 256
Magnuson, Axel Emfred "Jimmy" 352
Magnuson, Florentine (Kruse) 352
Malloy, C. P. 129
Mandy, S. P. 358
Mandy, Mrs. S. P. 358
Mangeliers, Otto 76
Mangeliers, Rosa (Kresta) 76

Marchant, Dr. Juliett 109, 239
Mares, Desideria 358
Marsh children 22
Marsh, Mrs. 153
Marsh, W. S. 321
Martin, Floy Mae (Scott) 289
Martin, Francis M. 289
Martin, Fred J. 161, 289
Martin, Janette 233, 289
Martin, "Pepper" 279
Martinez, Lenora 237, 245
Martinez, Mary 245
Martinez, Tommie 245
Martyn, James 24
Marvick Dairy Farm 368
Mason's Cafe 360
Mason, Alma 354
Mason, Ella 180
Mason, Ethel Marie 234
Mason, Jess T. 234, 265, 368
Mason, Lola 234
Masonic Lodge 236, 262, 268, 269, 296, 308, 362
Massey, Charles D. (ferry) 346
Massey, Joe B. 348
Masterson, N. T. 138
Mata, Carman Balli (Carazos) 245
Mata, Ignacio 245
Mata, Jose 245
Mata, Leonardo 245
Mathews, Fleeta 329
May Day festival 330, 332
Mayfield, Marion 333
Mayo, Osi 287
McBurney, Francis "Frank" 67
McBurney, Lucy 67
McBurney, Minnie (Plum) 67, 84
McBurney, William 67, 116
McCauley, Mrs. J. P. 358
McCloud, Reverend 64
McClung, Mattie 355
McCollough, Bessie (see Neugebauer) 316
McCormick, Belle (also see Deane) 61, 156
McCormick, Dan 61, 156
McCoy, Dr. H. T. 109

McCoy, Naomi (Daily) 353
McCoy, Sam A. 353
McCrory, W. S. 265
McCullough, Charlie 54
McCullough, R. B. 358
McCullough, Mrs. R. B. 358
McDaniel, Rev. George E. 148
McDearnor's Sanitarium 164
McDonald, John 43
McDowell, Charles "Buddy" 316
McDowell, W. D. 316
McDurman Sanitarium 164
McEvain, George 36
McEvers, Hugh 98, 104
McEvers, Mattie (also see Mrs. Savage) 98, 168
McEvers, Rhoda Elizabeth (see Kingsbury) 98, 159
McFarland, Texas 139
McGowen, R. S. 162
McGraw, Joe 350
McGraw, Michael Wayne 350
McGraw, Nora Lee (Glasgow) 350
McGraw, Thomas A. 350
McGraw, Tommy Lee 350
McIlhenny, Mrs. Sam 75
McKay, Coach 227
McKissick, D. H. 306, 340, 342
McKnight, Elizabeth 137
McKnight, Gertrude 137
McKnight, Minnie 137
McKnight, Robert 137
McKnight, Robert A. 137
McLaughlin, J. J. 321
McLean, Clifton Olive 310
McLean, Edgar L. 310
McLean, Edith 310
McLean, Harrison, 82, 84, 136, 310
McLean, Harrison, Jr. 310
McLean, Ira M. 310
McLean, Mary Lou 310
McLean, Ward L. 310
McLean, William Carrol 310
McLeod, Rev. J. F. 90, 91
McMaster & Pomeroy 131, 132, 179, 200, 201, 204, 211, 244, 272, 275, 290, 305, 327, 347, 365

Index 467

McMaster, Credella 157, 218, 233
McMaster, David Clarkson 157, 158
McMaster, Emma Alice (Webb) 106, 112, 157, 167, 217-218
McMaster, (baby) Emma 106
McMaster, Gertrude (see Pomeroy) 108, 110, 111, 112, 115, 131, 146, 154, 158
McMaster, Irma (see Williams) 154, 218
McMaster, Myrtle 157, 161
McMaster, Myrtle Lillian 110, 112, 154, 218, 232, 355
McMaster, W. Clyde 106, 110, 112, 116, 129-132, 157, 199-202, 204, 208, 211, 217-218, 223, 259, 272, 274, 275, 300, 304-306, 313, 341, 342, 351, 354, 368
McMurry, Claude P. "Mac" 314, 315, 363, 368
McMurry, Robert Charles 314
McMurry, Wanda Rae 315
McMurry, Wilma (Plaisance) 314
McMurry's Service Station 315
McNair, Maxie 332
McNay, Bertha Shore (Farrow) 161, 251
McNay, Charnock Boyd "C.B." 50, 138-139, 161, 245, 251, 275
McNay, Elizabeth Araverne 161, 229
McNay, Laurel Eugene "L.E." 161, 252
McNay, Lavera E. 161
McNay, Lockridge D. 161, 252
McNeil's mercantile 74
McPherson, Kansas 34, 35, 36, 42. See also Kansas, State of
McWhorter, Dr. James Edison 149, 163, 239
Mead, W. A. 58
Meador family 148
Meador, Ann Elizabeth 148
Meador, Benjamin Franklin I 148, 163, 348
Meador, B. F. "Frank" II 146, 348
Meador, Horace 163

Meador, Joe 163
Meador, Reba (Estes) 348
Meador, Rex 163
Meador, Wallace Warwick 324
Medicine 110, 238-240
Memorial Baptist Church 359
Menard, Alfred 23
Mercer, Rev. W. A. 144
Methodist 91, 92, 95, 118, 144, 156, 170, 216, 223, 229, 272
Methodist, Deepwater 65, 67
Methodist, La Porte 66, 74
Methodist, Pasadena 64, 67, 78, 85, 86, 91, 92, 95, 118, 144, 156, 170, 322, 340, 364
Methodist Episcopal Church, South 66
Metropolitan Milk (see Pomeroy Dairy) 76, 86
Mexia, Texas 51, 82
Mexicans 68, 117, 130, 171, 180, 244, 245, 317, 329, 342, 364
Mexican Church of Pasadena 358
Meyer, Charles 247
Meyer, D. B. 236
Meyer, Hedwig Paula (Vieweger) 275
Meyer, Isabell 275
Meyer, John August 252, 275
Meyer, John Maximillian "Johnny" 231, 270, 282-283, 361
Meyer, O. E. "Perk" 361
Meyer, Sylvia (Wilson) 361
Mickey Mouse 279
Middle Bayou 8, 16, 24, 154
Middleton's Grocery 351
Midland Bridge Co. 179
Midwives 239
Migratory workers 124, 133, 141, 244, 329
Milam, Texas 320
Milby High School 365
Milby, Charles 99
Miller, Belle Credella 98
Miller, Betty L. 98
Miller, Bob 98
Miller, Bud 98, 252
Miller, Egbert P. 161

Miller, Ira L. 98, 181
Miller, Jake D. 98, 116, 137, 181
Miller, Kirby J. 98
Miller, K. Jack 233
Miller, Thomas L. "Tom" 98, 251
Miller, V. W. 293
Mills, Rev. John W. Jr. 298
Mills, R. Q. Sr. 308
Mills, R. Q. Jr. 308
Missionary Strawberries 320
Missouri, State of 113, 137
Mitchell's Store 361, 362
Mitchell, Betty (Williams) 266, 361, 362
Mitchell, Blanche 177
Mitchell, W. Lee 266, 307, 359, 361, 368
Moberly, W. L. 162, 348
Mock, James 36
Mock, Mrs. James 36
Moechel, Jason Robert 156, 218, 319
Moechel, J. Robert Jr. 156-157
Moechel, Josephine 156-157
Moechel, Renee Marie 156-157, 355
Moechel, Yvonne 156-157
Mohr family 23
Moller, Mr. 53
Monteith, Walter E. 250, 304
Montgomery, Collin 301
Montgomery, Dewitt Talmage "D.T." 301
Montgomery, Fred Sigfred "Sig" 301, 328
Montgomery, Lois May (Snelling) 301
Montgomery, Louise 301
Montoya, Felicitos 317
Montoya, Francisco 244
Montoya, Frajeda 244
Montoya, Juan 244
Montoya, Maria 244
Montoya, Secundio 244
Montoya families 316
Moody, Arthur Bently 295-296
Moody, A. B. Jr. 295
Moody, Daisey Dean 295

Moody, Gertrude Isabel (Dauson) 295, 296
Moody, Margaret Eva 295
Moore, Carter 337
Moore, Dr. 240
Moore, Dora Katherine 64
Moore, Emma Malvena (see Cruse) 64, 126, 208, 239
Moore, Oscar F. "the father" 62, 217
Moore, Oscar Flake "the son" 64
Moore, Floyd Melton 64
Moore, M. Emma (Robertson) 64, 217
Moore, Mr. 132
Moore, Marion Walker 64, 274
Moore, N. 58
Moore, Ora Jane 64
Moore, Oscar Riba 64
Moore, Ronnie 337
Moore, Sammie 64
Moore, Thomas Andrew 337
Moore, Mrs. T. A. 359
Moore, Thomas W. "Tom" 327, 336, 337, 348
Moore, Verda Eliz (see Kaul) 64, 83
Moore, W. W. 258
Moore, Zora Lee (see Kingsbury) 64, 110, 121
Moore family 121
Moore's Park (also see Poole's Rest) 190
Morgan (Charles) Ship Lines 8, 10, 11, 12, 13, 15, 17, 189
Morgan, "Col." James 3, 8, 18, 21, 23, 48, 180, 189
Morgan, "Com." Charles 8, 13, 15, 188-189
Morgan's Point 3, 8, 21, 23, 25, 48, 74, 82, 87, 99, 105, 154, 164, 196, 247, 260, 346
Morries, A. L. 359
Morries, Mrs. A. L. 359
Morris' Cove 23, 65
Morris, Joe 137
Morris, Kate 137
Morris, Margaret 326
Morris, Martha 137

Morris, Reina 137
Morris, Rosa 326
Morris, Ritson 23
Morris, W. A. 36
Morrison, Bessie 350, 351
Moruna, Felipe 244
Moruna, Finstia 244
Moruna, Francisco 245
Moruna, Lorenzo 244
Moruna, Santiago 244
Moss, Catherine 333
Movies 237-239, 279
Movie Theaters 237, 344, 359, 360
Mud Lake 23
Muecke, Amelia 322
Muecke, Bertha Mae (Weinberg) 322, 325
Muecke, Jewell G. 322
Muecke, Kenneth W. 322
Muecke, Louis A. 322
Muecke, Louis John Jr. 322, 325
Muecke, Myrta Ann 322
Muecke, Wesley M. 322
Muecke, Wesley Jr. 322
Muldoon's Saloon 74
Munger, Avilda (Witter) 30, 38
Munger, C. Russell "Russie" Jr. 30, 46-48, 54, 355
Munger, Charles R. 25, 28, 30, 45-47, 67, 52-55, 57, 58, 76, 86-87, 118, 122, 127, 132, 212
Munger, Edith 30, 47, 48
Munger's Bank 28
Munger's Desk 54
Munozes family 316
Murphy, Donna (see Kingsbury) 84
Murphy, Rev. P. M. 78
Murphy, Dr. W. W. 34
Myer, Sewall 249

N

N. G., H. & K. C. R. R. 30, 49
Nacogdoches, wooden ship 179
Napp, Ann 292
Napp, Donald Edward 292
Napp, Edward Frank "Hickey" 292
Nashold, Bessie 137

Nashold, Daniel E. 137
Nashold, Gladys 137
Nashold, Harry 137
Nashold, Helen 137
Nashold, Jeane 137
Nashold, Marion 137
Nation, Carrie 88, 105
Navigation District 249
Neagle, Francis M. "Harrisburg" 357
Neal, Huey A. 43
Neal, Marie 333
Nebraska Syndicate 49
Negroes 14, 22, 63, 138, 154, 155, 277, 354
Nelson family 59
Nelson, Beverly 361
Nelson, Capt. 23
Nelson, Cato N. 361
Nelson, Donald 361
Nelson, Harold 361
Nelson, Neal 361
Nelson, Nelwyn 361
Neugebauer, Andrew 316
Neugebauer, Bessie (McCollough) 316
New Deal economic policy 341, 352, 354
New Town, see La Porte, NT
New Washington 3, 25, 48
Newell, Allie Gertrude (see Brown) 181, 339
Newell, Annie Elizabeth 113
Newell, Banna Lee 113
Newell, Bertrum Francie "Bert" 113
Newell, Beulah Colesta 113
Newell, Earl Lester 113, 203, 322
Newell, Effie Eugene (see Howell) 113, 160
Newell, Ernest Theodore "Ted" 113, 185
Newell, Fontis Eugene 113, 181
Newell, Francis Devier 112, 113, 116, 132, 208, 219, 240
Newell, Ila Myrtle (see Holloway) 113, 217
Newell, Martha Jane (Osborne) 112-113

Newell, Thomas Vernon 113, 180-181, 183, 298
Newell, Wesley Osborne 113
Newspapers (see *Deepwater Enterprise, La Porte Chronicle, La Porte Herald, Pasadena Record, Pasadena Sun* and others)
Newton, J. E. 107
Newton, Kansas 28-30, 33, 36-38
New York & Tx Beef Preserving Co. 14
Nicholas, excursion boat 191, 192
Nichols, Addie 233
Nichols, Mattie 64
Nicholson, Rev. Peter 23, 64
Nicknames 328
Noftsyer, Albert N. 48, 53
Norris, M. F. 364
Norris, Mrs. M. F. 364
Norris Barber & Beauty Shop 364
Norsworthy terminal/tank farm 198, 199
North Carolina 145, 172
North Galveston, City of 27
North Galveston, Houston & Kansas City Railroad (see N.G., H. & K.C. RR)
Norton, Edward H. 58

O

Oak Park Subdivision 298
Oaklawn (ranch house) 20, 21
Oaklawn, Harrisburg & Ship Chan. Jitney 221
Oberholtzer, Dr. E. E. 229
Ohmstead, Preacher 64
"Old Ironsides" see U. S. S. *Constitution*
Old Southern Inn 233
Olive, George Marvin 162, 206, 216, 247
Olive, Grover Cleveland 206
Olive, Irma Gladys (see Shannon) 162, 216, 232, 311
Olive, Rose (May) 162, 216
Olive family 137
Olsen family 52

Olson family #2 162
Olson, Alpha Neppie 113
Olson, Edward A. 113, 201
Olson, Lottie 113
Olson, Rosa 113
Open Range 17, 139, 250
Oranges, see Satsuma 37, 47, 48, 122, 133
Orr, Emogene (see Bunkley) 334, 355
Ortiz, Cenobia 358
Osborne, Dr. Clarence F. 369
Ostendorf family 152
Otis, H. F. 42, 47
Otterside, Doris 309
Otterside, Melvin "Bubba" 309
Otterside, Melvin Ralph 309
Otterside, Thelma Myrtle (White) 309
Outhouses 246, 295, 296

P

Packard, Mr. 35
Paine, Herbert A. Sr. 99, 367
Paine, Herbert A. Jr. 351, 361, 366, 367
Painter, J. H. 340
Palmer, Bert 43
Palmer, Connie 137
Palmer, Edna 137
Palmer, Johnie 137
Palmer, Lucy 137
Palmer, S. S. 116, 137
Palmer, Will 43
Palms, A. 23
Pan Smerican Shipbuilding 179
Pancho Villa 171
Park Place, community of 184, 219, 256, 289
Parker, Rev. Alton L. 358
Parker, Evelyn L. (Kelley) 365
Parker, Howard William 365
Parks, Alice 125, 231
Parks, Bessie 125
Parks, Calvin Emerson 50, 58, 79, 95, 208
Parks, Carrie (see Phillips) 79, 125,

Index 471

177, 213, 227
Parks, Elmer Calven 125
Parks, Everett R. "Eli" 125
Parks, Flora Irene "the grandmother" 79
Parks, Flora Irene "the granddaughter" 125
Parks, Gladys Angeline 125, 332, 334
Parks, Ima I. 125-126, 185, 225, 351
Parks, Irma Leora (see Blakesley) 58, 64, 79, 125, 300
Parks, James Devere, Sr. 58, 79, 95, 116, 117, 132, 165, 175, 208, 229, 238, 240, 296, 311
Parks, J. D., Jr. 125, 270
Parks, J. E. 359
Parks, Mrs. J. E. 359
Parks, J. E., Jr. 359
Parks, Lenora "Nora" (Thurman) 79, 115
Parks, Leora (Gartney/Gwartney) 125, 185
Parks, Ralph Emerson 58, 79, 129-130, 185, 208-212, 226, 229, 236, 245, 247, 249, 352
Parks, William Sullivan "Will" 79, 125, 185, 275, 308, 309, 311, 322
Parks, W. S. "Muggins" Jr. 125, 339
Parks' Dairy 81, 95, 185
Parson family 42, 53
Pasadena, California 30
Pasadena, Texas Producers' Exchange 129, 159, 207, 211, 214, 271, 275
Pasadena, West (see West Pasadena)
Pasadena Acres 127, 141, 244
Pasadena Band 284, 285
Pasadena Band March 285
Pasadena Baptist Church (see Baptists) 358
Pasadena Barber Shop 267
Pasadena Cemetery, see Crown Hill Cemetery 106, 107, 208
Pasadena Citizen Ass'n 247
Pasadena Cleaners 362
Pasadena Drug Co. 213, 266, 267, 361
Pasadena Dry Goods Store 361
Pasadena Early Settlers Club 354
Pasadena (Telephone) Exchange 275
Pasadena Farm (see Santa Anna Farm 196, 225
Pasadena Fruit & Truck Growers Assn. 129
Pasadena Garage 271, 272
Pasadena Garden Club 354
Pasadena Grocery 361
Pasadena High School (also see High School) 155, 229, 230, 231, 250, 271, 273, 275, 283, 300, 301, 328, 330, 334, 348, 354
Pasadena Hospital & Clinic 369
Pasadena Ice and Fuel 211, 269, 362, 363
Pasadena Ice, Fuel and Transfer Co. 362
Pasadena Independent School Dist. (PISD) 62-64, 66, 76, 82, 83, 132, 257, 287, 303, 329, 334, 347, 348
Pasadena Light Company 247, 257
Pasadena Lumber Co. 272, 291, 364
Pasadena Missionary Baptist Church 78, 359
Pasadena National Farm Loan Association 141
Pasadena Pioneers' Club 354
Pasadena Public Library Association 153
Pasadena Pure Milk Dairy (Syfan) 308
Pasadena Record newspaper 264, 298
Pasadena Red Cross 180
Pasadena Ship Channel 298
Pasadena State Bank 207-209, 211, 213-214, 216, 248, 266, 287, 298, 315, 332, 333, 351, 361, 364
Pasadena Sun newspaper 298
Pasadena (Movie) Theater, 350, 360
Pasadena Volunteer Fire Department (see Fire Dept., Pasadena)
Pathe News 352
Patrick, Whitney 315, 316

Patterson, H. L. 246
Paulham, Louis, 145-151
Peden, E. A. 203
Pelly, community of 203
Peltz, Earl 136
Peltz, Erntine 136
Peltz, Harry 136
Peltz, Harry Jr. 136
Peltz, Lawrence 136
Peltz, Lester 136
Peltz, Milton 136
Pendleton, Robert Edward Sr. 293
Pendleton, Robert E. Jr. 293
Pendleton, W. N. "Bill" 293 325, 327
Pendleton, Zada Mae (Braswell) 293
Penn City, community 179, 282
Penn, John C. Jr. 249
Pennington, Virginia 313
Pennington, William "Bill" R. N. 235, 313
Pennington, Zelma 313
Pentecostal Church, see Assembly of God 144, 242, 291, 297, 358
People's State Bank 206
Permanent Waving 265
Perry, David 56
Perry, John L. 56, 66
Perry, Lucinda 56
Perry, Ray 56
Perry, Roy H. 56
Perryman, Alexander W. 206
Perryman Investment Co. 206
Pershing, Gen. John J. "Black Jack" 171
Peterson, Johanna (see Kruse) 59
Peterson, Peter J. 208
Petroleum Iron Works 318, 319
Pevoto, D. R. 358
Phillips, Caroline 283
Phillips, Carrie (Parks) 213, 283
Phillips, Charlie Vernon 283
Phillips, Culley "Tut" 283, 328
Phillips, Francis Janette 283
Phillips, Herman "Tee Tie" 283, 284, 328, 356, 357
Phillips, J. Barton 283

Phillips, Jesse Mae (Lewis) 283
Phillips, Lois 283
Phillips, Mary Alice (see Chambers) 283, 334
Phillips, Preston 213, 283, 296, 298
Phillips, Preston Arland 283
Phillips, Rodney 283, 356
Phillips, Weldon "Stoney 283, 284, 328, 350, 356, 357
Phillips Petroleum 310, 311, 329
Phleuger, Lena Flayer 75
Pickett, Henrietta 236
Pickett, Ida M. 236
Pickett, Luther 236, 327
Pickett, Mr. 236
Pickett, Ralph 104
Picnics 224, 225
Pierce, A. B. "Shanghi" 12, 13, 18, 19
Pillot's grocery store 241
Pinkston, W. Otis 344
Pipelines 290, 292, 293
Pitre, A. J. 353
Pitre, A. J. Jr. 353
Pitre, Jennings L. "Pete" 353
Pitre, Mrs. A. J. 353
Pitts, Bama E. (Scroggins) 114, 305
Pitts, Bernal Howard 43, 83, 143, 144, 201, 214, 221, 259, 271, 300, 362
Pitts, Bertram Ernest "Bert" 107, 226
Pitts, Charles Alfred 271, 363
Pitts, Charles Aubrey 216
Pitts, Cora Bell (Shine) 216, 354
Pitts, Eula May (Brockman) 46
Pitts, Glenn Hughes 271, 363
Pitts, Ira Cleveland 180
Pitts, Ira Leander "Lee" 35, 55, 63, 66, 69, 72, 107, 136, 319
Pitts, Jewel (see Conrad) 107, 114
Pitts, Julie Estell "Duckie" (see Towles) 272, 300, 328, 363, 369
Pitts, Lillian Rhoretta (see Dickerson) 46, 62, 69
Pitts, Lula Irene (see Jensen) 35, 72
Pitts, Mamie Ellen (Hughes) 221, 272

Index

Pitts, Naomi Catherine 363
Pitts, Oliver Claude 46, 114, 208, 236, 247, 305-307, 340, 342, 348, 352, 354
Pitts, Rewell Grady 83, 143, 144, 216, 363
Pitts, Thelma Lois 272, 363
Pitts, Vernon 363
Pitts, Victor Grady 216
Pitts, Wesley Howard "Sonny" 328, 363
Pitts children 72
Pitts' Service Station 271, 362
Pizzitola family 23
Plaisance, Avis 314-315
Plaisance, Donald 314
Plaisance, Douglas 314
Plaisance, Laura Lee 314, 334
Plaisance, Malcolm 314
Plaisance, Rowena/Raena "Ena" 314, 333
Plaisance, Wilma (see McMurry) 314
Plaisance family 314, 364
Planters & Mechanics National Bank 78
Pledger, Eletha 233
Plum, Alice 85
Plum, Ethel 85, 114
Plum, George 85
Plum, George Horace 84, 85, 95, 116
Plum, Tom H. 85, 94, 114, 116
Plunkett, Jessie 347
Poirrier, Al L. 311
Poirrier, Charlotte 311
Poirrier, Louis 311
Pokersville 4
Police 293-295, 306, 340, 342, 364
Poll Tax 247
Pollard, J. H. 58
Pollock, Eva 48
Pomeroy Dairy (Metropolitan Milk) 76, 81, 95, 107, 120, 241
Pomeroy Water Works 210, 253, 254, 326
Pomeroy, Anna Louise (Kresta) 76-78, 106-108, 111, 112, 121, 136, 146, 157, 159, 177, 232, 234, 239, 252, 257, 258, 278, 313, 326, 336, 371
Pomeroy, Bessie 234, 278, 286, 328, 336, 343
Pomeroy, Clyde D. 234, 254, 274, 278, 286, 327, 328, 335, 339, 344, 352, 357, 365
Pomeroy, Edward Payson 76, 77, 86, 93, 95, 100, 101, 106-107, 120, 122, 157, 158, 172, 238, 311
Pomeroy, Gertrude (McMaster) 157, 234, 240, 278
Pomeroy, John Edward 72, 77, 78, 96, 99, 102, 104, 106-108, 111, 129-135, 144-146, 151, 185, 199, 200-202, 204, 208, 211-212, 229, 233, 234-235, 241, 246, 248, 253-255, 259, 265, 271, 272, 274-275, 278, 284-285, 311, 313, 327, 336, 340, 344, 347, 348, 351, 354, 358, 371
Pomeroy, J. Edward, Jr. "Tubby" 131, 158, 159, 212, 241, 254, 274, 279, 286, 296, 328, 335, 336, 355
Pomeroy, Loise (Williams) 335, 336, 355
Pomeroy, Marguerite 157, 158, 212, 233, 278, 284, 343
Poole, Aubrey Harold 310
Poole, Dan 310
Poole, George Edward 309
Poole, George I. 309
Poole, Irvin 310
Poole, Marguerite 310
Poole, Maurine 310
Poole, Virgie M. 309
Poole, Virginia D. 309
Poole boy 280
Poole's Rest (also see Moore's) 190
Port Arthur, Texas 71, 195, 197
Port of Galveston 2
Port of Houston 3, 15, 170, 198, 261, 297, 339, 346
Portwood, Cora Iola (Wertz) 269
Portwood, Dr. Oscar Frank 269, 306, 326, 333, 361

Portwood, O. Frank Jr. 269, 361, 368
Portwood, Margie (Blakesley) 361
Post Office, Deepwater 56, 110, 161, 212
Post Office, Deer Park 49, 50, 57, 62, 87, 212
Post Office, Genoa 40, 162
Post Office, La Porte 40, 41, 162
Post Office, Pasadena 30, 40, 50, 57, 61, 62, 77, 95, 97, 118, 157, 162, 211-212, 267, 268, 286, 361
Post Office, Red Bluff 23
Post Office, South Houston 147
Porter, James E. "Red" 369
Porter, Mary Agnes (Garfield) 369
Powell, Ben 292
Powell, James D. "J. D." 292
Powell, Rachel 292
Powell, Stella 292
Poyser, Harmah 132
Poyner, Dr. I. Patrick 109, 206, 240
Powitzky, C. E. 366
Prairie fires 122
Presbyterians 162
Producers' Row 128
Prohibition 205, 241, 278, 321
Pugh, L. L. 102

Q

Quinn, Aldy E. 218-219, 226
Quinn, Asa Rogers "Abe" 218
Quinn, Bertha (Dickerson) 263
Quinn, Edna Alice (Rogers) 181, 218
Quinn, Fern (Dow) 218
Quinn, Glenn Colquit "Baldy" 218, 226, 263
Quinn, Irma Inez 218
Quinn, Ray Marian (see Thornton) 218
Quinn, Rex Clifton 218
Quinn, Samuel Adolphus Mabery 218
Quinn, Samuel Augustus "Sam" 141, 181, 218, 219, 237, 245, 321
Quinn, Vera L. (Jones) 219

R

R & K Dry Goods 360
Raddue, Fritz 322
Radio 255, 278, 279, 344, 347, 362
Railroads (also see individual) 3, 7, 9, 10, 14-16, 18, 21, 22, 24, 25, 27-33, 36, 37, 39, 40, 41, 43, 44, 47-50, 53, 56-59, 62, 68, 69, 75, 77, 79, 81, 88, 95, 107, 108, 126-129, 132, 141, 145, 147-149, 121, 152, 159, 161-164, 187, 188, 193, 196, 200, 207, 211-214, 222, 226, 236, 243, 255, 260, 267, 289, 297, 298, 310, 314, 322, 324, 327, 329, 367
Rainbow Girls 284
Rathbone, D. P. 360, 368
Rawlins, Alice 218
Rawlins, Josiah 117, 118, 218
Rawlins, Lonnie Edward 218
Rawlins, Marcus L. 218
Rawlins, Martha H. (Knapp, Bailey) 117, 118, 218
Rawlins, Ruth Aline (see Dearing) 218, 313
Rawlins, Warren Montgomery 104, 118, 218, 313
Ray, Steve 138
Ream Field 184
Red & White Grocery 267, 297
Red Bluff, Community of 23
Redwood, A. G. 42
Reed, Francis Helen 361
Reed, Grace 361
Reed, Matt F. 361, 368
Reeves, Ruby 333
Relief Bureau 341
Reno, Bill 361
Repsdorph family 75
Republic Oil Company 199
Retail Merchants Association 265
Reyes, Candilaria 245
Reyes, Juan 245
Reyes, Mike 245
Reyes, Roman 245
Rhinehart, Marshall 231
Rice (agricultural commodity) 34,

Index

82, 102, 131, 137, 138, 190, 216
Rice Hotel 124, 277, 279
Richards, W. E. 151
Richey, C. R. 36
Richey, John 34, 35, 36, 37, 326
Richland, Community of 37, 48, 87
Richmond, Community of 27, 188
Riggs, Gertrude 225
Riggs, Isadore (see Cargill) 225, 346
Riggs, Joseph Allison "Jay" 224, 225, 232, 282
Riggs, James Oliver Riggs, 225
Riley, Archie Columbus "Railroad" 236
Riley, Harry E. 236, 327
Riley, Mame "Mae" 236, 327
Ringling Brothers Circus 323
Rita Theater 360
Ritz Theater 279, 343
Rivera, Jesus 317
Roach, Jack 319
Road side stands 129
Robb, A. G. 36
Roberts, Blanche May (see Sippy) 207, 212, 221, 227
Roberts, Carrie Eugenia (Weston) 212, 268, 286
Roberts, Constance Zola (see Ervin) 212
Roberts, Dorothy 357
Roberts, Joseph Richard 212
Roberts, Leona Adell (see Burch) 212
Roberts, Minne Lee (see Burnett) 52
Roberts, Myrtle 357
Roberts, Olin 357
Robertson, Bob 271
Robertson, Blanche 185
Robertson, May B. (Van Dorn) 185
Robertson, Pearl (see Crenshaw) 73, 164
Robertson, Sidney G. 185
Robertson, Sidney J. 185
Robertson, William 23
Rocha, Anita 308
Rocha, Juan 308
Rocha, Leornor (Martinez) 308

Rocha, Louis 308
Rocha, Octavino 245, 308
Rocha, Pedro 308
Rochelle, Isabella 333
Rodenbough, W. E. 58
Rodman, Ruth 83
Rodriquez, Antonio 358
Roe, Lillian 334
Rogers, Jack 233
Roller, Barbara Jean 353
Roller, Charles William "Bill" 353
Roller, Leora Chambers 353
Roller, M. Luther 353
Roosevelt, President F. D. 341, 351, 352
Roosevelt, Teddy 64, 109
Rosales, Agili 245
Rosales, Alusa 245
Rosales, Dominga 245
Rosales, Jerza 245
Rosales, Maria 245
Rosales, Pedro 245
Rosales, Sara 245
Ross, Burnett 28
Ross, Ellen (Burnett) 52, 78, 87
Ross, Ethel 83-85, 112
Ross, J. E. 82
Ross, J. H. 82
Ross, James O. 28, 52, 78, 85, 87, 99, 106, 151
Ross, Mattie, 90
Ross, Minnie 85, 112
Ross, Pearl 28
Ross, Sullivan 90
Ross, Dr. W. B. 85, 107, 109
Rotary Club of Houston 367
Rotary Club of Pasadena 367
Round Point 24
Roxana Petroleum Corp. 289
Ruth, "Babe" 279
Rubenstein 360
Russell, F. B. 163

S

Sabo, Betty Lou 352
Sabo, Clara (Curtis) 352, 353
Sabo, Helen 352

Sabo, John 352, 353
Sabo, John George 353
Sabo, John H. 352
Sabo, Marie 352
Sabo, Mary (Gulyus) 352
Sabo, Michael "Mike" 352
Sabo, Michael "Mikey" 352
Saderwhite, Charlie 77-78
Saderwhite, Lucy 77-78
St. Ann's Catholic Church 285
Saibara, Seito 137
Sallee, J. W. 58
Sam Houston Hall/Colosium 277
Sam Houston State Teachers College 275, 293
Samuells, G. D. 129, 162, 176
San Jacinto, Community of 3, 9, 22, 23, 64, 156, 164, 191
San Jacinto Battle & grounds 2, 5, 6, 22, 69, 146, 190, 247, 252, 351
San Jacinto High School 316, 358
San Jacinto Monument 352
San Jacinto Inn 300
San Leon, community of 183-184, 322
Sanchez, Phillip 275
Sanchez, Sam 275
Sanchez, Tony 275
Sanchez family 275, 316
Sanders, Dorothy 359
Sanders, Vera 359
Santa Anna Farm (see Pasadena Farm) 225, 244, 346
Santa Anna, General 3, 25, 69, 156, 225
Santa Fe Railroad 25, 27
Satilla steamship 170
Satsuma Gardens 131, 133
Satsuma oranges 132-133
Savage, Mrs. (see McEvers) 168
Scannell, Channler H. 268
Scannell, John Joseph 268
Scannell, Rosa Lee (Gibbs) 268, 300
Sherman Produce Co. 130
Schmidt, J. H. 58
School, Deer Park 154, 216, 289, 329
School, Deepwater 154, 329

School, Genoa 52, 154, 311, 347, 348
School, La Porte 32, 46, 154, 329
School, Lynchburg 154, 216, 329
School, Middle Bayou 24, 154
School, Morgan's Point 154
School, Pasadena 46, 54, 60, 63, 66, 72, 74, 76, 77, 82-84, 110-111, 115, 122, 152, 154, 164, 170, 250, 271, 273, 275, 281, 285, 328, 329, 334, 336, 339, 346, 354
School, Red Bluff 23
School, South Houston 147, 329, 347, 348
School Board/Trustees 64, 66, 82, 84, 110-111, 115, 153, 161, 162, 253, 264, 308, 311, 335-337, 347-348, 364
School Building 47, 53, 56, 60, 64, 65, 72, 74, 78, 82, 84, 92-94, 117-118, 144, 162, 213, 220, 227-231, 281, 340, 353, 354
School Colors 282
School Districts consolidation 347, 348
Schwandee, Joseph P. 181
Scott, Annie Laurie (White) 309
Scott, Mr. 269
Scott, Thomas A. 293, 298
Scott, William DeWitt 309
Scott, William Hadley 309
Scopes, John 255
Scroggins, Bama (see Pitts) 107, 114
Scroggins, T. D. 236
Seabrook, community of 65, 66, 75, 81, 116, 149, 151, 154, 159, 227, 246, 247, 260, 285, 322, 329
Seabrook Electric Railway 247
Seawall (at Galveston) 164
Senreau, Edward P. 23
Sens Road 169
Severtson, Surd 36
Seymour, James Survey 35, 39
Sewer system 296
Shannon, David Winifred "Dave" 311
Shannon, Dilla V. 311

Shannon, Gertrude Mae (Chambers) 311
Shannon, Irma G. (Olive) 311, 316
Shannon, Oley E. 311
Shannon, Oscar Cleaver 311, 316
Shannon, Vina M. 311
Shaw, Albert Howard 316
Shaw, Betty Ann 316
Shaw, Billy Carroll 286
Shaw, Buna Constance "Connie" 288
Shaw, Edna Elizabeth (Killough) 288, 316
Shaw, Mary Francis 288
Shaw, Ray 288
Shaw, Robert K. "Bobby" 288, 365
Shaw, Thomas Theodore "Theo" 286, 288, 316, 322, 339, 350
Shaw, Thomas Thuel 288
Shaw, Judge W. N. 64
Shell Petroleum Refinery 288, 289, 291, 293, 295, 306, 314, 315, 329, 337, 341, 344, 352-355
Shelton, Elvie "Seep" 236, 328
Shelton, Jimmy 236
Shelton, John Payton "Jap" 236, 328, 336
Shelton, Lilly Pearl 236
Shelton, Maxine 236
Shelton, Toka Lee (Fields) 336
Shelton, William J. 206, 236
Shelton, William Lloyd "Bear Track" 236, 328
Sherman, J. M. 301, 335
Sherman, Mae Hill 301, 335
Sherman, Sidney 188
Sherman, Wanda 301, 333, 334
Sherrill, Hazel 333
Sherrill, Willie Mae 333
Shine, Cora Bell (see Pitts) 98, 216
Shine, Emma Francis (Jones) 99
Shine, James Irby 99, 116, 216
Shine, John Oscar 99, 208, 216
Shine, John Taylor 99, 106, 116, 216
Shine, Pearl (Anderson) 216
Shine family 121
Shine's Restaurant 274, 313
Shipbuilding 179, 224

Shoulders, Addie V. 67
Shoulders, John 67
Shoulders, Lollie 67
Shoulders, Mattie 67
Shoulders, Renie 67
Shoulders, Robby McNider 67
Shoulders, Ruby E. 67
Shoulders, Scipio 67
Shoulders, Scipio Jr. 67
Simms-Sinclair Refinery 139, 200
Sims Bayou 5, 6, 8, 9, 10, 15, 16, 18, 21, 37, 179, 189, 198, 200, 256-258, 324
Sims, Jennah, 364
Sims, Louy V. 359, 364
Sims, Louy Vernon 364
Sims, Thelma 364
Sinclair Refinery 201, 212, 216, 218-219, 226, 240-241, 245-246, 258, 261, 287-289, 307-312, 317, 320, 321, 328, 329, 337, 342, 343, 346, 348, 352-353, 364, 365
Sinclair Gulf Refinery 201
Sippy, Blanche May (Roberts) 212, 240, 288
Sippy, Dorothy 288
Sippy, Jeanette 288
Sippy, Lawrence Nelson 212, 221, 288
Sippy, Nathalie 288
Sisson, Cecil 176, 261
Skyes, Ben 307
Slagle, Charles 44
Slagle, Elias 42, 44
Slagle, Jesse 44
Slagle, Orlin 42
Slagle, Salomie 42
Slagle family 61, 97
Slaten, Charles Elick 314
Slaten, James 314
Slaten, James Samuel "Sam" 314
Slaten, M. Eugene 314
Slaten, Mary Brady (Boulton) 314, 326
Slaten, Mary Elizabeth "Beth" 314
Slaten, Thomas Ray 314
Smith, Gov. Alfred E. 278, 279

Smith, Bertie (see Florrow) 310
Smith, Bessie 219
Smith, Birdie Mae 355
Smith, Clara 310
Smith, F. Aaron "Ike" 310
Smith, Henry 310
Smith, Kate 157
Smith, Lelisa 148
Smith, Loire 148
Smith, Louis F. "Greasy" 148, 172, 296
Smith, Lozene 148
Smith, Merriweather Woodson 4, 188
Smith, Mollie 148
Smith, Sally 310
Smith, Vera 310
Smith, W. Earl 310
Smith, Rev. W. F. 78
Smythe, Mae 233, 355
Smythe, Lillian 233-234, 260, 355
Smythe Sadie 233-234, 355
Sneed, Lillian 355, 367
Sneed, Mildred 333
Snift, A. B. 58
Snow/Freeze 48, 75, 146, 250
Son Brothers Circus 323
Sour Lake, community/oil field 195, 199
South Houston, City of 116, 145-147, 149-151, 154-155, 162-164, 172, 181, 212, 226, 239, 282, 296, 314, 315, 323-325, 329, 345, 348, 349, 352, 368
South Houston Baptist Church 155
South Houston Commercial Club 163
South Houston Electric Co. 324
South Houston Fireworks Factory (see Texas FWF)
South Houston Hotel 147
South Houston Iron Works 148
South Houston Times newspaper 163
South Houston-La Porte Rd. 169, 314, 315, 325
South Texas National Bank 51
Southern Motors Mfg Ass'n Ltd 222

Southern Pacific RR 58, 68, 107, 149, 236, 315
Southwestern Bell Telephone 257, 275, 294
Spacie, Ellen 67
Spacie, Emma "Elenor" 67
Spacie, William W. "Will" 67
Spacie, William Jr. 67, 104
Spencer Highway (also S.H.-La P. Rd) 315, 324, 325
Spencer, Commissioner R. H. 325
Spindletop 88, 193-195, 197-198
Spooner, Mr. 29
Spraggins, Fred 307
Sportt, Ethel (Williams) 335
Sprott, Jimmy B. 335
Stable, C. L. 99
Stafford, Belle Adell (Hills) 218
Stafford, Bob 10, 16, 18
Stafford, Eulas 218
Stafford, Leonard J. 218
Stafford, Marybell 218
Stafford, May Effie 218
Stafford, Ralph L. 141, 218, 231, 282, 355, 366
Stafford, William O. 218
Stafford, Winogene (see Cloutier) 355
Stafford Lumber Co. 365, 366
Stafford's Point 188
Stake, Mrs. E. A. 326
Star Monthly magazine 103
Starkeys 79, 138
Starkey, Bessie O. 58, 161
Starkey, Bryon 114
Starkey, Hershal Gregg 58, 114-115
Starkey, Josiah H. 58, 74, 79, 161
Starkey, LaVerne 58
Starkey, Laura P. 58
Starkey, Luther E. 58
Starkey, Mary (Harwell) 114-115
Starkey, Mary E. 58
Starkey, Spencer A. 58, 114, 116
Starkey, Sula A. 114, 116
Starkey, Walter Y. 58
Starkey, Wilford 58
Starnes, James Q. "Jimmy" 143, 144, 161

Index

Starnes, Lometta 161
Starnes, Minnie 78, 161
Starnes, Oscar 76, 161
Starnes, Roy 161
Starnes, Sidney 143, 144, 161
State Bank & Trust Co. 208-209
State National Bank 209
Steel, Mr. 143-144
Steele, Alfonso 146-147
Stephens, Everett 181
Stephenson, Homer 247
Sterling Highway/Ave. (La Porte Rd) 297, 301, 325, 340, 351, 359, 360, 362, 364-366
Sterling, Ross 197, 203, 261, 278, 297, 344
Stewart, Betty 289
Stewart, James B. "Jim" 289, 307
Stewart, Miss 153
Stone and Webster Engineering Co. 151
Stowers, Mrs. James 326
Strait, Arthur 316
Strait, Charles Earl 316
Strait, Christine 316
Strait, Clearance 316
Strait, Clyde James 315
Strait, Florence 316
Strait, Leonard King 316
Strait, Mary (McKinney) 315
Strait, Mary Louise 316
Strait, William Everett "Billy" 316
Strawberries 34, 37, 70, 75, 76, 102, 103, 111, 114, 118-132, 138, 141, 144, 151, 185, 203, 205, 209, 214, 243, 244, 250, 259, 290, 308, 313, 314, 316-321, 342, 351, 362, 371
Strengths, Eric 118
Strope, Allia M. (Loomis) 159
Strope, John H. 159
Strope, Julia Loomis (see King) 159
Stroud, Aida A. (Hill) 353
Stroud, George Russell 353
Stroud, G. Russell Jr. 353
Stroud, Mannie Mae 353
Stucco House 291
Stuchbery, "Aunt" Rill 355, 356

Stuchbery, James Eugene "Stutts" 355, 356
Stuchbery, Thomas Richard 356
Stucky, Mrs. J. I. 326
Subdivisions 245, 246, 257, 261, 298, 299, 301, 351
Suburban motorcar (see Bayshore Suburban Motor Car) 259-260
Suburban Record newspaper 298
Sugar cane 134
Sugar cane mills 136
Summit, community of 17, 28, 31
Sunday School 46, 47, 64, 117, 334
Sunset Coal & Wood Co. 241
Swedish/Sweden 52, 59, 60, 180
Sweeney, Ann 137
Sweeney, Earl 137
Sweeney, Ernest 137
Sweeney, John W. 137
Sweeney, Katie 137
Swimming holes 103, 144, 225
Swimming Pool 354
Sydnor, Seabrook 65
Syfan, Charles Edward Jr. 289, 307
Syfan, Moessie 307
Syfan, Josephine 308
Syfan, Mae Evelyn (see Warren) 232, 308
Syfan, Wilabie (see Larson) 289, 307
Syfan's Dairy (see Pas. Pure Milk) 275, 307, 308
Sylvan Beach 56, 78, 105, 129, 152, 162, 164, 176, 190, 209, 211, 259-261, 290, 295, 300, 343, 346
Sylvan Beach Special 177
Sylvan Grove 38, 56, 78
Sylvan Hotel/Sylvan Beach Hotel 39, 74, 191-192

T

Tabb's Bayou 197, 199
Tabor, L. O. "Bobbie" 318
Tabor, Lawrence G. 236, 318, 319, 327
Tabor, Mildred (see Hay) 181, 232, 289, 318, 319, 327, 333. 344
Tabor, Rex 231, 318

Tabor, Thelma 318, 319
Tabor, Vina (Barnes) 318, 335
Tackaberry, Dr. A. L. W. 268
Tacker, Alvin L. "Sonny" 288
Tacker, Dorothy S. 288, 327, 352
Tacker, Edith I. 288
Tacker, G. M. 306
Tacker, Harry Jefferson "Bear" 288, 301, 308
Tacker, Ruth Iline (Johnson) 288
Tacker's Dairy 308
Tatar, Eva 366
Tatar, Herbert "Herb" 366
Tatar, Leonard B. 366
Tatar, Seymour M. 366
Taylor's Lake 23
Taylor, Clara E. 281
Teas, Edward 132
Telephone 75, 77, 98, 121, 246, 257, 268, 275
Television 279
Tennant, J. H. 30
Tennis 227
Tex Dreifuss (ferry boat) 345, 347
Texas City, community of 164, 172, 197, 280, 308, 309
Texas Company 122, 132, 194-198
Texas Chemical Co. 201
Texas Fireworks Co. (S. Hou. FW Co.) 163, 164, 296, 324, 325
Texas Fruit Company 58
Texas Ice Company 127
Texas Ice & Fuel 269, 363
Texas Portland Cement Co. (see Lone Star Cement Co.) 132, 199, 200
Thayer, Gov. 25
Thomas, D. Lamar "Top" 287, 328
Thomas, Ella 293
Thomas, Ezekiel 5
Thomas, George W. 293
Thomas, James Cumberland "J. C." 259, 287, 304, 341, 364
Thomas, J. C. Jr. 287
Thomas, Jessie Dee (Young) 287
Thomas, Juanita "Skitter" 287, 328, 334

Thomas, Rebecca Jane (see Allen) 5
Thomason, Elma (see Griffin) 310
Thomason, Jobe Smith 310
Thomason, Sue Francis 310
Thomasson, Archie G. 121
Thomasson, Dagma 121
Thomasson, Nettie D. 121
Thompson, Arvie 98
Thomasson, Edwin 98
Thompson, Fern 98
Thompson, Grace 98
Thompson, L. M. 66
Thompson, O. F. 348
Thornton, Alma (see Jones) 137
Thornton, B. B. 294
Thornton, George C. 181, 218, 237, 297-298, 305
Thornton, Glennera "Ginny" 237
Thornton, Glenora 333
Thornton, L. Ward 137
Thornton, Ray Marian (Quinn) 181, 218, 237
Thornton, Sarah Caroline 137, 157
Thornton, Whit Brownelle 129, 137, 143, 144, 206, 211-212, 237, 248, 265
Thornton, William H. 137, 151
Thorp, Mr. & Mrs. 162, 275
Thurman, Clara (see Wilson) 52, 72, 115, 168
Thurman, Francis Lenora (see Parks) 52, 115
Thurman, Josephine (see Atkinson) 52, 115
Thurman, Martha Angeline 72
Thurman, Roy 52, 72
Tiller, Silma 300
Tilley, B. B. 294
Tilley, Arthur Carl 95, 180, 273, 298
Tilley, Cecil H. 95
Tilley, Charles Albert 95, 180
Tilley, Charles Henry 95, 106, 116, 157
Tilley, Mary F. 95
Tilley, Ola O. 95
Tilley's Garage 273
Tilley's Mercantile Store 95-97, 103, 110, 153, 157, 211, 214, 298, 361

Index

Tingle, A. D. 275
Tingle, A. D. Jr. 275
Tingle, Billy V. 275
Tingle, Boyd 275, 357
Tingle, Jack M. 275
Tingle, Juanita 275, 287, 333, 334
Tingle, Kenneth E. 275
Tingle, Mary 275, 287, 334
Tingle, Minnie (Goode) 275
Tips, Gus W. 366
Tobacco crop 53, 81, 82
Tofte, Mrs. H. H. 221
Tognacioli, Mrs. John 326
Tokens 126, 318, 320
Toppers (strawberries) 126, 320
Towles, Samuel Basil 369
Towels, Julie E. (Pitts) 369
Townsend, Mr. 335
Track (sports) 281
Traffic light signal 222
Trains (see individual railroads)
Trains, Excursion 31, 49, 57, 129, 259
Treadwell, Roy 325
Trifon, C. 247
Tipton, Bill 353
Tipton, Charles 353
Tipton, J. E. 353
Tipton, Lenora Buss 353
Trolleys 105, 219
Truck Growers Assistance Holiday 84
Truelove, Charles E. 206
Truelove, Minnie Lu 206
Tullis, J. J. 348
Twyford Automobile Co. 163

U

Ulmer, Percy 306-307
Ulmer, Mrs. Percy 306
Unincorporation 258
Union Baptist Association 88, 90
Union Congregation Church 64
Union Sunday School 78
Universal Shipbuilding Co. 179, 224
U-Boat 171

V

Vanderson family 53, 105
Vanderson, Nettie 53
Van Dorn, Bessie 98
Van Dorn, Elnor Agnes 98
Van Dorn, Hazel A. 98
Van Dorn, Ivy 98
Van Dorn, Lois 98
Van Dorn, Maybelle (see Robertson) 98
Van Dorn, Raymond Oliver 98
Van Dorn, Richard 98
Van Dorn, Tyra 98
Van Dorn, William 98
Van Dorn, William F. 98, 116, 132
Vance, Reverend Marvin S. 368
Vasmer, Ernest H. 108, 152
Vaugh, Gertrude 137
Vaugh, Grace 137
Vaugh, Marshall 137
Vaugh, Myrom C. 137
Vaugh, Myrtle 137
Vauters, C. E. 162
Veatch, Dr. Everett Parker 369
Vick, Andrew J. 32, 50-52, 68
Vick, Augustus Theodore "A. T." 257, 275, 309
Vick, Gilbert Marvin 309, 368
Vick, Sue B. (Marshall) 309
Vick's Dairy 309
Victoria, Texas 139
Vince, Allen 5
Vince, William 2, 4
Vince, Wm. Survey 4, 5, 25, 27, 33, 35, 39, 44
Vince's Bayou 2, 4, 6, 10, 22, 35, 41, 42, 53, 91, 97, 99, 103, 106, 131, 132, 136, 167-168, 200, 211, 226, 237, 244, 258, 261, 263, 274, 296, 298, 307, 310, 316, 322, 327
Vince's Bridge 156

W

Wafer, Albert W 47, 48.
Wafer, John T. (F.?) 34, 41, 43, 46

Wafer, Margarett J. 47
Wagoner, W. H. 129, 197, 198
Walker, Hazel 369
Walker, Leslie Lewis "Shorty" 148, 172
Walker, Thomas Bryant "T. B." 369
Wall, Barbara 357
Wall, C. P. 357
Wall, "Cy" 357
Wallace, Homer 107
Wallace, James G. or D.? 342
Wallace, Russel 107
Wallman, Aldoph F. 113, 116
Wallman, Ella 113
Wallman, Ester 113
Wallman, Eva 113
Wallman, Fred 113
Wallman, Freda 113
Wallman, Henry 113
Wallman, Hilda 113
Wallman, Matilda 113
Wallman, Ruth 113
War Between the States (Civil War) 12, 27, 277
Ward, Alvin A. 259, 294
Ward, Stafford 23
Warner, Reverend S. W. 65, 78
Waring, Fred 262, 263
Warren, Gentry Alvin 307, 308
Warren Mae Evely (Syfan) 307
Warren, Ruby Davis (see Brammer) 307
Water wells 44, 95, 102, 131-132, 138, 190, 192, 200, 201, 211, 254, 274, 290, 305, 313, 344, 347
Watermelons 103, 129, 133, 242, 326
Waterworks 296, 324, 340
Watkins, George A. "Watty" 226, 279
Watson, Gus A. 211, 236, 241, 263, 301, 366
Watson, J. L. 74
Way, C. H. 36
Waycott, Anna Jane (Allen/Glass) 219, 308
WEAY radio station 344

Webb, "Doc" D. L. 167, 218
Webb, Ethel Mary (Sonnier) 370
Webb, John Statts 370
Webb, Laura 370
Webb, Sarah 167, 218
Webb Co. (store) 362
Webster, community of 31, 63, 137, 164, 357
Webster, Charles W. 34, 37
Webster, F. B. 37
Webster, Ollie 36
Websterville, Tx also see Webster 31
Weinberg, Bert 322
Wells Fargo 97
Werner, E. E. 148
Wesney, Dolores Jane 353
Wesney, John George "Jack" 352
Wesney, Julius 352
Wesney, Mary (Sabo) 352
Wesney, Mary Marguerite 353
Wesney, Patricia Gail 353
West, Jack 201
West, Jim 251
West Pasadena 62, 67, 69, 107, 142, 254, 258, 261-263, 298, 312, 364-366
West, Simeon H. 32, 33, 36, 37, 49, 87, 289
Western Land Co. 144, 147, 149
Western Union 95, 159
Westheimer, Sid 106
Westheimer, Livery & Funeral Co. 106
WEV radio station 255
Wharf 15, 18, 56, 299
Wheeler, Preston "Bert" 300
Whitaker, Alton Ruth 332-334
Whitaker, Clarence 356
White, Annie Lauris (see Scott) 309
White, Billy 309
White, Claude 309
White, Doris 309
White, E. A. 132
White, Garrett 144
White, Gary 143
White, Hadley 280, 308, 309
White, Hill P. 366

Index 483

White, Kizzie 280, 308, 309
White, Josaphine 309
White, Thelma Murtle (see Otterside) 309
White, Thomas C. "Tommy" 280, 309
White, T. C. Jr. 309
White, Tilman 355
White, William B. 309
White wash paint 102
White's dairy 308
Whitman, Annette 272
Whitman, Arthur G. 272, 357, 364, 368
Whitman, Emmett E. 272
Whitman, Ralph Garrison 272
Whitten, C. L. 118, 130
Whitten, Lizzie 118, 130
Whoopee, 299-302, 314
Whoopee Inn 300, 313
Willard, Francis (Close) 292, 336
Willard, Jimmie 292
Williams, Mrs. Agnes 326
Williams, Alfred G. 275
Williams, Alma (Mason) 354
Williams, Amos J. 216
Williams, Anna Bell 275
Williams, Ardell (Della ?) 79
Williams, Arsula "Sula" (Conn) 77-78, 94
Williams, Betty 227, 266
Williams, Billie 359
Williams, Bryon Curtis "Twig" 275
Williams, Bryon Fred "Barney" 62, 83, 275
Williams, Carey 270
Williams, Chester A. 77, 79, 104, 236
Williams, Cornelius "Neal" 114
Williams, Cynthia (Hutchinson) 79
Williams, Delia "D" 333
Williams, Ed 316
Williams, Ethel 335, 336
Williams, Everett M. 217, 265, 287, 301, 354
Williams, Fleeta 153
Williams, Irene 316

Williams, Irma (McMaster) 217-218, 252
Williams, James Walter 77-78, 208
Williams, Jennie Elvira (see Hughes) 320, 362
Williams, Jimmie L. 275
Williams, John R. 62, 208, 216, 266
Williams, Lillie A. 213, 216
Williams, Loise (see Pomeroy) 286, 333, 335, 336
Williams, Lula I. 275
Williams, Mae 316
Williams, Marie 316
Williams, Mary E. (Hutchinson) 213, 216, 266
Williams, Mattie Ella (Cammack) 62, 66, 72, 78
Williams, Nettie Irene 275
Williams, Ray C. Sr. 62, 83, 121, 179, 217-218, 224-225, 248, 358
Williams, Ray C. Jr. "R. C." 217, 287
Williams, Ruth A. 225, 229, 231, 286, 293, 333, 361
Williams, Truett H. 275
Williams, Walter F. 79, 116, 124, 180, 208, 236, 245, 266, 268, 305, 306, 311, 320, 341, 361, 362
Williams, William Benjamin "Ben" 62, 66, 77, 78, 79, 82, 84, 86, 91, 94, 110, 113, 116, 216, 274, 296, 311
Williams, W. C. "Professor" 153-154
Williams, Mrs. W. C. 153, 154
Williams, William Carey "Willie" 270, 325
Williams, William Roy 79, 180
Williams, Wynona Jean 275
Williams, Zeola Annie (Harwell) 114
Williams' Grocery 266, 267
Williams' Mercantile 266, 286
Willis, Mr. 263
Wilson, Clara (Thurman) 115, 168, 240, 355
Wilson, Estelle 168, 240, 301, 332, 334
Wilson, Mrs. Mary 326
Wilson, Merle "Mud" 259, 328

Wilson, Sylvia (see Meyer) 168, 238, 270, 332, 361
Wilson, Thurman "Little Foots" 168, 232, 238, 239, 271, 282, 328,
Wilson, W. L. "Foots" 106, 115, 121, 144, 168, 206, 211, 224, 225, 248, 253, 269, 287, 326, 328, 362
Wilson, Walter 107, 168
Wilson, President Woodrow 171
Wine 3, 123, 321
Wirt, P. W. 53
Witt, Harry 263
Witt, Harry Jr. 263
Witt, Lillian "Kitty" 232, 263
Witt, Mary 231, 263
Witter, Arch 38
Wizoreck, Emil 136
Wizoreck, Emma Louise 136
Wizoreck, Eva 136
Wizoreck, Frida (see Laschinsky) 136
Wizoreck, Dr. Michael 136
Wolves 82
Wood, Dowe 311
Wood King 241
Woodmen of the World 153
Woods, C. S. 147
Work Projects Administration (WPA) 342, 345, 354
Worley, Coral 334
Worley, Jacob Archie "Arch" 288, 307
Worley, Mildred (Gray) 288
World War I, see Great War 170-171, 179-181, 184-186, 199, 201, 209, 219, 243, 244, 278
Wright, Marvin V. 53
Wright, "Babe" 334
Wright, Edweena 333, 334
Wright, Elizabeth 333
Wright, Jewell 363, 364
Wright, Morris Jesse Sr. 363, 364, 368
Wright, Morris J. Jr. 363
Wright, Quenton 304
Wright Brothers 145
Wright's Grain Co. 362-364
Wright's Nursery 53, 298

Y

Yarnell, Alva 42
Yarnell, Ethel 42
Yarnell, Harly 42
Yarnell, Lennie 42
Yarnell, Leon J. 42, 66
Yarnell, Mary 42
Ye Old college Inn 300
Yeamans, Edna 310
Yeamans, Olin 310
Yeamans, R. E. 310
Yeamans, Mrs. R. E. 310
Yellow fever "Yellow Jack" 5, 65
Yerkes, Emile F. 98
Yerkes, Mabel M. 98
Yerkes, Mr. & Mrs. 98
York, A. M. "Colonel" 25, 31, 32, 39, 49
York, J. H. 25, 31, 49, 75
Young's Bakery 333, 334
Young, Adella (Krenek) 334, 335
Young, Alton De 299
Young, Frank M. 334
Young, Robert L. 206
Youngblood, Addie 334
Youngblood, W. O. 294

Z

Zepedas family 316
Zimmerman, Rev. O. F. 92
Zlomke, Alvin 50
Zlomke, Amelia 50
Zlomke, Bertha 50
Zlomke, Ervin 50
Zlomke, John 50, 185
Zlomke, Leopold 50
Zlomke, Lydia 50, 115
Zlomke, Walter 185
Zlomke, William 50, 146-147
Zuber, William 146, 147

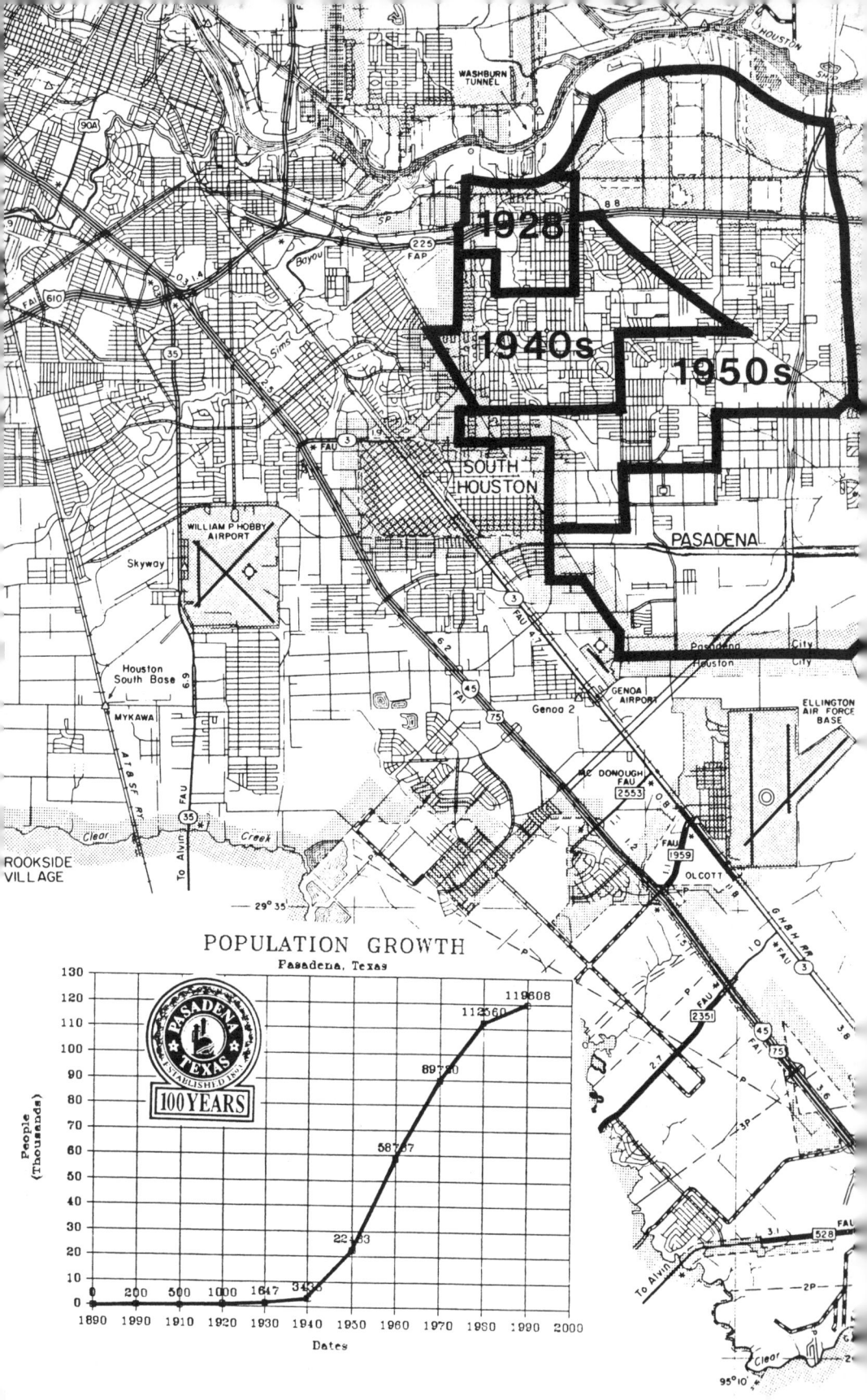